European Union Public Law

European Union Public Law
CASES AND MATERIALS

Damian Chalmers

CAMBRIDGE
UNIVERSITY PRESS

CAMBRIDGE UNIVERSITY PRESS
Cambridge, New York, Melbourne, Madrid, Cape Town, Singapore, São Paulo, Delhi, Tokyo, Mexico City

Cambridge University Press
The Edinburgh Building, Cambridge CB2 8RU, UK

Published in the United States of America by Cambridge University Press, New York

www.cambridge.org

First published 2010
Reprinted 2011

Printed in the United Kingdom at the University Press, Cambridge

A catalogue record for this publication is available from the British Library

ISBN 978-0-521-18123-5 Paperback

Contents

v

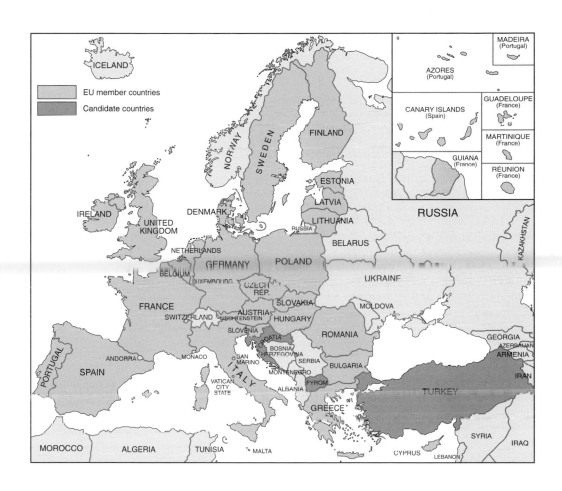

Abbreviations

AFSJ	Area of Freedom, Security and Justice
BER	Block Exemption Regulation
BSE	bovine spongiform encephalopathy
CAP	Common Agricultural Policy
CESR	Committee of European Securities Regulators
CFI	Court of First Instance
CFSP	Common Foreign and Security Policy
CISA	Schengen Implementing Convention
COR	Committee of the Regions
COREPER	Committee of Permanent Representatives
COSAC	Conference of Community and European Affairs Committees of Parliaments of the European Union
CT	Constitutional Treaty
DCT	Draft Constitutional Treaty
DG	Directorate-General
EAW	European Arrest Warrant
EC	European Communities
ECB	European Central Bank
ECHR	European Convention on Human Rights
ECN	European Competition Network
ECOWAS	Economic Community of West African States
ECSC	European Coal and Steel Community
ECtHR	European Court of Human Rights
ECU	European Currency Unit
EDC	European Defence Community
EDP	excessive deficit procedure
EEA	European Economic Area
EEC	European Economic Community
EFSA	European Food Safety Authority
EFTA	European Free Trade Area
EMI	European Monetary Institute
EMS	European Monetary System
EMU	economic and monetary union
ENP	European Neighbourhood Policy
EO	European Ombudsman
ERDF	European Regional Development Fund
ERM	exchange rate mechanism

ERT	European Round Table
ESC	Economic and Social Committee
ESCB	European System of Central Banks
ESDP	European Security and Defence Policy
ESecC	European Securities Committee
ESF	European Social Fund
EUCFR	European Union Charter of Fundamental Rights
EURATOM	European Atomic Energy Community
EUROPOL	European Police Office
FSA	Financial Services Authority
FSAP	Financial Services Action Plan
IGC	intergovernmental conference
ISO	International Standards Organisation
JHA	Justice and Home Affairs
MCA	monetary compensation amount
MEP	Member of the European Parliament
MEQR	measure of equivalent effect
MiFiD	Markets in Financial Instruments Directive
NAAT	no appreciable affectation of trade
NCA	national competition authority
NCB	national central bank
NGO	non-governmental organisation
OHIM	Office for Harmonisation in the Internal Market
OLAF	European Anti-Fraud Office
OMC	open method of coordination
PJCC	police and judicial cooperation in criminal matters
QMV	qualified majority voting
SEA	Single European Act
SGEI	services of general economic interest
SIA	Schengen Implementing Agreement
SIS	Schengen Information System
TEU	Treaty on European Union
TEU(M)	Treaty on European Union (Maastricht)
TFEU	Treaty on the Functioning of the European Union
WTO	World Trade Organization

Table of Cases

European Court of Justice: numerical order

European Ombudsman Decisions

European Court of Human Rights

National Courts

European Court of Justice: alphabetical order

European Court of Justice: Opinions

Table of Treaties, Instruments and Legislation

Treaties and Analogous Instruments

EU Legislation and Policy Documents

National Legislation and Policy Documents

Table of Equivalents

TREATY ON EUROPEAN UNION

Lisbon Treaty numbers and their Amsterdam and Pre-Amsterdam equivalents (Amsterdam and Pre-Amsterdam is TEU unless specified otherwise)

Lisbon	Amsterdam	Pre-Amsterdam	Lisbon	Amsterdam	Pre-Amsterdam
1	1	A	29	15	J.5
2			30	22	J.12
3	2	B	31	23	J.13
4	10 EC	5 EC	32	16	J.6
5	5 EC	3b EC	33	18	J.8
6	6	F	34	19	J.9
7	7	F.1	35	20	J.10
8			36	21	J.11
9			37	24	J.14
10	191(1) EC	138a	38	25	J.15
11	191(1) EC	138a	39		
12			40	47	M
13	3, 5, 7, 8, 10 EC	C, D 4, 4a. 5 EC	41	28	J.18
14	189/190/192/197 EC	137, 138, 138b, 140 EC	42	17	J.7
15	4	D	43		
16	202/203/205 EC	145, 146, 148 EC	44		
17	211/214/217 EC	155, 158, 161 EC	45		
18			46		
19	220/221/224 EC	164, 165, 168 EC	47	281 EC	210 EC
20	11/11A EC		48	48	N
	27A–27E, 40–40B, 43–45		49	49	O
21	3	C			
22			50		
23			51	311 EC	239 EC
24	11	J.1	52	299(1) EC	227(1) EC
25	12	J.2	53	51	Q
26	13	J.3	54	52	R
27			55	53	S
28	14	J.4		314 EC	248 EC

TREATY ON THE FUNCTIONING OF THE EUROPEAN UNION

Lisbon Treaty numbers and their Amsterdam and Pre-Amsterdam equivalents (Amsterdam and Pre-Amsterdam is EC Treaty unless specified otherwise)

Lisbon	Amsterdam	Pre-Amsterdam	Lisbon	Amsterdam	Pre-Amsterdam
1			49	43	52
2			50	44	54
3			51	45	55
4			52	46	56
5			53	47	57
6			54	48	58
7	3 TEU	C TEU	55	294	221
8	3(2)	3(2)	56	49	59
9			57	50	60
10			58	51	61
11	6	3c	59	52	63
12	153(2)	129a	60	53	64
13			61	54	65
14	16	7d	62	55	66
15	255	191a	63	56	73b
16	286	213b	64	57	73c
17			65	58	73d
18	12	6	66	59	73f
19	13	6a	67	61	73i
20	17	8		29 TEU	K.1 TEU
21	18	8a	68		
22	19	8b	69		
23	20	8c	70		
24	21	8d	71	36 TEU	K.8 TEU
25	22	8e	72	64(1)	73l(1)
26	14	7a		33 TEU	K.4 TEU
27	15	7c	73		
28	23	9	74		
29	24	10	75	60	73g
30	25	12	76		
31	26	28	77	62	73j
32	27	29	78	63(1, 2), 64(2)	73k(1, 2), 73l(2)
33	135	116	79	63(3, 4)	73k(3, 4)
34	28	30	80		
35	29	34	81	65	73m
36	30	36	82	31 TEU	K.3 TEU
37	31	37	83	31 TEU	K.3 TEU
38	32	38	84		
39	33	39	85	31 TEU	K.3 TEU
40	34	40	86		
41	35	41	87	30 TEU	K.2 TEU
42	36	42	88	30 TEU	K.2 TEU
43	37	43	89	32 TFEU	K.4 TEU
44	38	46	90	70	74
45	39	48	91	71	75
46	40	49	92	72	76
47	41	50	93	73	77
48	42	51	94	74	78

Lisbon	Amsterdam	Pre–Amsterdam	Lisbon	Amsterdam	Pre–Amsterdam
95	75	79	147	127	109p
96	76	80	148	128	109q
97	77	81	149	129	109r
98	78	82	150	130	109s
99	79	83	151	136	117
100	80	84	152		
101	81	85	153	137	118
102	82	86	154	138	118a
103	83	87	155	139	118b
104	84	88	156	140	118c
105	85	89	157	141	119
106	86	90	158	142	119a
107	87	92	159	143	120
108	88	93	160	144	121
109	89	94	161	145	122
110	90	95	162	146	123
111	91	96	163	147	124
112	92	98	164	148	125
113	93	99	165	149	126
114	95	100a	166	150	127
115	96	101	167	151	128
116	96	101	168	152	129
117	97	102	169	153(1, 3, 4, 5)	129a
118			170	154	129b
119	4	3a	171	155	129c
120	98	103a	172	156	129d
121	99	103	173	157	130
122	100	103a	174	158	130a
123	101	104	175	159	130b
124	102	104a	176	160	130c
125	103	104b	177	161	130d
126	104	104c	178	162	130e
127	105	105	179	163	130f
128	106	105a	180	164	130g
129	107	106	181	165	130h
130	108	107	182	166	130i
131	109	108	183	167	130j
132	110	108a	184	168	130k
133			185	169	130l
134	114	109c	186	170	130m
135	115	109d	187	171	130n
136			188	172	130o
137			189		
138	111(4)	109(4)	190	173	130p
139			191	174	130r
140	121(1), 122(2), 123(5)	109j, 109k, 109l	192	175	130s
141	123(3), 117(2)	109l(3), 109f(2)	193	176	130t
142	124(1)	109m(1)	194		
143	119	109h	195		
144	120	109i	196		
145	125	109n	197		
146	126	109o	198	182	131

Lisbon	Amsterdam	Pre-Amsterdam	Lisbon	Amsterdam	Pre-Amsterdam
199	183	132	251	221(2), (3)	165
200	184	133	252	222	166
201	185	134	253	223	167
202	186	135	254	224	168
203	187	136	255		
204	188	136a	256	225	168a
205			257	225a	168a
206	131	110	258	226	169
207	133	113	259	227	170
208	177/178	130u/130v	260	228	171
209	179	130w	261	229	172
210	180	130x	262	229a	172
211	181	130y	263	230	173
212	181a	130y	264	231	174
213			265	232	175
214			266	233	176
215			267	234	177
216			268	235	178
217	310	238	269		
218			270	236	179
219	111(1, 3, 5)	109(1, 3, 5)	271	237	180
220	302, 303, 304	229, 230, 231	272	238	181
221			273	239	182
222			274	240	183
223	190(4, 5)	138(3)	275		
224	191(2)	138(3)	276		
225	192(2)	138b	277	241	184
226	193	138c	278	242	185
227	194	138d	279	243	186
228	195	138e	280	244	187
229	196	139	281	245	188
230	197(2)–(4)	140	282	8	4a
231	198	141	283	112	109a
232	199	142	284	113	109b
233	200	143	285	246	188a
234	201	144	286	247	188b
235			287	248	188c
236			288	249	189
237	204	147	289		
238	205(1, 3)	148(1, 3)	290	202	145
239	206	150	291	202	145
240	207	151	292		
241	208	152	293	250	189a
242	209	153	294	251	189b
243	210	154	295		
244			296	253	190
245	213	157	297	254	191
246	215	159	298		
247	216	160	299	256	192
248	217(2)	161	300	257/258/263	193/194/198a
249	218(2)	162(2)	301	258(1), (2), (4)	194(1), (2), (4)
250	219	163	302	259	195
			303	260	196

Lisbon	Amsterdam	Pre-Amsterdam	Lisbon	Amsterdam	Pre-Amsterdam
304	262	198	332		
305	263(2), (3), (4)	198a(2), (3), (4)	333		
306	264	198b	334		
307	265	198c	335	282	211
308	266	198d	336	283	212
309	267	198e	337	284	213
310	268/270	199/201a	338	285	213a
311	269	200	339	287	214
312			340	288	215
313	272(1)	203	341	289	216
314	272(2–10)	203	342	290	217
315	273	204	343	291	218
316	271	202	344	292	219
317	274	205	345	295	222
318	275	205a	346	296	223
319	276	206	347	297	224
320	277	207	348	298	225
321	278	208	349	299(2)–(4)	227
322	279	209	350	306	233
323			351	307	234
324			352	308	235
325	280	210	353		
326			354	309	236
327			355	299(2)–(6)	227
328			356	312	240
329			357	313	247
330			358		
331					

Electronic Working Paper Series

ARENA Working Papers: www.sv.uio.no/arena/

Constitutionalism Web (CONWeb) Papers:
www.qub.ac.uk/schools/SchoolofPoliticsInternationalStudiesandPhilosophy/
Research/PaperSeries/ConWEBPapers/

Centre for Advanced Study in Social Sciences (CEACS) Working Papers:
www.march.es/ceacs/ingles/Publicaciones/working/working.asp

Center for Culture, Organization and Politics Working Papers:
http://socrates.berkeley.edu/~iir/culture/papers.html

Jean Monnet Papers: www.jeanmonnetprogram.org/papers/index.html

European Research Papers Archive: http://olymp.wu-wien.ac.at/erpa/

European Integration Online Papers: http://eiop.or.at/eiop/

EUI Online Papers: www.iue.it/PUB/

Federal Trust Constitutional Online Papers: www.fedtrust.co.uk/constitutionalpapers

Ius Gentium Conimbrigae Working Papers: www.fd.uc.pt/hrc/pages_en/papers.htm

Lucas Pires Working Papers on Constitutionalism: www.fd.unl.pt/jc/work_pap.htm

Max Planck Institut für Gesellschaftsforschung (MPIfG) Working Papers:
www.mpi-fg-koeln.mpg.de/pu/workpapers_en.html

Mannheim Zentrum für Europäische Sozialforschung (MZES) Working Papers:
www.mzes.uni-mannheim.de/frame.php?oben=titel_e.html&links=n_publikationen_e.
php&inhalt=publications/wp/workpap_e.php

Nuffield College Working Papers in Politics: www.nuffield.ox.ac.uk/Politics/papers/

Queens Papers on Europeanisation:
www.qub.ac.uk/schools/SchoolofPoliticsInternationalStudiesandPhilosophy/
Research/PaperSeries/EuropeanisationPapers/

University of Edinburgh Europa Institute Mitchell Working Papers: www.law.ed.ac.uk/mitchellworking
papers

1

European Integration and the Treaty on European Union

CONTENTS

1 INTRODUCTION

This chapter sets out the central features of the European integration process, which provides the historical and political context for EU law. It also introduces some of the central concepts, ideas and developments in EU law.

Section 2 explores how all EU law is centred around an interplay between two central themes. The first is the addressing of many contemporary problems through a new form of transnational law. The second is the development of the ideals of Europe and European union. These ideals bestow a distinctive quality to the EU legal system and lay the ground for many of its debates. The European ideal conceives of Europe as the central place of progress, learning and civilisation, placing faith in humanity and her capacity to improve. Its dark side is its arrogance and its dismissal of 'un-European' ways of life or thought as violating these virtues. The idea of European union sets up a political community in competition with the nation-state but one, nevertheless, through which government policy is carried out.

Section 3 considers the establishment of the three Communities, the European Economic Community (EEC), the European Coal and Steel Community (ECSC) and the European Atomic Energy Community (EURATOM), by the Treaties of Paris and Rome. It sets out the central institutions: the Commission, the Parliament, the Council and the Court of Justice. It also considers the central policies established by these institutions, most notably the common market. This section also compares two developments of the 1960s that set out the two dominant models of political authority in EU law. In 1966, the Luxembourg Accords were agreed. This provided all national governments with a veto over the adoption of any law. The model was an intergovernmental one, with political authority and democracy vested in the nation-state. In 1963, in *Van Gend en Loos*, the Court of Justice declared that the EC Treaty constituted a new sovereign legal order for the benefit of its citizens. The model was a supranational one, in which authority is vested not in national institutions but the rights of European citizens.

Section 4 considers how, after a period of stagnation, European integration regained momentum with the adoption of the Single European Act (SEA) in 1986. This established the internal market: an area without internal frontiers in which there is free movement of goods, services, persons and capital. It also unlocked the decision-making processes by allowing for significant amounts of legislation to be adopted free from the national veto. The European Parliament was granted significant legislative powers for the first time.

Section 5 considers the Maastricht Treaty and the Treaty on European Union (TEU). The central mission of this treaty, signed in 1991, was to establish an economic and monetary union. However, it also established a three pillar structure. The first pillar, the EC Treaty, was dominated by supranational features, whilst the other two pillars, the Common Foreign and Security Policy and Justice and Home Affairs, were dominated by intergovernmental procedures. The TEU formalised a large number of new EU competences. It also significantly extended majority voting and the powers of the European Parliament.

Section 6 considers the Treaty of Amsterdam. Convened to deal with unfinished business from Maastricht, it was the first treaty to address increasingly popular antipathy against the European integration process. Its central policy was the establishment of the area of freedom, security and justice. The main features of this were the abolition of internal border controls between all Member States other than the United Kingdom and Ireland; the establishment of a common supranational immigration and asylum policy; and police cooperation and judicial cooperation in criminal policy. The Treaty made majority voting the dominant procedure. It also began to introduce national safeguards, most notably limited rights for national parliaments and a detailed Protocol on the subsidiarity principle, the principle which governs when the Union, acting within its competences, is better equipped to legislate than the Member States. This principle provides that the European Union should only act when Member States cannot realise their objectives acting unilaterally and by reason of the nature or scale of the action, these objectives are better realised through Union action.

Section 7 considers the enlargement of the European Union. Initially agreed between six states, the Union had grown to fifteen Member States by the mid-1990s. Almost all were prosperous and almost all came from Western Europe. The 2004 and 2007 accessions brought the number of Member States to twenty-seven with most of the new states being from Central and East Europe and having a post-communist past. This has made the Union a genuinely pan-European organisation but it has made it much more heterogeneous, posing new preferences and challenges, and raising the question of whether it is possible to have a 'one size fits all' EU law.

Section 8 considers the processes that were tried to deal with the challenges of a lack of popular enthusiasm for the Union and of enlargement. In 2000, the Treaty of Nice was agreed. This agreed limited institutional reforms to deal with the anticipated enlargements. These were perceived as insufficient. A suggestion was made to debate a wide-ranging recasting of the institutional settlement in open session by a Convention made up not just of national governments and the Commission, but also MEPs and national parliamentarians. It was to be approved by referendums across a number of Member States. This process led to the Constitutional Treaty in 2004. This was, however, rejected by referendums in the Netherlands and France.

Section 9 considers the Treaty of Lisbon, which was an attempt to rescue the process of institutional reform following the collapse of the Constitutional Treaty. The Lisbon Treaty recasts the Treaties around two treaties, the Treaty on European Union and the Treaty on the Functioning of the European Union (TFEU). Whilst special institutional arrangements are made for foreign and defence policy, all other policies are brought within a supranational framework. The Lisbon Treaty increases the powers of the Parliament and the Court of Justice and increases the areas subject to majority voting. It also introduces new safeguards to protect national autonomy. The competences of the Union are catalogued. The powers of national parliaments are increased. The subsidiarity principle is strengthened and a new principle of non-violation of national constitutional identities is established.

2 EUROPE AND THE EUROPEAN UNION

This book is about the European Union. The European Union is, amongst other things, a legal system established to deal with a series of contemporary problems and realise a set of goals that individual states felt unable to manage alone. That idea is conveyed by the word 'Union'. However, one can have a union of many things and actors. The distinctive feature of the European Union is that it claims to be a union that is *European*. Its mission is to lay claim to the development of the European ideal and the European heritage. The opening words of the Preamble to the Treaty on European Union establishing the European Union state:

> RESOLVED to mark a new stage in the process of European integration undertaken with the establishment of the European Communities,
> DRAWING INSPIRATION from the cultural, religious and humanist inheritance of Europe, from which have developed the universal values of the inviolable and inalienable rights of the human person, freedom, democracy, equality and the rule of law...

Laying claim to the ideals of Europe and the European heritage is, of course, contentious. Some may disagree with these ideals or to the European Union claiming ownership of them. Yet if one is to understand EU law, one has to realise that at its core is a constant interplay between two agendas: the development of these ideals and the government of the problems of contemporary Europe. Elements of both permeate all the chapters of this book. In some areas, there is a tension, imbalance or dysfunction between the two. In other areas, each is being revised in the light of concerns provoked by the other. However, the balance is never static. It is constantly changing as political beliefs change, the European Union's institutional settlement evolves and the challenges of the outside world alter. However, each development is not considered anew. They are considered in the light of a long legacy: be this the history of the European ideal, the institutional settlement of the European Union or a policy whose inception and development goes back many years.

Different chapters of this book consider different legal problems and goals. Yet it is worth pausing at the beginning of the book to consider some of the central elements of this European inheritance, both to understand what it means to call something European and so that we know the sort of venture upon which the European Union is embarked. If discussion of the Ancient Greeks and Charlemagne seems rather removed from that of discussion of the single European market, it is, however, worth considering what broader vision of life that market is tapping into. Does it change anything by calling itself a European market and does it change anything that has emerged within a particular trajectory of European integration?

(i) The idea of Europe

There is nothing fixed about the meaning of the term 'Europe'. It has been used for a variety of purposes, often as a form of self-justification. Its roots, like many things, are curious. The first references to 'Europe' depict it as a woman and the sun. The most famous early reference to Europe is that found in Greek mythology. Europa was a Phoenician woman seduced by the Greek god Zeus to come from Lebanon to Crete.[1] Europa was also, however, a Phoenician word that referred to the setting sun. From this, Europe was associated in Ancient Greece with the idea of 'the West'. Originally used to designate the lands to the west of Greece, usage shifted as the Ancient Greek territorial centre of gravity changed with incursions into modern Turkey and Iran. In his wars, Alexander the Great used it to denote non-Persians and it became associated with the lands in Greece and Asia Minor (today's Turkish Mediterranean coastline). Following this, the term was to lie largely dormant for many centuries. The Roman Empire and Christianity dominated in the organisation of political life, and neither had much use for the term.

Europe re-emerged as an important political idea from the eighth century AD onwards. It was here that it began to acquire many of the associations that we currently make when we use the word 'European'. In part, it became an expression of a siege mentality. The advance of Islam from the South and the East led to Europe being associated with resistance to the religion. An army of Franks, which fought against the Moors, was referred to as a 'European army'.[2] At this time Europe also became associated with the idea of Western Christianity. The Frankish Empire stretched across much of West Europe under the rule of Charlemagne in the ninth century AD. He styled himself the father of Europe and sought to impose a political

---

[1] D. De Rougemont, *The Idea of Europe* (New York, Macmillan, 1965) 6–19.
[2] D. Lewis, *God's Crucible: Islam and the Making of Europe 570–1215* (New York, Norton, 2008).

system across the region, based on communication between a large number of political and administrative centres. Alongside this, common economic practices were developed: shared accounting standards, price controls and a currency. Finally, he also sought to build a common Christian culture, which fostered learning, Christian morality, the building of churches and the imposition of a single interpretation of Christianity.[3]

These elements are all associated with a European identity. However, it was only from the twelfth century onwards that Europe was used to refer to a place whose inhabitants enjoyed a shared way of life based on Christian humanism, revolving around images of God and Christ portrayed as human.[4] Alongside particular religious beliefs, Europe also became associated with a particular form of political economy, namely that of rural trade. Increasingly, the rural town became the centre of the local economy. Trade relations between towns expanded across Europe, so that from the fifteenth century onwards, trade flourished between the Italian ports in the south and Flanders in the North, in which the role of the merchant was pivotal. The final feature of this European region was the persecution of non-Christians, be they pagans or followers of other faiths, such as Judaism or Islam. Those whose conduct offended the central values of Christianity were also maltreated, such as heretics and homosexuals, as were those perceived as socially unproductive, in particular, lepers.

Developments in the sixteenth and seventeenth centuries were to set out the dominant institutional context for the subsequent evolution of the European idea. The establishment of the modern nation-state consolidated power in centralised, impersonal bureaucracies and led to certain core policies, such as tax, law and order and foreign policy being the exclusive competence of these bureaucracies.[5] This hegemony of the nation-state over political life led to Europe acquiring new associations in the eighteenth and nineteenth centuries. It became, increasingly, an 'aesthetic category, romantic and nostalgic', associated with utopian ideals. Authors such as Rousseau and Kant saw Europe as an expression of certain ideals: be it a social contract between nations or as a form of perpetual peace. Europe was also considered to represent a shared aesthetic tradition:[6] be this a common form of high culture, institutionalised through the growth of elite tourism in Europe at that time, or that of a historical civilisation, distinguishing it from the New World and justifying its colonialism.

The final twist came in the twentieth century and derives from the United States' involvement in Europe. The role of the United States in two World Wars, the Cold War and in the regeneration of Europe after the Second World War heavily influenced European identity.[7] The idea of Europe as a historically entrenched community has been reinforced in other ways. The other association has been of Europe as the Eastern borderlands of the United States.

---

[3] The most extensive exposition is to be found in R. McKitterick, *Charlemagne: The Formation of a European Identity* (Cambridge, Cambridge University Press, 2008).

[4] J. Le Goff, *The Birth of Europe* (Oxford, Blackwell, 2005) 76–80.

[5] C. Tilly (ed.), *The Formation of Nation-States in Europe* (Princeton, NJ, Princeton University Press, 1975); G. Poggi, *The Development of the Modern State: A Sociological Introduction* (Stanford, CA, Stanford University Press, 1978); M. Mann, 'The Autonomous Power of the State: Its Origins, Mechanisms and Results' (1984) 25 *European Journal of Sociology* 185; H. Spruyt, *The Sovereign State and its Competitors: An Analysis of Systems Change* (Princeton, NJ, Princeton University Press, 1994).

[6] A. Chebel d'Appollonia, 'European Nationalism and European Union' and J. Tully, 'The Kantian Idea of Europe: Critical and Cosmopolitan Perspectives' in A. Pagden (ed.), *The Idea of Europe: From Antiquity to the European Union* (Cambridge, Cambridge University Press, 2002). Recent examples of this tradition are Z. Bauman, *Europe: An Unfinished Adventure* (Cambridge, Polity, 2004); U. Beck, *Cosmopolitan Europe* (Cambridge, Polity, 2005).

[7] G. Delanty, *Inventing Europe: Idea, Identity, Reality* (Basingstoke, Macmillan, 1995) 115–55.

For those reverting to market democracy after forty-five years of communism, a 'return to Europe' means a turn to the West and to values that are associated, unashamedly, with the United States, namely those of free markets and constitutional democracy. In today's Western Europe, Europe has acquired an alternate meaning, in that its values are similar but different to those of the United States. Although there is a shared commitment to markets and constitutional democracy, these take a different form from those in the United States. There is an emphasis on the social market and on supposedly 'European' values, such as opposition to the death penalty, which are not present in the United States.

J. Habermas and J. Derrida, 'February 15, or, What Binds Europeans Together: Plea for a Common Foreign Policy Beginning in Core Europe' in D. Levy *et al., Old Europe, New Europe, Core Europe: Transatlantic Relations after the Iraq War* (London, Verso, 2005) 5, 10–12

... the spread of the ideals of the French revolution throughout Europe explains, among other things, why politics in both of its forms – as organizing power and as a medium for the institutionalization of political liberty – has been welcomed in Europe. By contrast, the triumph of capitalism was bound up with sharp class conflicts, and this fact has hindered an equally positive appraisal of free markets. That differing evaluation of politics and markets may explain Europeans' trust in the civilizing power of the state, and their expectations for it to correct market failures.

The party system that emerged from the French revolution has often been copied. But only in Europe does this system also serve an ideological competition that subjects the socio-pathological results of capitalist modernization to an ongoing political evaluation. This fosters the sensitivities of citizens to the paradoxes of progress. The contest between conservative, liberal and socialist agendas comes down to the weighing of two aspects: Do the benefits of a chimerical progress outweigh the losses that come with the disintegration of protective, traditional forms of life? Or do the benefits that today's processes of 'creative destruction' promise for tomorrow outweigh the pain of modernity's losers?

In Europe, those affected by class distinctions, and their enduring consequences, understood these burdens as a fate that can be averted only through collective action. In the context of workers' movements and the Christian socialist traditions, an ethics of solidarity, the struggle for 'more social justice', with the goal of equal provision for all, asserted itself against the individualist ethos of market justice that accepts glaring social inequalities as part of the bargain. Contemporary Europe has been shaped by the experience of the totalitarian regimes of the twentieth century and by the Holocaust – the persecution and annihilation of European Jews in which the National Socialist regime made the societies of the conquered countries complicit as well. Self-critical controversies about the past remind us of the moral basis of politics. A heightened sensitivity to injuries to personal and bodily integrity reflects itself, among other ways, in the fact both the Council of Europe and the EU made the ban on capital punishment a condition for membership.

Since the eighth century, the idea of Europe has thus been that it is a place where there are multiple political communities with a shared way of life. This way of life is based on a commitment to progress, civilisation, learning and culture. It is based on a belief in the value of humanity and humankind's capacity to better itself and to resolve any problems. The hubristic nature of this indicates its dark sides. Europe historically posited itself as the centre of the world for all these things. It has been its job to civilise others, to spread progress or human values. There is also an intolerance of things 'non-European'. For if they are not European, there is a chance that they do not represent the good things Europe represents. At its worst, this arrogance and intolerance has led to racism and colonialism, yet it is also present in the European integration process. Time and again, the *sui generis* nature or specialness of the process is emphasised as a form of particularly enlightened cooperation between nations. There is an assumption about the desirability of the policies, as otherwise why would so many states agree to them? There is also a concern, as we shall see, that the policies should always be the very best. Opponents of integration can, thus, often be dismissed as unreasonable or nationalistic (e.g. un-European). It may be, however, that they simply disagree with the policy or the procedure, or that they believe there exist other forms of value or life beyond the European ideal.

(ii) The idea of 'European union'

Whilst related, the idea of European union has different associations from that of Europe. After all, many self-avowed Europeans oppose European union! Independent proposals for a 'united Europe' first emerged at the end of the seventeenth century. However, they were still firmly confederal in nature. Ultimate authority was vested in the state, with pan-European structures acting as little more than a fetter upon the autonomy of the states. In 1693, the English Quaker William Penn wrote *An Essay Towards the Present and Future Peace of Europe*. Penn suggested that a European Parliament should be established, consisting of representatives of the Member States. The primary purposes of this Parliament would be to prevent wars breaking out between states and to promote justice. A more far-reaching proposal was put forward by John Bellers in 1710. Bellers proposed a cantonal system based upon the Swiss model whereby Europe would be divided into 100 cantons, each of which would be required to contribute to a European army and send representatives to a European Senate.

The first proposal suggesting a Europe in which the state system was to be replaced by a system within which there was a sovereign central body came from the Frenchman Saint-Simon. This proposal was published in a pamphlet in 1814, entitled *Plan for the Reorganisation of the European Society*. Saint-Simon considered that all European states should be governed by national parliaments, but that a European Parliament should be created to decide on common interests. This Parliament would consist of a House of Commons peopled by representatives of local associations and a House of Lords consisting of peers appointed by a European monarch. Saint-Simon's views enjoyed considerable attention during the first part of the nineteenth century. Mazzini, the *éminence grise* of Italian nationalism, allied himself with Proudhon and Victor Hugo in declaring himself in favour of a United Europe. Yet, the nineteenth century represented the age of the nation-state and the relationship between that structure and that of a united Europe was never fully explored.

The balance was altered by the First World War, which acted as a stimulus for those who saw European union as the only means both to prevent war breaking out again between the nation-states and as a means of responding to increased competition from the United States, Argentina and Japan. Most prominent was the pan-European movement set up in the 1920s by the Czech Count Coudenhove-Kalergi.[8] This movement not only enjoyed considerable support amongst many of Europe's intellectuals and some politicians, but was genuinely transnational,

---

[8] N. Coudenhove-Kalergi, *Pan-Europe* (New York, Knopf, 1926). An excellent discussion can be found in C. Pegg, *Evolution of the European Idea 1914–1932* (Chapel Hill, NC, University of North Carolina Press, 1983).

having 'Economic Councils' both in Berlin and in Paris. During the 1920s, the idea of European unity received governmental support in the shape of the 1929 Briand Memorandum. This Memorandum, submitted by the French Foreign Minister to twenty-six other European states, considered the League of Nations to be too weak a body to regulate international relations, and proposed a European Federal Union, which would better police states, whilst not 'in any way affect the sovereign rights of the States which are members of such an association'. This proposal, despite being strongly confederal in that it acknowledged the authority of the nation-states, was still regarded as too radical and received only a lukewarm response from the other states.

A further shock, in the form of the Second World War, was needed to arouse greater governmental interest in the idea of a united Europe. The coming into being and development of first, the European Communities, followed by the European Union, are explored in greater depth in the rest of this chapter. It is useful to consider for a moment how the creation of this political organisation with law-making powers, with the idea of Europe as its justification and its purpose, changed the geo-political context in which the idea of Europe was formulated. On the one hand, the European Union has become an independent centre in its own right for the generation of understandings about Europe and European values and symbols. The European Union has, therefore, tried to replicate the symbols and tools of nationhood at a pan-European level, be it through the (re)discovery of European flags, anthems, Cities of Culture or common passports.[9] This understanding of Europe, as a competing alternative to the nation-state, has been replicated by 'Euro-sceptic' groups, who see Europe as a centralised, monolithic entity which crushes local communities and self-government.[10] On the other hand, the idea of European union has become a justification for national government policy, as the Union becomes a vehicle through which national governments pursue and articulate their understanding of the national interest. On such a view, Europe does not act as a competitor to the nation-state but, rather, as a vehicle through which nation-states articulate their understandings of themselves and their place in the world through asking themselves how European they are or how they relate to Europe.[11] The extract below considers the case of Finland, in which the authors argue that by placing itself within the European Union many Finns were able to resolve a prior dichotomy about whether Finland was more 'Western' or more Russian.

M. Malmborg and B. Stråth, 'Introduction: The National Meanings of Europe' in M. Malmborg and B. Stråth (eds.), *The Meaning of Europe* (Oxford and New York, Berg, 2002) 1, 20

Finland's national history has been characterized by a strong awareness of being either on the brink of Europe or on the margins of Russia or somewhere in between ... Meinander traces two basic conceptions of Finnish national identity: the Fennoman that stresses the indigenous features of Finnish culture and sees Finland as a cooperative borderland between the West and Russia, and the liberal that

---

[9] C. Shore, *Building Europe: The Cultural Politics of European Integration* (London and New York, Routledge, 2000).

[10] A flavour is provided in M. Holmes (ed.), *The Eurosceptical Reader* (Basingstoke, Macmillan, 1996).

[11] For an extremely scholarly account of this see J. Diez Medrano, *Framing Europe: Attitudes to European Integration in Germany, Spain and the United Kingdom* (Princeton, NJ, Princeton University Press, 2003).

is akin to the Russian *zapadniki* in the sense that it prescribes close integration with the Western and European cultures.[12] For the Fennomans, Russia was in a cultural sense never outside Europe, but the feeling of standing at the edge of Europe was reinforced by the Russian revolution, the Finnish civil war and the foundation of the Soviet Union, which effectively precluded any acknowledgement of the eastern layers of Finnish identity. The Finnish notion of Europe became increasingly polarized not least due to the experiences of Finland being left very much alone in the Second World War. Forced into a policy of friendly neutrality with the Soviet Union after the war Finland rediscovered its role as a mediator between East and West. The Finns began to admit that Russia, even in its Soviet manifestation, was a part of European civilization.

The accession to the EU in 1995 was supported by a feeling that the Finns had at last found an answer to two centuries of uncertainty and identity-searching. Finland had, as it were, ultimately found a synthesis of its two historical roles, to be both on the brink of Western Europe and serve as a bridge-builder toward a Europe that stretched to include Russia and Slavonic Europe. EU membership implies both an improvement of national security and an emotional homecoming.

The idea of European union has thus come to carry three associations. First, it is associated with the establishment of a political community or tier of government in competition with that of the nation-state. Any Union policy, procedure or institution is thus always evaluated for its effects on the autonomy of national administrations. Secondly, it is associated with government policies that could not be secured by the nation-state alone (e.g. environment or trade liberalisation). They are, however, policies of the governments of the day and, inevitably, they will benefit some constituencies and disadvantage others.[13] Opposition to European union is often therefore opposition to the government of the day or a dominant policy process. The third association is that European union provides a context for debates about the nature of the state and national identity. It acts as a point of comparison; but also, by joining the European Union, a state commits itself to a particular vision of political community. This vision of 'what we are' is always likely to be contentious.

3 EARLY DEVELOPMENT OF THE EUROPEAN COMMUNITIES

(i) From the Treaty of Paris to the Treaty of Rome

The origins of the current European Union lie in a crisis provoked by the establishment of the Federal Republic of Germany. In 1949, the Ruhr, then under the administration of the International High Commission, was due to be handed back to the Federal Republic, along with the Saar. French fears of emerging German industrial might were compounded by Germany's increasing share of European steel production. The French response was a plan drafted by the

---

[12] H. Meinander, 'On the Brink or In Between? The Conception of Europe in Finnish Identity' in M. Malmborg and B. Stråth (eds.), *The Meaning of Europe* (Oxford and New York, Berg, 2002).

[13] N. Fligstein, *Euro-Clash: The EU, European Identity, and the Future of Europe* (Oxford, Oxford University Press, 2008), especially ch 8.

French civil servant, Jean Monnet, which was known as the Schuman Plan, after the French Finance Minister, Robert Schuman.[14]

Robert Schuman, Declaration of 9 May 1950[15]

Europe will not be made all at once or according to a single plan. It will be built through concrete achievements which first create a *de facto* solidarity. The coming together of the nations of Europe requires the elimination of the age-old opposition of France and Germany. Any action which must be taken in the first place must concern these two countries. With this aim in view, the French Government proposes that action be taken immediately on one limited but decisive point. It proposes that Franco-German production of coal and steel as a whole be placed under a common High Authority, within the framework of an organisation open to the participation of the other countries of Europe.

The pooling of coal and steel production should immediately provide for the setting up of common foundations for economic development as a first step in the federation of Europe, and will change the destinies of those regions which have long been devoted to the manufacture of munitions of war, of which they have been the most constant victims.

The solidarity in production thus established will make it plain that any war between France and Germany becomes not merely unthinkable, but materially impossible. The setting up of this powerful productive unit, open to all countries willing to take part and bound ultimately to provide all the member countries with the basic elements of industrial production on the same terms, will lay a true foundation for their economic unification.

This Plan formed the basis of the Treaty of Paris in 1951, which established the ECSC.[16] This Treaty entered into force on 23 July 1952 and ran for fifty years.[17] It set up a common market in coal and steel, which was supervised by the High Authority, a body independent from the Member States and composed of international civil servants, which had considerable powers to determine the conditions of production and prices for coal and steel.[18] The High Authority was, in turn, supervised by a Council, which consisted of Member State representatives. The Treaty of Paris was signed by only six states: the BENELUX States (Netherlands, Belgium and Luxembourg), Italy, France and Germany. The United Kingdom had been invited to the negotiations, but refused to participate, as it opposed both the idea of the High Authority and the remit of its powers.[19]

---

[14] W. Diebold, *The Schuman Plan: A Study in International Cooperation* (Oxford, Oxford University Press, 1959).

[15] European Parliament, *Selection of Texts concerning Institutional Matters of the Community for 1950–1982* (Luxembourg, Office for Official Publications of the European Communities, 1982) 47.

[16] On the negotiations, see P. Gerbet, 'The Origins: Early Attempts and the Emergence of the Six (1945–52)' in R. Pryce (ed.), *The Dynamics of European Union* (London, Croom Helm, 1987); R. Bullen, 'An Idea Enters Diplomacy: The Schuman Plan, May 1950' in R. Bullen (ed.), *Ideas into Politics: Aspects of European History 1880–1950* (London, Croom Helm, 1984).

[17] The ECSC expired on 23 July 2002. Decision of the representatives of the Member States meeting within the Council on the consequences of the expiry of the European Coal and Steel Community [2002] OJ L194/35.

[18] A good history is D. Spierenburg and R. Poidevin, *The History of the High Authority of the European Coal and Steel Community: Supranationality in Operation* (London, Weidenfeld & Nicholson, 1994).

[19] E. Dell, *The Schuman Plan and the British Abdication of Leadership in Europe* (Oxford, Clarendon, 1995); C. Lord, '"With But Not Of"': Britain and the Schuman Plan, a Reinterpretation' (1998) 4 *Journal of European Integration History* 23.

In 1950, during negotiations for the Treaty of Paris, the Korean War began. The United States, perceiving an increased threat from Stalin's Soviet Union, pressed for German rearmament and its entry into NATO, something which was inimical to the French.[20] As a response, the French Defence Minister, Pléven, proposed a European Defence Community. There would be a European army under a European Minister of Defence, administered by a European Commissariat. Once again, Britain was invited to join, but it declined on the basis that it preferred an expansion of NATO to the establishment of a European Defence Community (EDC). Nevertheless, a treaty establishing the EDC was signed between the same six states which had signed the ECSC in 1952. However, the EDC failed. A less integrationist French government under Mendès-France assumed power and French reverses in South-East Asia made France wary about ceding military sovereignty. In 1954, the French National Assembly refused to ratify the treaty.[21]

The failure of the EDC marked a moment of considerable political fluidity. The BENELUX states were increasingly worried by the nationalist policies of the Mendès-France government in France, in particular, its attempt to upgrade bilateral relations with Germany. In 1955, the Belgian Foreign Minister, Henri-Paul Spaak, suggested that there should be integration in a limited number of sectors, notably transport and energy. This worried the Netherlands as it threatened to restrict its efficiencies, particularly in the transport sector. The Dutch government responded by reactivating the 1953 Beyen Plan, which proposed a common market that would lead to economic union. A meeting of foreign ministers was held in Messina, Italy, in 1955. The British were invited, in addition to the six ECSC Member States, but did no more than send a Board of Trade official. Despite considerable French scepticism, a Resolution was tabled, calling for an Intergovernmental Committee under the chairmanship of Spaak to be set up to examine the establishment of a common market. As a carrot to the French, it was agreed that this should be done in tandem with examining the possibility of integration in the field of atomic energy. British objections to the supranational elements required for a common market entailed that they were unable to participate in the project.

The Spaak Report, published in 1956, laid the basis for the Treaty Establishing the European Economic Community (EEC Treaty). The Report made a pragmatic distinction between matters affecting the functioning of the common market, which would require a supranational decision-making framework and some supranational supervision of Member States' compliance with their obligations, and more general matters of budgetary, monetary and social policy, which would remain within the reserved competence of the Member States. Where these policies had a significant effect on the functioning of the common market, however, Member States should endeavour to coordinate these policies. An intergovernmental conference (IGC) was convened in Venice, with the Spaak Report as the basis for negotiations. The result was the signing of the Treaties of Rome in 1957 between the Six: Germany,

---

[20] T. Schwartz, 'The Skeleton Key: American Foreign Policy, European Unity, and German Rearmament, 1949–54' (1986) 19 *Central European History* 369.

[21] On this ill-fated enterprise, see E. Fursdon, *The European Defence Community: A History* (London, Macmillan, 1980); R. Cardozo, 'The Project for a Political Community (1952–4)' in R Pryce (ed.), *The Dynamics of European Union* (London, Croom Helm, 1987); R. Dwan, 'Jean Monnet and the Failure of the European Defence Community' (2001) 1 *Cold War History* 141.

France, Italy and the BENELUX states. Doubts about difficulties in French ratification led to two treaties being signed, one establishing the EEC, the other EURATOM. The treaties duly entered into force on 1 January 1958.[22]

(ii) The EEC Treaty

The dominant aim of the EEC Treaty was the establishment of a common market. This can be divided into a number of different elements. The first was the customs union, which required the abolition of all customs duties or charges having equivalent effect on the movement of goods between Member States and the establishment of a common external tariff. Secondly, the common market extended beyond the customs union to include the 'four freedoms', so that restrictions on the movement of goods, workers, services and capital were also prohibited by the EC Treaty. Furthermore, a procedure was put in place for harmonising national laws whose differences were preventing the establishment and functioning of the common market. Thirdly, a competition policy was set up to ensure that private market barriers and cartels did not undermine the prohibition on state barriers. Fourthly, state intervention in the economy, such as that in the form of state aids and public undertakings, was closely regulated. Fifthly, Member States' fiscal regimes on goods were regulated so that they could not discriminate against imports. Sixthly, a common commercial policy was established to regulate the Community's trade relations with third states. Finally, provision was made for more general cooperation in the field of economic policy in order that broader economic policy-making did not disrupt the common market.

A number of other policies were established. Arguably, the most famous is the Common Agricultural Policy. At the time, agriculture accounted for about 20 per cent of the European labour force and the memory of the severe deflation in the agricultural sector during the 1930s recession had led to considerable government intervention in the sector. A separate policy was, therefore, required in order to Europeanise the system of state intervention currently in place. A further policy included in the EEC Treaty was a common transport policy. As with agriculture, this required a separate heading due to the heavy intervention by states in their transport sectors. The EEC Treaty also contained a limited social policy, whose central feature was the establishment of a principle of equal pay for work of equal value for men and women.[23] Finally, an association policy was included to provide for the economic and social development of dependent or formerly dependent territories of the Member States.

The most remarkable feature of the EEC Treaty was the institutional arrangement set up to realise these objectives. There were four central institutions. The Commission, a body independent from the Member States, was responsible, inter alia, for proposing legislation and checking that the Member States and other institutions complied with the Treaty and any secondary legislation. The Assembly, later to develop into the European Parliament, was composed, initially, of national parliamentarians. It had the right to be consulted in most fields of legislative activity and was the body responsible for holding the Commission to account. The Council was

---

[22] The literature on the negotiations is voluminous. See E. di Nolfo (ed.), *Power in Europe? Britain, France, Germany, Italy, and the Origins of the EEC, 1952–1957* (Berlin and New York, de Gruyter, 1992); E. Serra (ed.), *The Relaunching of Europe and the Treaties of Rome* (Baden Baden, Nomos, 1989).

[23] C. Barnard, 'The Economic Objectives of Article 119' in T. Hervey and D. O'Keeffe (eds.), *Sex Equality Law in the European Union* (Chichester, John Wiley, 1996) 321, 322–4.

the body in which national governments were represented. It had the power of final decision in almost all areas of EEC activity. It voted by unanimity or (in only a few areas initially) by a weighted form of voting, known as Qualified Majority Voting (QMV). Finally, the European Court of Justice was established to monitor compliance with the Treaty. Matters could be brought before it, not only by the Member States but also by the supranational Commission, or be referred to it by national courts.

(iii) De Gaulle and the Luxembourg Accords

1958 marked not only the coming into force of the Treaties, but also Charles de Gaulle becoming President of France.[24] De Gaulle was well known for his opposition to the development of any supranational organisation and for his support for a Europe of nation-states, based upon intergovernmental cooperation. As early as 1961, De Gaulle attempted to subvert the supranational qualities of the EEC Treaty through the Fouchet Plan. This proposed a European Political Community whose remit would cover not only economic, but also political and social affairs. It would be based on intergovernmental cooperation, with each state retaining a veto. This failed to gain the support of the other Member States.[25] Tensions were raised further in 1963 when De Gaulle vetoed the accession of the United Kingdom which, along with Denmark, Norway and Ireland, had applied for membership in 1961.

Matters came to a head in 1965. The Commission had made three proposals: first, increased powers for the Assembly; secondly, a system of 'own resources' so that the Communities were financially independent and not dependent on national contributions; and finally, a series of financial regulations, which would allow the common agricultural policy to make progress. France favoured the third proposal, but was strongly opposed to the first two. The Commission insisted on a 'package deal', however, where Member States accepted either all or none. When negotiations broke down, the French walked out of the Council in June 1965, refusing to take part in further EEC business. De Gaulle came under considerable domestic criticism for this drastic move.[26] Yet the Commission was also perceived as having adopted a very high-handed approach. The crisis was eventually defused in January 1966 in Luxembourg, but in a way that would cast a shadow over the development of the EEC for the next twenty years. The Luxembourg Accords, as they came to be known, were an 'agreement to disagree'. If a Member State raised 'very important interests' before a vote in the Council was taken, it was agreed that the matter would not be put to a vote. In essence, it gave every Member State a veto in all fields of decision-making.

Whilst this veto was developed at the behest of France, once in place it was subsequently deployed equally freely by all the Member States.[27] 'Very important interests' were invoked at

---

[24] An excellent overview of this period is N. Ludlow, *The European Community and the Crises of the 1960s: Negotiating the Gaullist Challenge* (Abingdon, Routledge, 2006).

[25] P. Gerbet, 'The Fouchet Negotiations (1960–2)' in R. Pryce, *Dynamics of Political Union* (London, Croom Helm, 1987); N. Ludlow, 'Challenging French Leadership in Europe: Germany, Italy and the Netherlands and the Origins of the Empty Chair Crisis of 1965' (1999) 8 *Contemporary European History* 231.

[26] On De Gaulle's Europe see W. Loth (ed.), *Crises and Compromises: The European Project, 1963–9* (Baden Baden, Nomos, 2001); C. Parsons, *A Certain Idea of Europe* (Ithaca, NY, Cornell University Press, 2003).

[27] W. Nicholl, 'The Luxembourg Compromise' (1984) 23 *JCMS* 35. For a modern perspective see J.-M. Palavret *et al.* (eds.), *Visions, Votes and Vetoes: Reassessing the Luxembourg Compromise 40 Years On* (Brussels, Peter Lang, 2006).

every turn, even where the interest in question was insignificant.[28] This chilled the legislative process.[29] The Commission, aware of the need for the assent of all the Member States, became a passive body reluctant to generate controversy.

Despite this, significant institutional developments did take place. At the signing of the Treaty of Rome, the Convention relating to Certain Institutions Common to the European Communities established a single Court and a single Assembly for the three Communities. In 1963, it was agreed that the other institutions, the Council and the Commission, should be merged, and this took place with the Merger Treaty in 1965.[30] In 1970, the Communities were provided with their own budget and autonomous revenue stream with the Own Resources Decision.[31] Finally, it was agreed in 1976 that there should be direct elections for the European Parliament.[32] These were first held in 1979 and have since been held at five-year intervals.

(iv) Emergence of two visions of political authority

The most significant development to take place during this time was, however, in the Court of Justice. For it was here that an alternate vision of political community – a supranational one – was first developed. It took place in *Van Gend en Loos*, arguably the most important decision ever given by that institution and one of the most revolutionary ever given by a court. The facts were arcane. Van Gend en Loos was charged an import duty on chemicals imported from Germany by the Dutch authorities. It considered this to be in breach of what is now Article 30 TFEU, which prohibits customs duties or charges having equivalent effect being placed on the movement of goods between Member States. It sought to invoke the provisions in legal proceedings before a Dutch tax court, the Tariefcommissie. The question for the Court of Justice was whether a party could invoke and rely on provisions of Community law in proceedings before a national court. The Court's answer was that it could.[33]

Case 26/62 *Van Gend en Loos* v *Nederlandse Administratie der Belastingen* [1963] ECR 1

The first question of the Tariefcommissie is whether Article [30 TFEU] has direct application in national law in the sense that nationals of Member States may on the basis of this Article lay claim to rights which the national court must protect.

To ascertain whether the provisions of an international treaty extend so far in their effects it is necessary to consider the spirit, the general scheme and the wording of those provisions.

---

[28] In 1985, they were invoked by Germany to prevent a 1.8 per cent decrease in the price of colza, a cooking oil grain. M. Vasey, 'The 1985 Farm Price Negotiations and the Reform of the Common Agriculture Policy' (1985) 22 *CMLRev.* 649, 664–6.

[29] Legislative progress has taken longer to agree, paradoxically, where there was no possibility of veto. The Accords effect seems to have been therefore mainly on the Commission's willingness to make significant legislative proposals. J. Golub, 'In the Shadow of the Vote? Decision Making in the European Community' (1999) 53 *International Organization* 737.

[30] P.-H. Houben, 'The Merger of the Executives of the European Communities' (1965) 3 *CML Rev.* 37.

[31] Decision 70/243/EEC [1970] OJ English Spec. edn (I) 224.

[32] Decision 76/287/EEC [1976] OJ L278/1. Until 1979 it consisted of representatives of national Parliaments.

[33] Here we are concerned with what *Van Gend en Loos* tells us about European constitutional law in broad terms. The details of the Court's rulings as regards supremacy and as regards direct effect are considered more fully in Chapters 5 and 7, respectively.

The objective of the EEC Treaty, which is to establish a common market, the functioning of which is of direct concern to interested parties in the community, implies that this Treaty is more than an agreement which merely creates mutual obligations between the contracting States. This view is confirmed by the preamble to the Treaty which refers not only to governments but to peoples. It is also confirmed more specifically by the establishment of institutions endowed with sovereign rights, the exercise of which affects Member States and also their citizens. Furthermore, it must be noted that the nationals of the States brought together in the Community are called upon to cooperate in the functioning of this Community through the intermediary of the European Parliament and the Economic and Social Committee.

In addition the task assigned to the Court of Justice under Article [267 TFEU][34] the object of which is to secure uniform interpretation of the Treaty by national courts and tribunals, confirms that the States have acknowledged that Community law has an authority which can be invoked by their nationals before those courts and tribunals. The conclusion to be drawn from this is that the Community constitutes a new legal order of international law for the benefit of which the States have limited their sovereign rights, albeit within limited fields, and the subjects of which comprise not only Member States but also their nationals. Independently of the legislation of Member States, Community law therefore not only imposes obligations on individuals but is also intended to confer upon them rights which become part of their legal heritage. These rights arise not only where they are expressly granted by the Treaty, but also by reason of obligations which the Treaty imposes in a clearly defined way upon individuals as well as upon the Member States and upon the institutions of the Community.

There are two remarkable features about this terse, dense passage. The first is a claim about power. It is contained in the statement that: 'the Community constitutes a new legal order of international law for the benefit of which the States have limited their sovereign rights, albeit within limited fields'. This is a vision of the EU, legally at least, as a supranational organisation that exists not merely autonomously from the national legal orders but over and above them. For the Treaty has created not merely a legal order that is independent but also one claiming to be sovereign. And if legal sovereignty is understood to be a claim to ultimate legal authority then a reversal of traditional understandings of legal authority is being asserted. National legal systems no longer form the central building block for legal authority within Europe. Rather, legal authority flows from the Treaty with national legal systems having to adapt as sub-units to it.

The second is a claim about the nature of political community within Europe. It lies in the justification: the Treaty exists to benefit not merely the governments but also the peoples of Europe. This characterises the EU legal community as a wider, more plural legal community than other international legal communities. If traditional international law governs mutual obligations between states, EU law recognises other subjects: private parties, be they EU citizens, non-EU nationals or corporations. These are to hold a direct relationship with EU law through its conferring both rights and obligations on them. It suggests that the constituent power of the

---

[34] Article 267 TFEU (ex Article 234 EC) enables national courts and tribunals to refer questions of the interpretation of Community law to the Court of Justice. The relationships between national courts and the Court of Justice are considered in detail in Chapter 7.

European Union resides at least in part in the peoples of Europe themselves. That constituent power may use the intermediary of the state to confer authority on the European Union, but it does not necessarily have to. The Court in *Van Gend en Loos* does not say this explicitly, but it clearly suggests that the founding myth of the European Union may be legally constructed so that the Union may be seen as an agreement between the peoples of Europe that binds their governments, and not simply as an agreement between the governments of Europe that binds its peoples.

It is worth setting this vision alongside the vision of political community that was presented by De Gaulle, as they represent, in reality, the two poles between which European integration has been mediated. At a press conference on 15 May 1962, he declared:

> These ideas (supranationalism) might appeal to certain minds but I entirely fail to see how they could be put into practice, even with six signatures at the foot of a document. Can we imagine France, Germany, Italy, the Netherlands, Belgium, Luxembourg being prepared on matters of importance to them in the national or international sphere, to do something that appeared wrong to them, merely because others had ordered them to do so? Would the peoples of France, of Germany, of Italy, of the Netherlands, of Belgium, or of Luxembourg ever dream of submitting to laws passed by foreign parliamentarians if such laws run counter to their deepest convictions? Clearly not.[35]

It is too crude to see this view as an expression of nationalism for nationalism's sake or an unwillingness to share power. At its heart is a vision that democracy rests upon certain social and political institutions and forms of political community which must have a certain pedigree and strength if democracy is to be sustained. Currently, these qualities exist only at the level of the nation-state. On such a view, supranationalism – be it decisions of the Court of Justice, majority voting by national governments or proposals by the Commission – is invariably a threat to democracy insofar as it limits the autonomy and power of these national institutions, and has insufficient institutions and forms of political community of its own to fall back upon.[36]

The tension between these two visions of political authority and political community permeate in an ongoing manner nearly every chapter of this book. In the 1960s and 1970s, the vesting of one vision, the Gaullist one, in the political institutions through the Luxembourg Accords, and another one, that of a pan-European political community, in the Court of Justice, led to a highly unfortunate dynamic.[37] The Court gave a series of integrationist judgments, expanding its 'constitutional' jurisprudence, developing treaty-making powers for the Community, expanding the Treaty provisions on sex equality, the economic freedoms and the competition provisions. When juxtaposed with the inertia of the legislature, this led to the development of an unplanned deregulatory bias under which national policies were prohibited or tightly restricted by the Court, without there being any substitute EU legislation available to take their place.[38]

---

[35] This can be found in D. Weigall and P. Stirk, *The Origins and Development of the European Community* (Leicester, Leicester University Press, 1992) 134.

[36] One of the most articulate and scholarly expositions of this is D. Miller, *On Nationality* (Oxford, Oxford University Press, 1995).

[37] On how this manifested itself institutionally see J. Weiler, 'The Community System: The Dual Character of Supranationalism' (1981) 1 *YBEL* 267.

[38] F. Scharpf, 'Negative and Positive Integration in the Political Economy of European Welfare States' in G. Marks *et al.*, *Governance in the European Union* (London, Sage, 1996).

Yet if this tension can give rise to difficulties, others have noted that within it lies the European Union's uniqueness and genius: namely it has to confront these poles and resolve them in a way that creates a new type of legal authority and political community.

J. Weiler, 'In Defence of the Status Quo: Europe's Constitutional Sonderweg' in J. Weiler and M. Wind (eds.), *European Constitutionalism Beyond the State* (Cambridge, Cambridge University Press, 2003) 19–22

There are, it seems to me, two basic strategies for dealing with the alien ... One strategy is to remove the boundaries. It is the spirit of 'come, be one of us'. It is noble since it involves, of course, elimination of prejudice, of the notion that there are boundaries that cannot be eradicated. But the 'be one of us', however well intentioned, is often an invitation to the alien to be one of us, by being us. Vis-à-vis the alien, it risks robbing him of his identity. Vis-à-vis oneself, it may be a subtle manifestation of both arrogance and belief in my superiority as well as intolerance. If I cannot tolerate the alien, one way of resolving the dilemma is to make him like me, no longer an alien. This is, of course, infinitely better than the opposite: exclusion, repression, and worse. But it is still a form of dangerous internal and external intolerance.

The alternative strategy of dealing with the alien is to acknowledge the validity of certain forms of non-ethnic bounded identity but simultaneously to reach across boundaries. We acknowledge and respect difference, and what is special and unique about ourselves as individuals and groups; and yet we reach across differences in recognition of our essential humanity. What is significant in this are the two elements I have mentioned. On the one hand, the identity of the alien, as such, is maintained. One is not invited to go out and, say, 'save him' by inviting him to be one of us. One is not invited to recast the boundary. On the other hand, despite the boundaries which are maintained, and constitute the I and the Alien, one is commanded to reach over the boundary and accept him, in his allenship, as oneself. The alien is accorded human dignity. The soul of the I is tended to not by eliminating the temptation to oppress but by learning humility and overcoming it.

The European current constitutional architecture represents this alternative, civilizing strategy of dealing with the 'other'. Constitutional tolerance is encapsulated in that most basic articulation of its meta-political objective in the preamble to the EC Treaty ...: 'Determined to lay the foundations of an ever closer union among the *peoples* of Europe'. No matter how close the Union, it is to remain a union among distinct peoples, distinct political identities, distinct political communities. An ever closer union could be achieved by an amalgam of distinct peoples into one which is both the ideal and/or the de facto experience of most federal and non-federal states. The rejection by Europe of that One Nation ideal or destiny is ... intended to preserve the rich diversity, cultural and other, of the distinct European peoples ...

[I]n the Community, we subject the European peoples to constitutional discipline even though the European polity is composed of distinct peoples. It is a remarkable instance of civic tolerance to accept being bound by precepts articulated not by 'my people' but by a community composed of distinct political communities ...

Constitutional actors in the Member States accept the European constitutional discipline not because, as a matter of legal doctrine, as is the case in the federal state, they are subordinate to a higher sovereignty and authority attaching to norms validated by the federal people, the constitutional demos. They accept it as an autonomous voluntary act, endlessly renewed on each occasion, of subordination, in the discrete areas governed by Europe, to a norm which is the aggregate expression of other wills, other political identities, other political communities. Of course, to do so creates in itself a different type of political community, one unique feature of which is that very willingness to accept a binding discipline which is rooted in and derives from a community of others. The Quebecois are told: in the name of the people of Canada, you are obliged to obey. The French or the Italians or the Germans are told: in the name of the peoples of Europe, you are invited to obey ...

This process operates also at Community level. Think of the European judge or the European public official who must understand that, in the peculiar constitutional compact of Europe, his decision will take effect only if obeyed by national courts, if executed faithfully by a national public official with whom he belongs to a national administration which claims from them a particularly strong form of loyalty and habit. This, too, will instil a measure of caution and tolerance.

(v) The early enlargements

The United Kingdom was all too aware that the establishment of a common market left it economically isolated. Therefore, from 1956 onwards, it pushed for the establishment of a free trade area with other European States, which culminated in its setting up of the European Free Trade Area (EFTA) with Austria, Denmark, Norway, Sweden, Switzerland and Portugal in 1960. By 1961, however, states within the EEC were experiencing faster economic growth rates than Britain and the latter's failure to prevent South Africa's expulsion from the Commonwealth, following the Sharpeville massacres, brought home Britain's relative decline on the international stage.

As discussed earlier,[39] the French President, De Gaulle, vetoed the British entry in 1963. Four years later, the United Kingdom, plus Ireland, Denmark and Norway, reapplied. The application was once again vetoed by De Gaulle. This use of the veto left France increasingly isolated and French policy changed in 1969 with the resignation of De Gaulle. The Six agreed in the Hague to open negotiations with the applicants, with a view to extending membership. The United Kingdom, Denmark and Ireland formally became members on 1 January 1973.[40] However, following a referendum, where 53 per cent voted against membership, Norway did not accede to the EEC.

The next state to join was Greece. Greece applied for membership in 1975, following its establishment of a democratic government. Accession was attractive for both parties. For the Greeks, accession was not only economically attractive, but symbolised modernisation and democratic stability. For the Member States, Greece was important geo-politically during the Cold War because of its strategic location in the Aegean. Membership was, therefore, seen as tying Greece more firmly to the West. The Greek Act of Accession was completed in 1979, with Greece becoming a Member in 1981.

Like Greece, Spain and Portugal emerged from dictatorships and isolationism in the mid-1970s. They made applications to join the Communities only two years after Greece, in 1977.

---

[39] See p. 13.
[40] U. Kitzinger, *Diplomacy and Persuasion: How Britain Joined the Common Market* (London, Thames & Hudson, 1973); C. O'Neill, *Britain's Entry into the European Community, Report on the Negotiations of 1970–1972* (London, Frank Cass, 2000).

Yet, accession was more problematic in their cases. Whilst both saw the Community as a fulcrum through which to achieve economic modernisation and end their relative international isolation, the size of the agricultural sector in Spain resulted in initial French resistance to entry due to the likely negative effects on the French agricultural sector. It was, therefore, not until 1985 that an Act of Accession was signed, with Spain and Portugal becoming Members in 1986.

4 THE SINGLE EUROPEAN ACT AND BEYOND

(i) Run-up to the Single European Act

The recession of the early 1980s led national governments to confront their relative economic decline and prompted a relaunch of the integration process, as a way of combating this decline. A Solemn Declaration on European Union was adopted by the Heads of Government in 1983. This proposed few concrete reforms, but declared that there should be a 'renewed impetus' towards completion of the internal market, in particular the removal of obstacles to the free movement of goods, services and capital.[41]

This Declaration occurred against the backdrop of a number of significant developments. 1983 marked the collapse of the Keynesian economic policies which had been adopted in France. This collapse led to some convergence between national governments that economic policy-making had to focus on 'supply-side' measures which stimulated competition and trade. Market integration did both, and therefore fitted this new consensus.[42] Alongside this, since the 1970s, transnational pressure groups had begun to locate themselves in Brussels. The number of these groups expanded in the early 1980s, leading to the growth of an organised industrial constituency that was increasingly rallying for European solutions.[43] From the early 1980s onwards, major industrialists mobilised through organisations such as the European Round Table (ERT) and UNICE. These groups lobbied aggressively across Europe, arguing for the completion of the common market as a means of promoting European competitiveness.[44] Finally, direct elections had also produced a more aggressive European Parliament. Under the chairmanship of Alfiero Spinelli, it produced a draft Treaty on European Union, which proposed a fully federal Europe with common foreign, macro-economic and trade policies and a developed system of central institutions.[45]

---

[41] For critical comment see J. Weiler, 'The Genscher-Colombo Draft European Act: The Politics of Indecision' (1983) 6 *Journal of European Integration* 129.

[42] On the convergence of national government preferences see K. Middlemas, *Orchestrating Europe: The Informal Politics of European Union 1973–1995* (London, Fontana, 1995) 115–35; A. Moravcsik, *The Choice for Europe: Social Purpose and State Power from Messina to Maastricht* (Ithaca, NY, Cornell University Press, 1998) ch. 5; J. Gillingham, *European Integration 1950–2003: Superstate or New Market Economy* (Cambridge, Cambridge University Press, 2003) ch. 9.

[43] N. Fligstein and J. McNichol, 'The Institutional Terrain of the European Union' in W. Sandholtz and A. Stone Sweet (eds.), *European Integration and Supranational Governance* (Oxford, Oxford University Press, 1998) 59, 75–80; N. Fligstein and P. Brantley, 'The Single Market Program and the Interests of Business' in B. Eichengreen and J. Frieden (eds.), *Politics and Institutions in an Integrated Europe* (Berlin, Springer, 1995).

[44] W. Sandholtz and J. Zysman, '1992: Recasting the European Bargain' (1989) 42 *World Politics* 95, 116; M. Cowles, 'Setting the Agenda for a New Europe: The ERT and EC 1992' (1995) 33 *JCMS* 527; Middlemas, above n. 42, 136–40.

[45] [1984] OJ C77/33. For comment, see R. Bieber *et al.*, *An Ever Closer Union: A Critical Analysis of the Draft Treaty Establishing the European Union* (Luxembourg, Office for Official Publications of the European Communities, 1985).

These developments all pressed towards further European integration, but were fragmented and uncoordinated. The final piece in the jigsaw fell into place with the appointment of a new Commission in late 1984, headed by the charismatic former French Finance Minister, Jacques Delors. Delors, in lobbying for the post, had already seized upon the goal of market unity as the principal task of the new Commission to be achieved by the end of 1992. In November 1984, he gave the national governments four choices for recapturing momentum: monetary policy, foreign policy and defence, institutional reform or the internal market.[46] All agreed that the internal market was the way forward.

The Commission was instructed by the Member States to consider the practical steps necessary to realise this. In truth, the idea had been kicking around the Commission for a few years. In 1981, the German Commissioner, Karl-Heinz Narjes, had looked into the idea of creating an 'internal market' in which there were no barriers to the exchange of goods, services and labour, but this had met with opposition from the French Government in 1982.[47] The new British Commissioner, Lord Cockfield, took up Narjes' work, and in June 1985, presented the White Paper on Completion of the Internal Market to the Heads of Government at Milan.[48] The paper was a clever piece of work, suggesting that 279 measures were necessary to realise the internal market. Member States were not, therefore, committing themselves to an open-ended set of obligations, but to a finite and limited project. The project was also cast as largely a technical mission rather than having broader panoramas of greater integration.[49] For all this, the goal of the internal market was unattainable whilst unanimity voting prevailed in the Council. Any change in this was firmly opposed by Britain, Denmark and Greece. Notwithstanding this, the Italian government called for a conference to amend the Treaties. Despite their opposing stance, all three states attended. The result was the signing of the Single European Act in 1986.

(ii) The Single European Act

The principal achievements of the SEA appeared limited and modest at the time. They were described as a victory for minimalism,[50] and both the Commission and the Parliament were relaxed about the Act.[51] Much of the SEA was therefore about giving formal recognition to pre-existing policies and institutions. Provision was made for express competences in health and safety at work, economic and social cohesion, research and development and environmental protection. A Title was added on European Cooperation in the Sphere of Foreign Policy codifying intergovernmental cooperation in foreign policy. The European Council, the meetings of Heads of Government, was formally acknowledged.[52] However, there had been regular summits from 1961 and it was agreed in 1974 that these should meet twice a year to discuss

---

[46] Middlemas, above n. 42, 141.

[47] N. Fligstein and I. Mara-Drita, 'How to Make a Market: Reflections on the Attempt to Create a Single Market in the European Union' (1996) 102 *American Journal of Sociology* 1, 11–13.

[48] European Commission, *Completing the Internal Market*, COM(85)310 final.

[49] W. Sandholtz and J. Zysman, '1992: Recasting the European Bargain' (1989) 42 *World Politics* 95, 114–15.

[50] G. Bermann, 'The Single European Act: A New Constitution for the European Community?' (1989) 27 *Columbia Journal of Transnational Law* 529; A. Moravcsik, 'Negotiating the Single European Act' (1991) 45 *IO* 19.

[51] C.-D. Ehlermann, 'The Internal Market Following the Single European Act' (1987) 24 *CMLRev.* 361.

[52] Article 2 SEA. On the early evolution of the European Council, see S. Bulmer, 'The European Council's First Decade: Between Interdependence and Domestic Politics' (1985) 23 *JCMS* 89; S. Bulmer and W. Wessels, *The European Council* (London, Macmillan, 1987); J. Werts, *The European Council* (North Holland, Elsevier, 1992).

internal difficulties within the European Communities, broader issues about the future of European integration, and the place of the European Communities in the world order.

There were two reforms, which marked the SEA as possibly the most significant institutional reform of them all. The first was the commitment to establish the internal market by 31 December 1992. The internal market is now set out in Article 26(2) TFEU:

> The internal market shall comprise an area without internal frontiers in which the free movement of goods, persons, services and capital is ensured in accordance with the provisions of the Treaties.

The second was institutional reform to realise this objective. A new legislative procedure, the cooperation procedure, was introduced, which provided for qualified majority voting (QMV) in the Council and increased powers for the European Parliament.[53]

Neither reform seemed particularly radical at the time. The internal market project seemed to be no more than a restatement of the old dream of establishing a common market. In fact, it seemed a paler version, as it was unclear whether it extended to policies clearly caught by the common market, such as competition policy, commercial policy, non-discrimination and economic policy.[54] The new voting procedures did not apply to core areas such as taxation and freedom of persons, and its effect upon the Luxembourg Accords was uncertain, particularly as the United Kingdom, Greece and Denmark insisted upon a Declaration being appended to the SEA claiming that nothing within it affected Member States' rights to invoke the Accords.

However, the SEA confounded expectations and brought about the most radical change in the history of the European Union's fortunes. It changed both the legislative and political culture of the Union. In legislative terms, Member States became less tolerant of each others' attempts to invoke the Luxembourg Accords. This was reflected in the 1987 Council Decision on the 'vote to go to a vote', where it was agreed that if a simple majority of Member States voted to go to a formal vote, then a vote should be taken.[55]

The legislative processes became energised. By the end of 1990, all the measures contained in the White Paper had been formally proposed by the Commission.[56] By the end of 1992, almost 95 per cent of the measures had been enacted and 77 per cent had entered into force in the Member States.[57] Alongside this, the Commission had vastly understated the legislative output of the European Communities. Legislative output increased to 2,500 binding acts per year by 1994;[58] 53 per cent of the legislative measures adopted in France in 1991 were inspired by its Treaty obligations and 30 per cent of all Dutch legislation during the early 1990s implemented EU legislation.[59]

---

[53] This legislative procedure no longer exists as it has been completely superseded by the co-decision procedure.

[54] P. Pescatore, 'Some Critical Remarks on the Single European Act' (1987) 24 *CMLRev.* 9, 11.

[55] Council Rules of Procedure, art. 5 [1987] OJ L291/27.

[56] *Twenty Fourth Report on the General Activities of the European Communities 1990* (Luxembourg, Office for Official Publications of the European Communities, 1991) 53. For an insight into how the Commission operated during this period see G. Ross, *Jacques Delors and European Integration* (London, Polity, 1995).

[57] *Twenty Sixth General Report on the Activities of the European Communities 1992* (Luxembourg, Office for Official Publications of the European Communities, 1993) 35.

[58] W. Wessels, 'An Ever Closer Fusion? A Dynamic Macropolitical View on Integration Processes' (1997) 35 *JCMS* 267, 276.

[59] G. Mancini, 'Europe: The Case for Statehood' (1998) 4 *ELJ* 29, 40.

(iii) The road to Maastricht

This transformation in law-making discussed above brought about a change in political culture. As the technical façade of the White Paper was exposed, highly divisive questions became more salient. These included such matters as the relationship between state and market, the role of central government actors and the appropriate method to regulate non-economic public goods, such as public health or the environment.[60]

This led to tensions on three fronts: all were opposed by the British Government, which perceived them as interventionist and centralising.

The first front concerned the degree of regulation needed to complete the internal market. In a speech to the European Parliament in July 1988, the Commission President, Jacques Delors, observed that it could lead to 80 per cent of Member State economic legislation being passed as Community law. The second front concerned the social dimension of the EC. From 1986, the Commission tried to link the development of a Community social policy to the realisation of the internal market, on the grounds that some harmonisation of social legislation was necessary for the attainment of the latter. In May 1989, the Commission proposed a Community Charter of Fundamental Social Rights. This was adopted by all of the Member States, apart from Britain, at the Strasbourg European Council in December 1989.[61]

The third front was economic and monetary union (EMU). As early as 1987, the Commission indicated that due to the uncertainty generated by national currency stability, the gain anticipated for the single market could not be fully realised without some form of economic and monetary union.[62] Insofar as it was perceived to contribute to monetary stability, it also tied in with the anti-inflationary policies adopted by most Member States.[63] Monetary union was also a Trojan horse. It fitted with the aspirations of those, notably President Mitterand of France and President Kohl of Germany, who saw 1992 as being the cantilever to open the door to greater political integration. The question of economic and monetary union was, therefore, placed on the agenda of the Hanover Summit, in June 1988. At Hanover, the Heads of State asserted that 'the Single European Act confirmed the objective of progressive realisation of economic and monetary union'.[64] The Delors Committee, a committee of central bank governors chaired by the Commission President, Jacques Delors, was mandated to examine the concrete steps required to realise this goal.

In June 1989, the Delors Report on economic and monetary union was submitted to the Heads of State in Madrid.[65] This Report suggested a gradualist approach to monetary union, which was to be completed in three stages. The first stage should consist of achievement of the internal market, liberalisation of all capital movements and all Member States becoming members of the Exchange Rate Mechanism. The second stage required the establishment of an independent European Central Bank, convergence of national economies and a gradual

---

[60] J. Weiler, 'The Transformation of Europe' (1991) 100 *Yale Law Journal* 2403, 2477; R. Dehousse, 'Integration v. Regulation? On the Dynamics of Regulation in the Community' (1992) 30 *JCMS* 383.

[61] Conclusions of Strasbourg European Council, *EC Bulletin* 12–1989, 1.1.1.

[62] T. Padoa-Schipoa *et al.*, *Efficiency, Stability and Equity: A Strategy for the Evolution of the Economic System of the European Community* (Oxford, Oxford University Press, 1987).

[63] W. Sandholtz, 'Choosing Union: Monetary Politics and Maastricht' (1993) 47 *IO* 1.

[64] Conclusions of Hanover European Council, *EC Bulletin* 6–1988, 1.1.1–1.1.5.

[65] Conclusions of Madrid European Council, *EC Bulletin* 6–1989, 1.1.11.

assumption of the national central bank functions by the European Central Bank. The final stage would necessitate the European Central Bank fully taking over national central bank functions and assuming a monopoly over the money supply.[66] Faced with the opposition of all the other Member States and the threatened resignation of both her Chancellor of the Exchequer and Foreign Secretary, Mrs Thatcher grudgingly adopted the Report and it was agreed that the first stage should begin on 1 July 1990. The outmanoeuvring of Mrs Thatcher was completed at Strasbourg, where it was agreed that an intergovernmental conference should be held to amend the Treaties, with a view to economic and monetary union.

Presidents Kohl and Mitterand, the German and French Presidents, considered that economic and monetary union would not be sustainable without further political integration, and launched an initiative to that effect in April 1990.[67] In June 1990, it was agreed that a separate conference should be held on political union.[68] They culminated in the signing of the Treaty on European Union, at Maastricht, on 10 December 1991.[69]

5 THE TREATY ON EUROPEAN UNION

(i) A tripartite institutional settlement

The Treaty on European Union (TEU) was a very different Treaty from the SEA. If the latter required considerable legal integration, this was simply the byproduct of the establishment of an internal market. The TEU marked very definitely a change in tone. It created a new form of political project, which included, to be sure, an amount of arcane detail, but also marked out a new form of polity, which has its own set of political values and political communities. This shift is reflected in the first article of the current TEU, which builds on and rearticulates what was agreed at Maastricht.

> **Article 1 TEU**
>
> By this Treaty, the HIGH CONTRACTING PARTIES establish among themselves a EUROPEAN UNION, hereinafter called 'the Union' on which the Member States confer competences to attain objectives they have in common.
>
> This Treaty marks a new stage in the process of creating an ever closer union among the peoples of Europe, in which decisions are taken as openly as possible and as closely as possible to the citizen.

---

[66] The German Central Bank, the Bundesbank, applied strong pressure for the Report to follow the German model of monetary policy-making as the price for its support. It was also adamant that the transition should be a gradual one. M. Artis, 'The Maastricht Road to Monetary Union' (1992) 30 *JCMS* 299.

[67] On the Franco-German role in the negotiations leading to Maastricht see C. Mazzucelli, *France and Germany at Maastricht: Politics and Negotiations to Create the European Union* (New York, Garland, 1997).

[68] Conclusions of the Dublin European Council, *EC Bulletin* 6–1990, 1.11. Political union was added as an afterthought to economic and monetary union and negotiations were not well prepared. R. Corbett, 'The Intergovernmental Conference on Political Union' (1992) 30 *JCMS* 271.

[69] The most detailed analysis of the negotiations is F. Laursen and S. Vanhoonacker, *The Intergovernmental Conference on Political Union: Institutional Reforms, New Policies and International Identity of the European Community* (Dordrecht, Martinus Nijhoff, 1992).

The Commission and the Parliament pressed for the Union to be governed by a single institutional, supranational structure. In two fields, a practice of intergovernmental cooperation had emerged that was to prove difficult to displace. The first was foreign policy. All Member States, other than the Belgians and the Dutch, wanted to keep it this way and were opposed to bringing foreign and defence policy within the EC supranational framework. The second field was that of Justice and Home Affairs, a ragbag field focused on combating international crime and policing asylum and migration of non-EU nationals. In 1985 and 1990, two agreements were signed at Schengen, in Luxembourg, between all the Member States, excluding Ireland and the United Kingdom.[70] These Conventions provided for the abolition of frontier checks between parties and a common external frontier. To realise this, the 1990 Convention provided for intergovernmental cooperation in the fields of migration of non-EU nationals, crime and policing. Whilst many Member States wanted to see this brought within the EC framework, the British, Irish, Greeks and Danes were adamant that this was an area where the national veto should be maintained.

The Union was, therefore, to be composed of three pillars. The first was that of the European Community, the second, Common Foreign and Security Policy (CFSP), and the third, Justice and Home Affairs (JHA).[71] These three pillars were, in principle, to constitute a single institutional framework.[72] The overarching, unitary provisions were weak, however. There was a unitary legal framework in that any understanding of one pillar could only be had by reference to the TEU as a whole.[73] Beyond that, only two provisions united the three pillars. The European Council was given a pre-eminent, coordinating role for all three pillars. Its position as the body with ultimate political authority and the body which was responsible for visioning and coordinating all EU activities was, for the first time, formalised.[74] In addition, the unique position of the Member States and the commitment to respect fundamental rights were recognised as a constituent element of each pillar.[75]

The institutional balance within each pillar was, however, very different. The Parliament and the Court of Justice were only minimally associated with either the second or third pillars.[76] If the EC pillar was characterised by some parliamentary and judicial controls, these were largely absent at either a national or EU level and, instead, were to be dominated by executive government. Whilst the Commission was associated quite strongly with the work of the third pillar on Justice and Home Affairs, it was almost completely excluded from the second pillar. Even between the two intergovernmental pillars, there was a mismatch, with one being more clearly Europeanised than the other. The question of legal personality was also mixed. The EC had had legal personality since 1957, and retained this. By contrast, the European Union was to have no legal personality. Whilst the EC had treaty-making powers in its field of competence, there was no equivalent power in the fields of CFSP and JHA.[77]

---

[70] This is now to be found at [2000] OJ 2000 L239/19. Iceland and Norway are also associated members.

[71] Allegedly, the idea was first suggested by a French negotiator, Pierre de Boissieu, and was constructed around the metaphor of a temple based on three pillars, Middlemas, above n. 42, 188.

[72] Article 3 TEU (M).

[73] A. v. Bogdandy and M. Nettesheim, 'Ex Pluribus Unum: Fusion of the European Communities into the European Union' (1996) 2 *ELJ* 267, 279–81; D. Curtin and I. Dekker, 'The EU as a Layered International Organization: Institutional Unity in Disguise' in P. Craig and G. de Búrca (eds.), *The Evolution of EU Law* (Oxford, Oxford University Press, 1999).

[74] Article 4 TEU (M).

[75] Article 6 TEU(M).

[76] For a reassertion of this see Case C-160/03 *Spain* v *Eurojust* [2005] ECR I-2077.

[77] D. Curtin, 'The Constitutional Structure of the Union: A Europe of Bits and Pieces' (1993) 30 *CMLRev.* 17.

There was a political price to be paid for these three pillars: a commitment to a further IGC to reconsider this in 1996.

(ii) The new competences

The EC was granted express competences in the fields of visas for non-EU nationals, education, culture, public health, consumer protection, the establishment of trans-European networks in transport, energy and telecommunications, industrial policy and development cooperation. There were two fields which evoked particular controversy.

The first was economic and monetary union. The Treaty followed the three stage structure of the Delors Report, with the third stage of economic and monetary union beginning on 1 January 1999.[78] Economic and monetary union allocated responsibility for various aspects of economic policy to different institutions. The third stage involved monetary policy becoming the responsibility of an independent European Central Bank, established in Frankfurt, which was to be exclusively responsible for authorising the issue of the new European currency, the euro, and for the setting of short-term interest rates. Constraints were also to be placed on national fiscal policy through the limiting of the size of the deficits that governments could run. A procedure was established: the excessive deficit procedure, whereby governments participating in the euro could be heavily penalised if they ran an excessive deficit. This proved too constraining for two Member States, Denmark and the United Kingdom, and Protocols were agreed reserving their right not to participate in the third stage of EMU.

The other area to prove particularly problematic was that of social policy. There was strong support amongst all Member States, apart from Britain, for an extension of the social policy provisions to all areas of labour law and social protection for workers. The British government opposed this on the grounds that this was purely a matter of national concern and it did not fit in with that government's views of a deregulated labour market. The compromise was a Protocol, which authorised all the Member States, apart from the United Kingdom, to establish an Agreement on Social Policy that would bind only those Member States, but would allow them access to existing EU machinery and resources.

(iii) The quest for Union 'democracy'

As there was a sense of putting a new political system in place, Maastricht gave far more serious consideration to the 'democratic' nature of the European Union and its need to seek political legitimacy. A variety of strategies were introduced.

The first was to increase parliamentary input into the legislative processes. A new legislative procedure was introduced, the co-decision procedure, which gave the European Parliament more powers by allowing it, in certain sectors, to veto legislation. The place of national parliaments was recognised for the first time, albeit in a fairly minimal manner. A Declaration was attached to the TEU committing governments to greater involvement of their national parliaments in the integration process and to ensuring these receive legislative proposals in

---

[78] It was initially envisaged that the third stage could begin as early as 31 December 1996 if the convergence criteria were met by sufficient Member States, Article 109j(3) EC. At the Cannes Summit, in 1995, it was agreed that the date for the third stage should be 1 January 1999, *EU Bulletin* 6–1995, 1.11.

good time. Alongside this, there was an attempt to pluralise the decision-making process. New stakeholders were introduced, most notably the Committee of the Regions which, whilst only being given consultative powers, created a voice for the European regions within the Community policy process.

The TEU was also concerned with administrative accountability. To that end, an Ombudsman was established to consider acts of maladministration by the EU institutions. Provision was also made for considering whether the decision-making procedures could be made more transparent and, for the first time, the question of freedom of information was formally acknowledged.

Most symbolic of the sentiment that a new centre for democratic participation was being created was the institution of European Union citizenship. Citizens were granted new rights to free movement and to access to social benefits in other Member States. New possibilities for democratic participation at both local and European level were created. European citizenship also created new patterns of inclusion and exclusion between Europeans and non-Europeans, insofar as these rights were only granted to Member State nationals as EU citizens. Most controversially, citizenship has traditionally been used to foster new political allegiances, as it suggests a common political identity between its members, which to some seemed to compete with that claimed by the nation-state.

The democratic turn, however, was not just about strengthening the credentials of the centre. By the time the TEU was signed, the European Union was churning out more legislation, more intensely, in more fields, than ever before. This was placing unheralded pressures on national, regional and local government. There were also concerns as to how to police and limit the activities of the Union. We have seen how special arrangements were put in place for the United Kingdom in social policy and for it and Denmark in EMU. As well as these, other Member States began to ring-fence their laws. Ireland and Denmark, thus, respectively obtained Protocols protecting their abortion law and legislation on ownership of second homes from EU law. To manage these tensions more generally, a new principle was introduced: the subsidiarity principle. In areas where both it and the Member States had powers, the Union was only to act if the objectives of the proposed action could not be sufficiently achieved by the Member States and by reason of its scale or effects the action could be better achieved by the Community.

6 THE 1990s: THE DECADE OF SELF-DOUBT

(i) Ratification of the Treaty on European Union

On 2 June 1992, the Danes voted against ratification of the TEU by 50.7 to 49.3 per cent. This shook the process to the core as the Treaty could not enter into effect unless all Member States ratified it. To boost the credibility of the ratification process, President Mitterand decided to hold a referendum in France. Although an easy 'yes' vote had been predicted, it soon became a very close contest, with only 51 per cent of the vote being in favour of ratification. The Treaty was salvaged at Edinburgh, in December 1992. The other Member States considered the Treaty to be non-negotiable, but something had to be done to allow the Danish government to say that the Treaty it was proposing for a second referendum was substantially different from the initial Treaty. The route taken was a Decision 'interpreting' the Treaty giving the Danish government guarantees about the autonomy of its citizenship and defence as well as setting out in more detail the subsidiarity principle.[79] This gave the Danish government the necessary breadth to hold a second referendum. This was duly held in May 1993, with 56 per cent voting in favour of ratification.

However, the damage had been done. The political aura of inevitable integration and the assumption of popular support for it had been tarnished. The first Danish referendum signalled the beginning of a bitter legislative fight in the British Parliament, in which ratification was fought for by both the British Labour Party and a minority of the then ruling Conservative party. The legislation was only adopted in July 1993 – a year and a half after the Treaty had been agreed – and only after the government had put a gun to its rebels' heads, by passing it as a motion of confidence, with the consequence that if it had fallen, the government would have had to resign.[80]

The drama of ratification of the Treaty was now re-enacted in the courts. Challenges to the Treaty were made before the British, French, Danish and Spanish courts.[81] It was the challenge before the German Constitutional Court, in October 1993, which was to have the most far-reaching consequences.[82] In its judgment, the German Constitutional Court placed markers on the nature and limits of European integration. It ruled that democratic legitimacy is constituted above all at a national level. Within this setting, the constitutionality of the European Union rests on its being an organisation with limited powers operated in a democratically account-able fashion. Further integration would only be possible if it did not fundamentally undermine national self-government.

The TEU entered into force on 1 November 1993 but the environment was now heavily polarised. Public support for the European Union had diminished[83] and deep divisions had emerged between national governments about which direction to take.[84] Member States had, however, committed themselves at Maastricht to a further IGC in 1996.[85] Negotiations only began in earnest in the latter half of 1996 with the Irish government presenting a draft Treaty to the other Member States in December 1996.[86] The Treaty of Amsterdam was signed on 2 October 1997.

---

[79] D. Howarth, 'The Compromise on Denmark and the Treaty on European Union: A Legal and Political Analysis' (1994) 31 *CMLRev.* 465.

[80] R. Rawlings, 'Legal Politics: The United Kingdom and Ratification of the Treaty on European Union' (1994) *PL* 254 and 367; D. Baker, A. Gamble and S. Ludlum, 'The Parliamentary Siege of Maastricht: Conservative Divisions and British Ratification' (1994) 47 *Parliamentary Affairs* 37.

[81] *R* v *Secretary of State for Foreign and Commonwealth Affairs, ex parte Rees-Mogg* [1994] QB 552 (Britain); *Re Treaty on European Union* (Decision 92–308), Journel Officiel de la République Française 1992, 5354 (France); *Re Treaty on European Union* [1994] 3 CMLR 101 (Spain).

[82] *Brunner* v *European Union* [1994] 1 CMLR 57.

[83] Opinion polls showed that those who considered the European Union a 'good thing' had dropped from 72 per cent in 1990 to 48 per cent in autumn 1996. Eurobarometer, *Public Opinion in the EU*, Report No. 46, Autumn 1996 (Luxembourg, Office for Official Publications of the European Communities, 1997).

[84] A summary of all the positions taken by the Member States at the 1996 Intergovernmental Conference can be found at http://europa.eu.int/en/agenda/igc-home/ms-doc.

[85] See p. 25.

[86] Conference of the Representatives of the Governments of the Member States, *The European Union Today and Tomorrow: Adopting the European Union for the Benefit of Its Peoples and Preparing It for the Future, A General Outline for a Draft Revision of the Treaties*, CONF 2500/96.

(ii) The Treaty of Amsterdam

(a) The Area of Freedom, Security and Justice

If the central monuments of the SEA and Maastricht were the internal market and EMU, respectively, then the Area of Freedom, Security and Justice (AFSJ) occupied a similar place for the Treaty of Amsterdam. The AFSJ is now set out in the following terms.

Article 67 TFEU

1. The Union shall constitute an area of freedom, security and justice with respect for fundamental rights and the different legal systems and traditions of the Member States.
2. It shall ensure the absence of internal border controls for persons and shall frame a common policy on asylum, immigration and external border control, based on solidarity between Member States, which is fair towards third-country nationals. For the purpose of this Title, stateless persons shall be treated as third-country nationals.
3. The Union shall endeavour to ensure a high level of security through measures to prevent and combat crime, racism and xenophobia, and through measures for coordination and cooperation between police and judicial authorities and other competent authorities, as well as through the mutual recognition of judgments in criminal matters and, if necessary, through the approximation of criminal laws.
4. The Union shall facilitate access to justice, in particular through the principle of mutual recognition of judicial and extrajudicial decisions in civil matters.

To realise the AFSJ, the Treaty of Amsterdam first integrated the Schengen Agreements into the legal framework of the TEU. A Protocol Integrating the Schengen Acquis into the framework of the European Union was adopted, which made the Schengen Acquis part of EU law.[87] Secondly, the AFSJ reallocated decision-making between the first and third pillars. Immigration, asylum and the rights of non-EU nationals were brought within EC legislative competences, whilst policing and judicial cooperation on criminal matters remained subject to the predominantly intergovernmental procedures of the third pillar. Finally, the AFSJ re-oriented the EU more explicitly around certain ideals. This was marked most strongly in the new Article 6 TEU, which stated that the Union was to be founded on the 'principles of liberty, democracy, respect for human rights and fundamental freedoms, and the rule of law'. These ideals were further institutionalised in two ways First, the EC acquired a general legislative competence to combat discrimination on grounds that related to sex, race or ethnic origin, religion or belief, disability, age or sexual orientation. Secondly, provision was made for a Member State to have its rights suspended under the TEU or to be expelled from the European Union, where it was deemed that the Member State had seriously and persistently breached these ideals.

---

[87] The acquis is the name for the existing body of law that has been adopted up until now, in this instance under the Schengen procedures.

(b) Further supranational 'democratisation'

The Treaty of Amsterdam led to a significant extension of QMV. It was the first time a majority of legal bases now provided for QMV.[88] Qualitatively, QMV was extended to important new fields, including employment, countering social exclusion, equality of opportunity and treatment for men and women, public health, transparency, fraud and freedom of establishment. In terms of parliamentary accountability, it also led to a considerable extension of the European Parliament's powers. The scope of the co-decision procedure was extended considerably. The European Parliament was also, for the first time, given some involvement in the third pillar. Alongside this, more attention was paid to the role of national parliaments within the integration process. A Protocol on National Parliaments was adopted, which extended their guarantees. All consultation documents would now be sent to them and there would be a six-week period between proposals being announced and their being placed on the legislative agenda, in order to allow national parliaments to consider them. Administrative accountability was strengthened by the principle of transparency being formally incorporated into the EC Treaty with a qualified right of access to EC documents being granted to every citizen of the Union and natural or legal person having its registered office in a Member State.

(c) Differentiated integration

A new Title on Employment was added to the EC Treaty and, with a change of government in the United Kingdom, the Protocol on Social Policy was abolished, and social policy was placed on the same footing as all other first pillar policies. However, Amsterdam was more noteworthy for reflecting the multiplicity of tensions surrounding the pace, direction and form of European integration that had emerged since Maastricht. A Protocol on the Application of the Principles of Subsidiarity and Proportionality was agreed, which entrenched in Treaty law the Declarations agreed at Edinburgh that had enabled Denmark to hold a second referendum on the Maastricht Treaty.

It was clear, however, that a 'one size fits all' approach was becoming harder to manage as disagreements about the fields and intensity of the integration process became more entrenched. Provision was made, therefore, for a majority of Member States to engage, as a last resort, in 'enhanced cooperation':[89] adoption of EU laws amongst themselves where agreement was not possible involving all the EU Member States. Alongside this, country specific opt-outs proliferated at Amsterdam. The United Kingdom and Ireland obtained Protocols preserving their right to decide whether to opt-in to individual pieces of legislation on immigration, asylum and other policies concerning free movement of persons, as well as Protocols preserving their rights to impose frontier controls on persons coming from other Member States. In like vein, Denmark negotiated a Protocol stating that it would only be bound by such legislation under its general obligations in international law, as a Schengen signatory, and not by virtue of EU law.

There were also a series of soft opt-outs. A Protocol had been adopted which established a presumption of no asylum for EU nationals in other Member States. Belgium adopted a Declaration stating it would not follow this presumption but would treat each case on its merits.

---

[88] A. Maurer, 'The Legislative Powers and Impact of the European Parliament' (2003) 41 *JCMS* 227, 229.
[89] See pp. 113–16 for more detail on this.

Germany, Luxembourg and Austria sought Declarations in a different field. These states were concerned that their systems of public banking might be compromised by EU competition law, and therefore sought Declarations to the contrary.

7 RECASTING THE BORDERS OF THE EUROPEAN UNION

The shape of the European Union was modified by two events at the end of the 1980s. The success of the SEA entailed that exclusion from the world's largest trading bloc posed significant economic risks for neighbouring states. At the same time, communism collapsed in Central and Eastern Europe. Many states, previously antagonistic to the European Union, now embraced the market-orientated ideals it symbolised and saw membership as the anchor around which changes in their societies could be made.

The process of expansion began with the EFTA states (Norway, Sweden, Finland, Iceland, Austria, Liechtenstein and Switzerland). In 1991, the Treaty of Oporto was signed, establishing the European Economic Area (EEA).[90] The EFTA states were required to adopt all EU legislation in the fields of the internal market, research and development policy, social policy, education, consumer protection and environmental protection in return for access to the internal market.

In June 1993, the European Union agreed that membership be offered to Austria, Finland, Sweden and Norway.[91] Referendums were necessary in all four states prior to accession. In Austria and Finland, comfortable majorities voted in favour of membership. However, that in Sweden was narrow. The Norwegians voted narrowly against membership. The three new Member States acceded to the TEU on 2 January 1995.

More challenging was the question of possible membership of the former communist states of Central and Eastern Europe. By the early 1990s, twelve of these states had applied for membership.[92] This would almost double the size of the Union, with a corresponding reduction of political influence for existing Member States. It would create a financial burden on current members as the applicants were poorer than the Western European states and many had large agricultural populations, which could press claims for support from the EU Budget. Nevertheless, in Lisbon 1992, the European Union stated that any European state whose government was based on the principle of democracy could apply to accede.[93] A year later, at Copenhagen, the European Union went a step further and agreed that the states of Central and Eastern Europe could become members of the European Union once able to satisfy the obligations of membership. These obligations required new states to have:

- stable institutions guaranteeing democracy, the rule of law, human rights and respect for and protection of minorities;

---

[90] Although Switzerland signed the Treaty, following a referendum it decided not to ratify it. In 2002, agreements were signed between the European Union and Switzerland in the fields of free movement of persons, agriculture, transport, public procurement, mutual recognition and scientific and technological cooperation [2002] OJ L114/1. The most detailed analysis of the Treaty can be found in T. Blanchet *et al.*, *The Agreement on the European Economic Area* (Oxford, Clarendon Press, 1994).

[91] M. Jorna, 'The Accession Negotiations with Austria, Finland, Sweden and Norway: A Guided Tour' (1995) 20 *ELRev.* 131; F. Granell, 'The European Union's Enlargement Negotiations with Austria, Finland, Norway and Sweden' (1995) 33 *JCMS* 117.

[92] These were Bulgaria, Cyprus, the Czech Republic, Estonia, Hungary, Latvia, Lithuania, Malta, Poland, Romania, Slovenia and Slovakia.

[93] Conclusions of the Lisbon European Council, *EC Bulletin* 6-1992, 1.4.

- a functioning market economy as well as the capacity to cope with competitive pressures and market forces within the Union;
- the ability to assume the obligations of membership, including both adherence to the aims of the Union and adoption of all existing EU legislation;
- the legislative and administrative capacity to transpose EU legislation into national legislation and to implement it effectively through appropriate administrative and judicial structures.[94]

In 1994, it was agreed that a 'structured relationship' should be established between the European Union and the countries of Central and Eastern Europe to prepare the latter for membership. In July 1997, following the Treaty of Amsterdam, the Commission stepped up the process with the launch of its 2000 Agenda programme. In a 1,300 page document, it assessed how far the applicant states met the criteria agreed in Copenhagen. On the basis of that progress report, it recommended the opening of membership negotiations with the Czech Republic, Poland, Hungary, Slovenia, Estonia and Cyprus, with a view to accession by 2003. The discussions began in March 1998. However, limiting negotiations to a selection of applicant states proved hopelessly divisive, and in January 2000, Bulgaria, Romania, Latvia, Lithuania, Malta and Slovakia were also invited to participate. Between 1997 and 2002, the Commission published annual reports on each applicant. In Copenhagen, in December 2002, the Member States agreed that all these states, other than Bulgaria and Romania, should become Members of the European Union from 1 May 2004. These latter two states acceded to the Union on 1 January 2007, bringing membership of the Union to twenty-seven.

The expansion of the European Union from twelve states to twenty-seven in just over twelve years has not simply made the Union bigger. It has also transformed it. It can now claim to be an organisation that is genuinely pan-European rather than predominantly West European. A corollary of this is considerable diversity. Economically, the GDP per capita (even after rescaling it to account for purchasing power parity) of Luxembourg is seven times that of Bulgaria.[95] There are also significant differences in legal and political culture. Traditionally, trust in the new Member States in democratic institutions, political parties, trade unions and private enterprises is low. There are also lower levels of civic responsibility but higher levels of solidarity with the socio-economically disadvantaged.[96] This is not to be decried but, inevitably, reshapes the common political and legal space established by the European Union as new members bring in new ways of doing things.[97]

Management of this diversity has come up in relation to the question of continued enlargement. Three states have been granted candidate status: Croatia, the Former Yugoslav Republic of Macedonia (FYROM) and Turkey.

The most unproblematic has been Croatia. It was agreed to open accession negotiations in 2004 and these duly began at the end of 2005. These have passed relatively smoothly. Whilst there is a border dispute with Slovenia still to be resolved, the Commission noted at the end of

---

[94] This last condition was added at Madrid in December 1995.

[95] See http://epp.eurostat.ec.europa.eu/cache/ITY_OFFPUB/KS-SF-08-112/EN/KS-SF-08-112-EN.PDF

[96] J. Zielonka, 'How New Enlarged Borders will Reshape the European Union' (2001) 39 *JCMS* 507, 513–15.

[97] The fourth largest party in the 2009–14 European Parliament is therefore the Polish Civic Platform party and the new President, Jerzy Buzek, is one of its members. Czech and Polish Constitutional Courts have already given seminal judgments causing us to rethink our understandings of the authority of EU law. See pp. 191–3, 212–13 and 222.

2008 that negotiations had begun in twenty-one out of thirty-five Chapters, and that it hoped to publish a timetable for completion of the negotiations by the end of 2009 with the 'perspective of membership a reality'.[98] By contrast, whilst FYROM was granted candidate status only a year later than Croatia in 2005, accession negotiations have still not begun, with the Commission report in 2008 suggesting that significant progress still had to be made on all the Copenhagen criteria.[99]

Tensions have crystallised most acutely in the debate about possible Turkish membership of the European Union. Formal EU-Turkey relations go back over forty years to the signing of an Association Agreement in 1963. In 1987, Turkey applied for membership of the European Union. This application lay dormant, but fears over alienating Turkey led to a rapprochement in the mid-1990s, which resulted in the establishment of a customs union between Turkey and the European Union in 1995. It was clear that this was likely to be insufficient. In 1999, the Member States recognised Turkey's eligibility for membership and agreed this should be assessed according to the Copenhagen criteria. Turkey was pressed to reform its Criminal Code, strengthen its judiciary, secure the rights of association, expression and religion more effectively and reduce the role of the military in the government of the country. In December 2004, it was agreed that Turkey had made the necessary political reforms, and that accession negotiations would open in October 2005. In December 2006, negotiations between the Union and Turkey were disrupted over the refusal by Turkey to admit ships or planes flying the Cypriot flag into its ports or airports. This refusal was influenced by a perception that the European Union was not doing enough to improve the lot of the Turkish Cypriot community in the north of Cyprus. As a consequence, the European Union decided that there would be no negotiations in eight fields[100] and it would not consider negotiations in any field closed until this matter was resolved. Whilst negotiations have continued since, they have done so slowly, with negotiations opened on only eight out of thirty-five Chapters.

Debate about Turkish membership also goes to wider questions about the identity of the European Union. Turkey would be the largest state to join the Union since 1957. It would be the first predominantly Islamic state and would extend the Union's borders far into Asia.[101] In 2007, public surveys suggested that only 31 per cent of EU citizens were in favour of Turkish membership with 55 per cent against.[102] Analysis suggests that the economic costs or benefits of Turkish membership play only a small role. Instead, views are shaped by the perception by those opposed to Turkish membership that Turkey is too culturally different from the European Union, or the perception that the Union should be a liberal order capable of embracing all those who sign up to its values by those supportive of Turkish membership.[103] These views have as much to do with (mis)conceptions about European identity as about the nature of Turkey: whether Europe should still be seen as a Christian club, an

---

[98] European Commission, *Enlargement Strategy and Main Challenges 2008–9*, SEC(2008)674, 4.

[99] European Commission, *The Former Yugoslav Republic of Macedonia 2008 Progress Report*, SEC(2008)2695.

[100] These were free movement of goods, right of establishment and freedom to provide services, financial services, agriculture and rural development, fisheries, transport policy, customs union and external relations.

[101] European Commission, *Staff Working Paper on Issues arising from Turkey's Membership Perspective*, COM(2004)656.

[102] A. Ruiz-Jiménez and J. Torreblanca, *European Public Opinion and Turkey's Accession: Making Sense of Arguments For and Against* (Brussels, Centre for European Policy Studies, 2007) 8–9.

[103] *Ibid.* 16–23.

evangelising force for liberal values, or, as some have argued, a place not to minimise differences but to mediate between them.[104]

Another issue raised by enlargement is whether it is possible with twenty-seven states to press forward with common policies across so many different fields. Majone, in particular, has argued that this is increasingly unrealistic and that we will increasingly witness arrangements involving some Member States but not others.

G. Majone, 'Unity in Diversity: European Integration and the Enlargement Process' (2008) 33 *European Law Review* 457, 470–1

An association established to provide excludable public goods is a *club*. Two elements determine the optimal size of a club. One is the cost of producing the club good – in a large club this cost is shared over more members. The second element is the cost to each club member of a good not meeting precisely his or her individual needs or preferences. The latter cost is likely to increase with the size of the club. Therefore the optimal size is determined by the point at which the marginal benefit from the addition of one new member, i.e. the reduction in the per capita cost of producing the good, equals the marginal cost caused by a mismatch between the characteristics of the good and the preferences of the individual club members ...

Think now of a society composed, not of individuals but of independent states. Associations of independent states (alliances, leagues, confederations) are typically voluntary, and their members are exclusively entitled to enjoy certain benefits produced by the association, so that the economic theory of clubs is applicable. In fact, since excludability is more easily enforced in such a context, many goods which are purely public at the national level become club goods at the international level. The club goods in question could be collective security, policy coordination, common technical standards, or tax harmonization. In these and many other cases, countries which are not willing to share the costs are usually excluded from the benefits of inter-state cooperation. Now, as an association of states expands, becoming more diverse in its preferences, the cost of uniformity in the provision of such goods – harmonization – can escalate dramatically. The theory predicts a growing number of voluntary associations to meet the increased demand of club goods more precisely tailored to the different requirements of various subsets of more homogeneous states. It will be noted that the model sketched here is inspired by a pluralist philosophy quite different from the one-dimensional philosophy of enhanced cooperation as discussed in a previous section. It is not a question of states working closely together for the sake of the Union. Rather, the underlying idea is that variety in preferences should be matched by a corresponding variety in institutional arrangements.

... 'integration à la carte' and 'variable geometry' come closest to the situation modelled by the economic theory of clubs. The expression 'variable geometry' has been used in several meanings. In the meaning most relevant here, it refers to a situation where a subset of member states undertake some project, for instance an industrial or technological project in which other members of the Union are not interested, or to which they are unable to make a positive contribution. Since, by assumption, not all Member States are willing to participate in all EU programmes, this model combines the criterion of differentiation by country, as in multi-speed integration, and by activity or project – as in integration à la carte ...

---

[104] E. Balibar, 'Europe as Vanishing Mediator' (2003) *Constellations* 312, 332–3.

Majone presents a world in which all states can freely and equally choose between different policies. The enlargement process suggests a twist to this, however. Recent entrants have not been able to join on an equal basis but on others' terms. The club goods described by Majone have therefore taken the form of newer states not being allowed full access to all the entitlements of membership. The most discussed example of this concerned free movement of persons. Both the 2004 and 2007 entrants were subject to '2+3+2' regimes where their own nationals would only be granted in EU law the same rights to live and work in other EU states as other EU nationals seven years after their entry into the Union.[105] A more wide-ranging regime was put in place for Bulgarian and Romanian accession. Both states are subject to a Cooperation and Verification Mechanism for three years from entry under which the Commission is to monitor their legal obligations and more general performance in a number of fields. If there is a deterioration in the economic situation in those states or the Commission considers that they fail to meet their legal obligations or their commitments to improve performance, the Commission may adopt measures against these states, notably suspending their rights.[106]

As well as this, entry of the new Member States to certain fields of EU policy is being closely policed. In December 2007, all new EU Member States acceded to the Schengen Convention, with the exception of three, Cyprus, Romania and Bulgaria, for whom provision was made to join when ready. Membership of the euro-zone has proved more challenging. Both Slovenia and Lithuania applied for membership from 1 January 2007. Whilst Slovenia was allowed to join and adopt the euro as its currency, Lithuania was blocked by the Commission and other Member States on the grounds that its level of inflation was too high. This move was perceived as divisive and unfair by a number of the new Member States as Lithuania met all the other criteria, which at the time was not true of a number of existing members of the euro-zone. On 1 January 2008, Malta and Cyprus also joined the euro-zone, and Slovakia on 1 January 2009, taking its overall number to sixteen.

8 THE CONSTITUTIONAL TREATY

(i) The European Union Charter of Fundamental Rights and Freedoms and the Treaty of Nice

The achievements of the Treaty of Amsterdam were seen at the time as limited.[107] There were two areas, in particular, that were seen as 'unfinished'. First, there had been much discussion about whether the European Union should have its own Bill of Rights. Whilst references were introduced to fundamental rights and provision was made for expulsion of Member States for gross violations, a self-standing Bill of Rights was seen by some Member States as a step too far. The second matter not addressed head on was the institutional pressures generated by possible enlargement of the Union. A Protocol was therefore signed, agreeing that a conference be

---

[105] S. Currie, '"Free" Movers? The Post Accession Experience of Accession: 8 Migrant Workers in the United Kingdom' (2006) 31 *ELRev.* 207.

[106] Indeed, in 2008, Commission concerns with Bulgarian maladministration led it to suspend payments of €220 million structural funds to Bulgaria. European Commission, *On the Management of EU Funds in Bulgaria*, COM(2008)496. For comment see 'The European Union and Bulgaria: The New Colonialism', *The Economist*, 19 March 2009.

[107] K. Hughes, 'The 1996 Intergovernmental Conference and EU Enlargement' (1996) 72 *International Affairs* 1; A. Teasdale, 'The Politics of Qualified Majority Voting in Europe' (1996) *Political Quarterly* 101, 110–15.

convened at least one year before membership of the European Union reached twenty, to carry out a comprehensive review of the composition and functioning of the institutions.

Attention turned, first, to an EU Bill of Rights. The Member States, meeting at Cologne in 1999, agreed that an EU Charter of Fundamental Rights should be established cataloguing such rights. Instead of this being left to intergovernmental negotiations, a special Convention was established to agree the Charter.[108] Chaired by Roman Herzog, formerly the German President, the Convention was composed of fifteen representatives of national governments, thirty representatives of national parliaments, sixteen representatives of the European Parliament and one representative of the Commission. It met in open session, decided upon matters by consensus rather than by voting, and received extensive representations from civil society. Parliamentarians were not only more numerous in the Convention than government representatives, but also more vocal. A total of 805 amendments were put forward by parliamentarians whilst only 356 were put forward by government representatives.[109] It constituted a move away from negotiations between governments to a new form of deliberative decision-making. It was also successful in terms of its outcome: the Convention drafted the European Union Charter of Fundamental Rights and Freedoms which was wide-ranging in the entitlements it recognised. The Charter was adopted by the Convention in October 2000.

On the second matter, institutional reform, discussions began in the same month as the Treaty of Amsterdam came into force: 1 May 1999. There was agreement that negotiations should be exclusively concerned with recasting the institutional settlement so that it would function more efficiently and accommodate new states who might join the Union. Notwithstanding its technicality, this task was a challenging one, for it was a redistributive task involving reallocation of votes or influence within the EU institutions, entailing that for every winner there would be an equivalent loser.

With every state having a veto, no previous IGC had realised its ambitions for management of internal reform. This was also the case for the Treaty of Nice. The Treaty was finally signed on 11 December 2000, after over ninety hours of acrimonious, direct negotiations between the Heads of Government.[110] Even within governmental circles, the agreement was seen as limited and unsatisfactory. Agreement was not reached on many of the items for discussion: most notably the legal status of the EU Charter of Fundamental Rights and Freedoms. Instead, limited reforms were made to the four main institutions, the Commission, the Council, the Parliament and the Court of Justice. QMV was extended into thirty-one further areas, but almost all of these were procedural and were concerned with the appointment of EU officials. The reforms were not only insubstantial but the Treaties were now a confusing and incoherent mess. The Union had now a bewildering gamut of competences, governed by an array of legislative procedures, producing a range of legal instruments. There were thirty-eight combinations of 'possible voting modalities in the Council and participation opportunities of the European Parliament of which 22 were "legislative"'.[111] Whilst, therefore, there did not seem to be many

[108] See G. de Búrca, 'The Drafting of the EU Charter of Fundamental Rights' (2001) 26 *EL Rev.* 126.

[109] A. Maurer, 'The Convention, the IGC 2004 and European System Development: A Challenge for Parliamentary Democracy', 7 in *Democracy and Accountability in the Enlarged European Union*, Joint Conference of SWP and the Austrian Academy of Sciences, 7–8 March 2003, www.swp-berlin.org/common/get_document.php?asset_id=689 (accessed 20 July 2009).

[110] M. Gray and A. Stubb, 'The Treaty of Nice: Negotiating a Poisoned Chalice?' (2001) 395 *JCMS* 5.

[111] W. Wessels, 'The Millenium IGC in the EU's Evolution' (2001) 39 *JCMS* 197, 201.

strong reasons to vote against the Treaty of Nice, there did not seem to be many reasons to vote for it. In June 2001, the Irish voted 53.87 per cent against ratification of the Treaty of Nice.[112] A Declaration was added that nothing in the TEU affected Irish military neutrality, something that had been raised as a concern amongst a small number of Irish voters. On the basis of this, a second referendum was held in September 2002, and the Treaty of Nice was approved by 62.89 per cent of the vote.[113]

(ii) The Constitutional Treaty

Dissatisfaction with the substance and the process of Nice had emerged prior to the Irish referendum. At Nice, the Member States announced that there would be yet another IGC in 2004 to consider the significant issues that had not been resolved. These comprised delimitation of powers between the European Union and the Member States; the status of the EU Charter of Fundamental Rights; simplification of the Treaties; and setting out more fully the role of national parliaments in the European architecture. As important as the substance was the process. There was considerable dissatisfaction with this intractable process of closed negotiations between governments running up against deadlines that seemed to be brought by every IGC. In a Declaration at Nice, the Member States called, therefore 'for a deeper and wider debate about the future of the European Union' which would involve 'wide-ranging discussions with all interested parties: representatives of national parliaments and all those reflecting public opinion, namely political, economic and university circles, representatives of civil society, etc.'.[114]

This Declaration had been preceded by a significant debate between political leaders about the nature of institutional reform that had been begun by Joschka Fischer, the German Foreign Minister, at the Humboldt University in Berlin in 2000. Fischer considered that European integration had to have a *finalité*, an end-point, and that this should be a European Constitution:

> These three reforms – the solution of the democracy problem and the need for fundamental reordering of competences both horizontally, i.e. among the European institutions, and vertically, i.e. between Europe, the nation-state and the regions – will only be able to succeed if Europe is established anew with a constitution. In other words: through the realisation of the project of a European Constitution centred around basic, human and civil rights, an equal division of powers between the European institutions and a precise delineation between European and nation-state level. The main axis for such a European Constitution will be the relationship between the Federation and the nation-state.[115]

A number of Heads of Government picked up on this theme. Within two months, Jacques Chirac, the French President, talked of a 'first European Constitution'. Tony Blair, the British Prime Minister, suggested that there should be a new statement of principles about the Union. And in June 2000, Paavo Lipponen, the Finnish Prime Minister, suggested that a special Convention be established to launch a 'constitutionalisation process'.[116]

---

[112] K. Gilland, 'Ireland's (First) Referendum on the Treaty of Nice' (2002) 40 *JCMS* 527.

[113] The Treaty of Nice came into force on 2 February 2003.

[114] Declaration 23 to the Treaty of Nice on the Future of the Union.

[115] J. Fischer, 'From Confederacy to Federation: Thoughts on the Finality of European Integration', Humboldt University, Berlin, 12 May 2000, available at www.jeanmonnetprogram.org/papers/00/joschka_fischer_en.rtf (accessed July 2009).

[116] P. Norman, *The Accidental Constitution: The Story of the European Convention* (Brussels, Eurocomment, 2003) 11–24.

The debate re-emerged a year later, in December 2001, at Laeken in Belgium when Member States had to think about the preparations for the 2004 IGC. There was agreement that the institutional tinkering witnessed at Amsterdam and Nice was neither sufficient to equip the Union for the challenges it faced nor sufficient to engage popular enthusiasm. Instead, what was necessary was a process of democratic regeneration. Such an effort would not only require wide-ranging institutional reform. It was also a process that could not be managed just by an IGC. Accordingly, an extraordinary process was called for. The draft Treaty would be formulated by a Convention, named the Future of Europe Convention, which would be modelled on the Convention used to draft the EU Charter of Fundamental Rights.

Chaired by Giscard d'Estaing, the former French President, the Convention would comprise 105 members from national governments, parliaments, MEPs and the Commission. The accession states would be involved as would civil society. The Convention would meet in plenary session, with all members present, once a month. It was the final decision-making body, responsible for adopting any agreed text. Its decisions were to be taken in public by consensus rather than by vote.

The Convention opened in February 2002. Although its initial mandate was merely to identify options for the subsequent IGC, knowing that a vast majority of the Convention was willing to reach an ambitious agreement, Giscard discarded this idea at the first session stating that its purpose should be a single proposal opening the way for a 'Constitution for Europe'.[117] Sixteen months later, he presented this proposal, the Draft Constitutional Treaty, with much pomp and fanfare to the Member States. The IGC following the Convention was short. There was only one significant item in the Draft Constitutional Treaty which was subject to significant amendment. Spain and Poland were unhappy about the voting rights accorded to them in the EU law-making process. However, after a change of government in Spain and a series of small but important amendments to the text, the Member States changed their position and signed the Constitutional Treaty, at a ceremony in Rome, in October 2004.

To mark both the significance of the Constitutional Treaty and the spirit of democratic renewal, ten Member States arranged for referendums to determine whether or not they should ratify it. The first was held in Spain, where the Treaty was approved by 72 per cent of those who voted. However, in the next referendums, held in France (on 29 May 2005) and in the Netherlands (three days later, on 1 June 2005), the Treaty was roundly rejected, with 55 per cent voting against it in France and 62 per cent voting against it in the Netherlands. Analysis of the reasons for the 'No' vote in the Netherlands and France showed the Constitutional Treaty had little hold or meaning for public debate. Despite voters being reasonably well-informed about the details of the Constitutional Treaty, the reasons for their vote had little to do, in most cases, with its legal details. Opponents were protesting against globalisation, the consequences of the 2004 enlargement, fears about Turkish membership of the Union, and in the Netherlands there was anger amongst voters at the perceived power of the large Member States in the Union.[118]

---

[117] P. Magnette, 'In the Name of Simplification: Coping with Constitutional Conflicts in the Convention on the Future of Europe' (2005) 11 *ELJ* 432, 436.

[118] Flash Eurobarometer 171 and 172, *European Constitution: Post-Referendum Survey in France and in The Netherlands*. This was notwithstanding that 88 per cent of the French and 82 per cent of the Dutch still had positive perceptions of the Union in the period after the referendum. European Commission, *The Period of Reflection and Plan D*, COM(2006)212, 2.

In short, citizens did not buy into the need to create a new form of political community to which they would have loyalty and affinity and which had to be 'democratically regenerated' by them. Part of the reason is that such loyalty or affinity is challenging to generate. Bartolini has observed that it is 'an affective or emotional relationship to the organization or group that one belongs to, and makes it difficult (if not impossible) to contemplate the possibility of abandoning such a group or organization'. He notes that it is built upon the identity, solidarity and trust that exist between members of a group.[119] The development of such elements required much effort within the national context. Most notably, Bartolini has observed that the cultural, economic, coercion and politico-administrative boundaries of any modern state generally coincide and reinforce each other.[120] That is to say, there is a *national* system of law and order, a *national* community with its own myths and symbols, a *national* welfare system, a *national* economy and a *national* administration. For better or worse, this reinforcement generates common identities. By contrast, such elements are almost completely absent in the EU context.[121] To assume that they could be generated by a Convention of 105 people and a ballot was always optimistic. Instead, the absence of these elements gave the process a somewhat surreal feel with both academics and observers noting that much of the debate at the Future of Europe Convention was dominated by a disembodied, elite discourse marked by the absence of significant disagreement.[122]

By the end of June 2005, ratification of the Constitutional Treaty had reached an impasse. A significant majority of Member States, eighteen, had ratified the Treaty, with Luxembourg also having held a positive referendum. Of the remaining seven Member States, six (Czech Republic, Denmark, Ireland, Poland, Portugal and the United Kingdom), were scheduled to hold their own referendums. Of these, there was a significant chance of a 'No' vote in all bar Portugal. When combined with the French and Dutch 'No' votes, this not only suggested that there would be eight states unable to ratify the Treaty. It also suggested a scenario in which, out of the ten states holding referendums, the overwhelming majority, seven, might have voted against the project. The popular vote was out on the European Union.

9 THE LISBON TREATY

(i) The road to Lisbon

The Union was faced not with a single recalcitrant state, such as Denmark and Ireland, as with previous amending Treaties. It was instead confronted with a deep divide in which two-thirds of Member States wished to press ahead whilst one-third did not. A period of reflection was called for by the European Council which lasted until late 2006, when the Finnish government prepared the ground by engaging in a series of consultations on how to achieve institutional reform. Alongside this, a series of prominent politicians, acting under the umbrella of the organisation

---

[119] S. Bartolini, *Restructuring Europe: Centre Formation, System Building, and Political Structuring Between the Nation State and the European Union* (Oxford, Oxford University Press, 2005) 31.

[120] *Ibid.* 410.

[121] For a not dissimilar argument see P. Schmitter, 'Making Sense of the EU: Democracy in Europe and Europe's Democratization' (2003) 14 *Journal of Democracy* 71.

[122] Norman, above n. 116, 326–38; G. Stuart, *The Making of Europe's Constitution* (London, Fabian Society, 2003) 19–24. C. Skach, 'We the Peoples? Constitutionalising the European Union' (2005) 43 *JCMS* 149.

named the Action Committee for European Democracy, began to publish articles in the press indicating that the time for listening was over and that the time for action had begun.[123]

In March 2007, at the fiftieth anniversary of the Treaty of Rome, the German government obtained a commitment from the other Member States to place 'the European Union on a renewed common basis before the European Parliament elections in 2009'.[124] In other words, they had committed to a deadline for ratifying a new treaty.

The German government's strategy for reaching an agreement was to close the gap between the Member States in a highly structured manner. 'Political agreement' on the central points of disagreement was reached in closed, confidential negotiations between ministries, named 'sherpas'. Only when political agreement was reached on the main points would the second stage, an IGC, be opened. Its tasks, however, would be limited by the mandate of the political agreement, and so restricted to translating the political agreement into legal detail and resolving any ambiguities. States wishing to introduce new points or reopen old debates would run the risk of being accused of having breached the existing political agreement, and therefore of having acted in bad faith. The process was thus to be a relatively confined affair subject to few external risks or interventions. In terms of substance, the strategy involved the use of the Constitutional Treaty as a starting point, along with the question of what had to be offered to make the Treaty acceptable to those national governments constituting the recalcitrant one-third. Ultimately, for these states, the Treaty was not a question of reform, but a series of individual concessions.

The Heads of Government met between 21 and 23 June 2007 to conclude the first stage of the process. The outcome was a sixteen-page mandate that was to provide the basis for an IGC that the Heads of Government indicated was to be completed by December 2007 and was to be confined to the terms of the mandate. It also indicated that the new Treaty was to follow the text of the Constitutional Treaty unless otherwise specified by the mandate. The subsequent IGC was, consequently, highly limited. By 19 October a text had been agreed informally between the Member States. On 13 December 2007, the new text, the Treaty of Lisbon was formally signed.

The conclusion of the Treaty was a significant coup. It involved amendments to all of the articles in the TEU and to 216 provisions in the EC Treaty.[125] There were, moreover, significant differences that had to be bridged between the twenty-seven Member States, each with their own distinct agenda and constituencies. Yet this negotiating triumph came at a cost. In particular, it created a double bind. If the Treaty of Lisbon differed significantly from the Constitutional Treaty, its nature of reform was more closed and more accelerated than any other to date. There was a lack of transparency and an exclusion of national parliaments that still remains to be justified. If the Treaty of Lisbon was not substantially different from the Constitutional Treaty, that would open negotiators to charges of arrogance for ignoring the referendum results in France and the Netherlands.

[123] See www.iue.it/RSCAS/research/ACED/MissionStatement.shtml (accessed 18 July 2009).
[124] EU Council, Declaration on the occasion of the fiftieth anniversary of the signature of the Treaty of Rome, Brussels, 25 March 2007, para. 3.
[125] Statewatch, www.statewatch.org/news/2007/oct/eu-refrom-treaty-tec-external-relations-3-5.pdf (accessed 20 July 2009).

(ii) The Treaty of Lisbon[126]

(a) Two treaties of equal value: the Treaty on European Union and the Treaty on the Functioning of the European Union

The Treaty of Lisbon created two new treaties to replace the previous framework.[127] One, confusingly, is named the Treaty on European Union (TEU). The central items set out by it are as follows:

- the mission and values of the European Union: respect for the rule of law, the principle of limited powers, respect for national identities and upholding democracy and fundamental rights;
- the democratic principles of the Union and providing for the active contribution of national parliaments to the functioning of the European Union;
- a neighbourhood policy, whereby the Union is to develop a special relationship with neighbouring countries;
- the composition and central functions of the EU institutions;
- detailed provisions on the Union's external action in the TEU, in particular both its Common Foreign and Security Policy and its common security and defence policy;
- procedures are set out for amendment of the two Treaties;
- legal personality for the Union;
- provisions governing asymmetric integration; these include the circumstances in which a Member State may leave or be expelled from the Union and when states may engage in enhanced cooperation, the procedure whereby some Member States may develop EU legislation amongst themselves where there is not sufficient will for that legislation to be adopted by all Member States.

The second treaty is the Treaty on the Functioning of the European Union (TFEU). This sets out the explicit competences of the Union and, with the exception of external action, the detailed procedures to be used in each policy field. In legislative style, it is similar therefore to the existing EC Treaty. There is, however, one significant adaptation taken from the Constitutional Treaty: the competences and their nature are catalogued at the beginning of the TFEU.[128]

Article 3 TFEU

1. The Union shall have exclusive competence in the following areas:
   (a) customs union;
   (b) the establishing of the competition rules necessary for the functioning of internal market;
   (c) monetary policy for the Member States whose currency is the euro;

---

[126] As with discussion of other Treaty amendments in this chapter, the section below covers only the most salient features with detailed discussion left to subsequent chapters.

[127] On the Treaty of Lisbon see P. Craig, 'The Treaty of Lisbon: Process, Architecture and Substance' (2008) 33 *ELRev.* 137; M. Dougan, 'The Treaty of Lisbon 2007: Winning Minds not Hearts' (2008) 45 *CMLRev.* 617; Y. Devuyst, 'The European Union's Institutional Balance After the Treaty of Lisbon: "Community Method" and "Democratic Deficit" Reassessed' (2008) 39 *Georgetown Journal of International Law* 247. A thoughtful and detailed assessment is provided by House of Lords European Union Committee, *The Treaty of Lisbon: An Impact Assessment* (London, HL,10th Report, Session 2007–08, 2008).

[128] The discussion is set out in more detail in Chapter 5 at pp. 206 *et seq.*

(d) the conservation of marine biological resources under the common fisheries policy;

(e) common commercial policy.

2. The Union shall also have exclusive competence for the conclusion of an international agreement when its conclusion is provided for in a legislative act of the Union or is necessary to enable the Union to exercise its internal competence, or insofar as its conclusion may affect common rules or alter their scope.

Article 4 TFEU

1. The Union shall share competence with the Member States where the Treaties confer on it a competence which does not relate to the areas referred to in Articles 3 and 6.

2. Shared competence between the Union and the Member States applies in the following principal areas:

(a) internal market;

(b) social policy, for the aspects defined in this Treaty;

(c) economic, social and territorial cohesion;

(d) agriculture and fisheries, excluding the conservation of marine biological resources;

(e) environment;

(f) consumer protection;

(g) transport;

(h) trans-European networks;

(i) energy;

(j) area of freedom, security and justice;

(k) common safety concerns in public health matters, for the aspects defined in this Treaty.

3. In the areas of research, technological development and space, the Union shall have competence to carry out activities, in particular to define and implement programmes; however, the exercise of that competence shall not result in Member States being prevented from exercising theirs.

4. In the areas of development cooperation and humanitarian aid, the Union shall have competence to carry out activities and conduct a common policy; however, the exercise of that competence shall not result in Member States being prevented from exercising theirs.

Article 5 TFEU

1. The Member States shall coordinate their economic policies within the Union. To this end, the Council shall adopt measures, in particular broad guidelines for these policies. Specific provisions shall apply to those Member States whose currency is the euro.

2. The Union shall take measures to ensure coordination of the employment policies of the Member States, in particular by defining guidelines for these policies.

3. The Union may take initiatives to ensure coordination of Member States' social policies.

> **Article 6 TFEU**
>
> The Union shall have competence to carry out actions to support, coordinate or supplement the actions of the Member States. The areas of such action shall, at European level, be:
> (a) protection and improvement of human health;
> (b) industry;
> (c) culture;
> (d) tourism;
> (e) education, vocational training, youth and sport;
> (f) civil protection;
> (g) administrative cooperation.

Each treaty is to have 'the same legal value'.[129] It is however unclear what this means. Is each to be interpreted in the light of the other? If that is the case, it could lead to the more detailed TFEU being given an expanded remit as a result of the broader mission of the TEU. Or does it mean that each curtails the other? In this case, many of the broader provisions of the TEU will be little more than rhetorical as they will be curtailed by the substance of the TFEU.

(b) Enhancing the democratic credentials of the Union

A different ethos permeates the Lisbon Treaty than the Constitutional Treaty. The latter was concerned to establish an autonomous pan-European constitutional democracy. The Constitutional Treaty therefore carried a number of procedures and symbols associated with constitutional democracy. At the most ephemeral level, there was provision for a European Union flag, anthem, motto and holiday. The Constitutional Treaty also contained all the tools of an autonomous European constitutional democracy. There was a primacy clause asserting the precedence of EU law over national law within the limits of the Treaty. A Bill of Rights of sorts was established with the incorporation of the EU Charter of Fundamental Rights, and EU Regulations and Directives were to become known as 'laws' or 'framework laws'. The Union was to have its own legal personality and Foreign Minister. Whilst the exact working out of these provisions resulted in much curtailed powers than those enjoyed by most liberal democratic states, they did convey the imagery of statehood.

The Treaty of Lisbon, in the words of the mandate to the IGC, abandoned the 'constitutional concept'.[130] Almost all the above provisions were removed by the Treaty of Lisbon. The provision establishing the primacy of EU law over national law and the detailed elaboration of the Charter were removed from the main text of the Treaty. A Declaration was instead attached setting out the primacy of EU law and a provision added requiring the Union to respect the rights, freedoms and principles in the Charter. Union legislative measures were to return to their traditional designation as Regulations and Directives, and the Foreign Minister was to be known as the High Representative. To be sure, sixteen Member States signed a Declaration stating that the symbols of the Union (the flag, the anthem, the motto, the provision on the

---

[129] Article 1(2) TFEU.
[130] EU Council, IGC 2007 Mandate, Brussels, 26 June 2007, para. 1.

euro as the European Union currency and the holiday) would remain as 'symbols to express the sense of community of the people in the European Union and their allegiance to it'.[131] Yet the fact that this was hidden away as a remote Declaration signed by a bare majority of states indicated constitutionalism's fall from grace.

If the constitutional conceit was abandoned by Lisbon, there was still a concern that the democratic qualities of the Union should have a more autonomous presence so that a Frankenstein should not be created which develops large numbers of laws and administers lives in an undemocratic way. This ethos is rooted around a twin set of principles.

The first is that the European Union is founded upon and must respect a set of liberal values that are shared across the Union and form part of a common identity. The nature and content of these values are set out in the first substantive provision of the TEU.

Article 2 TEU

The Union is founded on the values of respect for human dignity, freedom, democracy, equality, the rule of law and respect for human rights, including the rights of persons belonging to minorities. These values are common to the Member States in a society in which pluralism, non-discrimination, tolerance, justice, solidarity and equality between women and men prevail.

These values are not rhetorical, nor do they form some general aspirational goal. Instead, they are to be recognised by the Union, must not be violated by it, and the Union commits itself to external policing by the European Court of Human Rights.[132] The commitment to respect fundamental rights was not uncontroversial. It begs questions as to which values were to be protected and whether they would be used to bootstrap new roles for the European Union. These concerns were strongly articulated by the British and Polish governments and a Protocol was therefore added, which stated that the Charter did not extend the ability of any court to declare Polish or British measures incompatible with EU fundamental rights law. As these states had particular concerns about the development of EU social rights, the Protocol provided that Title IV of the Charter, in which most of these rights were incorporated, was only justiciable in these states insofar as the latter provided for them in national law.

The other set of principles is a more explicit commitment by the Union to democracy. The Lisbon Treaty, in particular, requires the Union to respect two forms of democracy: representative democracy and participatory democracy.[133] These principles are not just constraints that the Union must not violate. They are also a statement of its qualities. The idea of the European Union being a representative democracy was challenged before the German Constitutional Court in a challenge to the ratification of the Lisbon Treaty. Whilst allowing for the ratification of the Treaty, in that it only provided for limited powers to be conferred on the European Union, the German Constitutional Court agreed that the European Union was not a democracy when measured against national standards. It considered representative democracy, the principle of a legislator based upon one person per vote, as the heart of a democratic system. It also

---

[131] Declaration 52 to the Treaty of Lisbon on the symbols of the European Union.
[132] Article 6(1) TEU. This is dealt with in much more detail in Chapter 6 at pp. 259–62.
[133] Article 10 TEU.

considered the Union to be characterised by what it termed 'excessive federalisation'. By this, it meant the principle, as in federal systems, of equality between the constituent elements. In the case of the European Union, this meant equality of votes between the nation-states.

---

2 BvE 2/08 *Gauweiler* v *Treaty of Lisbon*, **Judgment of 30 June 2009**

280. Measured against requirements in a constitutional state, the European Union lacks, even after the entry into force of the Treaty of Lisbon, a political decision-making body which has come into being by equal election of all citizens of the Union and which is able to uniformly represent the will of the people. What is also lacking in this connection is a system of organisation of political rule in which a will of the European majority carries the formation of the government in such a way that the will goes back to free and equal electoral decisions and a genuine competition between government and opposition which is transparent for the citizens, can come about … contrary to the claim that Article 10.1 TEU Lisbon seems to make according to its wording, the European Parliament is not a body of representation of a sovereign European people. This is reflected in the fact that it, as the representation of the peoples in their respectively assigned national contingents of Members, is not laid out as a body of representation of the citizens of the Union as an undistinguished unity according to the principle of electoral equality.

281. Also in their elaboration by the Treaty of Lisbon, no independent people's sovereignty of the citizens of the Union in their entirety results from the competences of the European Union. If a decision between political lines in the European Parliament receives a narrow majority, there is no guarantee of the majority of votes cast representing a majority of the citizens of the Union. Therefore the formation, from within Parliament, of an independent government vested with the competences that are usual in states would meet with fundamental objections. Possibly, a numerical minority of citizens existing according to the ratio of representation could govern, through a majority of Members of Parliament, against the political will of an opposition majority of citizens of the Union, which does not find itself represented as a majority. It is true that the principle of electoral equality only ensures a maximum degree of exactness as regards the will of the people under the conditions of a system of strict proportional representation. But also in majority voting systems, there is a sufficient guarantee of electoral equality for the votes at any rate as regards the value counted and the chance of success, whereas it is missed if any contingent that is not merely insignificant is established.

282. For a free democratic fundamental order of a state …, the equality of all citizens when making use of their right to vote is one of the essential foundations of state order …

288. It is true that the democracy of the European Union is approximated to federalised state concepts; measured against the principle of representative democracy, however, it would to a considerable degree show excessive federalisation. With the personal composition of the European Council, of the Council, the Commission and the Court of Justice of the European Union, the principle of the equality of states remains linked to national rights of determination, rights which are, in principle, equal. Even for a European Parliament elected with due account to equality, this structure would be a considerable obstacle for asserting a representative will of the parliamentary majority with regard to persons or subject-matters. Also after the entry into force of the Treaty of Lisbon, the Court of Justice, for instance, must always be staffed according to the principle 'one state, one judge' and under the determining influence of the Member States regardless of their number of inhabitants. The functioning of the European Union continues to be characterised by the influence of the negotiating governments and the subject-related administrative and formative competence of the Commission even though the

rights of participation of the European Parliament have been strengthened on the whole. Within this system, the parliamentary influence has been consistently further developed with Parliament's being accorded the right to veto in central areas of legislation. With the ordinary legislative procedure, the Treaty of Lisbon makes a norm what is already factually decisive under the currently applicable law in many areas: in the co-decision procedure, a directive or a regulation cannot be adopted against the will of the European Parliament.

289. The deficit of European public authority that exists when measured against requirements on democracy in states cannot be compensated by other provisions of the Treaty of Lisbon and to that extent, it cannot be justified.

290. The European Union tries to compensate the existing considerable degree of excessive federalisation in particular by strengthening the citizens' and associations' rights aimed at participation and transparency, as well as by enhancing the role of the national parliaments and of the regions. The Treaty of Lisbon strengthens these elements of participative democracy aimed at procedural participation. Apart from the elements of complementary participative democracy, such as the precept of providing, in a suitable manner, the citizens of the Union and the 'representative' associations with the possibility of communicating their views, the Treaty of Lisbon also provides for elements of associative and direct democracy (Article 11 TEU Lisbon). They include the dialogue of the institutions of the Union with 'representative' associations and the civil society as well as the European citizens' initiative. The European citizens' initiative makes it possible to invite the Commission to submit any appropriate proposal on the regulation of political matters. Such an invitation is subject to a quorum of not less than one million citizens of the Union who have to be nationals of a 'significant number of Member States' (Article 11.4 TEU Lisbon). The citizens' initiative is restricted to issues within the framework of the powers of the Commission and it requires concretisation of its procedures and conditions under secondary law by a regulation…

293. Also the institutional recognition of the Member States' Parliaments by the Treaty of Lisbon cannot compensate for the deficit in the direct track of legitimisation of the European public authority that is based on the election of the Members of the European Parliament. The status of national parliaments is considerably curtailed by the reduction of decisions requiring unanimity and the supranationalisation of police and judicial cooperation in criminal matters. Compensation, provided for by the Treaty, by the procedural strengthening of subsidiarity shifts existing political rights of self-determination to procedural possibilities of intervention and judicially assertable claims of participation; this was concurringly emphasised in the oral hearing.

294. Neither the additional rights of participation, which are strongly interlocked as regards the effects of their many levels of action and in view of the large number of national parliaments, nor rights of petition which are associative and have a direct effect vis-à-vis the Commission are suited to replace the majority rule which is established by an election. They are intended to, and indeed can, ultimately increase the level of legitimisation all the same under the conditions of a *Staatenverbund* (association of States) with restricted tasks.

The view of the German Constitutional Court is not simply that the European Union is not yet sufficiently democratic. It is that it can never be fully democratic. For the Union to realise the standard of democracy set by the German Constitutional Court, it would have to turn itself into a unitary state. One would need a single legislative assembly in which representation in the dominant chamber was not allocated according seats per Member State but simply on the basis of European citizenship. As we shall see, the only directly elected body, the European Parliament, is not the dominant chamber, and there is no prospect of seats being allocated other than on a national basis. Indeed, the idea of national allocation (or excessive federalisation in the language of the German Constitutional Court) permeates all EU decision-making structures. To eradicate it is not only politically unrealistic but would create a beast unrecognisable from the current European Union.

The judgment is thus a powerful indictment of the European Union. Whilst used by the German Constitutional Court to limit the tasks which can be granted to the Union,[134] it also begs questions about the legitimacy of the European Union when acting within its aegis. For, if the Union can only look at best for what the German Constitutional Court terms 'democratic supplementation'[135] there is a challenge to justify why it should have wide-reaching authority over our lives or precedence over national laws or local traditions.

(c) Supranationalisation of the Union

The Lisbon Treaty kept the new explicit competences enumerated by the Constitutional Treaty: energy, intellectual property, space, humanitarian aid, sport and civil protection. In addition, it added a further one: that of climate change. Yet there was already competence to carry out activity here under other legal bases, and the Union had already taken significant measures in all these fields. The most important reform was not a formal extension of EU powers but an abolition of the three pillar structure established at Maastricht. All three pillars were brought into a single framework. Whilst provision was made for the Common Foreign and Security Policy to continue to be treated discretely, activities governed by the third pillar, namely policing and judicial cooperation in criminal matters, were now to be governed by the same procedures as those traditionally applied to EC activities. This reform had two important implications. The first was a significant extension of the supranational qualities and procedures of the Union to govern more extensively the sensitive fields of policing and criminal justice. The second was the extension of the so-called flexibility provision which permits legislation to be adopted to realise broad EU objectives if no more specific legal provision allows this. As the previous procedure applied only to the EC Treaty, the new procedure has a wider remit as it applies not merely to Community but to all Union activity.

Member States sought to draw some of the teeth from the unification of the pillars through the insertion of a new proviso stating that national security remains the sole responsibility of each Member State. The flexibility provision was amended so that it cannot be used as a legal base for matters relating to common and foreign security, and a Declaration was inserted stipulating that it could not be used to enable de facto amendment of the Treaties. In addition, specific provision was made for the United Kingdom and Ireland. A Protocol was introduced which amends and extends that granted at Amsterdam. In addition to being free to decide whether or not to participate in individual pieces of legislation on visas, asylum, immigration and other policies related to free movement of persons, they had now a parallel entitlement in the fields of policing and judicial cooperation in criminal justice. If either Member State chooses not to participate, it would not be bound by that legislation.

---

[134] See pp. 194–8.
[135] This term is used at para. 272 of the judgment, above n. 82.

(d) Recasting the institutional setting

The Constitutional Treaty was largely about institutional reform. Its proposals were adopted largely unscathed in the Treaty of Lisbon. QMV was extended to about fifty new areas. Provision was also made for legislative procedures based on the unanimity vote in the Council to be altered to QMV without the need for an IGC. In terms of the powers of the European Parliament, the co-decision procedure, which grants it a veto, has been applied to forty new areas. In addition, it has been granted significant powers of assent, most notably with regard to Article 352 TFEU and anti-discrimination, whereby its agreement must be obtained before any legislative proposal can become law. The Treaty of Lisbon also extended the powers granted to national parliaments. They were given additional time to consider legislative proposals and increased powers to call for a proposal to be reviewed on the ground that it does not comply with the principle of subsidiarity, which provides that EU measures should only be adopted if the objectives of the action cannot be sufficiently achieved by Member States and by reason of their scale or effects can be better realised through Union action.

This increase in QMV and European Parliament powers led to the introduction of some caveats. 'Brake' procedures were added where national governments could insist that the matter be discussed at European Council level – and therefore be subject to unanimity – if a measure touched fundamental aspects of their social security or criminal justice systems. The French government, in particular, was concerned that market liberalising measures might in some way undermine national public services. A Protocol on Services of General Interest was therefore added which stated that nothing in the Treaties affected the competence of Member States to provide, commission or organise non-economic services of a general interest.

Internal reforms were also made to the EU institutions. Commission membership is slimmed down to comprise, from 2014, a number corresponding to two-thirds of the number of the Member States. The President of the Commission was also given the unilateral power to dismiss individual Commissioners. With regard to the European Parliament, the cap on the number of MEPs in the European Parliament, 732, is retained. The central change to the Council was the introduction of a new formula for QMV in which there will be a qualified majority if 55 per cent of states representing at least 65 per cent of the population vote for it, and at least four states are required to vote against a measure for it to be blocked. Finally, the European Council was finally recognised as a formal EU institution.

There were also a number of institutional innovations. First, a President of the European Council elected by the European Council for a once renewable two and a half year period is established. Her job will be to drive forward and prepare the work of that institution. Secondly, a High Representative of the European Union is established. A member of both the Council and the Commission, her duty is to represent the Union in matters relating to the Common Foreign and Security Policy and ensure the consistency of the Union's external action. Finally, provision is made for citizens' initiatives whereby the Commission is obliged to consider proposals for legal measures made by petitions of one million citizens who are nationals of a significant number of Member States.

(iii) Ratification of the Lisbon Treaty

The ratification of the Lisbon Treaty was to follow the new ethos set out by that Treaty. This was to be no big pan-European constitutional moment in which, through referendums, the peoples of Europe participated in the creation of a new pan-European constitutional democracy. Instead, ratification was to take place, discretely, through national processes, which were in most cases national parliamentary ones. Indeed, Hungary set a record by ratifying the Lisbon Treaty four days after its signature. Only one state, Ireland, was to have a referendum, and this was because it was constitutionally required to do so.

If the ethos and symbolism of the Lisbon Treaty were different from the Constitutional Treaty, for the overwhelming majority of states, the institutional detail and extension of supranational competences were not significantly so.[136] This begged the question as to what weight was being given to the referendum results in the Netherlands and France and for the promises to hold referendums in the five other states which had promised to do so and had never held a referendum.

The question was particularly challenging for two very different reasons. The first relates to the nature of the Constitutional Treaty process. As has been said, this process had (unsuccessfully) been about mobilising popular loyalty, affection and support for the European integration process. The route chosen was to garner these elements around a particular document, the Constitutional Treaty. European publics were asked to bless a text that had been developed in a civil and plural manner. This was always an optimistic strategy, but, alongside this, it conveys the message to all that this text has a significance of the highest order. If the substance of this text is now to be adopted not only through different processes but through processes that seem to fly against previous wishes, a climate of mistrust is unsurprising. The second relates to the nature of the European Union. Selling institutional reform to the public is hard work in any circumstances, as procedures seem arcane and there is no obvious large policy goal, such as the single market or EMU, around which debate can be mobilised. The European Union is particularly difficult, for, as the German Constitutional Court pointed out, its procedures are hybrid ones, oscillating between being similar but not identical to those found in national democracies and intergovernmental ones. Ratification was not therefore straightforward.

On 12 June 2008, the Irish referendum on the Lisbon Treaty was held; 53.4 per cent of the voters rejected it. Subsequent analysis of the 'No' vote suggested lack of information about the Lisbon Treaty as an important determinant, as well as concerns about perceived threats to Irish abortion laws and neutrality, as well as possible conscription to a pan-European army. None of these were countenanced by the Lisbon Treaty amendments. The only amendment that weighed heavily was the possible loss of an Irish Commissioner generated by the reduction of the Commission.[137]

In response, in December 2008, national governments agreed that they would take a Decision upon the entry into force of the Lisbon Treaty providing that the Commission would retain

---

[136] For a thoughtful comparison see House of Commons, *EU Reform: A New Treaty or an Old Constitution*, Research Paper 07/64 (London, House of Commons, 2007). Ireland and the United Kingdom obtained opt-outs from the most significant extension of supranational competences, policing and judicial cooperation in criminal matters, something not granted to them by the Constitutional Treaty.

[137] The main research for the Irish government was carried out by Milward Brown IMS, Post Lisbon Treaty Research Findings, available at http://angl.concourt.cz/angl_verze/cases.php (accessed 20 July 2009).

one Commissioner from each Member State.[138] This will, of course, prevent its being reduced to two-thirds of the number of Member States, and is, in effect, an amendment to the Lisbon Treaty. In June 2009, the Member States set out three sets of guarantees in a European Council Decision that nothing in the Lisbon Treaty would:

- affect the scope or applicability of the rights to life, protection of the family or in respect of education as set out in the Irish Constitution;
- change in any way, for any Member State, the extent or operation of EU competence in respect to taxation;
- prejudice the security and defence policy of any Member State, provide for the creation of a European army or conscription, or affect a state's right to decide whether or not to participate in a military operation.[139]

On the basis of this, the Irish government held a second referendum on 2 October 2009. The Lisbon Treaty was approved by 67 per cent of the vote. However, this was not the end of the process. The Czech government extracted a final concession before ratification. The same guarantees granted to Poland and the United Kingdom in respect of the EU Charter of Fundamental Rights were to be granted to it.

The tawdriness to the conclusion of this process contrasts markedly with the fanfare surrounding the beginning of the Future of Europe Convention; for the Heads of Government took the opportunity in the Decisions on Ireland to bring in a series of general amendments and interpretations to the Treaty of Lisbon on the size of the Commission, its ambit on taxation and its impact on national security and defence policies. In addition, at the June 2009 summit, they passed a further Solemn Declaration on Workers' Rights, Social Policy and Other Issues.[140] Whilst only repeating the wording of the Treaty of Lisbon, it emphasised the responsibility of Member States for delivery of education and health, and importance of local autonomy in the provision and organisation of services of general economic interest: a message that EU law is to interfere as little as possible in these fields as well. Whatever the substantive merits of the case, the status of these is unclear. They are not formal amendments that have gone through appropriate EU or national processes or through any form of deliberation. Their legality and relationship to the Lisbon Treaty is uncertain. And it may be that this casualness with procedure will come back to haunt the Member States if, for example, the size of the Commission is challenged before a court.

The Irish referendums carried another message for those interested in European integration. The lack of knowledge about the process and the power of the 'myths' surrounding the Treaty of Lisbon illustrated the lack of depth of popular interest in the process, and the difficulty of mobilising popular loyalty for the project. This raises doubts about how democratically legitimate the process can ever be, and raises immediate concerns to make sure that the process is properly contained.

To this end, the process was challenged before national constitutional courts, most notably those in the Czech Republic[141] and Germany.[142] Both constitutional courts focused on whether excessive powers had been granted to the Union, albeit that the bases were different. For the Czech Constitutional Court, this derived from the Czech Republic being a democratic state

---

[138] Conclusions of the Brussels European Council, 11/12 December 2008, I.2, EU Council, 17271/1/08 Rev. 1.

[139] Conclusions of the Brussels European Council, 18/19 June 2009, Annex 1, EU Council 11125/2/09/Rev. 2.

[140] *Ibid.* Annex 2.   [141] Pl ÚS 19/08 *Treaty of Lisbon*, Judgment of 26 November 2008, available at www.usoud.cz/clarek; Pl ÚS 29/09 Treaty of Lisbon II, Judgment of 3 November 2009.

[142] 2 BvE 2/08 *Gauweiler* v *Treaty of Lisbon*, Judgment of 30 June 2009.

based upon the rule of law. This entailed that unlimited powers could not be transferred to another body such as the European Union. For the German Constitutional Court, it lay in the principle of self-determination incorporated in the right of each German citizen to vote in the Bundestag (the German Parliament). This entailed that the competences central to Germany's constitutional identity were not transferred to the EU level, as the latter lacked sufficient democratic structures to safeguard this principle.

In both instances, the language used by the courts was similar in tone to that used by the national constitutional courts vetting the Maastricht Treaty. Yet this time, both courts went a step further than simply placing a marker over the integration process. Whilst allowing for ratification of the Lisbon Treaty, both expressed concerns about individual provisions, thereby holding out the possibility of future review. Both also expressed concerns about the vagueness and possibility for abuse of the simplified revision procedure. The German Constitutional Court, in particular, considered that any revision using that procedure was a formal amendment, which would be open to constitutional review and would need ratification by both German parliamentary chambers, the Bundestag and the Bundesrat. There were further concerns from both courts. The Czech Constitutional Court was unhappy about the lack of clarity surrounding the Union's treaty-making powers and the German Constitutional Court was concerned about the vagueness and breadth of the flexibility provision. Whilst these amounted to grumblings in both cases rather than opposition, these grumblings suggested that use of these procedures is likely to be subject to particular scrutiny by these courts.

This brings us to the final paradox of the Treaty of Lisbon. It started as a process intended to open up European integration to greater popular participation. It has been allowed to be realised by the most intergovernmental body of the Union, the European Council, and by national constitutional courts. The price exacted by these bodies is a far more active control over European integration in the future. The European Council has taken it upon itself to interpret the Treaties and national constitutional courts have suggested that they are more amenable to challenges to EU acts on the grounds that these are ultra vires. Neither the European Council nor the courts are majoritarian institutions. Yet, it is they who have taken on the burden of the safeguarding of the European ideal, whilst, in the case of the German Constitutional Court at least, seriously questioning its democratic credentials.

FURTHER READING

S. Bartolini, *Restructuring Europe: Centre Formation, System Building, and Political Structuring Between the Nation State and the European Union* (Oxford, Oxford University Press, 2005)

G. Delanty, *Inventing Europe: Idea, Identity, Reality* (Basingstoke, Macmillan, 1995)

M. Dougan, 'The Treaty of Lisbon 2007: Winning Minds Not Hearts' (2008) 45 *Common Market Law Review* 617

N. Fligstein, *Euro-Clash: The EU, European Identity and the Future of Europe* (Oxford, Oxford University Press, 2008)

J. Gillingham, *European Integration 1950–2003: Superstate or New Market Economy* (Cambridge, Cambridge University Press, 2003)

J. Le Goff, *The Birth of Europe* (Oxford, Blackwell, 2005)

G. Majone, *Dilemmas of European Integration: The Ambiguities and Pitfalls of Integration by Stealth* (Oxford, Oxford University Press, 2005)

K. Middlemas, *Orchestrating Europe: The Informal Politics of European Union 1973–1995* (London, Fontana, 1995)

A. Milward, *The Reconstruction of Western Europe 1945–51* (London, Methuen, 1984)

A. Moravcsik, *The Choice for Europe: Social Purpose and State Power from Messina to Maastricht* (Ithaca, NY, Cornell University Press, 1998)

A. Pagden (ed.), *The Idea of Europe: From Antiquity to the European Union* (Cambridge, Cambridge University Press, 2002)

F. Scharpf, *Governing in Europe: Effective and Democratic?* (New York, Oxford University Press, 1999)

C. Shore, *Building Europe: The Cultural Politics of European Integration* (London and New York, Routledge, 2000)

J. Zielonka, *Europe as Empire: The Nature of the Enlarged European Union* (Oxford, Oxford University Press, 2006)

2

The EU Institutions

CONTENTS

1 INTRODUCTION

This chapter looks at the institutional settlement that governs the European Union.

Section 2 considers the organisation and powers of the European Commission. An independent administration, the Commission is the central institution for proposing legislation and for securing national government compliance with that legislation. It has been delegated significant law-making powers and is responsible for many of the executive tasks of the Union.

The wide-ranging nature of the Commission's powers has led to considerable specialisation within the Commission and to its delegating significant administrative powers to specialised agencies. It has also resulted in the Commission being dependent on national administrations for much of the administration of the Union whilst having a responsibility for supervising the latter's performance. The consequence is an executive order with extensive powers, marked by specialisation and mutually reinforcing relations between different administrative actors, which escapes accountability to either pan-European or national democratic constituencies.

Section 3 considers the Council of Ministers. The Council is composed of national ministers and has the final power of decision over almost all fields of EU law. Much debate centres on the level of national influence within the Council, in particular whether a measure is decided by unanimity or by qualified majority voting (QMV) and the weighting of national votes within QMV. In practice, most Decisions are taken without a vote and this shifts the question to how influence is exercised and the quality of debate that takes place. The Council's power is limited by its specialisation and by its floating membership. This has led to its being particularly dependent on the Committee of Permanent Representatives (COREPER), which prepares the Council's work, takes many of its Decisions and mediates with ministries back in the national capitals to formulate common positions.

Section 4 considers the European Council. This comprises the Heads of Government; the central roles of the European Council are to provide political direction to the Union and to resolve disputes that have otherwise proved intractable. It has historically been beset by a lack of infrastructure and a perceived lack of continuity, as the Presidency of the Council and of the European Council rotates between Member States every six months. The Lisbon Treaty creates a new fixed post of President of the European Council to prepare and to ensure follow-up to the meetings. If the European Council is to have an increased presence, its Decisions are likely to constrain and frame the workings of the rest of the institutional settlement. This will not only make the Union more of an intergovernmental and less of a supranational organisation, but, insofar as EU law constraints are likely to act less strongly on the European Council, may undermine many of the checks and balances that have been put in place.

Section 5 looks at the European Parliament. The Parliament does not have a general power of legislative initiative nor a monopoly over the adoption of laws. In addition, there are no European political parties and Members of European Parliament (MEPs) are not elected on a pan-European 'one citizen one vote' principle, but on the basis of quotas allocated to each Member State. This has led to questions about the democratic credentials of the Parliament. Notwithstanding this, it is the forum where there is most open public debate about EU decision-making. The Parliament has significant powers over law-making, the Budget and holding the executive to account. In this, it has the qualities of a reviewing parliament: one in which the executive does not hold a majority and whose influence derives from its ability, usually in committees, to review the proposals and activities of the executive. Whilst its formal legislative powers vary according to the nature of the legislative procedure, in all procedures Parliament has used its powers of amendment to significant effect. Similarly, it is the central institution where questions are asked, petitions considered and enquiries held about the other EU institutions.

2 THE COMMISSION

(i) The Commission bureaucracy

The Commission is often described as a single body with the sole agenda of promoting European integration. The reality is more complex. It employs more than 25,500 permanent staff, performs a wide number of tasks and has a wide array of relationships with a multiplicity of actors. Although in legal terms it is a single body, it is best to see the Commission as composed of three tiers: the College of Commissioners, the Directorates-General (DGs) and the Cabinets.

(a) The College of Commissioners

Formally, the Commission consists of twenty-seven Commissioners, with one Commissioner from each Member State.[1] These Commissioners make up the College of Commissioners. The Commission is appointed for a five-year term.[2] Once appointed, the Commissioners are allocated portfolios by the President.[3] Each Commissioner is then the primary person responsible for all the work of the Commission that falls within that policy area. The Commissioners are to be persons whose 'independence is beyond doubt'.[4] They are required not to seek or take instructions from any government or any other body and a duty is imposed on Member States to respect this principle. In addition, Commissioners must not find themselves in a position where a 'conflict of interest' arises. They must not, therefore, engage in any other occupation during their period of office. If any Commissioner fails to observe these rules, the Court of Justice may, on application by either the Council or the Commission, compulsorily retire that Commissioner.[5]

The Lisbon Treaty introduced one exception to this principle of independence. This concerns the office of the High Representative of the European Union for Foreign Affairs and Security Policy. Responsible for the conduct of the EU Common Foreign and Security Policy and its security and defence policy, she is a member of the Commission and one of the twenty-seven Commissioners.[6] However, she takes part in the work of the European Council,[7] chairs the Foreign Affairs Council[8] and acts under the mandate of the Council.[9] The intention of this 'double hat' is to create a more integrated and coordinated external policy,[10] as well as to give the Union a more salient international profile. Straddling the Commission and the Council,

---

[1] Article 17(4) TEU. It was initially anticipated that from 1 November 2014 the Commission should comprise only two-thirds that number: Article 17(5) TEU. In December 2008, as allowed by the Lisbon Treaty, the European Council took a Decision that the principle of one Commissioner from each Member State should continue after that date. EU Council, Presidency Conclusions 11 and 12 December 2008, para. 2 EU Council 17271/1/08.

[2] Article 17(3) TEU.

[3] The portfolios for the 2004–09 Commission were institutional relations and communication strategy; enterprise and industry; transport; administrative affairs and anti-fraud; justice, freedom and security; information society; environment; economic and monetary affairs; regional policy; fisheries; budget; science and research; education and culture; health and consumer protection; enlargement; development and humanitarian aid; taxation and customs union; competition; agriculture and rural development; external relations and European neighbourhood policy; internal market and services; employment, social affairs and equal opportunities; external trade; and energy. At the time of writing, they had not been allocated for the 2009–14 Commission.

[4] Article 17(3) TEU.

[5] Article 245 TFEU.

[6] Article 17(4) TEU.

[7] Article 15(2) TEU.

[8] Article 18(3) TEU.

[9] Article 18(2) TEU.

[10] Article 18(4) TEU.

she is subject to a double chain of accountability. She is appointed, by QMV, by the European Council with the agreement of the President of the Commission.[11] She is dismissed in the same manner[12] and so is the only member of the Commission who cannot be dismissed unilaterally by the President of the Commission.[13]

More generally, the independence of individual Commissioners must be seen in relative terms. Chosen because of distinguished and well-connected prior careers, they have a list of professional and political contacts, with over two-thirds chosen from a party in government at the time of appointment.[14]

> Usually, they are members – and appointees – of the major parties in their member state and continue some involvement with national politics after becoming Commissioners. Frequent trips to speak before (and to lecture to) national audiences are common. Again, the metaphor of gate-keeping is perhaps most useful: Commissioners are an easy and efficient way for the Commission to maintain a link with member state governments and domestic political systems. They will know what legislative proposals are politically acceptable in national capitals, while at the same time being in an ideal position to communicate to national elites the requirements of efficient European policy-making.[15]

Commissioners are also granted wriggle-room by only the most severe breaches of this principle being subject to sanction. In *Cresson*, the French Commissioner, Edith Cresson, had hired her dentist to be her personal adviser on a contract as a visiting scientist, notwithstanding that her chef de cabinet had seen this person as ill-qualified for any post.[16] Disciplinary proceedings were subsequently brought to withdraw some of her pension entitlements on the grounds that her actions were incompatible with her duties. The Court of Justice stated Commissioners were required to ensure that the general interest of the European Union took precedence at all times over both national and personal interests. However, slight deviations from this principle did not have to be censured. Censure was available only where the breach was of sufficient gravity. This will be the case, as was the case here, if the action by the Commissioner was manifestly inappropriate. There was little elaboration on what this phrase means, but it seems to suggest that only the most outrageous conduct will lead to legal sanction.

The other feature of the College is the principle of *collegiality*. The Commission is collectively responsible for all Decisions taken and all Commission Decisions should be taken collectively. In principle, these Decisions should take place at the weekly meetings of the Commission by a simple majority vote of the College. Meetings of each Commissioner's Cabinet (staff) occur two days before the weekly meeting. If there is agreement, it will be formally adopted as an 'A' item and there will be no formal discussion of the matter at the meeting. However, the reality is that there is little discussion within the College about the majority of the Commission's business. A 2008 study of legislative proposals between 2000 and 2004 found that only 17.4 per cent

---

[11] Article 18(1) TEU.

[12] Article 17(6) TEU.

[13] However, if the Parliament passes a motion of censure over the whole Commission, she must resign with the other Commission members: Article 17(8) TEU.

[14] A. Wonka, 'Technocratic and Independent? The Appointment of European Commissioners and its Policy Implications' (2007) 14 *JEPP* 169, 178.

[15] T. Christiansen, 'Tensions of European Governance: Politicised Bureaucracy and Multiple Accountability in the European Commission' (1997) 4 *JEPP* 73, 82; A. Smith, 'Why Commissioners Matter' (2003) 41 *JCMS* 137, 143–5.

[16] Case C-432/04 *Commission* v *Cresson* [2006] ECR I-6387.

even made it to the agenda of the meeting.[17] Of these, very few are discussed. Between 2000 and 2003, of 1,344 Decisions, there was a vote on only 11 and there was discussion on less than 3 per cent.[18]

The Commission deploys two procedures for conducting the majority of its business. The first is the 'written procedure'. Under this procedure, a proposal, a *greffe*, is adopted by the Commissioner responsible for the relevant portfolio. After the proposal has been approved by the Legal Service and associated Directorates-General, it is then circulated to the Cabinets of the other Commissioners. If there is no objection, the proposal is adopted as a Commission Decision. The 'ordinary' written procedure gives the Cabinets five working days to consider the proposal. The expedited written procedure must be authorised by the President. In such circumstances, the Cabinets are only given three working days. The second procedure is internal delegation. The Commission can delegate a straightforward 'act of management' to particular members.[19] What constitutes such an act is not clear. A Decision requiring undertakings to submit to a Commission investigation into anti-competitive practices was considered to be an act of management, which could be delegated. By contrast, a Decision finding a violation of EC competition law was not considered to be administrative in nature and was considered to be too wide a power to be delegated.[20]

(b) The President of the Commission

The President is proposed by the European Council, acting by QMV, and elected by the Parliament.[21] The only Commissioner without a portfolio, the President is the most powerful of all the Commissioners.[22] He has five important roles.

- He is involved in the appointment of the other Commissioners. With the Heads of Government, he nominates the other Commissioners, who are subject to a collective vote of approval by the Parliament and then appointed by the European Council by QMV.[23]
- He decides on the internal organisation of the Commission. This involves not only that the President allocates the individual portfolios at the beginning of the term, but that he can also shift the portfolios of Commissioners during their term of office.
- Individual Commissioners are responsible to him. The President can request individual Commissioners to resign.[24]
- He is to provide 'political guidance' to the Commission. At its most formal, this involves chairing and setting the agenda for the weekly meetings of the Commission. More substantively, it means proposing the political priorities of the Commission through pushing forward one proposal rather than another for adoption by the Commission.
- He has a roving policy brief. Although this causes tensions with the individual Commissioner concerned, the President may seek to take over a particular issue and drive Commission policy on that issue.

---

[17] A. Wonka, 'Decision-making Dynamics in the European Commission: Partisan, National or Sectoral?' (2008) 15 *JEPP* 1145, 1151.
[18] European Commission, *A Constitution for the Union*, COM(2003)548 final, Annex I.
[19] This practice was upheld in Case 5/85 *Akzo* v *Commission* [1986] ECR 2585.
[20] Case C-137/92 P *Commission* v *BASF* [1994] ECR I-2555.
[21] Article 17(7) TEU.
[22] The current President is a Portuguese national, Manuel Barroso.
[23] Article 17(7) TEU.
[24] Article 245 TFEU.

The President may be interested in the particular issue because it may be of such seminal importance to that term of the Commission or because there is strong disagreement between the Commissioner and the President over an issue. In the early 1990s, for example, Jacques Delors worked closely with the British Commissioner, Lord Cockfield, on the internal market because it was so central to the Commission's work at that time. He also intervened extensively, however, on social and environmental issues because he was unhappy with the work of the two Commissioners in those fields.[25] The President can also reserve important policy issues for himself. For example, in the mid-1990s, President Santer decided that he would assume responsibility for institutional reform. Finally, the President has an important representative role. He represents the Commission at meetings involving the Heads of Government and must account to other institutions when there is a questioning of the general conduct of the institution or a particular issue raises broader questions.

The power of the President has grown in recent times. Initially, there was no power to 'hire and fire'. Although it reflects the practice since 2004,[26] the power granted by the Lisbon Treaty for the President to fire individual Commissioners unilaterally is likely to loom over Commissioners. Awareness of it may lead them to anticipate his preferences or be particularly susceptible to his intervention. This will create particular challenges for the Commission as it reaches the end of its term. If the President wishes to be renominated, she will be especially keen to ensure her 'team' does not offend the players with the power to reappoint her, namely the national governments and the Parliament, with all the corollary implications for the independence of the Commission.

(c) The Directorates-General

The majority of Commission employees work for the DGs. DGs are the equivalent of Ministries within a national government. In the current Commission, there are forty DGs. These are divided into four groupings: policies,[27] external relations,[28] general services[29] and internal services.[30] Whilst these all fall within the portfolio of at least one Commissioner and are answerable to (at least) that Commissioner, with forty DGs and twenty-seven Commissioners, there is no neat dovetailing. Furthermore, DGs' duties are to the Commission rather than the Commissioner and individual Commissioners have complained about the autonomy they enjoy and the lack of loyalty they show.[31]

---

[25] G. Ross, *Jacques Delors and European Integration* (Oxford and New York, Oxford University Press, 1995).

[26] This is currently contained in the Code of Conduct that all Commissioners must sign on taking office. European Commission, *Code of Conduct for Commissioners*, SEC(2004)1487/2, 1.2.1.

[27] Currently these are economic and financial affairs; enterprise and industry; competition; employment, social affairs and equal opportunities; agriculture and rural development; energy and transport; environment; research; information society and media; joint research centre; fisheries and maritime affairs; internal market and services; regional policy; taxation and customs union; education and culture; health and consumer protection; justice, freedom and security.

[28] These are trade; development; enlargement; humanitarian aid; external relations and EuropeAid.

[29] These are communication; European Anti-Fraud Office; Eurostat; publications office and Secretariat General.

[30] These are personnel and administration; bureau of European policy advisers; informatics; European Commission data protection officer; infrastructures and logistics (Brussels and Luxembourg); internal audit service; budget; interpretation; legal service; translation; office for administration and payment of individual entitlements.

[31] D. Curtin and M. Egeberg, 'Tradition and Innovation: Europe's Accumulated Executive Order' (2008) 31 *West European Politics* 639, 657.

The variety of fields and roles in which the Commission is engaged results in there being little cohesion between the different DGs.[32] Put simply, the interests, backgrounds and values of those officials working for the Environment DG are likely to be very different from those working in the Competition DG. In addition to this, the work of each DG may focus on very different tasks. The bulk of the work of the Environment DG will be concentrated around the proposal and enforcement of legislation. By contrast, in the fields of education and culture the European Union has no law-making powers. The work of officials in that DG focuses on the development of programmes, administration of Community funding, and bringing different public and private actors together. This leads to different DGs having quite distinct cultures. This distinctiveness is reinforced by poor central coordinating mechanisms, which lead (arguably) to insufficient exchange between the DGs and to poor policy coherence because different DGs are often working in very different directions.[33]

(d) The Cabinets

If the College of Commissioners represents the political arm of the Commission and the DGs represent the administrative arm, between them sit the Cabinets. Formally appointed by the President, each Cabinet is the Office of a Commissioner. Composed of seven to eight officials,[34] the Cabinets act, first, as the interface between the Commissioner and the DGs under her aegis. They enable liaison between the two, and they help the Commissioner with formulating priorities and policies. They also act as the eyes and ears for the Commissioner, keeping her informed about what is happening elsewhere in the Commission. Finally, they combine with other Cabinets to prepare the weekly meetings for the College of Commissioners.

These tasks place the Cabinets in a very strong position within the Commission. The preparation of the meetings between the Commissioners forecloses a great deal of debate in the College, because in reality much is negotiated between the Cabinets. Similarly, by acting as the interface between the Commission and the DG, they inevitably become gate-keepers to the Commissioner, who must be negotiated with by DG officials wishing to put forward particular ideas. Their role is, thus, controversial. DGs have seen them at times as Machiavellian, bypassing normal procedures and sabotaging perfectly acceptable proposals.[35]

(ii) Powers of the Commission

The powers of the Commission are now systematised in a single Article.

---

[32] L. Cram, 'The European Commission as a Multi-Organization: Social Policy and IT Policy in the EU' (1994) 1 *JEPP* 195.

[33] L. Hooghe, *The European Commission and the Integration of Europe* (Cambridge, Cambridge University Press, 2001) 201–5.

[34] The President's Cabinet is larger, with eleven officials.

[35] J. Peterson, 'The Santer Era: The European Commission in Normative, Historical and Theoretical Perspective' (1999) 6 *JEPP* 46.

Article 17 TEU

1. The Commission shall promote the general interest of the Union and take appropriate initiatives to that end. It shall ensure the application of the Treaties, and of measures adopted by the institutions pursuant to the Treaties. It shall oversee the application of Union law under the control of the Court of Justice of the European Union. It shall execute the budget and manage programmes. It shall exercise coordinating, executive and management functions, as laid down in the Treaties. With the exception of the common foreign and security policy, and other cases provided for in the Treaties, it shall ensure the Union's external representation. It shall initiate the Union's annual and multiannual programming with a view to achieving interinstitutional agreements.
2. Union legislative acts may only be adopted on the basis of a Commission proposal, except where the Treaties provide otherwise. Other acts shall be adopted on the basis of a Commission proposal where the Treaties so provide.

Whilst this bringing together of the Commission's powers is very welcome, it still makes sense to consider them in the light of the different roles of the Commission, particularly as reference still has to be had to other parts of the Treaties in relation to certain powers.

(a) Legislative and quasi-legislative powers

The Commission has direct legislative powers in only two limited fields: ensuring that public undertakings comply with the rules contained in the Treaty[36] and determining the conditions under which EU nationals may reside in another Member State after having worked there.[37] It has more significant powers in the field of delegated legislation, where the Council can confer quasi-legislative powers upon it.

The remit of these quasi-legislative powers has been interpreted very broadly. Whilst the Council cannot delegate the essential elements of a policy to the Commission, it can delegate any other legal powers to the Commission.[38] The delegation of quasi-legislative powers to the Commission is also very widespread. Provision for delegation is estimated to be present in about 20 per cent of all legislation. The figure is still higher where legislation

---

Article 290 TFEU

1. A legislative act may delegate to the Commission the power to adopt non-legislative acts to supplement or amend certain non-essential elements of the legislative act.
2. The objectives, content, scope and duration of the delegation of power shall be explicitly defined in the legislative acts. The essential elements of an area shall be reserved for the legislative act and accordingly shall not be the subject of a delegation of power.

---

[36] Article 106(3) TFEU.
[37] Article 45(3)(d) TFEU.
[38] Article 290(1) TFEU. This codifies judicial practice. Joined Cases T-64/01 and T-65/01 *Afrikanische Fruchtcompanie* v *Council* [2004] ECR II-521.

either authorises expenditure or was adopted by QMV, with it being used in 66 per cent of all expenditure-authorising legislation and in 67 per cent of legislation adopted under the single market procedures.[39] Highly significant matters have also been delegated. The measure prompting the bovine spongiform encephalopathy (BSE) crisis, the prohibition on the export of beef and bovine products from the United Kingdom, was instigated under powers granted to the Commission to make veterinary and zootechnical checks on live animals and products with a view to the completion of the internal market.[40] The measure had huge implications for animal welfare, public health, public finances and the livelihood of farmers across the Union. These were so big that they prompted a political crisis across the Union.[41]

Since the early 1960s, the exercise of these powers has been monitored by committees composed of representatives of the national governments.[42] In certain circumstances, these committees can refer a matter to the Council, one of the primary legislative bodies in the Union, to overrule the Commission. This process, known as comitology, is dealt with in more detail in Chapter 3.[43] It is sufficient to note here that members of these committees represent governmental interests and, insofar as they are experts, also monitor the technical quality of the Commission's work. Even to secure these interests, these are quite modest controls, with an eschewal of the more rigorous types of control that are present in the United States to control similar delegated powers.[44]

Such widespread delegation raises questions of democratic accountability.[45] One justification is that the laborious nature of the primary law-making procedures can result in pressing decisions not being taken sufficiently quickly. Another is policy credibility. Primary legislatures may neither have the expertise nor be able to take a sufficiently long-term view of matters, because of fears about electoral accountability. Finally, it can be argued that the grant of legislative powers to the Commission in highly technical areas liberates other institutions, allowing them to spend more time on what 'matters'. Yet, even if these were accepted, they do not provide a blank cheque to the Commission to legislate in so many areas.[46] The Lisbon Treaty has therefore introduced increased parliamentary[47] and judicial controls.[48] It remains to be seen how effectively these will work.

---

[39] R. Dogan, 'Comitology: Little Procedures with Big Implications' (1997) 20 *WEP* 36. Similar findings are made in F. Franchino, 'Delegating Powers in the European Community' (2004) 34 *BJPS* 269.

[40] The measure was Decision 96/239/EC [1996] OJ L78/47. The principal basis for it was Directive 90/425/EEC, article 10(4) [1990] OJ L224/29.

[41] See J. Neyer, 'The Regulation of Risks and the Power of the People: Lesson from the BSE Crisis' (2006) 4 *EIOP* No. 6.

[42] The limits of comitology as a check on the Commission are perhaps reflected in its being something that was originally proposed by the Commission to garner acceptance for its proposals in agriculture. J. Blom-Hansen, 'The Origins of EU Comitology System: A Case of Informal Agenda-Setting by the Commission' (2008) 15 *JEPP* 208, 213–18.

[43] See pp. 117–24.

[44] These include time limits on delegation, appeal procedures, public hearings and requirements for explicit legislative approval. F. Franchino, 'Delegating Powers in the European Community' (2004) 34 *BJPS* 269.

[45] M. Cini, 'The Commission: An Unelected Legislator?' (2002) 8(4) *Journal of Legislative Studies* 14.

[46] G. Majone, 'Two Logics of Delegation: Agency and Fiduciary Relations in EU Governance' (2001) 2 *EUP* 103. F. Franchino, 'Efficiency or Credibility? Testing the Two Logics of Delegation to the European Commission' (2002) 9(5) *JEPP* 1; M. Pollack, *The Engines of European Integration: Delegation, Agency and Agenda-Setting in the EU* (Oxford, Oxford University Press, 2003) 101–7.

[47] Article 290(2), (3) TFEU. For further analysis see pp. 120–2 in Chapter 3.

[48] Article 263(4) TFEU. See pp. 414–15.

(b) Agenda-setting

The Commission has responsibility for initiating the policy process in a number of ways. It first decides the legislative programme for each year.[49] Secondly, in most fields, it has a monopoly over the power of legislative initiative.[50] Thirdly, it also has the power of financial initiative. The Commission starts the budgetary process by placing a draft Budget before the Parliament and the Council.[51] Finally, the Commission is responsible for stimulating policy debate more generally. The most celebrated example of this was the White Paper on Completion of the Internal Market, which set out an agenda and timetable for completing the internal market by the end of 1992.[52]

The matter will be assigned to the DG within whose field the proposal seems to fall most clearly. The DG will appoint a senior official as rapporteur. This rapporteur will be responsible to a 'management board' of senior officials within the DG. He is responsible for internal consultation with other interested DGs and for external consultation with outside parties. The external consultation will take place in expert committees, consisting of national officials and experts, and advisory committees composed of different sectional interests (e.g. industry, consumer and environmental groups and trade unions). The proposal has then to be vetted by the Commission Legal Service for its legality. It will then be adopted by a lead Commissioner with responsibility for the portfolio, who will choose whether to put it before the other Commissioners.

Very few proposals are put forward by the Commission using its own initiative. It enjoys, instead, a gate-keeper role, where different interests (national governments, industry, NGOs) come to it with legislative suggestions. Taking 1998 as an example, the Commission estimated that 35 per cent of its proposals were adapting legislation to new economic, scientific or social data; 31 per cent were because of international obligations imposed on it, 12 per cent were tasks required by the Treaty where it enjoyed no discretion; and 17 per cent were responding to requests by national governments, EU institutions or economic operators. Only 5 per cent were taken at its own behest.[53]

This results in the Commission being far more politicised than a traditional civil service. It becomes a marketplace for the development of ideas and accommodation of interests, with a variety of parties, both public and private, seeking to influence it.[54] In addition, it is both an agenda-setter and a veto-player. Nothing can happen without the Commission deciding to make a proposal in the first place and it can frame the terms of debate and legislation. It also gives the Commission significant influence in the subsequent debates. Because it can withdraw a proposal at any time, parties cannot ignore its views even after the proposal has been made. However, its power should not be overestimated. Its influence depends upon a number of variables. Central is institutional context. In areas where a unanimity vote by Member States is not required, the Commission can act as a broker between some actors and to outmanoeuvre

---

[49] For 2009, see European Commission, *Commission Work Programme for 2009*, COM(2008)712.

[50] The main exception is in Common Foreign and Security Policy where it has only an ancillary role. In this field initiatives or proposals may be made by any Member State, the High Representative or the High Representative with Commission support: Article 30(1) TEU.

[51] Article 314(2) TFEU.

[52] COM(85)310 final.

[53] House of Lords European Union Committee, *Initiation of EU Legislation* (22nd Report, 2007–08 Session, HL, London) 15.

[54] G. Peters, 'Agenda-Setting in the European Community' (1994) 1 *JEPP* 9.

others.[55] In some areas, it can induce other institutions to adopt its proposal as the 'lesser evil' by threatening to use other powers at its disposal, such as bringing a Member State before the Court of Justice, which would lead to more draconian consequences.[56] There is also a temporal dimension. If the Commission is impatient, its influence is weakened, as it has to accept more readily the views of the other institutions. The reverse is true if the other institutions are impatient for a measure to be adopted.[57]

The traditional justification for the Commission's powers was that its autonomy would result in its being best able to represent the common European interest.[58] Over time, this justification has come to carry less weight. The transfer of competences to the European Union has not always resulted in a corresponding transfer of powers to the Commission. Increasingly, therefore, national governments have taken an interest in agenda-setting and limiting the Commission's discretion.[59] A range of measures have also been taken to place institutional constraints on this important power.

First, the Council, through its Presidency, sets out legislative timetables of six months each, which the Commission is expected to follow. More wide-ranging, since 2002, the European Council, representing the Heads of Government, seeks to determine the legislative agenda of the Union, agreeing and revising annual and tri-annual legislative programmes every year.[60] The second measure is that both the Parliament and the Council can ask the Commission to make a proposal.[61] In 2003, the Commission gave an undertaking to 'take account' of such requests and reply 'rapidly and appropriately'.[62] The third measure is introduced by the Lisbon Treaty and is the citizens' initiative. This requires the Commission to consider petitions for proposals where these come from at least one million citizens from a significant number of Member States.[63] The details of these procedures have yet not been worked out, but it is undoubtedly intended to make the process less technocratic and more populist. In addition, there are now well-established procedures which require the Commission to consult widely and consider the impacts of a significant legislative proposal before it adopts it.[64]

It is doubtful whether this is sufficient. Formally, the Commission is the central agenda-setter for the European Union and a feature of democracies is popular contestation about future political direction. As we shall see, the democratic credentials of both the Council and Parliament can be questioned. Further, neither makes requests for initiatives that often.[65] Whilst the citizens' initiative is an attempt to open the process, there is a danger of its being captured by small interest groups, particularly as only 0.5 per cent of the EU population have to sign

---

[55] S. Schmidt, 'Only an Agenda-Setter? The Commission's Power over the Council of Ministers' (2000) 1 *EUP* 37.

[56] S. Schmidt, 'The European Commission's Powers in Shaping Policies' in D. Dimitrakopoulos (ed.), *The Changing Commission* (Manchester, Manchester University Press, 2004).

[57] M. Pollack, 'Delegation, Agency and Agenda Setting in the European Community' (1997) 51 *IO* 99, 121–4.

[58] K. Featherstone, 'Jean Monnet and the "Democratic Deficit" in the European Union' (1994) 32 *JCMS* 149, 154–5.

[59] G. Majone, *Dilemmas of European Integration: The Ambiguities and Pitfalls of Integration by Stealth* (Oxford, Oxford University Press, 2005) 51–3.

[60] See p. 77.

[61] Articles 225, 241 TFEU respectively.

[62] Interinstitutional Agreement on Better Law-Making [2003] OJ C321/1, para. 9. This duty has been strengthened by the Lisbon Treaty which now formally requires the Commission to give reasons if it does not accede to their requests: Articles 225 and 241 TFEU.

[63] Article 11(4) TEU.

[64] This is dealt with in more detail in the chapter on governance. See pp. 373–8.

[65] There are no figures from the Council but only six requests were, for example, made by the Parliament between 2004 and 2007: House of Lords European Union Committee, *Initiation of EU Legislation*, above, n.53, 27–32.

the petition; and there also remains the question of how responsive the Commission will be to these petitions. Follesdall and Hix have suggested that as the Commission holds a power, the power to initiate legislation, that is usually granted only to governments in democratic states, then one should have votes for the President of the Commission in the same way that there are votes for domestic government.

A. Follesdall and S. Hix, 'Why there is a Democratic Deficit in the EU: A Response to Majone and Moravcsik' (2006) 44 *Journal of Common Market Studies* 533, 554

...the Commission's designated role regarding the European interest should not be formulated in such a way as to imply that the content of this term is uncontested, or that the Commission is the only institution able and willing to identify and pursue it. Now that the basic policy-competence architecture of the EU has been confirmed – in terms of the regulation of the market at the European level and the provision of spending-based public goods at the national level – the role of the Commission is not fundamentally different from other political executives.

The purely Pareto-improving functions of the Commission, such as the merger control authority or the monitoring of legislative enforcement, could easily be isolated in new independent agencies. Then, the expressly 'political' functions of the Commission, in terms of defining a work programme for five years, initiating social, economic and environmental laws, and preparing and negotiating the multi-annual and annual budgets, should be open to rigorous contestation and criticism. Such criticism should not be interpreted as euroscepticism or anti-federalism, but rather as an essential element of democratic politics at the European level...

Related to these two ideas, an institutional mechanism needs to be found for generating debate and contestation about politics *in*, not only *of*, the EU. The most obvious way of doing this is contestation of the office of the Commission President – the most powerful executive position in the EU. For example, there could be a direct election of the Commission President by the citizens or by national parliaments. Alternatively, a less ambitious proposal would be for government leaders to allow a more open battle for this office without any further treaty reform. Now that the Commission President is elected by a qualified-majority vote (after the Nice Treaty), a smaller majority is needed in the European Council for a person to be nominated. This led to a dramatic increase in the number of candidates in the battle to succeed Romano Prodi and a linking of the nomination of a candidate to the majority in the newly elected European Parliament. However, the process could have been much more open and transparent – with candidates declaring themselves before the European elections, issuing manifestos for their term in office, and the transnational parties and the governments then declaring their support for one or other of the candidates well before the horse-trading began.

(c) **Executive powers**

The Commission is responsible for ensuring that the European Union's revenue is collected and passed on by national authorities and that the correct rates are applied. It is also responsible for overseeing and coordinating a large part of EU expenditure, be this structural, agricultural or social funds. Secondly, it is responsible for administering EU aid to third countries. Thirdly, the High Representative, who, it will be remembered, is also a Commissioner, is to represent the Union for matters relating to the Common Foreign and Security Policy. Notably, she will conduct political dialogue with third parties on the Union's behalf and express the Union's position in international organisations and at international conferences.[66] To that end, she will be assisted by a European External Action Service, which will comprise officials from the Council Secretariat of the Council and the Commission.[67] It is worth noting that there is some ambiguity about the organisations in which the High Representative is to represent the European Union. This is explicitly stated to be the case for the United Nations, the Council of Europe and the OECD.[68] The Treaties are silent on the WTO, the international organisation in which the Union has been historically most active, and it is the Commission which has traditionally represented the Union here. Finally, the Commission handles applications for membership of the European Union by carrying out an investigation of the implications of membership and submitting an opinion to the Council.[69]

(d) Supervisory powers

The Commission acts as the 'conscience of the Union'. First, the Commission enjoys certain regulatory powers. It can declare illegal state aids provided by Member States[70] or measures enacted in favour of public undertakings which breach the Treaty.[71] It has also been granted powers to declare anti-competitive practices by private undertakings illegal and to fine those firms,[72] as well as the power to impose duties on goods coming from third states, which are benefiting from 'unfair' trade practices, such as dumping or export subsidies.[73]

Secondly, it may bring Member States before the Court of Justice for breaching EU law.[74] It uses this power extensively.[75] The Commission is also responsible for monitoring compliance by Member States with judgments of the Court of Justice. It can bring those Member States which it considers to have failed to comply back before the Court to have them fined. This was done seven times in 2007.[76]

Couching it in these terms leads to the process being seen as one of enforcement. To be sure, when the matter is finally litigated before the Court that is what takes place. Yet, as the statistics show, only in a very small proportion of cases does the process get that far. Such a view also obscures the policy-choices involved in the development of local procedures to comply with, transpose and apply EU law. Instead, as Curtin and Egeberg have argued,[77] a far more synergistic relationship often emerges. The responsibility of national administrations for applying, transposing and administering EU law, with Commission responsibility for oversight

---

[66] Article 27(1), (2) TEU.
[67] Article 27(3) TEU.
[68] Article 220 TFEU.
[69] Article 49 TEU.
[70] Article 108(2) TFEU.
[71] Article 106(3) TFEU.
[72] Regulation 1/2003/EC, articles 7 and 23 respectively [2001] OJ L1/1.
[73] In relation to dumping see Regulation 384/96/EC [1996] OJ L56/1, especially articles 7–9.
[74] Article 258 TFEU.
[75] At the end of 2006, for example, the Commission had instigated proceedings in 2,518 cases. European Commission, *Twenty Fourth Annual Report on Monitoring the Application of Community Law*, COM(2007)398, 3. The number was not given for the following year.
[76] Article 260(2) TFEU. European Commission, *Twenty Fifth Annual Report on Monitoring the Application of Community Law*, COM(2008)777, 3.
[77] See also G. della Cananea, 'The European Union's Mixed Administrative Proceedings' (2004) 68 *Law and Contemporary Problems* 197; H. Hofmann and A. Türk, 'Conclusion: Europe's Integrated Administration' in H. Hofmann and A. Türk (eds.), *EU Administrative Governance* (Edward Elgar, Cheltenham, 2006).

and coordination of the process, leads to an ongoing engagement between the Commission and its national counterparts, which revolves more around resolving common interests than around antagonism. This institutional engagement and spirit generates a new executive order, which is neither simply European nor simply national.

D. Curtin and M. Egeberg, 'Tradition and Innovation: Europe's Accumulated Executive Order' (2008) 31 *West European Politics* 639, 649–50

Since the Commission does not possess its own agencies at the member state level, it (and EU-level agencies) seems to establish a kind of partnership with those national bodies responsible for the application of EU legislation as well as some involvement in the development of EU policies. Such bodies may be found among national agencies that are already somewhat detached from their respective ministerial departments.

The term 'Europe's integrated administration' takes on board the situation where in contemporary European integration processes the traditional distinction of direct and indirect administration has become blurred, with the levels being interwoven to form a more unitary pattern of 'integrated administration'. The EU level is also involved in implementing activities undertaken by member state authorities, while member states' administrations are involved in creating EU legislation and implementing acts. Case studies within five different policy fields have shown that national agencies in fact seem to act in a 'double-hatted' manner, constituting parts of national administrations while at the same time becoming parts of a multi-level Union administration in which the Commission in particular forms the new executive centre. As parts of national administrations, serving their respective ministerial departments, agency officials play a crucial role in transposition of EU legislation as well as in Council working parties and comitology committees. However, when it comes to the application of EU legislation in particular, agencies also cooperate rather closely with their respective directorates in the Commission, often by-passing their ministerial departments.

Not surprisingly, in this situation agencies may face competing policy expectations from their two 'masters' that may be hard to reconcile. A questionnaire study showed that the importance of the 'parent ministry' partly depends on its organisational capacity in the field and the extent to which the legislative area is politically contested. Obviously, the role of the Commission will tend to vary as well depending on, for example, the relative strength of the DG involved. Also, lack of knowledge and novelty make national agencies in new member states more receptive to inputs from the Commission. 'Double-hattedness' entails new patterns of cooperation and conflict in executive politics, evoking conflicts that cut across national boundaries as well. It could also be expected to lead to more even implementation across countries compared to indirect implementation, although not as even as if the Commission had its own agencies or if the application of EU law was in the hands of EU-level bodies.

The presence of such an executive order poses a number of challenges. Most fundamentally, it raises, as Curtin and Egeberg note in the remainder of their article, real questions about accountability. A world in which national administrations justify themselves to and are held to account by a Commission can not only create mixed loyalties, but also loosen the duty of those national administrations to account to other parts of their government and to their domestic constituencies. This is particularly worrisome if the relationship with the Commission is essentially a cosy one based on mutual trust, as then it becomes not so much a duty to hold oneself to account to another master as a duty not to hold oneself out too strongly to account at all.

(iii) Regulatory agencies and the Commission

The concentration of so many functions in the Commission has placed pressure on its resources. A preference has emerged for delegating specialised and time-consuming tasks to independent agencies and offices rather than for using the Commission as a repository for further regulatory competences. This preference took on a new intensity following two scandals in the late 1990s: first, the BSE scandal in which the Commission had been found to cover up knowledge relating to the risks of BSE and new variant Creutzfeldt–Jakob disease; and secondly, evidence of mismanagement by the Santer Commission. In 1999, a Task Force for Administrative Reform recommended that the Commission was administering too much and more needed to be delegated to specialised agencies.[78] This theme was taken up a year later in the Commission White Paper on Governance, which advocated the creation of independent EU regulatory agencies in any field marked by specialisation and complexity, and where a single public interest predominates.[79]

To date, twenty-two Community agencies, plus a further six executive agencies,[80] have been established. The remit of Community agencies ranges over a wide area from fundamental rights, environment and external frontiers to pharmaceuticals, trade marks and air safety. Their powers vary considerably. Some, like the European Environment Agency or the European Institute for Gender Equality, do little more than provide information and commission studies on their fields. There are two, the Office for Harmonisation of the Internal Market and the Community Plant Variety Office, which grant intellectual property rights (trade marks and plant variety rights respectively).

The most wide-ranging power granted to a number of agencies is to provide expert opinion, which will either guide other EU institutions in deciding whether to authorise a product or activity or inform legislation they wish to develop in this field. Agencies having one or both of these powers include the European Food Safety Authority (EFSA),[81] the European Aviation Safety Authority (EASA), the European Chemicals Agency (ECHA), the European Medicines Agency (EMEA), the European Railway Agency (ERA) and the European Network and Information Security Agency (ENISA). Whilst EU institutions are not bound by these Opinions in adopting legislation or granting authorisations, there is invariably a duty to consult the agency before doing this.[82] It can then depart from the agency's Opinion only on grounds of safety where it can provide an alternative, equally authoritative, contradictory opinion. This is difficult and, in practice, the Commission has always followed agency Opinions. The consequence has been that the latter has become the central institution for determining which food may be marketed in the European Union. This is not uncontroversial as it allows both the acquisition of new EU capacities and the taking of important decisions behind the cloak of 'expertise'.

---

[78] European Commission, *Reforming the Commission*, COM(2000)200, Part I, 6.
[79] European Commission, *European Governance: A White Paper*, COM(2001)428, 24.
[80] Executive agencies differ from other agencies in that they are more managerial in nature, being responsible for the administration of an EU programme. Their mandate is set out in Regulation 58/2003/EC [2003] OJ L11/1.
[81] The central powers of EFSA are set out in Regulation 178/2002/EC [2002] OJ L31/1.
[82] Case T-13/99 *Pfizer Animal Health* v *Council* [2002] ECR II-3305. See pp. 380–2.

M. Shapiro, 'The Problems of Independent Agencies in the United States and the European Union' (1997) 4 *Journal of European Public Policy* 262, 281–2

The standard, overt rationale for the creation of EU agencies is that they ought to be partially or wholly independent of the Commission because they are 'managerial', perform 'technical' tasks or are engaged in 'information' gathering and analysis only. In the US it may make sense to say that managerial, technical, informational functions should be separated from the regular cabinet departments or ministries because those departments are part of the Executive Branch which is political. Both in the sense that it is headed by a democratically elected President and in the sense that the President is his political party's leader. This is the get-technology-out-of-politics theme. But the separation of powers in the EU is entirely different. The Commission-Council separation is itself a supposed separation of technocracy (the Commission) from intergovernmental politics (the Council). Therefore, to assert a managerial-technical-informational rationale for separating the agencies from the Commission is, in a certain sense, absurd. It is the assertion that the technical ought to be separated from the technical.

Is all this managerial-technical-informational talk simply a smoke screen for the more fundamental argument that, because Europeans don't like the technocrats in Brussels and fear concentrating even more governance there, if we want more EU technocrats, we need to split them up and scatter them about Europe? I think the answer to this question is largely yes but not entirely.

A second motive is, I believe, a kind of 'neo-functionalism'. If currently direct routes to further political integration of the Union are blocked, following Haas's old arguments about the World Health Organisation and the UN, further growth can be achieved indirectly through the proliferation of small, limited jurisdictions, allegedly 'technical agencies' that will appear politically innocuous. That is why it is not enough to say that the agencies are not in Brussels. It must also be said that they are merely technical or informational.

A third motive is about technocracy. The member state composed management boards were no doubt a political necessity. But by stressing the technical and informational functions of these agencies, by making each highly specialised to a particular technology and by incorporating large components of scientific personnel, there is undoubtedly the hope that the technocrats will take over these agencies from the politicians. And the technocrats for each of these agencies, it is hoped will create Europe-wide epistemic communities whose technical truths transcend intergovernmental politics. As Americans say 'there is no Republican or Democratic way to pave a street', Europeans may be able to say there is no French or Greek way. Thus, while the proffered technocratic rationales do not really explain why the agencies should be independent of the Commission, they do explain why the agencies should each take a small slice of allegedly technical-informational activity. That kind of organisation is most likely, over time, to assure the internal dominance within each agency of its transnational technocrats over its national politicians.

3 THE COUNCIL OF MINISTERS

(i) Powers and workings of the Council

The Council of Ministers, alongside the European Council, is the institution that represents national governments. Its powers are rather unsatisfactorily set out in the TEU.

> ### Article 16(1) TEU
>
> The Council shall, jointly with the European Parliament, exercise legislative and budgetary functions. It shall carry out policy-making and coordinating functions as laid down in the Treaties.

In fact, ranged across the Treaties, the Council's powers are multifaceted and varied. They include the following:

- In areas of policy where responsibility lies with the Member States, such as general economic policy, the Council acts as a forum within which Member States can consult with each other and coordinate their behaviour.[83]
- It can take the other institutions before the Court for failure to comply with EU law[84] or for failure to act when required by EU law.[85]
- It can request the Commission to undertake studies or submit legislative proposals.[86]
- It prepares the work for the European Council meetings and ensures their follow-up.[87]
- It frames the Common Foreign and Security Policy and takes the decisions necessary for defining and implementing it on the basis of the general guidelines and strategic lines defined by the European Council.[88]
- It has power of final decision on the adoption of legislation in most areas of EU policy.

The last power is particularly significant. Whilst, as we shall see, it is shared with the Parliament in certain fields, it leads to the Council being perceived, as Article 16(1) TEU suggests, as the most important institution in the law-making process. The Council comprises a minister from each Member State, who is authorised to commit the government of that state on that matter.[89] Environmental ministers will, thus, sit in the Environmental Council and agriculture or fisheries ministers in the Agriculture and Fisheries Council. Since 2002, it has been agreed that more than one minister from each Member State may sit in a Council meeting, particularly where an issue crosses different ministerial portfolios.[90] Most Councils meet formally between once a month and once every two months. Prior to the Lisbon Treaty, the Council sat in nine configurations:

- General Affairs and External Relations;
- Economic and Financial Affairs;
- Justice and Home Affairs;
- Employment, Social Policy and Consumer Affairs;
- Competitiveness;
- Transport, Telecommunications and Energy;
- Agriculture and Fisheries;
- Environment;
- Education, Youth and Culture.

---

[83] Article 121 TFEU.   [84] Article 225 TFEU.
[85] Article 265 TFEU.   [86] Article 241 TFEU.
[87] Article 16(6) TEU.   [88] Article 26(2) TEU.
[89] Article 16(2) TEU.
[90] The rules for the Council are set out in Decision 2002/682/EC, EURATOM adopting the Council's Rules of Procedure [2002] OJ L230/7. See also Decision 2009/878/EU establishing a list of Council configurations [2009] OJ L315/46.

Whilst these configurations are fewer than those which existed previously, decision-making is still perceived as fragmented by the specialised nature of the different Council configurations. Furthermore, the floating membership of each Council, with the constant changing of ministers and governments and its occasional nature (namely that it only met once a month), was felt to weaken any sense of collective identity. The Lisbon Treaty therefore provides for the European Council to adopt a Decision by QMV on all Council configurations other than General Affairs and Foreign Affairs.[91] Moreover, there is clearly a feeling that this should be urgently revisited with it being provided that, pending such a European Council Decision, the General Affairs Council may take such a Decision by simple majority vote.[92]

The other 'innovation' to enable this is the strengthening of the General Affairs Council. Since 2002, the General Affairs and External Relations Council, composed of foreign ministers, has met alternately as the General Affairs Council and as the External Relations Council. As the former, it considers matters that affect a number of EU policies and is responsible for coordinating work done by the other Council configurations, and for handling dossiers submitted by the European Council. The Lisbon Treaty formalises this by establishing two different configurations: the General Affairs Council and the Foreign Affairs Council, thereby increasing the number of configurations to ten. The former is to ensure that the different Council configurations all row in the same direction and that this direction is the one ordained by the European Council, the institution comprising the Heads of Government and State. To this end, the General Affairs Council is to secure consistency in the work of the different Council configurations and to prepare and ensure the follow-up to meetings of the European Council, in liaison with the Presidents of the European Council and the Commission.[93]

It is questionable whether this will be sufficient to overcome the current difficulties of fragmentation. The initial draft for the Constitutional Treaty proposed a permanent General and Legislative Affairs Council based in Brussels composed of Ministers of Europe, which would assume the role performed by the General Affairs Council.[94] This proposal was rejected by the national governments, who were concerned that such a Council might become too autonomous and powerful. Yet, the original initiative suggests that foreign ministers meeting every now and then in Brussels may not have the required level of interest and resources to do the job expected of them. The other concern is whether, given the jealousy that national ministers exercise over their portfolios, the General Affairs Council will have the necessary authority. Will, for example, a powerful economics minister listen to his foreign minister?

(ii) Decision-making within the Council

The first form of voting is the *simple majority* vote. Under this system, each Member of the Council has one vote, and fourteen votes are required for a measure to be adopted. This procedure is used in only a few areas, principally procedural ones, as it fails to protect national interests and undue weight is given to the interests of small states at the expense of larger ones. The only area of real significance that is subject to a simple majority vote is the decision to convene an intergovernmental conference to amend the TEU.[95] The converse of simple

---

[91] Article 236(a) TFEU.
[92] Protocol No. 10 on Transitional Provisions, Article 4.
[93] Article 16(6) TEU.   [94] Article 23(1) DCT.
[95] This is taken by the European Council, Article 48(3) TEU. The others are adoption of the Council's own rules of procedure (Articles 240(3) and 235(3) TFEU for European Council) and request for the Commission to undertake studies or submit proposals (Article 241 TFEU).

Table 2.1   Votes and population sizes of Member States

State	Votes	Population
Germany	29	82 million
United Kingdom	29	59.4 million
France	29	59.1 million
Italy	29	57.7 million
Spain	27	39.4 million
Poland	27	38.6 million
Romania	14	22 million
Netherlands	13	15.8 million
Greece	12	10.6 million
Czech Rep	12	10.3 million
Belgium	12	10.2 million
Hungary	12	10 million
Portugal	12	9.9 million
Sweden	10	8.9 million
Austria	10	8.1 million
Bulgaria	10	7.7 million
Slovakia	7	5.4 million
Denmark	7	5.3 million
Finland	7	5.2 million
Lithuania	7	3.7 million
Ireland	7	3.7 million
Latvia	4	2.4 million
Slovenia	4	2 million
Estonia	4	1.4 million
Cyprus	4	0.8 million
Luxembourg	4	0.4 million
Malta	3	0.4 million

majority voting is voting by *unanimity.* Every Member State has a veto on any legislation being considered. It must actively vote against a measure for it to be vetoed; abstention is insufficient. Unanimity voting is used in those areas of the TEU which are more politically sensitive. Its requirement is still widespread in the Treaty.[96] The final form of voting frequently used is that of QMV. This is a weighted system of voting, under which each Member State is allocated a number of votes. If the measure is proposed by the Commission, it requires 255 out of 345 possible votes to be adopted and at least fourteen states must vote for it. In the rare circumstances where a measure is not proposed by the Commission, it requires 255 votes, but at least two-thirds of the Member States must vote for it. In either case, any Member State can ask to verify that states representing at least 62 per cent of the total EU population supported it. The respective votes and population sizes are shown in Table 2.1.

[96] The Annex at the end of Chapter 3 contains a list of the different legislative competences of the European Union and the procedures and voting requirements used.

The weighting of votes seeks to form a delicate balance between preserving individual national voices and reflecting the different population sizes of the Member States. Since 2004, however, the majority of EU Member States have been 'small' states with populations of less than 10 million. One has the perverse situation where the fourteen smallest Member States have a combined population of 55.4 million citizens, about two-thirds of the German population, but combined, they have 88 votes, over three times the number of votes of Germany. This is not the only anomaly, as each state's voting strength depended as much upon its perseverance in Treaty negotiations as anything else. France has, therefore, equal votes to Germany, despite having a population only two-thirds the size of the latter. An almost identical situation exists between Belgium and the Netherlands even if the latter does have one more vote. The most overrepresented states, however, are Poland and Spain. These have only two votes less than Germany, despite populations less than half its size.

The debate was hotly contested, both at the Future of Europe Convention and during the negotiations for the Lisbon Treaty. The larger Member States wished a weighting more based on population. Despite an absence of evidence that this has ever happened,[97] smaller Member States were worried that such a criterion would allow a small number of large Member States to veto any measure, as the four largest Member States comprise just over 50 per cent of the population. There was provision that existing arrangements would prevail until November 2014.

Article 16(4) TEU

As from 1 November 2014, a qualified majority shall be defined as at least 55% of the members of the Council, comprising at least fifteen of them and representing Member States comprising at least 65% of the population of the Union.

A blocking minority must include at least four Council members, failing which the qualified majority shall be deemed attained.[98]

The new formula gives greater power to the larger Member States by introducing a population requirement as a central threshold for the first time. It provides safeguards for the smaller Member States by providing that at least fifteen states must vote for it. They are protected against the large state veto by the requirement that at least four states must vote against the measure, although it must be said it is unlikely to be difficult for two large Member States to find two smaller states to join them if they try hard enough.[99]

Poland was particularly unhappy with the new formula. It benefits disproportionately from the status quo and was thus hit hard by the new weighting for QMV. A transitional regime was therefore agreed. As can be seen, the new formula does not begin to bite until 1 November 2014. Between that date and 31 March 2017, however, a Member State can ask for the existing

---

[97] M. Mattila and J. Lane, 'Why Unanimity in the Council? A Roll-Call Analysis of Council Voting' (2001) 2 *EUP* 31.
[98] This is also reproduced in Article 238(3) TFEU.
[99] On the differences in respective influence between the Treaty of Nice and the new formula see D. Cameron, 'The Stalemate in the Constitutional IGC' (2004) 5 *EUP* 373, 383.

formula to be used.[100] This is likely to lead to the existing formula prevailing until the latter date as states with a winning majority under it will want it to prevail, as will states who would wish to block a measure under it.

Perhaps even more significantly, a Decision was added indicating a new blocking minority.[100a] From 1 November 2014 to 31 March 2017, if Member States representing three-quarters of the population or of the number of states to form a blocking minority indicate their opposition to a measure, the Council shall do all in its power to reach 'a satisfactory solution' – a euphemism for resolving the matter through unanimity. Translated, that means that during that period, only 33.75 per cent of states or states representing 26.25 per cent of the EU population have to indicate their opposition to a measure for it not to be adopted. From 1 April 2017, the position is even more drastic. The figure becomes 55 per cent of the blocking minority. This means only 24.75 per cent of the states or states representing 19.25 per cent of the population have to oppose a measure for it not to be adopted. On current figures, this is eight states or three states representing 20 per cent of the population. To put this in perspective, Germany alone currently has about 17.5 per cent of the EU population. This Decision makes it significantly easier for Member States, particularly those with large populations, to block measures than under the current regime.

The debate about vote weighting may be overblown. Historically, the distinction between unanimity and QMV was seen as axiomatic to the climate of negotiation. Under unanimity, it was argued that Member States, aware of their veto, are inclined to have a heightened sense of self-interest and to look for matching concessions.[101] In circumstances where Member States do not have a veto, they are aware of the possibility of outmanoeuvring. A climate of problem-solving prevails, with Member States looking far more towards constructing common solutions and being less protective of their initial positions.[102] Whilst these differences in style may exist on occasion, more recent, empirical studies have suggested the differences to be less stark. Prior to 2004, Wallace and others calculated that votes were taken in the Council on only about 25 per cent of matters discussed, even under QMV, with the majority of voting concentrated in two sectors, agriculture and fisheries, where redistributive issues play a powerful role.[103] This figure seems to have reduced even further since 2004, with Mattila suggesting that in 2004 and 2005, 82 per cent of items decided by QMV were passed without contestation.[104] The quid pro quo for this culture of consensus is that individual concerns are, where possible, simply incorporated into the text. The 2004 enlargement led, for example, to the length of legislative documents increasing by approximately 15 per cent.[105]

---

[100] Protocol to the Treaty of Lisbon on Transitional Provisions, Article 3(2).

[100a] This is now contained in Decision 2009/857/EC relating to the implementation of Article 9C(4) TEU and Article 205(2) TFEU [2009] OJ L314/73.

[101] F. Scharpf, 'The Joint Decision Trap: Lessons from German Federalism and European Integration' (1988) 66 *Public Administration* 239. A good introduction to the different types of interaction in the Council is H. Wallace, 'The Council: An Institutional Chameleon?' (2002) 15 *Governance* 325.

[102] F. Hayes-Renshaw and H. Wallace, *The Council of Ministers* (Basingstoke, Macmillan, 1997) 256–8.

[103] M. Mattila, 'Contested Decisions: Empirical Analysis of Voting in the Council of Ministers' (2004) 43 *EJPR* 29; F. Hayes-Renshaw, W. van Aken and H. Wallace, 'When and Why the Council of Ministers of the EU Votes Explicitly' (2006) 44 *JCMS* 161, 165.

[104] M. Mattila, 'Voting and Coalitions in the Council after Enlargement' in D. Naurin and H. Wallace (eds.), *Unveiling the Council of the European Union: Games Governments Play in Brussels* (Basingstoke, Palgrave, 2008).

[105] E. Best and P. Settembri, 'Legislative Output after Enlargement: Similar Number, Shifting Nature' in E. Best *et al.* (eds.), *The Institutions of the Enlarged European Union: Change and Continuity* (Cheltenham, Edward Elgar, 2008).

In a world of consensus-seeking, the key dynamic, a study by Beyers and Dierickx suggests, is not the form of vote taken, but the presence of central players and smaller players.[106] Coalitions cluster around central players, who have the resources and networks to articulate common views and mediate between positions. These tend to be the large Member States and the Commission. Other states see themselves as having to mediate with these and rarely negotiate with other partners. Negotiations are, thus, usually driven by a few key players.

This focus on consensus has led to concerns about the quality of debate in the Council. Since 2002, parts of Council meetings have been opened to the public. This would include the initial presentation of certain legislative proposals by the Commission to the Council, the ensuing debate and the votes and explanation of votes. The form of public access was, however, of a limited kind, as it involved only the provision of a room in which the public could watch via live feed.[107] The Lisbon Treaty has opened up all deliberations and votes on legislative acts to the public.

Article 16(8) TEU

The Council shall meet in public when it deliberates and votes on a draft legislative act. To this end, each Council meeting shall be divided into two parts, dealing respectively with deliberations on Union legislative acts and on non-legislative activities.

This approach generates two types of response. One response sees this reform as overdue. In particular, it will allow national publics and parliaments to hold governments more fully to account and possibly generate greater interest in and understanding of the law-making process. Such a view would presumably wish this access to extend to non-legislative activities as well. The other response is to see this provision as containing risks. It may lead to grandstanding by individual ministers for the benefit of their home constituencies, thereby obstructing problem-solving. Furthermore, as it would only be the formal meetings that are made public, there is a fear that the real decision-making processes will be driven elsewhere, out of sight, with the Council becoming no more than a ratifying body designed, more than anything else, for public show.[108]

(iii) Management of the Council: the Presidency, the Secretariat and COREPER

The Presidency of the Council rotates between groups of three Member States for eighteen months at a time on the basis of equal rotation.[109] The Presidency has a number of duties:

- it arranges and chairs Council meetings and sets the agenda for them;[110]
- it represents the Council both before the other EU institutions and in the world more generally;

---

[106] J. Beyers and G. Dierickx, 'The Working Groups of the Council of the European Union: Supranational or Intergovernmental Negotiations?' (1998) 36 *JCMS* 289.

[107] Only those proposals that were governed by the ordinary legislative procedure were subject to this access.

[108] For an indication of the two views see House of Lords European Union Committee, *The Treaty of Lisbon: An Impact Assessment* (10th Report, 2007–08 Session, TSO, London) 56–47.

[109] Article 16(9) TEU, Article 236(b) TFEU. The sequence is set out in Decision 2007/5/EC, EURATOM determining the order in which the office of the President is held [2007] OJ L1/11. See also Decision 2009/881/EU on the exercise of the Presidency of the Council [2009] OJ L315/50.

[110] Decision 2002/682/EC, article 20. Each Member State will chair the Council for six months: Decision 2009/881/EU, article 1(2).

- it acts as a 'neutral broker' between other Member States in order to secure legislation;
- it sets the legislative agenda for its six-month term of office. This will be done in consultation with the Commission and the Presidencies preceding and succeeding it.

There is some debate about the power of the Presidency. It has been argued that the short term of office and the need not to appear too partisan restrict it to an essentially clerical role.[111] Certainly, these features prevent the Presidency from hijacking the agenda of the Council to further national priorities. Nevertheless, a study of eight Presidencies found that whilst these had to stay within the mandates set by their predecessors or the Commission, they have a soft power in the form of discretion to steer or shape these agendas.[112] If they had been given only a vague mandate to realise a task, they could choose, instead, to make it a priority for their Presidency. Unanticipated events, such as 9/11, also provide opportunities for agenda-setting. As they require new forms of response from the Union, reliance is placed on the Presidency to organise that response and set out the framework for future action. Conversely, they also seem to have some influence when negotiations are closed. At this moment, they have to bring views together and whilst this must be done even-handedly, empirical studies show that decisions reached during state Presidencies are usually closer to what they want than decisions taken outside them.[113]

Whilst the Presidency sets out the overall framework for Council meetings, the mundane details are carried out by the Secretariat.[114] Based in Brussels, the central functions of the Secretariat are conference organisation and committee servicing. It produces documents, arranges translation, takes notes and organises meeting rooms. It performs this role also for the European Council.[115] It also provides advice to the Council on the legality of its actions and will represent the Council before the other institutions. It will thus be the Council Secretariat who will litigate on behalf of the Council in the Court of Justice or represent the Council before Parliament committees. A new role provided by the Lisbon Treaty is that it will contribute to the External Action Service that will assist the High Representative in fulfilling her mandate.[116]

However, the central body in the preparation of Council meetings is COREPER. The formal duties of COREPER are merely to prepare the work of the Council and carry out any tasks assigned to it.[117] It has no power to take formal decisions other than ones on Council procedure.[118] It is divided into COREPER I, which is composed of deputy permanent representatives and is responsible for issues such as the environment, social affairs, the internal market and transport. COREPER II consists of permanent representatives of ambassadorial rank responsible for the more sensitive issues, such as economic and financial affairs and external relations.

---

[111] A. Tallberg, 'The Agenda-Shaping Powers of the EU Council Presidency' (2003) 10 *JEPP* 1; B. Crum, 'Can the EU Presidency Make its Mark on Interstate Bargains? The Italian and Irish Presidencies of the 2003–4 IGC' (2007) 14 *JEPP* 1208.

[112] E. Bailleul and H. Versluys, 'The EU Rotating Presidency: "Hostage Taker" of the European Agenda?', paper presented at EUSA Conference, 30 March 2005. A similar conclusion is reached by study of the Presidency of Environmental Councils: A. Warntjen, 'Steering the Union: The Impact of the EU Presidency on Legislative Activity' (2007) 45 *JCMS* 1135.

[113] R. Thomson, 'The Council Presidency of the European Union: Responsibility with Power' (2008) 46 *JCMS* 593, 604–11.

[114] Article 240(2) TFEU.

[115] Article 235(4) TFEU.

[116] Article 27(3) TEU.

[117] Article 16(7) TEU, Article 240(1) TFEU.

[118] Case C-25/94 *Commission v Council (FAO Fisheries Agreement)* [1996] ECR I-1469.

Each meets weekly. Successive reports have found COREPER essential both to alleviating Council workload and coordinating its work.[119]

The heart of COREPER's power lies in its setting the agenda for Council meetings and its dividing that agenda into 'A' and 'B' matters. 'A' items are technical matters, on which there is agreement. These are nodded through in the Council meeting, without discussion. 'B' items, by contrast, are considered more contentious, requiring discussion. COREPER, therefore, decides on what the Council is to decide on. An 'A' item is effectively decided by COREPER, and a 'B' item by the Council of Ministers. In this, the overwhelming majority of items are 'A' items. A study in the early 1990s found that of 500 items placed on the Agricultural Council agenda, ministers discussed only 13 per cent of them.[120]

In this, COREPER does not act as a loose cannon, but as a conduit for informing national capitals of the work of the European Union and for enabling national positions to be properly defended.[121] It is, thus, assisted by about 250 Working Groups of national civil servants. A Commission proposal is first passed to these Groups for analysis. These Groups provide Reports which set the agenda for COREPER meetings by indicating points on which there has been agreement within the Working Group (Roman I points) and points which need discussion within COREPER (Roman II points). It is best to see COREPER as the tip of complex networks of national administrations working together to agree legislation.[122] Even in this light, COREPER raises some concerns. There is disagreement about whether representatives always articulate national interests or whether they are concerned with solving problems and reaching agreement, wherever possible.[123] The other concern raised by COREPER is government by 'moonlight'. Meetings of the COREPER are not public. Its minutes are not published and it is not accountable to any parliamentary assembly. To be sure, many decisions taken in any national government are taken by civil servants, but it is the unprecedented extent of COREPER's influence that raises particular concerns about accountability and transparency.

4 THE EUROPEAN COUNCIL

The European Council comprises the Heads of Government of the Member States, its President and the President of the Commission.[124] It is a separate institution from the Council of Ministers. It is to meet at least four times per year, although additional meetings can be convened if necessary.[125] The Lisbon Treaty sets out a change of gear for the European Council. For the first time it is formally recognised as an institution of the European Union.[126] It is no longer, formally at least, confined to setting out guidelines for the Union, but is now to define its directions and priorities.

---

[119] *Report on the European Institutions by the Committee of Three to the European Council* (Tindemans Report) (Brussels, EC Council, 1979) 49–54; *Report from the Ad Hoc Committee on Institutional Affairs to the European Council* (Dooge Report), *EC Bulletin* 3-1985, 3.5.1.

[120] M. v. Schendelen, '"The Council Decides": Does the Council Decide?' (1996) 34 *JCMS* 531.

[121] F. Hayes-Renshaw, C. Lequesne and P. Lopez, 'The Permanent Representatives of the Member States of the European Union' (1989) 28 *JCMS* 119, 129–31.

[122] D. Bostock, 'Coreper Revisited' (2002) 40 *JCMS* 215, 231–2.

[123] Cf. J. Lewis, 'National Interests: COREPER' in J. Peterson and M. Shackleton (eds.), *The Institutions of the European Union* (Oxford, Oxford University Press, 2002); F. Häge, 'Committee Decision-making in the Council of the European Union' (2007) 8 *EUP* 299.

[124] Article 15(2) TEU

[125] Article 15(3) TEU.

[126] Article 13 TEU.

> ### Article 15(1) TEU
>
> The European Council shall provide the Union with the necessary impetus for its development and shall define the general political directions and priorities thereof. It shall not exercise legislative functions.

This agenda-setting is limited by the final sentence, which indicates that the European Council is not to trespass on the Commission's traditional prerogatives to propose legislation. Instead, the suggestion is that it is now to steer, direct and prompt the general course of the Union far more actively than previously. To support this enhanced role, greater organisational support is provided for it and it is made more accountable than previously.

(i) Powers of the European Council

The first set of powers enjoyed by the European Council may be described as constitution-making powers. It makes decisions about the future shape and membership of the European Union. It is the European Council, therefore, which makes the decision to suspend the membership of a state.[127] Whilst not taking the formal decision, it is the European Council which sets the criteria to be met by a state wishing to join the Union.[128] Perhaps the most important power enjoyed by the European Council is the power to instigate Treaty reform. Following the Lisbon Treaty, there are now two procedures for this. In the ordinary revision procedure, after consulting other EU institutions, it can call, by simple majority, either a convention along the lines of the Future of Europe Convention or an intergovernmental conference. These will put forward amendments which have to be ratified by all Member States in accordance with their constitutional requirements.[129]

More controversial is the simplified revision procedure. On the one hand, this allows the European Council, after consulting the other EU institutions, to amend Part III of the TFEU on Internal Policies of the European Union, although any such amendment must not increase EU competences. Any amendment cannot enter into force until ratified by all Member States in accordance with their constitutional requirements.[130] On the other, it creates what is known as a *passerelle*, which allows for amendment of the requirement of unanimity to that of QMV and adaptation of any legislative procedure to that of the ordinary legislative procedure in the TFEU and in Title V of the TEU (which governs external action).[131] Any amendment here must be notified to national parliaments and if any national parliament indicates its opposition, the amendment must be dropped.

The proponents of the simplified revision procedure argue that it is necessary to give the European Union some flexibility and responsiveness.[132] Whilst this argument can be made for QMV, as it allows the Union to take action without the shadow of the national veto, it is less convincing in the case of the ordinary legislative procedure. This gives the Parliament a

---

[127] Article 7(3) TEU.
[128] Article 49 TEU.
[129] Article 48(2)–(4) TEU.
[130] Article 48(6) TEU.
[131] Article 48(7) TEU. There is an exclusion for anything that has defence or military implications.
[132] House of Lords European Union Committee, *The Treaty of Lisbon: An Impact Assessment*, above n. 108, 37–8.

veto over legislation, and it is unclear how adding a further veto-player adds flexibility.[133] Its opponents worry that, avoiding traditional revision procedures, it could be a process for integration by stealth. In its judgment on the Lisbon Treaty, the German Constitutional Court noted that the use of the simplified revision procedure for Part III of the TFEU gave the possibility to amend 172 Articles of primary law in unpredictable ways. Whilst expressing concern over this, it reserved its full ire for the *passerelle*. It noted that with any transfer to QMV or to the ordinary legislative procedure, it would be difficult to predict the degree of power being granted to the European Union and the loss of influence for an individual Member State. Given the implications of this both for the integration process and for local democracy, the German Constitutional Court considered it an insufficient guarantee that national parliaments could simply make their opposition known. More was required. It would only be compatible with the German Basic Law if the precise amendment was approved by a German law approved by both German legislative assemblies.[134]

The second form of power enjoyed by the European Council is less controversial. These are the powers relating to organisation. Within the limits set by the Treaties, the European Council can determine the composition of the Parliament and the Commission.[135] It appoints its own President and the President of the Commission, the Commission, the High Representative, and the Executive Board of the European Central Bank.[136] To be sure, this is often done in tandem with other EU institutions but almost every non-elected office involves appointment by the Council.[137] Even judges of the Court of Justice, while not appointed by the European Council, are appointed by common accord of the governments of the Member States, which is essentially the same thing.[138]

The third form of power, alluded to more explicitly in Article 15(1) TEU, is informal agenda-setting powers. In some fields this is explicitly mandated,[139] but the European Council will agree programmes of legislation across all areas of EU policy. In such instances, a division of labour takes place, in which the European Council will usually set out broad principles and ask the Commission to develop an Action Plan to implement these principles. This role of agenda-setting transcends the formal Treaty structures and takes place in fields that fall outside formal EU competence. The pre-eminent example is the 'Lisbon process', but this is something that has nothing to do with the Lisbon Treaty. In 2000, at Lisbon, the European Council committed the Union to becoming, by 2010, 'the most competitive and dynamic knowledge-based economy in the world, capable of sustainable economic growth with more and better jobs and greater social cohesion'.[140] To do this, it recognised it would have to carry out a number of tasks that did not fall within EU competences, most notably in the fields of welfare reform and macro- and micro-economic policy. Nevertheless, every spring, under the umbrella term of the Lisbon Strategy for Growth and Jobs, the European Council sets priorities and reviews national Action Plans set by individual Member States but assessed in the light of Commission reports and guidelines that have been agreed at EU level.

---

[133] See pp. 103–5.
[134] 2 BvE 2/08 *Gauweiler* v *Treaty of Lisbon*, Judgment of 30 June 2009, paras. 311–21.
[135] Articles 14(2) and 17(5) TEU respectively.
[136] Articles 15(5), 17(7) (both President and Commission as a whole), 18(1) TEU and 283(2) TFEU respectively.
[137] The most significant exception is the Ombudsman: who is elected by the European Parliament, Article 228(1), (2) TFEU.
[138] Article 19(2) TEU.
[139] Article 68 TFEU (freedom, security and justice); Article 148 TFEU (employment).
[140] Conclusions of the Presidency, *EU Bulletin* 3–2000, 1.5.

Fourthly, the European Council has problem-solving powers. Heads of Government have the domestic authority to resolve issues which have reached an impasse within the Council of Ministers. In particularly sensitive fields, the European Council is deployed not merely where there is no resolution but where a Member State feels insufficient sensitivity is being shown to its prerogatives. In the field of Common Foreign and Security Policy (CFSP), where there is provision for QMV, a Member State may refer the matter to the European Council for 'vital and stated' reasons.[141] The other problem-solving power is the so-called 'brake procedure' introduced by the Lisbon Treaty. This allows a member of the Council to refer a legislative proposal to the European Council if it affects important aspects of its social security system[142] or fundamental aspects of its criminal justice system.[143]

Finally, the European Council has a particularly prominent role in the CFSP. It defines and identifies the strategic objectives and interests of the CFSP and sets out guidelines.[144] It also acts as a forum where Member States can consult each other about matters of general interest in this field.[145]

(ii) Organisation of the European Council

There is mismatch between the time spent by Heads of Government in the European Council and its wide-ranging tasks. For many years it was unclear whether it had the resources to discharge the more extensive responsibilities demanded of it. Thus, despite the European Council formally being pre-eminent in the Lisbon process, it was, in practice, the Commission or individual Councils that did much of the work. Since 2002, the General Affairs and External Relations Council has performed a similar role to that performed by COREPER for the Council of Ministers. This role is to ensure overall coordination of policy between the different Council of Ministers configurations and to set the agenda for the European Council. The General Affairs and External Relations Council also agrees items to be adopted without discussion and those that need further debate. If the item requires discussion, it will prepare an outline paper setting out the issues to be discussed and the options available.[146]

This has been formalised by the Lisbon Treaty, with the new autonomous General Affairs Council having this role.[147] Yet, experience since 2002 begs the question whether foreign ministers have, alongside all their other responsibilities, the authority and resources either to coordinate policy or to prepare meetings sufficiently. Alongside this, the question of continuity was a problem, as, with the rotating Council Presidencies, every six months a new Member State came forward to chair European Council meetings.

To that end, the Lisbon Treaty creates a new office, that of President of the European Council. Elected by the European Council by QMV for a two and a half year term that may be

---

[141] Article 31(2) TEU.
[142] Article 48 TFEU.
[143] Articles 82(3) and 83(3) TFEU.
[144] Articles 22 and 26 TEU.
[145] Article 32 TEU.
[146] Decision 2002/682/EC, EURATOM, article 2(3).
[147] Article 16(6) TEU. It is working with the Commission and the President of the European Council on this.

renewed once,[148] the President will sit as an additional member of the European Council.[149] Her tasks are to:

- chair and drive forward the work of the European Council whilst endeavouring to facilitate consensus and cohesion within it;
- ensure the preparation and continuity of the work of the European Council in cooperation with the President of the Commission, and on the basis of the work of the General Affairs Council;
- present a report to the Parliament after each of the meetings of the European Council;
- ensure the external representation of the Union on issues concerning its Common Foreign and Security Policy, without prejudice to the powers of the High Representative.[150]

The mission of the President has both an ex ante and an ex post dimension. Ex ante, she is to organise, coordinate and secure direction for the European Council, building alliances and facilitating agendas. Ex post, she is mandated to secure follow-up, seeing that European Council Decisions are implemented. Her success will be dependent on a number of factors. While setting the policy agenda for the European Union and building consensus around this looks like a significant task, there is no provision made for the President to have a significant administration of her own. There is also the question of her relationship with the different Member States. Since she is expected to be the handmaiden of national governments, there will inevitably be a tension between the larger Member States, which will expect her to pay more attention to their greater economic weight and larger populations, and the smaller Member States, which will expect her to treat all Member States equally regardless of size. Finally, there is her relationship with the supranational institutions, notably the Commission. They are expected to cooperate with each other, but the essential structure of the relationship is a competitive one. Each will have an agenda setting role and will be keen to assert its preferences and prerogatives.

(iii) The European Council within the EU institutional settlement

Although recognised by the SEA,[151] the European Council is often treated as something apart from the EU institutional settlement. Its relationship to the wider institutional settlement or as part of it has not been researched in detail. This might be in part because it started as an informal summit, or because it did not conform to the same legal strictures as other parts of the Union. Even before being raised to that formal status by the Lisbon Treaty, it is a central part of the institutional settlement with significant powers.[151a]

The first question is how the exercise of European Council power shifts influence within the European Union. If it exercises a powerful guiding hand, it also has the potential to direct the Union. As the extract below illustrates, notwithstanding that voting is usually done by unanimity and sometimes by QMV, it is the body where large state influence is most to the fore.

---

[148] Article 15(5) TEU.   [149] Article 15(2) TEU.   [150] Article 15(6) TEU.   [151] Article 2 SEA.
[151a] This positioning is reflected in the European Council publishing its Rules of Procedure in the *Official Journal*: Decision 2009/882/EU adopting the European Council Rules of Procedure [2009] OJ L315/51.

J. Tallberg, 'Bargaining Power in the European Council' (2008) 46 *Journal of Common Market Studies* 685, 690–1

In Europe of today, gun-boat diplomacy is not an option and aggregate structural power affects negotiations in considerably more subtle ways. The interviews suggest that resources and capabilities rarely are actively deployed in the bargaining process. Rather, asymmetries in aggregate structural power matter indirectly, by affecting a state's range of alternatives, the resources it can commit to an issue and the legitimacy of its claims to influence.

A large home market makes a state more influential in economic negotiations, military capabilities enable a state to exercise leadership in the EU's foreign and security policy and population size grants voice in an EU conceiving of itself as a democratic community.

According to the interviewees, national executives representing structurally advantaged states are allowed greater latitude in the negotiations. Jean-Claude Juncker explains: 'If you are representing a medium-sized country, you can never say "Denmark thinks…". You can only say "I would submit to your considerations, if not…". Those who are speaking for greater Member States, by opening their mouth and by referring to their national flag, they are immediately indicating that, behind their words, you have to accept size and demography. "La France pense que…" and "Deutschland denkt…" that is something different'. Göran Persson, former prime minister of Sweden, points to a parallel dynamic: 'If you are the prime minister of a country with five to ten million people, you simply cannot monopolize 20 per cent of the time devoted to the conclusions.' Furthermore, differences in structural power are perceived to affect the legitimacy of wielding the veto. According to one prime minister, it is a simple reality of politics that 'Luxemburg can issue a veto once in a decade and Britain once per week'. By the same token, the veto of large Member States is perceived to carry more weight than that of the small or medium-sized states, according to David O'Sullivan, former secretary general of the Commission: 'The veto of Cyprus is not the same as the veto of Germany.' Interviewees also testify that large Member States may get away with tactics that otherwise are considered inappropriate, such as exploiting the inadequate preparation of an issue to push through their own proposal, or launching entirely new initiatives at the negotiation table.

As a result, the interests of the larger Member States tend to set the framework for European Council negotiations. Where the interests of France, Germany and the UK conflict, they nevertheless set the terms within which agreements must be sought. Where these states see eye-to-eye on an issue, or even have arrived at pre-agreements, it is extremely difficult to achieve outcomes that diverge from this position. Frequently cited examples in recent years of France, Germany and the UK dominating negotiations and outcomes in the European Council include the provisions on a semi-permanent president of the European Council in the 2004 Constitutional Treaty, the deal in December 2005 on the new financial perspective for 2007–13 and the political agreement in July 2007 on the subsequent Lisbon Treaty.

In the remainder of the article, Tallberg notes that the situation is not as simple as, the bigger and richer you are, the more powerful you are. He notes that the Presidency always enjoys a particular power. The personal authority of individuals matters, and on specific issues where a state has a particular interest it will acquire more authority. This simply raises further questions about how Decisions are reached and the relative legitimacy of Decisions reached in the European Council vis-à-vis those in other EU institutions, particularly when the former impact on the latter. This is addressed half-heartedly by the Lisbon Treaty. The European Council can now be subject to review by the Court of Justice[152] and the Presidents must submit reports after each meeting to the Parliament.[153] Yet it is far-fetched to imagine the circumstances in which a court would strike down a Decision by twenty-seven Heads of Government, and how seriously the latter will take any critical views of the Parliament is also open to question. More interestingly, other controls such as duties of transparency or a duty to account to national parliaments before and after any meeting are missing. The test of whether formalising the position of the European Council is simply returning decision-making to intergovernmental negotiations will be to observe whether such negotiations are developed.

5 THE EUROPEAN PARLIAMENT

(i) Composition of the European Parliament

The European Parliament was initially set up as the European Assembly and was only formally recognised as a Parliament in the Single European Act (SEA).[154] Prior to 1979, it consisted of representatives from national assemblies or parliaments. Since then, MEPs have been elected by direct universal suffrage at five-yearly intervals.[155] There are a number of features which distinguish the Parliament from its national counterparts.

The seats are not evenly distributed on the basis of population.[156] The Parliament is composed of 736 members, but citizens in smaller Member States are better represented than citizens in larger Member States. Luxembourg, with a population of 400,000 citizens, has one MEP for roughly every 65,500 citizens. Germany, by contrast, with a population of 82 million citizens, has one MEP for approximately every 828,000 citizens. The 2009 cohort of MEPs were elected before the Lisbon Treaty. This provides a different formula for future elections. The Parliament should not exceed 750 members. Representation will be on the basis of degressive proportionality, whereby the principle of per head representation is combined with the principle that the larger the population of a Member State, the lower the weighting per head. Additionally, no state should receive fewer than six MEPs and no state may have more than 96 MEPs.[157] In October 2007, the Constitutional Affairs Committee of the Parliament made a distribution of seats for each national territory on the basis of this principle and negotiations proceeded on the basis of these calculations. This was accepted with one small amendment.[158] Whilst the principle of degressive proportionality curbs the horse trading of prior times, it

---

[152] Articles 263 and 265 TFEU.

[153] Article 15(6)(d) TEU.

[154] Article 3 SEA.

[155] Decision 76/787/EEC [1976] OJ L278/1. On the history of the European Parliament since the establishment of the Common Assembly in the ECSC see B. Rittberger, *Building Europe's Parliament: Democratic Representation Beyond the Nation-State* (Oxford, Oxford University Press, 2005) chs. 3–6.

[156] The respective numbers are: Austria 17, Belgium 22, Bulgaria 16, Czech Republic 22, Cyprus 6, Denmark 13, Estonia 6, Finland 13, France 72, Germany 99, Greece 22, Hungary 22, Ireland 12, Italy 72, Latvia 8, Lithuania 12, Luxembourg 6, Malta 5, the Netherlands 25, Poland 50, Portugal 22, Romania 33, Slovakia 13, Slovenia 7, Spain 50, Sweden 18, United Kingdom 72.

[157] Article 14(2) TEU.

[158] Declaration No. 4 to the Lisbon Treaty on the composition of the European Parliament. Italy was awarded an extra seat. It was also agreed that the President of the European Parliament will count towards the total. The future allocation of seats will be 96 (Germany), 74 (France), 73 (United Kingdom, Italy), 54 (Spain), 51 (Poland), 33 (Romania), 26 (the Netherlands), 22 (Greece, Portugal, Belgium, Czech Republic, Hungary), 20 (Sweden), 19 (Austria), 18 (Bulgaria), 13 (Denmark, Slovakia, Finland), 12 (Ireland, Lithuania), 9 (Latvia), 8 (Slovenia), 6 (Luxembourg, Malta, Cyprus, Estonia).

should be noted that it is still a long way from equal representation of citizens, and Luxembourgeois votes continue to be more valuable than German ones.

There are no uniform procedures for election. Common procedures were used for the first time in the 2004 elections with MEPs elected by proportional representation. However, states can decide on the particular system of proportional representation they wish to use. They can establish constituencies as they see fit and can require parties to achieve 5 per cent of the vote before they are allocated seats.[159] Furthermore, the Parliament cannot challenge the administration of these elections even where it believes that Member States have not followed their own electoral procedures or some dubious practice has taken place. National law is taken as the exclusive basis for verifying this.[160] Finally, as mentioned previously, there are no European political parties. MEPs are elected as representatives of national political parties. This has made elections 'second order national contests'.[161] Voters vote on domestic issues and turn-outs tend to be lower than for national elections.[162] Instead, most MEPs sit in European party groupings.[163] There are seven groupings, of which the two largest are the European Peoples' Party (right of centre parties) and the Progressive Alliance of Socialists and Democrats (left of centre parties).[164] These groupings are important in the organisation of the Parliament.[165] Studies have shown that these groupings affect voting behaviour, with MEPs within groupings acting reasonably cohesively.[166] That said, voting behaviour is still considerably less cohesive than in national parliaments and party groupings are unable to affect the way national delegations cast their votes in key votes.[167]

These traits generate concerns about both the representative and deliberative capacities of the Parliament. Concerns about the former lie in the idea that a representative democracy depends upon the presence of a 'people' (*demos*) or collective sense of 'Us' to represent.[168] Without this common sense of 'Us', it is argued, there is no reason for losers of any vote to accept the view of the majority, for they do not see themselves as part of a common political community with whose decisions they must comply.[169] Concerns about the latter stem from political parties, media and civil society all being organised along predominantly national lines. This prevents a debate which is plural, transparent and vigorous.

---

[159] Decision 2002/772/EURATOM/EC, concerning the election of the members of the European Parliament by direct universal suffrage [2002] OJ L283/1.

[160] Joined Cases C-393/07 and C-9/08 *Italy* v *Parliament*, Judgment of 30 April 2009.

[161] M. Franklin *et al.*, 'Uncorking the Bottle: Popular Opposition to European Unification in the Wake of Maastricht' (1994) 32 *JCMS* 455, 470. On this debate see B. Crum, 'Party Stances in the Referendum on the EU Constitution' (2007) 8 *EUP* 61, 63–4

[162] Turn-out was just over 43 per cent despite voting being compulsory in some Member States.

[163] On the evolution of these see A. Kreppel, *The European Parliament and the Supranational Party System* (Cambridge, Cambridge University Press, 2002).

[164] For the 2009–14 Parliament, the groupings are European Peoples' Party (265 MEPs); Progressive Alliance of Socialists and Democrats (184 MEPs); Alliance of Liberals and Democrats for Europe (84 MEPs); the Greens and European Free Alliance (55 MEPs); European Conservatives and Reformists (54 MEPs); European United Left and Nordic Green Left (35 MEPs); Europe of Freedom and Democracy (35 MEPs). There are 27 non-attached MEPs.

[165] Membership of a grouping also entitles a national party to funding. Regulation 2004/2003/EC on the regulations governing political parties at European level and the rules regarding their funding [2003] OJ L297/1.

[166] S. Hix, A. Noury and G. Roland, 'Power to the Parties: Cohesion and Competition in the European Parliament' (2005) 35 *BJPS* 209.

[167] D. Judge and D. Earnshaw, *The European Parliament* (Basingstoke, Palgrave, 2003) 149–55.

[168] J. Weiler, 'Does Europe Need a Constitution? Reflections on Demos, Telos and the German Maastricht Decision' (1995) 1 *ELJ* 219, 225.

[169] F. Scharpf, *Governing in Europe: Effective and Democratic?* (Oxford, Oxford University Press, 1999) 7–20.

D. Grimm, 'Does Europe Need a Constitution?' (1995) 1 *European Law Journal* 282, 293–4, 296–7

The democratic nature of a political system is attested not so much by the existence of elected parliaments ... as by the pluralism, internal representativity, freedom and capacity for compromise of the intermediate area of parties, associations, citizens' movements and communication media. Where a parliament does not rest on such a structure, which guarantees constant interaction between people and State, democratic substance is lacking even if democratic forms are present.

... At European level, though, even the prerequisites are largely lacking. Mediatory structures have hardly been even formed here yet. There is no Europeanised party system, just European groups in the Strasbourg parliament, and apart from that, loose cooperation among programmatically related parties. This does not bring any integration of the European population, even at the moment of European elections. Nor have European associations or citizens' movements arisen, even though cooperation among national associations is further advanced than with parties. A search for European media, whether in print or broadcast, would be completely fruitless. This makes the European Union fall far short not just of ideal conceptions of a model democracy but even of the already deficit situation in Member States ...

The absence of a European communication system, due chiefly to language diversity, has the consequence that for the foreseeable future there will be neither a European public nor a European political discourse. Public discourse instead remains for the time bound by national frontiers, while the European sphere will remain dominated by professional and interest discourses conducted remotely from the public. European decisional processes are accordingly not under public observation in the same way as national ones. The European level of politics lacks a matching public. The feedback to European officials and representatives is therefore only weakly developed, while national politicians orient themselves even in the case of Council decisions to their national publics, because effective sanctions can come only from them. These circumstances give professional and technical viewpoints, particularly of an economic nature, excessive weight in European politics, while the social consequences and side-effects remain in the dark. This shortcoming cannot be made up for even by growing national attention to European policy themes, since the European dimension is just what is lacking there.

If this is true, the conclusion may be drawn that the full parliamentarisation of the European Union on the model of the national constitutional State will rather aggravate than solve the problem. On the one hand it would loosen the Union's ties back to the Member States, since the European Parliament is by its construction not a federal organ but a central one. Strengthening it would be at the expense of the Council and therefore inevitably have centralising effects. On the other hand the weakened ties back to the Member States would not be compensated by any increased ties back to the Union population. The European Parliament does not meet with any European mediatory structure in being: still less does it constitute a European popular representative body, since there is yet no European people. This is not an argument against any expansion of Parliament's powers. That might even enhance participation opportunities in the Union, provide greater transparency and create a counterweight to the dominance of technical and economic viewpoints. Its objective ought not, however, to be full parliamentarisation on the national model, since political decisions would otherwise move away to where they can be only democratically accountable.

The suspicion that this assessment is a front for the idea that democracy is possible only on the basis of a homogeneous 'Volksgemeinschaft' [ethnic community] is, after all that, baseless. The requirements for democracy are here developed not out of the people, but out of the society that wants to constitute itself as a political unit. It is true that this requires a collective identity, if it wants to settle its conflicts non-violently, accept majority rule and practise solidarity. But this identity need by no means be rooted in ethnic conflict, but must also have other bases. All that is necessary is for the society to have formed an awareness or belonging together that can support majority decisions and solidarity efforts, and for it to have the capacity to communicate about its goals and problems discursively. What obstructs democracy is accordingly not the lack of cohesion of Union citizens as a people, but their weakly developed collective identity and low capacity for transnational discourse. This certainly means that the European democracy deficit is structurally determined. It can therefore not be removed by institutional reforms in any short term. The achievement of the democratic constitutional State can for the time being be adequately recognised only in the national framework.

(ii) Powers of the European Parliament

Most people consider parliaments as law-makers and their influence is often measured by their power over the making of policy and legislation. Strong parliaments are responsible for making policy and law, whilst weaker parliaments can only influence them.[170] Parliaments also exercise power over the executive. In stronger parliamentary systems, executive power is derived from the legislature. The legislature appoints the executive and sets the conditions for the exercise of its powers.[171] In weaker systems, parliaments exercise powers of scrutiny over the executive and it is accountable to them. Finally, parliaments traditionally have powers over the finances of a state. Once again, these vary according to the strength of the parliament, with the stronger parliaments having control over both revenue (money coming in) and expenditure (money going out). These are all mentioned in the description of the Parliament's powers set out in Article 14 TEU.

Article 14(1) TEU

The European Parliament shall, jointly with the Council, exercise legislative and budgetary functions. It shall exercise functions of political control and consultation as laid down in the Treaties. It shall elect the President of the Commission.

In evaluating the Parliament as a parliament, it is also worth considering it against two styles of parliament. Dann has termed these the debating parliament and the working parliament. The former, of which the British House of Commons is an example, is characterised by the government having a majority in it, and its central role being most of the time to debate government policy. On the other hand, with a working parliament, of which the US Congress is an example, the legislature is separate from the executive. It centres around reviewing the work of the executive and this is usually done by strong committees. In this regard, Dann notes that the Parliament is very much a working parliament. The extract below set outs the structure and work of the committees.

---

[170] P. Norton, *Legislatures* (Oxford, Oxford University Press, 1990) 179.

[171] P. Raworth, 'A Timid Step Forwards: Maastricht and the Democratisation of the European Community' (1994) 19 *ELRev.* 16.

P. Dann, 'European Parliament and Executive Federalism: Approaching a Parliament in a Semi-Parliamentary Democracy' (2003) 9 *European Law Journal* 549, 564–5

First, their role in acquiring information, discussing and analysing it, and finally formulating the political position of the European Parliament is absolutely central. The committees have the right to interrogate the Commission and to hold hearings with special experts. Building on these instruments, the committees can (and do) acquire specific expertise in their fields. On this basis, it is their task to file reports for the plenary, thereby formulating and pre-determining most of the final outcomes. These powers are a sword with two sharp sides: they not only facilitate the European Parliament's role in legislative procedures, but also contribute to the European Parliament's ability to competently scrutinise the executive, especially when it comes to implementation.

There is a second aspect which allows the committees to play such a pivotal part in the institution: their internal structure. They are not only small, but also specialised and oriented in their scope towards the division of subject matters in the Commission. Of salient importance is their special leadership structure. This consists of a chairman and a *rapporteur*. The latter is responsible for presenting a matter to the committee, drafting the report for the committee and arguing it in plenary and with other institutions. Therefore a highly influential figure, he is chosen in a complicated and hotly contested procedure. Besides, this position creates clear responsibilities, giving the committee a distinct voice to communicate to the inside (between different committees and party groups) as well as to the outside (to other institutions). It renders the committee especially suited to negotiate with other institutions through an expert representative. It also contributes to the European Parliament's chances to fit into the consensus system of the EU, where different institutions have to constantly negotiate.

There is one more parameter to qualify a parliament as working or debating type and that is the size and organisation of its staff: whereas the *working parliament* can acquire its expertise and level of scrupulous scrutiny of the executive only because of the support of an extensive staff, the *debating parliament* traditionally has very little of it. Its approach is based more on the rhetorical skill of the single parliamentarian to surprise the government and disclose its weakness in debate than on counter-weighing governmental bureaucracies.

Looking at the European Parliament, the staff is yet another factor which underlines its basic nature as a working parliament. Compared to the US Congress of course, it looks petty. But compared to all national parliaments in Europe, it has one of the largest staffs. The EP staff is organised on different levels: on an individual level, every MEP has at least one full time assistant which she can freely employ. On a party level, every party group in the EP is ascribed a number of assistants according to their size and the number of languages spoken. Finally, there is the General Secretariat of the European Parliament in Luxembourg which provides further assistance for the parliamentarians.

Altogether, the staff of the European Parliament totals 4,100 persons. In sum: the European Parliament is also in respect to its oversight function clearly a working parliament with well-structured committees having prominent rights, providing an infrastructure to seriously scrutinise the executive, and with the number and organisation of the staff displaying once again the basic character of the European Parliament as a working parliament.

The party groups exert their strongest influence over determining the composition of Parliament committees. Although committee membership is intended to reflect the ideological and territorial composition of the full Parliament,[172] the chairs of the committees are determined by negotiation between the groups.[173] Thus, for the 2009 Parliament, there are twenty-two committees. Of these, eighteen are chaired either by a MEP belonging to the European Peoples' Party or to the Progressive Alliance of Socialists and Democrats.[174]

(a) Legislative powers of the European Parliament

On their face, the legislative powers of the Parliament seem weaker than national parliaments. The Parliament has no monopoly of adoption over any legislative proposal nor power of initiative in any significant field of policy-making. Instead, its legislative powers vary according to the legislative procedure adopted and this will depend on the policy field in question. There are two dominant procedures: the consultation procedure and the ordinary legislative procedure. Under the former, the Parliament is consulted on a proposal and has the right to propose amendments. Under the latter, in addition to these rights, the Parliament can veto any proposal. It also has the power to negotiate joint texts in a committee, the Conciliation Committee, with the Council. Bald statements of its powers do not capture the significance of its input and this is addressed in more detail in Chapter 3.

The Parliament does have, however, informal, general powers of agenda-setting under both procedures. One route is for it to request the Commission to submit a proposal.[175] The route for this is an 'Own Initiative' report. The relevant committee of the Parliament will draw up a report. The Parliament will then vote on it in plenary session, adopting a Resolution requesting the Commission to act. The request to submit a proposal is deployed in a limited manner. This is not true of the other route for agenda-setting available under both legislative procedures, which is to propose amendments to Commission proposals. Between 1999 and 2007, about 87 per cent of Commission proposals under the ordinary legislative procedure (known then as the co-decision procedure) were subject to amendment and about 54 per cent of those involving the consultation procedure.[176] The procedure involves the Parliament committee providing a report, which is then ratified by plenary session, and has been used to gain the Parliament significant influence. It is estimated that 19 per cent of its amendments under consultation[177] and up to 83 per cent under the ordinary legislative procedure are accepted. [178]

(b) Powers over the Executive

Parliament has a variety of tools to hold the other EU institutions to account. It has powers of appointment and dismissal, powers of litigation and powers of enquiry.

---

[172] G. Mcelroy, 'Committee Representation in the European Parliament' (2006) 7 *EUP* 5.

[173] S. Bowler and D. Farrell, 'The Organizing of the European Parliament: Committees, Specialization and Co-ordination' (1995) 25 *BJPS* 219.

[174] www.europarl.europa.eu/members/expert/committees.do?language=EN (accessed 1 August 2009). All the other groupings other than the grouping of Europe of Freedom and Democracy (the most Euro-sceptic grouping) have one chair.

[175] See p. 62.

[176] R. Kardasheva, 'The Power to Delay: The European Parliament's Influence in the Consultation Procedure' (2009) 47 *JCMS* 385, 392.

[177] *Ibid.* 394–5.

[178] European Parliament, *Activity Report for 5th Parliamentary Term*, PE 287.644, 14. Figures are only available for this procedure for the 1999–2004 period. On the reasons for this influence see pp. 105–7.

Powers of appointment and dismissal The Parliament is exclusively responsible for appointing the European Ombudsman[179] and can apply for her to be dismissed by the Court of Justice if she no longer fulfils the conditions required for the performance of her duties or is guilty of serious misconduct.[180] Of greater political significance are the Parliament's powers over the appointment of the Commission. The Parliament has a double power of approval. It must approve the President of the Commission, who has been nominated by the Heads of Government. If the nomination is accepted, it must also approve the College of Commissioners nominated by the President of the Commission and the Heads of Government.[181] Since 1999, the term of the Commission has been synchronised with that of the Parliament. This has allowed the Parliament to use its powers of assent extremely effectively. All prospective Commissioners are subject to questioning by Parliament committees before assent is given to their appointment. They must answer questions about their professional past, their views on European integration and their legislative agenda for their term in office.

That Parliament will use its power of assent if it is not satisfied with the views of individual Commissioners was demonstrated by the events of 2004. The Parliament was unhappy with three nominees, in particular. It disapproved of the Italian nomination, Rocco Buttiglione, because of his views on women and homosexuality. It was also unhappy with the Latvian nominee, Ingride Udre, because of allegations surrounding corruption in her party. Finally, it was unconvinced that the Hungarian nominee, László Kovács, had sufficient knowledge about the Energy portfolio allocated to him. When it became clear that there was not a majority for the Commission because of these nominations, Barroso, the Commission President, had to arrange for the Italian and Latvian nominations to be replaced, and Kovács was allocated the Taxation and Customs Union portfolio instead.

The Parliament also has important powers to dismiss the Commission. If a motion of censure is passed by a two-thirds majority of the votes cast representing a majority (i.e. more than 368) of the total members of the Parliament, the Commission is obliged to resign as a body.[182] This is an 'all or nothing' power. It does not allow the Parliament to criticise or dismiss individual Commissioners. Nevertheless, it was threatened against the Santer Commission in 1998 following allegations of corruption and maladministration against some of its members.[183] The Commission resigned the day before a vote would have been taken sacking the entire College. Following this, a Framework Agreement was made between the Commission and Parliament which allows the Parliament to hold individual Commissioners more to censure. Under the 2005 version of the agreement, if the Parliament expresses no confidence in an individual Commissioner, the President must either sack the individual or justify not doing so to the Parliament.[184]

---

[179] Article 228(1) TFEU.

[180] Article 228(2) TFEU.

[181] Article 17(7) TEU.

[182] Article 17(8) TEU, Article 234 TFEU.

[183] D. Judge and D. Earnshaw, 'The European Parliament and the Commission Crisis: A New Assertiveness?' (2002) 15 *Governance* 345.

[184] The agreement is available at http://ec.europa.eu/dgs/secretariat_general/relations/relations_other/docs/framework_agreement_ep-ec_en.pdf (accessed 1 June 2009).

Powers of litigation   The Parliament has unlimited powers to challenge the acts of the EI institutions before the Court of Justice as well as their failure to act where they are legally required to do so.[185] Prior to the Treaty of Nice, legal acts could only be challenged where they transgressed on the Parliament's prerogatives. Parliamentary litigation focused around securing greater institutional powers for itself. It would, therefore, litigate to try to secure those legal procedures which ensured it the greatest amount of influence and challenge legislation which delegated significant law-making powers to the Commission.[186] That strategy continues, but since the Treaty of Nice, Parliament has used its unlimited *locus standi* to challenge those acts which it cannot veto, but where it is unhappy with the policy being adopted, notably where it feels there has been a violation of fundamental rights.[187]

Powers of enquiry   EU citizens and residents of the European Union are entitled to petition the Parliament.[188] In 1987, the Parliament set up a Committee of Petitions, consisting of MEPs, to consider the petitions. In 2008, the Committee received 1,886 petitions.[189] These petitions either express views on an issue, such as human rights or animal welfare, or seek redress for a particular grievance, which may have been caused by an EU institution, national authority or private body. The process serves a number of functions. In cases where a political issue is raised, it allows the possibility for a hearing to be organised by the Parliament, thereby securing a voice for parties who might otherwise be disenfranchised. In cases where maladministration by an EU institution is alleged, the Parliament may take the matter up itself. In cases where a failure of a Member State is alleged, it will ask the Commission to take the matter up with the Member State concerned.

In addition, Parliament has the power to ask questions of or receive reports from most of the EU institutions. The European Commission, European Central Bank and Ombudsman must all submit annual reports to the Parliament.[190] In addition, the President of the European Council must report to the Parliament after each of its meetings.[191] Whilst there is no formal obligation to do so, it is also customary for the state holding the Presidency of the Council to present the proposed work of the Council during its Presidency before the Parliament. Commissioners are also required to reply to questions put by parliamentary members.[192] A convention has also grown whereby the Council will answer questions put to it by members of the Parliament.[193] A corollary of this is that the Council and the European Council have a right to be heard by the Parliament.[194] Finally, the President of the European Central Bank and members of the Executive Council may, at the request of the Parliament, or on their own initiative, be heard by the competent committees of the Parliament.[195]

---

[185] Articles 263 and 265 TFEU.

[186] M. McCowan, 'The European Parliament before the Bench: ECJ Precedent and EP Litigation Strategies' (2003) 10 *JEPP* 974.

[187] See e.g. Joined Cases C-317/04 and C-318/04 *Parliament* v *Commission (European Network and Information Security Agency)* [2006] ECR I-4721; Case C-540/03 *Parliament* v *Council (family reunification)* [2006] ECR I-5769.

[188] Article 20(2)(d) TEU and Articles 24 and 227 TFEU.

[189] European Parliament, *Report on the Deliberations of the Committee of Petitions during the Parliamentary Year 2008*, A6–00232/2009.

[190] Articles 249, 284(3), 228 TFEU.

[191] Article 15(6)(d) TEU.

[192] Article 230 TFEU.

[193] It is formally obliged to answer questions in the field of CFSP: Article 36 TEU.

[194] Article 230 TFEU.

[195] Article 284(3)TFEU.

(c) Financial powers of the Parliament

Parliament has significant powers over the EU Budget and, in this field, is the central player with the Council. Expenditure is set through a five-year multi-annual framework for expenditure setting out the limits on total expenditure, and ceilings for each heading of expenditure are to be set by the Council after obtaining the consent of the Parliament.[196] Annual budgets are then set each year. These have to be in balance, comply with the multi-annual framework and be based on individual institutions' estimates of expenditure. Within these constraints, the Commission sets a draft Budget, which may then be adopted by the Council. The Parliament then has the right to veto the Budget should it wish.[197]

6 OTHER INSTITUTIONS[198]

(i) The Court of Auditors

Comprising twenty-seven members appointed for a six-year term, the duty of the Court of Auditors is to audit the revenue and expenditure of the European Union.[199] The audit is to be based on the records of the Union and if necessary, performed on the spot on the premises of any body that manages EU revenue or receives any payments from the EU Budget.[200] Despite these investigative powers, it has no powers to prosecute for fraud, but is obliged to report any irregularity to the appropriate body. For these purposes, the Court of Auditors is required to liaise with national audit bodies or, where appropriate, with national departments. The Court of Auditors can submit observations or deliver opinions on specific matters at the request of the other EU institutions and it can also assist the Parliament and the Council in exercising their powers of control over the implementation of the EU Budget. However, its greatest voice comes from the annual report it publishes on EU finances at the end of each financial year.[201] The Parliament can only give a discharge to the Commission in respect of implementation of the Budget on the basis of this report.[202] These reports have been trenchant in their criticism of the management of the EU finances. In the 2008 Report, for example, on spending in 2007, the Court of Auditors found that there were insufficient controls by both the Commission and the Member States for managing the risk of irregularity and illegality in a number of fields, which included all the majority fields of expenditure.[203]

(ii) The Committee of the Regions and the Economic and Social Committee

Established to give regional authorities greater input in the decision-making process, the Committee has 344 members, appointed for a five-year renewable term.[204] Historically,

---

[196] Article 312(1), 2 TFEU.
[197] Article 314 TFEU. A process of conciliation takes place similar to that in the ordinary legislative procedure.
[198] Other EU institutions not directly involved in law-making or governing the European Union are considered in other chapters. The Court of Justice is considered in Chapter 4.
[199] Article 287(1) TFEU.
[200] Article 287(3) TFEU.
[201] Article 287(4) TFEU.
[202] Article 319(1) TFEU.
[203] The Annual Report can be found at [2008] OJ C286/1.
[204] Article 305 TFEU.

the Committee has just had advisory status, with its being consulted on Commission legislative proposals. In some fields this is mandatory,[205] but there still remain a number of areas with an important regional dimension, such as the internal market, competition, industrial policy and consumer protection, for which no consultation is required. The Committee has been relatively unsuccessful in this role, with its opinions carrying limited weight with the other EU institutions,[206] and the most powerful regions of the Union preferring to deal with the other EU institutions directly rather than act through the Committee.[207] The Lisbon Treaty granted the Committee of the Regions new powers as a litigator. It can now take the other EU institutions to court if it believes they violate the subsidiarity principle. This principle states that the Union must only add legislation insofar as the objectives of the measure cannot be achieved by the Member States acting unilaterally and by reason of their scale or effect can better be realised at EU level. The potential policing effect of this is mitigated by its only being able to do this in the limited fields where consultation of the Committee is mandatory,[208] and it is to be noted that the Court of Justice has yet to strike down a measure for violating the subsidiarity principle.[209]

The Economic and Social Committee (ESC) is to represent civil society within the decision-making processes. There are 344 members appointed for a five-year renewable term[210] and these are divided into three Groups: Group I comprises employers; Group II consists of employees and trade unions; Group III represents variable interests, a heterogeneous group representing farmers, small businesses, the crafts, the professions, cooperatives and non-profit associations, consumer and environmental organisations, associations representing the family, women, persons with disabilities and the academic community. The ESC's central role is to provide Opinions on legislative initiatives. In some fields, consultation with the ESC is compulsory, whilst in others it is optional. Its impact appears to be minor[211] and this, together with a perception that it is overly corporatist, led fifty-seven MEPS in 2007 to call for its abolition.[212]

---

[205] Most notably education (Article 165(2) TFEU); culture (Article 167(5) TFEU); public health (Article 168(4) TFEU); trans-European networks (Article 172 TFEU); and economic and social cohesion (Article 178 TFEU).

[206] R. McCarthy, 'The Committee of the Regions: An Advisory Body's Tortuous Path to Influence' (1997) 4 *JEPP* 439.

[207] T. Borźel, *States and Regions in the European Union* (Cambridge, Cambridge University Press, 2002) 73.

[208] Protocol on the application of the principles of subsidiarity and proportionality, Article 8. See also Article 263(3) TFEU.

[209] See pp. 364–5.

[210] Article 302 TFEU.

[211] Cf. S. Weatherill and P. Beaumont, *EC Law: The Essential Guide to the Legal Workings of the European Community* (3rd edn, Harmondsworth, Penguin, 1999).

[212] European Parliament, Written Declaration pursuant to Rule 116 of the Rules of Procedure by Nils Lundgren and Hélène Goudin on the abolition of the Economic and Social Committee, 0078/2007.

FURTHER READING

D. Curtin and M. Egeberg, 'Tradition and Innovation: Europe's Accumulated Executive Order' (2008) 31 *West European Politics* 639

D. Earnshaw and D. Judge, *The European Parliament* (2nd edn, Basingstoke, Palgrave, 2008)

D. Geradin *et al.* (eds.), *Regulation through Agencies in the EU* (Cheltenham, Edward Elgar, 2006)

F. Hayes-Renshaw and H. Wallace, *The Council of Ministers* (2nd edn, Basingstoke, Macmillan, 2006)

H. Hofmann and A. Türk (eds.), *EU Administrative Governance* (Cheltenham, Edward Elgar, 2006)

L. Hooghe, *The European Commission and the Integration of Europe* (Cambridge, Cambridge University Press, 2001)

M. Pollack, *The Engines of European Integration: Delegation, Agency and Agenda-Setting in the EU* (Oxford, Oxford University Press, 2003)

B. Rittberger, *Building Europe's Parliament: Democratic Representation Beyond the Nation-State* (Oxford, Oxford University Press, 2005)

A. Warntjen, 'Steering the Union: The Impact of the EU Presidency on Legislative Activity' (2007) 45 *Journal of Common Market Studies* 1135

A. Wonka, 'Decision-making Dynamics in the European Commission: Partisan, National or Sectoral?' (2008) 15 *JEPP* 1145

3

Union Law-making

CONTENTS

1 INTRODUCTION

This chapter considers the different forms of law and regulatory acts in EU law, the legislative and regulatory procedures deployed to enact them and the debate about the democratic legitimacy of the European Union. It is organised as follows.

Section 2 looks at the allocation of legislative or regulatory authority in EU law. A legal base for each field of EU law sets out the legislative procedure and legal or regulatory instruments that may be adopted in that field. In cases of contestation reference will be had to the predominant aim and content of the measure to determine the base. If the measure is inextricably and equally associated with more than one base the Court of Justice will then apply a formal hierarchy between legal bases.

Section 3 discusses the types of legislation in EU law. There are four types of binding legislative instrument in EU law: Regulations, Directives, Decisions and international agreements. Two problems to have emerged are that the legislative instruments have been used interchangeably and that there was traditionally no hierarchy between different types of legislative instrument. The latter was addressed by the Lisbon Treaty, which drew a hierarchy between legislative acts (acts adopted under the legislative procedures set out in the Treaty) and non-legislative acts. However, no hierarchy is provided between the different types of non-legislative act: delegated acts and implementing acts.

Section 4 considers the central legislative procedures. The ordinary legislative procedure grants Parliament the power of veto and Council, acting by qualified majority voting (QMV), the power of assent over any Commission proposal. Parliament rarely exercises its veto under this procedure. By contrast, it proposes extensive amendments, a significant proportion of which are accepted. Under the assent procedure Parliament has the power of assent, a requirement for it actively to approve a proposal before it becomes law. Under the consultation procedure, Parliament is merely consulted on a Commission proposal with the Council taking the final decision. Increasingly, the formal features of the legislative procedures have been blurred by the development of trilogues. These are informal meetings between representatives from the three institutions, usually taking place before the Council first considers the proposal, in which agreement is sought on the proposal.

Section 5 discusses enhanced cooperation. This enables as few as nine Member States to adopt EU laws between themselves where there is not a sufficiently high threshold for general legislation applicable across the Union. The procedural and substantial restraints on use of these procedures are stringent and no legislation has yet been adopted under them. Instead, groups of Member States have resorted to international agreements outside the structures of the Treaties. These are then either incorporated into EU law as a measure binding just those states (e.g. the Protocol integrating the Schengen Acquis) or they are subsequently made into an EU instrument as other Member States join because of the costs of exclusion (e.g. Prüm Convention).

Section 6 considers comitology. These are the procedures that govern delegated law-making by the Commission. There are four procedures: the advisory procedure, management procedure, regulatory procedure and regulatory procedure with scrutiny. Whilst their features differ, a central feature of all, other than the first one, is that a committee of national government representatives considers a draft Commission legislative act and considers whether it should be referred to the Council to adopt a different decision. In practice, almost nothing is referred and this has led to a debate about whether the interaction is an enlightened form of deliberate problem-solving, in which the different actors take on board each other's views, or whether it is simply an administrative club. In recent years, the Parliament has acquired increased powers to monitor and control the extent of delegated law-making.

Section 7 discusses the democratic deficit in the European Union. Concern about the democratic qualities of EU law-making follows a number of axes. There are, first, debates about whether the central supranational institutions have too much power at the expense of national actors. There are, secondly, concerns about whether executives and civil servants have too much power at the expense of representative institutions. Attention has, thirdly, focused on the checks and balances within the system and the efficacy of these. A final feature is the quality of public debate surrounding the EU institutions and whether it is sufficiently vigorous and plural.

2 ALLOCATION OF LEGISLATIVE PROCEDURES

The European Union has no general law-making power. Instead, its legislative powers are to be found in specific Treaty provisions, which authorise it to make laws in particular fields. Prior to the entry into force of the Treaty of Lisbon, it was possible to identify twenty-two different legislative procedures in EU law.[1] The Treaty has reduced it down to four legislative procedures, which are now set out in Article 289 TFEU.

Article 289 TFEU

1. The ordinary legislative procedure shall consist in the joint adoption by the European Parliament and the Council of a regulation, directive or decision on a proposal from the Commission. This procedure is defined in Article 294.
2. In the specific cases provided for by the Treaties, the adoption of a regulation, directive or decision by the European Parliament with the participation of the Council, or by the latter with the participation of the European Parliament, shall constitute a special legislative procedure.

The ordinary legislative procedure was known as the co-decision procedure prior to the Treaty of Lisbon. Whilst this procedure has been emphasised as being the central legislative procedure, this may be something of a misnomer. As Figure 3.1 shows, it has never been the most frequently deployed of all the legislative procedures.[2]

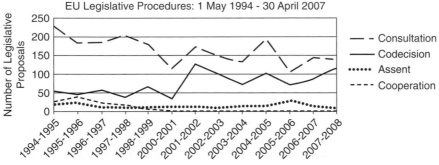

Figure 3.1   EU legislative procedures, 1 May 1994 to 30 April 2007

---

[1] *European Convention, Legislative Procedures (including the Budgetary Procedure): Current Situation*, CONV 216/02, Annex I.

[2] Figure 3.1 is taken from R. Kardasheva, *Legislative Package Deals in EU Decision-Making 1999–2007* (PhD, London School of Economics and Political Science, 2009) 16. The data was obtained from the European Parliament Legislative Observatory (OEIL). All procedures were taken into account (including procedures completed, lapsed or withdrawn and procedures under way). The period pictured runs from 1 May 1994 to 30 April 2007.

The term 'special legislative procedure' is also something of a misnomer, as, in reality, it covers two procedures. These are dealt with in more length later in the chapter but, briefly, they are the consultation procedure and the assent procedure.[3] Both the ordinary legislative procedure and the consultation procedure were extended to about forty new fields by the Lisbon Treaty. Perhaps the most interesting extension was that of the assent procedure. It was only extended to a few new competences, but these were significant ones and one, the flexibility provision in Article 352 TFEU, is one of the most frequently used. It is likely to play an increasingly prominent role alongside the other two procedures.

The choice of procedure is determined by a legal base set out in the TEU and TFEU. This legal base (e.g. Article 114 TFEU on the internal market) entitles the Union to legislate in the given field and sets out the scope for EU legislation in the area. It also determines the legislative procedures and the types of laws that can be adopted. In turn, this determines the respective powers and influences of the different EU institutions and the influence of national governments within the law-making process.[4] Often, the choice of legal base for the adoption of a provision will not be self-evident, with the different institutions seeking to use the legal basis that provides the procedure most advantageous to them. Unsurprisingly, as different procedures privilege different actors, this has led to both EU institutions and Member States vigorously litigating the choice of legal base.[5]

Prior to the Lisbon Treaty, the relationship between the three pillars had become a vexed issue as the Court of Justice had aggressively expanded the Community pillar at the expense of the other two. This led to much legislation being based on the procedures in that pillar at the expense of the procedures in the other two pillars.[6] This debate has been resolved by the abolition of the pillar structure in favour of a structure built around the two Treaties, the TEU and TFEU. The relationship between them is set out in Article 1 TEU and Article 1(2) TFEU, which both state that the Treaties are to have 'the same legal value'. This suggests that a single test will operate across the two Treaties to determine the appropriate legal base for a measure. The test used by the Court in the field of the Community pillar prior to the Lisbon Treaty, where it had to operate a single test, was to look at the predominant aim and content of the measure, and ascribe it accordingly to the appropriate legal base.[7] However, a single legal measure will often address multifarious matters (e.g. in respect of an environmental matter, single market as well as penal questions will arise). To decide that it is more about one than another is a highly contrived exercise, which inevitably involves a select foregrounding of certain features of the measure at the expense of others.

An example of the Court's reasoning is the *Recovery of Indirect Taxes* judgment. The Commission and Parliament challenged the adoption of Directive 2001/44/EC, which provided for the mutual assistance between Member States in the recovery of unpaid indirect taxation. The Council had adopted it under what is now Article 113 TFEU, which concerned

---

[3] The cooperation procedure mentioned in Figure 3.1 was abolished at Lisbon and after the coming into force of Maastricht was rarely deployed.

[4] R. Barents, 'The Internal Market Unlimited: Some Observations on the Legal Basis of Community Legislation' (1993) 30 *CMLRev.* 85, 92.

[5] H. Cullen and H. Charlesworth, 'Diplomacy by Other Means: The Use of Legal Basis Litigation as a Political Strategy by the European Parliament and Member States' (1999) 36 *CMLRev.* 1243.

[6] See, in particular, Case C-176/03 *Commission v Council (Environmental Crimes)* [2005] ECR I-7879.

[7] For a more recent restatement of the principles set out below see Case C-155/07 *Parliament v Council (EIB Guarantees)* [2008] ECR I-8103.

harmonisation of indirect taxes,[8] rather than under what is now Article 114 TFEU, the internal market provision. The latter requires the use of the ordinary legislative procedure, which provides for QMV in the Council and a veto for the Parliament. The former, by contrast, provides for a unanimity vote in the Council and a reduced role for the Parliament. If tax measures could be agreed by QMV, recalcitrant states could be outmanoeuvred and bargained down. If the process were to be subject to a veto, fiscal integration would be held hostage to the wishes of the least integrationist Member State.

Case C–338/01 *Commission v Council (Recovery of Indirect Taxes)* [2004] ECR I–4829

54. ...the choice of the legal basis for a [Union] measure must rest on objective factors amenable to judicial review, which include in particular the aim and the content of the measure.

55. If examination of a [Union] measure reveals that it pursues a twofold purpose or that it has a twofold component and if one of these is identifiable as the main or predominant purpose or component whereas the other is merely incidental, the act must be based on a single legal basis, namely that required by the main or predominant purpose or component...

56. By way of exception, if it is established that the measure simultaneously pursues several objectives which are inseparably linked without one being secondary and indirect in relation to the other, the measure must be founded on the corresponding legal bases...

57. However, no dual legal basis is possible where the procedures laid down for each legal basis are incompatible with each other...

58. In the present case, the procedures set out under [Article 113 TFEU], on the one hand, and that set out under [Article 114 TFEU], on the other, mean that the latter article cannot be applied...in order to serve as the legal basis for a measure such as Directive 2001/44. Whereas unanimity is required for the adoption of a measure on the basis of [Article 113 TFEU], a qualified majority is sufficient for a measure to be capable of valid adoption on the basis of [Article 114 TFEU]...

59. So far as concerns the scope of Article [114 TFEU], which the Commission and Parliament argue ought to have been used as the legal basis for the adoption of Directive 2001/44, it must be pointed out that it is clear from the very wording of Article [114(1) TFEU] that that article applies only if the Treaty does not provide otherwise.

60. It follows that, if the Treaty contains a more specific provision that is capable of constituting the legal basis for the measure in question, that measure must be founded on such provision. That is, in particular, the case with regard to Article [113 TFEU] so far as concerns the harmonisation of legislation concerning turnover taxes, excise duties and other forms of indirect taxation.

61. It must also be pointed out that Article [114(2) TFEU] expressly excludes certain areas from the scope of that article. This is in particular the case with regard to 'fiscal provisions', the approximation of which cannot therefore take place on the basis of that article...

67. ...the words 'fiscal provisions' contained in Article [114(2) TFEU] must be interpreted as covering not only the provisions determining taxable persons, taxable transactions, the basis of imposition, and rates of and exemptions from direct and indirect taxes, but also those relating to arrangements for the collection of such taxes...

76. ...it must be held that Directive 2001/44 does relate to 'fiscal provisions' within the meaning of Article [114(2) TFEU], with the result that Article [114 TFEU] cannot constitute the correct legal basis for the adoption of that directive.

---

[8] It also based it on a now defunct provision, Article 93 EC, which relates to realisation of the common market.

The Court will thus look at the predominant aim and content of a measure to decide the legal base. To ascertain this, it will look at the principles on which it is based and its ideological content rather than its effects. In *Framework Directive on Waste*,[9] the Commission challenged the adoption of the Directive under the predecessor to Article 192(1) TFEU, the environmental base, arguing that it should have been based on what is now Article 114 TFEU, the internal market provision.[10] The Court disagreed. It noted that the central tenets of the Directive were those of environmental management. Instead of securing the internal market objectives of free movement of waste, the Directive implemented the ecological principles that environmental damage should be rectified at source and that waste should be disposed of as close as possible to the place of production in order to keep transport to a minimum.

If two objectives are so inextricably and equally associated that the Court cannot ascertain the predominant purpose of a measure, it moves to a different test in which it operates a formal hierarchy between the different legal bases, looking to the relationship specified in the Treaties between each. Article 114 TFEU, the internal market provision, enjoys a precedence over Article 192(2) TFEU, the provision governing EU environmental action, on, inter alia, measures primarily of a fiscal nature, because the latter indicates that it is 'without prejudice to Article 114'. At the bottom of the pecking order of legal bases sits Article 352 TFEU, the flexibility provision that allows the Union to take measures to meet its objectives, where no other legal base provides the requisite power. This is because this provision stipulates that it can only be used where the Treaties have not provided the necessary powers elsewhere. As such, all other legal bases enjoy precedence over it.[11]

However, it will be rare that a measure pursues inextricably and equally associated objectives. In *Linguistic Diversity in the Information Society*, the Court had to consider a Decision which set up a programme to promote linguistic diversity in the information society. It had been adopted under what is now Article 173(3) TFEU, the legal base for industrial policy. The Parliament challenged this, arguing that it should have been based on what is now Article 166(5) TFEU, the legal base for culture. The Court stated that the fact that a measure had twin objectives was insufficient to bring it outside the 'predominant purpose' rule. Each component had to be equally essential to the measure and each had to be indissociable. In this instance, the predominant purpose was industrial. The beneficiaries of the programme were, almost exclusively, small and medium-sized enterprises, who might lose competitiveness because of the costs associated with linguistic diversity.[12]

Neither rule is easy to apply to particular sets of circumstances. The 'predominant aim and content' rule assumes each legal base is characterised by a distinctive set of principles, through which it is possible to identify all legislation founded on it.[13] This is rarely the case, and the Court has to engage in highly selective analysis to justify a particular legal base for a measure. The 'inextricably associated' rule, if applied literally, is so narrow that it is almost meaningless. Yet it has been applied in some cases, suggesting that, sometimes, for ulterior motives, the Court simply wishes to discard the 'predominant purpose' rule. It is wise not to be too critical

---

[9] Case C-155/91 *Commission v Council (Framework Directive on Waste)* [1993] ECR I-939.

[10] At the time the former provided only for consultation of the Parliament and unanimity voting in the Council.

[11] Case C-295/90 *Parliament v Council (revision of Judgment)* [1992] ECR I-4193.

[12] Case C-42/97 *Parliament v Council (Linguistic Diversity in the Information Society)* [1999] ECR I-869.

[13] D. Chalmers, 'The Single Market: From Prima Donna to Journeyman' in J. Shaw and G. More (eds.), *New Legal Dynamics of the European Union* (Oxford, Clarendon, 1995) 55, 69–71.

of the Court. While differing legal bases exist, uncertainty will persist and result in continued litigation. Weatherill has observed that this is a problem which is likely to remain whatever test is adopted by the Court. The underlying difficulty is the byzantine structure of the Treaties, with their proliferation of legal bases.[14]

3 EU LEGISLATION

(i) Types of legislative act in EU law

All legislative acts must be published in the Official Journal and enter into force twenty days after publication or on the date specified in the instrument.[15] The central provision setting out the types of legislative act is Article 288 TFEU.

> ### Article 288 TFEU
>
> To exercise the Union's competences, the institutions shall adopt regulations, directives, decisions, recommendations and opinions.
>
> A regulation shall have general application. It shall be binding in its entirety and directly applicable in all Member States.
>
> A directive shall be binding, as to the result to be achieved, upon each Member State to which it is addressed, but shall leave to the national authorities the choice of form and methods.
>
> A decision shall be binding in its entirety. A decision which specifies those to whom it is addressed shall be binding only on them.
>
> Recommendations and opinions shall have no binding force.

The provision is not exhaustive and international agreements with non-EU states, although not mentioned in Article 288 TFEU, are regarded as secondary legislation, binding both the Union and the Member States.[16] A 2004 study found Regulations were the most widely used of all, accounting for 31 per cent of all legislation. Decisions addressed to a party accounted for a further 27 per cent, with Decisions not addressed to anybody accounting for 10 per cent of all measures. Directives and international agreements each accounted for 9 per cent of all legislation.[17] The different legislative instruments have different traits.

Regulations are the most centralising of all EU instruments and are used wherever there is a need for uniformity. As they are to have general application, they do not apply to individual sets of circumstances, but to an 'objectively determined situation and produce(s) legal effects with regard to categories of persons described in a generalised and abstract manner'.[18] The other hallmark of Regulations is their direct applicability. From the date that they enter into force,

---

[14] S. Weatherill, 'Regulating the Internal Market: Result Orientation in the House of Lords' (1992) 17 *ELRev.* 299, 312–13.

[15] Article 297(1) TFEU.

[16] Article 216(2) TFEU.

[17] A. v. Bogdandy, F. Arndt and J. Bast, 'Legal Instruments in European Union Law and their Reform: A Systematic Approach on an Empirical Basis' (2004) 23 *YBEL* 91, 97.

[18] Joined Cases 789/79 and 790/79 *Calpak v Commission* [1980] ECR 1949.

they automatically form part of the domestic legal order of each Member State and require no further transposition. Indeed, it is normally illegal for a Member State to adopt implementing legislation because such measures might contain changes which affect the uniform application of the Regulation[19] or obscure from citizens the fact that it is the Regulation which is the direct source of their rights and obligations.[20] However, there is a caveat. In some cases, Regulations will require national authorities to adopt implementing measures. If there is such a requirement, a failure to implement the Regulation will be a breach of EU law.[21]

Directives are binding as to the result to be achieved. They leave the choice as to form and methods used to implement it to the discretion of Member States. Although, like other legislative instruments, a Directive comes into force twenty days after publication or on the date stipulated in the Directive, it will give a deadline (usually eighteen or twenty-four months after publication) by which Member States must transpose its obligations into national law.

Decisions are binding upon those to whom they are addressed. For this reason the addressee must be notified of any Decision.[22] The majority of Decisions are addressed to Member States, with only a small number addressed to private parties, with almost all of the latter being in the field of competition law, where the Commission can impose fines on parties or require them to desist from certain practices. The Lisbon Treaty introduces an amendment by stipulating that Decisions which specify those to whom they are addressed shall be binding only on them. In this, it seems to be making a distinction found in Germany, which distinguishes these types of Decisions from Decisions which have no addressee ('*Beschluss*'). If the former are seen more as directions to particular individuals, the latter impose general obligations which bind the Union as an organisational entity, and Member States as part of that entity. However, as they are not addressed to private parties, they are thought not to impose obligations on them.[23]

International agreements will only have legal effects within EU law for that part of the agreement that falls within Union competence. Their legal effects will also depend upon the phrasing of the agreement. If these agreements impose precise obligations, they will not require implementation by either Member States or EU institutions but will enter directly into force in EU and national law. More vaguely phrased provisions will necessitate implementation. Interpretation of the provisions of an international agreement will be carried out in the light of the object and purpose of that agreement. Provisions identically worded to EU law provisions may be interpreted differently, on the ground that the objective of the agreement differs from that of the Treaties.[24]

The justification for this wide array of legislative instruments is that the founders of the Treaties wanted EU law to have different legal bite in different policy fields and that in some they wished the legislator to have discretion on this matter. This rationale has been undermined by the legislative instruments being substitutable for one another. One finds Regulations which substitute for Decisions, in that they apply to individual sets of circumstances rather than generally.[25] There are, conversely, Directives which look like Regulations because they

---

[19] Case 39/72 *Commission* v *Italy (premiums for slaughtering cows)* [1973] ECR 101.
[20] Case 34/73 *Variola* v *Amministrazione delle Finanze* [1973] ECR 981.
[21] Case 128/78 *Commission* v *United Kingdom (failure to implement regulation 1463/70 on recording equipment in road transport)* [1978] ECR 2429.
[22] Article 297(2) TFEU.
[23] v. Bogdandy *et al.*, above n. 17, 103–6.
[24] The seminal case on international agreements is Case 104/81 *Hauptzollamt Mainz* v *Kupferberg* [1982] ECR 3641.
[25] See e.g. Joined Cases 41/70–44/70 *International Fruit Company* v *Commission* [1971] ECR 411.

are so detailed that they vitiate the discretion granted to Member States and must be transposed into national law verbatim.[26] Finally, Decisions without addressees act as a substitute for Directives in that they require Member States to realise certain results without specifying the means. In no instance has any of this been declared illegal.

(ii) The hierarchy of norms

The other difficulty has traditionally been that of no hierarchy of norms, where one type of instrument is taken to trump another. This is particularly problematic as 69 per cent of Regulations are delegated legislation, adopted by the Commission under powers granted to it by the other institutions.[27] The Future of Europe Convention felt that the functions of primary legislation and delegated legislation were different.[28] The function of the former should be to set out the essential elements of an area, whilst the latter's role was to fill in the detail. This was not simply for the sake of legislative clarity, but also to enable a clear separation of powers. The legislature should be focused exclusively on the central policy choices, whilst the executive should be responsible for administering the technical detail.

The Lisbon Treaty introduces a distinction, therefore, between legislative and non-legislative measures. Legislative acts are those adopted by the procedures set out in Article 289 TFEU.[29] The legislator may, however, grant to the Commission the power to take two types of measure: 'delegated' acts and 'implementing' acts. The former are described as 'non-legislative' in nature and it is safe to assume this is also true of the latter. There is thus clearly a hierarchy between them and all legislative acts. The role of delegated measures is to supplement or amend certain non-essential elements of the legislative act. The role of implementing measures is to set out uniform conditions for implementing EU legally binding acts.[30] Each must identify itself in its title as either a 'delegated' or 'implementing' measure.[31]

The distinction between delegated and implementing acts matters because the former are subject to additional controls by the Council and Parliament that the latter are not.[32] The distinction is, however, obscure. Hoffmann has observed that implementing acts are traditionally thought of as:

> rule interpretation, rule application, rule setting/evaluation, approval of funds, the extension/ new specification of funding programmes and information management. They ranged from single-case decisions to the adoption of acts 'supplementing' or 'amending non-essential elements' of a legislative act.[33]

This all fits within the definition for implementing acts set out by the Lisbon Treaty. It also fits within that for delegated acts. It is not clear how the two will be distinguished. Clearly, delegated acts are meant to have a broader sweep than implementing acts. Yet this is incredibly elastic and begs a further question: is this new concept of delegated legislation actually substituting

---

[26] Case 38/77 *ENKA* v *Inspecteur der Invoerrechten* [1977] ECR 2203.
[27] v. Bogdandy *et al.*, above n. 17, 99.
[28] *Final Report of Working Group IX on Simplification*, CONV 424/02.
[29] Article 289(3) TFEU.
[30] They are set out in Articles 290(1) and 291(2) TFEU.
[31] Articles 290(3) and 291(4) TFEU.
[32] Article 290(2) TFEU. See p. 121.
[33] H. Hoffmann, 'Legislation, Delegation and Implementation under the Treaty of Lisbon: Typology Meets Reality' (2009) 15 *ELJ* 482, 495.

measures by the Commission for laws that should be adopted by the Parliament and Council by virtue of their breadth, salience or importance?[34]

(iii) Soft law

Recommendations and Opinions are mentioned in Article 288 TFEU, but have no binding force. They must be viewed alongside a variety of other instruments, which include resolutions and declarations, action programmes and plans, communications by the Commission, Conclusions of the representatives of the Member States meeting in Council, guidelines and inter-institutional arrangements. These measures all come under the generic heading of 'soft law': 'rules of conduct which, in principle, have no legally binding force but which nevertheless may have practical effects'.[35] These instruments are an integral part of the Union legal order, reportedly accounting for 13 per cent of all EU law.[36] They are used for a variety of purposes.

Commitments about the conduct of institutions   These are commonly used to organise the relations between the institutions. A good example is the Joint Declaration on Practical Arrangements for the Co-Decision Procedure, which sets out the *modus vivendi* for one of the main EU legislative procedures and the institutions' understanding of their rights and duties under it.[37]

Commitments to respect certain values   Soft law, most notably Declarations, is used to commit EU institutions to pursuing certain values. Declarations are not merely commitments to future conduct, but also seek to redefine the political identity of the Union. The most obvious example is the Joint Declaration by the European Parliament, the Council and the Commission on Fundamental Rights, where the institutions were asserting for the first time that observance of fundamental rights norms was a goal of the EU institutions, thereby admitting that it was not merely concerned with economic integration, but also had an incipient civil identity.[38]

Programming legislation   The instrument, *par excellence*, for this is the Action Plan. Action Plans set out objectives and timetables for particular EU policies, which are used to justify specific legislation and which provide a wider background against which this legislation is understood and interpreted. A good example is the Commission Action Plan for European renewal in the field of freedom, security and justice, issued in 2005.[39] The Action Plan identifies ten priorities for freedom, security and justice for the period up to 2010. These include developing policies for fundamental rights and citizenship, the establishment of a common asylum area, managing migration, and developing an integrated management of the external borders of the Union. It also lists over 200 measures, some legislative and others administrative, some binding and others not, to be adopted to meet these priorities.

---

[34] For powerful criticism see *ibid.* 491–9.

[35] F. Snyder, 'The Effectiveness of European Community Law: Institutions, Processes, Tools and Techniques' (1993) 56 *MLR* 19, 32. For an exhaustive discussion see L. Senden, *Soft Law in European Community Law* (Oxford and Portland, Hart, 2004) ch. 5.

[36] v. Bogdandy *et al.*, above n. 17, 97.

[37] [2007] OJ C145/2.

[38] [1977] OJ C103/1.

[39] COM(2005)184.

Regulatory communications   In areas such as nuclear energy and competition, the Commission will issue Opinions as an informal way of indicating to undertakings whether they are complying with EU law. It will also issue notices, setting out its general enforcement policy on what infractions it will or will not pursue.[40]

Model law-making   The most controversial use of soft law is for 'model law-making', where guidelines or recommendations setting out best practice for Member States are adopted. In some areas of EU law, harmonising measures involving the setting of common standards through Regulations, Directives and Decisions are excluded. In such fields, norm-setting is done exclusively through soft law.[41] Yet, soft law is also used in many fields where there is the option of harmonising measures. The Secretariat at the Future of Europe Convention identified three circumstances where the former is likely to be preferred:

- where the area of work is closely connected with national identity or culture, e.g. culture or education;
- where the instruments for implementing national policies are so diverse and/or complex that harmonisation seems disproportionate in relation to the objectives pursued, e.g. employment;
- where there is no political will for EC legislation amongst the Member States, but there is a desire to make progress together.[42]

As it has no coercive force and no system of sanctions to underpin it, the effect of soft law on its subjects' behaviour is uncertain. It seems, at the very least, that soft law frames institutional expectations and opens actors to diverse forms of peer pressure.[43] There has been a recent fierce debate over the value of soft law. The arguments on each side have been well set out by Trubek, Cottrell and Nance.[44] Some of the criticisms of soft law they observe are that:

- it lacks the clarity and precision needed to provide predictability and a reliable framework for action;
- soft law cannot really have any effect, but is a covert tactic to enlarge the Union's legislative hard law competence;
- soft law bypasses normal systems of accountability;
- soft law undermines Union legitimacy because it creates expectations, but cannot bring about change.

---

[40] See e.g. Commission Notice on agreements of minor importance which do not appreciably restrict competition [2001] OJ C368/13.

[41] The fields include Common Foreign and Security Policy (Article 24(1) TEU); economic policy (Article 121(2) TFEU); employment (Article 148(2) TFEU); education, vocational training, youth and sport (Article 165(4) TFEU); culture (Article 167(5) TFEU); most areas of public health (Article 168(4), (5) TFEU); industry (Article 173(3) TFEU); space (Article 189(2) TFEU); tourism (Article 195(2) TFEU); civil protection (Article 196(2) TFEU); administrative cooperation (Article 197(2) TFEU).

[42] *European Convention, Coordination of National Policies: The Open Method of Coordination*, WG VI WD015, Brussels, 26 September 2002.

[43] M. López-Santana, 'The Domestic Implications of European Soft Law: Framing and Transmitting Change in Employment Policy' (2006) *JEPP* 481, 494–6.

[44] D. Trubek *et al.*, 'Hard and Soft Law in European Integration' in J. Scott and G. de Búrca (eds.), *New Governance and Constitutionalism* (Oxford and Portland, Hart, 2005).

They argue, however, that soft law has some advantages over traditional law:

- Hard law tends toward uniformity of treatment while many current issues demand tolerance for significant diversity among Member States.
- Hard law presupposes a fixed condition based on prior knowledge while situations of uncertainty may demand constant experimentation and adjustment.
- Hard law is very difficult to change yet in many cases frequent change of norms may be essential to achieve optimal results.
- If actors do not internalise the norms of hard law, enforcement may be difficult; if they do, it may be unnecessary.

From this, it would appear that much depends on the nature of the field. In areas where uniformity is not important and there is a need for experimentation, soft law would seem to have important advantages. Yet even in these fields, some of the criticisms of soft law still persist: namely the manner in which it has been used to expand EU involvement, its blurring of institutional rules,[45] and its lack of concern with asymmetries of power, so that compliance with soft law only tends to occur when it suits vested interests.[46]

4 EU LEGISLATIVE PROCEDURES

(i) Ordinary legislative procedure

(a) Central features of the ordinary legislative procedure

The ordinary legislative procedure (previously known as the co-decision procedure) is set out in Article 294 TFEU. Its central elements are set out below.

Article 294 TFEU

1. Where reference is made in the Treaties to the ordinary legislative procedure for the adoption of an act, the following procedure shall apply.
2. The Commission shall submit a proposal to the European Parliament and the Council.

First reading

3. The European Parliament shall adopt its position at first reading and communicate it to the Council.
4. If the Council approves the European Parliament's position, the act concerned shall be adopted in the wording which corresponds to the position of the European Parliament.
5. If the Council does not approve the European Parliament's position, it shall adopt its position at first reading and communicate it to the European Parliament.
6. The Council shall inform the European Parliament fully of the reasons which led it to adopt its position at first reading. The Commission shall inform the European Parliament fully of its position.

---

[45] Commission Communications have been criticised for enabling the Commission to enshrine a particular interpretation of EU law without proper judicial control. S. Lefevre, 'Interpretative Communications and the Implementation of Community Law at National Level' (2004) 29 *ELRev.* 808.

[46] See, in particular, Senden, above n. 35, 477–98.

Second reading

7. If, within three months of such communication, the European Parliament:
   (a) approves the Council's position at first reading or has not taken a decision, the act concerned shall be deemed to have been adopted in the wording which corresponds to the position of the Council;
   (b) rejects, by a majority of its component members, the Council's position at first reading, the proposed act shall be deemed not to have been adopted;
   (c) proposes, by a majority of its component members, amendments to the Council's position at first reading, the text thus amended shall be forwarded to the Council and to the Commission, which shall deliver an opinion on those amendments.
8. If, within three months of receiving the European Parliament's amendments, the Council, acting by a qualified majority:
   (a) approves all those amendments, the act in question shall be deemed to have been adopted;
   (b) does not approve all the amendments, the President of the Council, in agreement with the President of the European Parliament, shall within six weeks convene a meeting of the Conciliation Committee.
9. The Council shall act unanimously on the amendments on which the Commission has delivered a negative opinion.

Conciliation

10. The Conciliation Committee, which shall be composed of the members of the Council or their representatives and an equal number of members representing the European Parliament, shall have the task of reaching agreement on a joint text, by a qualified majority of the members of the Council or their representatives and by a majority of the members representing the European Parliament within six weeks of its being convened, on the basis of the positions of the European Parliament and the Council at second reading.
11. The Commission shall take part in the Conciliation Committee's proceedings and shall take all necessary initiatives with a view to reconciling the positions of the European Parliament and the Council.
12. If, within six weeks of its being convened, the Conciliation Committee does not approve the joint text, the proposed act shall be deemed not to have been adopted.

Third reading

13. If, within that period, the Conciliation Committee approves a joint text, the European Parliament, acting by a majority of the votes cast, and the Council, acting by a qualified majority, shall each have a period of six weeks from that approval in which to adopt the act in question in accordance with the joint text. If they fail to do so, the proposed act shall be deemed not to have been adopted.
14. The periods of three months and six weeks referred to in this Article shall be extended by a maximum of one month and two weeks respectively at the initiative of the European Parliament or the Council.

The length of this provision makes the procedure look intimidating. It is best to think of the procedure as a series of four key features.

Joint agreement   Joint adoption of legislation by the Council and Parliament can happen at three junctures during the procedure:

- First reading by the Parliament: the Commission makes a proposal. The Parliament issues an Opinion on it (the first reading). The Council can adopt the act by QMV if either the Parliament has made no amendments or it agrees with its amendments.
- Second reading by the Parliament: if there is no agreement after the first reading the Council can adopt a 'common position'. If it is adopting the Commission proposal, it does this by QMV. If it makes amendments of its own, it does this by unanimity. This common position is referred back to the Parliament for a second reading. If the Parliament does nothing for three months or agrees with the common position, the measure is adopted. Alternately, it may propose amendments. If the amendments have been approved by the Commission, they may be adopted by the Council by QMV. If, however, the Commission expresses a negative view of the Parliament's amendments, these have to be adopted by unanimity in the Council.
- Third reading: if there is no agreement following the second reading, a Conciliation Committee is established. It has six weeks to approve a joint text. This text must be adopted within six weeks, by both the Council by QMV and the Parliament, to become law.

Double veto of the Parliament   The ordinary legislative procedure grants the Parliament a veto over legislation. The veto can be exercised at the second reading if the Parliament decides to reject the common position of the Council. The other possibility is at the third reading after the Conciliation Committee has provided a joint text on which it must vote. Technically speaking, it is not a veto that is being exercised here, but Parliamentary assent. It must positively agree to it at this point for it to become law.

Assent of the Council   A measure will only become law if the Council agrees to it. The number of votes required will either be QMV or unanimity. If the measure has been approved by the Commission or by the Conciliation Committee, it will be QMV.[47] If the Council is proposing its own amendments, it must act by unanimity to adopt these amendments.

The Conciliation Committee   As mentioned under 'Joint agreement' above, this is convened following the Parliament's second reading, where the Council is unable to accept the amendments proposed by the Parliament. Modelled on the German Mediations Committee,[48] it comprises twenty-seven members from the Council and twenty-seven MEPs. The Council members vote by QMV and the MEPs by simple majority.

(b) Legislative practice and the ordinary legislative procedure

Looking at the European Parliament, the most dramatic power it enjoys appears to be the veto. However, it has made only limited use of this. Between 1 May 1999 and 1 July 2009, Parliament only used the veto three times in 916 procedures, less than 0.33 per cent of the time.[49] There are a number of reasons for this. The veto can bring the worst outcome because, often, from the Parliament's perspective, imperfect EU legislation is better than no legislation.

---

[47] Prior to Lisbon, there were a limited number of fields where unanimity was required in the Council, most notably culture.

[48] N. Foster, 'The New Conciliation Committee under Article 189b' (1994) 19 *ELRev*. 185.

[49] These statistics are from the EU Council's Consilium website, www.consilium.europa.eu/uedocs/cmsUpload/090622-bilan_general.pdf (accessed 4 September 2009).

Regular exercise of the veto would also be bad politics. Other parties also will not communicate with the Parliament if, in the end, its position is inflexible as there is nothing to talk about. This will be true not just of the Commission and the Council, but also of lobbyists, such as those in industry and NGOs, who will no longer see it as an effective opportunity structure. For the Parliament, it is not the veto which is important, but the shadow of the veto. By threatening to thwart other parties' objectives, it can secure input for itself. They have to listen to its policy preferences and it can secure influence for itself to realise outcomes it desires. This role is reinforced by a quirk in the legislative procedure. If the Commission agrees with the Parliament, it is easier for the Council to accept parliamentary amendments than to produce its own.

Article 293(1) TFEU

Where, pursuant to the Treaties, the Council acts on a proposal from the Commission, it may amend that proposal only by acting unanimously, except in the cases referred to in paragraphs 10 and 13 of Articles 294, in Articles 310, 312 and 314 and in the second paragraph of Article 315.[50]

Acceptance of amendments proposed by the Parliament only requires a QMV in the Council, whilst it requires unanimity to produce its own. To be sure, the Commission must agree with the Parliament's suggestions but, importantly, it cannot propose amendments of its own without withdrawing the proposal and starting again. Parliament is the only institution that has the opportunity to 'improve' the text. This has led to a number of authors talking of its being a 'conditional agenda-setter'; provided it sticks within the limit of what is acceptable to the other two institutions, it can seize the agenda.[51] Statistics seem to bear this out. The last statistics prepared by any of the institutions were in 1 May 2004 by the European Parliament. It found 23 per cent of parliamentary amendments were accepted by both of the other institutions in an unqualified form. A further 60 per cent were accepted in some compromise form. In other words, 83 per cent of parliamentary suggestions are taken on in some form in the legislation.[52]

There are, however, different forms of amendment. Some just dot 'i's; others radically change policy; some clump amendments together, whilst others are put through at the behest of the Council or the Member States. Careful research by Kardasheva, which looked at 470 proposals between 1999 and 2007, found that parliamentary input was high. It amended 87 per cent of the proposals, with amendments per proposal varying from 1 to 322. Instead of looking at formal amendments, Kardasheva identified 1,567 issues raised by the Parliament (discrete matters that were not tidying up exercises) and found parliamentary success in 65.2 per cent of the cases − a high rate.[53]

---

[50] These last four provisions are budgetary provisions.
[51] G. Tsebelis, 'The Power of the European Parliament as a Conditional Agenda Setter' (1994) 88 *American Political Science Review* 128; G. Tsebelis and G. Garrett, 'Legislative Politics in the European Union' (2000) 1 *EUP* 9; G. Tsebelis, C. Jensen, A. Kalandrakis and A. Kreppel, 'Legislative Procedures in the European Union: An Empirical Analysis' (2001) 31 *BJPS* 573.
[52] European Parliament, *Activity Report for 5th Parliamentary Term*, PE287.644, 14.
[53] Kardasheva, above n. 2, 242–4.

The position of the Commission under the ordinary legislative procedure is curious. On the face of it, its influence diminishes as the procedure continues. As it plays no active role in the Conciliation Committee, it would be possible for the Council and Parliament to rearrange its proposals at that point.[54] In practice, its influence remains significant. This is because very few proposals require conciliation.[55] In the majority of instances, agreement is reached at first or second reading. At this point in the procedure, the Commission influence is considerable. Both the Council and the Parliament are working from its proposal and, in practice, it is very difficult for them to deviate from the proposal without the Commission's acquiescence. Almost all successful parliamentary amendments require the Commission's agreement. Very few are adopted by the Council where there has not been prior approval by the Commission. Earlier studies found that there was an 88 per cent probability that a parliamentary amendment would be rejected by the Council if the Commission rejected it, whilst there was an 83 per cent probability that it would be accepted if the Commission approved it.[56]

A further counter-intuitive feature of the procedure is the effectiveness of the Conciliation Committee. The Committee would appear to have little mandate, as any Decision requires the subsequent approval of both Parliament and Council and it might be thought that, by the time it meets, institutional positions would be so entrenched there would be little possibility of movement and agreement. Yet, in almost all procedures,[57] the Committee had been able to propose a joint text accepted by both the Parliament and the Council. This might be because the Council is able to behave more proactively and recapture the agenda within the Committee, as it is able to make its own amendments and accept amendments by QMV.[58] An alternative might be that, as parties are aware of each other's positions, negotiation is easier. New amendments are not continually being thrown in, but there is a stable set of issues on which discussion can proceed.[59] Whatever the reason, the effect is an increase in the influence of COREPER, as it is members of COREPER, not Council ministers, who sit in the Conciliation Committee. COREPER is not just preparing the meeting here, but also adopting the joint text.

(c) First reading and the trilogue

All the evidence discussed in the previous section suggests a picture significantly different from that provided by a simple reading of Article 294 TFEU, which would emphasise the role

---

[54] C. Crombez, 'The Codecision Procedure in the European Union' (1997) 22 *Legislative Studies Quarterly* 97.

[55] In the eighteen months to 30 June 2009 only 6 out of 203 proposals went to conciliation. EU Council, Consilium, above n. 49.

[56] G. Tsebelis *et al.*, 'Legislative Procedures in the European Union: An Empirical Analysis' (2001) 31 *BJPS* 573. For a case study see C. Burns, 'Codecision and the European Commission: A Study of Declining Influence?' (2004) 11 *JEPP* 1.

[57] Between 1 July 1999 and 30 June 2009, 112 proposals went successfully through conciliation. Only three failed. Above, n. 49.

[58] G. Tsebelis, 'Maastricht and the Democratic Deficit' (1997) 52 *Aussenwirtschaft* 26, 43–5.

[59] A. Rasmussen and M. Shackleton, 'The Scope for Action of European Parliament Negotiators in the Legislative Process: Lessons of the Past and for the Future', paper presented at 9th Biennial EUSA Conference, 31 March 2005. Rasmussen also has found that the Committee has tried to adopt positions that it knows are acceptable to both sides rather than asserting its own position. A. Rasmussen, 'The EU Conciliation Committee: One or Several Principals' (2008) 9 *EUP* 7.

of the parliamentary veto and the assent of the Council. Yet, even this understates the extent to which the balance of power is determined by a shared legislative culture, which has emerged with the evolution of the ordinary legislative procedure.

In 1999, the institutions adopted a Joint Declaration on practical arrangements for the procedure. This was updated by a 2007 Joint Declaration.[60] This Joint Declaration formalises two developments that have become a central part of institutional practice and have reshaped understandings in this area: the commitment to reach agreement at first reading and the trilogue.

The Joint Declaration commits the institutions to clear the way, where appropriate, for the adoption of the act concerned at an early stage of the procedure.[61] This is understood to mean that, wherever possible, they should try to secure agreement at first reading.[62] In the early days of this arrangement, they were only partially successful, with only about 28 per cent of the total agreed at first reading between 1 May 1999 and 30 June 2004.[63] Enlargement has had a significant effect on these figures, however. Concerns about the difficulties of getting twenty-seven states rather than fifteen to agree have led to an impetus to get agreement by first reading, so that between 1 July 2004 and 30 June 2009, 379 out of 484 dossiers, or 78.3 per cent, were agreed at first reading.[64]

This telescopes the procedure. It forecloses spaces for public debate, notably the second and third reading. It also changes the opportunity structures available as it means parties that wish to seek influence have to do so as early as possible. For first reading is no longer what it says: an opportunity for initial consideration. It is rather usually nearer to the moment of final decision. This clearly benefits parties that are well-organised, in the know and above all, have connections with the Commission, as in the period prior to first reading, the Commission's presence is particularly powerful.

This position is exacerbated by the dominance of the trilogue. Trilogues first emerged in 1995 to prepare the work of the Conciliation Committee.[65] A trilogue is composed of three parties: two or three MEPs, normally from the respective committee, a Deputy Permanent Representative, normally from the state holding the Presidency, and a senior Commission official. The job of the trilogue is to act as a forum where each side can explain its position to the other and, if possible, where agreement can be reached. They now operate at all stages of the procedure: before all the readings, after the Council common position and before the Conciliation Committee. Kardasheva has estimated that trilogues take place, in some form, on 76 per cent of Commission proposals under the ordinary legislative procedure.[66] Their value to the EU institutions is set out in the Joint Declaration.

---

[60] [1999] OJ C148/1 and [2007] OJ C145/2.
[61] *Ibid.* para. 4.
[62] *Ibid.* para. 11.
[63] European Parliament, *Activity Report for 5th Parliamentary Term*, PE287.644, 12–13.
[64] EU Council, Consilium, above n. 49.
[65] On the trilogue see M. Shackleton, 'The Politics of Codecision' (2000) 38 *JCMS* 325, 334–6; M. Shackleton and T. Raunio, 'Codecision since Amsterdam: A Laboratory for Institutional Innovation and Change' (2003) 10 *JEPP* 171, 177–9.
[66] Kardasheva above n. 2, 25.

> **Joint Declaration on Practical Arrangements for the [Ordinary Legislative] Procedure [2007] OJ C145/2**
>
> 7. Cooperation between the institutions in the context of codecision often takes the form of tripartite meetings ('trilogues'). This trilogue system has demonstrated its vitality and flexibility in increasing significantly the possibilities for agreement at first and second reading stages, as well as contributing to the preparation of the work of the Conciliation Committee.
> 8. Such trilogues are usually conducted in an informal framework. They may be held at all stages of the procedure and at different levels of representation, depending on the nature of the expected discussion. Each institution, in accordance with its own rules of procedure, will designate its participants for each meeting, define its mandate for the negotiations and inform the other institutions of arrangements for the meetings in good time.
> 9. As far as possible, any draft compromise texts submitted for discussion at a forthcoming meeting shall be circulated in advance to all participants. In order to enhance transparency, trilogues taking place within the European Parliament and Council shall be announced, where practicable.

The growth of the trilogue has implications for the balance of power between institutions.[67] In instances, where the trilogue is successful, Parliament and COREPER are acting as genuine co-legislators. It also has implications for the democratic quality of law-making within codecision. The trilogue is the biggest challenge to democratic legitimacy, for it centralises power in those actors who represent the Council and Parliament at the trilogue. Farrell and Héritier note, therefore, that small parties within the European Parliament are excluded by the trilogue, as they are never represented at it and the committee structure and its attendant public debates within the European Parliament are bypassed. They also noted that trilogues reinforce the power of COREPER, as they result in even less being decided by the Council of Ministers.[68] There is, in all this, a sidelining of checks and balances and a lack of formality and transparency. A division is made between formal and substantive decision-making, with the locus of substantive decision-making being hidden away. Whilst formal decision-making takes place in the Council or in parliamentary committees, in many instances substantive decisions are vested in these informal arrangements. The formal procedures do no more than rubber stamp the agreements. Only very well-connected actors have the opportunity to lobby these informal processes because only they can know where they are taking place or who is important within them. Furthermore, only they will have the resources to arbitrage between these centres of power, lobbying both central protagonists in the trilogue and other important actors in the Council, the Parliament and the Commission.

---

[67] On the trilogue see H. Farrell and A. Héritier, 'Interorganizational Negotiation and Intraorganizational Power in Shared Decision Making: Early Agreements under Codecision and their Impact on the European Parliament and the Council' (2004) 37 *Comparative Political Studies* 1184; F. Häge and M. Kaeding, 'Reconsidering the European Parliament's Legislative Influence: Formal vs. Informal Procedures' (2007) 29 *Journal of European Integration* 341.

[68] Farrell and Héritier, above n. 67, 1200–4.

(ii) Special legislative procedures

(a) Consultation procedure

The consultation procedure follows three stages:

(a) the Commission submits a proposal to the Council;
(b) the Council consults the Parliament;
(c) the Council adopts the measure, either by qualified majority or by unanimity, depending upon the field in question.

The most salient feature of the consultation procedure is the duty to consult the Parliament. In *Roquette Frères*, the Court of Justice stated that consultation was an expression of the cardinal principle of institutional balance:

> [Consultation] … allows the Parliament to play an actual part in the legislative process of the Community, such power represents an essential factor in the institutional balance intended by the Treaty. Although limited, it reflects at Community level the fundamental democratic principle that the peoples should take part in the exercise of power through the intermediary of a representative assembly. Due consultation of the Parliament in the cases provided for by the Treaty therefore constitutes an essential formality disregard of which means that the measure concerned is void.[69]

From this principle of institutional balance, the Court has crafted a number of mutual obligations between Parliament and the Council. On the one hand, the Council is obliged to reconsult Parliament if the text is amended. This ensures that the text adopted by the Council does not differ substantially from the one on which the Parliament has been consulted, unless these amendments correspond essentially to the wishes of the Parliament.[70] By contrast, Parliament must not abuse its right of consultation. In *General Tariff Preferences*,[71] the Council sought to consult Parliament on a proposal to extend the Regulation on General Tariff Preferences, which gave preferential tax treatment to imports from less developed countries, to the states which had emerged from the collapse of the Soviet Union. The request was made in October 1992 and the dossier was marked 'urgent' by the Council, but the full decision was postponed until a further debate in January 1993, on the grounds that the Parliament's Committee on Development was not happy about including these states. The Council adopted the Regulation in December 1992, without further consultation, on the grounds that the matter was urgent. The Court noted that there was a duty on the Council to consult the Parliament but, correspondingly, duties of mutual cooperation also governed relations between the EU institutions. It noted that Parliament had failed to discharge these duties by refusing to take heed of the urgency of the file and by having regard to what the Court considered to be extraneous factors.

Parliament's powers under the consultation procedure are clearly more limited than under the ordinary legislative procedure. The Council is not required to take account of the Parliament's views and the lack of leverage over the Council also harms Parliament's relations with the Commission. As Parliament's views count for so little, there are no incentives for the Commission to coordinate or even consult with it. This marginalisation is further increased by

---

[69] Case 138/79 *Roquette Frères* v *Council* [1980] ECR 3333.
[70] Case C-65/90 *Parliament* v *Council (Cabotage II)* [1992] ECR I-4593.
[71] Case C-65/93 *Parliament* v *Council (General Tariff Preferences)* [1995] ECR I-643.

the fact that the Council is not required to wait until Parliament has been consulted, before it considers a proposal. The Court has even stated that the Council is making good use of time if it considers the matter pending consultation of the Parliament.[72]

Yet, it is wrong to argue that the Parliament's presence does not matter. At the very least, parliamentary hearings bring greater transparency to the process and provide an arena for actors whose voice might otherwise have been excluded to express their views. In addition, Parliament does make significant inputs of its own. It submits amendments to about 54 per cent of proposals and about 19 per cent of its amendments are accepted – not an insignificant proportion.[73] Notwithstanding the *General Tariff Preferences* judgment, it has acquired this influence by exercising a power to delay. It does this by inviting the Commission to withdraw a proposal or to accept amendment, and when the latter refuses, referring it back to a parliamentary committee to consider its response to this.

R. Kardasheva, 'The Power to Delay: The European Parliament's Influence in the Consultation Procedure' (2009) 47 *Journal of Common Market Studies* 385, 404–5

The power to delay allows the EP [European Parliament] to enjoy important benefits in the legislative system. First, through delay the Parliament manages to force concessions from the Council and the Commission. Delay allows the Parliament to see many of its preferences incorporated in the final legislative texts. Second, delay opens the door for informal negotiations between the Council and Parliament. While informal negotiations have become a typical element of Council–Parliament legislative work under co-decision, there are few incentives for Member States to seek informal contacts in consultation. However, when the EP delays its opinion and Member States need an urgent decision the Council has an incentive to speed up the procedure through informal contacts. Third, delay gives the consultation procedure two readings. Formally, the consultation procedure consists of only one reading. However, by delaying its final vote, the EP gains an additional reading. The EP makes its position on the Commission proposal known, but the plenary refrains from issuing an opinion. Once aware of the EP's preferences, the Council and Commission negotiate with MEPs and adjust their positions in order to speed up the decision-making process. Thus, through delay, the EP transforms the simple consultation procedure into a decision-making procedure with two readings.

However, these features exert only a limited effect upon the broader institutional settlement, which revolves around the Commission-Council axis. Both the Commission and the Council are executive-dominated and the current safeguards for national parliamentary input are weak.[74] There is still the question of which 'executive' holds the balance of power in these procedures. Everything hinges on the vote required in the Council. If a unanimity vote is required, power would seem to remain in the hands of individual national governments, as any government can veto the measure. However, the position is more complicated. Twenty-six national governments do not have the power to push through a measure if

---

[72] Case C-417/93 *Parliament v Council (consultation with Parliament)* [1995] ECR I-1185.

[73] R. Kardasheva, 'The Power to Delay: The European Parliament's Influence in the Consultation Procedure' (2009) 47 *JCMS* 385, 392–4.

[74] See pp. 126–32.

one national government resists it. Power is, therefore, concentrated in the government that is most resistant to the measure, as it holds the decision on whether or not to go forward.[75] Yet power is also strongly vested in the Commission here. As the Council can only amend its proposals by unanimity,[76] its proposals have a 'take it or leave it quality' given that it will be rare that there will be consensus on the part of, or the resources available for, the Member States to put forward an alternative proposal that secures the agreement of all of them.

(b) Assent procedure

The assent procedure is the procedure in which Parliament enjoys greatest formal powers and brings together a number of heterogeneous procedures:

- The Commission does not enjoy a monopoly of initiative. Depending on the field, a proposal can also be made by the Parliament, Member States or the European Council.
- The proposal may come direct to the Parliament. Alternatively, there may be other institutions that have either to be consulted or to give their consent to the proposal first. The procedures depend on the legal base in question.
- The Parliament will then have to consent to the measure. There are no time limits on it to do so.
- In some instances, the Council or the European Council then has to consent to the measure before it can become law.

The uniting features of all these procedures, which allow them to be classified under the assent procedure umbrella, are first that in all cases Parliament has to affirm a legislative proposal before it can be adopted. This is different from the ordinary legislative procedure in that Parliament must actively say 'yes' to a proposal whereas the latter merely gives it a veto. Secondly, it has an indefinite time in which to do this. There must be a strong majority in Parliament in favour of immediate action, therefore, if a measure is to be agreed.

The assent procedure was downplayed before the Treaty of Lisbon as it was largely used for a limited number of institutional matters related to the European Central Bank and the Parliament itself. This is no longer the case. It now governs significant fields, which include EU anti-discrimination policy,[77] significant parts of EU criminal justice policy,[78] the budget,[79] many international agreements[80] and, perhaps most prominently, the flexibility principle, which allows measures to be taken to realise Union objectives where there is no other legal base and which, historically, has been deployed about thirty times per annum.[81]

The procedure is likely to be a prominent procedure. However, it is to be wondered if, in practice, it will differ that much from the ordinary legislative procedure. Agreement will be sought to be reached after the initial proposal through a trilogue with all parties aware that the proposal requires the cooperation of each to make it law.

---

[75] On this see *Report by the Ad Hoc Group Examining the Question of Increasing the Parliament's Powers* (Vedel Report), *EC Bulletin* Supplt. 4/72; Committee of Three, *Report on the European Institutions* (Luxembourg, Office for Official Publications of the European Communities, 1980) 74–5.

[76] Article 293(1) TFEU.

[77] Article 19(1) TFEU.

[78] Articles 82, 83(1), (6), 86(1), (4) TFEU.

[79] Articles 311 and 312 TFEU.

[80] Article 218(6) TFEU.

[81] Article 352 TFEU. For a fuller list see the Annex at the end of this chapter.

5 ENHANCED COOPERATION

Enhanced cooperation grew out of a debate that emerged prior to the Treaty of Amsterdam in which deep-seated differences between Member States about both the pace and ideological direction of integration emerged. It was agreed that some Member States should not be held back from developing common laws between themselves, should they so wish, and enhanced cooperation was established to enable this. It allows EU laws to be developed by as few as nine Member States where there is not a sufficient voting threshold for general legislation. Lowering the threshold in this way intrudes on general EU law-making as it raises the possibility of a 'hard core Europe', which develops laws for itself, excluding other Member States and creating a two-tier Union.[82] To prevent this, the provisions on enhanced cooperation put in place a number of safeguards.

Article 20 TEU

1. Member States which wish to establish enhanced cooperation between themselves within the framework of the Union's non-exclusive competences may make use of its institutions and exercise those competences by applying the relevant provisions of the Treaties, subject to the limits and in accordance with the detailed arrangements laid down in this Article and in Articles 326 to 334 TFEU.

   Enhanced cooperation shall aim to further the objectives of the Union, protect its interests and reinforce its integration process. Such cooperation shall be open at any time to all Member States, in accordance with Article 328 TFEU.

2. The decision authorising enhanced cooperation shall be adopted by the Council as a last resort, when it has established that the objectives of such cooperation cannot be attained within a reasonable period by the Union as a whole, and provided that at least nine Member States participate in it. The Council shall act in accordance with the procedure laid down in Article 329 TFEU.

Article 326 TFEU

Any enhanced cooperation shall comply with the Treaties and Union law. Such cooperation shall not undermine the internal market or economic, social and territorial cohesion. It shall not constitute a barrier to or discrimination in trade between Member States, nor shall it distort competition between them.

---

[82] On the debate see A. Stubb, 'The 1996 Intergovernmental Conference and the Management of Flexible Integration' (1997) 4 *JEPP* 37; F. Tuytschaever, *Differentiation in European Union Law* (Oxford and Portland, Hart, 1999) 1–48; E. Phillipart, 'From Uniformity to Flexibility: The Management of Diversity and its Impact on the EU System of Governance' in G. de Búrca and J. Scott (eds.), *Constitutional Change in the EU: From Uniformity to Flexibility?* (Oxford and Portland, Hart, 2000).

> ### Article 327 TFEU
>
> Any enhanced cooperation shall respect the competences, rights and obligations of those Member States which do not participate in it. Those Member States shall not impede its implementation by the participating Member States.

The provisions suggest a total of six substantive constraints:

- there must be nine Member States;
- it must not be in a field where the Union has exclusive competence;
- the measure must only be adopted as a matter of last resort;
- enhanced cooperation must comply with other EU law;
- it must not undermine the internal market or economic or social cohesion; in particular, it must not constitute a barrier to or discrimination in trade between Member States or distort competition between them;
- it must respect the rights, competences and obligations of other Member States.

These alone would suggest enhanced cooperation could only occur in very restricted circumstances. However, additional procedural constraints have been put in place, which grant vetoes to a number of actors. Any enhanced cooperation must be notified to the Commission, which must decide whether to put forward a proposal on it, giving its reasons if it does not.[83] The Parliament and Council must then assent to it, with the Council making the Decision by unanimity.[84]

The value of the measure is further eroded to the participating states by its being deemed not to be part of the EU legislative acquis.[85] Furthermore, they do not have freedom to negotiate between themselves as they must allow non-participating states to participate in the deliberations leading up to the adoption of legislation even if they cannot vote on it.[86] Finally, non-participating states can free-ride by waiting to see the effects of the measure and then joining later. Any state that did not take part initially can apply subsequently and is free to participate subject to verification that it meets the conditions for participation.[87]

In the light of this, it is unsurprising that for all the institutional and academic energy devoted to these procedures, there has yet to be a measure adopted under them.[88] Instead, resort had been made to arrangements outside this framework, some within the EU legal framework, and in some cases outside. These arrangements have thrown up real concerns both about fragmentation of the Union and about protecting the integrity of the Union's decision-making processes.

---

[83] Slightly different procedures apply in CFSP. The proposal is notified to the Council. It obtains an Opinion from the Commission and the High Representative. Parliament is also notified. The Council then makes a Decision by unanimity with only it and not the Parliament having a veto in this field: Article 329(2) TFEU.

[84] Article 329(1), (2) TFEU.

[85] Article 20(4) TEU.

[86] Articles 20(3) TEU and Article 330 TFEU.

[87] This is to be done by Commission authorisation in all fields other than CFSP. In CFSP it is done by the Council in consultation with the High Representative: Article 331 TFEU.

[88] On the one attempt to do so, see M. O'Brien, 'Company Taxation, State Aid and Fundamental Freedoms: Is the Next Step Enhanced Co-operation?' (2005) 30 *ELRev.* 209.

The central example of 'variable geometry' within the EU legal framework, in which only some Member States participate, is the Protocol on the Schengen Acquis integrated into the framework of the European Union. The Schengen Conventions of 1985 and 1990 were international agreements concluded between thirteen of the EU-15 Member States, Norway and Iceland. They provide for the abolition of frontier checks, a common external frontier and cooperation in the fields of migration of non-EU nationals, crime and policing. All Member States are currently signatory to them except Ireland, United Kingdom, Cyprus, Bulgaria and Romania.[89] The Protocol integrates the measures agreed under the Schengen Acquis into EU law. It also defines the relationship between participating and non-participating states. Article 4 of the Protocol provides that non-participants may request to take part in any part or all of the acquis, so long as all other Member States consent. This is, of course, in contrast, to the procedures on enhanced cooperation, which require simple satisfaction of the conditions of participation.[90]

In the fields covered by the Schengen Protocol, certain Member States can therefore be excluded from subsequent involvement. Yet, this begs the question of the relation between this Protocol and the general provisions on immigration, asylum, policing and frontier controls, which form part of the Treaties and to which all Member States are party. How could it be that a Member State can be excluded from a field of policy that also forms part of EU law to which it is party? The relationship between the Protocol and the rest of the Treaties was considered in two cases brought by the United Kingdom against two measures: one establishing the European Agency for the Management of Operational Cooperation at the External Borders of the Member States (Regulation 2007/2004/EC), and the other introducing common security features and biometric identifiers into passports.[91] These had been adopted under the Schengen Protocol, thereby excluding the United Kingdom, even though Article 77(2) TFEU provides for the Union to develop legislation on external borders and the United Kingdom is party to that.

Case C-77/05 *United Kingdom* v *Council* [2007] ECR I-11459

77. ...by analogy with what applies in relation to the choice of the legal basis of a [Union] act, it must be concluded that in a situation such as that at issue in the present case the classification of a [Union] act as a proposal or initiative to build upon the Schengen acquis...must rest on objective factors which are amenable to judicial review, including in particular the aim and the content of the act...

83. It should be recalled...that both the title of the Schengen Agreement and the fourth recital in its preamble and Article 17 of the agreement show that its principal objective was the abolition of checks on persons at the common borders of the Member States and the transfer of those checks to their external borders. The importance of that objective in the context of the Schengen Agreements is underlined by the place occupied in the Implementing Convention by the provisions on the crossing of external borders, and by the fact that, under Articles 6 and 7 of that convention, checks at external borders are to be carried out in accordance with uniform principles, with the Member States having to implement constant and close cooperation in order to ensure that those checks are carried out effectively.

---

[89] Cyprus is acceding in 2010. Romania and Bulgaria are to join when 'ready'. No date has been set.
[90] Article 331 TFEU.
[91] See also Case C-137/05 *United Kingdom* v *Council* [2007] ECR I-11593.

84. It follows that checks on persons at the external borders of the Member States and consequently the effective implementation of the common rules on standards and procedures for those checks must be regarded as constituting elements of the Schengen acquis.

85. Since...Regulation No 2007/2004 is intended, as regards both its purpose and its content, to improve those checks, that regulation must be regarded as constituting a measure to build upon the Schengen acquis...

This reasoning is open to criticism. It would seem that there are two possible legal bases: the Protocol and Article 77(2) TFEU. The responsibility of the Court was to mediate a conflict between these bases, which, as we have seen above, it does elsewhere. In this case it did not do this but deemed it sufficient for the matter to fall within the aegis of the Protocol for it to declare that the Protocol should prevail over other parts of the Treaty. No reasons were given for this, and it is a peculiar view of European integration, in which fragmentation and exclusion are chosen over commonality and inclusion.

The other feature to emerge is the conclusion of international agreements between limited numbers of states, who know others will subsequently join them as there will be significant exclusionary costs if they do not. Once this occurs, the international agreement is then subsequently transformed into an EU law, be it as a Regulation, Directive or Decision. This was indeed the template set out by the Schengen Protocol and it was followed in 2005 by the Prüm Convention.[92] Signed between Austria, Belgium, France, Germany, Luxembourg, the Netherlands and Spain, this provides for greater exchange of DNA, fingerprint and vehicle data between security agencies than was previously possible. It is controversial at a number of levels: notably there are no common rules on collection of the data or (arguably) sufficient common rules on its protection.[93] Other security agencies were, of course, eager to have access to this pool of data as they saw it as a huge resource.

In 2008, the Prüm Convention was made part of EU law binding all Member States.[94] The difficulty with this is not simply the feeling that other states were bounced into something that, all things being equal, they might not have chosen, but also the short-circuiting of public debate. A document was agreed between seven interior ministries with little public debate in their own countries. It was then presented as a *fait accompli* to the EU legislative process in such a way that few amendments could be made, given the momentum behind the process.

---

[92] Prüm Convention, EU Council Doc. 10900/05. For an interesting analysis, see R. Bossong, 'The European Security Vanguard? Prüm, Heiligendamm and Flexible Integration Theory', LSE/Challenge Working Paper, January 2007, available at www.2.lse.ac.uk/internationalRelations/centresandunits/EFPU/EFPUhome.aspx (accessed 5 November 2009).

[93] House of Lords European Union Committee, *Prüm: An Effective Weapon Against Terrorism and Crime?* (Session 2006–07, 18th Report, London, SO).

[94] Decision 2008/615/JHA on the stepping up of cross-border cooperation, particularly in combating terrorism and cross-border crime [2008] OJ L209/1; Decision 2008/616/JHA on the implementation of Decision 2008/615/JHA on the stepping up of cross-border cooperation, particularly in combating terrorism and cross-border crime [2008] OJ L210/12.

6 COMITOLOGY

(i) Comitology procedures

We saw in Chapter 2 that not merely 'technical', but highly significant questions are delegated to the Commission and that this delegation is also widespread.[95] In 2008 alone, the Commission undertook 2,022 measures.[96] Although this is not considered to be law-making under the Treaty, the measures are regulatory acts which still have legally binding effects and would be called delegated legislation in any other jurisdiction. The Commission adopts measures here under a set of procedures, known as comitology, in which it works in tandem with a committee of representatives of national governments whose role is to oversee it.[97] At the end of 2008, there were 270 committees in operation.[98] The role of the committee varies according to the procedure used and is set out in Decision 1999/468/EC.[99] Comitology establishes four central procedures: the advisory procedure, the management procedure, the regulatory procedure and the regulatory procedure with scrutiny. Each procedure gives the committee different powers. At the end of 2008, twenty-three advisory procedures, fifty-nine management procedures, eighty-three regulatory procedures and four regulatory procedures with scrutiny were in operation.[100] The criteria for determining which procedure is to be used is set out in article 2 of Decision 1999/468/EC.

Decision 1999/468/EC, article 2

1. Without prejudice to paragraph (2), the choice of procedural methods for the adoption of implementing measures shall be guided by the following criteria:

   (a) management measures, such as those relating to the application of the common agricultural and common fisheries policies, or to the implementation of programmes with substantial budgetary implications, should be adopted by use of the management procedure;

   (b) measures of general scope designed to apply essential provisions of basic instruments, including measures concerning the protection of the health or safety of humans, animals or plants, should be adopted by use of the regulatory procedure; where a basic instrument stipulates that certain non-essential provisions of the instrument may be adapted or updated by way of implementing procedures, such measures should be adopted by use of the regulatory procedure;

---

[95] See pp. 59–60.

[96] European Commission, *Report on the Working of the Committees during 2008*, SEC(2009)913, 6.

[97] For an excellent analysis of the evolution of comitology over the years see C. Bergström, *Comitology: Delegation of Powers in the European Union System* (Oxford, Oxford University Press, 2005).

[98] *Report on the Working of the Committees*, above n. 98, 4.

[99] [1999] OJ L184/23 as amended by Decision 2006/512 [2006] OJ L200/11. For discussion see K. Lenaerts and A. Verhoeven, 'Towards a Legal Framework for Executive Rule-making in the EU? The Contribution of the New Comitology Decision' (2000) 37 *CMLRev*. 645. There is a further procedure, the safeguard procedure, which operates in the field of external trade: article 6. Only two committees are established under it, however, and it is not discussed further here.

[100] A further 100 committees operated under a mix of procedures and were therefore difficult for the Commission to categorise. *Report on the Working of the Committees*, above n. 98, 5–6.

(c) without prejudice to points (a) and (b), the advisory procedure shall be used in any case in which it is considered to be the most appropriate.

2. Where a basic instrument, adopted in accordance with the [ordinary legislative procedure] provides for the adoption of measures of general scope designed to amend non-essential elements of that instrument, inter alia by deleting some of those elements or by supplementing the instrument by the addition of new non-essential elements, those measures shall be adopted in accordance with the regulatory procedure with scrutiny.

The procedure under which the Commission has the most freedom on paper is the advisory procedure. Under this procedure, the role of the committee is to 'advise' the Commission, with the Commission required to give 'utmost account' to the view of the committee but, having done that, being ultimately free to disregard it.

Decision 1999/468/EC, article 3

1. The Commission shall be assisted by an advisory committee composed of the representatives of the Member States and chaired by the representative of the Commission.
2. The representative of the Commission shall submit to the Committee a draft of the measures to be taken. The committee shall deliver its opinion on the draft, within a time-limit which the chairman may lay down according to the urgency of the matter, if necessary by taking a vote.
3. The opinion shall be recorded in the minutes; in addition, each Member State shall have the right to ask to have its position recorded in the minutes.
4. The Commission shall take the utmost account of the opinion delivered by the committee. It shall inform the committee of the manner in which the opinion has been taken into account.

In all the other procedures, the committee has a fire-warning role. It has to decide whether or not the Commission draft should be referred to the Council. With the management procedure, the committee, if it is unhappy with a Commission draft, can, by QMV, refer the matter to the Council. It needs a QMV majority in favour of referral. The Council then has up to three months to adopt another Decision.

Decision 1999/468/EC, article 4(3), (4)

3. The Commission shall...adopt measures which shall apply immediately. However, if these measures are not in accordance with the opinion of the committee, they shall be communicated by the Commission to the Council forthwith. In that event, the Commission may defer application of the measures which it has decided on for a period to be laid down in each basic instrument but which shall in no case exceed three months from the date of such communication.[101]
4. The Council, acting by qualified majority, may take a different decision within the period provided for by paragraph 3.

---

[101] Decision 1999/468/EC, article 8.

There was concern that the majority of committee members could disapprove of the Commission draft, but it would still be adopted. To that end, the Commission issued a Declaration on adoption of the Decision stating that, with regard to the management procedure, it would never go against 'any predominant position which might emerge against the appropriateness of an implementing measure'.[102]

This danger does not exist in the regulatory procedure, where the committee must positively agree to the Commission draft by QMV. If it fails to do this, the draft is referred to the Council, which has up to three months to take a decision of its own.

Decision 1999/468/EC, article 5(3)–(6)

3. The Commission shall, without prejudice to article 8,[103] adopt the measures envisaged if they are in accordance with the opinion of the committee.
4. If the measures envisaged are not in accordance with the opinion of the committee, or if no opinion is delivered, the Commission shall, without delay, submit to the Council a proposal relating to the measures to be taken and shall inform the European Parliament.
5. If the European Parliament considers that a proposal submitted by the Commission pursuant to a basic instrument adopted in accordance with the [ordinary legislative procedure] exceeds the implementing powers provided for in that basic instrument, it shall inform the Council of its position.
6. The Council may, where appropriate in view of any such position, act by qualified majority on the proposal, within a period to be laid down in each basic instrument but which shall in no case exceed three months from the date of referral to the Council. If within that period the Council has indicated by qualified majority that it opposes the proposal, the Commission shall re-examine it. It may submit an amended proposal to the Council, re-submit its proposal or present a legislative proposal on the basis of the Treaty. If on the expiry of that period the Council has neither adopted the proposed implementing act nor indicated its opposition to the proposal for implementing measures, the proposed implementing act shall be adopted by the Commission.

The regulatory procedure contains its own perversity, which is the difference between the voting thresholds in the committee and those in the Council. A QMV majority must actively *support* the measure in the committee for it not to be referred to the Council. By contrast, a QMV majority in the Council must actively *oppose* the measure or support an alternative for the Commission draft not to become law. This leaves a space for the Commission to adopt measures unchecked. This is best illustrated by giving an example where fourteen out of twenty-seven Member States oppose a measure. They do not make a QMV majority but they do form a blocking minority. In such circumstances, the measure would be referred by the committee as a QMV majority would not be in support. The measure could still be adopted, however, as there is not a QMV majority opposing it or formulating an alternative. A Commission measure could therefore become law even if a majority of Member States oppose it. To be sure, given the Commission's Declaration in relation to the management committee, it is unlikely it would ever

---

[102] [1999] OJ C203/1.
[103] See p. 120.

pursue the measure in such circumstances, but it may, however, where there is a substantial minority against the measure, as it can point to a simple majority being in favour.[104]

(ii) The Parliament and comitology

The other issue raised in the regulatory procedure is the role of the Parliament. The ordinary legislative procedure, of course, provides for measures to be adopted by the Council and the Parliament. The Parliament had become increasingly uneasy during the 1990s about delegating powers to the Commission that it thought would be better exercised by the ordinary legislative procedure (at that time, the co-decision procedure). It was, therefore, agreed that regulatory measures based on a parent instrument adopted under the ordinary legislative procedure would be notified to the Parliament and it could object through a Resolution if it considered they exceeded the implementing power granted by the parent instrument. Under article 8 of Decision 1999/468/EC, the Commission committed itself to reconsider the measure taking the Parliament's Resolution into account. The Decision did not require the Commission to withdraw the measure but only to give reasons for its decision. In subsequent years, Parliament continued to feel its prerogatives were being ignored and this culminated in a 2005 exchange where the Commission admitted over fifty instances where it had failed to respect Parliament's rights under comitology.[105]

Following this exchange, the regulatory procedure with scrutiny was introduced. The procedure only applies to instruments which are perceived as 'amending' their parent instruments, where the latter had been adopted under the ordinary legislative procedure. Regulatory procedure with scrutiny begins the same way as the regulatory procedure, with the Commission submitting a draft to the committee which expresses an opinion on it. The process is convoluted after that but boils down to two processes depending on whether the committee agrees with the Commission draft or not.

If the committee agrees with the draft, either the Council or Parliament can veto the draft, but only on the grounds that it is too sweeping and therefore either exceeds the implementing powers granted to the Commission or breaches the subsidiarity or proportionality principles. If they fail to act, it is adopted.[106]

If the committee disagrees with the draft, the same possibilities exist except that this time the Council can decide to oppose the measure *for any reason* and this pre-empts any consideration by the Parliament, which only looks at the draft if the Council is inclined to accept it. The Council has two months to make its opposition known and the Parliament four months after that. If they both fail to indicate their opposition, the measure will be adopted.[107]

Both the Parliament and the Council have high thresholds to meet to register their opposition: an absolute majority of members and a QMV majority respectively. However, in 2008, seven measures were vetoed by one or other of these institutions on the grounds that the

---

[104] For a case study where this happened in relation to the regulation of genetically modified organisms see D. Chalmers, 'Risk, Anxiety and the European Mediation of the Politics of Life' (2005) 30 *ELRev.* 649.

[105] K. Bradley, 'Halfway House: The 2006 Comitology Reforms and the European Parliament' (2008) 31 *WEP* 837, 842–3.

[106] Decision 2006/512/EC, article 5a(3).

[107] *Ibid.* article 5a(4). For discussion see G. Schusterschitz and S. Kotz, 'The Comitology Reform of 2006: Increasing the Power of the European Parliament without Changing the Treaties' (2007) 3 *European Constitutional Law Review* 68.

Commission was exceeding its powers, just under 10 per cent of the measures proposed for regulatory procedure with scrutiny in that year.

It is the Council that has benefited most from the procedure, not the Parliament, vetoing all but one of them.[108]

The place of these procedures has been changed by the coming into force of the Lisbon Treaty, which grants additional powers to the Council and Parliament to place constraints on the Commission with regard to delegated measures.

Article 290(2) TFEU

Legislative acts shall explicitly lay down the conditions to which the delegation is subject; these conditions may be as follows:
(a) the European Parliament or the Council may decide to revoke the delegation;
(b) the delegated act may enter into force only if no objection has been expressed by the European Parliament or the Council within a period set by the legislative act.

Both the Council and Parliament will now have the opportunity to block the measure. This power is also to exist across other areas of legislative activity, not just across the ordinary legislative procedure. The other feature of Article 290(2) TFEU is the possibility it provides to both institutions to revoke a delegation. Up until now, this could only be done through deploying the formal legislative procedures to amend the parent instrument: so if it had been adopted by ordinary legislative procedure, it had to be amended by that procedure. Article 290(2) TFEU suggests more truncated procedures may be set for revocation of a delegation, which, importantly, do not require a Commission proposal for an amendment but can be done at either of the other institutions' behest. Consequently, the Commission may be exercising its powers under the shadow of the sword with the possibility that if it does something institutionally unpopular it will suffer the consequences.

The procedure in Article 290(2) TFEU only applies to delegated acts and not to implementing acts.[109]

Article 291(3) TFEU

...the European Parliament and the Council, acting by means of regulations in accordance with the ordinary legislative procedure, shall lay down in advance the rules and general principles concerning mechanisms for control by Member States of the Commission's exercise of implementing powers.

---

[108] Seventy-one measures were adopted. *Report on the Working of the Committees*, above n. 98, 6–7.
[109] The absence of an equivalent provision to Article 291(3) TFEU in Article 290 TFEU has led some authors to suggest that comitology is prohibited for delegated measures. We disagree. The absence of such a provision does not constrain the other institutions from introducing provisions any more than its absence in the earlier Treaties, and it would be difficult to see how they could police the measures otherwise; cf. K. Lenaerts and M. Desomer, 'Towards a Hierarchy of Legal Acts in the EU' (2005) 11 *ELJ* 744, 755.

This begs the question how Article 290(2) TFEU affects the different procedures set out in Decision 1999/468/EC. Implementing measures will continue to be subject to the same comitology regime, but for delegated measures the only procedure definitely covered by Article 290(2) TFEU is the regulatory procedure with scrutiny, as the jurisdiction of both extends to amending non-essential parts of the parent instrument. For the other procedures it is opaque; and this is extremely concerning, given that the regulatory procedure with scrutiny applies to less than 2 per cent of all the committees.

(iii) Dynamics of comitology and its concerns

Despite this debate on checks and balances, it is not clear that the other institutions either have the resources to police the Commission or that the committees have the inclination to refer the matter to the Council. In 2008, the committees gave 2,185 opinions but only seven references were made to the Council.[110] The central constraints lie in the interactions between the Commission and the committee. In pioneering work, Joerges and Neyer studied the interaction between the Commission and two such committees, the Standing Committee on Foodstuffs (StCF) and the Scientific Committee on Foodstuffs (SCF). They found that comitology did not consist of national checks on Commission decision-making but was, rather, a more fluid settlement centred around deliberative problem-solving in which actors took on board each other's suggestions, and concern focused on finding the optimal solution rather than representing different interests.

C. Joerges and J. Neyer, 'Transforming Strategic Interaction into Deliberative Problem-Solving: European Comitology in the Foodstuffs Sector' (1997) 4 *Journal of European Public Policy* 609, 618–20

Whereas the comitology system in the foodstuffs sector is far too small an arena to allow generalization, it is nevertheless indicative of how this relationship can work in practice and what its deficiencies might be. Three elements are of particular importance:

(a) The proposals which the Commission presents to the StCF are in general the result of extensive consultations with individual national administrations and independent experts. Particularly in committees like the StCF which act under qualified majority voting, proposals not only reflect the Commission's interest but also what it assumes to be in the interest of *more than a qualified majority* of the other parties involved. This becomes of crucial importance as the effectiveness of any measure adopted depends on member states transposing the measure adequately into their national legal systems without leaving too many opportunities for evasion and – more importantly – not invoking safeguard procedures. However, in an institutional environment without effective means of hierarchical enforcement, this is only likely to happen if delegates see their own legitimate concerns acknowledged and protected in decision-making.

(b) The importance of the SCF in supporting certain arguments does not derive from any formal power to decide issues of conflict (it has only an advisory status) but from the legal fiction of its scientific expertise and neutrality. To be sure, member states are well aware that the SCF is sometimes used by

---

[110] *Report on the Working of the Committees*, above n. 98, 6–109.

the Commission as an instrument for furthering its interests and, furthermore, that its experts do not always comply with the norm of objectivity. Moreover, the bovine spongiform encephalopathy (BSE) case has highlighted the fact that even scientific institutions can easily be captured by certain interest groups and instrumentalized for political purposes by the Commission. The Scientific Veterinary Committee was not only chaired by a British scientist; the available records of attendance also show the preponderance of UK scientists and officials, meaning that the Committee tended to reflect current thinking at the British Ministry of Agriculture, Fisheries and Food. Why do member state delegates nevertheless adhere to the fiction of objective science? To understand this, one needs to consider the functions of legal fictions: scientific findings are supposed to be accepted by all the parties concerned; science-based discourses have the power to discipline arguments; and they allow a clear distinction between legitimate and illegitimate arguments in cases of conflict over competing proposals. Therefore, the fact that the opinions of the SCF have never been seriously challenged by the StCF may be grounded less in the objectivity of its opinions than in the function of scientific discourses as a mechanism that is helpful in overcoming politically constituted preferences by relying on the fiction of objective science.

(c) International negotiations concerning common solutions to problems of interdependence generally involve two modes of interaction: strategic bargaining to maximize particular utilities at the expense of others and deliberative problem-solving to maximize collective utilities. Empirically, it is important to realize that the relative intensity of both modes may vary, and identify the conditions which influence them. Whereas the mainstream literature on international negotiations does not acknowledge the possibility of deliberative problem-solving but conceptualizes international negotiations as a pursuit of domestic policy goals by different means, recent contributions to the literature on epistemic communities highlight conditions where the grip which national politicians have on delegates is rather weak. The most prominent conditions mentioned are uncertainty about the distributive effects of certain policies, long-term interaction among delegates, as well as their mutual socialization into a community with common problem definitions and collectively shared approaches to dealing with them.

Under such conditions governments may be unaware of what their preferences are, or delegates, perceiving themselves as part of a transnational problem-solving community, may be able to change their governments' perceptions of interests or even simply bypass them. The condition of high uncertainty about the distributional effects of certain policies is surely not always met; often governments have clear perceptions of the costs that certain policy options might impose on them. However, in negotiations in the StCF – and even more so in the SCF – the particular economic costs of policies cannot be explicitly discussed, and information is primarily provided on nondistributional issues. *Ceteris paribus*, therefore, the knowledge of delegates about adequate problem-solving strategies will increase with the duration of negotiations, whereas their *relative* knowledge about economic effects will decline. This change in the perceptions and preferences of delegates becomes increasingly important for shaping national preferences as their informational advantage over their national administration increases over time. It is also important to note that negotiations sometimes last for years among nearly the same set of delegates. Moreover, delegates have frequent contacts outside the sessions of the Standing Committee, and have often previously met working on the preparation of a legislative proposal in negotiations about its adoption in Council working groups. During the course of this collaboration, delegates not only learn to reduce differences between national legal provisions but also to develop converging definitions of problems and philosophies for their solution. They slowly proceed from being representatives of national interests to being representatives of a Europeanized inter-administrative discourse characterized by mutual learning and an understanding of each other's difficulties in the implementation of specific solutions.

Subsequent studies have reaffirmed this characterisation. A study of Scandinavian officials found that whilst the overwhelming majority of those sitting on the committees saw themselves as government representatives, there was also a strong perception that they saw themselves both as independent experts and as persons acting on behalf of the collective European interest. Above all, there was a strong esprit de corps and loyalty to the committee and other members of the committee, which was particularly marked amongst those who participated most intensively on the committee.[111]

Understandings of comitology as an interactive network of administrators and experts rather than as a check on the Commission's powers have provoked a fierce debate about its democratic qualities.[112] There have been two central concerns. One is that its language is too technocratic. Delicate political and social questions are reduced to questions of expertise and risk assessment.[113] The other is that its make-up is insufficiently pluralistic. Administrators may 'up their game' by having to respond to other administrators' arguments but, as Gerstenberg and Sabel artfully put it, this may only 'improve government performance and renovate the role of the bureaucrat without much changing the role of the citizen'.[114] The rights of audience or participation of private parties before these committees, for example, are notoriously unclear.[115] Joerges has observed, in defence of the processes, that they contain many checks and balances that are generally unappreciated.

C. Joerges, 'Deliberative Supranationalism: A Defence' (2001) 5(8) *European Integration online Papers (EIoP)* 8–9

...comitology...interested us because of its links not just with the bureaucracies but also with the polities of the Member States, because of its complex internal structure in which government representatives, the representatives of social interests and 'the' economy all interact. Risk regulation in the internal market seemed to us to document the weaknesses of expertocratic models adequately, because the normative, political and ethical dimensions of risk assessments resist a merely technocratic treatment. Admittedly, in the debates about the tensions between the ideals of democracy and the constraints of the 'knowledge society', Columbus' egg has not been sighted so far. My mere status as a citizen does not qualify me for a qualitatively convincing (to me at least) technical decision, nor can it be seen how 'all' the citizens affected by such decisions are really to participate in them. What is true of risk policy is present as a problem in practically every corner of modern law. And what is true of

---

[111] J. Trondal, 'Beyond the EU Membership-Non Membership Dichotomy? Supranational Identities among National EU Decision-Makers' (2002) 9 *JEPP* 468. This has been found in other surveys: see J. Blom-Hansen and G. Brandsma, 'The EU Comitology System: Intergovernmental Bargaining *and* Deliberative Supranationalism?' (2009) 47 *JCMS* 719.

[112] R. Dehousse, 'Comitology? Who Watches the Watchmen?' (2003) 10 *JEPP* 798.

[113] J. Weiler, 'Epilogue, "Comitology" as Revolution: Infranationalism, Constitutionalism and Democracy' in C. Joerges and E. Vos (eds.), *EU Committees: Social Regulation, Law and Politics* (Oxford and Portland, Hart, 1999) 339, 345–6.

[114] O. Gerstenberg and C. Sabel, 'Directly-Deliberative Polyarchy: An Institutional Ideal for Europe' in C. Joerges and R. Dehousse (eds.), *Good Governance in Europe's Integrated Market* (Oxford, Oxford University Press, 2002) 289, 320.

[115] F. Bignami, 'The Democratic Deficit in European Community Rulemaking: A Call for Notice and Comment in Comitology' (1999) 40 *Harvard International Law Journal* 451.

risk policy in an EU Member State in which (relatively) dense communicative processes gu...
ongoing political debate is true *a fortiori* for such a polymorphic entity as the EU.

The much-maligned comitology has the advantage over agencies of the American pattern in that it structures risk policy pluralistically, that national bureaucracies have to face up to the positions of their neighbour states, and that interests and concerns in Member States cannot be filtered out. Committees can be observed closely by the wider public and such politicisation has proved to be effective. This seems to be the situation: any conceivable argument can be brought to bear in the committee system. It tends to offer *fora* for pluralistic discussions. Its links with the broader public do, however, remain dependent on the attention that an issue attracts and on the insistence of the actors concerned on public debate.

This may be so, but it requires rather a lot to be taken on trust and there is the broader question of how others would know if what was said to be happening within the committees *was* actually happening. Since 1999, there have therefore been attempts to make the procedure more transparent. Public access to the documents and discussions of the committees is granted on the same basis as to other Commission documents.[116] The Commission has established a register of draft measures placed before the committees and of the agendas and voting records of the committees.[117] Disturbingly, an independent study found that this was something of a hollow commitment: 95 per cent of draft measures and 35 per cent of agendas were not published.[118]

The Lisbon Treaty also suggested that less trust was to be placed in these procedures. It is far easier to challenge them judicially. An individual may now challenge any 'regulatory act' simply if it directly concerns her.[119] This will be the case wherever the measure directly prejudices her legal rights.[120] The consequence is that it will be relatively easy for private parties to challenge delegated legislation. It remains to be seen whether this is a panacea for opening up comitology. Litigation is notoriously ad hoc and threatens the rationales for delegation in the first place, namely policy credibility and efficiency. Furthermore, judges are also non-majoritarian actors and poor substitutes for pluralistic processes if that is the centre of the concern.

7 THE 'DEMOCRATIC DEFICIT' AND THE LEGISLATIVE PROCESS

The question of democratic legitimacy, the 'democratic deficit' in Euro-speak, has dominated debate surrounding the Union's legislative processes. Such debate typically criticises EU law-making in three ways. First, there are concerns about the quality of representative democracy. Such concerns focus both on the parliamentary input in the processes and the extent to which EU law-making undermines parliamentary democracy at a national and regional level.

---

[116] See Decision 1999/468/EC, article 7(2). On public access to the work of the Commission see pp. 384–94.

[117] *Ibid.* article 7(5).

[118] G. Brandsma *et. al.*, 'How Transparent are EU "Comitology" Committees in Practice' (2008) 14 *ELJ* 819, 833.

[119] Article 263(4) TFEU. For other legislative measures, a private party must also show that it is of individual concern to her. This is quite a restrictive hurdle to meet. See pp. 413–28.

[120] Case C-486/01 P *Front National* v *Parliament* [2004] ECR I-6289.

Secondly, there are concerns about the quality of participatory democracy. EU law-making has been accused of being insufficiently plural, of not listening to enough interested parties, and of giving too great weight to some interests. Finally, concerns have been expressed about the quality of deliberative democracy: the quality of public debate that surrounds and informs the law-making processes. Here, it is often argued that law-making processes are far too characterised by strategic negotiation between interests rather than public debate between citizens.

(i) Representative democracy and national parliaments

Representative democracy was seen by the German Constitutional Court in its judgment on the Lisbon Treaty as central to any democratic system:

> The citizens' right to determine, in equality and freedom, public authority with regard to persons and subject-matters through elections and other votes is the fundamental element of the principle of democracy. The right to free and equal participation in public authority is anchored in human dignity…It belongs to the principles of German constitutional law that are laid down as non-amendable.[121]

A similar sentiment is expressed in Article 10(1) TEU which states that the functioning of the European Union is to be founded on representative democracy. It would seem, therefore, to be as central a filament of the Union's mission as it is to the German constitutional state. If so, it appears to fail miserably on two counts.

First, the institutions set out in the Treaty as embodying this idea are not clearly representative institutions.

> ### Article 10(2) TEU
>
> Citizens are directly represented at Union level in the European Parliament. Member States are represented in the European Council by their Heads of State or Government and in the Council by their governments, themselves democratically accountable either to their national Parliaments, or to their citizens.

Governments, be they sitting in the Council or European Council, are not seen as representative institutions. Indeed, the history of representative democracy is a history of the development of institutions to curb and hold accountable the growth of executives. Notwithstanding its direct elections, doubts can also be held over the European Parliament for the reasons given by the German Constitutional Court. Citizens are not represented equally in it. There is low interest and involvement in it. And, finally, there is little popular commitment to it.

The second reason is even more of an indictment. Administrators dominate EU law-making. It is the Commission which proposes legislation. The proposal is negotiated by national officials in COREPER and it is adopted by government ministers in the Council. Swathes of delegated legislation are adopted by the Commission with national administrators through comitology.

---

[121] 2 BvE 2/08 *Gauweiler* v *Treaty of Lisbon*, Judgment of 30 June 2009, para. 211.

strong, powerful

The European Union seems, therefore, to violate the most central foundation of democracy as seen by itself and the German Constitutional Court. This is a swingeing condemnation. And indeed it is largely the Euro-sceptic case. The solution does not seem simply to be to increase the powers of the European Parliament, as for the reasons just outlined it can only partially alleviate concerns about representation.

eight

The 'representative deficit' has focused in recent years, instead, on the role of national parliaments in the law-making processes.[122]

Following the Lisbon Treaty, the Treaties do provide for an increased role for national parliaments. Significantly, this is in a separate provision, suggesting that they are not to be at the heart of the Union, but are instead to remain secondary players. It outlines, inter alia, their contribution to the law-making process.

Article 12 TEU

National Parliaments contribute actively to the good functioning of the Union:

(a) through being informed by the institutions of the Union and having draft legislative acts of the Union forwarded to them in accordance with the Protocol on the role of national Parliaments in the European Union;

(b) by seeing to it that the principle of subsidiarity is respected in accordance with the procedures provided for in the Protocol on the application of the principles of subsidiarity and proportionality...

(f) by taking part in the interparliamentary cooperation between national Parliaments and with the European Parliament, in accordance with the Protocol on the role of national Parliaments in the European Union

---

The first form of power is involvement in the pre-legislative and legislative processes to secure influence for individual parliaments in the decision-making process. The Protocol on the Role of National Parliaments seeks to realise this in a number of ways:

- All draft legislative acts will be sent directly to national parliaments, rather than to national governments to pass onto national parliaments.[123]
- National parliaments will also be sent the annual legislative programme, as well as any policy or legislative planning instrument.[124]
- All agendas and minutes of Council meetings will be sent to national parliaments.[125]
- An eight-week period will elapse between a draft legislative act being sent to national parliaments and its being placed on the agenda of the Council.[126]

---

[122] A. Maurer and W. Wessels (eds.), *National Parliaments on their Ways to Europe: Losers or Latecomers?* (Baden Baden, Nomos, 2001).
[123] Protocol on the role of national parliaments in the European Union, Article 2.
[124] *Ibid.* Article 1.
[125] *Ibid.* Article 5.
[126] *Ibid.* Article 4.

The central intention is that the provision of this information will allow parliaments to exercise influence over their national government in the Council in such a way that it can become a vehicle for their views. Two types of procedure have emerged for the expression of this influence. The *document-based* procedure does not mandate the national minister to take a position. Instead, on important proposals, it requires the minister not to agree to any proposal until a parliamentary committee has scrutinised it and published its findings. The other is the *mandate-based* system, whereby the national parliament authorises the government to take a position and the national government cannot deviate from that, or must provide reasons if it intends to do so.[127]

Auel and Benz have argued that the most suitable procedure depends also on the nature of government-parliament relations. They observed that in the United Kingdom, the document-based system worked well, as the party which was in government also usually had a large majority in parliament. If the mandate-based system were to be used, the party in government would just fill the committee with sympathetic MPs. However, the document-based system had allowed the parliamentary committees to be relatively non-partisan, mobilising them as points for civil society and expertise to coalesce around. In turn, this reputation enables some influence. By contrast, the mandate-based system has traditionally worked well in Denmark, as coalition governments in which all the main parliamentary parties are represented has been a feature of the post-war settlement. The mandate-based procedure allows all coalition partners as well as public debate to inform the position of the minister, thereby ensuring the position has not only parliamentary but also wider government support.[128]

For all this, the limits of each procedure indicate how difficult it is to exercise indirect influence over negotiations involving so many players. The document-based system relies on the idea of soft influence. The parliamentary committee understands that the government needs room to negotiate but rather seeks to bring out issues and interests to the fore that have not been publicly debated or thought through. Its weakness, however, lies in its lack of constraint. The mandate-based system secures a far more direct parliamentary influence on negotiations. Its problem lies in its lack of flexibility. It can lead to governments being disempowered in negotiations and awareness of this often leads the parliament to soften the mandate or use it highly selectively.

There are further difficulties, whichever procedure is used. It is often difficult for national parliaments to formulate a position. As national parliaments often have few supporting staff, contacts with the relevant minister and ministry might be minimal.[129] In this regard, it is doubtful whether the eight-week period national parliaments are given to consider drafts is sufficient to enable effective input into the process.[130] To put this in perspective, the Commission

---

[127] Austria, Belgium, Bulgaria, Cyprus, France, Germany, Ireland, Italy, Luxembourg, Netherlands, Portugal, Slovakia, Spain and the United Kingdom all adopt document-based systems. Denmark, Estonia, Finland, Latvia, Lithuania, Poland, Romania, Slovakia, Slovenia and Sweden use mandate-based systems. Other Member States use a mix of the two. COSAC, *Eighth Biannual Report: Developments in European Union Procedures and Practices relevant to Parliamentary Scrutiny* (Luxembourg, COSAC, 2007) 7–9.

[128] K. Auel and A. Benz, 'The Politics of Adaptation: The Europeanization of National Parliamentary Systems' (2005) 11 *Journal of Legislative Studies* 372.

[129] For criticisms see *Future of Europe Convention, Final Report of the Working Group IV on the Role of National Parliaments*, CONV 353/02, 4–5.

[130] House of Lords European Union Committee, *The Treaty of Lisbon: An Impact Assessment* (Session 2007–08, 10th Report, London, SO) paras. 11.50–11.53.

allows a period of eight weeks for private parties to make submissions in its consultative procedures.[131] Considering that national parliaments represent a wider array of interests and are charged with more significant responsibilities, giving them the same time period to intervene seems unjustified.

In addition to influence via their national governments, all national parliaments have direct relations with the Commission. Since 2006, the latter has instigated a procedure whereby it sends its proposals directly to national parliaments, who also return their opinions straight to the Commission.[132] Between September 2006 and the end of 2008, the Commission received 368 opinions from 33 national assemblies in 24 Member States. This is an impressive number, particularly as 200 opinions were given in 2008 alone.[133] However, whilst the number of opinions were substantial, four chambers (the Czech Senate, the German Bundesrat, the French Senate and the UK House of Lords) were responsible for 54 of the 200 in 2008. These are all second chambers, and their predominance suggests a danger of asymmetric representation where assemblies with stronger capacity or interest are more actively involved. The quality of opinion is also variable. The Portuguese Assembly of the Republic gave 65 opinions in 2008, but all were positive on the Commission proposal and none contained specific comments. The final observation made by the Commission was that parliamentary comments tended to follow those of the respective national governments.[134]

The second set of powers provided for national parliaments in the legislative process is to police the legislative process for compliance with the subsidiarity principle: the principle whereby the European Union is only to legislate if the objects of a measure cannot be realised by Member States acting unilaterally and could by reason of their scale or effects be better realised by EU action.[135] National parliaments seem to have a particularly important role in the process. It is the powers of national and regional parliaments that are most encroached upon by EU legislation. They seem to be among the biggest stakeholders in determining where its limits should be set.

Detailed provision is made for them in the Protocol on the application of the principles of subsidiarity and proportionality.

Protocol on the application of the principles of subsidiarity and proportionality, Article 6

Any national Parliament or any chamber of a national Parliament may, within eight weeks from the date of transmission of a draft legislative act, in the official languages of the Union, send to the Presidents of the European Parliament, the Council and the Commission a reasoned opinion stating why it considers that the draft in question does not comply with the principle of subsidiarity.

---

[131] European Commission, General Principles and Minimum Standards for Consultation of Interested Parties by the Commission, COM(2002)704, 21.

[132] European Commission, *A Citizens' Agenda:- Delivering Results for Europe*, COM(2006)211 final.

[133] European Commission, *Annual Report on Relations between the European Commission and Nation Parliaments*, COM(2009)343, 4.

[134] *Ibid.* 6.

[135] Protocol on the role of national parliaments in the European Union, Article 3.

The national parliaments of each Member State are also given two votes, which are shared out between chambers in the case of a bicameral system. Opinions suggesting a violation of the subsidiarity principle are then tallied up. If at least eighteen out of the current fifty-four votes suggest that it does (fourteen in the case of Article 76 TFEU), then the institution that proposed the measure may decide to withdraw it.

Protocol on the application of the principles of subsidiarity and proportionality, Article 7(2)

Where reasoned opinions on a draft legislative act's non-compliance with the principle of subsidiarity represent at least one third of all the votes allocated to the national Parliaments…, the draft must be reviewed. This threshold shall be a quarter in the case of a draft legislative act submitted on the basis of Article 76 TFEU on the area of freedom, security and justice.

After such review, the Commission or, where appropriate, the group of Member States, the European Parliament, the Court of Justice, the European Central Bank or the European Investment Bank, if the draft legislative act originates from them, may decide to maintain, amend or withdraw the draft. Reasons must be given for this decision.

Concern was expressed that national parliaments could issue only a 'yellow card' to the Union legislature, requiring it to reconsider a proposal, and not a 'red card', requiring it to abandon it. Criticism was also expressed that there is only optional involvement of regional assemblies, who will be consulted if the respective national parliament so decides.[136] Furthermore, national parliaments have no direct powers to protect their prerogatives under the procedures through bringing annulment actions before the Court of Justice, but must rely on national governments to do so.[137] These criticisms are, however, formalistic. It is politically inconceivable that the Commission or national governments could ignore opposition from one-third or one-quarter of national parliaments. Apart from anything else, it is doubtful whether a QMV majority will be available in many circumstances where that number do oppose.

A bigger challenge is the threshold of opposition required: that of one-third or one-quarter of national parliamentary chambers. Typically, EU legislation will not violate some bright red line drawn by all national parliaments, but will threaten some tradition, which is cherished in a particular Member State. This is regardless of whether they are measures prohibiting the use of snuff in Sweden, or imperial weights and measures in the United Kingdom, or measures allowing cheese to be marketed as feta not from Greece or beer to be marketed in Germany despite not being in accordance with German purity laws. A feature of these is that they are idiosyncratic. Their value is deeply felt in the state in question, but much less so elsewhere. It will be difficult, in such circumstances, for the national parliament of that state to persuade the parliaments in other states that there has been a breach of subsidiarity.

---

[136] For criticism, see House of Lords European Union Committee, *Strengthening National Parliamentary Scrutiny of the EU* (Session 2004–05, 14th Report, London, SO) paras. 183–203.

[137] Protocol on the application of the principles of subsidiarity and proportionality, Article 8. S. Weatherill, 'Better Competence Monitoring' (2005) 30 *EL Rev.* 23, 40.

In spite of this, the Member States decided a further procedure was necessary after the failure of the ratification of the Constitutional Treaty. The 'orange card' procedure was therefore introduced by the Lisbon Treaty.

Protocol on the application of the principles of subsidiarity and proportionality, Article 7(3)

Furthermore, under the ordinary legislative procedure, where reasoned opinions on the non-compliance of a proposal for a legislative act with the principle of subsidiarity represent at least a simple majority of the votes allocated to the national Parliaments…, the proposal must be reviewed. After such review, the Commission may decide to maintain, amend or withdraw the proposal.

If it chooses to maintain the proposal, the Commission will have, in a reasoned opinion, to justify why it considers that the proposal complies with the principle of subsidiarity. This reasoned opinion, as well as the reasoned opinions of the national Parliaments, will have to be submitted to the Union's legislator, for consideration in the procedure:

(a) before concluding the first reading, the legislator (the European Parliament and the Council) shall consider whether the legislative proposal is compatible with the principle of subsidiarity, taking particular account of the reasons expressed and shared by the majority of national Parliaments as well as the reasoned opinion of the Commission;

(b) if, by a majority of 55% of the members of the Council or a majority of the votes cast in the European Parliament, the legislator is of the opinion that the proposal is not compatible with the principle of subsidiarity, the legislative proposal shall not be given further consideration.

This new procedure seems unnecessary. It is almost inconceivable that the Commission would take forward a proposal where over half the national parliaments opposed it. As national governments are accountable to national parliaments, it is almost as unimaginable that such a proposal would receive a QMV majority in the Council. On its own terms, the procedure is somewhat bizarre. It only applies to the ordinary legislative procedure. Yet, if there is a problem with Commission discretion, surely it would generally affect the institution's role in all legislative procedures. The other odd feature is that a positive majority is needed to vote a measure incompatible with the subsidiarity principle. This is a high threshold as it means that a measure could be adopted, despite the fact that a majority of national parliaments and half the members of the Council (including all the large Member States) thought EU legislation should not be developed on the matter in question.

The Protocol looks as if it also might be the making of the Conference of Community and European Affairs Committees of Parliaments of the European Union (COSAC). Established in 1989, COSAC is a forum in which national parliaments and the European Parliament meet biannually to discuss the business of the forthcoming Council Presidency and to exchange information and best practice.[138] Since 2007, COSAC has become a more proactive and salient forum for securing the subsidiarity principle. It coordinates checks by national parliaments

---

[138] Its position is formalised in the Protocol on the role of national parliaments in the European Union, Article 10. See also Article 12(f) TEU.

where Commission proposals appear to touch particularly on national sensitivities. In 2008, three exercises were conducted on Commission proposals for legislation on terrorism; organ transplants; and amending the Framework Directive prohibiting discrimination. This led to forty-five opinions by national parliaments on the two proposals.[139] COSAC has also set itself up as a forum for national parliamentary concerns. All commit themselves to an early exchange of information through communicating any particular subsidiarity concerns to each other through COSAC.[140]

(ii) Participatory democracy and republicanism

The challenges of representative democracy for the European Union lie in its not being a single political community which can lay claim to the primary political allegiances of its members in the same way as the nation-state. It is also a community of states and this leads to many of the features that obstruct the Union's claims to representative democracy: notably the weakness of the European Parliament's credentials and the heavy presence of national administrations in EU law-making.

Those relying exclusively on this to indict the Union have to explain, however, what arrangements should then exist for dealing with transnational issues. These issues can arise in at least three ways. First, they can arise because one state imposes externalities on another, such as pollution crossing from the territory of one into the other's environment. Secondly, they can arise because we can wish to create new collective goods, such as international trade, communications or transport links, which are perceived as enriching all parties' lives. Finally, they can arise because we feel responsibilities not just to those in our national territory but to others outside: that it is unacceptable to stand by and watch the suffering of others.

Traditional arrangements have either relied on one or a few states imposing their model on others to realise these goals (the colonial or neocolonial model) or on international treaties concluded between national administrations (the Westphalian model). The former excludes every state not involved in the development of the model and does not even consider what democratic controls exist within the state enacting the model. The latter is government by bureaucratic fiat, as these treaties are invariably developed by cartels of national civil servants with possibly the odd facilitation by an international civil servant. Indeed, it is positively perverse for those who criticise the European Union because it is executive-oriented or does not sufficiently involve national parliaments to hark back nostalgically to this intergovernmental model. It leads to an even higher executive dominance and even greater parliamentary exclusion.

In the absence of a less imperfect alternative, concerns about insufficient representative democracy in the European Union point to two things. First, they suggest scepticism about what it should do. If it is harder to 'democratise' transnational decision-making than national decision-making, this points to our considering carefully when to deploy the former. Secondly, they point to the Union having to look more acutely to other sources of democratic legitimation to justify its law-making powers. These are set out in Articles 10 and 11 TEU.

---

[139] European Commission, *Annual Report*, above n. 135, 5–6.
[140] COSAC, *Tenth Biannual Report: Developments in European Union Procedures and Practices relevant to Parliamentary Scrutiny* (Paris, COSAC, 2008) 17–18.

> **Article 10(3) TEU**
>
> Every citizen shall have the right to participate in the democratic life of the Union. Decisions shall be taken as openly and as closely as possible to the citizen.

> **Article 11 TEU**
>
> 1. The institutions shall, by appropriate means, give citizens and representative associations the opportunity to make known and publicly exchange their views in all areas of Union action.
> 2. The institutions shall maintain an open, transparent and regular dialogue with representative associations and civil society.

Three particular features of the Union enable a quality of engagement to take place in which political institutions of the Union engage with each other and with the Union's citizenry in a culture of mutual respect.

First, the Union institutionalises a principle of 'constitutional tolerance'.[141] It leads nationals of Member States to accept and acknowledge a shared destiny with strangers and the values of strangers without trying to change them. A British citizen is required to recognise that the French citizen has rights and interests that she must not impinge upon and that she brings something different, but equally valuable, to the Union political community of which the British citizen is part. This is, as Müller has observed, a potentially very deep-seated form of tolerance, for it is born out of the idea that a state must be a liberal democracy and have a particular memory of the destructiveness of conflict to be a member of the European Union. This embeds a culture where only certain claims which accept the presumptive validity of difference are politically acceptable.[142]

Secondly, the Union is built around the creation of common institutions to realise shared projects (e.g. the single market, the area of freedom, security and justice, a common environmental policy). These institutions have an elevating effect, as they require citizens to come together to realise common goods; to act and negotiate in the public interest recognising each other's needs and arguments rather than acting in a self-interested manner. They require citizens to act in a public rather than a private manner.[143]

Thirdly, the institutional settlements of the Union prevent concentrations of power and foster pluralism.[144] Power is not centred in any one set of institutions, but is spread across the supranational institutions and national governments. Each has its own constituencies and

---

[141] J. Weiler, *The Constitution of Europe* (Cambridge, Cambridge University Press, 1999) especially 332–48; M. Poiares Maduro, *We, the Court: The European Court of Justice and the European Economic Constitution* (Oxford, Hart, 1998) 166–74; J. Lacroix, 'For a European Constitutional Patriotism' (2002) 50 *Political Studies* 944.

[142] J.-W. Müller, 'A European Constitutional Patriotism? The Case Restated' (2008) 14 *ELJ* 542, 554.

[143] On the ethics of participation see R. Bellamy and R. Warleigh, 'From an Ethics of Integration to an Ethics of Participation' (1998) 27 *Millennium* 447; P. Magnette, 'European Governance and Civic Participation: Beyond Elitist Citizenship?' (2003) 51 *Political Studies* 1.

[144] N. McCormick, 'Democracy, Subsidiarity and Citizenship in the European Commonwealth' (1997) 16 *Law and Philosophy* 331; K. Nicolaidis, 'Conclusion: The Federal Vision Beyond the Federal State' in K. Nicolaidis and R. Howse (eds.), *The Federal Vision: Legitimacy and Levels of Governance in the United States and the European Union* (Oxford, Oxford University Press, 2001).

each represents different interests. This allows a voice to be given to a variety of identities and interests. The most careful analysis of Union practice is that of Héritier.

A. Héritier, 'Elements of Democratic Legitimation in Europe: An Alternative Perspective' (1999) 6 *Journal of European Public Policy* 269, 274–6

2.2.1 Mutual horizontal control and 'distrust'

At each step of the European policy process, from the first tentative drafts to the formal decision-making process, policy-making is characterized by a distrustful and circumspect observation of the mutual policy proposals made by the involved actors. The participants controlling each other are generally experts and/or decision-makers from the different member states, responding to each other's policy proposals with counterproposals backed up by expertise. The mutual distrust signifies an enormous potential for control and a chance to hold actors accountable for individual policy moves which need to be defended in substantive terms. This is the virtuous side of the slowness, and indeed potential deadlock, inherent in the European decisional process. This phenomenon is so widespread, permeating virtually the entire fabric of the decision making process across issue areas, that individual policy examples are superfluous…

The dark side of mutual control and distrust is – considering that European decision-making does not usually rely on the majority principle – of course stalemate, where a decisional process is stalled because the participants are exclusively engaged in controlling and fending-off policy initiatives presented by other actors involved. 'Distrust leads to forgone opportunities' unless it is overcome by constructive bargaining.

2.2.2 Bargaining democracy

Fortunately, bargaining constitutes the complementary side of mutual horizontal control and distrust. It is present in all aspects of European policy-making, given the presence of actors with diverse interests and a concrete need for consensual decision-making. Consensus is achieved through negotiating in the course of which compromises are formulated, compensation payments made, and package deals struck.

Actors negotiating may be representatives from territorial units or delegates from functional organizations, such as associations. Thus, in negotiating sectoral questions, such as in regional and social policy under the 'partnership principle', delegates from functional organizations are predominantly involved. During the input phase bargaining mostly takes place at the supranational level. If legislative details need to be specified during the output phase they occur at the national/subnational level as well. Bargaining democracy creates input-legitimation since it prevents individual interests from being outvoted and thereby forces actors to take multiple interests into account. This is reflected in the more equitable outcomes of bargaining processes. By virtue of precisely this fact it also constitutes a source of output-legitimation. The underlying process mechanism is consensus-building with the help of compromises, compensation payments, and package deals.

2.2.3 Pluralistic authorities in a 'composite polity'

The multiple political and jurisdictional authorities which exist in the European Union at the vertical and horizontal level have generated more opportunities for individual citizens and corporate actors to address an authority and voice their concern in the case of a specific policy issue. In practice, this means the opportunity to exit from a specific avenue of decision-making which has proved less than promising and to test prospects in another arena. Thus, a citizen or corporate actor may address his or her representative in parliament at the national or European level, the national or the European Ombudsman, and the national courts or the European Court of Justice. These increased opportunities at the European Union level – as compared with their nation state counterparts – create leverage to press for political action.

This model is a republic model of democracy. It is an ideal and, as with any ideal that looks for its realisation in institutional practice, institutional elements identified as having positive traits also carry a negative underbelly. Arguments can be made, therefore, countering each of these claims about EU law-making.

We turn, first, to the question of constitutional tolerance. The Union may require nationals to recognise the rights and identities of foreigners, but one has to consider the extent and nature of this duty as it only applies to foreigners 'like us'. Recognition of Europeans has undoubtedly reinforced non-recognition of 'non-Europeans', who are excluded from the powerful EU law-making regimes and not granted the same legal entitlements as EU citizens. More generally, the Union can be characterised as a cartel of elites, who act together to disenfranchise others' subjects within their respective territories.[145] This view is simplistic, but studies show that about 70 to 75 per cent of accredited interest groups are business-oriented.[146]

Similarly, it is argued that the European Union induces parties to act in a public-spirited manner to realise public projects. However, there is something speculative in this statement. The art of lobbying is a black art and Brussels is full of lobbyists acting exclusively to realise their clients' interests. It is difficult to see what public spirit is being realised here. More substantively, as Héritier points out later in the article quoted above, models concerned with day-to-day checks and balances are not well designed for setting out strategic visions and common goals, as they fragment decision-making and lead to multiple veto points.[147]

Finally, the argument that the European Union diffuses power and encourages pluralism can be turned on its head. De Areilza has noted that institutional differentiation only diffuses power where different constituencies are confined to specific institutional settings. Otherwise, it benefits two kinds of powerful interest. One is that which can arbitrate between different institutional settings: lobbying MEPs, lunching with a Commissioner, visiting the office of national governments or litigating before national courts. The transnational nature of the Union means that these are likely to be actors that are well-resourced, well-connected and transnational in scope. The other is locally vested interests, which can act as veto-players: blocking something in the Council that will undoubtedly be for the greater good, but does not favour their narrow interests. It can thus act to concentrate power and, in many circumstances, make the process more opaque.[148]

The concern with the closed nature of decision-making led to the Lisbon Treaty establishing one innovatory mechanism of participatory democracy, that of the citizens' initiative.

Article 11(4) TEU

Not less than one million citizens who are nationals of a significant number of Member States may take the initiative of inviting the European Commission, within the framework of its powers, to submit any appropriate proposal on matters where citizens consider that a legal act of the Union is required for the purpose of implementing the Treaties.

[145] This is the essence of the consociational model. P. Taylor, *International Organization in the Modern World: The Regional and the Global Process* (London, Pinter, 1993) ch. 1.

[146] D. Coen, 'Empirical and Theoretical Studies in EU Lobbying' (2007) 24 *JEPP* 333, 335.

[147] A Héritier, 'Elements of Democratic Legitimation in Europe: An Alternative Perspective' (1999) 6 *JEPP* 269, 277–8.

[148] J. de Areilza, *Enhanced Cooperation in the Treaty of Amsterdam: Some Critical Remarks*, Jean Monnet Working Paper 13/98, http://centers.law.nyu.edu/jeanmonnet/papers/index.html (accessed 5 November 2009).

The ethos of the citizens' initiative is to instil, albeit in a limited way, some direct democracy into the Union.[149] An advantage of initiatives is that they enable citizens to make the political system responsive to individual issues of particular interest to them. This remedies a feature of representative democracy, which requires citizens to vote for candidates who stand on a platform of issues, some of which the citizen may disagree with even if she still prefers the candidate.

weaken

The concerns about citizens' initiatives are that they can enfeeble other parts of the political settlement, which allow more space for reflection and checks and balances. This has been countered to some extent by the Commission's not being required to follow a citizens' initiative. The other concern is that they can be manipulated by special interests or are used particularly by politically engaged elites. As such, they become a vehicle for dominating the Commission's attention and agenda. However, at the moment all this is speculation. All will depend on the details of the conditions which will be set out in EU legislation[150] and how EU citizens respond to it.

FURTHER READING

C. Bergström, *Comitology: Delegation of Powers in the European Union System* (Oxford, Oxford University Press, 2005)

C. Burns, 'Codecision and the European Commission: A Study of Declining Influence?' (2004) 11 *Journal of European Public Policy* 1

R. Dehousse, 'Comitology? Who Watches the Watchmen' (2003) 10 *Journal of European Public Policy* 798

H. Farrell and A. Héritier, 'Formal and Informal Institutions under Codecision: Continuous Constitution Building in Europe' (2003) 16 *Governance* 577

H. Hoffmann, 'Legislation, Delegation and Implementation under the Treaty of Lisbon: Typology Meets Reality' (2009) 15 *European Law Journal* 482

C. Joerges and E. Vos (eds.), *EU Committees: Social Regulation, Law and Politics* (Oxford and Portland, Hart, 1999)

R. Kardasheva, 'The Power to Delay: The European Parliament's Influence in the Consultation Procedure' (2009) 47 *Journal of Common Market Studies* 385

B. Kohler Koch and B. Rittberger (eds.), *Debating the Democratic Legitimacy of the European Union* (Lanham, Rowman & Littlefield, 2007)

A. Maurer and W. Wessels (eds.), *National Parliaments on their Ways to Europe: Losers or Latecomers?* (Baden Baden, Nomos, 2001)

J-W. Müller, 'A European Constitutional Patriotism? The Case Restated' (2008) 14 *European Law Journal* 542

L. Senden, *Soft Law in European Community Law* (Oxford and Portland, Hart, 2004)

---

[149] The duties on the Commission to consult on legislative and non-legislative measures are addressed in the chapter on governance. See pp. 373–9.
[150] Article 24 TFEU.

ANNEX

Treaty on the Functioning of the European Union

Legal bases covered by the ordinary legislative procedure

Article 14: services of general economic interest

Article 15(3): limitations on citizens' right of access to documents

Article 16: rules relating to data protection

Article 18: rules to prohibit discrimination on grounds of nationality

Article 19(2): incentive measures to support action taken by the Member States to combat discrimination

Article 21(2): measures to facilitate the right of citizens to move and reside freely within the Union

Article 24: citizens' initiative

Article 33: customs cooperation

Article 43(2): common organisation of agricultural markets

Article 46: freedom of movement for workers

Article 48: measures relating to social security for Community migrant workers

Article 50(1): freedom of establishment

Article 51(2): excluding application of Chapter 2, Title IV (Right of establishment) provisions to certain activities

Article 52(2): coordinating provisions providing for special treatment of foreign nationals on grounds of public policy, public security or public health

Article 53(1): mutual recognition of diplomas, certificates, other formal qualifications, etc, and self-employment and coordination of these provisions between Member States

Article 56(2): extending provisions of Chapter 3, Title IV (Services) to third country nationals

Article 59(1): liberalisation of specific services

Article 64(2): measures on the free movement of capital

Article 75: framework for administrative measures relating to movement of capital (e.g. freezing of funds) in order to combat terrorism and related activities

Article 77(2): common visa policy; management of external borders and the free movement of third country nationals

Article 78(2): common policy for asylum, subsidiary protection and temporary protection of third country nationals

Article 79(1), (2)(b), (c), (d), (3), (4), (5): measures relating to the common immigration policy; the definition of the rights of third country nationals; removal and repatriation; combating trafficking in persons; readmission agreements

Article 79(2)(a): entry and residence, long-term visas; residence permits; family reunion

Article 81: judicial cooperation in civil matters with cross-border implications; mutual recognition and enforcement of judgments, rules of evidence, access to justice, etc.

Article 82: judicial cooperation in criminal matters having cross-border dimension with provisions for minimum rules for rights of accused, victims and admissibility of evidence

Article 83(1): minimum rules for definition of certain serious crimes

Article 83(2): minimum rules regarding definition of criminal offences in areas concerned

Article 84: prevention of crime

Article 85: structure, operation, field of action and tasks of Eurojust

Article 87(2)(a)–(c): collection, etc. of information; training of staff; common investigative techniques for police cooperation

Article 88: structure, operation, field of action and tasks of Europol

Article 91: rules relating to transport policy

Article 100: provisions relating to sea and air transport

Article 114: approximation of national provisions which have as their object the establishment and functioning of the internal market

Article 116: elimination of distorting conditions of competition in the internal market resulting from national provisions

Article 118: laws for uniform intellectual property rights

Article 121: rules for monitoring the economic policies of Member States

Article 129: amending certain provisions of the Statute of the European System of Central Banks and of the European Central Bank

Article 133: measures for the use of the euro as the single currency

Article 149: incentive measures for cooperation between Member States in the field of employment

Article 153(1)(a) (e), (h), (2): support for Member State activities in relation to workers' rights; minimum standards and cooperation for the achievement of these rights

Article 157(3): equality of men and women in the workplace

Article 164: regulations for the European Social Fund

Article 165: development of quality education and sport

Article 166: content and organisation of vocational training

Article 167: contribution to development of Member State cultures and respect for national and regional diversity

Article 168: public health, including enablement of monitoring, detecting and combating cross-border threats to health

Article 169: measures to ensure consumer protection in respect of health, safety and economic interests

Article 172: trans-European networks for transport, telecommunications and energy

Article 173: ensuring the competitiveness of industry

Article 175: necessary specific actions outside structural funds

Article 177: tasks, priority objectives and organisation of structural funds

Article 178: implementing regulations relating to the European Regional Development Fund

Article 182(1), (5): multi-annual framework programme setting out all the activities of the Union and the scientific and technological objectives of the Union; establishing the measures necessary for the implementation of the European research area

Article 188: adoption of supplementary programmes

Article 189: European space policy for promotion of scientific and technical progress, industrial competitiveness and the implementation of the Union's policies

Article 192: common environmental policy, including the setting up of general action programmes

Article 194: preservation and improvement of the Union's energy policy

Article 195: promoting the competitiveness of the Union in the tourism sector

Article 196: civil protection in the event of disasters

Article 197(2): improving administrative cooperation

Article 207(2): framework for implementing the common commercial policy

Article 209: measures for the implementation of the development cooperation policy

Article 212: financial, technical and economic cooperation, including financial assistance, to third countries excluding developing countries

Article 214: framework for humanitarian aid

Article 224: regulations for political parties at European level (including rules for their funding)

Article 257: establishment of specialised courts to hear and determine specific area disputes at first instance

Article 281: amending the Statute of the European Court of Justice at the request of the Court and after consultation with the Commission, or after a proposal with the Commission and in consultation with the Court

Article 291: rules and general principles concerning mechanisms for control by Member States of the Commission's exercise of implementing powers

Article 298: provisions for European public service

Article 322(1): financial rules determining the budget procedure and checks and balances of financial actors

Article 325: combating fraud

Article 336: staff regulations of EU officials

Article 338: measures for the production of statistics

Legal bases covered by the consultation procedure

Article 21(2): measures concerning social security or social protection in relation to the right of citizens to move and reside freely

Article 22: citizens' right to vote in municipal and European Parliament elections

Article 23: protection of EU citizens in third countries

Article 62: adoption of measures which constitute a step backwards in EU law for liberalisation of capital to and from third countries

Article 72: administrative cooperation

Article 77(3): adoption of provisions concerning passports, identity cards, residence permits, etc. for common immigration policy

Article 81(3): measures concerning family law with cross-border implications

Article 87(3): measures concerning operational cooperation between the police and other criminal law enforcement authorities

Article 89: conditions for relevant criminal law enforcement authorities of one Member State to operate in other Member States

Article 95: prohibition of discrimination in relation to transport services

Article 103: anti-competitive measures

Article 109: appropriate regulations for state aid

Article 113: harmonisation of legislation relating to indirect taxation to the extent necessary for the internal market and for avoiding distortion of competition

Article 115: approximation of laws relating to the internal market when Article 114 not deployed

Article 118: language arrangements in relation to intellectual property rights

Article 126(14): replacement of and detailed rules for application of the Protocol on the excessive deficit procedure

Article 127: conferring specific tasks upon the European Central Bank concerning policies relating to the prudential supervision of credit institutions

Article 128: harmonising the denominations and technical specifications of all coins intended for circulation

Article 129(4): adopting certain provisions of the Statute of the European System of Central Banks and of the European Central Bank

Article 140(2): reporting on Member State derogation and finding conditions for abrogation

Article 148: guidelines for employment policies

Article 150: establishment of advisory Employment Committee to coordinate employment and labour policies

Article 153(1)(c), (d), (f), (g): social security of workers; collective defence of workers; protection post contract termination

Article 160: establishing the Social Protection Committee to coordinate social protection strategies

Article 182: adoption of special multi-annual framework activity programmes

Article 188: establishment of joint undertakings or any other structure necessary for the efficient execution of EU research, technological development and demonstration programmes

Article 192(2): environmental measures relating to fiscal provisions; town and country planning, land use, quantitative management of water resources; choice between energy sources

Article 194: energy provisions of a primarily fiscal nature

Article 203: detailed rules for association of countries and territories within the Union in certain circumstances

Article 218: certain agreements between the Union and third countries and international organisations

Article 219: formal agreements for the euro in relation to currencies of third states

Article 246: appointment of Commission member if vacancy caused by resignation, compulsory retirement or death

Article 262: conferring jurisdiction on the Court of Justice in disputes relating to creation of European intellectual property rights

Article 286: adoption of list of Court of Auditors

Article 308: amendment of the Statute of the European Investment Bank

Article 311: adopting a Directive relating to the system of own resources of the Union

Article 322(2): determining methods whereby the budget revenue provided relating to the Union's own resources are to be made available to the Commission; determining measures to meet cash requirements

Article 332: decision of which bodies, if not the Member States, should bear the expenditure resulting from implementation of enhanced cooperation

Article 349: adoption of specific measures relating to listed insular regions (e.g. Canary Islands) of the Union

Legal bases covered by the assent procedure

Article 19(1): combating discrimination

Article 25: measures to strengthen citizens' rights

Article 82(2)(d): adoption of decisions on miscellaneous aspects of criminal procedure

Article 83(1): identification of other particularly serious crime

Article 86: establishment of the European Public Prosecutor from Eurojust and extending his powers

Article 218(6): association agreements; agreement on accession to European Convention of Human Rights; agreements with important budgetary implications and those governed by legislative procedures where Parliament consent needed

Article 223: election procedures for the European Parliament

Article 226: exercise of right of enquiry for suspected maladministration by EU institutions

Article 311: implementation of the Union resource system

Article 312: laying down a multi-annual financial framework

Article 329: granting authorisation to proceed with enhanced cooperation

Article 352: flexibility provision

4

The EU Judicial Order

CONTENTS

1 INTRODUCTION

This chapter considers the judicial order within the European Union, comprising the Court of Justice and national courts and tribunals, and the institutional relations of this judicial order.

Section 2 considers the Court of Justice of the European Union. The institution comprises three courts: the Court of Justice, the General Court and the European Union Civil Service Tribunal.

A feature of EU law is that there is a joint responsibility between national courts and the Union courts for the interpretation and maintenance of EU law. Section 3 considers the central institutional features of this judicial order, which is governed by Articles 267 and 274 TFEU. The Court of Justice has an exclusive responsibility to declare EU measures invalid and to provide authoritative interpretations of EU law across the Union, whilst national courts have a monopoly over the adjudication of disputes. A further feature of this order is that its only subjects are courts. Institutional relations between them are not governed by a system of appeal by individuals but a reference from a national court to the Court of Justice on a point of EU law. The Court of Justice has sought to expand the subjects of this judicial order by allowing many bodies to refer, which would be considered regulatory or administrative bodies rather than courts under national law. It also allows any body to make a reference irrespective of national precedents or hierarchies. This has created a judicial order, the relationship of which to the administration is often far from clear and which is marked by a lack of hierarchy or specialisation.

Section 4 looks at the roles played by the preliminary reference procedure, the central institutional link between courts in the Union, in securing the EU legal order and judicial order. It argues that the preliminary reference procedure is pivotal, first, to the development of EU law through national courts, which set out the emerging questions to be addressed by the Court of Justice. Secondly, it is the central form of judicial review of EU institutions through individuals challenging implementation of an EU measure before a national court, which then questions the legality of the EU measure in a reference. Thirdly, it is central to preserving the autonomy and unity of EU law. Finally, it facilitates national courts in resolving disputes that involve EU law.

Section 5 looks at how relations between the courts are managed to secure these roles. This has been done, first, through the Court holding that its judgments bind all authorities in the Union, not just the referring court. Secondly, relations between the parties are managed during the reference period through the grant of interim measures by national courts. Whilst this will be used to suspend national law wherever the effectiveness of EU law requires it, the test for suspending EU measures or national measures implementing them is more restrictive: it is only if the application is urgent and the applicant would suffer irreparable damage. Suspension must be weighed against the broader Union interest in keeping the measure in place.

Section 6 looks at how the workload of the Court of Justice has been regulated. Far more cases are referred than the Court can decide each year. The strategy for managing for this is threefold. First, national courts are prevented from referring judgments in only very limited circumstances. Secondly, the central route for managing workload is the use of Chambers by the Court of Justice so that over three-quarters of cases are decided by Chambers of three or five judges. Finally, certain cases are prioritised by the use of two procedures, the accelerated and urgent procedures. Management of relations between national courts and the Court of Justice has been only partially successful.

2 THE COURT OF JUSTICE OF THE EUROPEAN UNION

The Treaties provide for the Union to have its own Court of Justice of the European Union to ensure that the law is observed in the interpretation and application of the Treaties. .

> **Article 19 TEU**
>
> 1. The Court of Justice of the European Union shall include the Court of Justice, the General Court and specialised courts. It shall ensure that in the interpretation and application of the Treaties the law is observed.
>
>   Member States shall provide remedies sufficient to ensure effective legal protection in the fields covered by Union law.
>
> 2. The Court of Justice shall consist of one judge from each Member State. It shall be assisted by Advocates-General.
>
>   The General Court shall include at least one judge per Member State.
>
>   The Judges and the Advocates-General of the Court of Justice and the Judges of the General Court shall be chosen from persons whose independence is beyond doubt and who satisfy the conditions set out in Articles 253 and 254 TFEU. They shall be appointed by common accord of the governments of the Member States for six years. Retiring Judges and Advocates-General may be reappointed.
>
> 3. The Court of Justice of the European Union shall, in accordance with the Treaties:
>   (a) rule on actions brought by a Member State, an institution or a natural or legal person;
>   (b) give preliminary rulings, at the request of courts or tribunals of the Member States, on the interpretation of Union law or the validity of acts adopted by the institutions;
>   (c) rule in other cases provided for in the Treaties.

The Court of Justice is thus composed of three courts: the Court of Justice, the General Court and, currently, only one specialised court, the European Civil Service Tribunal.

(i) The Court of Justice

As Article 19(1) TEU makes clear, the Court of Justice is made up of twenty-seven judges, one from each Member State. These are appointed for a renewable period of six years and are required to be persons whose independence is beyond doubt and who are either suitable for the highest judicial office in their respective countries or 'jurisconsults of recognised competence'.[1] The judges elect the President from amongst themselves for a three-year term.[2] Her central responsibility is to determine the case list and allocate cases to different Chambers.[3] A new system of appointment was introduced by the Lisbon Treaty to prevent the over-politicisation of the process.[4] Previously, a panel comprising members of the Court of Justice and members of national supreme courts ruled on the suitability of candidates, and governments could only appoint candidates after consulting this Panel.[5]

---

[1] See also Article 253 TFEU. This is done on a three-yearly cycle, so that every three years half the Court is replaced.

[2] Article 253(3) TFEU. The current President is Greek, Judge Skouris.

[3] The President also chairs the Grand Chamber and is responsible for interim measures.

[4] On this debate see P. Kapteyn, 'Reflections on the Future of the Judicial System of the European Union after Nice' (2001)20 *YBEL* 173, 188–9.

[5] Article 255 TFEU. It is doubtful whether this is sufficient, however, to secure a Court that is representative of the diversity within the Union. I. Solanke, 'Diversity and Independence in the European Court of Justice' (2009) 15 *CJEL* 89.

Fears have been expressed that the ability to renew the term of office might compromise the independence of the judges. In 1993, the European Parliament proposed that judges should be elected by the Parliament for a non-renewable term of nine years, a suggestion endorsed by the Court of Justice.[6] In practice, this has not posed a problem, possibly because the Court works under the principle of collegiality, in which a single judgment is given. This prevents Member States pointing to sympathetic dissenting opinions of their national judge to undermine the authority of a judgment, with judges of the Court also arguing that it allows for a considerable exchange of views and differing national legal traditions to filter through to the judgment.[7] This has been countered by some who argue that because the judgment is built on compromise, this affects the quality of its reasoning, with the Court often seeming not to counter a point or consider a question.[8]

The Court is assisted by eight Advocates General.[9] The same procedure and conditions of appointment apply to these as to judges of the Court of Justice. The role of the Advocate General is to make, in open court, impartial and independent submissions on any case brought before the Court.[10] She acts not as a legal representative of one of the parties, but as a legal representative of the public interest. These Opinions are adopted in advance of the judgment to allow the Court sufficient time to consider them. They often provide a more detailed analysis of the context and the argument than is found in the judgment of the Court itself. However, they are not binding on the Court, although they are often referred to by the Court of Justice in its judgments. Furthermore, even when the conclusions reached are similar, it is difficult to know whether the reasoning is the same, given that the Opinion is often discursive in nature, whilst the judgment itself is very terse.

For reasons of workload, cases are rarely decided by the full Court. Indeed, it is only to sit in full session in cases of 'exceptional importance' or where it is to rule that a senior EU official (e.g. Commissioner, Ombudsman, or Member of the Court of Auditors) is to be deprived of office for not meeting the requisite conditions. In 2008, no cases were assigned to the full Court. Instead, the majority of cases are heard by Chambers of either three or five judges, with 65 judgments/Opinions being given by Chambers of three judges, and 259 by Chambers of five judges. Alongside these, a Member State or EU institution party to the proceedings can request a case to be heard by a Grand Chamber of thirteen judges. This occurred in 66 cases in 2008.[11]

---

[6] Rothley Report, European Parliament Session Doc. A3–0228/93. The Court of Justice's views are in *Report of the European Court of Justice for the 1996 Intergovernmental Conference*, Proceedings of the Court 15/95, 11.

[7] See e.g. F. Jacobs, 'Advocates General and Judges in the European Court of Justice: Some Personal Reflections' in D. O'Keeffe and A. Bavasso (eds.), *Judicial Review in European Union Law, Liber Amicorum Lord Slynn*, vol. I (The Hague, Boston and London, Kluwer Law International, 2000).

[8] W. Bishop, 'Price Discrimination under Article 86: Political Economy in the European Court' (1981) 44 *MLR* 282, 294–5.

[9] Article 252 TFEU. On the Advocates General see T. Tridimas, 'The Role of the Advocate General in Community Law: Some Reflections' (1997) 34 *CMLRev.* 1349. Also the magisterial study of N. Burrows and R. Greaves, *The Advocate General and EC Law* (Oxford, Oxford University Press, 2007).

[10] Article 252 TFEU.

[11] The rules on the full Court and the Grand Chamber are set out in Article 251 TFEU and Protocol on the Statute of the Court of Justice, Article 16. This number is greater than the 333 judgments given by the Court in 2008 as it takes no account of joinder of cases. *Annual Report of the Court of Justice 2008* (Luxembourg, Office for Official Publications of the European Communities, 2009) 90.

Whilst Article 19(1) TEU suggests a general jurisdiction for the Court of Justice over both Treaties, this is subject to three forms of exclusion:

- It has no jurisdiction in the field of the Common Foreign and Security Policy.[12]
- In judicial cooperation in criminal matters and police cooperation, it has no jurisdiction to review the validity or proportionality of operations carried out by the police or other law-enforcement services of a Member State or the exercise of the responsibilities incumbent upon Member States with regard to the maintenance of law and order and the safeguarding of internal security.[13]
- If measures are taken to expel a Member State, the Court of Justice can rule on the procedure but not the substance of the grounds for expulsion.[14]

The Court's jurisdiction is further restricted by the rules on *locus standi* which determine the circumstances in which parties can bring actions before it. Matters can come before it in a variety of ways:

- preliminary references from national courts: national courts may, or in some cases must, refer the point of EU law to the Court of Justice which is necessary to enable them to decide the dispute. The Court of Justice will give judgment on the point of EU law, which the national judge will apply to the dispute in hand;[15]
- enforcement actions brought by the Commission or Member States against other Member States: the Commission, or in rare cases another Member State, can bring a Member State before the Court of Justice for a declaration that the latter is in breach of EU law;[16]
- sanctions for failure to comply with Court judgments:[17] if a Member State fails to comply with a Court of Justice judgment, the Commission can bring it back before the Court in order to have it fined for its behaviour;
- judicial review of EU institutions by other EU institutions and judicial review of the Parliament or Council by Member States;[18]
- Opinions on the conclusion of international agreements: the Council, Parliament, Commission or any Member State can ask for an Opinion of the Court as to whether the Union has lawfully concluded a draft treaty. If the Court rules that the international agreement is illegal, it can only enter into force if the treaty is first amended;[19]
- appeals from the General Court on points of law;[20]
- the Council may confer jurisdiction on the Court with regard to disputes concerning the application of European intellectual property rights.[21]

---

[12] Article 24(1) TEU, Article 275 TFEU. It can, however, rule on the limits relative to other parts of the Treaties: Article 40 TEU.

[13] Article 276 TFEU.

[14] Article 269 TFEU.

[15] Article 267 TFEU.

[16] Articles 258 and 259 TFEU.

[17] Article 260 TFEU.

[18] Article 263(2) and 265(1) TFEU; Protocol on the Statute of the Court of Justice, Article 51. There are limited exceptions for national actions against Council exercise of delegated powers, Council measures authorising state aids and Council measures defining the common commercial policy. These go to the General Court.

[19] Article 218(11) TFEU.

[20] Article 256(1) TFEU.

[21] Article 262 TFEU.

These procedures are discussed in far more detail in subsequent chapters. Combined, they make a substantial docket. In 2008, the Court of Justice disposed of 567 cases and gave 333 judgments.[22] Despite this considerable output, it struggles to cope with the number of cases that are submitted to it: 767 cases were still pending at the end of 2008.[23]

(ii) The General Court

The General Court (formerly known as the Court of First Instance) is composed of twenty-seven judges. Unlike the Court of Justice, it is not confined to a single judge from each Member State, but must comprise at least one judge from each Member State.[24] The General Court can sit in full Court if it considers the circumstances require or because of the importance of the case.[25] It almost always sits in Chambers of three or five judges. One of the judges will act as Advocate General. A single judge can give judgments in actions brought by private parties, but the circumstances in which this can occur are extremely restricted. The case must raise only questions already clarified by established case law and must not cover certain fields, notably state aids, competition, mergers, agriculture and trade with non-EU states.[26]

The General Court's jurisdiction has expanded over the years and it now has the power to receive the following cases:

- judicial review by individuals of actions or illegal action by EU institutions or action for non-contractual damages against the EU institutions;[27]
- actions by Member States against the Commission, the European Central Bank and the European Council;[28]
- matters referred to the Court of Justice under an arbitration clause;[29]
- appeals from decisions of the Office for Harmonisation in the Internal Market.[30] This agency is responsible for the grant of the Community trademark and anybody adversely affected by its decisions can appeal these to the General Court;
- appeals from decisions of the European Civil Service Tribunal.[31]

Jurisdiction over these matters results in the General Court being the central administrative court. It has thus become the key actor in the development of administrative principles of due process. As much competition law and external trade law develops through challenges by private parties adversely affected by EU measures, it is also the central judicial institution in these fields as well as in the field of the Community trade mark, where a similar process takes place with challenges to decisions by the Office for Harmonisation of the Internal Market.

---

[22] *Annual Report*, above n. 11, 87–8.
[23] *Ibid.* 94–5.
[24] Article 19(2) TEU.
[25] Rules of Procedure of the Court of First Instance, article 14(1). Available at http://curia.europa.eu/jcms/upload/docs/application/pdf/2008-09/txt7_2008-09-25_14-08-6_431.pdf (accessed 2 August 2009).
[26] *Ibid.* article 14(2).
[27] Articles 263(4), 265(3), 268 and 340(2) TFEU.
[28] Articles 263 and 265 TFEU. Protocol on the Statute of the Court of Justice, article 51. There is a limited exception for challenges against Commission authorisation of enhanced cooperation. These go to the Court of Justice.
[29] Article 272 TFEU.
[30] Regulation 40/94/EC on the Community trade mark [2004] OJ L70/1, article 63.
[31] Article 256(2) TFEU.

In 2008, actions against EU institutions accounted for 44.2 per cent of cases and trade mark cases 31.78 per cent.[32] The General Court is struggling even more than the Court of Justice to keep up with its docket. At the end of 2008, 1,178 cases were pending and the duration of proceedings was (depending on the type of action) between 20.4 and 38.6 months.[33] These delays are so serious that they have led to decisions being overturned on the grounds that they violated the applicant's fundamental right to have the case heard within a reasonable period of time.[34] Notwithstanding this, there is also provision for it to receive preliminary rulings in fields to be specified.[35] Although, as yet, no field has been transferred under this heading, the provision is important for what it promises. For it suggests that over the years, the jurisdiction and size of the General Court could be expanded.

There is a right to appeal from the General Court to the Court of Justice within two months of notification of the decision. The appeal must be on points of law,[36] but this right to appeal exists not just for parties to the dispute but also for Member States and EU institutions where the decision directly affects them.[37] Even if the Court of Justice finds that the General Court has misapplied EU law, it will only uphold an appeal if the mistake of law relates to the operative part of the judgment. Even if EU law is misapplied in the operative part of the judgment, the appeal will not be successful if the operative part is shown to be well-founded for other legal reasons.[38] In 2008, the Court of Justice considered seventy-seven appeals and found for the appellant, fully or partially, in twenty-three of these.[39] These statistics tell only part of the story as differences on significant and controversial areas of law have emerged between the two courts.[40]

If the Court of Justice finds the appeal to be well founded, it will quash the decision of the General Court. It then has the discretion to give the final judgment or to refer the matter back to the General Court. If it adopts the latter course of action, the General Court is bound by the Court of Justice's decision on the point of law.[41] The General Court takes the view that it is only bound by the judgments of the Court where its decision has been quashed by the Court of Justice and the matter is referred back, or where the principle of *res judicata* operates, that is to say, where a dispute involving the same parties, the same subject-matter and the same cause of action had already been decided by the Court of Justice.[42] Nevertheless, the circumstances in which the General Court will not follow judgments of the Court of Justice will be rare, as this would generate considerable instability.

---

[32] *Annual Report*, above n. 11, 173, 211.

[33] *Ibid.* 179.

[34] Case C-185/95 P *Baustahlgewerbe* v *Commission* [1998] ECR I-8417; Case C-385/07 P *Grüne Punkt DSD* v *Commission*, Judgment of 16 July 2009.

[35] Article 256(3) TFEU.

[36] Article 256(1) TFEU.

[37] Protocol on the Statute of the Court of Justice, article 56.

[38] Case C-30/91 P *Lestelle* v *Commission* [1992] ECR I-3755; Case C-226/03 P *José Martí Peix* v *Commission* [2004] ECR I-11421.

[39] *Annual Report*, above n. 11, 188, 211.

[40] There have been strong differences, for example, over the rules on *locus standi* of private parties to challenge EU acts, Case T-177/01 *Jégo-Quéré* v *Commission* [2002] ECR II-2365; Case C-263/02 P *Commission* v *Jégo-Quéré* [2004] ECR I-3425.

[41] Protocol on the Statute of the Court of Justice, article 61.

[42] Case T-162/94 *NMB France* v *Commission* [1996] ECR II-427.

(iii) The European Union Civil Service Tribunal

There is provision for work of the General Court to be transferred to specialised courts. The rules on the organisation for each court are likely to be different, as they will be governed by the legislation establishing it. In all cases, members must be independent and fit for judicial office. There must also be the possibility of appeal to the General Court.[43] To date, only one has been established, the European Union Civil Service Tribunal, which hears disputes between employees of the EU institutions and the institutions themselves.[44]

3 ARCHITECTURE OF THE EU JUDICIAL ORDER

It is wrong to see the judicial application of EU law as all about the activities of the three courts set out in Article 19 TEU. These are important but, as we have seen in Chapter 1 and will see in much more detail in Chapter 7,[45] EU law gives individuals the right to invoke EU law provisions before national courts in certain circumstances and imposes a whole host of duties on national courts when this happens. These are more numerous, have greater resources and are more accessible to individual litigants. There is, thus, a shared responsibility between them and the three Union courts for the application and development of EU law. This is a shared responsibility that has been made explicit by the Treaty of Lisbon with its introduction in Article 19(1) TEU of the requirement that Member States must provide remedies sufficient to ensure effective legal protection in the fields covered by EU law.

(i) Preliminary reference procedure and the EU judicial order

If EU law provides for its administration by a judicial order that comprises not just the three Union courts but all the courts and tribunals in the Member States, there are only two provisions that govern the nature of this judicial order and the duties it imposes on the different courts.

The first is Article 274 TFEU. This grants the Court of Justice exclusive jurisdiction where the Treaties provide for the Union to be a party to the proceedings.

Article 274 TFEU

Save where jurisdiction is conferred on the Court of Justice of the European Union by the Treaties, disputes to which the Union is a party shall not on that ground be excluded from the jurisdiction of the courts or tribunals of the Member States.

---

[43] Article 257 TFEU.

[44] Decision 2004/752/EC, EURATOM establishing the European Union Civil Service Tribunal [2004] OJ L333/7. It has similar problems to the other courts with, at the end of 2008, 217 cases pending and a mean waiting time of 19.7 months: *Annual Report*, above n. 11, 220–2.

[45] See pp. 268-71.

The European Union will be a party to the proceedings where one of the EU institutions is either plaintiff or defendant. It will be a defendant in cases where judicial review or damages are being sought against an act or omission of one of the institutions. The only circumstances where it will be a plaintiff are either where one EU institution is seeking judicial review against another institution(s) or the Commission is bringing enforcement actions or an action for damages against a Member State for non-compliance with EU law.

If Article 274 TFEU sets out the scenarios on which national courts cannot rule, Article 267 TFEU sets out their relationship with the Court of Justice in the contexts where they can adjudicate.

Article 267 TFEU

The Court of Justice of the European Union shall have jurisdiction to give preliminary rulings concerning:
(a) the interpretation of the Treaties;
(b) the validity and interpretation of acts of the institutions, bodies, offices or agencies of the Union.

Where such a question is raised before any court or tribunal of a Member State, that court or tribunal may, if it considers that a decision on the question is necessary to enable it to give judgment, request the Court to give a ruling thereon.

Where any such question is raised in a case pending before a court or tribunal of a Member State against whose decisions there is no judicial remedy under national law, that court or tribunal shall bring the matter before the Court.

If such a question is raised in a case pending before a court or tribunal of a Member State with regard to a person in custody, the Court of Justice of the European Union shall act with the minimum of delay.

Two initial features of the procedure are striking. First, subject to Article 274 TFEU, national courts have a monopoly of adjudication over disputes that come before them that involve EU law. Article 267 TFEU sets out circumstances when they may or must refer points of EU law to the Court of Justice and these judgments are binding on them. It is national courts, however, who decide the dispute. They decide not only points of national law that may be pertinent but, even more centrally, they decide the facts to the dispute and, on the basis of this, they decide how to apply EU law to the dispute.[46] In *WWF*, a challenge was made to the transformation of the military airport in Bolzano, Italy, into one for commercial use because there had been a failure to carry out an environmental impact assessment.[47] The airport authorities argued that the facts presented by the national court were inaccurate and that the national court, being confined to considering questions of law, had exceeded its jurisdiction by considering these questions of fact. The Court dismissed these arguments. It noted that it was for the national court, not itself, to ascertain the facts and that it was not its role to examine whether the reference had been made in accordance with national laws on court jurisdiction and procedure.

---

[46] Case 104/79 *Foglia* v *Novello* [1980] ECR 745.
[47] Case C-435/97 *WWF* v *Autonome Provinz Bozen* [1999] ECR I-5613.

The second feature is that Article 267 TFEU is a court to court procedure, with national courts acting as gate-keepers to the Court.[48] It grants private parties no direct access to the Court of Justice, nor can they appeal decisions of the national courts to the Court of Justice. The Court has thus characterised the procedure as:

> a non-contentious procedure excluding any initiative of the parties who are merely invited to be heard in the course of this procedure.[49]

There are circumstances when the parties can, on paper at least, oblige a national court to refer.[50] In addition, they may submit written observations and may make oral representations of between 15 and 30 minutes long, depending upon the nature of the proceedings, to the Court.[51] This limited role reflects, however, their not being the centre of proceedings. Instead, centre stage is taken by the reference from the national court. This will take the form of a question or number of questions about EU law. These must be accompanied by a statement setting out the factual and legal context of the dispute.

Information Note on References from National Courts for a Preliminary Ruling, OJ 2009, C 297/1

22. ...The order for reference must be succinct but sufficiently complete and must contain all the relevant information to give the Court and the interested persons entitled to submit observations a clear understanding of the factual and legal context of the main proceedings. In particular, the order for reference must:
   - include a brief account of the subject-matter of the dispute and the relevant findings of fact, or, at least, set out the factual situation on which the question referred is based;
   - set out the tenor of any applicable national provisions and identify, where necessary, the relevant national case-law, giving in each case precise references (for example, a page of an official journal or specific law report, with any internet reference);
   - identify the European Union law provisions relevant to the case as accurately as possible;
   - explain the reasons which prompted the national court to raise the question of the interpretation or validity of the European Union law provisions, and the relationship between those provisions and the national provisions applicable to the main proceedings;
   - include, if need be, a summary of the main relevant arguments of the parties to the main proceedings.

This statement frames the dispute. The Court of Justice cannot look behind it and will, indeed, sometimes look to it, rather than the explicit questions set out by the national court, in providing the judgment it gives.[52]

---

[48] Private parties not allowed to appear before the national court will not, therefore, be allowed to intervene before the Court of Justice: Case C-181/95 *Biogen* v *SmithKlineBeecham* [1996] ECR I-717.
[49] Case C-364/92 *SAT Fluggesellschaft* v *Eurocontrol* [1994] ECR I-43.
[50] See pp. 174–8.
[51] Protocol on the Statute of the Court of Justice, articles 20, 23.
[52] Case C-365/02 *Lindfors* [2004] ECR I-7183. T. Tridimas, 'Knocking on Heaven's Door: Fragmentation, Efficiency and Defiance in the Preliminary Reference Procedure' (2003) 40 *CMLRev.* 9, 21–6.

The wording of Article 267 TFEU is thin. It sets out a procedure but tells us little more about the mutual relations and duties surrounding this procedure. It has been left to the Court of Justice to craft its own vision of an EU judicial order and set out this provision as the spine of that judicial order. It has done this through a three stage argument. First, it sets out that the European Union is an autonomous legal order. Secondly, an autonomous legal order requires that all courts in the Union interpret EU law in a uniform manner. Thirdly, to enable this, Article 267 TFEU provides a direct relationship between national courts and the Court of Justice. It is to be interpreted and developed in the light of the needs of the Union legal order and its need for a coordinated judicial order in which EU law is given the same effect across the Union.

This reasoning emerged in *Rheinmühlen*, in which the question arose whether national courts were prevented from being able to refer by rulings from superior courts, which would normally bind them. Rheinmühlen received a subsidy to export barley outside the Union. When he failed to do this, the German authorities sought to recover the subsidy. The Hesse Finance Court considered that the authorities were entitled to recover the full subsidy, but, on appeal, the Federal Finance Court ruled that the authorities were entitled only to recover part of the subsidy. The matter was referred back to the Hesse court, which considered that the Federal court's ruling was inconsistent with the EU Regulation on the matter. It referred the question as to whether it still had a discretion to refer, unfettered by the ruling of the superior domestic court.

Case 166/73 *Rheinmühlen-Düsseldorf* v *Einfuhr- und Vorratstelle für Getreide* [1974] ECR 33

2. [Article 267 TFEU] is essential for the preservation of the Community character of the law established by the Treaty and has the object of ensuring that in all circumstances this law is the same in all States of the Community.

   Whilst it thus aims to avoid divergences in the interpretation of Community law which the national courts have to apply, it likewise tends to ensure this application by making available to the national judge a means of eliminating difficulties which may be occasioned by the requirement of giving Community law its full effect within the framework of the judicial systems of the Member States.

   Consequently any gap in the system so organized could undermine the effectiveness of the provisions of the Treaty and of the secondary Community law.

   The provisions of [Article 267 TFEU], which enable every national court or tribunal without distinction to refer a case to the court for a preliminary ruling when it considers that a decision on the question is necessary to enable it to give judgment, must be seen in this light.

3. The provisions of [Article 267 TFEU] are absolutely binding on the national judge and, in so far as the second paragraph is concerned, enable him to refer a case to the Court of Justice for a preliminary ruling on interpretation or validity.

   This Article gives national courts the power and, where appropriate, imposes on them the obligation to refer a case for a preliminary ruling, as soon as the judge perceives either of his own motion or at the request of the parties that the litigation depends on a point referred to in the first paragraph of [Article 267 TFEU].

4. It follows that national courts have the widest discretion in referring matters to the Court of Justice if they consider that a case pending before them raises questions involving interpretation, or consideration of the validity, of provisions of Community law, necessitating a decision on their part.

It follows from these factors that a rule of national law whereby a court is bound on points of law by the rulings of a superior court cannot deprive the inferior courts of their power to refer to the Court questions of interpretation of Community law involving such rulings.

It would be otherwise if the questions put by the inferior court were substantially the same as questions already put by the superior court.

On the other hand the inferior court must be free, if it considers that the ruling on law made by the superior court could lead it to give a judgment contrary to Community law, to refer to the Court questions which concern it.

If inferior courts were bound without being able to refer matters to the Court, the jurisdiction of the latter to give preliminary rulings and the application of Community law at all levels of the judicial systems of the Member States would be compromised.

The only circumstance in which the Court of Justice will have regard to national hierarchies is where the judgment of the lower court making the reference has been overturned on appeal by a more senior national court.[53] However, this appeal must relate to a point of national law that does not relate to the reference. For the Court of Justice has held that if the decision to refer has been appealed, the lower court is not bound by that appeal. The autonomous nature of Article 267 TFEU means that it has only to draw inferences from that appeal if it wishes, and it is free to maintain or withdraw the reference in such circumstances, irrespective of the wishes of the higher court.[54]

(ii) Subjects of the EU judicial order

Within the framework of Article 267 TFEU, it is crucial to be a court or tribunal. These and the Court of Justice are the only bodies recognised by the provision. National courts and tribunals become both opportunity structures for those seeking access to the Court of Justice and independent actors in their own right with new powers to ask questions of the Court of Justice and influence the contours of EU law across the Union. This begs the question, however, of what is to be considered a court or tribunal for these purposes. Throughout the Union, a variety of professional, regulatory and arbitral bodies, which are not formally designated as courts under national law, adjudicate upon EU law. It would be problematic, in terms of the uniformity of EU law, if some were entitled to refer, but not others.

In *Broeckmeulen*, therefore, the Court of Justice ruled that the uniformity of EU law required that a Union definition be provided for what constituted a court or tribunal for the purposes of Article 267 TFEU.[55] This should be a broad definition, which should include many bodies that were not formally courts within the national legal system. Thus, the Court held that an appeal committee within the Dutch professional body, regulating entry of doctors to the profession, constituted a court because it determined individual rights under EU law, acted under governmental legal supervision and employed quasi-legal procedures. Over the years, the Court has refined the

---

[53] Case 65/81 *Reina* v *Landeskreditbank Baden-Württemburg* [1982] ECR 33; Case C-309/02 *Radlberger Getränkegesellschaft* v *Land Baden-Württemberg* [2004] ECR I-11763.

[54] Case C-210/06 *Cartesio*, Judgment of 16 December 2008.

[55] Case 246/80 *Broeckmeulen* v *Huisarts Registratie Commissie* [1981] ECR 2311.

qualities necessary for a body to be a court. Bodies must be independent, be established by law and have a compulsory jurisdiction, and be taking a decision of a judicial nature.[56]

The criterion of independence has been held to have an external and internal dimension.[57] Externally, the body must be protected against intervention or pressure liable to jeopardise the independent judgment of its members as regards proceedings before them. There must also be safeguards protecting its independence. In *Gabalfrisa*, the Court considered the Tribunales Ecónomico-Administrativos, which reviewed the decisions of the tax authorities in Spain, to be courts.[58] Although members of these bodies were appointed and dismissed by the minister, there was considered to be a clear separation of functions between them and the tax authority.[59] By contrast, in *Syfait*, the Court did not consider the Greek competition authority to be a court even though it was formally independent, as there were insufficient guarantees against dismissal of its members by the Minister for Economic Development.[60] Internally, the body must be impartial between the parties. It must have no organisational links with any of the parties appearing before it and no interest in the outcome of the proceedings before it.[61]

Secondly, not only must the body be deciding the Union rights of the parties, but it must also have a compulsory jurisdiction over the activities in question. This means that a private body, most notably arbitration panels, cannot be a court for the purposes of Article 267 TFEU, as parties opt-in to such arrangements.[62] The last criterion is that the body must be taking decisions of a judicial nature. This leads to bodies having a floating status in which the nature of the proceedings determines whether they will be able to refer. The Court has been unclear about what constitutes a decision of a judicial nature, preferring the opposite strategy of stating that the decision must not be of an administrative nature. Courts allocating the surname to a child,[63] or registering a company[64] have been held not to be in a position to make a reference as these are considered to be administrative decisions. By contrast, if a court hears an appeal against such a decision, its decision will be considered to be of a judicial nature.[65]

The consequence of these criteria is that a whole number of public bodies have been found to be courts, notwithstanding that they are not part of the formal judiciaries of their Member States. They include immigration adjudicators,[66] professional disciplinary bodies,[67] bodies established to review public contracts[68] and tax adjudicators.[69] Whilst a case can be made for a uniform definition of a

---

[56] See Case C-210/06 *Cartesio*, Judgment of 16 December 2008.

[57] Case C-506/04 *Wilson* v *Ordre des avocats du barreau de Luxembourg* [2006] ECR I-8613.

[58] Joined Cases C-110/98–C-147/98 *Gabalfrisa* [2000] ECR I-1577.

[59] In recent years, the Court seems to have toughened up the guarantees necessary. Case C-246/05 *Häupl* v *Lidl* [2007] ECR I-4673.

[60] Case C-53/03 *Syfait and Others* v *GlaxoSmithKline AEVE* [2005] ECR I-4609.

[61] Case C-24/92 *Corbiau* v *Administration des Contributions* [1993] ECR I-1277; Case C-516/99 *Schmid* [2002] ECR I-4573.

[62] Case 102/81 *Nordsee Deutsche Hochseefischerei* v *Reederei Mond Hochseefischerei* [1982] ECR 1095; Case C-125/04 *Denuit and Cordonier* [2005] ECR I-923.

[63] Case C-96/04 *Standesamt Stadt Niebüll* [2006] ECR I-3561.

[64] Case C-182/00 *Lutz* [2002] ECR I-547.

[65] Case C-210/06 *Cartesio*, Judgment of 16 December 2008; Case C-14/08 *Roda Golf & Beach Resort*, Judgment of 25 June 2009.

[66] Case C-416/96 *El Yassini* v *Secretary of State for the Home Department* [1999] ECR I-1209.

[67] Case 246/80 *Broeckmeulen* v *Huisarts Registratie Commissie* [1981] ECR 2311.

[68] Case C-54/96 *Dorsch* v *Bundesbaugesellschaft Berlin* [1997] ECR I-4961; Case C-92/00 *HI* v *Stadt Wien* [2002] ECR I-5553.

[69] Case C-17/00 *De Coster* v *Collège des bourgmestre et échevins de Watermael-Boitsfort* [2001] ECR I-9445.

court in that it leads to an equal possibility of reference from across the Union, the rationale for the criteria used in that definition is not clear and the Court has been attacked on two fronts.

First, a rationale for a wide definition is that it is important that any body that decides EU law rights should be able to refer. If not, individuals will have to challenge the decision before a body that can refer. This adds expense and time to the process of referral and provides a disincentive for parties to seek a referral. Such a view would allow private bodies to refer and would probably not be too worried about whether the decision is of a judicial nature, as all that matters is a denial of rights and not the manner in which this happens.[70] Such a critique is, however, open to a floodgates argument in that it would allow an extensive number of poorly trained actors to overload the Court of Justice's docket.

The other criticism, made very effectively by Advocate General Colomer, is that the current definition is too wide.[71] He argues that a strategic decision was taken in Article 267 TFEU to create a conversation between courts, which would shape the development of EU law. Administrative and regulatory agencies, independent parts of the executive but nevertheless part of it, should not be part of that conversation. Colomer also notes many practical consequences of a wide definition. It allows bodies with no legal training to formulate references and statements. It has led to restrictions being placed on referrals by courts, notably the uncertain test that they be doing something of a judicial nature. Most crucially, he argues, it allows administrative actors to disrupt stable domestic judicial hierarchies and systems of judicial precedent by making a reference if they do not agree with these.

(iii) Structure of the EU judicial order

The Union court structure is different from national systems of administration of justice. These are characterised by compartmentalisation and decentralisation. There are specialised courts for particular areas, such as tax, intellectual property law, labour law and social security, and distinctions may be made between private law courts and administrative ones. Multitiered systems of appeal result in only a very small proportion of cases reaching the more senior courts. The preliminary reference procedure, by contrast, allows all courts and tribunals within the Union, no matter how high or low, to make a reference to a single court: the Court of Justice. The Union court structure is, therefore, a flat court structure of 'first, and then equals', in which all national courts are granted equal possibilities to make a reference to the Court and no national law can disenfranchise any national court of the possibility of making a reference.

K. Alter, 'The European Court's Political Power' (1996) 19 *West European Politics* 458, 466–7

While EC law supremacy posed a threat to the influence and authority of high courts and implied a significant compromise of national sovereignty, lower courts found few costs and numerous benefits in making their own referrals to the ECJ and in applying EC law. Being courts of first instance, lower-court judges were used to having another court hierarchically above them, and to having their judgments

---

[70] G. Bebr, 'Arbitration Tribunals and Article 177 of the EEC Treaty' (1985) 22 *CMLRev.* 489.

[71] See his Opinions in Case C-17/00 *De Coster* v *Collège des bourgmestre et échevins de Watermael-Boitsfort* [2001] ECR I-9445; Case C-205/08 *Alpe Adria Energia*, Opinion of AG Colomar of 25 June 2009.

re-written by courts above. They also did not have to worry about how their individual actions might upset legal certainty or the smooth functioning of the legal system. Thus, they were more open to sending to the ECJ broad and provocative legal questions about the reach and effects of European law in the national legal order. There were also many benefits for lower courts in taking advantage of the ECJ and in invoking EC law. It allowed lower courts to circumvent the restrictive jurisprudence of higher courts, and to re-open legal debates which had been closed, and thus to try for legal outcomes of their preference for policy or legal reasons. For example, recourse to EC law allowed pro-women industrial tribunals to circumvent the Employment Appeals Tribunal and the Conservative government, to get legal outcomes which helped them to promote equal pay for men and women. Having an ECJ decision also magnified the influence of the lower-court decisions in the legal process, as the decision became part of established legal precedence, and it sometimes led to journal articles on decisions which otherwise would not have been publicly reported, but which were able to decisively contribute to the development of national law. Having an ECJ decision behind a lower-court decision also made its reversal by a higher court less likely. Thus, it actually bolstered the legal power and influence of the lower courts. For a lower court, the ECJ was akin to a second parent where parental approval wards off sanction. When a lower court did not like what it thought one parent (a higher national court) would say, or it did not agree with what one parent said, it would ask the other parent (the ECJ). Having the other parent's approval decreased the likelihood of sanctions for challenging legal precedence or government policy. If the lower court, however, did not think that it would like what that other parent might say, it could follow the 'don't ask and the ECJ can't tell' policy and not make a referral.

The different strategic calculations of national courts vis-à-vis the ECJ created a competition-between-courts dynamic of legal integration; this fed the process of legal integration and came to shift the national legal context from under high courts. The limitations on interpretation of national law created by high courts provoked lower courts to make referrals to the ECJ. This enabled lower courts to deviate from established jurisprudence or to obtain preferred new legal outcomes. In so using EC law and the ECJ to achieve outcomes, lower courts created opportunities for the ECJ to expand its jurisdiction and jurisprudence, and, in some cases they actually goaded the ECJ to expand the legal authority of EC law even further. In this respect, one can say that lower courts were the motors of EC legal integration into the national order, and legal expansion through their referrals to the ECJ.

This structure is also relatively untested. This might seem a bizarre thing to say about a procedure that was in the Treaty of Rome and has given rise to 6,318 references by the end of 2008, including many of the Court of Justice's seminal judgments.[72] Yet prior to the entry into force of the Treaty of Lisbon, restrictions were placed on the references that could be made in the fields of immigration, asylum, civil justice and policing and criminal justice. In the case of policing and criminal justice, Member States could choose whether to let their courts refer and which courts could refer.[73] In the case of the other fields, only courts against whose decision there was no judicial remedy could refer. Combined, this restricted the possibilities for reference so that in 2008, only twenty-six references were made in all these fields combined.[74]

---

[72] *Annual Report*, above n. 11, 106.
[73] The procedures were in Article 68 EC and Article 35 TEU(M) respectively.
[74] *Annual Report*, above n. 11, 84.

Article 267 TFEU abolishes this exception and allows any national court or tribunal to refer in these fields in just the same way as in other fields. The abolition of this exception and the exposure of these fields to the full force of EU judicial structures are likely to change the workload and salience of the Court of Justice. Many of the fields traditionally exposed to these procedure, be they environmental, financial services, transport or broadcasting law, are, of course, significant but they are for the most part played out in national ministries and regulatory agencies rather than by courts. This has led to preliminary references being concentrated in limited fields perceived as technical in nature. A study carried out between 1998 and 2003 thus found that 47 per cent of the cases decided were on agriculture, VAT or the economic freedoms.[75] By contrast, the new fields – immigration, asylum and crime – constitute the daily bread-and-butter of national judicial systems in a way that other areas of EU law (with the exception of anti-discrimination law) do not. To give one example, in the United Kingdom, 390 out of 847 of all the applications for judicial review (46 per cent) that were considered were on immigration, asylum or crime.[76] The number of cases heard in any of these fields dwarfs those in other fields of EU law. They also frequently touch on civil liberty and public order sensitivities, which leads to any decision being potentially highly contentious. It remains to be seen if the procedure will meet this challenge.

4 FUNCTIONS OF THE PRELIMINARY REFERENCE PROCEDURE

The institutional role of the Court of Justice was discussed at length at the signing of the Treaty of Nice. The Court of Justice submitted a discussion paper there to the intergovernmental conference. In this paper the Court described the goal of the preliminary reference procedure as being:

> to guarantee respect for the distribution of powers between the Community and its Member States and between the Community institutions, the uniformity and consistency of Community law and to contribute to the harmonious development of the law within the Union.[77]

Extrapolating from this, the preliminary reference procedure can be said to contribute to the development of the EU legal and judicial orders in four ways.

The first is the development of EU law. It enables the Court to develop new interpretations of EU law, resolve uncertainties, correct injustices and enunciate principles. Secondly, in its statement, the Court talks of the maintenance of the institutional balance. By this it means that EU institutions do not trespass on each other's prerogatives and that the same is also true of the relationship between EU institutions and national institutions. EU institutions do not encroach in matters that are reserved to the domestic field and national institutions respect the autonomy and rules of the Union legal system. The preliminary reference procedure secures this through judicial review by private parties. Private parties can use it to challenge national behaviour through a ruling from the Court that exposes illegality by their courts, legislature or administration. Alternatively, a reference can be made which questions the legality of actions or omissions

---

[75] D. Chalmers, 'The Court of Justice and the Constitutional Treaty' (2005) 4 *ICON* 428, 455.

[76] Ministry of Justice, *Judicial and Court Statistics 2007* (London, Statistical Office, 2008) 27.

[77] European Court of Justice, *The Future of the Judicial System of the European Union* (Luxembourg, 1999) 21. Available at www.curia.eu.int/en/instit/txtdocfr/autrestxts/ave.pdf

by the EU institutions. Thirdly, the Court talks of the preliminary reference procedure as being necessary for the uniformity and consistency of EU law.[78] This is partly about coordination. Historically, decisions of the national courts of one Member State do not bind those of another. Without the possibility of access to a court whose authority is accepted by all actors, divergent interpretations of EU law would arise in the different national jurisdictions. The reference procedure also has a circulatory power in that it makes all Union courts part of a single judicial order and legal territory. A consequence of the reference procedure is that litigation in one Member State is now equally legally significant for the legal systems of all the other Member States, insofar as the Court of Justice judgment coming out of it will affect all the judiciaries. Litigation in the Netherlands, therefore, is as important as litigation in the United Kingdom for determining how EU law will govern life in the United Kingdom. Fourthly, the preliminary reference procedure has an administration of justice function. It enables national courts to decide disputes that involve EU law by allowing them to tap into the expertise of the Court of Justice.[79]

(i) Development of EU law

The reference procedure is significant quantitatively and qualitatively. Of the 767 cases pending at the end of 2008, 395 (about 51 per cent)[80] were preliminary references and almost all the significant rulings concerning EU law, other than those concerning the remit of the powers of the EU institutions, have come via the preliminary reference procedure. National courts act, therefore, as the gate-keepers to most of the central legal questions that move the EU legal order forward. However, they do more than this, as they formulate the questions that must be addressed. In this sense, they are agenda-setters, as, whilst the Court chooses how it responds to the question, they decide and frame what the Court can adjudicate upon.

The procedure is important for the development of EU law in another sense. The monopoly of adjudication provided to national courts indicates a division of functions, in which the Court of Justice is to steer the Union legal order, setting out its fundamental principles and limits and determining the legality of Union measures, whilst national courts are responsible for its day-to-day health. For the functions of the Court of Justice are exceptional in that they will not arise in most disputes involving EU law. In these disputes, it is the national courts and national legal systems that have hegemony over development of EU law: giving it a local reality, interpreting its principles, making sense of the practical relationship between it and national law.

(ii) Judicial review of EU institutions

Article 267 TFEU allows the Court of Justice to rule on the validity of EU legislation and administrative acts of the EU institutions.[81] Typically, the individual will challenge the national

---

[78] This was picked up early on in R. Buxbaum, 'Article 177 of the Rome Treaty as a Federalizing Device' (1969) 21 *Stanford Law Review* 1041. It has also been noted in a number of extra-judicial comments made by members of the Court: G. Mancini and D. Keeling, 'From CILFIT to ERT: the Constitutional Challenge Facing the Court' (1991) 11 *YBEL* 1, 2–3; G. Tesauro, 'The Effectiveness of Judicial Protection and Co-operation between the National Courts and the Court of Justice' (1993) 13 *YBEL* 1, 17.

[79] Although see Case 166/73 *Rheinmühlen-Düsseldorf* v *Einfuhr- und Vorratstelle für Getreide* [1974] ECR 33.

[80] *Annual Report*, n. 11 above, 95.

[81] Joined Cases 133/85–136/85 *Rau* v *Bundesanstalt für Landwirtschaftliche Marktordnung* [1987] ECR 2289.

measure implementing the EU act before a national court. The national court will then refer the question of whether the EU measure, which provides the legal authorisation for the national measure, is lawful or not.

In this way, the national court acts alongside the direct action procedures, which explicitly provide for individuals to challenge the acts of EU institutions.[82] Its relationship with these provisions is a complicated one as the Court sees it as part of a system of remedies. In *Jégo-Quéré*, the Commission adopted a Regulation setting a minimum mesh size for nets. Jégo-Quéré, a French company, fished for whitebait, a very small fish. The new minimum mesh sizes were now too big to allow it to do so effectively. It could not challenge the measure before a national court, as the Commission Regulation provided for no implementing measures to be taken, with the consequence that there was no national law to challenge. It sought to challenge the Regulation directly before the Court under Article 263(4) TFEU.[83] The Court held that they lacked standing, but that there were corollary duties on national authorities to allow individuals to challenge these acts before national courts, who could then refer the matter to the Union Courts.

Case C-263/02 P *Commission* v *Jégo-Quéré* [2004] ECR I-3425

29. It should be noted that individuals are entitled to effective judicial protection of the rights they derive from the Community legal order, and the right to such protection is one of the general principles of law stemming from the constitutional traditions common to the Member States. That right has also been enshrined in Articles 6 and 13 of the ECHR.

30. By Articles [263 and 268 TFEU]..., on the one hand, and by Article [267 TFEU], on the other, the Treaty has established a complete system of legal remedies and procedures designed to ensure review of the legality of acts of the institutions, and has entrusted such review to the Community Courts. Under that system, where natural or legal persons cannot, by reason of the conditions for admissibility laid down in the fourth paragraph of Article [263 TFEU], directly challenge Community measures of general application, they are able, depending on the case, either indirectly to plead the invalidity of such acts before the Community Courts under Article [268 TFEU] or to do so before the national courts and ask them, since they have no jurisdiction themselves to declare those measures invalid, to make a reference to the Court of Justice for a preliminary ruling on validity ...

31. Thus it is for the Member States to establish a system of legal remedies and procedures which ensure respect for the right to effective judicial protection...

32. In that context, in accordance with the principle of sincere cooperation laid down in Article [4 TEU], national courts are required, so far as possible, to interpret and apply national procedural rules governing the exercise of rights of action in a way that enables natural and legal persons to challenge before the courts the legality of any decision or other national measure relative to the application to them of a Community act of general application, by pleading the invalidity of such an act...

---

[82] On these see pp. 414–37.
[83] See pp. 424–5.

The Court of Justice thus states that there is a duty on national courts to allow individuals to challenge the legality of EU acts before them with the presumption that these will then in turn refer the question to the Court of Justice.[84] In this, the Court of Justice sees the preliminary reference procedure as the central instrument for judicial review of EU acts. For private parties are not required to meet any restrictive *locus standi* requirements to do this, whereas if they seek direct access to the Court of Justice under Article 263(4) TFEU, the requirements are highly restrictive. However, subsequently in the judgment, the Court limits the force of this position by indicating that there will be no sanction if national courts fail to do this. In particular, it will not step in to give private parties direct access to the Court under Article 263(4) TFEU.

By contrast, the preliminary reference procedure cannot be used to review an EU measure where a party had *locus standi* to challenge a measure directly before the Court of Justice under Article 263(4) TFEU but failed to bring the action within the necessary time limits. In *TWD*, a German textile company sought to challenge a 1985 Commission Decision declaring a German subsidy to it to be incompatible with the EU law on state aids by asking for a preliminary reference from a German court in 1992.[85] The applicant was only barred from bringing a direct action as the time limits for such an action, under Article 263(5) TFEU, are within two months of the Decision becoming known to it. The Court refused, stating that once the time limit had expired legal certainty required that the national court be bound by the Commission Decision and could not, therefore, raise the question of its validity.[86]

Two months is a short period and most cases are different from *TWD* as parties will not be clear whether they have standing or not. In *Atzeni*, the Court tempered the limitation, therefore.[87] It stated that the exclusion would only apply where the applicant was explicitly identified in an EU institution and clearly had standing under Article 263 TFEU. In other circumstances, where parties are not identified or only identified in a general manner, there is no time-frame on challenging an EU act before a court. Whilst the motivations behind this reasoning are clear, it still does not avoid the problem of legal uncertainty and it might be here that national courts could impose their own limitation periods provided these are not too restrictive.

(iii) Preserving the unity of EU law

The unity of the Union legal system rests on the idea that the Union legal system is an autonomous legal system that must be interpreted and applied in a uniform way across the Union.[88] This has required that the Court of Justice set out the corpus of EU law on which it can give judgments under Article 267 TFEU. If particular provisions of EU law could not be referred, both the uniformity and autonomy of the legal order would be compromised, as, without authoritative guidance, national courts would give divergent interpretations and the sense of being part of the same legal jurisdiction would be compromised.

Although Article 267 TFEU only gives the Court the power to give rulings on the Treaties and acts of the EU institutions, the Court has consequently interpreted its power more broadly

---

[84] Case 314/85 *Firma Fotofrost v Hauptzollamt Lübeck-Ost* [1987] ECR 4199. See pp. 162–3.
[85] Case C-188/92 *TWD Textilwerke Deggendorf v Germany* [1994] ECR I-833.
[86] D. Wyatt, 'The Relationship between Actions for Annulment and References on Validity after TWD Deggendorf' in J. Lonbay and A. Biondi (eds.), *Remedies for Breach of EC Law* (Chichester, John Wiley, 1997).
[87] Joined Cases C-346/03 and C-529/03 *Atzeni and Others v Regione autonoma della Sardegna* [2006] ECR I-1875.
[88] Case C-195/06 *Kommaustria v ORF* [2007] ECR I-8817.

to include anything which forms part of the EU legal order, even if it is neither a provision of the Treaties nor a piece of secondary legislation, be that international agreements to which the Union has succeeded the Member States[89] or general principles of law and fundamental rights when there was no explicit reference to these in the Treaties.[90]

A feature of international agreements and fundamental rights is that they form part of the EU legal order but they also have an existence outside it. The Court has held that it will still give rulings on such provisions, notwithstanding that they apply to situations governed by both domestic and EU law. In that regard, it will rule on a provision even where it will mostly be invoked as a matter of national law and only occasionally as a matter of EU law. In *Hermès*, the Court considered a provision of the WTO Agreement on Trade Related Intellectual Property Rights which concerned enforcement of intellectual property rights. This largely fell within national competence.[91] The Court nevertheless held that, insofar as the provision could potentially cover situations which fell within the scope of EU law, most notably where intellectual property rights generated by EU law were infringed, the provision required a uniform interpretation.

The Court has been concerned to secure not just uniformity of application of EU law but also an interpretive unity. This has led it to accept references on matters that do not fall within EU legal competences but where there is, nevertheless, a reference to EU law. Whilst it has no general power to give rulings on provisions of national law,[92] the Court will, thus, give rulings wherever the latter refers to the contents of provisions of EU law or adopts similar solutions to those found in EU law.[93]

In *Dzodzi*, a Togolese woman challenged a decision by the Belgian authorities refusing her a residence permit following the death of her Belgian husband, a situation governed exclusively by Belgian law.[94] The Belgian law stated, however, that the spouses of Belgian nationals should be treated in the same way as spouses of other EU nationals, whose treatment was governed by EU law. In other words, the standard for Belgian law was to be that set in EU law. The Court ruled it to be in the Union legal interest that it give a ruling, on the grounds that every EU provision should be given a uniform interpretation, irrespective of the circumstances in which it is to be applied, in order to forestall future differences in interpretation.[95]

This concern to secure uniform interpretation has generated its own legal uncertainties. For it raises the question of how explicit the reference to EU law must be for the Court to be able to give a reference. In *Dzodzi*, there was an explicit reference. This was not the case in *Les Vergers du Vieux Tauves*.[96] The Belgian government had transposed a Directive which restricted the

---

[89] Joined Cases 267/81–269/81 *Amministrazione delle Finanze dello Stato* v *SPI* [1983] ECR 801.

[90] See e.g. Case 11/70 *Internationale Handelsgesellschaft* v *Einfuhr- und Vorratstelle für Getreide und Futtermittel* [1970] ECR 1125.

[91] Case C-53/96 *Hermès International* v *FHT Marketing* [1998] ECR I-3603; Joined Cases C-300/98 and C-302/98 *Parfums Christian Dior* v *Tuk Consultancy* [2000] ECR I-11307; Case C-431/05 *Merck Genéricos – Produtos Farmacêuticos* v *Merck* [2007] ECR I-7001.

[92] Case 75/63 *Hoekstra* v *Bedrijfsvereniging Detailhandel* [1964] ECR 177.

[93] Case C-247/97 *Schoonbroodt* [1998] ECR I-8095; Case C-170/03 *Feron* [2005] ECR I-2299. For discussion, see S. Lefevre, 'The Interpretation of Community Law by the Court of Justice in Areas of National Competence' (2004) 29 *ELRev.* 501.

[94] Joined Cases C-297/88 and C-197/89 *Dzodzi* v *Belgium* [1990] ECR I-3673.

[95] Similar reasoning has been deployed to allow the Court to accept references on contracts that incorporate terms of EU law: Case C-88/91 *Federconsorzi* v *AIMA* [1992] ECR I-4035.

[96] Case C-48/07 *Les Vergers du Vieux Tauves*, Judgment of 22 December 2008.

taxes parent companies had to pay on dividends made by subsidiaries in other Member States. The Belgian law replicated, in parts, the language of the Directive, but the substance was wider and the Belgian law did not refer to it explicitly. It also applied to relations between Belgian parent companies and their subsidiaries, something that fell outside the Directive. The Court was asked to give an interpretation on the Belgian law in a case that involved only a Belgian parent company and its subsidiary. Notwithstanding the domestic nature of the case and the absence of an explicit reference, the Court considered it sufficient that the Belgian law was intended to transpose the Directive and there was some replication of the language. However, this is a very weak and uncertain nexus. It also loses sight of the initial rationale for intervention in such cases, namely unity of interpretation of EU law. As the Court acknowledged, the Belgian court need have only partial regard to its judgment in interpreting the provision but would also be able to look at the Belgian domestic legal context. There would be no guarantee, therefore, that its interpretation of its law would be the same as interpretations of identically worded provisions in other Member States.

The unity of EU law also has an institutional dimension in that the Court of Justice has understood it as suggesting that there needs to be one court with pre-eminent authority over the interpretation and validity of EU law.[97] This view is not uncontested by national courts.[98] We have already seen that by virtue of Article 274 TFEU, the power of judicial review over acts of the EU institutions is reserved to the Court of Justice. The Court has stated that national courts cannot declare EU measures invalid but must refer where this question arises.[99] In *Fotofrost*, a Commission Decision requiring import duties to be paid on binoculars imported from the eastern part of Germany was challenged before a Hamburg court on the grounds it conflicted with the 1957 Protocol on German Internal Trade, which allowed free trade between the two divided parts of Germany. The Hamburg court asked the Court of Justice whether it could declare the Commission Decision invalid.

Case 314/85 *Firma Fotofrost v Hauptzollamt Lübeck-Ost* [1987] ECR 4199

13. In enabling national courts, against those decisions where there is a judicial remedy under national law, to refer to the Court for a preliminary ruling questions on interpretation or validity, [Article 267 TFEU] did not settle the question whether those courts themselves may declare that acts of Community institutions are invalid.

14. Those courts may consider the validity of a Community act and, if they consider that the grounds put forward before them by the parties in support of invalidity are unfounded, they may reject them, concluding that the measure is completely valid. By taking that action they are not calling into question the existence of the Community measure.

15. On the other hand, those courts do not have the power to declare acts of the Community institutions invalid. As the Court emphasized...in Case 66/80 *International Chemical Corporation* v *Amministrazione delle Finanze* (1981) ECR 1191, the main purpose of the powers accorded to the Court

---

[97] European Court of Justice, above n. 77, 17.
[98] See pp. 191–7.
[99] G. Bebr, 'The Reinforcement of the Constitutional Review of Community Acts under the EEC Treaty' (1988) 25 *CMLRev.* 667.

by Article [267 TFEU] is to ensure that Community law is applied uniformly by national courts. That requirement of uniformity is particularly imperative when the validity of a Community act is in question. Divergences between courts in the Member States as to the validity of Community acts would be liable to place in jeopardy the very unity of the Community legal order and detract from the fundamental requirement of legal certainty.

16. The same conclusion is dictated by consideration of the necessary coherence of the system of judicial protection established by the Treaty. In that regard it must be observed that requests for preliminary rulings, like actions for annulment, constitute means for reviewing the legality of acts of the community institutions. As the Court pointed out... in Case 294/83 *Parti Ecologiste 'Les Verts'* v *European Parliament* (1986) ECR 1339, 'in Articles [263 and 268], on the one hand, and in Article [267 TFEU], on the other, the Treaty established a complete system of legal remedies and procedures designed to permit the Court of Justice to review the legality of measures adopted by the institutions'.

17. Since Article [263 TFEU] gives the Court exclusive jurisdiction to declare void an act of a Community institution, the coherence of the system requires that where the validity of a Community act is challenged before a national court the power to declare the act invalid must also be reserved to the Court of Justice.

18. It must also be emphasized that the Court of Justice is in the best position to decide on the validity of Community acts. Under Article 20 of the Protocol on the Statute of the Court of Justice of the EEC, Community institutions whose acts are challenged are entitled to participate in the proceedings in order to defend the validity of the acts in question. Furthermore, under the second paragraph of Article 21 of that Protocol the Court may require the Member States and institutions which are not participating in the proceedings to supply all information which it considers necessary for the purposes of the case before it.

19. It should be added that the rule that national courts may not themselves declare Community acts invalid may have to be qualified in certain circumstances in the case of proceedings relating to an application for interim measures; however, that case is not referred to in the national court's question.

The inflexibility and strength of the requirement on national courts to challenge the validity of EU measures was illustrated in *Schul*.[100] A Dutch court of last resort asked whether it could strike down an EU instrument when an analogous instrument based on identical principles had already been struck down. The case in question concerned a charge levied on Brazilian sugar imported into the Netherlands on the basis of a Commission Regulation. An identical pricing structure was used as in a measure in the poultry sector ruled illegal by the Court of Justice, namely the Council had suggested one pricing structure (the representative price) and the Commission had exceeded its delegated power by using a different one (cif price). The Court of Justice stated that the uniformity of EU law and its procedural rules, in which all Member States and EU institutions have the right to make observations, entailed that only it could declare Union acts invalid. This was the case even where an analogous measure had already been struck down. Analogies could be misleading in that the factual and legal context surrounding each measure would necessarily be different.

---

[100] Case C-461/03 *Schul v Minister van Landbouw, Natuur en Voedselkwaliteit* [2005] ECR I-10513.

A very slight nuancing of the situation was allowed in *IATA*.[101] IATA, the central association representing airlines, challenged Regulation 261/2004/EC, which provided for compensation and assistance to passengers in the event of being denied boarding and of cancellation or long delay to long-haul flights. The English court was sceptical of the challenge and, indeed, the challenge was eventually unsuccessful. It therefore questioned the threshold at which it must refer to the Court of Justice. The latter stated it was not required to refer simply because one party challenged the validity of a measure. It should only refer if it considers an argument as to the invalidity of a measure, brought up either by itself or by one of the parties, to be well founded.

The annual Commission studies on the application of EU law have, however, not suggested any rebellion against *Fotofrost* by national courts.[102] This is, in part, because the practical application of the *Fotofrost* judgment is rather different from its rhetoric. National courts may still suspend acts through the granting of interim relief pending a reference to the Court of Justice.[103] A compact is thereby offered, whereby national courts may provisionally suspend the application of an act provided they refer the matter to the Court of Justice for a definitive ruling. They retain their power of review but at the cost of having to make a reference.

(iv) Dispute resolution

The monopoly of adjudication granted to the national court by Article 267 TFEU suggests dispute resolution for it. However, the stipulation in Article 267(2) TFEU that it only refer when the point of EU law is necessary to give a judgment has been interpreted to mean that a reference should only take place and the Court of Justice give a judgment where the latter meaningfully contributes to the resolution of the dispute. The Court of Justice will not give a ruling, therefore, if it considers it will not be used to determine a genuine dispute before the national court. This inevitably means that it will look at the litigation before the national court to verify whether a dispute is taking place. This position was tested for the first time in the *Foglia* saga. Foglia had contracted to sell Italian liqueur wine to Novello in France with the proviso that Novello would reimburse any taxes Foglia incurred, unless these were levied contrary to Community law. Foglia sought to recover the French taxes paid from Novello, equivalent to 148,000 Italian lire, who refused on the grounds that these had been levied contrary to Community law. The matter was brought before an Italian court which was asked to rule on the compatibility of the French taxes with EC law. The case had all the hallmarks of a test case. Both Foglia and Novello argued that the taxes were illegal, the amount of tax paid was derisory and Foglia indicated that he was participating in this case on behalf of Italian traders of this wine. The Court of Justice refused to give judgment in the initial reference on the grounds that there was no genuine dispute.[104] The Italian court re-referred the matter, asking what the roles of the national court and Court of Justice were in such matters.

---

[101] Case C-344/04 *R, ex parte IATA* v *Department for Transport* [2006] ECR I-403.

[102] See e.g. European Commission, *25th Annual Report on Monitoring the Application of Community Law*, COM(2008)777, Annex VI.

[103] Case C-465/93 *Atlanta Fruchthandelsgesellschaft and others (No. 1)* [1995] ECR I-3761; Case C-334/95 *Krüger* v *Hauptzollamt Hamburg-Jonas* [1997] ECR I-4517.

[104] Case 104/79 *Foglia* v *Novello* [1980] ECR 745.

Case 244/80 *Foglia* v *Novello (No. 2)* [1981] ECR 3045

14. With regard to the first question it should be recalled, as the Court has had occasion to emphasize in very varied contexts, that [Article 267 TFEU] is based on cooperation which entails a division of duties between the national courts and the Court of Justice in the interest of the proper application and uniform interpretation of Community law throughout all the Member States.

15. With this in view it is for the national court – by reason of the fact that it is seized of the substance of the dispute and that it must bear the responsibility for the decision to be taken – to assess, having regard to the facts of the case, the need to obtain a preliminary ruling to enable it to give judgment.

16. In exercising that power of appraisal the national court, in collaboration with the Court of Justice, fulfils a duty entrusted to them both of ensuring that in the interpretation and application of the Treaty the law is observed. Accordingly the problems which may be entailed in the exercise of its power of appraisal by the national court and the relations which it maintains within the framework of [Article 267 TFEU] with the Court of Justice are governed exclusively by the provisions of Community law.

17. In order that the Court of Justice may perform its task in accordance with the Treaty it is essential for national courts to explain, when the reasons do not emerge beyond any doubt from the file, why they consider that a reply to their questions is necessary to enable them to give judgment.

18. It must in fact be emphasized that the duty assigned to the Court by [Article 267 TFEU] is not that of delivering advisory opinions on general or hypothetical questions but of assisting in the administration of justice in the Member States. It accordingly does not have jurisdiction to reply to questions of interpretation which are submitted to it within the framework of procedural devices arranged by the parties in order to induce the Court to give its views on certain problems of Community law which do not correspond to an objective requirement inherent in the resolution of a dispute. A declaration by the Court that it has no jurisdiction in such circumstances does not in any way trespass upon the prerogatives of the national court but makes it possible to prevent the application of the procedure under [Article 267 TFEU] for purposes other than those appropriate for it.

19. Furthermore, it should be pointed out that, whilst the Court of Justice must be able to place as much reliance as possible upon the assessment by the national court of the extent to which the questions submitted are essential, it must be in a position to make any assessment inherent in the performance of its own duties in particular in order to check, as all courts must, whether it has jurisdiction. Thus the Court, taking into account the repercussions of its decisions in this matter, must have regard, in exercising the jurisdiction conferred upon it by [Article 267 TFEU], not only to the interests of the parties to the proceedings but also to those of the Community and of the Member States. Accordingly it cannot, without disregarding the duties assigned to it, remain indifferent to the assessments made by the courts of the Member States in the exceptional cases in which such assessments may affect the proper working of the procedure laid down by [Article 267 TFEU] …

28. On the one hand it must be pointed out that the court before which, in the course of proceedings between individuals, an issue concerning the compatibility with Community law of legislation of another Member State is brought is not necessarily in a position to provide for such individuals effective protection in relation to such legislation.

29. On the other hand, regard being had to the independence generally ensured for the parties by the legal systems of the Member States in the field of contract, the possibility arises that the conduct of the parties may be such as to make it impossible for the State concerned to arrange for an appropriate defence of its interests by causing the question of the invalidity of its legislation to be decided by a court of another Member State. Accordingly, in such procedural situations it is impossible to exclude the

> risk that the procedure under [Article 267 TFEU] may be diverted by the parties from the purposes for which it was laid down by the Treaty.
>
> 30. The foregoing considerations as a whole show that the Court of Justice for its part must display special vigilance when, in the course of proceedings between individuals, a question is referred to it with a view to permitting the national court to decide whether the legislation of another Member State is in accordance with Community law.

Foglia was extremely contentious. The power to refuse a reference established a hierarchical element between the Court of Justice and the national court, as it granted a power to the Court of Justice to review the national court's decision to refer. The enquiry into the existence of a genuine dispute by the Court of Justice would also require it to look behind the national court's reference and examine the factual background to the dispute. There was consequently debate about whether this violated the cooperative spirit of Article 67 TFEU or transgressed unduly on the national court's monopoly over fact-finding.[105] Whatever its merits, there are severe practical difficulties in applying *Foglia*.[106] The finding of an absence of a genuine dispute requires the Court to take an independent view of the facts of the case. Without its own fact-finding powers, however, the Court has little capacity to second-guess national courts.

Within this context, the Court has accepted test cases. In *Leclerc Siplec* v *TF1 Publicité*, Leclerc Siplec challenged a refusal by TF1, one of the major French television broadcasters, to televise an advertisement which sought to persuade viewers to purchase petrol from the forecourts of Leclerc's chain of supermarkets.[107] The reason for the refusal was a French law prohibiting television advertising of the distribution sector. Both parties to the dispute were in agreement about the domestic legal situation and the need for a reference. The Court accepted the reference. It noted that what was being sought was a declaration from the national court that the French law did not comply with EU law. The parties' agreement did not make the need for that declaration any less pressing or the dispute any less real. Whilst resolution of test cases is an important part of the judicial function, it is very difficult to distinguish them from hypothetical cases. In both, there is little conflict between the immediate parties to the dispute.

Since *Foglia*, the Court has also accepted cases where the national law of one Member State is challenged in the courts of another. In *Eau de Cologne*, Eau de Cologne, a cosmetics company, agreed to supply cosmetics to an Italian company, Provide.[108] The contract contained a warranty that the cosmetics would comply with Italian law. Provide repudiated the contract on the grounds that the cosmetics did not comply with Italian labelling laws. Eau de Cologne argued that they complied with the Directive regulating the matter. Under a choice of forum provision in the agreement, the matter was brought before a German court which referred

---

[105] For differing views see A. Barav, 'Preliminary Censorship? The Judgment of the European Court in Foglia v Novello' (1980) 5 *ELRev.* 443, 451–4; H. Rasmussen, *On Law and Policy in the European Court of Justice* (Dordrecht, Martinus Nijhoff, 1986) 465–97; D. Wyatt, 'Foglia (No.2): The Court Denies It has Jurisdiction to Give Advisory Opinions' (1982) 7 *ELRev.* 186; C. Gray, 'Advisory Opinions and the Court of Justice' (1983) 8 *ELRev.* 24.

[106] G. Bebr, 'The Existence of a Genuine Dispute: An Indispensable Precondition for the Jurisdiction of the Court under Article 177 EC?' (1980) 17 *CMLRev.* 525, 532.

[107] Case C-412/93 *Société d'Importation Edouard Leclerc-Siplec* v *TF1 Publicité SA and M6 Publicité SA* [1995] ECR I-179. M. O'Neill, 'Article 177 and Limits to the Right to Refer: An End to the Confusion?' (1996) 2 *European Public Law* 375.

[108] Case C-150/88 *Eau de Cologne* v *Provide* [1989] ECR 3891.

a question on the interpretation of the Directive. The Court accepted the genuineness of the dispute despite a number of factors, notably the seemingly trivial nature of the breach and the choice of forum which allowed a German court to adjudicate upon the compatibility of Italian legislation with EU law.

The *Foglia* line of reasoning survives. Instead of being used by the Court to review the motives of the parties, it is being used to review the contents of the reference and the quality of the national court's communications.[109] The Court will refuse to give a reference not merely where the dispute is hypothetical but where the factual and legal context to the dispute has not been properly explained. In *Plato Plastik* v *Caropack*, Plato Plastik produced plastic bags in Austria which it sold to Caropack, who sold them at supermarkets. Under the contract, Plato Plastik's statutory obligation to participate in a collection and recovery scheme was transferred to Caropack. Following prosecution by the Austrian authorities, Plato Plastik asked for confirmation from Caropack that it was participating in the scheme. Caropack refused, arguing that it could not absolve Plato Plastik of its statutory duties. The Austrian court referred the question whether the Austrian scheme for the collection and recovery of waste complied with Directive 94/62/EC on packaging waste. The Commission noted that both parties agreed on the law and were using the case to have the Austrian scheme declared illegal.

Case C–341/01 *Plato Plastik* v *Caropack* [2004] ECR I–4883

26. It has consistently been held that it is solely for the national court before which the dispute has been brought, and which must assume responsibility for the subsequent judicial decision, to determine in the light of the particular circumstances of the case both the need for a preliminary ruling in order to enable it to deliver judgment and the relevance of the questions which it submits to the Court. Consequently, where the questions submitted by the national court concern the interpretation of Community law, the Court of Justice is, in principle, bound to give a ruling...

27. However, the Court has also held that, in exceptional circumstances, it should examine the conditions in which the case was referred to it by the national court...The spirit of cooperation which must prevail in the preliminary ruling procedure requires the national court, for its part, to have regard to the function entrusted to the Court of Justice, which is to assist in the administration of justice in the Member States and not to deliver advisory opinions on general or hypothetical questions...

28. The Court has accordingly held that it has no jurisdiction to give a preliminary ruling on a question submitted by a national court where it is quite obvious that the interpretation or assessment of the validity of a Community rule sought by that court bears no relation to the facts or purpose of the main action, where the problem is hypothetical or where the Court does not have before it the factual or legal material necessary to enable it to give a useful answer to the questions submitted to it...

29. In order that the Court of Justice may perform its task in accordance with the EC Treaty it is essential for national courts to explain, when the reasons do not emerge beyond any doubt from the file, why they consider that a reply to their questions is necessary to enable them to give judgment...Thus the Court has also on various occasions stressed that it is important for the national court to state the

---

[109] T. Kennedy, 'First Steps Towards a European Certiorari' (1993) 18 *ELRev.* 121; D. Anderson, 'The Admissibility of Preliminary References' (1994) 14 *YBEL* 179, 186–8.

precise reasons for which it is in doubt as to the interpretation of Community law and which led it to consider it necessary to refer questions to the Court for a preliminary ruling...

30. In the present case, the action before the national court seeks, on an application by Plato Plastik, an order that Caropack must provide the latter with confirmation of its participation in the ARA system relating to the plastic bags delivered to it. It is not manifestly apparent from the facts set out in the order for reference that the dispute is in fact fictitious...The fact that the parties to the main proceedings are in agreement as to the interpretation of the Community provisions in question does not affect the reality of the dispute in the main proceedings...

31. Consequently, the argument that the dispute is fictitious cannot succeed.

There is a duty for the national court to explain the factual and legal context and also a duty to provide reasons why it considered it necessary to make a reference. These reasons must explain the national court's doubts but they must also provide some explanation of the reasons for the choice of the EU provisions to be interpreted and of the link between those provisions and the national legislation applicable to the dispute. Whilst this may lead the Court to limit its answers to only some of the questions referred,[110] in recent years the review has been extremely light-touch. The Court has therefore stated that it will only refuse to give a reference where it is 'quite obvious' that there is no dispute, the point of law referred bears no relationship to the dispute in question or that it has not been provided with the necessary factual and legal material. The 'quite obvious' test means that if there is the slightest doubt about any of these it will give a ruling. In *Stichting Zuid-Hollandse Milieufederatie*, for example, the Court accepted a question from a Dutch court about the Directive on biocides, notwithstanding that the litigation concerned legislation on another Directive, that on plant protection, on the grounds that the two Directives were closely related and governed by similar principles.[111] Furthermore, even if the statement of the factual and legal context is thin and ambiguous or the reference is posed in general and hypothetical terms, the Court will give judgment if it thinks it can relate the reference to a particular dispute[112] and if it thinks enough of the facts are provided for it to give a sufficiently informed judgment.[113]

5 MANAGEMENT OF THE EU JUDICIAL ORDER

We have seen in the last two sections that the Court of Justice has set out an EU judicial order, comprising both EU and national courts, the structure of which is underpinned by Article 267 TFEU. This has led to a division of duties where the Court of Justice has a monopoly over the review of EU institutions and what can be referred to it whilst national courts have a monopoly of adjudication over other disputes involving EU law that come before them, albeit that a reference to the Court of Justice entitles the Court of Justice to instruct them on how to interpret the point of EU law before them.

[110] Case C-380/05 *Centro Europa 7* v *Ministero delle Comunicazioni* [2008] ECR I-349.
[111] Case C-138/05 *Stichting Zuid-Hollandse Milieufederatie* v *Minister van Landbouw* [2006] ECR I-8339.
[112] Case C-537/07 *Gómez-Limón* v *INSS*, Judgment of 16 July 2009.
[113] Joined Cases C-295/04–C-298/04 *Vincenzo Manfredi and Others* v *Lloyd Adriatico Assicurazioni SpA and Others* [2006] ECR I-6619.

All this still leaves the question of how the procedure is managed to realise these different functions and whether it successfully realises this. There are three points of management. First, there are the effects of the Court of Justice judgments on the referring court and the wider judicial order. Secondly, the reference process has to be managed by the domestic court in the period when it refers and when it gives final judgment. Finally, the circumstances under which a referral is or is not made have to be managed.

(i) Binding effects of Court of Justice judgments

A judgment given by the Court of Justice binds the referring national court.[114] However, it is free to refer the question back to the Court of Justice if it is either dissatisfied with the ruling or is unclear about the meaning of the ruling. In such circumstances, in a form of judicial 'ping pong', the Court has tended simply to reiterate or extrapolate on its prior judgment.[115] There is also no meaningful sanction that is applied against national courts that do not follow the rulings.[116] That said, national compliance is very high. A cross-country study found implementation of the Court's rulings in 96.3 per cent of the cases studied.[117] Challenges to the authority of the Court were rarely in the form of direct non-observance but rather in less direct ways. A study of Austrian courts found that a variety of devices were used to evade rulings of the Court of Justice that were unpopular with the local court. These included narrow constructions of EC legal norms, arguing that the norm does not apply to the facts, weak remedies, *a contrario* reasoning and application of domestic, rather than EU, legal norms if it would lead to the same result.[118] The Court of Justice has tried to circumvent this in some instances by sending back rulings which are so detailed that they leave national courts little room for discretion in how they decide the dispute in hand. By contrast, in other cases, they have sought to defuse conflict by sending back rulings that are sufficiently vague to allow the national court considerable discretion in deciding how to resolve the dispute.[119]

There is, however, the question of the effects of the Court's judgments on the wider EU judicial community. The doctrines of *stare decisis* and precedent do not formally exist in EU law. Judgments of the Court only declare the pre-existing state of the law.[120] However, judgments having no broader effects would be highly unsatisfactory for the development of the Union legal order. It was felt to be particularly problematic where the Court declared an EU measure illegal. If the judgment only bound the parties concerned, it would lead to the instrument being invalid for them but binding upon everybody else, albeit open to challenge by everybody else. In *ICC*, therefore, the Court ruled that a judgment declaring an EU measure illegal bound all

---

[114] Case 52/76 *Benedetti* v *Munari* [1977] ECR 163.
[115] Joined Cases 28/62–30/62 *Da Costa* [1963] ECR 37; Case 244/80 *Foglia* v *Novello (No. 2)* [1981] ECR 3045.
[116] Case C-224/01 *Köbler* v *Austria* [2003] ECR I-10239.
[117] S. Nyikos, 'The Preliminary Reference Process: National Court Implementation, Changing Opportunity Structures and Litigant Desistment' (2003) 4 *EUP* 397, 410.
[118] B. Bepuly, 'The Application of EC Law in Austria', IWE Working Paper No. 39, Available at www.iwe.oeaw.ac.at
[119] The manner in which the Court has done this has been subject to some criticism. J. Snell, 'European Courts and Intellectual Property: A Tale of Zeus, Hercules and Cyclops' (2004) 29 *ELRev.* 178.
[120] Case 61/79 *Denkavit Italiana* [1980] ECR 1205. T. Koopmans, 'Stare Decisis in European Law' in D. O' Keeffe and H. Schermers (eds.), *Essays in European Law and Integration* (Deventer, Kluwer, 1982); A. Arnull, 'Owning Up to Fallibility: Precedent and the Court of Justice' (1993) 30 *CMLRev.* 247.

courts and authorities in the Union.[121] The binding force of Court judgments interpreting EU law, by contrast, was unclear for some time.[122]

In *Kühne*, the Court resolved this by holding that the statements of the law in its judgments bound all courts and administrative authorities in the Union. Kühne exported chicken legs, with part of the chicken's back still attached, to states outside the European Union. In a judgment involving other parties, the Court of Justice had ruled that these were to be classified as 'chicken legs' for the purposes of customs classification[123] Kühne then sought reimbursement from the Dutch authorities who had previously placed its goods in a customs classification on which higher customs duties were levied. The Dutch authorities observed that the matter had previously been decided by a Dutch court, which had decided against Kühne, and could not, therefore, be reopened. Kühne argued that they were bound to reconsider the matter in the light of the earlier Court of Justice judgment.

Case C–453/00 *Kühne & Heitz v Productschap voor Pluimvee en Eieren* **[2004] ECR I–837**

21. The interpretation which, in the exercise of the jurisdiction conferred on it by Article [267 TFEU], the Court gives to a rule of Community law clarifies and defines, where necessary, the meaning and scope of that rule as it must be or ought to have been understood and applied from the time of its coming into force…

22. It follows that a rule of Community law interpreted in this way must be applied by an administrative body within the sphere of its competence even to legal relationships which arose or were formed before the Court gave its ruling on the question on interpretation.

23. The main proceedings raise the question whether the abovementioned obligation must be complied with notwithstanding that a decision has become final before the application for review of that decision in order to take account of a preliminary ruling by the Court on a question of interpretation has been lodged.

24. Legal certainty is one of a number of general principles recognised by Community law. Finality of an administrative decision, which is acquired upon expiry of the reasonable time-limits for legal remedies or by exhaustion of those remedies, contributes to such legal certainty and it follows that Community law does not require that administrative bodies be placed under an obligation, in principle, to reopen an administrative decision which has become final in that way.

25. However, the national court stated that, under Netherlands law, administrative bodies always have the power to reopen a final administrative decision, provided that the interests of third parties are not adversely affected, and that, in certain circumstances, the existence of such a power may imply an obligation to withdraw such a decision even if Netherlands law does not require that the competent body reopen final decisions as a matter of course in order to comply with judicial decisions given subsequent to the decision. The aim of the national court's question is to ascertain whether, in circumstances such as those of the main case, there is an obligation to reopen a final administrative decision under Community law.

---

[121] Case 66/80 *International Chemical Corporation v Amministrazione Finanze* [1981] ECR 1191; Case 314/85 *Firma Fotofrost v Hauptzollamt Lübeck-Ost* [1987] ECR 4199.

[122] For contrasting views of the Advocates General, see Advocate General Darmon in Case 338/85 *Pardini v Ministerio del Commercio con l'Estero* [1988] ECR 204; Advocate General Van Gerven in Case 145/88 *Torfaen Borough Council v B & Q* [1989] ECR 765; Advocate General Lenz in Case 103/88 *Fratelli Constanzo v Milano* [1989] ECR 1839.

[123] Case C-151/93 *Voogd Vleesimport en -export* [1994] ECR I-4915.

26. As is clear from the case-file, the circumstances of the main case are the following. First, national law confers on the administrative body competence to reopen the decision in question, which has become final. Second, the administrative decision became final only as a result of a judgment of a national court against whose decisions there is no judicial remedy. Third, that judgment was based on an interpretation of Community law which, in the light of a subsequent judgment of the Court, was incorrect and which was adopted without a question being referred to the Court for a preliminary ruling in accordance with the conditions provided for in Article [267 TFEU]. Fourth, the person concerned complained to the administrative body immediately after becoming aware of that judgment of the Court.

27. In such circumstances, the administrative body concerned is, in accordance with the principle of cooperation arising from Article [4 TEU], under an obligation to review that decision in order to take account of the interpretation of the relevant provision of Community law given in the meantime by the Court. The administrative body will have to determine on the basis of the outcome of that review to what extent it is under an obligation to reopen, without adversely affecting the interests of third parties, the decision in question.

Although *Kühne* only refers to the Court's judgment binding national administrative authorities, this has been interpreted as being binding on all national authorities. They are required to change national law as soon as possible after the judgment, making sure that they give full effect to individual rights under EU law.[124] These authorities include national judges, and they are, consequently, governed by the duties set out in the judgment.[125] Care has to be had when describing their binding effects. As the judgments are assumed to be declaring pre-existing law, their binding force applies to all relationships governed by the legal instrument since it entered into force. This poses, as the judgment acknowledges, real challenges for legal certainty. In most instances, this will be resolved by national limitation periods which will prevent disputes of a certain vintage being reopened. More challenging is the situation in *Kühne*, where a court or administrative authority has just given a decision which conflicts with a subsequent Court judgment. Legal certainty will prevent it being reopened unless four criteria are met: there is an administrative body that has the power to reopen the decision; the administrative decision in question has become final as a result of a judgment of a national court ruling at final instance; that judgment is based on a misinterpretation of EU law and the court failed to refer; the person concerned complained to the administrative body immediately after becoming aware of that decision of the Court.[126] These conditions are cumulative and restrictive. The Court has therefore held that the possibility of appeal would preclude reopening the matter.[127] It will be rare that they are met and the Court has insisted that there is no general obligation on courts to reopen cases simply because they conflict with subsequent Court judgments.[128]

---

[124] Case C-231/06 *NPO* v *Jonkman* [2007] ECR I-5149.

[125] Case C-212/04 *Adeneler and Others* v *ELOG (Ellinikos Organismos Galaktos)* [2006] ECR I-6057.

[126] However, the parties do not have to have raised it themselves before the court. Case C-2/06 *Kempter* [2008] ECR I-411.

[127] Joined Cases C-392/04 and C-422/04 *i-21 Germany* v *Bundesrepublik Deutschland* [2006] ECR I-8559.

[128] Case C-234/04 *Kapferer* v *Schlank & Schlick* [2006] ECR I-2585.

(ii) Management of the reference period and interim measures

There is a lengthy period between the time the reference is made by the national court and the adoption of a judgment by the Court of Justice. In 2008, this period was an average of 16.8 months.[129] In addition, there will be the period following the Court judgment when the matter must wait to go back before the national courts. National courts are required to manage the rights of the parties during this time through the grant of interim relief. This remedy of interim relief operates in different ways depending on whether interim relief is being sought against an autonomous provision of national law whose compatibility with EU law is being contested, or whether it is being sought against a national law implementing an EU law where the validity of the EU measure is being contested.

In the case of the former, the Court has ruled that the national court must do everything to secure the effectiveness of the Court's judgment. In *Factortame*, a challenge was made by a number of Spanish fishermen to the United Kingdom's Merchant Shipping Act 1988.[130] This Act made it very difficult for non-British boats to fish in British waters by imposing, most notably, a series of residence requirements as a precondition. The national court referred the matter to the Court of Justice. In the meantime, the House of Lords found that the applicants would suffer irreparable damage if interim relief was not granted as many fishermen would go bankrupt before judgment was delivered. As English courts had no jurisdiction to suspend the Act at that time, it referred the question whether national law should be set aside where its application would deprive a party of the enjoyment of rights derived from EU law. The Court of Justice ruled that it should. It ruled that national courts were under a duty to secure the full effectiveness of EU law. This required that they had to ensure the full effectiveness of any Court judgment on those rights. If the national court considers that the effectiveness of the final judgment might be otherwise undermined, it must grant interim relief. This works to the benefit of applicants claiming possible entitlements under EU law. They merely have to show that they would not be able to claim those rights if they won to make a strong case for interim relief.

The conditions for interim relief are much more restrictive where a reference is being sought that, in effect, challenges the validity of an EU measure. In such circumstances, the applicant must show they will suffer serious and irreparable damage and this has then to be weighed against the Union interest in not having the measure disapplied. In *Martini*, manufacturers in Italy, the Netherlands and the United Kingdom challenged Directive 2002/2/EC on the circulation and marketing of compound feeding stuffs for animals[131] This required manufacturers to indicate the quantities of feed materials used in the composition of the products with a tolerance of $\pm$ 15 per cent of the declared value and, when requested by a customer, to provide the exact percentages by weight of the feed materials making up a feeding stuff product. The Dutch court asked if the national implementing measure could be suspended pending judgment.

---

[129] *Annual Report*, above n. 11, 94.
[130] Case C-213/89 *R* v *Secretary of State for Transport, ex parte Factortame Ltd* [1990] ECR I-2433.
[131] This judgment consolidates a large number of cases, Joined Cases C-143/88 and C-92/89 *Zuckerfabrik Süderdithmarschen and Zuckerfabrik Soest* [1991] ECR I-415, Case C-465/93 *Atlanta Fruchthandelsgesellschaft and Others (No. 1)* [1995] ECR I-3761, Case C-68/95 *T. Port* [1996] ECR I-6065.

Joined Cases C–453/03, C–11/04, C–12/04 and C–194/04 *Martini* v *Ministero delle Politiche Agricole e Forestali* [2005] ECR I–10423

103. …references for preliminary rulings on the validity of a measure, like actions for annulment, allow the legality of acts of the Community institutions to be reviewed. In the context of actions for annulment, Article [279 TFEU] enables applicants to request enforcement of the contested act to be suspended and empowers the Court to order such suspension. The coherence of the system of interim legal protection therefore requires that national courts should also be able to order suspension of enforcement of a national administrative measure based on a Community regulation, the legality of which is contested.

104. The Court has, however, ruled that the uniform application of Community law, which is a fundamental requirement of the Community legal order, means that the suspension of enforcement of administrative measures based on a Community regulation, whilst it is governed by national procedural law, in particular as regards the making and examination of the application, must in all the Member States be subject, at the very least, to conditions which are uniform so far as the granting of such relief is concerned and which it has defined as being the same conditions as those of the application for interim relief brought before the Court…

105. The Court has pointed out in particular that, in order to determine whether the conditions relating to urgency and the risk of serious and irreparable damage have been satisfied, the national court dealing with the application for interim relief must examine the circumstances particular to the case before it and consider whether immediate enforcement of the measure which is the subject of the application for interim relief would be likely to result in irreversible damage to the applicant which could not be made good if the Community act were to be declared invalid…

106. As the court responsible for applying, within the framework of its jurisdiction, the provisions of Community law and consequently under an obligation to ensure that Community law is fully effective, the national court, when dealing with an application for interim relief, must take account of the damage which the interim measure may cause to the legal regime established by a Community measure for the Community as a whole. It must consider, on the one hand, the cumulative effect which would arise if a large number of courts were also to adopt interim measures for similar reasons and, on the other, those special features of the applicant's situation which distinguish it from the other operators concerned…

107. In particular, if the grant of interim relief may represent a financial risk for the Community, the national court must also be in a position to require the applicant to provide adequate guarantees, such as the deposit of money or other security…

108. The unavoidable conclusion in this regard is that national administrative authorities…are not in a position to adopt interim measures while complying with the conditions for granting such measures as defined by the Court.

These different tests result in applicants whose interests are prejudiced in very similar ways being treated very differently. This injustice results because the Court is giving priority to different systemic concerns: the effectiveness of EU law in one case and the cumulative effect of interim relief and the financial risks for the Union, in the other. We might wonder why these should have such priority, why different elements are emphasised in different cases and why the Court does not think these same arguments should apply analogously to national law.

This seemingly arcane question also strongly influences the type of litigant who goes to Luxembourg, and in not altogether desirable ways. The ready availability of interim relief, together with the presence of long delays in the reference system, serves to benefit litigants who can withstand delay.[132] The victory for them is simply obtaining the reference, as it will preserve their position for a couple of years. They have only to find their legal costs and hope that the position of their opponent weakens.[133] By contrast, in the second scenario, where interim relief is less likely, the applicant's position is greatly prejudiced. She will have to bear all the costs of the Union measure, however onerous, as well as the costs of litigation.

(iii) Managing the circumstances in which national courts refer

The central mechanism for determining when a reference should be made is set out in the distinction between Article 267(2) and 267(3) TFEU. The latter states that courts against whose decision there is no judicial remedy in national law are obliged to refer, where the point of EU law is necessary to decide the dispute in hand. All other courts fall within Article 267(2) TFEU and enjoy a discretion whether to refer. The obligation to refer extends not just to the highest courts in the land but also to any other court, where the party has been denied the possibility to take the matter further because they have been denied leave to appeal to a higher court. In *Lyckeskog*, Lyckeskog was prosecuted for importing rice into Sweden without paying customs duties. He appealed to the Swedish Court of Appeal, arguing that the relevant EU Regulation allowed this where the rice was for personal use. The Swedish Court of Appeal, whose decisions could be appealed to the Swedish Supreme Court, referred the question as to whether it fell within Article 267(3) TFEU for it to refuse Lyckeskog leave to appeal.

Case C–99/00 *Lyckeskog* [2002] ECR I–4839

14. The obligation on national courts against whose decisions there is no judicial remedy to refer a question to the Court for a preliminary ruling has its basis in the cooperation established, in order to ensure the proper application and uniform interpretation of Community law in all the Member States, between national courts, as courts responsible for applying Community law, and the Court. That obligation is in particular designed to prevent a body of national case law that is not in accordance with the rules of Community law from coming into existence in any Member State.

15. That objective is secured when, subject to the limits accepted by the Court of Justice…supreme courts are bound by this obligation to refer…as is any other national court or tribunal against whose decisions there is no judicial remedy under national law…

16. Decisions of a national appellate court which can be challenged by the parties before a supreme court are not decisions of a 'court or tribunal of a Member State against whose decisions there is no judicial remedy under national law' within the meaning of Article [267 TFEU]. The fact that examination of the merits of such appeals is subject to a prior declaration of admissibility by the supreme court does not have the effect of depriving the parties of a judicial remedy.

---

[132] On the difficulties and delays with the current preliminary reference procedure see p. 178.
[133] R. Rawlings, 'The Eurolaw Game: Some Deductions from a Saga' (1993) 20 *Journal of Law and Society* 309.

17. That is so under the Swedish system. The parties always have the right to appeal to the Högsta domstol against the judgment of a hovrätt, which cannot therefore be classified as a court delivering a decision against which there is no judicial remedy. Under Paragraph 10 of Chapter 54 of the Rättegångsbalk, the Högsta domstol may issue a declaration of admissibility if it is important for guidance as to the application of the law that the appeal be examined by that court. Thus, uncertainty as to the interpretation of the law applicable, including Community law, may give rise to review, at last instance, by the supreme court.

18. If a question arises as to the interpretation or validity of a rule of Community law, the supreme court will be under an obligation, pursuant to the third paragraph of Article [267 TFEU], to refer a question to the Court of Justice for a preliminary ruling either at the stage of the examination of admissibility or at a later stage.

Lyckeskog secures the universal jurisdiction of the Court of Justice. In principle, in every case, there should be a point at which individuals are able to demand a reference from a national court because there will be a moment where either leave to appeal is refused or the case is decided by the highest court in the land, and that court falls within Article 267(3) TFEU. Notwithstanding these points, there are drawbacks to such an interpretation, as it prevents national courts stopping proceedings becoming too drawn out, or matters not being referred to the Court of Justice because the sums involved are too small or the case is of very limited importance.

The distinction is not an immutable one, however. There are circumstances both when a lower court against whose decision there is a judicial remedy must refer and when a court against whose decision there is no judicial remedy must not refer.

The former circumstance has already been addressed. All national courts must refer if they consider that an EU measure may be invalid. This derives from the dictates of the uniformity of EU law, which require that EU measures cannot be declared invalid in one national territory in the Union but remain valid elsewhere. Only the Court of Justice has the power, therefore, to declare a Union measure invalid.[134]

By contrast, national courts against whose decision there is no judicial remedy are not compelled to refer if either the doctrine of *acte éclairé* or that of *acte clair* applies. The former allows a court not to refer if a materially identical matter has already been decided by the Court of Justice. The latter states that a question need not be referred if the provision in question is so clear that there is no reasonable doubt about its application.

In *CILFIT*, a group of textile firms challenged levies imposed by the Italian Ministry of Health on wool imported by them from outside the Union. The case centred on whether wool was an animal product as a Regulation prohibited levies imposed on 'animal products'. The dispute went up to the Italian Court of Cassation, the highest civil court in Italy. The Italian Ministry of Health argued that there was no need to make a reference to the Court of Justice as the question of law, namely whether wool is an animal product, was obvious.

---

[134] Case 314/85 *Firma Fotofrost* v *Hauptzollamt Lübeck-Ost* [1987] ECR 4199.

Case 283/81 *CILFIT* v *Ministry of Health* [1982] ECR 341

13. It must be remembered in this connection that... in Joined Cases 28 to 30/62 *Da Costa* v *Nederlandse Belastingadministratie* [1963] ECR 31 the Court ruled that: 'Although the third paragraph of [Article 267 TFEU] unreservedly requires courts or tribunals of a Member State against whose decision there is no judicial remedy under national law... to refer to the Court every question of interpretation raised before them, the authority of an interpretation under [Article 267 TFEU] already given by the Court may deprive the obligation of its purpose and thus empty it of its substance. Such is the case especially when the question raised is materially identical with a question which has already been the subject of a preliminary ruling in a similar case.'

14. The same effect, as regards the limits set to the obligation laid down by the third paragraph of [Article 267 TFEU], may be produced where previous decisions of the Court have already dealt with the point of law in question, irrespective of the nature of the proceedings which led to those decisions, even though the questions at issue are not strictly identical.

15. However, it must not be forgotten that in all such circumstances national courts and tribunals, including those referred to in paragraph (3) of [Article 267 TFEU], remain entirely at liberty to bring a matter before the Court of Justice if they consider it appropriate to do so.

16. Finally, the correct application of Community law may be so obvious as to leave no scope for any reasonable doubt as to the manner in which the question raised is to be resolved. Before it comes to the conclusion that such is the case, the national court or tribunal must be convinced that the matter is equally obvious to the courts of the other Member States and to the Court of Justice. Only if those conditions are satisfied may the national court or tribunal refrain from submitting the question to the Court of Justice and take upon itself the responsibility for resolving it.

17. However, the existence of such a possibility must be assessed on the basis of the characteristic feature of Community law and the particular difficulties to which its interpretation gives rise.

18. To begin with, it must be borne in mind that Community legislation is drafted in several languages and that the different language versions are equally authentic. An interpretation of a provision of Community law thus involves a comparison of the different language versions.

19. It must also be borne in mind, even where the different language versions are entirely in accord with one another, that Community law uses terminology which is peculiar to it. Furthermore, it must be emphasised that legal concepts do not necessarily have the same meaning in Community law and in the law of the various Member States.

20. Finally, every provision of Community law must be placed in its context and interpreted in the light of the provisions of Community law as a whole, regard being had to the objectives thereof and to its state of evolution at the date on which the provision in question is to be applied.

Read literally, the exception is so narrow so as to be almost meaningless.[135] There will be few national judges who have the capacity to compare the nuances and context of a provision in all languages of the Union.[136] Even the Court of Justice, with all the back-up of its

---

[135] H. Rasmussen, 'The European Court's *Acte Clair* Strategy in CILFIT' (1984) 9 *ELRev.* 242; F. Mancini and D. Keeling, 'From CILFIT to ERT: The Constitutional Challenge Facing the European Court' (1991) 11 *YBEL* 1, 4. For an argument that the exception should therefore be expanded see M. Broberg, '*Acte Clair* Revisited: Adapting the Demands of *Acte Clair* to the Demands of the Times' (2008) 45 *CMLRev.* 1383.

[136] For an attempt to do so see *Cunningham* v *Milk Marketing Board for Northern Ireland* [1988] 3 CMLR 815.

translating services, has struggled to come to terms with the interpretive difficulties posed by the authenticity of all the different language versions of EU law.[137] However, to concentrate on the formal limits of *CILFIT* is to miss its significance. *CILFIT* encourages national courts to decide seemingly non-controversial or technical matters of EU law themselves. To some, this creates a lacuna in judicial protection by providing circumstances where individuals will not have access to the Court of Justice.[138] To others, the doctrine of *acte clair* acts as a valve, defusing potential conflict between the higher national courts and the Court of Justice, by allowing the former to decide matters exclusively by themselves without engaging in any overt act of judicial rebellion.[139]

The practice of many senior national courts is irregular. Whilst the Belgian Constitutional Court has made seventy-one references, the Italian and Portuguese Constitutional Courts have made only one reference each, whilst the French Constitutional Council and German Constitutional Court have never made a reference.[140] However if *CILFIT* grants national courts some leeway for decision-making, it does so in a highly distorted manner. It requires the highest national court to hide behind semantic grounds as a reason for non-referral; that is, that the matter has already been decided or that the provision is so clear that it does not require interpretation. It does not permit national courts to put forward the far stronger reasons for non-referral, namely that there are important national constitutional values at stake that they wish to decide, or that to refer might lead to an abuse of the litigation process with one party needlessly drawing out the process.

Matters changed in *Köbler*.[141] Köbler was an Austrian professor who lost bonuses, to which he would otherwise have been entitled for his length of service in the university sector, because he had spent some years working outside Austria at a German university.[142] The Austrian Administrative Court, a court of last resort, wrongly ruled that this did not breach EU law and that it was not, therefore, obliged to refer. The Court ruled that an action for damages against the state would be available where it was manifestly apparent that a court had failed to comply with its obligations under Article 267(3) TFEU. This would be the case where it was evident that neither the doctrine of *acte clair* nor that of *acte éclairé* applied. In this instance, the Court ruled it was not obviously apparent, as the Austrian court had mistakenly, but in good faith, thought that the matter was covered by a previous ruling of the Court, which had held that the treatment was lawful. It contemplated, therefore, that it fell within the doctrine of *acte éclairé*.

In principle, this adds an incentive for courts to comply with their duties under Article 267 TFEU. National courts falling under Article 267(2) TFEU are as subject to appeal when they fail to apply EU law properly, as when they misapply domestic law. There is financial redress against the state if courts against whose decision there is no judicial remedy fail to refer, where it is obvious that they should. However, the duty might still only be a paper one.[143] The redress

---

[137] For difficulties with the different language versions of EU legislation see Case C-72/95 *Aanemersbedrijf P.K. Kraaijeveld* v *Gedeputeerde Staten van Zuid-Hooland* [1996] ECR I-5403.

[138] A. Arnull, 'Reflections on Judicial Attitudes at the European Court' (1985) 34 *ICLQ* 168, 172; A. Arnull, 'The Use and Abuse of Article 177 EEC' (1989) 52 *MLR* 622, 626.

[139] J. Golub, 'The Politics of Judicial Discretion: Rethinking the Interaction between National Courts and the European Court of Justice' (1996) 19 *WEP* 360, 376-7.

[140] *Annual Report*, above n.11, 104-5.

[141] Case C-224/01 *Köbler* v *Austria* [2003] ECR I-10239.

[142] This case is dealt with in more detail in Chapter 7 at pp. 308-11.

[143] J. Komárek, 'Federal Elements in the Community Judicial System: Building Coherence in the Community Legal System' (2005) 42 *CMLRev.* 9, 12-18.

is against the state, not against the court. It is not clear, short of legislation, what the other arms of government could do to redress a decision of a senior court. The incentives do not, therefore, fall directly on the court in question. Such an action would also require a court of first instance to rule negatively on the actions of the senior court. For it would require a new action to be brought before such a court, demanding that it rule that the latter had acted illegally. It seems implausible that many lower courts would do this.

Köbler is, therefore, more important for what it symbolises. This has been well described by Davies:

> Thus national court interpretations of Community law, while sometimes creative and purposive, take place in a grey area of semi-legitimacy, a sort of tolerated but not approved practice, where the assumption seems to be that ultimately any point of law will in fact make its way to the Court of Justice. Moreover, national final courts will have no interpretive competence at all.[144]

This view is strongly at odds with that of the judges of national courts, who see themselves as responsible for the administration of all law on their territories. Moreover, as a number of commentators have observed, it obstructs the goal of creating a Union court system, in which all courts in the Union identify themselves both as Union and national courts. By denying the contribution of national judges to the development of EU law, it emasculates and infantilises them.[145]

6 THE DOCKET OF THE COURT OF JUSTICE

Over the years, a number of features have emerged which have thwarted realisation of the objectives of the Union court order and throw into question how effectively the preliminary reference is managing it.[146]

Bottlenecking   At the end of 2008, there were 767 cases pending before the Court of Justice with the mean waiting time being 16.8 months. This has come down in recent years, with 840 cases pending and a mean waiting time of 23.5 months in 2004.[147] The reduction is due to very few cases (only 56 references at the end of 2008, for example) coming from the new Member States whilst the Court's capacity has increased with the addition of judges from those states.[148] However, this is, in part, down to long delays in the administration of justice in those states which means EU law cases are only just starting to feed through (there were only 18 references from these states to the end of 2006).

This will lead to a number of consequences. Important cases will get stuck in the queue behind other cases. In terms of the judicial review of the EU institutions, as it is difficult for national courts to grant it, it will lead to illegal EU measures persisting longer than they

---

[144] G. Davies, 'The Division of Powers between the European Court of Justice and National Courts' (2004) 3 *ConWeb* 19.

[145] *Ibid.*; P. Allott, 'Preliminary Rulings: Another Infant Disease' (2000) *ELRev.* 538, 542; H. Rasmussen, 'Remedying the Crumbling EC Judicial System' (2000) 37 *CMLRev.* 1071, 1092.

[146] On the evolution of the system over the years see C. Barnard and E. Sharpston, 'The Changing Face of Article 177 References' (1997) 34 *CMLRev.* 1113; C. Turner and R. Munoz, 'Revising the Judicial Architecture of the European Union' (1999–2000) 19 *YBEL* 1, 1–32.

[147] *Annual Report*, above n.11, 94–5.

[148] *Ibid.* 104–6.

should.[149] Finally, it is unsatisfactory in relation to dispute resolution. For many litigants, the redress simply arrives too late to be of much use to them. For others, conversely, the length of the procedure becomes an advantage. The delay becomes a litigation strategy that can be used to exert undue pressure on the other side.[150]

Legal pollution   The bottlenecking does not occur because the Court of Justice is a lazy court. It gave 333 judgments in 2008.[151] This compares favourably with national supreme courts in Western Europe who typically give considerably fewer than 100 judgments per year. This workload places enormous time and organisational pressures on the Court of Justice. Deadlines are tight, translation services stretched and time for judicial debate and reflection limited.[152]

Expertise   The Court is asked to adjudicate on a startling array of cases. In many other jurisdictions, these tasks would be divided between different courts. As a set of generalists, required to do all of them, it is becoming increasingly difficult for the Court to do any of them well, particularly given the time pressures it is under.

A skewed docket   The delays and contingencies of Article 267 TFEU result in its very rarely being used by litigants who are going to court for compensation. Instead, it is used predominantly by two types of litigant. There are those interested in judicial politics. This litigant is using the courts to bring about legal reform. She is not interested in compensation, but establishing a new legal principle. The second type of litigant is interested in regulatory or fiscal politics. Where large undertakings have ongoing relations with regulatory or fiscal authorities, one of the parties may use litigation to reconfigure the long-term basis for the relationship. Often the challenge is to a relatively small tax or piece of regulation, but the motive is to change the climate in which business is done. A study found that between 1994 and 1998, these two types of litigation accounted for 66.35 per cent of all references from the United Kingdom.[153] The difficulty with this is that it leads to an imbalance. Litigation is predominantly about the overturning of national regimes by discontented constituencies which are, otherwise, too isolated to mobilise change domestically.[154] If the Court accedes to only 10 per cent of these challenges, because of the one-way nature of the case, it comes across as a body consistently opposed to the domestic status quo.

These problems have been endemic for many years and there has been an ongoing debate about how to reform the preliminary reference procedure.[155] Early suggestions focused on

---

[149] See Joined Cases C-46/93 and C-48/93 *Brasserie du Pêcheur/Factortame III* [1996] ECR I-1029, which was referred in early 1993 and only decided three years later.

[150] R. Rawlings, 'The Eurolaw Game: Some Deductions from a Saga' (1993) 20 *Journal of Law and Society* 309.

[151] *Annual Report*, above, n.11, 88.

[152] J. Weiler, 'Epilogue, the Judicial après Nice' in G. de Búrca and J. Weiler (eds.), *The European Court of Justice* (Oxford, Oxford University Press, 2001).

[153] D. Chalmers, *The Much Ado about Judicial Politics*, Jean Monnet Working Paper No. 1/2000, 34, http://centers.law.nyu.edu/jeanmonnet/papers/index.html (accessed 5 November 2009).

[154] K. Alter, *The European Court's Political Power* (Oxford, Oxford University Press, 2009) 176 *et seq*. On the case of women's rights movements in different Member States see R. Cichowski, *The European Court and Civil Society: Litigation, Mobilization and Governance* (Cambridge, Cambridge University Press, 2007) ch. 3.

[155] A. Arnull, 'Refurbishing the Judicial Architecture of the European Community' (1994) 43 *ICLQ* 296; W. v. Gerven, 'The Role of the European Judiciary Now and in the Future' (1996) 21 *ELRev*. 211; D. Scorey, 'A New Model for the Communities' Judicial Architecture in the New Union' (1996) 21 *ELRev*. 224.

either establishing a system of regional courts,[156] which would create a new judicial layer between national courts and the Court of Justice, or developing specialised courts for complex, fact-intensive areas of EU law.[157] Neither of these has found favour.[158] Debate has instead distilled down to two alternatives. One alternative was that national courts decide more cases by themselves.[159] A suggestion was made that national courts submit draft answers with their references. If the Court agrees at an early stage that the draft answer is correct, it would simply state that it did not object to the suggested interpretation.[160] The other is that the Court of Justice decides more by engaging in more efficient case-management.[161] This would involve internal organisation of the Court through increased resort to Chambers, an increase in the jurisdiction of the General Court and an expansion of the translation services.[162] It would also be possible to have a mix of these two approaches.[163]

This was considered in most depth at the Treaty of Nice. A clear preference emerged for the second approach, namely that the problems were to be addressed by efficient management of its docket and internal distribution of its workload by the Court of Justice. This has involved a fourfold strategy.

First, there is only very limited control of references from national courts by the Court of Justice. As we have seen, the Court will not give a ruling if it is quite obvious there is no legal dispute, the factual and legal context to the dispute has not been provided in sufficient detail for the Court to be able to give an answer to the question, or the question referred is clearly not relevant to the dispute.[164] It will also not give a reference where this will undermine the *locus standi* conditions set out in other provisions of the Treaties.[165] It has also been noted, however, that this has led in recent times to very few references being refused. More significant is the rule in Article 104(3) of the Rules of Procedure that allows the Court to make an order referring

---

[156] J.-P. Jacqué and J. Weiler, 'On the Road to European Union, a New Judicial Architecture: An Agenda for the Intergovernmental Conference' (1990) 27 *CMLRev.* 185.

[157] P. Kapteyn, 'The Court of Justice of the European Communities after the Year 2000' in D. Curtin and T. Heukels (eds.), *Institutional Dynamics of European Integration, Liber Amicorum Schermers* (Dordrecht, Martinus Nijhoff, 1994) vol. I, 135, 141–5.

[158] Court of First Instance, 'Reflections on the Future Development of the Community Judicial System' (1991) 16 *ELRev.* 175.

[159] See Advocate General Jacobs in Case C-338/95 *Wiener v Hauptzollamt Emmerich* [1997] ECR I-6495.

[160] S. Strasser, *The Development of a Strategy of Docket Control for the European Court of Justice and the Question of Preliminary References*, Jean Monnet Working Paper No. 95/3, http://centers.law.nyu.edu/jeanmonnet/papers/index.html (accessed 5 November 2009).

[161] *Contribution by the Court of Justice and the Court of First Instance to the Intergovernmental Conference* (Luxembourg, Office for Official Publications of the European Communities, 2000). See also the earlier more extensive document issued by the European Court of Justice, above n. 77.

[162] British Institute of International and Comparative Law, *The Role and Future of the Court of Justice* (London, BIICL, 1996) 126–31. This is not unproblematic as the translation unit at the Court faces considerable strains. P. Mullen, 'Do You Hear What I Hear? Translation, Expansion and Crisis in the European Court of Justice' in M. Cowles and M. Smith (eds.), *The State of the European Union, vol. V, Risks, Reform, Resistance and Revival* (Oxford, Oxford University Press, 2000).

[163] *Report by the Working Party on the Future of the European Communities' Court System* (Brussels, European Commission, 2000) (Due Report). For discussion see A. Dashwood and A. Johnston (eds.), *The Future of the Judicial System of the European Union* (Oxford and Portland, Hart, 2001); P. Craig, 'The Jurisdiction of the Community Courts Reconsidered' in G. de Búrca and J. Weiler (eds.), *The European Court of Justice* (Oxford, Oxford University Press, 2001); H. Rasmussen, 'Remedying the Crumbling EC Judicial System' (2000) 37 *CMLRev.* 1071; A. Johnston, 'Judicial Reform and the Treaty of Nice' (2001) 38 *CMLRev.* 499.

[164] See pp. 167–8.

[165] Case C-188/92 *TWD Textilwerke Deggendorf v Germany* [1994] ECR I-833.

to its previous case law where the question is identical to one on which it has ruled, may be clearly deduced from existing case law, or where the answer 'admits of no reasonable doubt'. Twenty such orders were given in 2008. They involve only limited time savings, however, as the Court must still hear the Advocate General before making such an order.

Secondly, the central tool for efficient management of the Court is the Chamber system. The Treaty of Nice made provision, as we have seen, for preliminary references to be made to the General Court[166] and also for its possible expansion, as it introduced the provision that it comprise 'at least' one judge from each Member State.[167] There was the possibility of its becoming the central Union court with the Court of Justice only pronouncing on broad principles which affect the unity and consistency of EU law.[168] To date, however, this has not happened. Instead, reliance is placed upon the Chambers system of the Court of Justice. Between 2004 and 2008, 84.4 per cent of cases were heard by Chambers of either three or five judges.[169] This is not a new trend.[170] However, it does result in the Court becoming increasingly fragmented with individual judges acquiring special significance in the judgments upon which they rule. This is particularly concerning when important decisions are taken by Chambers of three judges, as only two judges have to agree for a judgment to be reached.[171]

Thirdly, the Court gives priority to ruling on certain types of case, notably where delay will lead to extremely adverse consequences. It does this by two procedures:

- the 'accelerated procedure': this allows a national court to request from the President of the Court that the matter be put to the Court as a matter of exceptional urgency. In such circumstances, the case will be prioritised and the time limits for observations restricted to not less than fifteen days;[172]
- the 'urgent procedure': this procedure is implicit in the amendment made by the Treaty of Lisbon, now set out in Article 267(4) TFEU, which provides that when a reference is made with regard to a person in custody, the Court shall act with the minimum of delay. It was anticipated by Decision 2008/79.[173] This procedure can either be requested by the national court or decided by the Court of its own motion. It is even more truncated than the accelerated procedure. No minimum time limits for submissions are set. Both the written procedure and the Opinion of the Advocate General can be dispensed with. To date, Opinions of Advocates General given under this procedure have not been published.

The procedures raise a number of different concerns. One of the challenges with the accelerated procedure is the high threshold of 'extreme urgency'. It is rarely used, with only thirty-four applications between 2004 and 2008, of which only two were successful.[174] The concerns

---

[166] Article 256(3) TFEU.
[167] Article 19(2) TEU.
[168] Weiler, above n. 152.
[169] *Annual Report*, above n. 11, 89.
[170] In 1999, for example, 177 out of 235 judgments were given by the Chambers. Statistics of judicial activity of the Court of Justice in 1999, http://curia.europa.eu/jcms/jcms/Jo2_7000 (accessed 12 August 2009).
[171] On concerns as to the effects of the pressures on the organisation of the Court see C. Timmermans, 'The European Union's Judicial System' (2004) 41 *CMLRev*. 393; H. Rasmussen, 'Present and Future European Judicial Problems after Enlargement and the Post-2005 Ideological Revolt' (2007) 44 *CMLRev*. 1661.
[172] It is set out in the Court's Rules of Procedure, article 104a.
[173] [2008] OJ L24/42. The procedure is now incorporated in the Court's Rules of Procedure, article 104b.
[174] *Annual Report*, above n. 11, 97. E. de la Serre, 'Accelerated and Expedited Procedures before the EC Courts: A Review of the Practice' (2006) 43 *CMLRev*. 783.

with regard to the urgent procedure are different. Six applications were made in the ten months of its use in 2008, of which three were successful. All the cases were in the fields of asylum, immigration and criminal law, for which there were twenty-six references in 2008.[175] It may thus apply in about one-quarter of the cases in these fields. These fields are, moreover, likely to take up a significant part of the Court's time following the reforms made by the Lisbon Treaty. There is thus a risk of displacing other important areas of activity. More serious are the procedural short-cuts being taken. Whilst it can be understood that the Court may wish to dispense with written submissions, the desire to dispense with an Advocate General's Opinion leads to concerns about what space there is for reflection here. And, put simply, the decision not to publish it cannot be justified on any basis whatsoever.

The jury is still out on whether these changes will reduce the current delays. In 1999, with fifteen judges, the Court gave 234 judgments. In 2008, with twenty-seven judges, it gave 333 judgments: a lower ratio of judgments per judge. Looked at from the point of view of number of cases per judge, they seem to be offering only modest efficiency gains, therefore. If the preliminary references were to increase, either because of more references from the new Member States or because of the increased jurisdiction of the Court, then it is clear that the problem of delay will be exacerbated. If the problem is not one merely of delay, but of a structural imbalance in the type of litigation arriving at the Court, then deciding more cases is likely to exacerbate existing problems. Resolution of more cases involving an ever more eclectic array of issues is likely both to stretch the Court's expertise and to dilute its capacity to act as a constitutional court. More generally, there are real concerns about the orderly development of EU law, where there is a single court rushing out around 400 judgments per year under increasingly tight deadlines. The potential for error and self-contradiction is considerable, and it will be increasingly difficult for national legal systems to keep up with and reflect on that amount of case law.

The refusal to countenance national courts making fewer references, as the article by Komárek sets out, also suggests a poorly articulated vision of the EU judicial order. It suggests that the Court of Justice should decide on everything that matters, and that virtually everything matters. It also suggests a vision where the preliminary reference procedure does not facilitate dispute resolution, but is the process at the centre of the dispute. Finally, in letting applicants force a reference, it contains a view of national courts as either incompetent or untrustworthy.

J. Komárek, 'In the Court(s) We Trust? On the Need for Hierarchy and Differentiation in the Preliminary Ruling Procedure' (2007) 32 *European Law Review* 467, 476

The attempt to attach fundamental status to every provision of EU law is contradicting the premise that EU law has become part of national law. If it has, then EU law can no longer be treated as 'supranational' law having some special force in each instance, rather must the weight of its rules reflect their actual nature.

Preliminary ruling procedure must be seen as a deviation from normal organisation of the judicial process, not as its natural component. This is because it allows obviating the existing hierarchy amongst the courts, which plays an important role in the rationalisation of the judicial process, and delays final

---

[175] *Annual Report*, above n. 11, 98 and 84 respectively.

resolution of the dispute, thus potentially bringing an element of injustice. Again, it is a question of how we want to see the EU judicial system: whether it really comprises national courts *as* European courts, or whether we use this label only for highlighting their obligations resulting from EU law. If we see it in the former sense, then we must accept that it means to see the EU judiciary as a judicial system without qualifications. Nice labels may only hide some (of course hard) choices we must inevitably make when we perceive national courts as 'Community courts of general jurisdiction'—thus fully competent to decide questions concerning interpretation of EU law. Insisting on all courts' possibility to refer to the Court of Justice questions their competence to give effective protection to individuals without the Court of Justice's assistance. At the same time, it implies that the Court should be involved in an everyday dispute settlement whenever a question of Community law arises, regardless of its importance for the EU legal system as a whole. The result is an unreasonable distribution of the Court of Justice's judicial capacity throughout the Union judicial system.

FURTHER READING

K. Alter, *The European Court's Political Power* (Oxford, Oxford University Press, 2009)

D. Anderson and M. Demetriou, *References to the European Court* (London, Sweet & Maxwell, 2002)

G. de Búrca and J. Weiler (eds.), *The European Court of Justice* (Oxford, Oxford University Press, 2001)

D. Chalmers, 'The Court of Justice and the Constitutional Treaty' (2005) 4 *ICON* 428

R. Cichowski, *The European Court and Civil Society: Litigation, Mobilization and Governance* (Cambridge, Cambridge University Press, 2007)

A. Dashwood and A. Johnston (eds.), *The Future of the Judicial System of the European Union* (Oxford and Portland, Hart, 2001)

J.-P. Jacqué and J. Weiler, 'On the Road to European Union, a New Judicial Architecture: An Agenda for the Intergovernmental Conference' (1990) 27 *Common Market Law Review* 185

J. Komárek, 'Federal Elements in the Community Judicial System: Building Coherence in the Community Legal System' (2005) 42 *Common Market Law Review* 9

H. Rasmussen, 'Remedying the Crumbling EC Judicial System' (2000) 37 *Common Market Law Review* 1071

R. Rawlings, 'The Eurolaw Game: Some Deductions from a Saga' (1993) 20 *Journal of Law and Society* 309

T. Tridimas, 'Knocking on Heaven's Door: Fragmentation, Efficiency and Defiance in the Preliminary Reference Procedure' (2003) 40 *Common Market Law Review* 9

C. Turner and R. Munoz, 'Revising the Judicial Architecture of the European Union' (1999–2000) 19 *Yearbook of European Law* 1

5

The Authority of EU Law

CONTENTS

1 INTRODUCTION

This chapter considers the authority of EU law. It is organised as follows.

Section 2 considers the claims by the Court of Justice that sovereignty is vested in the Treaties. This places ultimate legal authority in the Treaties and makes the Court of Justice the ultimate arbiter on the meaning and consequences of this authority. This has been given limited recognition by the national governments in a Declaration attached to the Treaty of Lisbon.

Section 3 considers the implications of these claims not being fully accepted by any national constitutional court. Whilst willing to grant the Treaties significant legal authority, all see their domestic constitutions, or some part of them, as sovereign. The authority of EU law rests, therefore, in the extent to which the claims of the Court of Justice are accepted by national constitutional courts and the principles on which the latter accept it. Instead of discussing sovereignty in abstract terms of whether EU law or domestic law is sovereign, it makes better sense to consider the extent to which the four different doctrines emanating from the sovereignty of EU law have been accepted.

Section 4 considers the first of these doctrines: the precedence of EU law over all national law, including national constitutions. There is almost no instance of a national constitutional court explicitly giving priority to a national law over EU law.

Section 5 considers the second doctrine: that EU law alone should determine the quality of legal authority of different norms. In particular, it is the claim of the Court of Justice that it should determine when there is a conflict between EU law and national law and what the consequences are of such a conflict. EU law sets out three different types of relationship between Member States and the European Union: exclusive competences, shared competences, and fields in which EU law cannot exclude national legislatures from law-making. These different models give rise to differing models of integration with differing scope for EU intervention.

Section 6 considers the third doctrine, namely that EU law can determine the remit of its own authority and the activities it governs. This is contained in the doctrine of conferred powers which states, first, that only EU law can determine the limits of EU law and, secondly, that the power of the Union is to be limited and contained. The latter has been challenged by the breadth of some of the provisions of the Treaties, notably the flexibility provision, Article 352 TFEU. This doctrine has been challenged by the constitutional courts of the Member States.

Section 7 considers the fourth doctrine, the fidelity principle, set out in Article 4(3) TEU. This sets out institutional duties on actors to ensure that the Union legal system functions effectively, such as requiring Member States not to obstruct EU policies. These institutional duties have been accepted by national constitutional courts subject to their not violating domestic constitutional constraints.

2 SOVEREIGNTY OF EU LAW

(i) The sovereign claims of EU law

Within standard conceptions of international law, states remain sovereign. They may have to exercise their sovereignty subject to the international treaty obligations they have created, but the domestic legal effects of any such obligations will be a matter for the national legal orders of each state to determine:

> in the context of the internal structure of a political society, the concept of sovereignty has involved the belief that there is an absolute power within the community. Applied to problems which arise in the relations between political communities, its function has been to express the antithesis of this argument – the principle that internationally, over and above the collection of communities, no supreme authority exists.[1]

In the 1950s, it was widely assumed that this, the traditional model of international law, would apply to the European Communities. Under this model, it is the states which are masters

---

[1] F. Hinsley, *Sovereignty* (Cambridge, Cambridge University Press, 1986) 158.

of the treaties and not the other way around. This means that, collectively, states were thought to be able to change the European Communities' powers, interpret their effects or even extinguish them if they so desired. Such a model would also have meant that the European Communities could not trump states' domestic, sovereign legal processes.[2]

This model was dramatically overturned by two judgments of the Court of Justice in the early 1960s that have been the starting point ever since in debates about the legal authority of EU law. First, the Court ruled in *Van Gend en Loos* that the EC Treaty did not merely regulate mutual obligations between Member States, but established what the Court called a 'new legal order of international law for the benefit of which the states have limited their sovereign rights'.[3] This was taken further in *Costa* v *ENEL*, decided shortly afterwards. An Italian law sought to nationalise the electricity production and distribution industries. Costa, a shareholder of Edison Volta, a company affected by the nationalisation, claimed that the law breached EC law. The Italian government claimed that the matter was one of Italian law as the Italian legislation post-dated the EC Treaty and, for that reason, should be held to be the applicable law.

Case 6/64 *Costa* v *ENEL* [1964] ECR 585

By contrast with ordinary international treaties, the EEC Treaty has created its own legal system which, on the entry into force of the Treaty, became an integral part of the legal systems of the Member States and which their courts are bound to apply.

By creating a Community of unlimited duration, having its own institutions, its own personality, its own legal capacity and capacity of representation on the international plane and, more particularly, real powers stemming from a limitation of sovereignty or a transfer of powers from the States to the Community, the Member States have limited their sovereign rights, albeit within limited fields, and have thus created a body of law which binds both their nationals and themselves.

The integration into the laws of each Member State of provisions which derive from the Community, and more generally the terms and the spirit of the Treaty, make it impossible for the States, as a corollary, to accord precedence to a unilateral and subsequent measure over a legal system accepted by them on a basis of reciprocity. Such a measure cannot therefore be inconsistent with that legal system. The executive force of Community law cannot vary from one State to another in deference to subsequent domestic laws, without jeopardizing the attainment of the objectives of the Treaty set out in Article [4(3) TEU] and giving rise to the discrimination prohibited by Article [18 TFEU].

The obligations undertaken under the Treaty establishing the Community would not be unconditional, but merely contingent, if they could be called in question by subsequent legislative acts of the signatories. Wherever the Treaty grants the States the right to act unilaterally, it does this by clear and precise provisions…Applications by Member States for authority to derogate from the Treaty are subject to a special authorization procedure… which would lose their purpose if the Member States could renounce their obligations by means of an ordinary law.

---

[2] See J. Weiler and U. Haltern 'The Autonomy of the Community Legal Order: Through the Looking Glass' (1996) 37 *Harvard Int'l LJ* 411, 417–19.

[3] Case 26/62 *Van Gend en Loos* v *Nederlandse Administratie der Belastingen* [1963] ECR 1. *Van Gend en Loos* is considered in more detail in Chapters 1 and 7.

> The precedence of Community law is confirmed by Article [288 TFEU], whereby a regulation 'shall be binding' and 'directly applicable in all Member States'. This provision, which is subject to no reservation, would be quite meaningless if a state could unilaterally nullify its effects by means of a legislative measure which could prevail over Community law. It follows from all these observations that the law stemming from the Treaty, an independent source of law, could not, because of its special and original nature, be overridden by domestic legal provisions, however framed, without being deprived of its character as Community law and without the legal basis of the Community itself being called into question.
>
> The transfer by the States from their domestic legal system to the Community legal system of the rights and obligations arising under the Treaty carries with it a permanent limitation of their sovereign rights, against which a subsequent unilateral act incompatible with the concept of the Community cannot prevail.

It would be difficult to overstate the radicalism of *Costa*. The claim that EU law enjoys some form of sovereignty means that the Union's legal power cannot be seen as deriving from the Member States, but must be understood instead as being autonomous and original. Not only is this absolute authority vested in the legal power of the Union. Everything – other laws and activities covered by EU law – takes subject to it. In short, it sets the legal framework for everything else around it. This is all very well, but these claims to sovereignty are just that: claims to legal authority. Legal authority rests, however, upon a relationship, in which the level of authority is accepted not just by the party seeking it but also by the parties subject to it.

The claims of the Court of Justice must be examined critically; not simply because they may be undesirable but also because they may represent only a partial statement of the authority of EU law. *Costa* may suggest a hierarchy of laws but these '[are] not rooted in a hierarchy of normative authority or in a hierarchy of real power'.[4] 'Real power' in the Union remains firmly with the national administrations. The execution or administration of EU law is overwhelmingly a matter for domestic authorities and national governments within Member States. Administrative actors are central to securing not just enforcement but also popular awareness and acceptance of the authority of EU law. In this regard, they were silent for forty years. This could be seen as tacit acceptance but it could also be seen as a lack of active support. A survey found that only in Luxembourg was there more awareness of the Court than of any of the other EU institutions.[5] It also found very little diffuse support for the Court so that citizens would support it even where they disagreed with its decisions. In Denmark, for example, such support was as low as 9.3 per cent in the early 1990s.[6]

---

[4] J. Weiler, 'Federalism Without Constitutionalism: Europe's Sonderweg' in K. Nicolaidis and R. Howse (eds.), *The Federal Vision: Legitimacy and Levels of Governance in the United States and the European Union* (Oxford, Oxford University Press, 2000) 57.

[5] On judicial politics see K. Alter, 'The European Union's Legal System and Domestic Policy: Spillover or Backlash?' (2000) 54 *International Organisation* 489; K. Alter and J. Vargas, 'Explaining Variation in the Use of European Litigation Strategies: European Community Law and British Gender Equality Policy' (2000) 33 *Comparative Political Studies* 452.

[6] J. Gibson and G. Caldeira, 'Challenges to the Legitimacy of the European Court of Justice: A Post Maastricht Analysis' (1998) 28 *British Journal of Political Science* 63.

This was initially addressed by the Constitutional Treaty. Article I-13 provided that within the competences conferred upon the Union, EU law would have primacy over the laws of the Member States. Following the failure of the Constitutional Treaty, this provision was seen as expressing too much political enthusiasm for the principle. Instead, at Lisbon, a Declaration was attached to the Treaties.

Declaration 17

The Conference recalls that, in accordance with well settled case law of the Court of Justice of the European Union, the Treaties and the law adopted by the Union on the basis of the Treaties have primacy over the law of Member States, under the conditions laid down by the said case law.

An Opinion of the Council Legal Service was also attached, which provides only sparse information.

Opinion of the Council Legal Service, EU Council Doc. 11197/07, 22 June 2007

It results from the case law of the Court of Justice that primacy of EC law is a cornerstone principle of Community law. According to the Court, this principle is inherent to the specific nature of the European Community. At the time of the first judgment of this established case law (Costa/ENEL, 15 July 1964, Case 6/64) there was no mention of primacy in the treaty. It is still the case today. The fact that the principle of primacy will not be included in the future treaty shall not in any way change the existence of the principle and the existing case law of the Court of Justice.

A minimalist interpretation is that these documents provide a reassurance of continuity that the tradition of primacy established since *Costa* is uninterrupted.[7] A more vigorous interpretation would note that this is the first time that the *Costa* case law has been explicitly endorsed and ratified by all Member States. Such ratification perhaps not only gives the interpretation greater legitimacy, but indicates that the primacy of EU law can no longer be relegated to merely being the view of the Court of Justice. Instead, primacy now represents the political consensus as to the status of EU law. Account will have to be taken of this political vindication by all courts within the Union when they apply the principle in future. If a national constitutional court were to deny the primacy of EU law, it would correspondingly be placing itself in an institutionally isolated position.

(ii) Sovereignty of EU law and domestic constitutional settlements

If the reception of the Court of Justice's case law by national administrations was important, the position of the national constitutional or senior courts was critical. This is because all Member States commit themselves to the rule of law. This commitment carries with it two

---

[7] Case 6/64 *Costa* v *ENEL* [1964] ECR 585.

requirements: first, the requirement that all be governed by the law of the land; and secondly, that this law will be determined authoritatively by an independent judicial system at the top of which sits a constitutional or senior court, whose judgments are binding on all actors, judicial and non-judicial, within their jurisdiction. This court has the last word, therefore, on who has legal authority, the extent of that authority and its consequences for the relevant Member State.

The formal authority of EU law is predominantly governed therefore by the relationship between the Court of Justice and national constitutional courts.[8] In particular, it will be settled by the nature of the claims made by the Court of Justice and the extent to which these are accepted by national constitutional courts. One of the most striking features of the EU legal system is that, despite being the ostensible guardians of their respective *national* constitutional settlements, these national constitutional courts have been generally willing to grant EU law a variant of the authority sought by the Court of Justice that is sufficiently proximate for the EU legal order to work closely along the lines suggested by the latter almost all the time.

B. de Witte, 'Direct Effect, Supremacy, and the Nature of the Legal Order' in P. Craig and G. de Búrca (eds.), *The Evolution of EU Law* (Oxford, Oxford University Press, 1999) 196–8

Among the original Six, no special efforts were required from the courts in the Netherlands and Luxembourg, where the supremacy of international treaty provisions over national legislation was accepted prior to 1957. Of the other four countries, the courts in Belgium reacted most promptly and loyally to the European Court's injunctions. A model of what national courts can achieve in the absence of clear constitutional guidelines is the 1971 judgment of the Belgian Cour de Cassation in the *Franco-Suisse Le Ski* case. Although the Belgian Constitution was silent on the domestic effect of international or European law (or precisely because of this absence of written rules) the Supreme Court adopted the principle of primacy as it had been formulated in *Costa*, and based on the nature of international law and (a fortiori) of EC law. The other Belgian courts soon followed the same line. In France, although the text of Article 55 of the Constitution recognised the priority of international treaties even over later French laws, the courts were surprisingly slow to accept that this constitutional provision could actually be used as a conflict rule in real cases and controversies. The Cour de Cassation taking the lead of all ordinary courts decided to cross the Rubicon in the 1975 *Cafés Jacques Vabre* judgment. The Conseil d'Etat (and the administrative courts subject to its authority) followed suit much later with the *Nicolo* decision (1989), after what must have been a very painful revision of established truths. One may note that one of the arguments used by the *commissaire* Frydman, when advising the Conseil in *Nicolo* to change its views on the supremacy of EC law, was that the supreme courts of surrounding countries (even those with ingrained dualist traditions) had long recognised this supremacy.

In Italy and Germany, the actual duties imposed on national courts by *Costa* went well beyond what the mainstream constitutional doctrine, at that time, was prepared to accept in terms of the domestic

---

[8] The literature is voluminous. The two best studies on the positions of the constitutional courts across the Union are M. Claes, *The National Courts' Mandate in the European Constitution* (Oxford and Portland, Hart, 2005); A. Albi, *EU Enlargement and the Constitutions of Central and Eastern Europe* (Cambridge, Cambridge University Press, 2005).

force of international treaty law. Yet the European Court suggested, by cleverly distinguishing EEC law from 'ordinary' international law, that the German and Italian courts might, with some creativity, find the constitutional resources needed for recognising the primacy of Community law. The message, in *Costa*, was primarily addressed to the Italian Constitutional Court. This court has gradually come to recognise the supremacy of Community law over national legislation, on the basis of its special nature which distinguishes it from other international treaties. A similar evolution took place in Germany...

Greece and Ireland, when they joined, had put their constitutions in order. Article 28 of the Greek Constitution, adopted prior to accession, recognises the primacy of international conventions over any national legislation. In Ireland, given the inability of the dualist constitutional tradition to cope with the demands of membership, a special EC clause was added to the Constitution (and adapted to later Treaty revisions) vouchsafing the direct effect and primacy of Community law.

In the United Kingdom, the supremacy question floated around for many years, until the *Factortame II* judgment, where the House of Lords for the first time disapplied a later Act of Parliament for being inconsistent with the EEC Treaty...

So, by and large, 'ordinary' supremacy of Community law, that is, supremacy over national legislation and sources of national law lower in rank than legislation, seems to be accepted in most Member States (primacy over national constitutional law is quite another matter...). But there are lingering doubts, even concerning 'ordinary' supremacy, in a long-standing Member State like Denmark. That country's constitution contains no rules on the relation between Community law and national law, and the doctrine of the primacy of EC law has never been expressly accepted by the courts. Indeed, it seems that there has not been, in the twenty-five years of Danish membership, a single court case involving a conflict between EC law and a later Danish Act of Parliament.

It has also been facilitated for almost all national courts to find their own ways of accepting the authority of EU law on terms and conditions drawn from their national constitutional settlements. Three broad approaches have emerged. These approaches may be called 'European constitutional sovereignty', 'national constitutional sovereignty' and 'constitutional tolerance'. Of these, it is the third which has been most widely adopted.

(a) European constitutional sovereignty

European constitutional sovereignty is where a constitutional court of a Member State unconditionally accepts the standpoint of the Court of Justice. This has the consequence that EU law is seen as being supreme, even over the national constitution. This position has not been taken by any national constitutional court. The closest is that of the Estonian Supreme Court. Prior to Estonia joining the European Union in 2004, a referendum was held approving an Amendment Act to the Estonian Constitution. Article 2 of this Act states that the Constitution applies taking account of obligations under EU law, suggesting the latter has precedence. The Constitutional Chamber of the Estonian Supreme Court was asked to interpret this provision in a case concerning the constitutional compatibility of Estonia joining the euro. Under Article 111 of the Estonian Constitution, only the Estonian Central Bank has the right to issue currency in Estonia. The Supreme Court held that Estonia was entitled to join the euro-zone, as the Treaties take precedence over its constitution.

> Opinion on the Interpretation of the Constitution No. 3-4-1-3-06, Opinion of 11 May 2006[9]
>
> 15. Pursuant to § 2 of the Constitution of the Republic of Estonia Amendment Act the Constitution applies taking account of the rights and obligations arising from the Accession Treaty. As a result of the adoption of the Constitution of the Republic of Estonia Amendment Act the European Union law became one of the grounds for the interpretation and application of the Constitution.
>
> 16. In the substantive sense this amounted to a material amendment of the entirety of the Constitution to the extent that it is not compatible with the European Union law. To find out which part of the Constitution is applicable, it has to be interpreted in conjunction with the European Union law, which became binding for Estonia through the Accession Treaty. At that, only that part of the Constitution is applicable, which is in conformity with the European Union law or which regulates the relationships that are not regulated by the European Union law. The effect of those provisions of the Constitution that are not compatible with the European Union law and thus inapplicable, is suspended. This means that within the spheres, which are within the exclusive competence of the European Union or where there is a shared competence with the European Union, the European Union law shall apply in the case of a conflict between Estonian legislation, including the Constitution, with the European Union law.

It is unsurprising that this approach has attracted so little support. It involves a constitutional court writing itself out of a job, as it surrenders its powers of judgment to the Court of Justice. Leaving aside the centralisation of power this involves, such a surrender sweeps aside all the checks and balances that constitutional courts are established to secure. The Estonian example is interesting, furthermore, because the acceptance of the Court of Justice's reasoning is not as unconditional as might appear. The Amendment Act granting EU law its authority over the constitution also has a defence provision, Article 1, which states that Estonia may only belong to the European Union in accordance with the 'fundamental principles of the Constitution of Estonia'.[10] EU law must take subject to certain constitutional provisions, which are seen as having a higher status. These are taken to include fundamental rights and retention of core competences for the Estonian state.[11] If this is so, the Estonian position is not so far from that of the courts which practise the notion of constitutional tolerance discussed below.

(b) Unconditional national constitutional sovereignty

National constitutional sovereignty is the opposite of European constitutional sovereignty. It insists upon the continuing and unconditional sovereignty of the national constitutional order. Whilst acknowledging that EU law may make special claims for itself, it denies that EU law is any different from other form of international law.

---

[9] See www.nc.ee/?id=663 (accessed 20 August 2009).

[10] The Act is available at http://proyectos.cchs.csic.es/europeconstitution/content/estonia-constitutional-provisions (accessed 20 August 2009).

[11] On Estonian judicial practice see J. Laffranque and R. D'Sa, 'Getting to Know You: The Developing Relationship between National Courts of the "Newer" Member States and the European Court of Justice, with particular reference to Estonia' (2008) 19 *European Business Law Review* 311.

Polish Membership of the European Union (Accession Treaty), **Polish Constitutional Court, Judgment K18/04 of 11 May 2005**

6. It is insufficiently justified to assert that the Communities and the European Union are 'supranational organisations' – a category that the Polish Constitution, referring solely to an 'international organisation', fails to envisage. The Accession Treaty was concluded between the existing Member States of the Communities and the European Union and applicant States, including Poland. It has the features of an international agreement, within the meaning of Article 90(1) of the Constitution. The Member States remain sovereign entities – parties to the founding treaties of the Communities and the European Union. They also, independently and in accordance with their constitutions, ratify concluded treaties and have the right to denounce them under the procedure and on the conditions laid down in the Vienna Convention on the Law of Treaties 1969. The expression 'supranational organisation' is not mentioned in the Accession Treaty, nor in the Acts constituting an integral part thereof or any provisions of secondary Community law.

7. Article 90(1) of the Constitution authorises the delegation of competences of State organs only 'in relation to certain matters'. This implies a prohibition on the delegation of all competences of a State authority organ or competences determining its substantial scope of activity, or competences concerning the entirety of matters within a certain field.

8. Neither Article 90(1) nor Article 91(3) authorise delegation to an international organisation of the competence to issue legal acts or take decisions contrary to the Constitution, being the 'supreme law of the Republic of Poland' (Article 8(1)). Concomitantly, these provisions do not authorise the delegation of competences to such an extent that it would signify the inability of the Republic of Poland to continue functioning as a sovereign and democratic State.

9. From an axiological perspective of the Polish Constitution, the constitutional review of delegating certain competences should take into account the fact that, in the Preamble of the Constitution, emphasising the significance of Poland having reacquired the possibility to determine her fate in a sovereign and democratic manner, the constitutional legislator declares, concomitantly, the need for 'cooperation with all countries for the good of a Human Family', observance of the obligation of 'solidarity with others' and universal values, such as truth and justice. This duty refers not only to internal but also to external relations.

10. The regulation contained in Article 8(1) of the Constitution, which states that the Constitution is the 'supreme law of the Republic of Poland', is accompanied by the requirement to respect and be sympathetically predisposed towards appropriately shaped regulations of international law binding upon the Republic of Poland (Article 9). Accordingly, the Constitution assumes that, within the territory of the Republic of Poland – in addition to norms adopted by the national legislator – there operate regulations created outside the framework of national legislative organs.

11. Given its supreme legal force (Article 8(1)), the Constitution enjoys precedence of binding force and precedence of application within the territory of the Republic of Poland. The precedence over statutes of the application of international agreements which were ratified on the basis of a statutory authorisation or consent granted (in accordance with Article 90(3)) via the procedure of a nationwide referendum, as guaranteed by Article 91(2) of the Constitution, in no way signifies an analogous precedence of these agreements over the Constitution.

12. The concept and model of European law created a new situation, wherein, within each Member State, autonomous legal orders co-exist and are simultaneously operative. Their interaction may not be completely described by the traditional concepts of monism and dualism regarding the relationship

between domestic law and international law. The existence of the relative autonomy of both, national and Community, legal orders in no way signifies an absence of interaction between them. Furthermore, it does not exclude the possibility of a collision between regulations of Community law and the Constitution.

13. Such a collision would occur in the event that an irreconcilable inconsistency appeared between a constitutional norm and a Community norm, such as could not be eliminated by means of applying an interpretation which respects the mutual autonomy of European law and national law. Such a collision may in no event be resolved by assuming the supremacy of a Community norm over a constitutional norm. Furthermore, it may not lead to the situation whereby a constitutional norm loses its binding force and is substituted by a Community norm, nor may it lead to an application of the constitutional norm restricted to areas beyond the scope of Community law regulation. In such an event the Nation as the sovereign, or a State authority organ authorised by the Constitution to represent the Nation, would need to decide on: amending the Constitution; or causing modifications within Community provisions; or, ultimately, on Poland's withdrawal from the European Union.

14. The principle of interpreting domestic law in a manner 'sympathetic to European law'…has its limits. In no event may it lead to results contradicting the explicit wording of constitutional norms or being irreconcilable with the minimum guarantee functions realised by the Constitution. In particular, the norms of the Constitution within the field of individual rights and freedoms indicate a minimum and unsurpassable threshold which may not be lowered or questioned as a result of the introduction of Community provisions.

Unconditional national constitutional sovereignty emphasises national self-determination and the need to put in place an active system of constitutional checks and balances on the development of EU law. It has only been adopted by Poland.[12] This is, in part, because unconditional national constitutional sovereignty inaccurately describes institutional practice. It is not simply that the Court of Justice has developed the filaments of a new constitutional order in its case law; it is that these doctrines have been applied, albeit pragmatically, by the overwhelming majority of national courts. To describe EU law as merely another form of international law is to dismiss not merely the views of the Court of Justice, but those of the broader Union judicial community.[13]

It is also a normatively contentious position, as it privileges the idea of the state unquestioningly. If a state began adopting, for example, racist legislation that conflicted with EU law, would this be right and would it equally be able still to claim membership of the Union legal order? It might be able to affirm national legal sovereignty but only at the expense of leaving the EU legal order.

As with the Estonian Supreme Court, the Polish Constitutional Court's judgment is, moreover, not such a strong statement of European or national sovereignty. For the judgment can

---

[12] For discussion see K. Kowalik-Bańczyk, 'Should We Polish It Up? The Polish Constitutional Tribunal and the Idea of Supremacy of EU Law' (2005) 6 *German Law Journal* 1355; W. Sadurski, '"Solange, Chapter 3": Constitutional Courts in Central Europe – Democracy – European Union' (2008) 14 *ELJ* 1, 18 *et seq.*

[13] Weiler and Haltern, above n. 2, 420–3; N. Walker, 'The Idea of Constitutional Pluralism' (2002) 65 *MLR* 317, 321–3.

read as a statement of cosmopolitan values, as it privileges all international law, including EU law, above all domestic law other than the Constitution.[14] Turned around, it accepts the primacy of EU law subject to constitutional courts (like all other national constitutional courts) and subject to its respecting international law: something which the Treaties commit the Union to do.[15] As such, albeit by a slightly different form of reasoning, it parallels the reasoning of constitutional tolerance set out below.

(c) Constitutional tolerance

The third approach is that of constitutional tolerance. This posits that while the authority and reach of EU law is ultimately for national constitutional courts to decide, these courts commit themselves to recognise the special status of EU law. However, they do so on the condition that it does not violate certain constraints of national constitutional law. Of the three approaches available to national constitutional courts, this is the position that has (thus far) been most frequently taken. This approach covers a spectrum of positions, and examples can be found, inter alia, in Denmark, Belgium, Italy, France, Czech Republic, United Kingdom and Slovenia.[16] The position of the German Constitutional Court is perhaps pre-eminent in formulating the meaning of constitutional tolerance. Articulated first in *Brunner*, a challenge to the Maastricht Treaty by a German Law Professor,[17] its most recent authoritative restatement was the judgment on the compatibility of the Lisbon Treaty with the German Basic Law.

The challenge was brought by a number of prominent parties, amongst which was Die Linke, a parliamentary group within the Bundestag (the German Parliament). The challenge focused on a number of articles of the Basic Law. It argued in the first place that there was a violation of the right to vote for members of the Bundestag, set out in Article 38, on the grounds that excessive powers had been transferred to the European Union from the Bundestag. This right to participate in representative democracy was also argued to be based on two further articles, Article 1(1) on the right to human dignity, and Article 20(2), which indicates that state authority emanates from the people and is exercised by them by means of elections and voting. This was important, as Article 79(3), the constitutional identity provision, stipulates that these two latter articles are inviolable and are not amendable. The last provision over which there was debate was Article 23(2), which provides inter alia that the German Federation will consent to such limitations upon its sovereign powers as will bring about and secure a peaceful and lasting order in Europe. The claimants claimed this provision was subject to the constraints placed on it by the other provisions.

---

[14] This has been explicitly stated by the Tribunal: Pl. 37/05 *Conformity of a Polish Statute with EU Law*, Judgment of 19 December 2006.

[15] Article 3(5) TEU.

[16] See *Carlsen* v *Rasmussen* [1999] 3 CMLR 854 (Denmark); Case 12/94, B6 *Ecole Européenne*, CA, 3 February 1994 (Belgium); *Admenta and Others* v *Federfarma* [2006] 2 CMLR 47 (Italy); Cahiers du Conseil Constitutionnel No. 17, 2004, www.conseil-constitutionnel.fr/cahiers/ (France); *R* v *MAFF, ex parte First City Trading* [1997] 1 CMLR 250 (United Kingdom); U-1-113/04 *Rules on the Quality Labelling and Packaging of Feeding Stuffs*, Judgment of 7 February 2007 (Slovenia); Pl ÚS 50/04 *Sugar Quota Regulation II*, Judgment of 8 March 2006, http://angl.concourt.cz/angl_verze/doc/p-50-04.php (accessed 22 August 2009) (Czech Republic).

[17] *Brunner* v *European Union* [1994] 1 CMLR 57.

2 BvE 2/08 *Gauweiler* v *Treaty of Lisbon*, Judgment of 30 June 2009

210. The right to vote is the citizens' most important individually assertable right to democratic participation guaranteed by the Basic Law. In the state system that is shaped by the Basic Law, the election of the Members of the German Bundestag is of major importance. Without the free and equal election of the body that has a decisive influence on the government and the legislation of the Federation, the mandatory principle of personal freedom remains incomplete. Invoking the right to vote, the citizen can therefore challenge the violation of democratic principles by means of a constitutional complaint (Article 38.1 sentence 1, Article 20.1 and 20.2 of the Basic Law). The right to equal participation in democratic self-determination (democratic right of participation), to which every citizen is entitled, can also be violated by the organisation of state authority being changed in such a way that the will of the people can no longer effectively form within the meaning of Article 20.2 of the Basic Law and the citizens cannot rule according to the will of a majority. The principle of the representative rule of the people can be violated if in the structure of bodies established by the Basic Law, the rights of the Bundestag are essentially curtailed and thus a loss of substance of the democratic freedom of action of the constitutional body occurs which has directly come into being according to the principles of free and equal election...

211. The citizens' right to determine, in equality and freedom, public authority with regard to persons and subject-matters through elections and other votes is the fundamental element of the principle of democracy. The right to free and equal participation in public authority is anchored in human dignity (Article 1.1 of the Basic Law). It belongs to the principles of German constitutional law that are laid down as non-amendable by Article 20.1 and 20.2 of the Basic Law in conjunction with Article 79.3 of the Basic Law...

218. From the perspective of the principle of democracy, the violation of the constitutional identity codified in Article 79.3 of the Basic Law is at the same time an infringement of the constituent power of the people. In this respect, the constituent power has not granted the representatives and bodies of the people a mandate to dispose of the identity of the constitution. No constitutional body has been accorded the competence to amend the constitutional principles which are essential pursuant to Article 79.3 of the Basic Law. The Federal Constitutional Court watches over this. With what is known as the eternity guarantee, the Basic Law reacts on the one hand to the historical experience of the free substance of a democratic fundamental order being slowly or abruptly undermined. However, it makes clear as well that the Constitution of the Germans, in correspondence with the international development which has taken place in particular since the existence of the United Nations, has a universal foundation which is not supposed to be amendable by positive law...

225. The constitutional mandate to realise a united Europe, which follows from Article 23.1 of the Basic Law and its Preamble...means in particular for the German constitutional bodies that it is not left to their political discretion whether or not they participate in European integration. The Basic Law wants European integration and an international peaceful order. Therefore not only the principle of openness towards international law, but also the principle of openness towards European law applies.

226. It is true that the Basic Law grants the legislature powers to engage in a far-reaching transfer of sovereign powers to the European Union. However, the powers are granted under the condition that the sovereign statehood of a constitutional state is maintained on the basis of an integration programme according to the principle of conferral and respecting the Member States' constitutional identity, and that at the same time the Member States do not lose their ability to politically and socially shape the living conditions on their own responsibility...

233. The Basic Law does not grant the German state bodies powers to transfer sovereign powers in such a way that their exercise can independently establish other competences for the European Union. It prohibits the transfer of competence to decide on its own competence (*Kompetenz-Kompetenz*)... Also a far-reaching process of independence of political rule for the European Union brought about by granting it steadily increased competences and by gradually overcoming existing unanimity requirements or rules of state equality that have been decisive so far can, from the perspective of German constitutional law, only take place as a result of the freedom of action of the self-determined people. According to the constitution, such steps of integration must be factually limited by the act of transfer and must, in principle, be revocable. For this reason, withdrawal from the European union of integration...may, regardless of a commitment for an unlimited period under an agreement, not be prevented by other Member States or the autonomous authority of the Union...

239. It is therefore constitutionally required not to agree dynamic treaty provisions with a blanket character or if they can still be interpreted in a manner that respects the national responsibility for integration, to establish, at any rate, suitable national safeguards for the effective exercise of such responsibility. Accordingly, the Act approving an international agreement and the national accompanying laws must therefore be such that European integration continues to take place according to the principle of conferral without the possibility for the European Union of taking possession of *Kompetenz-Kompetenz* or to violate the Member States' constitutional identity which is not amenable to integration, in this case, that of the Basic Law. For borderline cases of what is still constitutionally admissible, the German legislature must, if necessary, make arrangements with its laws that accompany approval to ensure that the responsibility for integration of the legislative bodies can sufficiently develop.

240. Apart from this, it must be possible within the German jurisdiction to assert the responsibility for integration if obvious transgressions of the boundaries take place when the European Union claims competences... and to preserve the inviolable core content of the Basic Law's constitutional identity by means of an identity review... The Federal Constitutional Court has already opened up the way of the *ultra vires* review for this, which applies where Community and Union institutions transgress the boundaries of their competences. If legal protection cannot be obtained at the Union level, the Federal Constitutional Court reviews whether legal instruments of the European institutions and bodies, adhering to the principle of subsidiarity under Community and Union law, keep within the boundaries of the sovereign powers accorded to them by way of conferred power... Furthermore, the Federal Constitutional Court reviews whether the inviolable core content of the constitutional identity of the Basic Law is respected... The exercise of this competence of review, which is rooted in constitutional law, follows the principle of the Basic Law's openness towards European Law, and it therefore also does not contradict the principle of loyal cooperation (Article 4.3 TEU); with progressing integration, the fundamental political and constitutional structures of sovereign Member States, which are recognised by Article 4(2) TEU, cannot be safeguarded in any other way. In this respect, the guarantee of national constitutional identity under constitutional, and the one under Union, law go hand in hand in the European legal area...

The judgment is a complex one that states a number of things and it is worth taking a moment to separate them out.

First, it asserts that sovereignty rests in the national constitution and that it is ultimately for the national constitutional court to determine the relative legal authority of EU law in accordance with national constitutional principles, which must be respected. *Gauweiler* is, however, not a bald restatement of national constitutional sovereignty.[18] It asserts that commitment to European integration is not just a matter of will but a constitutional requirement. The importance of this counter-weighing argument should not be understated. The German Constitutional Court commits itself to an openness to EU law, which will only be forgone in exceptional circumstances.

Secondly, the right to vote and the right to democratic participation for German citizens is a fundamental constitutional right. It is based on the formal right to vote for deputies in the German Bundestag, but it is also an expression of two other fundamental rights, which will be violated if it is breached. One is the right to human dignity. The other is the right of the German people, as the constituent power of the German Basic Law, to participate in the exercise of state authority, particularly by voting.[19] These principles are inviolable and European integration must take subject to them.

Thirdly, these principles might be breached in three ways. The first is if the Union breaches the principle of conferred powers (ultra vires review). This will be where it takes action that exceeds the powers conferred by the Treaties, but there is also a suggestion that it will occur if there is a breach of the principle of limited powers, and the Union seeks to exercise its powers too generally. The second is where the Union trespasses on the constitutional identity of a Member State (identity review). This will be the case where the Union legislates on a matter that is so central to the identity of a state that it should be legislated only at a national or sub-national level. Whilst ultra vires review and identity review are related, they are not the same thing. The former addresses the Union observing its own procedures and not legislating too widely. It could be violated if the Union breached its own procedures or legislated too broadly on politically uncontentious matters. Identity review is about things close to a state's heart. The Union could observe its own procedures, be legislating in a confined manner but still violate identity review by touching on a matter that was core to a state's constitutional identity. The third way in which the principle can be breached is if, even observing all this, the Union acts in an undemocratic matter. The German Constitutional Court accepted that the Union was not a representative democracy[20] but noted the presence of other substitutes and checks and balances. The Union must observe these.

3 ESTABLISHMENT OF A EUROPEAN SOVEREIGN ORDER

(i) The academic debate on the different claims to sovereign authority

The position of all national constitutional courts, whilst suggesting a disposition to accept the authority of EU law, is different from that of the Court of Justice, which argues for its sovereignty. How to mediate between these positions? For legal sovereignty clearly vests in the order that emerges from the reconciliation of these claims. To put it another way, EU law will only be sovereign to the extent that the national courts accept the Court of Justice's claims. Beyond that, national legal sovereignty will remain untouched.

---

[18] T. Schilling, 'The Autonomy of the Community Legal Order: An Analysis of Possible Foundations' (1996) 37 *Harvard Int'l LJ* 389; T. Hartley, 'The Constitutional Foundations of the European Union' (2001) 117 *LQR* 225.

[19] For criticism of this style of reasoning as too nationalistic see J. Weiler, 'Does Europe Need a Constitution? Demos, Telos and the Maastricht German Decision' (1995) 1 *ELJ* 219.

[20] See pp. 43–6.

A 'cottage industry' has developed around this question, with the two most prominent schools of thought being the pluralist school and the constitutionalist school.[21] The former sees the EU legal order and national legal orders as separate orders, which must accommodate themselves to each, whilst the latter emphasises a common set of normative principles which act as the basis for collective orientation.

Let us turn first to the pluralist school, whose earliest advocate was Neil MacCormick.

N. MacCormick, 'The Maastricht Urteil: Sovereignty Now' (1995) 1 *European Law Journal* 259, 264–5

... the most appropriate analysis of the relations of legal systems is pluralistic rather than monistic, and interactive rather than hierarchical. The legal systems and their common legal system of EC law are distinct, but interacting systems of law, and hierarchical relations of validity within criteria of validity proper to distinct systems do not add up to any sort of all-purpose superiority of one system over another. It follows also that the interpretative power of the highest decision-making authorities of the different systems must be, as to each system, ultimate. It is for the European Court of Justice to interpret in the last resort and in a finally authoritative way the norms of Community law. But, equally, it must be for the highest constitutional tribunal of each Member State to interpret its constitutional and other norms, and hence to interpret the interaction of the validity of EC law with higher level norms of validity in the given state system. Interpretative competence-competence is a feature of the highest tribunal of any normative system...

What this indicates is that acceptance of a pluralistic conception of legal systems entails acknowledging that not all legal problems can be solved legally. The problem in principle is not that of an absence of legal answers to given problems, but of a superfluity of legal answers. For it is possible that the European Court interprets Community law so as to assert some right or obligation as binding in favour of a person within the jurisdiction of the German court, while that Court in turn denies the validity of such a right or obligation in terms of the German Constitution. In principle, the same conflict is possible as between any Member State system and EC law. The problem is not logically embarrassing, because strictly the answers are from the point of different systems. But it is practically embarrassing to the extent that the same human beings are said to have and not to have a certain right. How shall they act? To which system are they to give their fidelity in action?

Resolving such problems, or more wisely still, avoiding their occurrence in the first place is a matter for circumspection and for political as much as legal judgment. The European Court of Justice ought not to reach its interpretative judgments without regard to their potential impact on national constitutions. National courts ought not to interpret laws or constitutions without regard to the resolution of their compatriots to take full part in European Union and European Community. If despite this conflicts come into being through judicial decision-making and interpretation, there will necessarily have to be some political action to produce a solution.

---

[21] It is worth noting that some argue strongly for exclusive reference to the Court's case law: J. Baquero Cruz, 'The Legacy of the Maastricht-Urteil and the Pluralist Movement' (2008) 14 *ELJ* 389. Others argue that the matter should be resolved by resort to universal principles of justice: P. Eleftheriadis, 'The European Constitution and Cosmopolitan Ideals' (2001) 7 *CJEL* 2. Neither of these arguments seems to address the exact terms of the dispute, however.

The advantages and disadvantages of a pluralistic approach lie in its intellectual elasticity. Legal authority is no longer exclusively vested in the state, but is enjoyed by a number of different institutions, which include the European Union, but also international organisations, regional government and even private organisations with strong norm-setting powers, such as professional or standardisation bodies. In such a world, there are possibilities for more diverse forms of self-government and greater checks and balances, with each order limiting the excesses of the other. Such accounts give ethical priority only to the legal order as they emphasise it is the autonomy of these legal orders that must be respected. It is not clear why we should do so, or whether all such orders are sufficiently similar in their features to make such recognition possible. Just as an elephant and a mouse are mammals but are, nonetheless, very different, so these various types of law may work in diverse ways and may be quite different beasts. Is a law passed through representative institutions really the same as a technical regulation passed by a bureaucracy such as the Commission?

Furthermore, pluralist accounts are weak on explaining the processes and norms of mutual accommodation.[22] Mutual accommodation is all very well, but there must be certain norms of mutual recognition and certain criteria for determining when it would be possible for one legal order to trump another.[23] When, for example, does something become a legal order that we must recognise? When does accommodating something in one legal order excessively violate the needs of another legal order?

Kumm seeks to address this by arguing for a common idea of constitutionalism that informs both the law of the Member States and EU law and is used to resolve disputes. He has identified four tenets central to this idea of constitutionalism. These are: commitment to the rule of law, protection of fundamental rights, federalism and a commitment to valuing the specific nature of the national community. It is these tenets, he suggests, which should be used to resolve disputes.

M. Kumm, 'The Jurisprudence of Constitutional Conflict: Constitutional Supremacy in Europe Before and After the Constitutional Treaty' (2005) 11 *European Law Journal* 262, 299–300

The *first* principle is formal and is connected to the *idea of legality*. According to the principle of the effective and uniform enforcement of EU law, further strengthened by the recent explicit commitment by Member States to the primacy of EU law, national courts should start with a strong presumption that they are required to enforce EU law, national constitutional provisions notwithstanding. *The presumption for applying EU law can be rebutted, however, if, and to the extent that, countervailing principles have greater weight.* Here there are three principles to be considered. The first is *substantive*,

---

[22] For an attempt to do so albeit by reference to constitutionalist language see M. Poiares Maduro, 'Contrapunctual Law: Europe's Constitutional Pluralism in Action' in N. Walker (ed.), *Sovereignty in Transition* (Oxford, Oxford University Press, 2003).

[23] C. Richmond, 'Preserving the Identity Crisis: Autonomy, System and Sovereignty in European Law' (1997) 16 *Law and Philosophy* 377; M. la Torre, 'Legal Pluralism as an Evolutionary Achievement of Community Law' (1999) 12 *Ratio Juris* 182; N. Walker, 'The Idea of Constitutional Pluralism' (2002) 65 *MLR* 317; N. Barber, 'Legal Pluralism and the European Union' (2006) 12 *ELJ* 306. For a response, see M. Loughlin, 'Ten Tenets of Sovereignty' in the same volume and D. Kostakopoulou, 'Floating Sovereignty: A Pathology or Necessary Means of State Evolution?' (2002) 22 *OJLS* 135.

and focuses on the effective *protection of fundamental rights of citizens*. If, and to the extent that, fundamental rights protection against acts of the EU is lacking in important respects, then that is a ground to insist on subjecting EU law to national constitutional rights review. If, however, the guarantees afforded by the EU amount to structurally equivalent protections, then there is no more space for national courts to substitute the EU's judgment on the rights issue with their own. Arguably the EU, and specifically the Court of Justice, has long developed substantially equivalent protections against violations of fundamental rights. At the very least the Constitutional Treaty, with its elaborate Charter of Fundamental Rights, should finally put an end to this issue. Even if some doubt that the Court of Justice can be trusted as an institution to take rights seriously, if the Charter of Fundamental Rights becomes the law of the land after ratification the guarantees it provides may not fall below the guarantees provided by the European Convention of Human Rights as interpreted by the ECHR. The second of the counter-principles is *jurisdictional*. It protects national communities against unjustified usurpations of competencies by the European Union which undermine the legitimate scope of self government by national communities. Call this principle the principle of *subsidiarity*. Here the question is whether there are sufficient and effective guarantees against usurpation of power by EU institutions. Much will depend on how the procedural and technical safeguards of the Constitutional Treaty will work in practice once the Treaty has been ratified. If the structural safeguards will succeed in establishing a culture of subsidiarity carefully watched over by the Court of Justice, then there are no more grounds for national courts to review whether or not the EU has remained within the boundaries established by the EU's constitutional charter. Lastly, there is the *procedural* principle of *democratic legitimacy*, the third counter-principle. Given the persistence of the democratic deficit on the European level – the absence of directly representative institutions as the central agenda-setters of the European political process, the lack of a European public sphere, and a sufficiently thick European identity even if the Constitutional Treaty will be ratified – national courts continue to have good reasons to set aside EU Law *when it violates clear and specific constitutional norms that reflect essential commitments of the national community*.

The principles elaborated by Kumm are taken from federal constitutional states and provide a nuanced matrix for resolving disputes between national constitutional courts and the Court of Justice. However, as Dani has observed, they pay only limited heed to the features of the Union:

> The choice for state constitutionalism as the EU form of power relies on a strong normative assumption: it is believed that the combination of fundamental rights protection, broad legislative powers and representative democracy devices provides the most effective and, probably, the only framework for ensuring the republican ideals of political inclusion, economic prosperity and social cohesion. In this respect, conversion narratives may be regarded not only as proofs of faith on the virtues of constitutionalism and state constitutions, but also as defences of a clear political strategy intended to preserve the European *modus vivendi*.[24]

[24] M. Dani, 'Constitutionalism and Dissonances: Has Europe Paid Off its Debt to Functionalism?' (2009) 15 *ELJ* 324, 343.

As Dani observes, the constitutionalist restatement is above all an ideological position that mistakes the genus and practice of European integration. On the one hand, the Union was established to deal with the consequences of state failure, namely that the states within their domestic constitutions failed to provide or could not provide certain goods to their citizens. On the other hand, an image of state constitutionalism assumes all players are pulling in a similar direction. It might be that EU policies and national policies have a different dynamic. He gives the example of industrial policy, where EU policy is about realising market integration whereas national policy is about addressing market failure. Dani argues therefore that mediation must be built around two functions: addressing state abuse when it occurs, even when it takes place within the domestic constitution, and allowing for structural dissonance, namely the possibility for significant difference in policy direction.

(ii) The ends and means for reconciling difference and moving to a European sovereign order

The Lisbon Treaty has introduced a new provision, which may be the vehicle through which the different judicial claims are mediated. For it introduces a new principle of judicial review, namely that EU law has violated the principle of self-government.

> ### Article 4(2) TEU
>
> The Union shall respect the equality of Member States before the Treaties as well as their national identities, inherent in their fundamental structures, political and constitutional, inclusive of regional and local self-government. It shall respect their essential State functions, including ensuring the territorial integrity of the State, maintaining law and order and safeguarding national security. In particular, national security remains the sole responsibility of each Member State.

The provision is, in part, an amalgamation of earlier provisions.[25] It also is, however, a significant extension. It synthesises them around an organising principle of self-government, which is detailed, placed at the forefront of the Treaties and subject to interpretation by the Court of Justice, which will be able to review EU measures against it. It also appears it will be a central instrument used by national constitutional courts. In *Gauweiler*, at paragraph 240 in the excerpt above, the German Constitutional Court stated that the possibility for it to review EU law to guarantee national constitutional identity went hand in hand with Article 4(2) TEU. It returned to the point at paragraph 339, where it stated:

> This establishment [of the inapplicability of an EU law to Germany] must also be made if within or outside the sovereign powers conferred, these powers are exercised with effect on Germany in such a way that a violation of the constitutional identity, which is inalienable pursuant to... the Basic Law and which is also respected by European law under the Treaties, namely Article 4.2 TEU, is the consequence.

---

[25] There were thus individual provisions requiring the national identities of the Member States to be respected: Article 6(3) TEU(M). For requirements that EU legislation in the area of freedom, security and justice should not affect national responsibilities for the maintenance of law and order and internal security, there were Articles 64(1) EC and 33 TEU(M).

For the German Constitutional Court, if an EU measure violates its *identity* review, it will also be illegal as a matter of EU law, as it will breach Article 4(2) TEU. Interpretations of Article 4(2) TEU will become the battleground or the meeting point, where the limits of the authority of EU law lie.

In this regard, it becomes important to consider the principles underlying the provision. The different elements of the academic debate outlined earlier are all present. There is the language of legal pluralism in that the prerogatives of different legal orders should be accommodated. Not only national identities must be respected, but also the fundamental structures of regional and local self-government. There is also the language of constitutionalism, with the reference in Article 4(2) TEU to respect for constitutional structures. Finally, there is the functional reference, in that respect must be had to essential state functions and to national security being the exclusive responsibility of each Member State.

Interestingly, these different elements have proved attractive to the different constitutional courts we have considered. The German Constitutional Court has addressed the question through the language of constitutionalism and constitutional identity. It has looked at how EU law might impinge on certain fundamental rights that it sees as central to German constitutional identity. The approach of the Polish Constitutional Court, by contrast, is closer to that associated with legal pluralism. It sees EU law and domestic law as two autonomous orders in which each must accommodate the other without compromising its own integrity. Finally, for all its rhetoric, the Estonian Constitutional Court is closest to the functionalist position. It accepts the sovereignty of EU law but, nevertheless, hives off certain, undisclosed key functions that it conceives as essential to Estonian statehood. The difference in nuance between these courts suggests that different courts will seek different things from the provision. This will make a 'common' interpretation very unlikely. Instead, the European sovereign legal order will, in all likelihood, be very asymmetric, with its being interpreted as meaning one thing and having one basis in one Member State and another thing, having another basis, in another.

Thought also has to be directed to where these debates will emerge. Debates take place at the meta-level over what is sovereign and who is to decide the question of sovereignty. This is the debate that has been addressed in the judgments above. It is known as the *Kompetenz-Kompetenz* debate: who is competent to decide on the competence and authority of EU law? This is quite an abstract debate, which does not address how legal relations are actually played out. It would be perfectly possible for a national court, for example, to assert domestic sovereignty but then state that it chooses to do whatever EU law tells it.[26] The reason for this is that the *Kompetenz-Kompetenz* debate, important as it is, does not address the legal substance of sovereignty and the doctrines it gives rise to. It is in the Court of Justice's claims and the national constitutional courts' acceptance of these claims that we see more clearly the level of authority of EU law.

The sovereignty of EU law makes four central claims about its authority and this leads to four different doctrines. First, EU law takes precedence over other law unless it expressly says otherwise. It cannot be disapplied in favour of any other form of law. If not, it would not have the absolute authority mentioned above (the doctrine of the primacy of EU law). The second is that EU law alone determines the quality of its legal authority. That is to say it determines

---

[26] This is to some extent what has taken place in Spain where the Spanish Constitutional Court has stated that the Spanish Constitution is sovereign but otherwise gives full effect to the case law of the Court of Justice: *Re EU Constitutional Treaty and the Spanish Constitution* [2005] 1 CMLR 981.

when there is a conflict between it and national law and what the consequences of that conflict are. This is a slightly different quality from primacy as it goes to the circumstances of any conflict and the legal consequences of EU law prevailing. The doctrine most associated with this principle is that of pre-emption. The third concerns the remit of EU legal authority. It is for EU law to determine which activities are governed by it and to what it can apply. If it cannot do this and this were to be determined elsewhere, its autonomy would be compromised (the doctrine of conferred powers). Finally, the sovereignty of EU law establishes a rule of law, to which all public institutions within the Member States are subject, including national courts. This involves specifying a series of institutional duties setting out what such institutions must do to make the European Union work as a fully effective legal system (the fidelity principle).

The remainder of this chapter looks at how these different doctrines are played out, both by the Court of Justice and the national courts.

4 THE PRIMACY OF EU LAW

The primacy principle in which EU law takes precedence over national law was first proclaimed in *Costa*. It is most neatly illustrated by the decision in *Internationale Handelsgesellschaft*, in which the Court famously ruled that EU law takes precedence over all forms of national law, including national constitutional law. The claimant brought an action before a German administrative court challenging the validity of a Regulation. The German court considered that the Regulation violated certain provisions of the German Constitution. The view of the Court of Justice was uncompromising.

Case 11/70 *Internationale Handelsgesellschaft* v *Einfuhr- und Vorratstelle für Getreide und Futtermittel* [1970] ECR 1125

3. Recourse to the legal rules or concepts of national law in order to judge the validity of measures adopted by the institutions of the Community would have an adverse effect on the uniformity and efficacy of Community law. The validity of such measures can only be judged in the light of Community law. In fact, the law stemming from the Treaty, an independent source of law, cannot because of its very nature be overridden by rules of national law, however framed, without being deprived of its character as Community law and without the legal basis of the Community itself being called in question. Therefore the validity of a Community measure or its effect within a Member State cannot be affected by allegations that it runs counter to either fundamental rights as formulated by the constitution of that State or the principles of a national constitutional structure.

The primacy of EU law applies not only to substantive conflicts, when a domestic norm conflicts with an EU law. It also has a jurisdictional dimension. It is not open to national law to determine which courts can hear conflicts. The primacy of EU law applies whenever a conflict appears before any court or body which is competent to take legal decision. In *Simmenthal*, an Italian system of fees for veterinary inspections of beef imports had already been held by the Court of Justice to breach EU law. An Italian magistrate asked the Court whether he was required to disapply the relevant Italian law. This was a power which at that time was enjoyed only by the Italian Constitutional Court as only it had the power of legislative review.

> ### Case 106/77 *Amministrazione delle Finanze dello Stato* v *Simmenthal* [1978] ECR 629
>
> 17. ... in accordance with the principle of the precedence of Community law, the relationship between provisions of the Treaty and directly applicable measures of the institutions, on the one hand and the national law of the Member States, on the other is such that those provisions and measures not only by their entry into force render automatically inapplicable any conflicting provision of current national law but – in so far as they are an integral part of, and take precedence in, the legal order applicable in the territory of each of the Member States – also preclude the valid adoption of new national legislative measures to the extent to which they would be incompatible with community provisions.
>
> 18. Indeed any recognition that national legislative measures which encroach upon the field within which the Community exercises its legislative power or which are otherwise incompatible with the provisions of Community law had any legal effect would amount to a corresponding denial of the effectiveness of obligations undertaken unconditionally and irrevocably by Member States pursuant to the Treaty and would thus imperil the very foundations of the Community...
>
> 21. ... every national court must, in a case within its jurisdiction, apply Community law in its entirety and protect rights which the latter confers on individuals and must accordingly set aside any provision of national law which may conflict with it, whether prior or subsequent to the Community rule.
>
> 22. Accordingly any provision of a national legal system and any legislative, administrative or judicial practice which might impair the effectiveness of Community law by withholding from the national court having jurisdiction to apply such law the power to do everything necessary at the moment of its application to set aside national legislative provisions which might prevent Community rules from having full force and effect are incompatible with those requirements which are the very essence of Community law.

On its face, primacy of EU law is the most direct expression of its sovereignty and, insofar as the latter is contested, one would have assumed it to be particularly contingent. Whilst it is difficult to imagine any national constitutional court, with the exception of the Estonian, ever allowing *Internationale Handelsgesellschaft* to be applied over its national constitution, it is almost impossible to find any recent example of a national measure being applied by a constitutional court over an EU measure.[27]

The first reason for this is that the constraints placed on the authority of EU law by national constitutional courts are exceptional ones. In principle, they are willing to grant EU law authority subject to its not violating certain national taboos. Their assertion of national sovereignty is rather an assertion of the power to put ultimate safeguards into action rather than an assertion of regular control of the application of EU law. This was reiterated in *Gauweiler*.

---

[27] Both the Cypriot Supreme Court and Polish Constitutional Tribunal refused to comply with the European Arrest Warrant which requires states to surrender individuals wanted in another state within forty-five days, *Attorney General of the Republic of Cyprus* v *Konstantinou* [2007] 3 CMLR 42; *Re Enforcement of a European Arrest Warrant* [2006] 1 CMLR 36. In each case, this was on the basis that measures then in the third pillar did not at the time have to be applied over national measures.

> **2 BvE 2/08** *Gauweiler* v *Treaty of Lisbon*, Judgment of 30 June 2009
>
> 331. With Declaration no. 17 Concerning Primacy annexed to the Treaty of Lisbon, the Federal Republic of Germany does not recognise an absolute primacy of application of Union law, which would be constitutionally objectionable, but merely confirms the legal situation as it has been interpreted by the Federal Constitutional Court...
>
> 337. The Basic Law's mandate of integration and current European law laid down in the treaties demand, with the idea of a Union-wide legal community, the restriction of the exercise of the Member States' judicial power. No effects that endanger integration are intended to occur by the uniformity of the Community's legal order being called into question by different applicability decisions of courts in Member States. The Federal Constitutional Court has put aside its general competence, which it had originally assumed, to review the execution of European Community law in Germany against the standard of the fundamental rights of the German constitution..., and it did so trusting in the Court of Justice of the European Communities performing this function accordingly... Out of consideration for the position of the Community institutions, which is derived from international agreements, the Federal Constitutional Court could, however, recognise the final character of the decisions of the Court of Justice only 'in principle'...
>
> 340. The Basic Law aims to integrate Germany into the legal community of peaceful and free states, but does not waive the sovereignty contained in the last instance in the German constitution. There is therefore no contradiction to the aim of openness to international law if the legislature, exceptionally, does not comply with the law of international agreements – accepting, however, corresponding consequences in international relations – provided this is the only way in which a violation of fundamental principles of the constitution can be averted... The Court of Justice of the European Communities based its decision in *Kadi*[28]... on a similar view according to which an objection to the claim of validity of a United Nations Security Council Resolution may be expressed citing fundamental legal principles of the Community... The Court of Justice has thus, in a borderline case, placed the assertion of its own identity as a legal community above the commitment that it otherwise respects. Such a legal figure is not only familiar in international legal relations as reference to the ordre public as the boundary of commitment under a treaty; it also corresponds, at any rate if it is used in a constructive manner, to the idea of contexts of political order which are not structured according to a strict hierarchy. Factually at any rate, it is no contradiction to the objective of openness towards European law, i.e. to the participation of the Federal Republic of Germany in the realisation of a united Europe... if exceptionally, and under special and narrow conditions, the Federal Constitutional Court declares European Union law inapplicable in Germany.

The other reason why constitutional courts rarely allow national law to take precedence over EU law relates to a feature of the latter, which is that it rarely prompts judicial conflicts. For only a small proportion of EU law has traditionally been invoked before domestic courts. One study found that just five areas of law – taxation, sex discrimination, free movement of goods, free movement of workers and intellectual property – accounted for 61 per cent of all reported litigation in the United Kingdom, and that just five Directives accounted for 73 per cent of the Directives that were invoked in British courts.[29] There is a quid pro quo in which the primacy of EU law is almost always accepted but, in return, it has traditionally been confined to fields that amount to only a small proportion of what is invoked before domestic courts.

[28] Joined Cases C-402/05 P and C-415/05 P *Kadi and Al Barakaat International Foundation* v *Council* [2008] ECR I-6351.
[29] D. Chalmers, 'The Positioning of EU Judicial Politics within the United Kingdom' (2000) 23 *WEP* 169, 178–83.

5 THE QUALITY OF EU LEGAL AUTHORITY

(i) Pre-emption and different models of European integration

If the doctrine of primacy is concerned with the hierarchy between EU law and national law, it is the doctrine of pre-emption which governs the question of when there is a conflict and what the consequences of a conflict are for EU law and national law.[30] This question is not a black and white one and covers a spectrum of types of conflict. These can be categorised into three general categories.

- field pre-emption: this is where EU law is considered to have a jurisdictional monopoly over a field; national laws, irrespective of whether they conflict with EU measures, can only be enacted with the authorisation of EU law;
- rule pre-emption: there is shared jurisdiction over a policy field; national measures can be adopted but will be set aside if they conflict with EU law;
- obstacle pre-emption: Member States are free to adopt national measures but must not adopt measures which obstruct the effectiveness of EU policies.[31]

All three categories address the question of how EU law and national law are to be arranged when they govern a single policy field. The debate about their relationship to each other (e.g. when a conflict arises and the consequences of that conflict) cannot take place separately, therefore, from the substantive debate on the respective places of EU and domestic law in that policy field: namely the extent to which policy is to be determined by the European Union alone or the Member States separately. Pre-emption is therefore also a debate about the allocation of different types of EU intervention. This is reflected in Article 2 TFEU, which not only codifies the doctrine of pre-emption for the first time but also sets out the different types of competence in the Treaties and, with that, the degree of EU intervention in that field.

Article 2 TFEU

1. When the Treaties confer on the Union exclusive competence in a specific area, only the Union may legislate and adopt legally binding acts, the Member States being able to do so themselves only if so empowered by the Union or for the implementation of acts of the Union.
2. When the Treaties confer on the Union a competence shared with the Member States in a specific area, the Union and the Member States may legislate and adopt legally binding acts in that area. The Member States shall exercise their competence to the extent that the Union has not exercised its competence. The Member States shall exercise their competence again to the extent that the Union has decided to cease exercising its competence.

---

[30] R. Schütze, 'Supremacy Without Pre-emption? The Very Slowly Emergent Doctrine of Pre-emption' (2006) 43 *CMLRev.* 1023, 1033. For early analyses see M. Waelbroeck, 'The Emergent Doctrine of Community Pre-emption: Consent and Re-delegation' in T. Sandalow and E. Stein (eds.), *Courts and Free Markets: Perspectives from the United States and Europe*, vol. II (Oxford, Oxford University Press, 1982); E. Cross, 'Pre-emption of Member State Law in the European Economic Community: A Framework for Analysis' (1992) 29 *CMLRev.* 447.

[31] This categorisation is taken from the excellent analysis by Schütze, above n. 30, 1038.

3. The Member States shall coordinate their economic and employment policies within arrangements as determined by this Treaty, which the Union shall have competence to provide.
4. The Union shall have competence, in accordance with the provisions of the Treaty on European Union, to define and implement a common foreign and security policy, including the progressive framing of a common defence policy.
5. In certain areas and under the conditions laid down in the Treaties, the Union shall have competence to carry out actions to support, coordinate or supplement the actions of the Member States, without thereby superseding their competence in these areas. Legally binding acts of the Union adopted on the basis of the provisions in the Treaties relating to these areas shall not entail harmonisation of Member States' laws or regulations.

The provision addresses the different but related tasks of determining when there is a conflict between EU law and national law and the quality of EU intervention in a particular field. Pre-emption, as an instrument for precluding national legislation, is only really addressed in the first two paragraphs, where the Union has exclusive or shared competences.[32] Instead, most of the provision is about setting out the scope of Union policy-making within the different fields, namely whether there should be a common policy, an EU policy complementary to national policies or any EU policy at all. The provision, therefore, is not just concerned with setting out a relationship between EU and national law, but also provides five different models of integration.

Possibly because it has been addressed at length by policy-makers in the making of the Treaties, it is the only doctrine where national constitutional courts have not intervened and where the authority of Court of Justice judgments is completely uncontested.

(ii) Exclusive competence

In fields of exclusive competence, only the Union may legislate, with Member States being able to legislate only if authorised by the Union or to implement EU measures. From a national perspective, this is the most draconian of competences as it involves a complete surrender of jurisdiction to the Union. There is *a priori* field pre-emption by the Union in these fields. For that reason, the fields of exclusive competence are rather limited. They comprise: the customs union; the competition rules necessary for the functioning of the internal market; monetary policy for the Member States whose currency is the euro; the conservation of marine biological resources under the common fisheries policy; and the common commercial policy.[33]

The philosophy or model of integration here is one of dual federalism. The European Union and Member States are co-equals with a division of power into mutually exclusive spheres, with the Union governing some and Member States others.[34] It is worth considering why we

---

[32] This has led some to argue that concerns about competence creep by the Union are perhaps overstated in most areas of policy. S. Weatherill, 'Competence and Legitimacy' in C. Barnard and O. Odudu (eds.), *The Outer Limits of European Union Law* (Cambridge, Cambridge University Press, 2009).

[33] Article 3 TFEU.

[34] R. Schütze, 'Dual Federalism Constitutionalised: The Emergence of Exclusive Competences in the EC Legal Order' (2007) 32 *ELRev.* 3.

would wish for such a model. One argument is that the competence simply does not exist unless there is an exclusive competence. There can be no customs union, therefore, without a single external tariff or single monetary policy without a single currency. The challenge with this argument is that it does not explain why the Union should preclude Member States from legislating when it has not set up the policy. A customs union does not exist without a common external tariff, but that is the case whether there are twenty-seven different tariffs or there are no tariffs at all. Another argument is a functional one. It argues that exclusivity is necessary for the policy to function optimally. The Court of Justice, for example, argued that exclusivity was necessary for the common commercial policy as different trade policies would compromise defence of a common Union interest.[35] The challenge to such an argument is that it is the argument which justifies common action in the first place. EU action is justified on the basis that it would enable a policy to function better, but this, as an advantage, has to be balanced against other advantages such as local autonomy.[36]

The justification for this model is further compromised by the fact that the central difference between exclusive competences and shared competences is that the Union has not legislated. In both cases, if it has legislated, Member States are precluded from legislating. In the absence of EU legislation, Member States are not precluded from legislating. Under this model, they simply need Union authorisation. The grant of wide authorisations led, in practice, to a *modus vivendi* where competence is effectively shared, with many national regimes still in place in fields such as fisheries and the common commercial policy, albeit placed under a duty to justify themselves to the Union.[37]

(iii) Shared competence

Fields of shared competence allow Member States to legislate to the extent that the Union has not legislated. The model is one of cooperative federalism, in which a shared responsibility is granted to both actors to realise a common policy. There is no fixed division here but they work together to realise this common goal, with the balance of responsibilities determined by the terms, limits and presence of EU legislation.[38] This model of integration applies to: the internal market; social policy; cohesion policy; agriculture and fisheries, excluding the conservation of marine biological resources; environment; consumer protection; transport; trans-European networks; energy; freedom, security and justice; and common safety concerns in public health matters.[39]

The modalities of shared competence were set out in *Commission* v *United Kingdom*. Here, the Commission brought an action against a British requirement that cars could be driven on British roads only if they were equipped with dim-dip lights.[40] The relevant Directive did not impose this as a requirement and, furthermore, it provided that any car which met its stipulations should be able to be driven on the roads. The Court of Justice found the British

---

[35] Opinion 1/75 *Re Understanding on a Local Costs Standard* [1975] ECR 1355.
[36] For a critique see Schütze, above n. 34.
[37] For example, national export restrictions have been allowed to be maintained in the field of the common commercial policy on such wide grounds as public policy: Case C-70/94 *Werner* [1995] ECR I-3189.
[38] R. Schütze, 'Co-operative Federalism Constitutionalised: The Emergence of Complementary Competences in the EC Legal Order' (2006) 31 *ELRev.* 167, 168–9.
[39] Article 4(2) TFEU.
[40] Case 60/86 *Commission* v *United Kingdom (dim-dip lighting devices)* [1988] ECR 3921.

requirement to be illegal. It stated that the intention of the Directive was to regulate exhaustively the conditions for lighting devices on cars. As this was now exhaustively regulated by EU law, Member States were prohibited from imposing additional requirements.

This relationship makes sense where there is a pressing need for uniformity with the conditions governed by EU legislation. Within the context of the internal market, the maintenance of differing national regimes can lead to distortions of competition and trade restrictions, with the consequence that the harmonisation process would be robbed of much of its effect. Even there, such a rule does create a regime which is both monolithic and inflexible; in which it is impossible to maintain national provisions that impose higher standards; and in which the only way of adapting legislation to new risks and technologies is through amending the EU legislation in question.[41]

In the other fields of shared competence, the need for uniformity seems less pressing and the ethos of cooperative federalism is that the relationship between EU and national law should be fluid and not fixed *a priori*. Some concession for this is made in Article 4 TFEU which provides for parallel competences in the fields of research and development, space, development and humanitarian aid. In these fields, the Union will be able to develop legislation, but that legislation will not prevent Member States enacting their own legislation, provided, one assumes, that it does not conflict with the EU legislation.[42]

In addition, in a number of areas of shared competence special provision is made for minimum harmonisation.[43] Here, Member States are not prevented from enacting more restrictive provisions. Litigation focuses on when the national legislation is more restrictive. In *Deponiezweckverband Eiterköpfe*, a landfill operator was refused permission to fill two sites with waste.[44] The reason was that the waste exceeded German limits on the proportion of organic waste that could be disposed of in landfill sites. By contrast, the Directive (on which the German law was based) set limits only for biodegradable organic waste. The operator argued that the national legislation was, therefore, unlawful. The Court of Justice disagreed. It stated that what was central was that the German legislation pursued the same objective as the Directive, namely the limitation of waste going into landfill. Insofar as it set limits for a wider range of waste, it was more stringent than the EU Directive and was, therefore, permissible.

No mention is made, however, of minimum harmonisation in Article 2(2) TFEU and the Court will, undoubtedly, have to address its relationship to the more specific provisions that provide for it. More generally, a case can be made for minimum harmonisation even in other fields, where it is felt that there are strong national public interests that should be allowed to be protected. This can be done by the relevant legislative instrument, which can provide for specific measures to be exempted or for more restrictive national measures to be permitted. However, this is not the default position and there can often be legislative oversight, in that the relationship between a new EU measure and a particularly important domestic public interest is not considered.

---

[41] S. Weatherill, 'Beyond Preemption? Shared Competence and Constitutional Change in the European Community' in D. O'Keeffe and P. Twomey (eds.), *Legal Issues of the Maastricht Treaty* (London, Chancery, 1994) 13, 18–19.

[42] Article 4(3), (4) TFEU.

[43] Notably criminal justice (Article 82(2) TFEU); social policy (Article 153(2)(b) TFEU); public health legislation on organs and blood (Article 168(4)(a) TFEU); consumer protection (Article 169 TFEU); environment (Article 193 TFEU).

[44] Case C-6/03 *Deponiezweckverband Eiterköpfe* [2005] ECR I-2753.

The Court has been sensitive to this and has departed from its standard position in circumstances where EU legislation fails to protect public interests that were previously safeguarded by national legislation. It has, on occasion, interpreted EU legislation narrowly, so that it is not deemed to regulate the field covered by national law, thereby allowing the national legislation to remain in place.[45] If this is not possible, in extreme circumstances, the Court will refuse to disapply the national legislation. *Commission* v *Germany* is an example.[46] Member States were required by Directive 79/409/EEC to designate the most suitable habitats in their territory for certain species of wild bird. Once designated, these habitats were to be preserved and appropriate steps taken to prevent their deterioration. The Directive envisaged no circumstances in which measures could be taken to reduce the size of the special protection areas and there was no provision for minimum harmonisation, as the Directive was based on Article 352 TFEU, the flexibility provision. Germany wished to build a dyke across one of its designated areas in the Leybucht region. It argued this was necessary for good ecological reasons. The coast would be washed away otherwise. Despite there being no provision, the Court held that it could reduce the size of the special protection area. It could do this, the Court ruled, because, exceptionally, there was in this case a general interest (protection of the coastline), which was superior to that represented in the Directive. The Court therefore ruled that the dyke could be built but must involve the smallest disruption possible to the protection area that was necessary to secure the coastline.

(iv) Other fields of competence

The three final types of competence relate to fields where the Union has no formal legislative competence and where, in a conflict between EU measures and national laws, national law is to have formal precedence. Each prescribes a different level of intervention for the Union.

The coordination of economic and employment policies set out in Article 2(3) TFEU suggests that the competence of the Union is limited to that of aligning national policies. It is not there to generate an independent policy of its own but to prevent Member States disrupting each other with their own policies. By contrast, the Union is to have its own Common Foreign and Security Policy. This is explicitly mentioned by Article 2(4) TFEU and is emphasised by the Treaties in the statement that it is moving towards framing a common defence policy, suggesting that the latter is not to be common, whereas the former is.

A Common Foreign and Security Policy suggests an independent Union policy, but does not confer the right to exclusivity, so this EU foreign and security policy is to sit alongside national ones, but commonality implies that the latter must operate within its framework. This relationship is not to be governed by pre-emption or adjudication, however. Finally, fields of supporting, coordinating and supplementing action set out in Article 2(5) TFEU sit in between these two positions. The Union is to do more than align. Yet it is unclear to what extent this can emerge into a common, autonomous policy. Union action must not only align national performance, but also improve it by supporting and supplementing actions. This implies some autonomy in considering what this improvement might mean, but it does not suggest sufficient autonomy to provide for different policy directions or priorities.

---

[45] Examples of this include Case C-11/92 *R* v *Secretary of State for Health, ex parte Gallaher Ltd* [1993] ECR I-3545.
[46] Case C-57/89 *Commission v Germany (conservation of wild birds)* [1991] ECR I-883.

Whilst Article 2 TFEU is quite clear about the different levels of intervention involved in each type of competence, there are no checks to secure this. Thus, to take one example, whilst Union competence is confined to coordinating national employment policies, Article 145 TFEU indicates that it and the Member States have to work towards a coordinated strategy for employment and particularly for promoting a skilled, trained and adaptable workforce and labour markets responsive to economic change. Whilst this does not increase Union powers, it does suggest certain normative requirements that could be interpreted as the basis for an EU policy.

A further criticism is of the *a priori* decision that there should be no EU legislation in these fields. One can understand concerns about competence creep, but these are fields where the Union and Member States acknowledge a shared purpose, in which there will be common action. To exclude EU legislation is to exclude a policy tool which may, in exceptional circumstances, be very useful. It is a dogmatic thing to do and perhaps concerns about competence creep could have been more easily addressed through establishing exceptional procedures, which would put in place checks and balances to ensure that this does not take place.

6 LIMITS OF EU LEGAL AUTHORITY

(i) Doctrine of conferred powers

A feature of the sovereignty of EU law is that EU law has the power to determine the remit of its authority and over which fields of activity it exercises that authority.[47] This also goes to the substantive power of the Union. If it exercises sovereign authority in very confined, technical fields, its power is very different and it is a very different beast than if it exercises that power over wide-ranging and politically significant fields of activity. Indeed, part of the secret of the reception of *Van Gend en Loos* and *Costa* was that the former concerned a very arcane tax on a specialised product, whilst in the latter the Court did not strike down the Italian law because it found no violation of EU law.

The remit of EU legal authority is governed by the principle of conferred powers which is set out in Article 5 TEU.

Article 5 TEU

1. The limits of Union competences are governed by the principle of conferral...
2. Under the principle of conferral, the Union shall act only within the limits of the competences conferred upon it by the Member States in the Treaties to attain the objectives set out therein. Competences not conferred upon the Union in the Treaties remain with the Member States.

Alongside this, reference is made to the same principle in Article 1 TFEU.

Article 1(1) TFEU

This Treaty organises the functioning of the Union and determines the areas of, delimitation of, and arrangements for exercising its competences.

---

[47] Opinion 1/91 *Re European Economic Area* [1991] ECR I-6079.

The principle of conferred powers expresses two complementary ideals.

The first is that it is the Treaties and only the Treaties that determine the material remit of EU legal authority. These Treaties, rather than any other consideration, determine what the European Union can and cannot do. EU institutions cannot act beyond them because they wish to, but, equally, informal political accommodation by national governments cannot determine the limits of EU law. They have to act within the parameters of the Treaties in determining the remit of EU law.

However, Article 5(2) TEU adds a twist by stating that Union competences are not conferred by the Treaties alone but by the 'Member States in the Treaties'. This suggests that the Treaties govern the powers of the Union and the obligations, responsibilities and powers it imposes on the subjects of EU law. They do not, however, found the European Union in some more profound sense. The power to establish it, change it or terminate it rests with the Member States. This self-evident political point is given further force by the provisions on admission and exit of Member States. Whilst there is a Union procedure for admission involving the three legislative institutions and requiring consent by both the Parliament and the Council for admission, the Treaties make clear that the conditions of admission and any adjustments to the Treaties are a matter not for the EU institutions, but between the applicant state and the other Member States.[48] The situation where a state wishes to leave the Union is even more stark. Whilst there is again a Union procedure to be followed, the Treaties make clear that the power to withdraw is for that Member State alone in accordance with its constitutional requirements.[49]

More axiomatically, the idea that it is the Treaties which determine the remit of EU legal authority is the doctrine that has been most contested by national constitutional courts. Whilst they would all accept that the Union cannot act beyond the limits of the powers set by the Treaties, there is a general belief that it is the domestic constitutional settlement which determins the remit of EU law, as the limits of any transfer are, above all, a matter of domestic constitutional law. This was expressed by the German Constitutional Court in *Gauweiler* above[50] but was articulated most forcefully by the Polish Constitutional Tribunal in its judgment on Polish accession to the European Union, where it denied that EU law had competence to determine its own limits.

Polish Membership of the European Union (Accession Treaty), Polish Constitutional Court, Judgment K18/04 of 11 May 2005

Member States maintain the right to assess whether or not, in issuing particular legal provisions, the Community (Union) legislative organs acted within the delegated competences and in accordance with the principles of subsidiarity and proportionality. Should the adoption of provisions infringe these frameworks, the principle of the precedence of Community law fails to apply with respect to such provisions.

---

[48] Article 49 TEU.

[49] Article 50 TEU. See G. Majone, *Dilemmas of European Integration: The Ambiguities and Pitfalls of Integration by Stealth* (Oxford, Oxford University Press, 2005) 209–16, especially 214–16.

[50] 2 BvE 2/08 *Gauweiler* v *Treaty of Lisbon*, Judgment of 30 June 2009 at para. 233.

The remit of EU law is therefore a field in which the Court of Justice makes assertions that are subject to contradiction by national constitutional courts. The consequence is that the former is making a prima facie case for the authority of EU law, which is then policed by the latter.

The second ideal is that of limited government. The European Union is to operate only in specific, confined fields. This was given concrete expression in the Treaty of Lisbon, which set out a catalogue of powers for the Union. The central provision, Article 2 TFEU, set out above, enumerates the fields of activity in which the Union has legal competence, the features of its legal authority in each of these fields, and the degree of Union intervention that is to take place. Articles 3 to 7 TFEU then set out which fields of activity fall within which type of competence.[51] The intention is that by specifying the different competences and their qualities in such a specified and concrete form, there will be less possibility for competence creep. The Union will be confined by the details of these provisions.[52]

The principle of limited government is also one that requires these limits to be clearly defined. This has not been articulated by the Court of Justice but has begun to be picked up by national constitutional courts. The Czech Constitutional Court, in particular, has made something of it. In ruling on the compatibility of the Lisbon Treaty with the Czech Constitution,[53] it stated that the following principle guided the limits of the powers which could be transferred to the Union and could be exercised by the Union:

> 93. The guiding principle is undoubtedly the principle of inherent, inalienable, non-prescriptible, and non-repealable fundamental rights and freedoms of individuals, equal in dignity and rights; a system based on the principles of democracy, the sovereignty of the people, and separation of powers, respecting the cited material concept of a law based state, is built to protect them.

From this, it went on later in its judgment to state:

> 135. However, the constitutional law limits for the transfer of powers contained in…the Constitution also indicate the need for clearer delimitation (and thus also definiteness and recognizability) of the transferred powers, together with sufficient review, which the Czech Republic, as a sovereign state, can exercise over the transfer of powers.

This led the Czech Constitutional Court to express particular concern over one provision, Article 216 TFEU. This grants the Union treaty-making powers wherever, inter alia, this is necessary to realise one of its objectives within the framework of its powers. The Czech Constitutional Court considered this a very vague formulation, and expressed concern about its lack of clarity. However, it held that it was not sufficiently unclear for the Lisbon Treaty to be held unconstitutional.[54]

---

[51] For these see pp. 40–2 in Chapter 1 and pp. 206–11 above.

[52] For debate see S. Weatherill, 'Competence Creep and Competence Control' (2004) 23 *YEL* 1; P. Craig, 'Competence: Clarity, Conferral, Containment and Consideration' (2004) 29 *ELRev.* 323; F. Mayer, 'Competences – Reloaded? The Vertical Division of Powers in the EU after the New European Constitution' (2005) 3 *ICON* 493.

[53] Pl ÚS 19/08 *Treaty of Lisbon*, Judgment of 26 November 2008 http://angl.concourt.cz/angl_verze/doc/pl-19-08.php (accessed 25 August 2009).

[54] At paras 184–6.

(ii) Flexibility provision

The Treaties contain numerous powers which have been expressly conferred upon the European Union, but in extraordinarily wide and undefined terms. Article 114 TFEU, for example, allows the Union to adopt measures for the approximation of national laws, which have as their object the 'establishment and functioning of the internal market'. Similarly, Article 192 TFEU allows for an astonishingly broad array of measures to be adopted in the field of environmental protection. The most problematic of these provisions, however, is the 'flexibility' provision, Article 352 TFEU.

Article 352(1) TFEU

If action by the Union should prove necessary, within the framework of the policies defined by the Treaties, to attain one of the objectives set out in the Treaties, and the Treaties have not provided the necessary powers, the Council, acting unanimously on a proposal from the European Commission and after obtaining the consent of the European Parliament, shall adopt the appropriate measures. Where the measures in question are adopted by the Council in accordance with a special legislative procedure, it shall also act unanimously on a proposal from the Commission and after obtaining the consent of the European Parliament.

Article 352 TFEU is significantly wider than its predecessor, Article 308 EC. The latter granted legislative powers whenever this was necessary to realise *Community* objectives. The new provision, by contrast, with the absorption of the Community into the Union, applies to a more extensive, ambitious set of objectives: those of *Union* objectives. The new provision is particularly controversial given the latitude with which the earlier provision was interpreted.[55]

R. Schütze, *From Dual to Cooperative Federalism: The Changing Structure of European Law* (Oxford, Oxford University Press, 2009) 136–8

What are the objectives of the European Community? The Treaty did not clearly define what its 'objectives' are. Its opening provisions refer to the – similar but not identical – concepts of 'tasks' and 'activities'. One influential current in the European law literature during the 1970s suggested that Article 308 could only be used to fill gaps inside those areas in which the Community had already been given a *specific* competence. Outside the expressly enumerated fields, it was impossible to assume the existence of an 'objective' since the Community legislator was not meant to regulate those areas in the first place. According to this view, Article 308's scope was to find a limit in the jurisdictional boundaries set by the 'activities' of the Community – a position which linked the notion of 'objective' in Article 308 to the areas listed in Article 3 EC. A gap in the Treaty could be identified only by comparing the extent of the specific legal entitlements *within* a policy field and the *specific* aims of the Community policy within that area.

---

[55] Most particularly with the German Länder who saw EU law encroaching on their autonomy in a manner that not even the German federal authorities were able to do. 'Forderungen der Länder zur Regierungskonferenz 1996', Drucksache 667/95 (Beschluß), 15 December 1995, 12–21.

A second academic camp favoured a much wider application of Article 308. This position was premised on a two-layered understanding of the enumeration principle, which draws on a conceptual distinction between *jurisdiction* and *competence*. Article 308 could be used to fill any gap between the Treaty's *aims* and its *powers*. The perhaps most comprehensive manifesto of this expansionist rationale argued that Article 308 was 'designed to bridge the discrepancy between the Community's jurisdiction – as defined by its objectives – and a partial *or complete absence of powers for their realisation*'. The provision would create a 'gap-less system of competences for achieving all Community objectives'. The Community's jurisdiction and its competence would, thus, coincide. Wherever a matter fell into the scope of the Treaty, the Community would have a legislative competence – at least a subsidiary one under Article 308 EC. The Community's competence was the sum of its objectives...

By the end of the 1970s, Article 308 had been allowed to tap into the global objectives of the Community set out in Article 2 EC. Ever since, conceptual limits to the Community's competence became hard to identify. If the Community could act to promote – for example – closer relations between the states, such a competence would be devoid of internal boundaries as all *common* legislation will, by definition, diminish legislative disparities and thereby increase the legal proximity between the Member States.

The textbook illustration for the dramatic expansion of Europe's competence sphere on the basis of Article 308 EC is provided by the Community's environmental policy. Stimulated by the political enthusiasm of the Member States after the Paris Summit, the Commission and the Council faced the legal problem that environmental policy was not an official Community activity. There was therefore no specific legal title offered by the Treaty. The way out of this dilemma had been suggested in the 1972 Paris Communiqué. It called on the Community institutions to make the widest possible use of all provisions of the Treaties, including Article 308. The Member States had thus themselves proposed an extensive interpretation of the Treaties' objectives to cause a 'small revision' of the Treaty by means of Article 308.

This 'constitutional' spirit would overcome the Treaty's textual boundaries. It can be gauged by the following commentary, in which Usher neatly captured the interpretative climate of legislative free style that would replace the missing Treaty amendment:

'[T]hose responsible for drafting Community environmental legislation appear to have found their own route for solving this dilemma. By about 1980, as exemplified in Council Directive 80/68 on the protection of ground water against pollution by certain dangerous substances, the recitals justify making use of [Article 308 EC] on the grounds of the necessity for Community action in the sphere of the environmental protection and improvement of the "quality of life", a phrase which is found neither in the recitals to the Treaty nor in its general introductory provisions... Nevertheless, over the years, the phrase the 'raising of the standard of living' was linked to improving the "quality of life" and by the time this Directive was adopted it could be stated that legislation was justified in terms of [Article 308 EC] on the basis that it improved the quality of life, *as if that were a Treaty objective.*' [56]

---

[56] J. Usher, 'The Gradual Widening of European Community Policy on the Basis of Articles 100 and 235 of the EEC Treaty' in J. Schwarze and H. Schermers (eds.), *Structure and Dimensions of European Community Policy* (Baden Baden, Nomos, 1988) 32–3.

It is not simply that this provision has been interpreted ambitiously. It has also been used extensively. De Búrca and de Witte reported, in 2002, that it had, by that date, served as the legal basis for about 700 EC legal acts.[57] In like vein, Schütze has observed that the provision has traditionally been deployed for about 30 legislative acts per annum.[58] The veto granted to national governments present in Article 352 TFEU and in its predecessor, Article 308 EC, has not been a sufficient safeguard to curb its use. This begs the question as to whether the even wider provision in Article 352 TFEU is closer to a general law-making power with insufficient constraints.

The Treaty of Lisbon has responded to this with the introduction of a number of constraints. Some of these are procedural. An extra veto player has been added in the form of the European Parliament and Article 352(2) TFEU requires all proposals based on the provision to be brought to the attention of national parliaments for them to consider whether these comply with the subsidiarity principle.[59] Article 352 TFEU introduces some new substantive constraints as well.

Article 352(3), (4) TFEU

3. Measures based on this Article shall not entail harmonisation of Member States' laws or regulations in cases where the Treaties exclude such harmonisation.
4. This Article cannot serve as a basis for attaining objectives pertaining to the common foreign and security policy and any acts adopted pursuant to this Article shall respect the limits set out in Article 40(2) TEU.[60]

Article 2 TFEU, it will be remembered, lists three fields where the Union does not have legislative competence. One of these is Common Foreign and Security Policy.[61] Article 352(2) TFEU repeats this, although it is worth noting that many fields of foreign policy are governed by the TFEU and it does have power to harmonise in these fields. These include trade and financial relations, sanctions, development and humanitarian aid. It can also not be used in some fields. The other two fields are those areas of employment and economic policy where the Union can only adopt guidelines and fields of coordinating, supplementary and supporting action. Article 352 TFEU cannot therefore be used in the fields, for example, of protection of human health, industry, culture, tourism or education.

So what can Article 352 TFEU be used for? Declaration 41 to the Lisbon Treaty states that the objectives pursued by Article 352 TFEU and mentioned in that provision refer to the objectives in what is now Article 3(2), (3) and (5) TEU.[62]

---

[57] G. de Búrca and B. de Witte, 'The Delimitation of Powers between the EU and its Member States' in A. Arnull and D. Wincott (eds.), *Accountability and Legitimacy in the European Union* (Oxford, Oxford University Press, 2002) 217.

[58] R. Schütze, 'Organized Change towards an "Ever Closer Union": Article 308 EC and the Limits to the Community's Legislative Competence' (2003) 22 *YBEL* 79.

[59] For more on this see pp. 361–7.

[60] This is a curious paragraph as it states that 'the implementation of the policies listed in Articles 3–6 TFEU shall not affect the application of the procedures and the extent of the powers of the institutions set out in the Chapter on CFSP'. It does not refer to Article 352 TFEU but the intent is that Article 352 TFEU must not trespass on the procedures there.

[61] Article 2(4) TFEU.

[62] The Declaration is confusing as it refers to the numbering of the Treaties before they were renumbered. Under the old numbering Article 2 was what is now Article 3, and this is referred to in the original Declaration. There was also, confusingly, reference to an Article 3(5) which did not exist in either Treaty in the original numbering. This is assumed to be the current Article 3(5) TEU.

> ## Article 3(2), (3), (5) TEU
>
> 2. The Union shall offer its citizens an area of freedom, security and justice without internal frontiers, in which the free movement of persons is ensured in conjunction with appropriate measures with respect to external border controls, asylum, immigration and the prevention and combating of crime.
> 3. The Union shall establish an internal market. It shall work for the sustainable development of Europe based on balanced economic growth and price stability, a highly competitive social market economy, aiming at full employment and social progress, and a high level of protection and improvement of the quality of the environment. It shall promote scientific and technological advance.
>
>   It shall combat social exclusion and discrimination, and shall promote social justice and protection, equality between women and men, solidarity between generations and protection of the rights of the child…
> 5. In its relations with the wider world, the Union shall uphold and promote its values and contribute to the protection of its citizens. It shall contribute to peace, security, the sustainable development of the Earth, solidarity and mutual respect among peoples, free and fair trade, eradication of poverty and the protection of human rights, in particular the rights of the child, as well as to the strict observance and the development of international law, including respect for the principles of the United Nations Charter.

This is the first time that an attempt has been made to confine Article 352 TFEU, but it still allows for an aggressive deployment. The objectives are wide-ranging, including social justice, intergenerational equity, full employment and the eradication of poverty. Declaration 42 is intended, however, to prevent this. It states that Article 352 TFEU:

> cannot serve as a basis for widening the scope of Union powers beyond the general framework created by the provisions of the Treaties as a whole and, in particular, by those that define the tasks and the activities of the Union. In any event, this Article cannot be used as a basis for the adoption of provisions whose effect would, in substance, be to amend the Treaties without following the procedure which they provide for that purpose.

At one level, this Declaration does no more than reiterate an earlier ruling of the Court of Justice that the provision cannot be used to amend the Treaties.[63] Yet the use of such detailed language and the emphasis by twenty-seven governments carries with it a powerful message. The procedure is not to be used expansively, and far more thought must be given to the limits of Union competence in the course of its deployment.

It will be interesting to see how much heed is given to this by the Court of Justice. In *Kadi*, the Court considered the question of when a measure pursued objectives related to the operation of the internal market (now set out in Article 3(3) TFEU). The facts were that, following the 9/11 attacks, the UN Security Council adopted Resolutions requiring states to freeze all the assets and funds of anyone it believed to be associated with Osama Bin Laden. The list of persons whose assets were to be frozen was updated by a UN Sanctions Committee. In 2001, Kadi and Al Bakaraat were put on this list and their assets frozen. The Union implemented the Resolution by a Regulation. This was based on Article 352 TFEU and two provisions that are

---

[63] Opinion 2/94 *Re Accession of the Community to the ECHR* [1996] ECR I-1759.

now succeeded by Article 215 TFEU, which provides sanctions, including interrupting economic and financial relations, to be taken against non-EU states. The challenge was that these referred exclusively to relations with non-EU states, and there was no mention of sanctions on private actors in them.[64] Whilst the Regulation allowed funds for food, medical treatment, mortgages and professional fees, it was otherwise sweeping. It was essentially a Regulation that determined what property an individual could have and whether they could have any property at all. Kadi challenged this before the General Court, who upheld the Regulation. The Court of Justice allowed the appeal on the grounds that the Regulation violated fundamental rights. Another of the grounds of appeal was that the Union did not have the competence to adopt the Regulation. This was dismissed by the Court of Justice.

Joined Cases C–402/05 P and C–415/05 P *Kadi and Al Barakaat International Foundation* v *Council* [2008] ECR I–6351

224. In this regard it may be recalled that... Article 352 TFEU, being an integral part of an institutional system based on the principle of conferred powers, cannot serve as a basis for widening the scope of [Union] powers beyond the general framework created by the provisions of the [TFEU] as a whole.

225. The objective pursued by the contested regulation may be made to refer to one of the objectives of the [Union] for the purpose of Article 352 TFEU, with the result that the adoption of that regulation did not amount to disregard of the scope of Community powers stemming from the provisions of the [TFEU] as a whole.

226. Inasmuch as they provide for [Union] powers to impose restrictive measures of an economic nature in order to implement actions decided on under the CFSP, [Article 215 TFEU is] the expression of an implicit underlying objective, namely, that of making it possible to adopt such measures through the efficient use of a [Union] instrument.

227. That objective may be regarded as constituting an objective of the Community for the purpose of Article [352 TFEU]...

229. Implementing restrictive measures of an economic nature through the use of a [Union] instrument does not go beyond the general framework created by the provisions of the [TFEU] as a whole, because such measures by their very nature offer a link to the operation of the common market, that link constituting another condition for the application of Article [352 TFEU]...

230. If economic and financial measures such as those imposed by the contested regulation, consisting of the, in principle generalised, freezing of all the funds and other economic resources of the persons and entities concerned, were imposed unilaterally by every Member State, the multiplication of those national measures might well affect the operation of the common market. Such measures could have a particular effect on trade between Member States, especially with regard to the movement of capital and payments, and on the exercise by economic operators of their right of establishment. In addition, they could create distortions of competition, because any differences between the measures unilaterally taken by the Member States could operate to the advantage or disadvantage of the competitive position of certain economic operators although there were no economic reasons for that advantage or disadvantage.

---

[64] This has since been rectified by the Treaty of Lisbon which introduces an entirely new provision allowing sanctions to be taken against non-state actors, Article 75 TFEU.

The key part of the reasoning is in paragraph 226, where the Court identifies the measures as having an economic nature. This allows it to make the link with the operation of the internal market. Any economic measure by its nature can be said to affect the competitive position of operators by granting or denying them a benefit. Whether it in fact does so is another matter, and the test is a notional one. It is beyond credulity that freezing the assets of a couple of hundred individuals distorts competition in any significant way in the world's largest economic bloc.

If the link with the internal market is interpreted so creatively in *Kadi* and still found to fall within the doctrine of conferred powers, this begs the question what will fall within the other fields, such as social justice or the area of freedom, security and justice. Housing law could, for example, fall within the former, whilst family and criminal law are clearly related to the latter. This raises the paradox that fields not mentioned in the Treaties are more at risk from Union intrusion than fields where provision is made only for supporting, coordinating or supplementary actions, as Article 352 TFEU involvement in the latter is excluded.

(iii) Protection of national constitutional identities

It also suggests that the Union may operate under a form of conferred powers, but this is very far from the model of limited powers or a model for determining what is sacred from a national point of view and what is not, both matters of concern for national constitutional courts. This led the German Constitutional Court in its assessment of the Lisbon Treaty to state that Article 352 TFEU had relaxed the doctrine of conferred powers, as the provision served 'to create a competence which makes action on the European level possible in almost the entire area of application of the primary law'.[65] If it were used, the German Constitutional Court added, this would require both German parliamentary chambers to approve formally any proposal under it before Germany would be able to agree to a proposal under it.

Even this was not sufficient: the German Constitutional Court went on to rule that there were a series of fields where Article 352 TFEU could not be used.

---

2 BvE 2/08 *Gauweiler* v *Treaty of Lisbon*, Judgment of 30 June 2009

251. Even if due to the great successes of European integration, a joint European public that engages in an issue-related cooperation in the rooms of resonance of their respective states is evidently growing…, it cannot be overlooked, however, that the public perception of factual issues and of political leaders remains connected to a considerable extent to patterns of identification which are related to the nation-state, language, history and culture. The principle of democracy as well as the principle of subsidiarity… therefore require to factually restrict the transfer and exercise of sovereign powers to the European Union in a predictable manner particularly in central political areas of the space of personal development and the shaping of the circumstances of life by social policy. In these areas, it particularly suggests itself to draw the limit where the coordination of circumstances with a cross-border dimension is factually required.

---

[65] 2 BvE 2/08 *Gauweiler* v *Treaty of Lisbon*, Judgment of 30 June 2009, paras. 326–7.

252. What has always been deemed especially sensitive for the ability of a constitutional state to democratically shape itself are decisions on substantive and formal criminal law, on the disposition of the police monopoly on the use of force towards the interior and of the military monopoly on the use of force towards the exterior, the fundamental fiscal decisions on public revenue and public expenditure, with the latter being particularly motivated, inter alia, by social-policy considerations, decisions on the shaping of circumstances of life in a social state and decisions which are of particular importance culturally, for instance as regards family law, the school and education system and dealing with religious communities.

For the German Constitutional Court, the European Union cannot pass legislation in five central fields of domestic life: the central features of criminal law, the deployment of the use of force, central budgetary issues, the central issues of social policy, and culturally important fields, in particular religion, education and family life. This is the most extensive and most explicit list of national reserved powers ever put forward. It has already been criticised. For example, why not include civil law or monetary laws, both of which have historically been important to state formation?[66]

This might be because the judgment takes the current status quo as the point of departure. The position of the Union is taken as a given but the German Constitutional Court has fired a shot across the bows about the fields into which it must not enter. This has been presaged by two decisions discussed below from France and Italy, which, whilst less clearly formulated, suggest that it must not trespass either on national constitutional symbols or the scope of national constitutional rights.

The issue of constitutional symbols was addressed by a 2005 Decision of the French Constitutional Council, in which it had to rule on the compatibility of the Constitutional Treaty with the French Constitution. Article 1 of the French Constitution provides that France is a secular republic. This has been interpreted as banning any display of religious symbols in schools, including the wearing of the cross or the veil by pupils. Article II-70 of the failed Constitutional Treaty provided that anyone may manifest their religious belief in public. There seemed, therefore, to be a straightforward conflict. However, the French Constitutional Council stated that the EU provision was intended to have the same scope and meaning as Article 9 ECHR, which allows restrictions to be imposed on the display of religious belief on grounds, inter alia, of public policy. This has been interpreted to give considerable weight to the principle of secularism in national constitutional traditions, leaving national authorities a considerable margin of discretion as to how to reconcile freedom of religion with secularism. On this basis, the Constitutional Council considered there to be no conflict between the Constitutional Treaty and the French Constitution.[67]

---

[66] D. Halberstam and C. Möllers, 'The German Constitutional Court says "*Ja zu Deutschland!*"' (2009) 10 *German Law Journal* No. 8.

[67] *Re EU Constitutional Treaty and the French Constitution*, French Constitutional Court [2005] 1 CMLR 750. For a similar style of reasoning by the Greek Constitutional Court, albeit in relation to the public status of universities, see M. Maganaris, 'Greece: The Principles of Supremacy of Community Law – The Greek Challenge' (1998) 23 *ELRev.* 179.

Whilst nothing is explicitly stated about the limits of EU law, the French Constitutional Council adopted an aggressive and some might say counter-intuitive interpretation of a Treaty provision and indicated that the Court of Justice would have to follow it. It was, in other words, asserting its hegemony over the meaning of the French constitutional order, and indicating that it would only tolerate Court of Justice involvement insofar as it took French understandings of that order as a given.

The other field where the Union must not trespass is that of constitutional rights or fundamental rights. As we shall see in the next chapter, the Court of Justice has stated that it is competent to rule on fundamental rights questions that fall within the aegis of EU law, and for that purpose has developed an autonomous EU law of fundamental rights. Following the Treaty of Lisbon, nothing must be done to restrict or adversely affect the rights set out in national constitutions.[68]

National constitutional courts have contested the Court of Justice's position. In the 1970s, both the German and the Italian constitutional courts indicated that they would not apply provisions of EU law that failed to respect the fundamental rights and values set out in their respective national constitutions.[69] In more recent times, some leeway has been given to the Court of Justice with both the German and Czech Constitutional Courts stating that, as EU law now contained sufficient fundamental rights guarantees of its own, they would not actively review EU legislation provided this general level of protection was maintained.[70]

However, they have never gone so far as to suggest that Court of Justice judgments bound them on fundamental rights and there is no instance of a national constitutional court accepting a judgment by the Court suggesting it had misinterpreted its constitution. National constitutional courts' monopoly over interpreting the meaning of rights set out in their constitutions was most explicitly stated in *Admenta*, a ruling by the Italian State Council.[71] The judgment concerned a 1991 law that allowed pharmaceutical companies to own municipal pharmacies in Milan. This was ruled unconstitutional on the grounds that, inter alia, it violated article 32 of the Italian Constitution, protecting the right to health insofar as it generated a conflict of interest in those selling the medicines. It was argued that this restriction violated EU law and it clearly fell within the aegis of EU law.[72] However, the State Council stated that under Italian law there were protected areas of law that existed outside EU law and in which Italian law was sovereign. One of these areas was fundamental rights. Even if the matter conflicted with EU law, this was not an issue, as fundamental rights were reserved for national law. There was no need for a referral, therefore, as in its view the matter was decided exclusively by the Italian Constitution.

Perhaps the most interesting question is whether the protection of national constitutional identities involves not just limits on the exercise of EU powers but some scrutiny of the democratic qualities of the Union. This was addressed in most detail in Pl US 50/04.[73] The Czech

---

[68] European Union Charter of Fundamental Rights, Article 53. See p. 242.

[69] See, respectively, *Internationale Handelsgesellschaft* [1974] 2 CMLR 540 and *Frontini v Ministero delle Finanze* [1974] CMLR 386. This has also been stated by the Czech Constitutional Court, Pl ÚS 50/04 *Sugar Quota Regulation II*, Judgment 8 March 2006, http://angl.concourt.cz/angl_verze/doc/p-50-04.php (accessed 22 August 2009).

[70] (1986) 73 BVerfGE 339 *Wünsche Handelsgesellschaft (Solange II)* [1987] 7 CMLR 225; Pl ÚS 66/04 *European Arrest Warrant*, Judgment of 3 May 2006, http://angl.concourt.cz/angl_verze/doc/pl-66-04.php (accessed 22 August 2009).

[71] *Admenta and Others v Federfarma* [2006] 2 CMLR 47.

[72] It was eventually held to fall within EU law but be lawful in Case C-531/06 *Commission v Italy*, Judgment of 19 May 2009.

[73] Pl US 50/04 *Sugar Quota Regulation II*, http://angl.concourt.cz/angl_verze/doc/p-50-04.php.

Constitutional Court annulled a series of government measures organising the sugar market on the grounds that competence for these had been transferred to the Union. In the judgment, it reflected on the relationship between EU and Czech law:

> In the Constitutional Court's view, this conferral of a part of its [the Czech Republic's] powers is naturally a conditional conferral, as the original bearer of sovereignty, as well as the powers flowing therefrom, still remains the Czech Republic, whose sovereignty is still founded upon Art. 1 para. 1 of the Constitution of the Czech Republic. In the Constitutional Court's view, the conditional nature of the delegation of these powers is manifested on two planes: the formal and the substantive planes. The first of these planes concerns the power attributes of state sovereignty itself, the second plane concerns the substantive component of the exercise of state power. In other words, the delegation of a part of the powers of national organs may persist only so long as these powers are exercised in a manner that is compatible with the preservation of the foundations of state sovereignty of the Czech Republic, and in a manner which does not threaten the very essence of the substantive law-based state. In such determination the Constitutional Court is called upon to protect constitutionalism (Art. 83 of the Constitution of the Czech Republic). According to Art. 9 para. 2 of the Constitution of the Czech Republic, the essential attributes of a democratic state governed by the rule of law, remain beyond the reach of the Constituent Assembly itself.

This formulation, repeated subsequently,[74] not only qualifies EU legal sovereignty as something that cannot extinguish the core functions of the Czech state. The Czech Constitutional Court will also intervene whenever the Union does not act according to the principles of a 'democratic law-based state'. The basis for this is that the constitutional identity of the Czech state rests upon these foundations and there can be no derogation whatsoever from these principles.

This test is more multifaceted than that in *Gauweiler*. The latter utilises a dualist logic in which representative democracy exists only at the national level and the majority of power must, correspondingly, be exercised there. As a consequence, the European Union is permitted to exercise only limited powers. The relationship between the logics of these two spheres is unexplored, with the consequence that no reason is provided why any power should be transferred to the Union, as any transfer is necessarily undemocratic. To maintain the stability of the reasoning, important notions such as national representative democracy and limited powers are left untested. Something called 'representative democracy' is taken as a sine qua non for democracy and, in like vein, the Union's extensive powers are assumed to be limited.

The reasoning of the Czech Constitutional Court, by contrast, is a unitary one. The idea of a democratic law-based state is not so troubled by a transfer of power to another democratic law-based state. The constitutional state acts as a fulcrum that both mediates power between, and provides a check on, other levels of government – a central republican principle. In addition, the idea of a democratic law-based state becomes a constitutive principle of all government. It can call for the transfer of competences between levels of government where one level is unable to meet the needs of its constituents. It also acts as a basis for each to review the actions of the other according to a common legal ethical syntax. Defined in such broad terms, it is not confined to questions of fundamental rights, but covers all questions that trouble

---

[74] Pl US 66/04 *European Arrest Warrant*, http://angl.concourt.cz/angl_verze/doc/pl-66-04.php.

public lawyers: checks and balances, principles of representation, accountability, deliberation and participation.

7 THE FIDELITY PRINCIPLE

A requirement on Member States simply not to breach EU law would be insufficient to secure the full effectiveness of the EU legal system. States are different from private actors in that they must not only comply with the law but are also under a positive duty to secure law and order within their territories. All legal systems confer responsibilities upon public bodies to ensure that the law is generally applied, policed and accessible, and that there are sufficient remedies for breach of the law. Known in the United States as the 'fidelity principle', the requirement is that 'each level and unit of government must act to ensure the proper functioning of the system of governance as a whole'.[75] In EU law, the principle is set out in Article 4(3) TEU.

Article 4(3) TEU

Pursuant to the principle of sincere cooperation, the Union and the Member States shall, in full mutual respect, assist each other in carrying out tasks which flow from the Treaties.

The Member States shall take any appropriate measure, general or particular, to ensure fulfilment of the obligations arising out of the Treaties or resulting from the acts of the institutions of the Union.

The Member States shall facilitate the achievement of the Union's tasks and refrain from any measure which could jeopardise the attainment of the Union's objectives.

The provision applies not only to the Member States, but also to the EU institutions, which must cooperate with national bodies to secure the full effectiveness of EU law.[76] It introduces two important modifications on its pre-Lisbon predecessor, Article 10 EC. First, it introduces the idea of 'mutual respect'. This suggests a countervailing principle, under which each institution must not only assist each other but must not transgress upon the prerogatives of the other. This would imply, for example, that if the duty of cooperation currently imposes a responsibility on national courts not to assess a potentially anti-competitive practice being considered by the Commission,[77] there may be a corollary obligation on the Commission to leave to national authorities assessment of practices more appropriately considered by them.[78] Secondly, the duty of cooperation applies to tasks that 'flow from the Treaties'. This is a more open-ended concept than the previous duty, which merely applied to tasks arising from fulfilment of Treaty obligations. Notably, it suggests that the duty of cooperation applies to projects such as the Lisbon Agenda, whose ambitions both build upon and extend beyond the Treaties.

The fidelity provision carries both negative and positive obligations for the EU institutions. The negative obligation is that these must not simply not take measures that conflict with substantive EU laws but also must not adopt measures which obstruct the effectiveness of EU

---

[75] D. Halberstam, 'The Political Morality of Federal Systems' (2004) 90 *Virginia L Rev.* 101, 104.

[76] Case 2/88 *Zwartveld* [1990] ECR I-3365.

[77] Case C-344/98 *Masterfoods* v *HB Ice Cream* [2000] ECR I-11369.

[78] This is already established by the Commission Notice on cooperation within the network of competition authorities [2004] OJ C101/43, para. 8.

policies in more indirect ways. The positive obligation is to take a number of measures that contribute to the realisation of Union policies. These negative and positive obligations are now set out in turn.

The central negative obligation is that once EU institutions have indicated a point of departure for common action, Member States are under a duty to abstain from any measure which could frustrate realisation of the objectives in the common action. In the field of external relations, if the Commission has been authorised to conclude an international agreement, therefore, Member States cannot enter independent bilateral agreements of their own on the subject in hand with the non-EU state concerned unless this is done with the cooperation of the EU institutions.[79] Internally, this duty applies with most force to Directives which have come into force but whose deadline for transposition has not yet expired. Whilst national authorities have until the latter date to adopt implementing legislation, the Court has indicated that they are under a duty prior to that to abstain from any measure that would compromise the objectives of the Directive.[80] The national legislature cannot pass legislation that would conflict with the Directive, and national courts, where this choice is open to them under national law, are not free to adopt interpretations that would conflict with it.

The positive obligations are multiple. First, national institutions are required to secure legal certainty for EU law. The Court of Justice has stated that Member States must implement their obligations 'with unquestionable binding force and with the specificity, precision and clarity necessary to satisfy that principle'.[81] Mere administrative practice will not be enough to meet a state's obligations. Measures must be in place which, whilst not necessarily legislation, are sufficiently binding that they cannot be changed at will. Such measures must be public so that citizens are able to identify their rights.[82]

Secondly, Member States must actively police EU law. In *Commission* v *France*, French farmers launched a violent campaign targeting the importation of Spanish strawberries.[83] Their action involved threatening shops, burning lorries carrying the goods and blockading roads. The French government took almost no action either to stop these protests or to prosecute offences committed as a result of them. While the acts stopping the import of Spanish strawberries were performed by *private* actors – the farmers – and while the relevant provision of EU law, Article 34 TFEU, imposed obligations only on *states* not to prevent the free movement of goods, the Court ruled that France had breached EU law. The state was required to adopt all appropriate measures to guarantee the full scope and effect of EU law. In taking measures that were manifestly inadequate, France had failed to do this. The requirement to police EU law, however, is not an absolute one: a Member State does not have to police EU law if this would result in public disorder which it could not contain. Similarly, it must not police EU law in such a way that it violates fundamental rights and civil liberties.[84]

Thirdly, Member States must penalise infringements of EU law under conditions, both procedural and substantive, that are analogous to those applicable to infringements of national law

[79] Case C-266/03 *Commission* v *Luxembourg* [2005] ECR I-4805.
[80] Case C-212/04 *Adeneler and Others* v *ELOG (Ellinikos Organismos Galaktos)* [2006] ECR I-6057. This is dealt with in much more detail on pp. 298–300.
[81] Case C-159/99 *Commission* v *Italy (conservation of wild birds)* [2001] ECR I-4007.
[82] Case C-313/99 *Mulgan and Others* [2002] ECR I-5719. The principle of legal certainty also requires that if Member States amend a law to comply with EU law, the amending measure must have the same legal force as the original measures: Case C-33/03 *Commission* v *United Kingdom (VAT on road fuel)* [2005] ECR I-1865.
[83] Case C-265/95 *Commission* v *France (Spanish strawberries)* [1997] ECR I-6959.
[84] Case C-112/00 *Schmidberger* v *Republic of Austria* [2003] ECR I-5659.

of a similar nature and importance.[85] In addition, national courts must ensure that, irrespective of the situation for breaches of national law, penalties for breach of EU law are effective, proportionate and dissuasive.[86] In *Berlusconi*,[87]Advocate General Kokott set out what these criteria mean:

> 88. Rules laying down penalties are *effective* where they are framed in such a way that they do not make it practically impossible or excessively difficult to impose the penalty provided for and, therefore, to attain the objectives pursued by Community law.
>
> 89. A penalty is *dissuasive* where it prevents an individual from infringing the objectives pursued and rules laid down by Community law. What is decisive in this regard is not only the nature and level of the penalty but also the likelihood of its being imposed. Anyone who commits an infringement must fear that the penalty will in fact be imposed on him. There is an overlap here between the criterion of dissuasiveness and that of effectiveness.
>
> 90. A penalty is *proportionate* where it is appropriate (that is to say, in particular, *effective* and *dissuasive*) for attaining the legitimate objectives pursued by it, and also necessary. Where there is a choice between several (equally) appropriate penalties, recourse must be had to the least onerous. Moreover, the effects of the penalty on the person concerned must be proportionate to the aims pursued.

Finally, Member States are under a duty to notify the Commission if they have any problems applying or enforcing EU law. In this regard, they cannot use Commission reservations, conditions or objections as a basis for derogating from EU law.[88]

Article 4(3) TEU has been described as an overarching provision 'drawing all relevant institutions into the job of effectively sustaining [Union] policy'.[89] This is true. However, the provision extends beyond that. It sets out the expectations of what a state must be capable of to sustain the obligations of membership. It set outs responsibilities of comity but, above all, it sets out expectations about the commitments and resources that states must both have and commit – be these effective judicial systems, proactive, well-resourced, non-corrupt policing or a clear and universal rule of law – for membership of the European Union.

For all this, the institutional actors, be they administrative, legislative or judicial, see themselves and are seen by EU law as domestic actors. This is significant because it suggests that they are embedded in a series of domestic constraints and relationships that shape who they are and which they cannot ignore. The heavy reliance of the Union on national authorities to apply and enforce EU law has, moreover, been seen by comparative scholars as an important democratic counterweight, which can curb the Union imposing excessive or repressive demands on local actors.[90]

---

[85] Case C-180/95 *Draehmpaehl* v *Urania Immobilienservice* [1997] ECR I-2195. They must also penalise them in an equivalent manner to breaches of other EU law provisions which are of a similar importance. Case C-460/06 *Paquay* v *Société d'architectes Hoet & Minne* [2007] ECR I-8511.

[86] Case 68/88 *Commission* v *Greece* [1989] ECR 2965; Case C-326/88 *Hansen* [1990] ECR I-2911; Case C-167/01 *Kamer van Koophandel en Fabrieken voor Amsterdam* v *Inspire Art* [2003] ECR I-10155.

[87] Joined Cases C-387/02, C-391/02 and C-403/02 *Berlusconi and Others* [2005] ECR I-3565.

[88] Case C-105/02 *Commission* v *Germany* [2006] ECR I-9659.

[89] S. Weatherill, 'Beyond Preemption? Shared Competence and Constitutional Change in the European Community' in D. O'Keeffe and P. Twomey (eds.), *Legal Issues of the Maastricht Treaty* (London, Chancery, 1994) 31. See also J. Temple Lang, 'Community Constitutional Law: Article 5 EEC Treaty' (1990) 27 *CMLRev.* 645.

[90] G. Bermann, 'Taking Subsidiarity Seriously: Federalism in the European Community and the United States' (1994) 94 *Colum. L Rev.* 331, 399; E. Young, 'Protecting Member State Autonomy in the European Union: Some Cautionary Tales from American Federalism' (2002) 77 *NYU L Rev.* 1612, 1736.

This ethos seems to be shared by national constitutional courts who have indicated that domestic actors' institutional duties under EU law are subject to those placed on them by the constitution and must not violate the constitution. Normally, this is done not by the constitutional court challenging EU law directly but rather by stating that the domestic implementing measure is illegal. Two examples will suffice to illustrate this.

In the first, the Hungarian Constitutional Court considered a 2004 Hungarian law which fined anybody engaged in speculation in agricultural products in the period prior to Hungarian accession to the European Union.[91] Speculation was assumed to have taken place where agricultural contracts were entered into after 1 January 2004 or where there was a sudden jump in the size of a farmer's inventories. The law was based on an EU Regulation designed to prevent profiteering as a consequence of the subsidies that would accrue to Hungarian farmers from EU membership and which would be based on the volume of their production. The difficulty was that both the Regulation and the Hungarian law came into force on 1 May 2004 and, therefore, were retroactive in that they punished acts that were lawful at the time they were committed.

Notwithstanding the identical phrasing of the EU Regulation and the Hungarian statute, the Constitutional Court treated it as a wholly internal matter. The Court made no reference to EU law. Instead, the Hungarian law was found to violate Article 2(1) of the Hungarian Constitution on the grounds that it violated the principle of legal certainty as it punished activities retroactively and there was no reason that those engaging in the activity could have known at the time that it would be punished.

The second example concerns consideration by the German Constitutional Court of the German law implementing the European Arrest Warrant.[92] The latter provided for the quasi-automatic surrender by a Member State to another Member State of somebody sought by the latter for the commission of a series of listed crimes. The surrender had to take place even if it were a surrendering state's own national, even if there were joint jurisdiction over the alleged criminal activities and even if these would not have been a crime in the surrendering state. Article 16(2) of the German Basic Law prohibited extradition of a German national, but provided an exception for extradition to other EU states, provided this complied with other constitutional requirements.

The German Constitutional Court found the German implementing measure violated a number of these. It found the possibility that a German national could be surrendered for an offence committed on German territory unconstitutional as it excluded a citizen's right to associate herself with a free, democratic polity, whose laws she had violated. The Constitutional Court also found insufficient judicial safeguards in the measure, as it considered any surrendering court would need to have all the facts before it in each case to make a proper assessment and to consider whether the fundamental rights of the individual would be respected in the requesting state. Finally, the German Constitutional Court considered that there was a breach of the principle of non-retroactivity insofar as a German could now be tried for something done in Germany which at the time was not illegal under German law.

---

[91] Decision 17/04 (V. 25) AB, www.mkab.hu/en/enpage3.htm (accessed 25 August 2009).
[92] *Re Constitutionality of German Law Implementing the Framework Decision on a European Arrest Warrant* [2006] 1 CMLR 16.

Both the German and Hungarian Constitutional Courts do not question directly the supremacy of EU law. Yet the domestic measures in both cases, particularly the Hungarian, accurately reflected the EU measure. In both cases, the constitutional courts refused to look at the wider EU context and the effects its ruling would have on the general operation of EU law. In this, there was an implicit suggestion that if EU law did not take account of the principles important to them, they would not have much regard for it. As Komárek has suggested, this debate is not, however, just about how amenable national constitutional courts are to EU law.[93] There is another issue, which is the distortion of institutional relations within the domestic settlement. In the Hungarian case, there was the problem of the legislature riding roughshod over both private autonomy and the power of judicial review. In the German case, there was the issue of German courts extraditing without sufficient regard to the relationship between German citizens and the political settlement. The defiance by the constitutional courts was therefore as much about protecting the checks and balances within their constitutional settlement as it was about asserting hegemony.

FURTHER READING

A. Albi, *EU Enlargement and the Constitutions of Central and Eastern Europe* (Cambridge, Cambridge University Press, 2005)

A. v. Bogdandy and J. Bast, 'The European Union's Vertical Order of Competences: The Current Law and Proposals for its Reform' (2002) 39 *Common Market Law Review* 227

M. Claes, *The National Courts' Mandate In the European Constitution* (Oxford and Portland, Hart, 2005)

M. Dani, 'Constitutionalism and Dissonances: Has Europe Paid Off its Debt to Functionalism?' (2009) 15 *European Law Journal* 324

J. Komárek, 'European Constitutionalism and the European Arrest Warrant: In Search of the Limits of "Contrapunctual Principles"' (2007) 44 *Common Market Law Review* 9

D. Kostakopoulou, 'Floating Sovereignty: A Pathology or Necessary Means of State Evolution' (2002) 22 *Oxford Journal of Legal Studies* 135

M. Kumm, 'The Jurisprudence of Constitutional Conflict: Constitutional Supremacy in Europe Before and After the Constitutional Treaty' (2005) 11 *European Law Journal* 262

R. Schütze, *From Dual to Cooperative Federalism: The Changing Structure of European Law* (Oxford, Oxford University Press, 2009)

N. Walker (ed.), *Sovereignty in Transition* (Oxford and Portland, Hart, 2003)

J. Weiler, 'Does Europe Need a Constitution? Demos, Telos and the Maastricht German Decision' (1995) 1 *European Law Journal* 219

---

[93] J. Komárek, 'European Constitutionalism and the European Arrest Warrant: In Search of the Limits of "Contrapunctual Principles"' (2007) 44 *CMLRev.* 9. For debate on this case law see also O. Pollecino, 'European Arrest Warrant and Constitutional Principles of the Member States: A Case Law-Based Outline in an Attempt to Strike the Right Balance between Legal Systems' (2008) 9 *German Law Journal* No. 10.

6

Fundamental Rights

CONTENTS

1 INTRODUCTION

This chapter considers EU fundamental rights law. It is organised as follows.

Section 2 considers Article 6 TEU, which sets out three dimensions to EU fundamental rights law. First, it describes a tension, because it grants the European Union an autonomous fundamental rights law, but these rights are to be derived from external sources, namely national constitutional traditions, the European Convention for the Protection of Human Rights and Freedoms (ECHR) and the European Union Charter of Fundamental Rights and Freedoms ('Charter'). Secondly, Article 6 TEU prescribes an institutional sensitivity to EU fundamental rights law. It is not to be used to enlarge Union competences. Finally, Article 6 TEU places the Union more firmly within the European human rights order by providing for the Union to accede to the ECHR.

Section 3 considers the rights contained within EU fundamental rights law. On the one hand, there are general principles of law derived from national constitutional traditions and the ECHR. These are non-codified and comprise civil rights, rights of defence, economic rights law and principles such as non-discrimination, legal certainty and proportionality. On the other, there is the Charter, which contains six types of right regarded as fundamental: rights to human dignity, freedoms, equality rights, solidarity rights, rights to justice and citizenship rights. Though wide-ranging, the Charter does not include certain important social rights. It makes a distinction between rights and principles, with the latter being judicially enforceable only in relation to legislation implementing them.

Section 4 considers the level of protection offered by EU law to the holders of these rights. Historically, as the ethos for protection of EU fundamental rights law has been unclear, debate has been shrouded in uncertainty about what level of protection would be appropriate. In recent years, there has been a formalistic deference to the norms set by national constitutions or the ECHR. This fails to question the processes of these settlements sufficiently and has resulted in the Court of Justice not engaging sufficiently with the ethical issues surrounding some of the cases.

Section 5 considers the institutions bound by EU fundamental rights law. EU institutions are bound by it but Member States are only bound where they implement Union measures. As this test does not cover all national measures, it gives actors the possibility to arbitrage by bringing measures within the aegis of EU law to test their fundamental rights ramifications. The other challenge of this test is that it is differently formulated from the one prior to the Lisbon Treaty, which covered national measures falling within the field of some areas of EU law. The application of EU fundamental rights law to national measures is one of the most contentious fields of EU law, because it requires the Union to be a 'community of values'. Yet, if national laws depart from these common values, pivotal choices made by national actors are called into question. The most wide-ranging challenge by national actors is the Protocol on the Application of the Charter to Poland and the United Kingdom, which provides that the Charter does not extend the ability of any court to find any of their laws incompatible with fundamental rights.

Section 6 considers the accession of the European Union to the ECHR, which was made possible by the Lisbon Treaty. Historically, this debate has taken place within the context of the Union becoming a more central actor for the protection of fundamental rights. The Treaties seek to restrict this by stating that accession will not affect Union competences or national derogations from the ECHR. The current level of protection demanded by the ECHR of the Union is lower than that for states, meaning a breach will only be found where the actions are manifestly deficient. It is to be seen whether accession will change this.

Section 7 considers the establishment of the Union fundamental rights policy. Historically, EU law has only required actors not to violate fundamental rights rather than to promote them. This was long argued to be insufficient and in 2007, a European Union Fundamental Rights Agency was established. This has the power to publish reports, collect data on fundamental rights and to issue opinions for the EU legislature. However, its remit to do this has been restricted by the EU institutions.

2 FUNDAMENTAL RIGHTS AND THE SCHEME OF THE TREATIES

Article 2 TEU states that respect for human dignity, freedom, equality and human rights are the values on which the European Union is founded. Notwithstanding this foundational status, references to fundamental rights are scarce and oblique in the Treaties. There is no catalogue of rights nor any direct statement on the legal bite of these rights or which actors are bound by them. However, the central provision is Article 6(1) TEU.

Article 6 TEU

1. The Union recognises the rights, freedoms and principles set out in the Charter of Fundamental Rights of the European Union of 7 December 2000, as adopted at Strasbourg, on 12 December 2007, which shall have the same legal value as the Treaties.

   The provisions of the Charter shall not extend in any way the competences of the Union as defined in the Treaties.

   The rights, freedoms and principles in the Charter shall be interpreted in accordance with the general provisions in Title VII of the Charter governing its interpretation and application and with due regard to the explanations referred to in the Charter, that set out the sources of those provisions.

2. The Union shall accede to the European Convention for the Protection of Human Rights and Fundamental Freedoms. Such accession shall not affect the Union's competences as defined in the Treaties.

3. Fundamental rights, as guaranteed by the European Convention for the Protection of Human Rights and Fundamental Freedoms and as they result from the constitutional traditions common to the Member States, shall constitute general principles of the Union's law.

This provision is, above all, a reference point marked by a series of allusions, all of which require further explanation.

The first point to note about Article 6 TEU is that EU fundamental rights law is based on a paradox. On the one hand, the sources for its fundamental rights come from outside the Treaty. Article 6(1) TEU refers to the Charter as one source and two further sources are provided in Article 6(3) TEU, the ECHR and national constitutional traditions. The norms governing the interpretation and application are also externally inspired. The third sentence of Article 6(1) TEU makes clear that these norms, partially at least, are to be governed by the principles set out in Chapter VII of the Charter. On the other hand, these instruments are not constitutive of the fundamental rights in EU law. They 'recognise', 'guarantee' or 'set out' these rights. These rights are seen as having a separate independent existence so that these instruments neither provide an exhaustive catalogue nor determine the formal legal status. This is done by EU law, which gives these rights, freedoms and principles (rather than the instruments in which they are contained) the same legal status as the Treaties.

The tension between this formal autonomy and substantive dependence was set out in *Kadi*. As will be remembered,[1] Kadi had been placed on a list by a UN Security Council Committee that alleged he was linked to Al Qaeda and severely curtailed the financial resources available to him. As a matter of international law, the UN Security Council Resolution establishing this

---

[1] See pp. 217–19.

Committee was binding on the European Union. Kadi argued, successfully, that it violated his fundamental rights. In particular he claimed that his being placed on the list violated the right to be heard and the right to effective judicial protection, as he had no way of challenging the basis on which he had been placed there.

Joined Cases C–402/05 P and C–415/05 P *Kadi and Al Barakaat International Foundation v Council* **[2008] ECR I-6351, Advocate General Poiares Maduro, Opinion of 23 January 2008**

44. …the Court should be mindful of the international context in which it operates and conscious of its limitations. It should be aware of the impact its rulings may have outside the confines of the [Union]. In an increasingly interdependent world, different legal orders will have to endeavour to accommodate each other's jurisdictional claims. As a result, the Court cannot always assert a monopoly on determining how certain fundamental interests ought to be reconciled. It must, where possible, recognise the authority of institutions, such as the Security Council, that are established under a different legal order than its own and that are sometimes better placed to weigh those fundamental interests. However, the Court cannot, in deference to the views of those institutions, turn its back on the fundamental values that lie at the basis of the [EU] legal order and which it has the duty to protect. Respect for other institutions is meaningful only if it can be built on a shared understanding of these values and on a mutual commitment to protect them. Consequently, in situations where the [Union's] fundamental values are in the balance, the Court may be required to reassess, and possibly annul, measures adopted by the [EU] institutions, even when those measures reflect the wishes of the Security Council.

The Court

281. In this connection it is to be borne in mind that the [Union] is based on the rule of law, inasmuch as neither its Member States nor its institutions can avoid review of the conformity of their acts with the basic constitutional charter, the [Treaties], which established a complete system of legal remedies and procedures designed to enable the Court of Justice to review the legality of acts of the institutions…

282. It is also to be recalled that an international agreement cannot affect the allocation of powers fixed by the Treaties or, consequently, the autonomy of the [EU] legal system, observance of which is ensured by the Court by virtue of the exclusive jurisdiction conferred on it by Article [19(3) TEU], jurisdiction that the Court has, moreover, already held to form part of the very foundations of the [Union]…

283. In addition, according to settled case law, fundamental rights form an integral part of the general principles of law whose observance the Court ensures. For that purpose, the Court draws inspiration from the constitutional traditions common to the Member States and from the guidelines supplied by international instruments for the protection of human rights on which the Member States have collaborated or to which they are signatories. In that regard, the ECHR has special significance…

284. It is also clear from the case law that respect for human rights is a condition of the lawfulness of [EU] acts… and that measures incompatible with respect for human rights are not acceptable in the [Union]…

285. It follows from all those considerations that the obligations imposed by an international agreement cannot have the effect of prejudicing the constitutional principles of the [Treaties], which include the principle that all [Union] acts must respect fundamental rights, that respect constituting a condition of their lawfulness which it is for the Court to review in the framework of the complete system of legal remedies established by the [Treaties].

There is a subtle but important difference between the reasoning of the Court of Justice and the Advocate General. The Court's position is highly formal. It emphasises both the autonomy of EU fundamental rights law and its central contribution to the idea of legality in the Union. The Advocate General, by contrast, looks at the substantive interplay of norms. He acknowledges that the Court has to engage with a variety of external sources to understand what fundamental values are, whilst taking responsibility for delivering a statement of EU law.

The second point to note about Article 6 TEU is its institutional sensitivity. The second sentence of Article 6(1) TEU states that the Charter shall not extend in any way the competences of the Union as defined in the Treaties. The Member States are aware that assertions of values by supreme courts in federal systems are not just statements about the value of these values, but also claims to a central competence to regulate them. Statements by the US Supreme Court allowing abortion in certain circumstances or prohibiting segregation in education are thus not just articulating political values. They are regulating abortion or certain dimensions of education at the expense of local authorities. There is therefore a particular sensitivity to judicial activism here. This is not merely expressed in general terms in Article 6 TEU but, as we shall see, certain Member States have a particular sensitivity over certain values being asserted aggressively against them.

The third feature to emerge from Article 6 TEU is the presence of external constraints on EU fundamental rights law. The requirement in Article 6(2) TEU for the Union to accede to the ECHR is a new requirement. It imposes an external accountability and, arguably, the presence of a higher law of fundamental rights. If the Court of Justice is to comply with the judgments of the European Court of Human Rights, this raises questions both about its relationship to that court and the relationship between EU law and the ECHR. Accession to the ECHR has other implications, however. Until now only states could accede to the ECHR. This possibility existed not only because states, with their considerable powers, can easily violate fundamental rights, but also because they allocate values. They set out a standard of what is right and wrong within a society. Allowing the Union to accede to the ECHR is therefore a double admission. It is a body that takes decisions, which increasingly affect human rights, but it is also a body that is increasingly involved in setting out visions of what is right and wrong for EU citizens.

3 THE SUBSTANCE OF EU FUNDAMENTAL RIGHTS LAW

Although it is the Charter which is mentioned first in Article 6 TEU, while national constitutional traditions and the ECHR are mentioned almost only as an afterthought as general principles of law in Article 6(3) TEU, the Charter builds on these, refers to them and is to be interpreted in the light of them.

(i) National constitutional traditions and the ECHR in EU fundamental rights law

The original Treaties contained no system of fundamental rights protection. The relatively limited scope of the EEC Treaty, with its focus on instituting a common market, provided limited opportunities for possible conflicts. If they did arise, states expected their national constitutions to be the best guarantee of protection of fundamental rights. The early case law of the Court of Justice reflected this line of thinking. In a series of judgments through to the mid-1960s, it refused to countenance arguments that the EU institutions had violated some right protected in national constitutions.[2] The Treaties contained no reference to these fundamental rights and, in the light of this, the Court resisted implications that it was responsible for the protection of these rights.

These assumptions were changed by *Van Gend en Loos* and *Costa* v *ENEL*.[3] The supremacy of EU law meant that national constitutional provisions could no longer be used to safeguard fundamental rights in all circumstances, as any EU legal provision took precedence over them. These judgments not only created this lacuna in protection, but also begged the question as to why this should be so. Even if the common market were to bring many benefits to the citizens of Europe, these were certainly not sufficient to legitimate the Treaties to such a degree that its citizens would be willing for it to exercise constitutional authority over them.[4] Human rights have, by contrast, since the Second World War, acquired 'symbolic pre-eminence' as an instrument for polity legitimation. They were a particularly powerful symbol in the context of European integration, for they were something archetypically European. They represented a common heritage, with the Union, as a self-styled European organisation, as the natural guardian of that heritage.[5] Protection of human rights offered a legitimation for EU constitutional authority that market integration did not.

A softening of the Court's case law emerged towards the end of the 1960s. In *Van Eick*, the Court stated that those administering EU institution staff disciplinary procedures were 'bound in the exercise of [their] powers to observe the fundamental principles of the law of procedure'.[6] The Court was more explicit in *Stauder*.[7] The case concerned a Commission Decision designed to reduce EU butter stocks, which allowed butter to be sold at a lower price to people who were on certain social welfare schemes. In order to claim the butter, the beneficiaries had to produce a coupon which, in the German and Dutch version of the Decision, had to indicate their name, whereas this was unnecessary in the French and Italian versions. Stauder, a German national, challenged the requirement that his name be on the coupon, claiming that it violated his right to respect for privacy. The Court indicated that the more liberal French and Italian version should be adopted because in this way the Decision would not prejudice the 'fundamental human rights enshrined in the general principles of [EU] law and protected by the Court'. In other words, if there were two legitimate interpretations of an EU law provision, the Court would adopt the one that did not violate fundamental rights.

Human rights still occupied no more than a second-order status. *Van Eick* and *Stauder*, whilst stressing the consonance between EU law and established notions of fundamental rights, did not grant these fundamental rights an organic status which would allow them to be used both as a basis for steering the actions of EU authorities and as a ground for judicial review. National courts were still, therefore, left with a choice between refusing to apply EU law and neglecting fundamental liberties enshrined in their national constitutions.[8] The matter came to

---

[2] Case 1/58 *Stork* v *High Authority* [1959] ECR 17; Joined Cases 36/59–38/59 and 40/59 *Geitling* v *High Authority* [1960] ECR 423; Case 40/64 *Sgarlata* v *Commission* [1965] ECR 215.

[3] Case 26/62 *Van Gend en Loos* v *Nederlandse Administratie der Belastingen* [1963] ECR 1; Case 6/64 *Costa* v *ENEL* [1964] ECR 585.

[4] A. Williams, *EU Human Rights Policies: A Study in Irony* (Oxford, Oxford University Press, 2004) 139.

[5] *Ibid.* 133–4.

[6] Case 35/67 *Van Eick* v *Commission* [1968] ECR 329.

[7] Case 29/69 *Stauder* v *City of Ulm* [1969] ECR 419.

[8] U. Scheuner, 'Fundamental Rights in European Community Law and in National Constitutional Law' (1975) 12 *CMLRev.* 171, 173–4.

a head in *Internationale Handelsgesellschaft*. There, a Regulation had awarded Internationale Handelsgesellschaft, a German trading concern, a licence to export maize on condition that it put down a deposit which would be forfeited if it failed to export the maize within the time stipulated in the licence. The latter failed to export the maize and, upon forfeiture of the deposit, challenged the Regulation before the administrative court in Frankfurt. The administrative court considered that the Regulation violated the provisions in the German Constitution protecting the freedom to trade. It therefore asked the Court of Justice whether the Regulation was valid.

Case 11/70 *Internationale Handelsgesellschaft v Einfuhr- und Vorratstelle für Getreide und Futtermittel* [1970] ECR 1125

3. Recourse to the legal rules or concepts of national law in order to judge the validity of measures adopted by the institutions of the [Union] would have an adverse effect on the uniformity and efficacy of [EU] law. The validity of such measures can only be judged in the light of Community law. In fact, the law stemming from the Treaty, an independent source of law, cannot because of its very nature be overridden by rules of national law, however framed, without being deprived of its character as [EU] law and without the legal basis of the [Union] itself being called in question. Therefore the validity of [an EU] measure or its effect within a Member State cannot be affected by allegations that it runs counter to either fundamental rights as formulated by the constitution of that State or the principles of a national constitutional structure.

4. However, an examination should be made as to whether or not any analogous guarantee inherent in [EU] law has been disregarded. In fact, respect for fundamental rights forms an integral part of the general principles of law protected by the Court of Justice. The protection of such rights, whilst inspired by the constitutional traditions common to the Member States, must be ensured within the framework of the structure and objectives of the [Union]...

The judgment establishes that fundamental rights form an integral part of EU law, although the Court went on to rule that there had been no violation of the fundamental right to trade in this instance. However, the genesis of EU law fundamental rights law was tainted due to its emergence within the context of a dispute about the supremacy of EU law. Disgruntled, Internationale Handelsgesellschaft pursued the matter further, before the German Constitutional Court.[9] The latter noted that at that time there was no catalogue of fundamental rights in EU law and the European Parliament did not have legislative powers. This prevented any assessment by it as to whether fundamental rights protection in EU law was similar to that within the German Basic Law. In the light of this, it ruled that in the case of a conflict between EU law and fundamental rights set out in the Basic Law, it would be the latter and not EU law that would take precedence. This challenge to the supremacy of EU law was supported by the Italian Constitutional Court, which also held that supremacy of EU law would not prevail where EU law violated fundamental principles of the Italian Constitution (including fundamental rights).[10]

Although apparently confrontational, the decisions of the German and Italian Constitutional Courts allowed the possibility of a dialectic to emerge. The implication of their judgments was

[9] *Internationale Handelsgesellschaft v Einfuhr- und Vorratstelle für Getreide und Futtermittel* [1974] 2 CMLR 540.
[10] *Frontini v Ministero delle Finanze* [1974] 2 CMLR 372.

that if EU law developed a sufficiently rigorous fundamental rights doctrine of its own, they would not apply their own constitutional norms, for the threat to fundamental rights would be averted by EU law putting in place its own checks, so that a conflict should (in theory at least) never happen. By 1986, in *Solange II*,[11] the German Constitutional Court considered this to be the case and reversed its approach to the review of Union acts in the light of fundamental rights. Though no catalogue of fundamental rights had yet been established, the German Constitutional Court considered that the protection of fundamental rights granted by the Court of Justice had reached a level that substantially coincided with that granted by the German Basic Law. As long as that was the case, the German Constitutional Court would no longer review the validity of specific Union acts in the light of national fundamental rights.

This has led to the accusation that the motivations for the development of fundamental rights were not those relating to protection of human dignity, but ulterior ones. They were to do with inducing national constitutional courts to accept the supremacy of EU law and, in particular, the ideological objectives of market integration.[12] Member States concerned about the liberalisation of the economy were to be soothed by the parallel development of a culture of rights in EU law.[13] Little direct evidence is offered to support this analysis, and it would not explain why the Court of Justice has looked at sources other than national constitutions to determine the content of EU fundamental rights law. In *Nold*, the Court stated that international human rights treaties were another source of fundamental rights in EU law.[14] Following *Nold*, the Court has recognised a number of human rights treaties as sources. Most importantly, in *Rutili*, it referred to the ECHR.[15] Whilst the Court has indicated that the ECHR has a particular status,[16] it has also looked broadly and in an open-ended way to incorporate other international human rights treaties as sources of fundamental rights: the International Covenant on Civil and Political Rights,[17] the UN Convention on the Rights of the Child,[18] the Community Charter of Fundamental Social Rights of Workers, and the European Social Charter.[19]

Relying on national constitutional traditions and international human rights treaties, the Court has recognised a number of categories of different rights.

Civil rights   These include the right to respect for family and private life;[20] protection of the child;[21] freedom of religion;[22] freedom of trade union activity;[23] freedom of expression;[24]

---

[11] Decision of the Bundesverfassungsgericht of 22 October 1986, *Wünsche Handelsgesellschaft (Solange II)* [1987] 3 CMLR 225.

[12] J. Coppell and A. O'Neill, 'The European Court of Justice: Taking Rights Seriously' (1992) 29 *CMLRev.* 669.

[13] J. Weiler and N. Lockhart, '"Taking Rights Seriously" Seriously: The European Court and Fundamental Rights Jurisprudence, Part I' (1995) 32 *CMLRev.* 51; J. Weiler and N. Lockhart, '"Taking Rights Seriously" Seriously: The European Court and Fundamental Rights Jurisprudence, Part II' (1995) 32 *CMLRev.* 579.

[14] Case 4/73 *Nold* v *Commission* [1974] ECR 491.

[15] Case 36/75 *Rutili* v *Ministre de l'Intérieur* [1975] ECR 1219.

[16] Case C-299/95 *Kremzow* v *Austria* [1997] ECR I-2629.

[17] Case 374/87 *Orkem* v *Commission* [1989] ECR 3283.

[18] Case C-540/03 *Parliament* v *Council (family reunification)* [2006] ECR I-5769.

[19] Case 24/86 *Blaizot* v *Belgium* [1988] ECR 379; Case 149/77 *Defrenne II* [1978] ECR 1365.

[20] Case 136/79 *National Panasonic* [1980] ECR 2033; Case C-249/86 *Commission* v *Germany (migrant workers)* [1989] ECR 1263.

[21] Case C-540/03 *Parliament* v *Council (family reunification)* [2006] ECR I-5769; Case C-244/06 *Dynamic Medien Vertriebs GmbH* v *Avides Media AG* [2008] ECR I-505.

[22] Case 130/75 *Prais* [1976] ECR 1589.

[23] Case 175/73 *Union Syndicale* [1974] ECR 917.

[24] Case C-260/89 *Elliniki Radiophonia Tiléorassi AE and Others* v *Dimotiki Etairia Pliroforissis* [1991] ECR I-2925; Case C-250/06 *United Pan-Europe Communications Belgium and Others* [2007] ECR I-11135.

protection of personal data;[25] access to basic data held about oneself;[26] equality;[27] protection from discrimination on grounds of sexual orientation;[28] the right to choose one's place of residence;[29] the right to free and informed consent before any medical procedure and the right to human dignity;[30] freedom from torture or subjection to inhuman and degrading treatment.[31]

Economic rights   Normally subject to provisos which may be imposed in the public interest and which restrict their exercise, these include the right to trade;[32] the right to own property;[33] and the right to carry out an economic activity.[34]

Rights of defence   These include the right to an effective judicial remedy;[35] the presumption of innocence;[36] the right to be informed in a criminal trial of the nature and cause of accusation against one;[37] the right to legal assistance and the right for all lawyer-client communications prepared for the purpose of defending oneself to be confidential;[38] the right to be heard in one's own defence before any measure is imposed;[39] and protection from self-incrimination.[40]

General principles of law   These include the principles of non-discrimination,[41] proportionality,[42] legitimate expectations[43] and non-retroactivity.[44] The meaning of these principles is discussed further in Chapter 10.

Most of these rights also find some reflection, as we shall see, in the Charter. However, the Lisbon Treaty poses some questions about their future development. Hitherto, this has been an organic process whereby the Court looks to sources it considers authoritative wherever these seem germane.[45] In some instances these are national constitutional traditions, in others the ECHR, and in yet other cases, other international human rights treaties. This is important because national constitutions are entrenched and the ECHR is a product of the post-Second World War era. As human rights have evolved since then, new international treaties have been concluded to reflect this. The Lisbon Treaty seems to preclude EU law, for the first time, from looking at these, as it suggests that, from now on, regard can only be had to national constitutional traditions and the ECHR. It would be a pity if this were the case.

---

[25] Case C-101/01 *Lindqvist* [2003] ECR-12971; Joined Cases C-465/00, C-138/01 and C-139/01 *Österreichischer Rundfunk* [2003] ECR I-4919.

[26] Case C-553/07 *College van Burgemeester en Wethouders van Rotterdam* v *Rijkeboer*, Judgment of 7 May 2009.

[27] Case C-43/75 *Defrenne* v *Sabena* [1976] ECR 455.

[28] Case C-117/01 *KB* v *National Health Service Pensions Agency* [2004] ECR I-541.

[29] Case C-370/05 *Festersen* [2007] ECR I-1129.

[30] Case C-377/98 *Netherlands* v *European Parliament and Council (Biotechnology Directive)* [2001] ECR I-7079.

[31] Case C-465/07 *Elgafaji* v *Staatsecretaris van Justitie*, Judgment of 17 February 2009.

[32] Case 240/83 *ADBHU* [1985] ECR 531.

[33] Case 44/79 *Hauer* [1979] ECR 3727.

[34] Case 230/78 *Eridania* [1979] ECR 2749.

[35] Case 222/84 *Johnston* v *Chief Constable of the Royal Ulster Constabulary* [1986] ECR 1651.

[36] Case C-344/08 *Rubach*, Judgment of 16 July 2009.

[37] Case C-14/07 *Weiss* v *Industrie- und Handelskammer Berlin* [2008] ECR I-3367.

[38] Case 155/79 *AM & S Europe Ltd* v *Commission* [1982] ECR 1575.

[39] Case 17/74 *Transocean Marine Paint* v *Commission* [1974] ECR 1063.

[40] Joined Cases 374/87 and 27/88 *Orkem & Solvay* v *Commission* [1989] ECR 3283.

[41] Case C-144/04 *Mangold* [2005] ECR I-9981.

[42] Case 11/70 *Internationale Handelsgesellschaft* v *Einfuhr- und Vorratstelle für Getreide und Futtermittel* [1970] ECR 1125.

[43] Joined Cases C–37/02 and C–38/02 *Di Lenardo and Dilexport* [2004] ECR I-6911.

[44] Case 63/83 *R* v *Kent Kirk* [1984] ECR 2689.

[45] As new Members joined the Union, fundamental rights evolved to incorporate their distinctive forms of human rights: F. Bignami, 'Creating European Rights: National Values and Supranational Interests' (2005) 11 *CJEL* 241.

(ii) European Union Charter of Fundamental Rights and Freedoms

The Charter emerged out of a two-fold impetus at the end of the 1990s. On the one hand, there was a desire to accord social rights the same status as other rights, notably civil liberties.[46] On the other, there was agreement that the fundamental rights in EU law should not be hidden away in the case law of the Court of Justice but should be more visible. In 1999, at the Cologne European Council, it was agreed therefore that a charter of fundamental rights should be established. The European Council believed that this charter should be an amalgam of rights. It should include the rights contained in the ECHR and those present in the constitutional traditions common to the Member States. It should also include the rights set out in the EU citizenship provisions, and economic and social rights as contained in the European Social Charter and the Community Charter of the Fundamental Social Rights of Workers.

This charter was to be drafted by a novel method, a Convention. This would be composed of representatives from national governments, the Commission, the European Parliament and national parliaments. Other EU institutions were to be given observer status. Human rights groups, regional bodies, trade unions and wider civil society were invited to make contributions.[47] Deliberations were to be held in public. The draft of the Charter was adopted by the Convention in October 2000 and was unanimously approved by the European Council at the Biarritz European Council. The question of the legal status of the Charter was to be left open. Moreover, this was not just a formal question. As this excerpt from Clapham presciently notes, debates about rights can confer legitimacy upon a political system and generate feelings of political community, but they can also polarise opinions and generate dissensus.

A. Clapham, 'A Human Rights Policy for the European Community' (1990) *Yearbook of European Law* 309, 311

Talking about human rights may sometimes bestow identity on Community citizens. This has a subjective dimension with citizens finding they have rights in common; as well as containing an objective perspective with the discovery of a common concern about the rights of others (inside or outside the Community). Where these rights move beyond 'God-given' or 'self evident' rights they result in an intense 'contract' or relationship with the right giver. Should the Community realize its role in distributing rights to Community citizens it could expect some increased loyalty. However such a symbiotic relationship could only occur should the Community respond to the demands of its citizens rather than reinforcing rights which are primarily geared to its own objectives.

Clearly, rights have an important role to play in the process of European integration, but, it must be said that they may well operate as a double-edged sword. Not only are they a cohesive force but they may well be divisive. Should the Community move to tackle questions such as divorce, contraception, abortion, blasphemy, surrogacy, etc., rights might no longer be handy tools for integration but vehicles of division and disintegration. Furthermore, not only will moral diversity have to be tolerated in the move towards unity, but it is clear that effective rights to challenge Community decisions or provisions could well slow up or completely ensnare new initiatives or progress at the Community level.

---

[46] Report of the Expert Group on Fundamental Rights, *Affirming Fundamental Rights in the European Union: Time to Act* (Brussels, European Commission, 1999) (Simitis Report).

[47] For discussion see G. de Búrca, 'The Drafting of the EU Charter of Fundamental Rights' (2001) 26 *ELRev.* 126: O. de Schutter, 'Europe in Search of its Civil Society' (2002) 8 *ELJ* 198, 206–12.

Leaving the status of the Convention open allowed the possibility of a wider array of rights being incorporated. It could always be argued that as these rights were not being made into 'legal' rights but only enunciated as statements of principle, their precise consequences did not have to be thought through. However, this did mean that substantive disagreement crystallised around the question of whether the Charter should have legal status or not.[48] As a consequence, at the Nice European Council, agreement on the legal status and consequences of the Charter could not be reached. Instead, it was 'proclaimed' by the Council, the Commission and the Parliament, with its final status to be resolved by the Constitutional Treaty.

This led to a period of hiatus. The Charter was not a formal legal instrument but it was an authoritative statement of the rights considered to be fundamental in the Union. Advocates General and the General Court began referring to it as a source of fundamental rights.[49] Under the Constitutional Treaty, it was inserted in Part II of the Treaty. This set out the provisions of the Charter but also constrained their remit and meaning in a manner that did not apply to other provisions of the Treaty.[50] Following the failure of the Constitutional Treaty in 2006, the Court of Justice also began to refer to the Charter as a source of fundamental rights.[51] In this, there has never been exclusive reliance on the Charter. The Court has always referred to it and an alternative source, invariably an international human rights treaty, as the basis for a right. Equally importantly, the Charter is not seen as a constitutive document but a statement of rights that are seen, in EU law at least, as fundamental.

This approach has been continued in Article 6(1) TEU, which states that the Union recognises the rights, freedoms and principles as set out in the Charter. The Charter was reproclaimed by the three EU institutions following the signing of the Lisbon Treaty.[52] It sets out its rights and principles under six headings, of which the central ones are set out below.

Rights to human dignity   Right to life; integrity of the person; prohibition of torture or inhuman and degrading treatment; prohibition of slavery or forced labour; prohibition on cloning or eugenics (articles 1–5).

Freedoms   Right to liberty and security; respect for private and family life; protection of personal data; right to marry and found a family; freedom of thought, conscience and religion; freedom of expression and information; freedom of assembly; freedom of the arts and sciences; right to education; freedom to choose an occupation and right to engage in work; freedom to conduct a business; right to asylum; right to property (articles 6–19).

Equality   Equality before the law; non-discrimination on sex, race, colour, ethnic or social origin, genetic features, language, religion or belief or political opinion, disability, sexual

---

[48] C. McCrudden, *The Future of the EU Charter of Fundamental Rights*, Jean Monnet Working Paper 13/01, http://centers.law.nyu.edu/jeanmonnet/papers/index.html (accessed 19 November 2009).

[49] See respectively Case C-173/99 *R v Secretary of State for Trade and Industry, ex parte BECTU* [2001] ECR I-4881, Advocate General Tizzano; Case T-177/01 *Jégo-Quéré v Commission* [2002] ECR II-2365.

[50] These constraints have been replicated by the Lisbon Treaty.

[51] Case C-540/03 *Parliament v Council (family reunification)* [2006] ECR I-5769; Case C-432/05 *Unibet v Justitiekanslern* [2007] ECR I-2271; Case C-275/06 *Promusciae v Telefónica de España* [2008] ECR I-271; Case C-12/08 *Mono Car Styling v Odemis*, Judgment of 16 July 2009; Joined Cases C-322/07 P, C-327/07 P and C-338/07 P *Papierfakbrik Koehler v Commission*, Judgment of 3 September 2009.

[52] The full text of the Charter can be found at [2007] OJ C303/1. The consolidated version differs from the 2000 version in that it includes some institutional amendments that had been included in the Constitutional Treaty.

orientation, birth; cultural, religious and linguistic diversity; equality between men and women; rights of the elderly, integration of persons with disabilities (articles 20–26).

Solidarity   Workers' right to information and consultation; right of collective bargaining; protection in the event of unfair dismissal; right to placement services; fair and just working conditions; prohibition on child labour; right to social security; right to health care; protection of the family; high level of environmental and consumer protection; access to services of general economic interest (articles 27–38).

Citizens' rights   Right to vote and stand in municipal and European Parliament elections; right to good administration; right to access to documents; right to refer matters to European Parliament and petition Ombudsman; freedom of movement and residence; right to diplomatic protection (articles 39–46).

Justice   Right to an effective remedy and a fair trial; presumption of innocence; right not to be tried or punished twice for same offence; principle of legality and proportionality of criminal offences (articles 47–50).

Few of these rights are absolute and many are conditioned by exceptions. Article 52(1) of the Charter sets out limits on how these exceptions may be invoked:

> **Charter, article 52(1)**
>
> Any limitation on the exercise of the rights and freedoms recognised by this Charter must be provided for by law and respect the essence of those rights and freedoms. Subject to the principle of proportionality, limitations may be made only if they are necessary and genuinely meet objectives of general interest recognised by the Union or the need to protect the rights and freedoms of others.

The rights were taken from three sources: rights recognised in the EU Treaty, rights recognised in the constitutions of the Member States, and international human rights treaties concluded by the Member States.[53] There are a number of noteworthy features.

First, the Charter incorporates a wider array of rights and freedoms possibly than any other human rights treaty. There are, thus, not just civil, political, economic and social rights, but protection of cultural and ecological interests as well. It can be seen as ambitious and nuanced, therefore, in what it considers humans need for a good life. However, there is also a concern about an inflation of the language of rights. The right of free access to a placement service is worthwhile no doubt (article 29 of the Charter) but it can hardly be seen as on the same level as the prohibition on slavery (article 5 of the Charter). To be sure, it might be argued that inclusion in a single document does not mean that they are being equated, but there is the question as to why they should be placed together at all and whether this might lead to phenomena such as similar methods of interpretation being applied to both.

Secondly, in the field of social rights, in particular, certain key rights are missing.[54] The right to nationality, the right to decent pay, the right to work and the right to housing are all not

---

[53] CHARTE 4473/00, 11 October 2000.

[54] J. Kenner, 'Economic and Social Rights in the EU Legal Order: The Mirage of Indivisibility' in T. Hervey and J. Kenner (eds.), *Economic and Social Rights under the EU Charter of Fundamental Rights* (Oxford, Hart, 2003) 1, 16–18.

included.[55] Certain other rights (for example, the right to marry, the right to collective bargaining, the right of workers to information and consultation, the right to protection against unfair dismissal, the right to social security and health care) are to be recognised only in accordance with the rules laid down by national or EU laws. National laws are to determine the content of these rights, so that instead of acting as a basis for review of EU and national practices, these are turned around to justify even egregious practices.[56]

Thirdly, the Charter suggests the indivisibility of these rights. Social, civil, political and environmental rights should all be treated equally as fundamental rights. Yet, it introduces this at the expense of introducing another distinction: that between rights and principles.

Charter, article 52(5)

The provisions of this Charter which contain principles may be implemented by legislative and executive acts taken by Institutions, bodies, offices and agencies of the Union and by acts of Member States when they are implementing Union law, in the exercise of their respective powers. They shall be judicially cognisable only in the interpretation of such acts and in the ruling on their legality.

Some provisions will be protected more absolutely than others. All institutional behaviour falling within the aegis of the Charter can be judicially reviewed against provisions that contain rights. By contrast, courts will only be able to look at principles in cases where institutions are implementing these principles rather than at activities that cut across them. The justification is that the sheer breadth of the Charter prevents a 'one size fits all' approach to protection. Courts are arguably not well-suited to determining the substance of wide-ranging socio-economic or environmental rights, e.g. when a right to sustainable development warrants protection, or when the level of health provision is so low that it violates the right of access to health care. More partial judicial control might be a price worth paying for having these recognised.

However, even if one accepts this ethos, the distinction was not considered at the original drafting of the Charter but only addressed subsequently: first, in the Constitutional Treaty, and then in the modified Charter proclaimed in 2007. As a consequence, the fundamental question of which provisions articulate rights and which principles was unaddressed. There are only three provisions which explicitly use the word 'principle': those on the principle of equality between men and women (article 23), sustainable development (article 37) and on the need for legality and proportionality of criminal offences (article 49). Of these, only the provision on sustainable development would seem in any way to generate problems with judicial enforcement. Reliance cannot be had therefore on the terminology of the Charter. Instead, it may be that provisions whose content is dependent upon their realisation by national or EU law would be considered to be principles.[57] Yet, many of the provisions to be implemented by national

---

[55] Albeit that the right to 'housing assistance' is provided for in article 34(3).

[56] D. Ashiagbor, 'Economic and Social Rights in the European Charter of Fundamental Rights' (2004) 1 *European Human Rights Law Review* 62.

[57] For example, the right to marry (article 9); the right to found educational establishments (article 14(3)); workers' right to information and consultation within their undertaking (article 27); the right to collective bargaining (article 28); social and housing assistance (article 34); the right to protection in the event of unjustified dismissal (article 30); and the right to health care (article 35).

law describe themselves as 'rights'.[58] There are also provisions where the Union commits itself to respect certain values in its policies, such as a high level of environmental protection or consumer protection or respect for services of a general economic interest.[59] These provisions would not seem to confer free-standing rights, but act merely to orient the policy in question. However, the question is surrounded by ambiguity.

4 STANDARD OF PROTECTION OF FUNDAMENTAL RIGHTS

It is all very well the Union developing a plethora of rights but this means little if they are just paper rights with no substance, which offer individuals little protection. Yet, if EU law is to demand a certain level of protection or a particular balance between different values, there must, at the very least, be a certain ethos which informs us why that level of protection or balance is adopted. Indeed, that is also the view of the Court of Justice. Since *Internationale Handelsgesellschaft*, it has indicated that EU fundamental rights law is to be interpreted according to an autonomous reasoning with the meaning of particular rights determined in the light of broader Union objectives.

There has been academic debate about the logic supporting this reasoning. Some authors have argued that it should be centred around the Western liberal tradition of protecting individual autonomy, so EU law should provide the standard which would secure the individual as high a level of protection as that offered by any Member State.[60] Others have convincingly argued that this is too formal and individualistic a conception of fundamental rights. Fundamental rights articulate basic choices about the structure of state and society. The Union should develop its own model here according to EU conceptions of right and wrong.[61] Commentary on the nature of such a model is, however, disappointingly vague. It has been argued that a feature might be a greater insistence on social rights and more scepticism of 'market rights' than in the United States.[62] Others have suggested that Europe's history of tragic events, most notably the Holocaust, would involve the development of a common set of choices concerned to avoid the suffering and pain associated with Europe's past and to give a voice to those suffering equivalent injustices today.[63]

It is not clear how such visions would inform the interpretation of rights across the board, and the Court has eschewed such an approach, with it being difficult to discern any general philosophy. Williams has argued that this lack of substance and intellectual vacuity is having powerful delegitimating effects by reducing the language of fundamental rights to a series of empty labels.[64]

---

[58] All the provisions mentioned above n. 57 (e.g. the right to marry, etc.), with the exception of article 34 on the right to housing assistance, do this.

[59] Articles 36, 37 and 38 respectively.

[60] L. Besselink, 'Entrapped by the Maximum Standard: On Fundamental Rights, Pluralism and Subsidiarity in the European Union' (1998) 35 *CMLRev.* 629.

[61] J. Weiler, 'Fundamental Rights and Fundamental Boundaries: On Standards and Values in the Protection of Human Rights' in N. Neuwahl and A. Rosas, *The European Union and Human Rights* (The Hague, Martinus Nijhoff, 1995) 51, 52–3; M. Avbelj, *The European Court of Justice and the Question of Value Choices*, Jean Monnet Working Paper 6/04, http://centers.law.nyu.edu/jeanmonnet/papers/index.html (accessed 19 November 2009).

[62] C. Leben, 'Is there a European Approach to Human Rights?' in P. Alston (ed.), *The EU and Human Rights* (Oxford, Oxford University Press, 1999) 69–98.

[63] K. Günther, 'The Legacies of Injustice and Fear: A European Approach to Human Rights and their Effects on Political Culture' in P. Alston (ed.), *The EU and Human Rights* (Oxford, Oxford University Press, 1999) 117–46.

[64] See also I. Ward, 'Making Sense of Integration: A Philosophy of Law for the European Community' (1993) 17 *Journal of European Integration* 101, 128–9 and 132–3.

A. Williams, *EU Human Rights Policies: A Study in Irony* (Oxford, Oxford University Press, 2004) 159–60

As the concern of the Community's institutions was to stave off criticism on the one hand and gain authenticity on the other, the phrase 'human rights' was used without regard to its full meaning or possibilities. Using the language of rights as a mythic construct was considered sufficient to justify the potential detractors of the Community and its Project. The resulting indeterminacy of human rights, the repeated failure to constitutionalise any definition of the term, ensured that the field was open to interpretation. Thus, the possibility of different human rights, discourses, practices and definitions emerging in different arenas inspired by different sources of law and philosophy became apparent. The most significant demonstration of the potential for variance was at the external/internal divide. In both realms, the failure to define what the Community meant by human rights or how they should be applied and promoted in any coherent fashion determined that other forces could influence their evolution.

...the mythic nature of the narrative has presented a debilitating factor in any attempt to rectify a perceived bifurcation. Due to its lack of substance, its lack of certainty, the narrative of founding principle has become a vapid construction, a wistful statement repeated as law without any certain content or appreciation of practice. It ignores the 'considerable differences' between the attitudes of the Member States to rights. It has been incapable of providing a framework for any kind of consistent human rights activity. Instead, the myth has lost its vitality and relevance and has left human rights to the vagaries of context and inherent discrimination.

The recognition of the Charter by the Lisbon Treaty alters this. Within the Charter, one can find four guiding principles that will inform the standard of protection by EU fundamental rights law.

The first is that there should be no undermining of the protections offered to the individual by either international treaties or national constitutions.

Charter, article 53

Nothing in this Charter shall be interpreted as restricting or adversely affecting human rights and freedoms as recognised, in their respective fields of application, by Union law and international law and by international agreements to which the Union or all the Member States are party, including the European Convention on Human Rights and Fundamental Freedoms, and by the Member States' constitutions.

Whilst this provision sets the context as to how EU fundamental rights should be interpreted, its guiding force is limited. It asserts a principle of non-violation. International treaties and national constitutions are to set out a 'bed of rights', below which the Union must not go. It is left to the other provisions to set out what the Union should do beyond this, and the more detailed relationship between EU fundamental rights and the ECHR and the national constitutions.

The second principle is that courts should have regard to the Explanations drawn up by the Secretariat to the Convention on the Charter in interpreting particular provisions.

Charter, article 52(7)

The explanations drawn up as a way of providing guidance in the interpretation of the Charter of Fundamental Rights shall be given due regard by the courts of the Union and the Member States.[65]

The purpose of this is to restrict judicial creativity, with the courts developing unanticipated interpretations with far-reaching consequences. It sets out a doctrine of original intent. However, this provision's significance is undercut by the Secretariat's Explanations being silent on the scope and content of each right, as they do no more than state its source (e.g. a particular international human rights treaty). However, this provision does encourage adjudicators to be backward-looking in their interpretation of the Charter. For the Explanations invariably seek to locate individual provisions as simply the culmination of the existing case law of the Court of Justice or existing international treaties. Over time there is thus a real danger that undue prominence will be given to dated interpretations, rather than to interpretations that meet the demands of an evolving society.

The third principle is more significant. It requires interpretations of the Charter to align themselves with those of the ECHR where they concern rights laid down in the ECHR.

Charter, article 52(3)

Insofar as this Charter contains rights which correspond to rights guaranteed by the Convention for the Protection of Human Rights and Fundamental Freedoms, the meaning and scope of those rights shall be the same as those laid down by the said Convention. This provision shall not prevent Union law providing more extensive protection.

This statement reflects the recent practice of the Court of Justice. It has stated that the ECHR has a special status in EU law. The consequence has been a reticence in judgments involving rights covered by the ECHR: it does not articulate new principles or values, but, instead, exercises a 'cut-out and paste' reliance on the case law of the European Court on Human Rights.[66] The most significant example was the *Family Reunification* judgment, where the Court considered the Charter's place in EU law for the first time. The European Parliament challenged three elements of the Directive on family reunification, which set out the conditions under which family members of non-EU nationals resident in the Union could join those nationals. The first provided that the unification with their family of a child aged 12 years or above arriving independently from their parents could be subject to an integration test.[67] The second was an exception to the general provision that children 16 years old or younger have a right to family

---

[65] This is now found in the Explanations relating to the Charter of Fundamental Rights [2007] OJ C303/17.

[66] The most extreme example of this is Case C-109/01 *Secretary of State for the Home Department* v *Akrich* [2003] ECR I-9607. The case law of the European Court of Human Rights is cited but not its reasoning, so the judgment makes no sense unless one refers back to the judgments of the latter. For an argument that there has been a shift recently, see B. Kunoy and A. Dawes, 'Plate Tectonics in Luxembourg: The *Ménage à Trois* between EC Law, International Law and the European Convention on Human Rights following the UN Sanctions Cases' (2009) 46 *CMLRev.* 73.

[67] These tests typically require knowledge of the language and history of the host state as well as demonstration of commitment to its values.

reunification. The exception provided that this rule did not apply to children who were already 15 years old at the time of the submission of the application. The third concerned a provision which stipulated that Member States could provide that non-EU nationals be lawfully resident for two years in their territories before their families join them. The Directive provided in its Preamble that it complied with the right to respect for family life as set out in the ECHR and the Charter.

Case C-540/03 *Parliament* v *Council (family reunification)* [2006] ECR I-5769

38. The Charter was solemnly proclaimed by the Parliament, the Council and the Commission in Nice on 7 December 2000. While the Charter is not a legally binding instrument, the Community legislature did, however, acknowledge its importance by stating, in the second recital in the preamble to the Directive, that the Directive observes the principles recognised not only by Article 8 of the ECHR but also in the Charter. Furthermore, the principal aim of the Charter, as is apparent from its preamble, is to reaffirm 'rights as they result, in particular, from the constitutional traditions and international obligations common to the Member States, the Treaty on European Union, the Community Treaties, the [ECHR], the Social Charters adopted by the Community and by the Council of Europe and the case law of the Court ... and of the European Court of Human Rights'...

52. The right to respect for family life within the meaning of Article 8 of the ECHR is among the fundamental rights which, according to the Court's settled case law, are protected in Community law... This right to live with one's close family results in obligations for the Member States which may be negative, when a Member State is required not to deport a person, or positive, when it is required to let a person enter and reside in its territory.

53. Thus, the Court has held that, even though the ECHR does not guarantee as a fundamental right the right of an alien to enter or to reside in a particular country, the removal of a person from a country where close members of his family are living may amount to an infringement of the right to respect for family life as guaranteed by Article 8(1) of the ECHR...

54. In addition, as the European Court of Human Rights held in *Sen* v *The Netherlands*, no. 31465/96, § 31, 21 December 2001, 'Article 8 [of the ECHR] may create positive obligations inherent in effective "respect" for family life. The principles applicable to such obligations are comparable to those which govern negative obligations. In both contexts regard must be had to the fair balance that has to be struck between the competing interests of the individual and of the community as a whole; and in both contexts the State enjoys a margin of appreciation' ...

55. In paragraph 36 of *Sen* v. *The Netherlands*, the European Court of Human Rights set out in the following manner the principles applicable to family reunification:
    (a) The extent of a State's obligation to admit to its territory relatives of settled immigrants will vary according to the particular circumstances of the persons involved and the general interest.
    (b) As a matter of well-established international law and subject to its treaty obligations, a State has the right to control the entry of non-nationals into its territory.
    (c) Where immigration is concerned, Article 8 cannot be considered to impose on a State a general obligation to respect the choice by married couples of the country of their matrimonial residence and to authorise family reunion in its territory.

56. The European Court of Human Rights has stated that, in its analysis, it takes account of the age of the children concerned, their circumstances in the country of origin and the extent to which they are dependent on relatives...

57. The Convention on the Rights of the Child also recognises the principle of respect for family life. The Convention is founded on the recognition, expressed in the sixth recital in its preamble, that children, for the full and harmonious development of their personality, should grow up in a family environment. Article 9(1) of the Convention thus provides that States Parties are to ensure that a child shall not be separated from his or her parents against their will and, in accordance with Article 10(1), it follows from that obligation that applications by a child or his or her parents to enter or leave a State Party for the purpose of family reunification are to be dealt with by States Parties in a positive, humane and expeditious manner.

58. The Charter likewise recognises, in Article 7, the right to respect for private or family life. This provision must be read in conjunction with the obligation to have regard to the child's best interests, which are recognised in Article 24(2) of the Charter, and taking account of the need, expressed in Article 24(3), for a child to maintain on a regular basis a personal relationship with both his or her parents.

59. These various instruments stress the importance to a child of family life and recommend that States have regard to the child's interests but they do not create for the members of a family an individual right to be allowed to enter the territory of a State and cannot be interpreted as denying States a certain margin of appreciation when they examine applications for family reunification.

This unflinching deference to the case law of the ECHR raises a concern that it is being used as cover for highly illiberal judgments or a failure to engage properly with the issues raised. In *Family Reunification*, the measures challenged were highly illiberal. The Court nevertheless held that they did not restrict the right to respect for family life. The restrictions on the entry of children under the age of 16 years were justified on the grounds that Member States were required to have regard, inter alia, to the interest of the child in the exercise of their discretion. Yet it is difficult to think of any circumstance, other than that of parental abuse, in which it is right to separate 12-year-old children from their parents. The other requirement of lawful residence was justified on the grounds that Member States were entitled to ensure that family reunification will take place on favourable conditions, after the sponsor has been residing in the host state for a period sufficiently long for it to be assumed that the family members will settle down well and display a certain level of integration. This is specious. It is unclear how separating a family for two years makes conditions easier for their settling down. It is rather likely to lead to family disintegration. Similarly, deferring entry for two years simply defers the time it takes the family to integrate. If the question was whether there was an issue about the seriousness of intent on the part of the family, this could be assessed by other means.

The other concern in the judgment is the undue faith placed in the ECHR's decision-making processes and judgment.[68] The ECHR covers forty-six states. It is committed to a less intense form of political integration and governs a more diverse array of situations than the European Union. It is not clear that the judgments of a court such as the European Court of Human Rights, operating in that context, should be accepted almost unquestioningly. A more preferable arrangement would be one of mutual justification: the EU Courts treat any judgment

---

[68] For a withering but highly persuasive critique see S. Greer and A. Williams, 'Human Rights in the Council of Europe and the EU: Towards "Individual", "Constitutional" or "Institutional" Justice?' (2009) 15 *ELJ* 462, 466–70.

given by the European Court of Human Rights as a persuasive suggestion. If the latter's judgment is not considered to protect adequately either the individual freedom or collective interest in question, then they can depart from it, but must give reasons for their choice.[69]

The fourth and final principle of interpretation is that EU fundamental rights law be interpreted in harmony with national constitutional traditions.

> ### Charter, article 52(4)
>
> Insofar as this Charter recognises fundamental rights as they result from the constitutional traditions common to the Member States, those rights shall be interpreted in harmony with those traditions.

National constitutional traditions are not, however, codified into a single legal instrument. Whilst one finds certain types of right (e.g. freedom of expression) recurring in different constitutions, it is difficult to synthesise an overall level of protection from this or to make statements about one level of protection being higher than the other.[70] Individual constitutional settlements reflect choices between conflicting value claims: freedom of expression versus privacy in libel cases; freedom of expression versus respect for religion in blasphemy cases, etc. One cannot talk of a baseline of protection or overall EU picture without having a hierarchy of values, so that, for example, freedom of expression will trump freedom of religion, etc.[71] Whilst national constitutional traditions have been used as the basis for identifying the presence of a particular right,[72] such use is not prevalent with regard to interpreting the substance of that right. Instead, EU law defers to the national constitution being challenged. The logic is one of ethical surrender rather than that of tracing a common constitutional reasoning.

An example is *Omega*. Omega ran a game under a franchise from a British company, Pulsar, whereby competitors attempted to shoot each other with laser guns. Sensory tags worn by competitors picked up whether they had been shot and 'killed' under the rules of the game. The Bonn police authority issued a prohibition order against Omega, on the grounds that the game simulated murder, and therefore constituted an affront to human dignity under paragraph 1(1) of the German Basic Law. Omega argued before the German court that the prohibition violated Article 56 TFEU, the provision on the freedom to provide services. The view of the German court was that the order would not violate Article 56 TEU if it protected the right to human dignity. It therefore asked the Court of Justice as to the meaning of this right in EU law. It also asked whether there had to be a common conception across the Union that games such as these violated human dignity before it could be invoked in the case in hand.

---

[69] N. Krisch, 'The Open Architecture of European Human Rights Law' (2008) 71 *MLR* 183; D. Halberstam and E. Stein, 'The United Nations, The European Union, and the King of Sweden: Economic Sanctions and Individual Rights in a Plural World Order' (2009) 46 *CMLRev.* 13.

[70] See p. 241.

[71] R. García, 'The General Provisions of the Charter of Fundamental Rights of the European Union' (2002) 8 *ELJ* 492, 508.

[72] See e.g. Joined Cases 374/87 and 27/88 *Orkem & Solvay v Commission* [1989] ECR 3283.

Case C–36/02 *Omega Spielhallen –und Automatenaufstellungs* v *Oberbürgermeisterin der Bundesstadt Bonn* [2004] ECR I-9609

33. …fundamental rights form an integral part of the general principles of law the observance of which the Court ensures, and…, for that purpose, the Court draws inspiration from the constitutional traditions common to the Member States and from the guidelines supplied by international treaties for the protection of human rights on which the Member States have collaborated or to which they are signatories. The ECHR has special significance in that respect…

34. … the Community legal order undeniably strives to ensure respect for human dignity as a general principle of law. There can therefore be no doubt that the objective of protecting human dignity is compatible with Community law, it being immaterial in that respect that, in Germany, the principle of respect for human dignity has a particular status as an independent fundamental right.

35. Since both the Community and its Member States are required to respect fundamental rights, the protection of those rights is a legitimate interest which, in principle, justifies a restriction of the obligations imposed by Community law, even under a fundamental freedom guaranteed by the Treaty such as the freedom to provide services…

37. It is not indispensable in that respect for the restrictive measure issued by the authorities of a Member State to correspond to a conception shared by all Member States as regards the precise way in which the fundamental right or legitimate interest in question is to be protected …

38. On the contrary…the need for, and proportionality of, the provisions adopted are not excluded merely because one Member State has chosen a system of protection different from that adopted by another State…

39. In this case, it should be noted, first, that, according to the referring court, the prohibition on the commercial exploitation of games involving the simulation of acts of violence against persons, in particular the representation of acts of homicide, corresponds to the level of protection of human dignity which the national constitution seeks to guarantee in the territory of the Federal Republic of Germany. It should also be noted that, by prohibiting only the variant of the laser game the object of which is to fire on human targets and thus 'play at killing' people, the contested order did not go beyond what is necessary in order to attain the objective pursued by the competent national authorities.

40. In those circumstances, the order…cannot be regarded as a measure unjustifiably undermining the freedom to provide services.

Omega can, of course, be applauded for its respect for national constitutional identities, in this instance the German one. Yet, this judgment is not simply about respecting the German constitutional autonomy, it also purports to set out a common EU fundamental rights law. In this regard, the substance of its vision on human dignity is completely empty, and the Court, by unquestioningly accepting the values of one state, may be accepting values as fundamental which other states find egregious.

Some authors have argued that reference to a multiplicity of sources for fundamental values and different courts (be it national constitutional courts, the Court of Justice or the European Court of Human Rights) having to justify their positions to one another leads to a marketplace of ideas in which fundamental rights can flourish.[73] This may be the case, but it has to be

---

[73] S. Douglas Scott, 'A Tale of Two Courts: Luxembourg, Strasbourg and the Growing European Human Rights Acquis' (2006) 43 *CMLRev.* 619; G. Harpaz, 'The European Court of Justice and its Relations with the European Court of Human Rights: The Quest for Enhanced Reliance, Coherence and Legitimacy' (2009) 46 *CMLRev.* 105.

questioned whether this is happening here.[74] It looks more like the Court of Justice is delegating the job of determining the content of EU fundamental rights law to other courts. Insofar as these judgments then resonate through EU law, there is an absence of safeguards where these courts make a mistake or hold values that are not widely shared. There is also a threat to the autonomy of EU law. The substance of article 52(3) and (4) of the Charter suggests that the content of the Charter must defer, in a dispute, to the ECHR provision or national constitutional provision governing that dispute. The latter should take precedence. In such circumstances, the threat to the supremacy of EU law looks compelling.[75]

5 FUNDAMENTAL RIGHTS AND THE INSTITUTIONAL SCHEME OF THE EUROPEAN UNION

A central concern of Article 6 TEU is that the Charter should not extend in any way the competences of the Union. This concern is also expressed in the Charter.

Charter, article 51(2)

This Charter does not extend the field of application of Union law beyond the powers of the Union or establish any new power or task for the Union, or modify powers and tasks in the other Parts of the Constitution.

One has to be clear, however, about how such an extension could be threatened. It is not possible for the EU legislative institutions to use Charter provisions as a legal base for legislation. The only possible route for this to happen is through judicial activity. The most obvious concern is that the Court of Justice might use the Charter to found new powers of judicial review for itself over activities that were thought to fall outside the Treaties. Another way would be if it were to interpret competences in the light of the Charter in such a way that they were to become 'stretched'. All these concerns go to the extent of review by the Court and its relationship with the other EU institutions and the Member States.

(i) Fundamental rights and the EU institutions

It is commonplace that fundamental rights are used as a basis for review whereby courts can strike down legislation or administrative acts that do not observe them. They are also used as an interpretive tool to shape the content of legislation and the scope of administrative discretion. In that regard, the Court of Justice has hitherto only been willing to grant social rights an interpretive function and has not been willing to strike down legislation for non-compliance with these. This interpretive role is not insignificant as it can be used to enlarge the scope and shape the ideological direction of legislation.

---

[74] This was astutely first spotted in M. Bronckers, 'The Relationship of the EC Courts with Other International Tribunals: Non Committal, Respectful or Submissive?' (2007) 44 *CMLRev.* 601.

[75] J. Liisberg, 'Does the EU Charter of Fundamental Rights Threaten the Supremacy of Community Law' (2001) 38 *CMLRev.* 1171, 1191. This article also provides an excellent summary of a parallel debate that took place at the time of the adoption of the Charter.

A good example is *Jaeger*. Directive 93/104/EC on the organisation of working time required amongst other things a minimum daily rest period of eleven consecutive hours per twenty-four-hour period. Jaeger was a doctor who worked in a hospital in the German town of Kiel. For about three-quarters of his working time, he was on-call. This required him to be present in the hospital to be available when needed. It was agreed that he performed services about 49 per cent of the time he was on call. The hospital considered that the time on call counted as a rest period for the purposes of the Directive. Jaeger believed it was work. The Court agreed with him.

Case C–151/02 *Landeshauptstadt Kiel* v *Jaeger* [2003] ECR I–8389

45. ...it should be stated at the outset that it is clear both from Article 118a of the EC Treaty... which is the legal basis of Directive 93/104, and from the first, fourth, seventh and eighth recitals in its preamble as well as the wording of Article 1(1) itself, that the purpose of the directive is to lay down minimum requirements intended to improve the living and working conditions of workers through approximation of national provisions concerning, in particular, the duration of working time...

46. According to those same provisions, such harmonisation at Community level in relation to the organisation of working time is intended to guarantee better protection of the safety and health of workers by ensuring that they are entitled to minimum rest periods—particularly daily and weekly—and adequate breaks and by providing for a ceiling on the duration of the working week...

47. In that context it is clear from the Community Charter of the Fundamental Social Rights of Workers, adopted at the meeting of the European Council held at Strasbourg on 9 December 1989, and in particular points 8 and 19, first subparagraph, thereof, which are referred to in the fourth recital in the preamble to Directive 93/104, that every worker in the European Community must enjoy satisfactory health and safety conditions in his working environment and must have a right, inter alia, to a weekly rest period, the duration of which in the Member States must be progressively harmonised in accordance with national practices.

48. With regard more specifically to the concept of 'working time' for the purposes of Directive 93/104, it is important to point out that at paragraph 47 of the judgment in *Simap*,[76] the Court noted that the directive defines that concept as any period during which the worker is working, at the employer's disposal and carrying out his activity or duties, in accordance with national laws and/or practices, and that that concept is placed in opposition to rest periods, the two being mutually exclusive.

49. At paragraph 48 of the judgment in *Simap* the Court held that the characteristic features of working time are present in the case of time spent on call by doctors in primary care teams in Valencia (Spain) where their presence at the health centre is required. The Court found, in the case which resulted in that judgment, that it was not disputed that during periods of duty on call under those rules, the first two conditions set out in the definition of the concept of working time were fulfilled and, further, that, even if the activity actually performed varied according to the circumstances, the fact that such doctors were obliged to be present and available at the workplace with a view to providing their professional services had to be regarded as coming within the ambit of the performance of their duties.

---

[76] Case C-303/98 *Simap* [2000] ECR I-7963.

The Court used the Community Charter of Fundamental Social Rights in this instance to give a wide interpretation of what constitutes work. Whilst it did not broaden Treaty competences, it did enlarge the meaning of the legislation and extend the duties upon Member States. It also recalibrated the balance between employer interests and employee needs in favour of the latter.

The use of fundamental rights to interpret EU legislation is also used to limit the circumstances in which EU legislation is struck down, as the Court will seek to secure a benign interpretation wherever possible, and only if that is not possible will it strike down the measure.

In *Osterreichischer Rundfunk*, the Austrian Court of Auditors required from all local authorities and public bodies details of the salaries and pensions of senior officials for the annual report that it submitted to the Austrian Parliament. It argued this was necessary to keep state finances in check. A number of these refused to submit the information, arguing that it violated Directive 95/46/EC on the protection of individuals with regard to the processing of personal data. In interpreting the obligations set out by the Directive, the Court was eager to interpret them in the light of Article 8 ECHR, upholding the right to respect for private life.

Joined Cases C-465/00, C-138/01 and C-139/01 *Osterreichischer Rundfunk* [2003] ECR I-4989

68. It should also be noted that the provisions of Directive 95/46, insofar as they govern the processing of personal data liable to infringe fundamental freedoms, in particular the right to privacy, must necessarily be interpreted in the light of fundamental rights, which, according to settled case law, form an integral part of the general principles of law whose observance the Court ensures...

70. Directive 95/46 itself, while having as its principal aim to ensure the free movement of personal data, provides in Article 1(1) that Member States shall protect the fundamental rights and freedoms of natural persons, and in particular their right to privacy with respect to the processing of personal data. Several recitals in its preamble...also express that requirement.

71. In this respect, it is to be noted that Article 8 of the Convention, while stating in paragraph 1 the principle that the public authorities must not interfere with the right to respect for private life, accepts in paragraph 2 that such an interference is possible where it is in accordance with the law and is necessary in a democratic society in the interests of national security, public safety or the economic well-being of the country, for the prevention of disorder or crime, for the protection of health or morals, or for the protection of the rights and freedoms of others.

72. So, for the purpose of applying Directive 95/46...it must be ascertained, first, whether legislation such as that at issue in the main proceedings provides for an interference with private life, and if so, whether that interference is justified from the point of view of Article 8 of the Convention...

91. If the national courts conclude that the national legislation at issue is incompatible with Article 8 of the Convention, that legislation is also incapable of satisfying the requirement of proportionality in... Directive 95/46. Nor could it be covered by any of the exceptions referred to in article 13 of that Directive, which likewise requires compliance with the requirement of proportionality with respect to the public interest objective being pursued. In any event, that provision cannot be interpreted as conferring legitimacy on an interference with the right to respect for private life contrary to Article 8 of the Convention.

The Data Protection Directive is thus to be interpreted in the light of the ECHR. On the one hand, this allows a more liberal application of the legislation. However, there is a danger that courts will look for mutual compatibility.[77] They will not merely interpret EU secondary legislation in the light of fundamental rights norms, but will also interpret fundamental rights norms in the light of the legislation being challenged, with the possibility of the safeguards offered by the latter being adjusted downwards to protect the legislation in question.

The principle also serves to reallocate risks between EU institutions and Member States. In adjusting their legislation to comply with EU measures, Member States must adopt interpretations of those measures which comply with EU fundamental rights norms. If they fail to do this, as *Österreichischer Rundfunk* shows, it is the Member State which is held accountable, not the EU legislature. This has the advantage that national administrations become guarantors of fundamental rights norms. To avoid being the targets of litigation, they will need to ensure that the legislation is not applied in any way that violates their understandings of fundamental rights. The judgment does, however, leave them between a rock and a hard place, as they have to choose between the apparent textual intent of a particular provision and compliance with an EU fundamental right. Adoption of either path is likely to leave them susceptible to legal challenge by individuals.

It is another matter when it comes to review of behaviour by the EU institutions. Whilst the General Court and Court of Justice are quite willing to strike down administrative acts by the Commission for not complying with EU fundamental rights law,[78] it is another matter when it comes to EU legislative acts. The Courts are pusillanimous here.[79] There is no instance of a Directive being struck down for failure to comply with fundamental rights. In recent times, there is only one instance of a Council Regulation being struck down and that was in *Kadi*. This, it will be remembered, was more of an administrative act as it listed individuals alleged to be associated with terrorist activities and froze their property. It was found to violate due process, in that the individuals never had the opportunity to make a case as to why they should not be listed, and the duty of judicial protection, as the listing could not be challenged before a court. Yet even there, the Court allowed the measure to be maintained for three months during the period in which Kadi could put his case before a court.

The lack of constraint is perhaps illustrated by the treatment of a commitment by the Commission to assess all proposals for their compatibility with the Charter.[80]

European Commission, *Application of the Charter of Fundamental Rights of the European Union*, SEC(2001)380/3

Any proposal for legislation and any draft instrument to be adopted by the Commission will ... as part of the normal decision-making procedures, first be scrutinised for compatibility with the Charter. Moreover, legislative proposals or draft instruments which have a specific link with fundamental rights will incorporate the following recital as a formal statement of compatibility...

---

[77] See Case C-101/01 *Lindqvist* [2003] ECR I-12971; Case C-553/07 *Rijkeboer*, Judgment of 7 May 2009.
[78] For a relatively recent example see T-185/05 *Italy* v *Commission* [2008] ECR II-3207.
[79] Particularly noteworthy examples of judicial feebleness are Case C-540/03 *Parliament* v *Council (family reunification)* [2006] ECR I-5769 (see pp. 243–5).
[80] H. Toner, 'Impact Assessments and Fundamental Rights Protection in EU Law' (2006) 31 *ELRev.* 316.

It would be easy for the Court to grant legal bite to such a procedural requirement. It necessitates less a direct involvement with the substance of the legislation but rather merely a requirement that legislators direct their attention to fundamental rights. Measures could therefore be struck down not merely where they violate a fundamental right but also where the EU institutions have failed to give due consideration to whether a measure potentially violates a fundamental right. Yet, in the eight years since this commitment, the Court has been silent. Consequently, commentators have suggested that the Commission's statement is no more than a paper requirement used to legitimise dubious practices, rather than improve fundamental rights compliance.[81]

(ii) Fundamental rights and the Member States

In the early years, fundamental rights were not used to review national action. In *Cinéthèque*, a judgment involving a challenge to French legislation prohibiting the marketing of any film shown in a cinema for a period between six and eighteen months after release, the Court stated that it had no jurisdiction to assess the compatibility of national law with the ECHR.[82] This position posed difficulties. Most administration regulated by EU law was carried out by national authorities. The coherence and unity of the EU legal order would be compromised if the EU institutions were subject to a regime in which they were bound by fundamental rights but these same rights did not bind implementing national authorities.[83]

In *Wachauf*, a German tenant farmer, upon expiry of his tenancy, requested compensation for the discontinuance of the production of milk for sale. German legislation, implementing an EU Regulation, provided that a milk producer could apply for compensation if he undertook to discontinue milk production definitively within a period of six months from the grant of the compensation. However, tenants were required to have the lessor's written consent to apply for compensation. Since Wachauf's landlord had withdrawn this consent, Wachauf was unable to receive the compensation. Wachauf argued that the German law violated his right to property, as the compensation was for something he had built up through working the land during his lease.

Case 5/88 *Wachauf v Germany* [1989] ECR 2609

18. The fundamental rights recognized by the Court are not absolute, however, but must be considered in relation to their social function. Consequently, restrictions may be imposed on the exercise of those rights, in particular in the context of a common organization of a market, provided that those restrictions in fact correspond to objectives of general interest pursued by the Community and do not constitute, with regard to the aim pursued, a disproportionate and intolerable interference, impairing the very substance of those rights.

---

[81] G. de Búrca and J. Aschenbrenner, 'The Development of European Constitutionalism and the Role of the EU Charter of Fundamental Rights' (2003) 9 *CJEL* 355, 366–8.

[82] Joined Cases 60/84 and 61/84, *Cinéthèque v Fédération Nationale des Cinémas Français* [1985] ECR 2605. See also Case 12/86 *Demirel v Stadt Schwäbisch Gmünd* [1987] ECR 3719.

[83] K. Lenaerts, 'Fundamental Rights to be Included in a Community Catalogue' (1991) 16 *ELRev*. 367, 368; J. Temple Lang, 'The Sphere in which Member States are Obliged to Comply with the General Principles of Law and Community Fundamental Rights Principles' (1991/2) *LIEI* 23, 28–9.

19. Having regard to those criteria, it must be observed that Community rules which, upon the expiry of the lease, had the effect of depriving the lessee, without compensation, of the fruits of his labour and of his investments in the tenanted holding would be incompatible with the requirements of the protection of fundamental rights in the Community legal order. Since those requirements are also binding on the Member States when they implement Community rules, the Member States must, as far as possible, apply those rules in accordance with those requirements...

22. The Community regulations in question...leave the competent national authorities a sufficiently wide margin of appreciation to enable them to apply those rules in a manner consistent with the requirements of the protection of fundamental rights, either by giving the lessee the opportunity of keeping all or part of the reference quantity if he intends to continue milk production, or by compensating him if he undertakes to abandon such production definitively.

Although the Court did not rule directly, there was a strong implication that the German legislation, insofar as it deprived tenants of compensation, violated their fundamental rights. It was also made clear that the German authorities were responsible as they had not exercised the discretion available to them in a manner that complied with EU fundamental rights norms. This last nuance allowed the Court to expand the reach of EU fundamental rights law. National compliance with fundamental rights was no longer merely about the coherence of the EU legal order and making sure the formulation and implementation of a legislative act were bound by the same norms. Rather, it was now about ensuring that national authorities exercised the discretion available to them in accordance with fundamental rights.

In *ERT*, ERT, a Greek radio and television company enjoying exclusive broadcasting rights under Greek law, sought an injunction against an information company and Mr Kouvelas, the Mayor of Thessaloniki, who had set up a rival television station. The respondents argued that ERT's exclusive rights infringed, inter alia, the right to free provision of services. The Greek government invoked what are now Articles 52 and 62 TFEU, which allow it to impose restrictions for reasons of public policy. ERT counter-argued that these could not be invoked, as the conduct violated Article 10 ECHR relating to freedom of expression.

Case C–260/89 *Elliniki Radiophonia Tiléorassi AE and Others* v *Dimotiki Etairia Pliroforissis* [1991] ECR I-2925

42. As the Court has held..., it has no power to examine the compatibility with the ECHR of national rules which do not fall within the scope of Community law. On the other hand, where such rules do fall within the scope of Community law, and reference is made to the Court for a preliminary ruling, it must provide all the criteria of interpretation needed by the national court to determine whether those rules are compatible with the fundamental rights the observance of which the Court ensures and which derive in particular from the ECHR.

43. In particular, where a Member State relies on the combined provisions of [Articles 52 and 62 TFEU] in order to justify rules which are likely to obstruct the exercise of the freedom to provide services, such justification, provided for by Community law, must be interpreted in the light of the general principles of law and in particular of fundamental rights. Thus the national rules in question can fall under

> the exceptions provided for by the combined provisions of [Articles 52 and 62 TFEU] only if they are compatible with the fundamental rights the observance of which is ensured by the Court.
>
> 44. It follows that in such a case it is for the national court, and if necessary, the Court of Justice to appraise the application of those provisions having regard to all the rules of Community law, including freedom of expression, as embodied in Article 10 ECHR, as a general principle of law the observance of which is ensured by the Court.

ERT expands the reach of EU fundamental rights law significantly. It provides that wherever a national measure, whatever its intent, restricts free movement it will be governed by EU fundamental rights norms, whether this free movement be of goods, services, capital or persons. Broadcasting laws, pornography laws, banning orders on hooligans or laws restricting individuals going abroad for assisted suicide – all would fall for assessment for their compliance with fundamental rights, insofar as they have the potential to restrict free movement between EU states.

However, the test is not a general one. In 2007, the Court stated that Member States were bound by fundamental rights norms when acting within the remit of the third pillar, but only when implementing EU law.[84] Prior to the coming into force of the Lisbon Treaty, two tests therefore existed. For measures falling within the first pillar, the test was whether the measure fell within the field of EC law, whilst for the third pillar it was whether it implemented an EU measure. The Lisbon Treaty now contains a single test, set out by the Charter.

> ### Charter, article 51(1)
>
> The provisions of this Charter are addressed to the institutions, bodies, offices and agencies of the Union with due regard for the principle of subsidiarity and to the Member States only when they are implementing Union law. They shall therefore respect the rights, observe the principles and promote the application thereof in accordance with their respective powers and respecting the limits of the powers of the Union as conferred on it in the Treaties.

The provision would seem to suggest a narrower test than *ERT*, as it suggests that only national implementing measures (not measures falling within the field of EU law) are to be reviewed. Yet ambiguity is provided by the Declaration of the Secretariat.[85] This draws a link between this provision and the existing case law of the Court of Justice, and suggests the latter can be incorporated within a wide notion of implementing measure.

---

[84] Case C-355/04 P *Segi* v *Council* [2007] ECR I-1657; Case C-354/04 P *Gestoras Pro Amnistía and Others* v *Council* [2007] ECR I-1579. See S. Peers, 'Salvation Outside the Church: Judicial Protection in the Third Pillar after the *Pupino* and *Segi* Judgments' (2007) 44 *CMLRev.* 883. A. Egger, 'EU Fundamental Rights in the National Legal Order: The Obligations of Member States Revisited' (2007) 25 *YBEL* 515.

[85] For a discussion see G. de Búrca, 'The Drafting of the EU Charter of Fundamental Rights' (2001) 26 *ELRev.* 126, 136–7.

Explanations (Charter, article 51)

As regards the Member States, it follows unambiguously from the case law of the Court of Justice that the requirement to respect fundamental rights defined in a Union context is only binding on the Member States when they act in the context of Community law (judgment of 13 July 1989, Case 5/88 *Wachauf* [1989] ECR 2609; judgment of 18 June 1991, *ERT* [1991] ECR I-2925...). The Court of Justice confirmed this case law in the following terms: 'In addition, it should be remembered that the requirements flowing from the protection of fundamental rights in the Community legal order are also binding on Member States when they implement Community rules...' (judgment of 13 April 2000, Case C-292/97 [2000] ECR I-2737, paragraph 37). Of course this principle, as enshrined in this Charter, applies to the central authorities as well as to regional or local bodies, and to public organisations, when they are implementing Union law.

It is stretching credulity to suggest that the two tests are the same and there is no difference between a measure that implements EU law and one that falls within the scope of EU law. This will have to be determined by the Court of Justice, but the matter was further muddied by the Czech Republic at the Lisbon Treaty.[86] It appended a Declaration emphasising its understanding that the Charter only applies to Member States when they are implementing EU law, but not when they are adopting and implementing national law independently from EU law.

Legal uncertainty is generated not simply by the nature of the test, which determines whether national measures are subject to EU fundamental rights law or not. It is also generated by the presence of a double test and the possibilities for arbitrage presented by this.[87] For, whether a measure is assessed for its legality for compliance with EU fundamental rights depends on whether the individuals choose to bring their activities within the reach of EU law or not.

The most celebrated instance of this is *SPUC* v *Grogan*. In 1986, the Irish Supreme Court ruled that it was against the Irish Constitution to help Irish women to have abortions by informing them of the identity and location of abortion clinics abroad. A number of Irish student unions provided the details of abortion clinics in the United Kingdom. This information was provided free. The Society for the Protection of the Unborn Child (SPUC) sought an undertaking that the student unions would cease to do this. The students invoked EU law, arguing their right to freedom of expression had been violated. SPUC countered, arguing that the measure fell outside the field of EU law, as it did not constitute a restriction on the freedom to provide services under what is now Article 56 TFEU.

Case C-159/90 *Society for the Protection of the Unborn Child (SPUC)* v *Grogan* [1991] ECR I-4685

22. ...the national court seeks essentially to establish whether it is contrary to Community law for a Member State in which medical termination of pregnancy is forbidden to prohibit students associations from distributing information about the identity and location of clinics in another Member State where

---

[86] Declaration 53 by the Czech Republic on the Charter of Fundamental Rights of the European Union.
[87] For strong criticism see P. Huber, 'The Unitary Effect of the Community's Fundamental Rights: The *ERT* Doctrine Needs to be Reviewed' (2008) 14 *EPL* 323.

medical termination of pregnancy is lawfully carried out and the means of communicating with those clinics, where the clinics in question have no involvement in the distribution of the said information...

24. As regards, first, the provisions of [Article 56 TFEU], which prohibit any restriction on the freedom to supply services, it is apparent from the facts of the case that the link between the activity of the students associations of which Mr Grogan and the other defendants are officers and medical terminations of pregnancies carried out in clinics in another Member State is too tenuous for the prohibition on the distribution of information to be capable of being regarded as a restriction within the meaning of [Article 56 TFEU]...

26. The information to which the national court's questions refer is not distributed on behalf of an economic operator established in another Member State. On the contrary, the information constitutes a manifestation of freedom of expression and of the freedom to impart and receive information which is independent of the economic activity carried on by clinics established in another Member State.

27. It follows that, in any event, a prohibition on the distribution of information in circumstances such as those which are the subject of the main proceedings cannot be regarded as a restriction within the meaning of [Article 56 TFEU]...

30. It was important to bear in mind that when national legislation fell within the field of application of Community law the Court, when requested to give a preliminary ruling, must provide the national court with all the elements of interpretation necessary in order to enable it to assess the compatibility of that legislation with the fundamental rights – as laid down in particular in the ECHR – the observance of which the Court ensures. However, the Court had no such jurisdiction with regard to national legislation lying outside the scope of Community law.

Fundamental rights are treated in a paradoxical manner.[88] On the one hand, EU law stresses the indivisibility of fundamental rights. On the other, it does not protect their indefeasibility. Fundamental rights are only to be protected if they fall within the field of EU law but not if they fall outside it. This leads to inequality before the law, with individuals in analogous situations being differently protected. It also provides incentives to cheat. The clear message in *Grogan*, for example, was that the students should offer to advertise, for a nominal fee, on behalf of the British abortion clinics, in order to bring themselves within the field of EU law.

(iii) National contestation of EU fundamental rights

The application of EU fundamental rights norms to national laws is one of the most sensitive fields in EU law. On the one hand, it has been argued it is central to the European Union's mission. If the nation-state gives individuals a sense of community, identification and cultural differentiation, the task of the Union is to tame and discipline the less attractive pathologies generated by these features: those of xenophobia, exclusionary practices and introspection. This would be done through:

> a commitment to the shared values of the Union as expressed in its constituent documents, a commitment, inter alia, to the duties and rights of a civil society covering discrete areas of public life, a commitment to membership in a polity which privileges exactly the opposites of nationalism – those human features which transcend the differences of organic ethno-culturalism.[89]

[88] P. Eeckhout, 'The EU Charter of Fundamental Rights and the Federal Question' (2002) 39 *CMLRev*. 945, 957–8; G. de Búrca, 'Fundamental Rights and the Reach of EC Law' (1993) 13 *OJLS* 283.
[89] J. Weiler, 'The Reformation of European Constitutionalism' (1997) 35 *JCMS* 97, 119.

If this assertion is very valuable, it is necessarily something very contentious. In all cases, upholding an EU fundamental right against a national law is stating that the national authorities have done something fundamentally wrong. Why else would we call it a fundamental right? It is invariably a condemnation of the character of the national polity. In some cases, the national authorities may be committing this sin by error but as often as not this Union judgment is setting out an assertion about a nation-state's firmly held beliefs. These might be egregious but they are generated by the same ties of community and of 'Them' and 'Us' as those that generate national senses of belonging.

The debate about the application of EU fundamental rights has therefore been characterised by two forms of national counter-reaction.

The first is resistance. There are cases of national protection of individual laws. Both Ireland and Malta have insisted, therefore, that their abortion laws are not to be touched by EU law.[90] Poland secured a Declaration at the Lisbon Treaty that the Charter does not affect in any way the right of Member States to legislate in the spheres of public morality, family law, protection of human dignity or respect for human physical and moral integrity.[91] The most wide-ranging challenge was made by the British and Polish governments. Concerned about judicial creativity and its effect on national choices, they secured a Protocol on the Application of the Charter to Poland and the United Kingdom. There was, furthermore, agreement at the European Council in October 2009 that the entitlements of this Protocol will extend to the Czech Republic at the conclusion of the next Accession Treaty with the next new Member State. The first provision of this Protocol states:

Protocol on the Application of the Charter to Poland and the United Kingdom, Article 1(1)

The Charter does not extend the ability of the Court of Justice of the European Union, or any court or tribunal of Poland or of the United Kingdom, to find that the laws, regulations or administrative provisions, practices or actions of Poland or of the United Kingdom are inconsistent with the fundamental rights, freedoms and principles that it reaffirms.

The Protocol does not give these two states an 'opt-out' from the Charter, as it allows both the courts of those states and the Court of Justice to rule on disputes occurring in those states. In those instances, the Charter can only be 'interpreted'. It cannot be extended. There were two particular areas of concern for those states. The first area was the 'solidarity' rights in Title IV of the Charter. These rights are largely concerned with labour protection, but also include wider social rights such as the right to health care and social assistance, as well as Union policies committing states to a high level of environmental and consumer protection. The states insisted on a provision that the Charter could not transform these into justiciable rights, if they were not already.

---

[90] Protocol on Article 40.3.3 of the Constitution of Ireland. A similar protection has been given for Malta, Protocol No. 7 Act of Accession 2003.

[91] Declaration 61 to the Treaty of Lisbon by the Republic of Poland on the Charter of Fundamental Rights of the European Union.

> ### Protocol on the Application of the Charter to Poland and the United Kingdom, Article 1(2)
>
> In particular, and for the avoidance of doubt, nothing in Title IV of the Charter creates justiciable rights applicable to Poland or the United Kingdom except insofar as Poland or the United Kingdom has provided for such rights in its national law.

The other area was the large number of provisions in the Charter which state that they are only to be recognised in accordance with the rules laid down by national laws.[92] There was a concern that 'national laws' would be understood as the general situation across the Union rather than the law in Poland or the United Kingdom, respectively. This would create problems for these states where their choices or level of protection differ markedly from the mean across the Union.

> ### Protocol on the Application of the Charter to Poland and the United Kingdom, Article 2
>
> To the extent that a provision of the Charter refers to national laws and practices, it shall only apply to Poland or the United Kingdom to the extent that the rights or principles that it contains are recognised in the law or practices of Poland or of the United Kingdom.

The Protocol is extremely clumsily worded. It makes a distinction between courts interpreting provisions and courts extending provisions that very few would recognise; a distinction which is likely to be inoperable. It is particularly inappropriate for the Charter, which describes itself as codifying human rights obligations present in other documents. There is nothing to stop the court in question 'extending' the right by having regard to these other instruments rather than the Charter. There is also a danger of interpretive chaos if the Court is being invited to provide a minimalist interpretation in references from Poland and the United Kingdom, but a different interpretation in references from other Member States. The situation in which the Court rules on the validity of Union measures forming the basis of national implementing measures is particularly murky. Is a Union measure to be struck down for twenty-five Member States but not for Poland and the United Kingdom on the basis that to do so would 'extend' the right being violated?

Notwithstanding these issues and contradictions, the chilling effect of the Protocol should not be underestimated. It is a clear indication to the Court of Justice, British and Polish courts to interpret the Charter restrictively. Insofar as it is unlikely that the Court of Justice will either accept that it 'extends' provisions in its judgments or that the same provision will be given two interpretations across the Union, a probable scenario is that it will just give very cautious interpretations. Indeed, when one looks at its interpretations of the substance of EU fundamental rights law, this seems already to be taking place.

The other strategy of opposition by national decision-makers to situations where national laws seem to be governed by EU fundamental rights law is avoidance. A tragic example is the case of *X* in Ireland.[93] X was a teenager who conceived after being raped. Her parents arranged

---

[92] See p. 240.
[93] *Attorney General* v *X* [1992] 2 CMLR 277.

for a termination at a British clinic but, as she was under 16 years old, notified the authorities of the reason for her trip abroad. The authorities refused to allow her to travel on the grounds that the Irish Constitution required them not to facilitate abortions. The matter was taken to the Irish Supreme Court. The case was legally similar to *Grogan*. It was covered by a point of EU law, namely the freedom to receive services in another Member State, and the Supreme Court should both have considered that and referred the matter to the Court of Justice for decision, as it was a court against whose decisions there was no judicial remedy under Article 267(3) TFEU. Instead, aware of both the terrible human tragedy of the case and of its considerable political implications for Ireland, the court chose to decide the case itself on the basis of Irish law. It held that, in the circumstances, abortion was compatible with the Irish Constitution, as the danger to the mother's life (X was suicidal) outweighed the case for protecting the foetus.

6 THE EUROPEAN UNION WITHIN THE EUROPEAN CONVENTION ON HUMAN RIGHTS

(i) The politics of Union accession to the ECHR

Article 6(2) TEU provides for European Union accession to the ECHR. A number of justifications can be found for this.

First, as the Union's activities have expanded, it has increasingly moved into fields where human rights concerns are frequently invoked. Examples include broadcasting, immigration, asylum, policing and judicial cooperation in criminal justice. In all fields, if an organisation setting norms applying across most of Europe were to be exempt from the safeguards of the ECHR, there would be a significant weakening of the latter.

Secondly, as the Union develops its own fundamental rights system, there is a concern that it might get things wrong. The ECHR acts as a safeguard on this. It acts as a check where the internal checks have failed or where a judgment has been reached that does not seem right.

The third reason is more contentious. It has more to do with the constitutionalisation of the Union. Union accession to the ECHR was first really pushed prior to the Treaty of Amsterdam. It was pushed by a number of Member States, who also proposed (unsuccessfully) the full incorporation of a European Bill of Rights into the TEU.[94] The debate was partly about strengthening fundamental rights protection within the Union. However, it was also about making protection of fundamental rights a central mission of the Union and, consequently, making the Union a central player in the development of fundamental rights in Europe. This posed questions about whether the Union was trying to oust the Council of Europe, the international organisation which had traditionally enjoyed that role. It also raised questions of competence creep, with the Union becoming the central locus for questions about fundamental rights rather than national settlements.

These last concerns have been carried forward in the Lisbon Treaty. Article 6(2) TEU makes clear that accession must not affect Union competences. A Protocol was also attached to the Treaties providing that special arrangements be made for participation by the Union in the Convention's control bodies and to ensure that proceedings by non-Member States and

---

[94] This was the position of Belgium, Finland, Italy, Spain and the German Länder. European Parliament, White Paper on the 1996 Intergovernmental Conference, vol. II (Brussels, European Parliament, 1997).

individual applications are correctly addressed to Member States and/or the Union.[95] The Protocol also emphasised that accession to the ECHR would not affect the situation of the Member States, particularly in relation to individual derogations from the Convention or choices of accession to particular Protocols of the ECHR.[96]

(ii) Obligations of the Union under the ECHR

The obligations of the Union under the ECHR are governed by the *Bosphorus* judgment. Bosphorus had leased two aircraft from Yugoslav National Airlines (JAT) and arranged for these to be subject to maintenance work in Ireland in 1993. At that time there were UN sanctions against the governments of Serbia and Montenegro. Acting under an EU Regulation, the Irish government impounded both aircraft. Bosphorus argued this contravened EU law as the Regulation violated the fundamental right of freedom to pursue a business. Following a reference by the Irish High Court, the Court of Justice ruled that it did not.[97] Bosphorus then took the Irish Government to the European Court of Human Rights, arguing that it had violated the right to property in Article 1 of Protocol 1.

No. 45036/98 *Bosphorus* v *Ireland*, Judgment of 30 June 2005

151. The question is therefore whether, and if so to what extent, that important general interest of compliance with Community obligations can justify the impugned interference by the Irish State with the applicant company's property rights.

152. The Convention does not, on the one hand, prohibit Contracting Parties from transferring sovereign power to an international (including a supranational) organisation in order to pursue cooperation in certain fields of activity… Moreover, even as the holder of such transferred sovereign power, that organisation is not itself held responsible under the Convention for proceedings before, or decisions of, its organs as long as it is not a Contracting Party…

153. On the other hand, it has also been accepted that a Contracting Party is responsible under Article 1 of the Convention for all acts and omissions of its organs regardless of whether the act or omission in question was a consequence of domestic law or of the necessity to comply with international legal obligations. Article 1 makes no distinction as to the type of rule or measure concerned and does not exclude any part of a Contracting Party's 'jurisdiction' from scrutiny under the Convention…

154. In reconciling both these positions and thereby establishing the extent to which a State's action can be justified by its compliance with obligations flowing from its membership of an international organisation to which it has transferred part of its sovereignty, the Court has recognised that absolving Contracting States completely from their Convention responsibility in the areas covered by such a transfer would be incompatible with the purpose and object of the Convention; the guarantees of the Convention could be limited or excluded at will, thereby depriving it of its peremptory character and undermining the practical and effective nature of its safeguards…

155. In the Court's view, State action taken in compliance with such legal obligations is justified as long as the relevant organisation is considered to protect fundamental rights, as regards both the substantive

---

[95] Protocol relating to Article 6(2) TEU on the Accession of the Union to the ECHR.
[96] The ECHR has five Protocols but not all are signed by all the Member States. Article 15(1) ECHR also allows states to make derogations from particular provisions in times of war or public emergency.
[97] Case C-84/95 *Bosphorus* [1996] ECR I-3953.

guarantees offered and the mechanisms controlling their observance, in a manner which can be considered at least equivalent to that for which the Convention provides... By 'equivalent' the Court means 'comparable'; any requirement that the organisation's protection be 'identical' could run counter to the interest of international cooperation pursued ... However, any such finding of equivalence could not be final and would be susceptible to review in the light of any relevant change in fundamental rights protection.

156. If such equivalent protection is considered to be provided by the organisation, the presumption will be that a State has not departed from the requirements of the Convention when it does no more than implement legal obligations flowing from its membership of the organisation.

   However, any such presumption can be rebutted if, in the circumstances of a particular case, it is considered that the protection of Convention rights was manifestly deficient. In such cases, the interest of international cooperation would be outweighed by the Convention's role as a 'constitutional instrument of European public order' in the field of human rights...

158. Since the impugned measure constituted solely compliance by Ireland with its legal obligations flowing from membership of the European Community ..., the Court will now examine whether a presumption arises that Ireland complied with the requirements of the Convention in fulfilling such obligations and whether any such presumption has been rebutted in the circumstances of the present case ...

165. ... the Court finds that the protection of fundamental rights by Community law can be considered to be, and to have been at the relevant time, 'equivalent' (within the meaning of paragraph 155 above) to that of the Convention system. Consequently, the presumption arises that Ireland did not depart from the requirements of the Convention when it implemented legal obligations flowing from its membership of the European Community (see paragraph 156 above).

166. The Court has had regard to the nature of the interference, to the general interest pursued by the impoundment and by the sanctions regime and to the ruling of the ECJ (in the light of the opinion of the Advocate General), a ruling with which the Supreme Court was obliged to and did comply. It considers it clear that there was no dysfunction of the mechanisms of control of the observance of Convention rights.

   In the Court's view, therefore, it cannot be said that the protection of the applicant company's Convention rights was manifestly deficient, with the consequence that the relevant presumption of Convention compliance by the respondent state has not been rebutted.

Having checked that the Union system of protection of fundamental rights is equivalent to that in the ECHR, the European Court of Human Rights held that actions against national measures governed by EU law would be upheld not if the measure breaches the ECHR, but only if it is 'manifestly deficient'.[98] This is a much weaker test than that applied to individual states under the ECHR. It appears that attention is paid to whether the judicial procedures worked within the Union rather than the substance of the breach. One has the feeling almost of a 'non-aggression pact' between the two European courts, whereby the Court of Justice will slavishly follow the case law of the European Court of Human Rights, whereas the latter will intervene only in cases of the most grotesque dysfunction. It may be that Union accession to the ECHR will change the reasoning of the European Court of Human Rights. It will no longer see itself as

---

[98] For criticism see C. Costello, 'The *Bosphorus* Ruling of the European Court of Human Rights: Fundamental Rights and Blurred Boundaries in Europe' (2006) 6 *Human Rights Law Review* 87; C. Eckes, 'Does the European Court of Human Rights Provide Protection from the European Community? The Case of *Bosphorus Airways*' (2007) 13 *EPL* 47.

having to mediate between two sets of international commitments, the ECHR and the TEU, but will rather say that this reasoning no longer applies now the Union is a member of the ECHR. It has to be treated like any other member and states cannot hide behind its obligations.

7 EU FUNDAMENTAL RIGHTS POLICY

Fundamental rights have not just been taken forward by the Court of Justice. In 1977, the Parliament, Commission and Council adopted a Joint Declaration on Fundamental Rights, in which they undertook to respect the ECHR in the exercise of their powers.[99] The commitment was one of constraint, however. The EU institutions were not to violate fundamental rights but, at the same time, these were not to become a central mission of the Union, pivotal to fashioning its political identity or orienting its activities. The Court of Justice confirmed the lack of a positive agenda for fundamental rights in Opinion 2/94, where it ruled there could be no accession to the ECHR, as there was no general human rights competence.[100] Alston and Weiler have characterised the approach of non-violation as negative integration, in that it indicates only a bald commitment not to breach fundamental rights rather than a commitment to realise them.[101] They argued that this led to a gap between rhetoric and reality, whereby the Union affirms the importance of many rights but did little to secure any of them. Concern with non-violation was marked by two further features: an inadequate information base, so that there was no real knowledge of what rights were being violated, and excessive reliance on judicial remedies.[102] Certainly by the early 1990s onwards, it was felt necessary to develop a human rights policy in two fields: external relations and accession.

(i) Fundamental rights and the external relations of the Union[103]

From the early 1990s, the European Union had begun to include human rights references in its trade and aid policies.[104] By the mid-1990s onwards, all trade and cooperation agreements had clauses committing both parties to respect human rights.[105] For example, the General Scheme of Preferences, which allows for certain goods from less developed countries to be imported free from customs duties or at lower tariffs, could also be suspended where beneficiary states failed to respect fundamental rights or basic labour standards.[106] Provision was also made for EU development projects to contribute to the promotion of human rights.[107] The Union has

---

[99] [1977] OJ C103/1.

[100] Opinion 2/94 *Re Accession of the Community to the ECHR* [1996] ECR I-1759.

[101] P. Alston and J. Weiler, '"An Ever Closer Union" in Need of a Human Rights Policy' (1998) 9 *EJIL* 658.

[102] Cf. A. v. Bogdandy, 'The European Union as a Human Rights Organization? Human Rights and the Core of the European Union' (2000) 27 *CMLRev.* 1307, 1319–20.

[103] For a fine overview see P. Leino, 'European Universalism? The EU and Human Rights Conditionality' (2005) 24 *YEL* 330.

[104] A. Brandtner and A. Rosas, 'Human Rights and the External Relations of the European Community: An Analysis of Doctrine and Practice' (1998) 9 *EJIL* 468.

[105] E. Riedel and M. Will, 'Human Rights Clauses in External Agreements' in P. Alston (ed.), *The EU and Human Rights* (Oxford, Oxford University Press, 1999).

[106] Regulation 980/2005/EC applying a scheme of generalised tariff preferences [2005] OJ L169/1, article 20(4). Preferences have been suspended to two states under this provision, Belarus and Myanmar.

[107] Regulation 975/1999/EC laying down the requirements for the implementation of development cooperation operations which contribute to the general objective of developing and consolidating democracy and the rule of law and to that of respecting human rights and fundamental freedoms [1999] OJ 1999 L120/1.

further applied these norms in fields closer to home. Its neighbourhood policy, which grants access to the EU market to neighbouring states in North Africa, the Middle East and Eastern Europe on the basis they engage in political and economic reforms, requires these states to respect human rights.[108] The arena in which the Union has sought most leverage for these is the enlargement process. The Copenhagen Criteria setting out the basis on which states can apply for membership include so-called political criteria, which require states to have, inter alia, stable institutions guaranteeing democracy, the rule of law, human rights and respect for and protection of minorities.[109] These criteria become the basis for Commission reports evaluating the state of human rights in all the applicant countries.[110] These reports have proved wide-ranging in their criticism of applicant state practices.[111]

This collage has been brought together by the Lisbon Treaty. Article 49 TEU provides that only states which respect the values set out in Article 2 TEU (which include respect for fundamental rights) may apply for membership of the Union. More generally, the formulation and application of fundamental rights norms in external relations policies have been brought together by a new provision in the Treaty of Lisbon.

Article 21 TEU

1. The Union's action on the international scene shall be guided by the principles which have inspired its own creation, development and enlargement, and which it seeks to advance in the wider world: democracy, the rule of law, the universality and indivisibility of human rights and fundamental freedoms, respect for human dignity, the principles of equality and solidarity, and respect for the principles of the United Nations Charter and international law.

2. The Union shall define and pursue common policies and actions, and shall work for a high degree of cooperation in all fields of international relations, in order to:
   (a) safeguard its values, fundamental interests, security, independence and integrity;
   (b) consolidate and support democracy, the rule of law, human rights and the principles of international law...

---

[108] European Commission, *Wider Europe – Neighbourhood: A New Framework for Relations with our Eastern and Southern Neighbours*, COM(2003)104 final. On this see P. Leino and R. Petrov, 'Between "Common Values" and Competing Universals: The Promotion of the EU's Common Values through the European Neighbourhood Policy' (2009) 15 *ELJ* 654.

[109] *EU Bulletin* 6–1993, 1.13.

[110] M. Nowak, 'Human Rights "Conditionality" in relation to Entry to, and Full Participation in the European Union' in P. Alston (ed.), *The EU and Human Rights* (Oxford, Oxford University Press, 1999); A. Williams, 'Enlargement and Human Rights Conditionality: A Policy of Distinction?' (2000) 25 *ELRev.* 601; C. Pinelli, 'Conditionality and Enlargement in Light of EU Constitutional Developments' (2004) 10 *ELJ* 354.

[111] Slovakia was initially denied pre-accession status in 1997 on the grounds of the quality of its political regime, and was then subject to sustained monitoring and criticism by the Commission. European Commission, *2002 Regular Report on Slovakia's Progress Towards Accession*, COM(2002)700. The 2008 reports on protection of human rights in the Former Yugoslav Republic of Macedonia and Turkey were damning: European Commission, *Progress Report on the Former Yugoslav Republic of Macedonia*, COM(2008)674, 15–21; European Commission, *Progress Report on Turkey*, COM(2008)674, 11–28. They were also wide-ranging. The one on Turkey condemned disproportionate use of force by police at public gatherings, honour killings, informal militias ('village guards'), the lack of resources and independence of human rights institutions, treatment of people with disabilities, and insufficient respect for cultural diversity and for the protection of minorities in accordance with European standards.

This codifies and brings together general practice in external relations. It does not, however, counter the dissatisfaction with the Union's practice in this area. It has been argued that it has been hypocritical for the Union to apply standards of scrutiny to other states that it does not apply to its own Member States.[112] It has also been argued that fundamental rights in external relations policy have been applied in a highly selective and uneven manner, and that negative opinions have often had counter-productive consequences.[113]

(ii) A domestic fundamental rights policy

A domestic human rights policy has proved less attainable. Beyond the injunction to EU institutions and Member States when implementing EU law not to violate fundamental rights, there is only one competence explicitly relating to fundamental rights.

Article 7 TEU

1. On a reasoned proposal by one-third of the Member States, by the European Parliament or by the European Commission, the Council, acting by a majority of four-fifths of its members after obtaining the consent of the European Parliament, may determine that there is a clear risk of a serious breach by a Member State of the values referred to in Article 2. Before making such a determination, the Council shall hear the Member State in question and may address recommendations to it, acting in accordance with the same procedure. The Council shall regularly verify that the grounds on which such a determination was made continue to apply.

2. The European Council, acting by unanimity on a proposal by one-third of the Member States or by the Commission and after obtaining the consent of the European Parliament, may determine the existence of a serious and persistent breach by a Member State of the values referred to in Article 2, after inviting the Member State in question to submit its observations.

3. Where a determination under paragraph 2 has been made, the Council, acting by a qualified majority, may decide to suspend certain of the rights deriving from the application of the Treaties to the Member State in question, including the voting rights of the representative of the government of that Member State in the Council. In doing so, the Council shall take into account the possible consequences of such a suspension on the rights and obligations of natural and legal persons. The obligations of the Member State in question under this Treaty shall in any case continue to be binding on that State.

4. The Council, acting by a qualified majority, may decide subsequently to vary or revoke measures taken under paragraph 3 in response to changes in the situation which led to their being imposed.

The voting thresholds for use of this provision are extremely high. Its use is likely to be highly restricted, if at all. In the one instance where they could have been used, Member States also preferred to go outside the formal procedures. In 2000, when the explicitly racist Freedom party joined the Austrian government, the other Member States entered into an extra-legal

---

[112] This is the central thesis of A. Williams, *European Union Human Rights Policy* (Oxford, Oxford University Press, 2004).

[113] For example, the treatment of Turkey during the 1990s, which led it to suspend relations with the European Union. See K. Smith, 'The Evolution and Application of EU Member State Conditionality' in M. Cremona (ed.), *The Enlargement of the European Union* (Oxford, Oxford University Press, 2003).

agreement in which they would have no bilateral contacts with the Austrian government. The matter was only resolved six months later, when a 'Committee of Wise Men' found both that the sanctions had inflamed nationalist feelings in Austria and that the Austrian government had a relatively good human rights record.[114]

The significance of the provision lies in the powers it bestows on the Union to monitor the Member States for compliance with fundamental rights. In this regard, a significant distinction exists between Article 7(1) and (2) TEU. The latter provision concerns the circumstances where a serious violation is found to exist and the ground is prepared for sanctions. The former concerns findings of a serious risk of a serious violation. It is an early warning system that is concerned with monitoring how the Member State is doing. This entails the Union acquiring an independent evidence-gathering and reporting capacity.

This capacity has been institutionalised with the establishment of the European Union Agency for Fundamental Rights.[115] The Agency has four central tasks:

- it has to collect, record, disseminate and compare data and research on fundamental rights and develop methods and standards to improve the comparability, objectivity and reliability of that data;
- at the request of EU institutions it can publish opinions for EU institutions and Member States implementing EU law;
- it is to publish both an annual report and thematic reports on fundamental rights issues in the areas of its activity, highlighting examples of good practice; and
- it is to mobilise public awareness of fundamental rights through promoting dialogue with civil society.[116]

The most powerful task of the Agency is the power to give opinions, notably on legislative proposals. The potential normative force of these opinions is unclear. In other fields, the Commission can only derogate from the opinions of the Agency, where it can provide a contrary opinion by a body of equal weight and can provide reasons for choosing one over the other.[117] The Commission, as a consequence, invariably follows the Agency's opinions. With fundamental rights teaching on all areas of EU law, the Fundamental Rights Agency is potentially a very powerful body. Yet the Regulation provides that the Agency can only provide opinions on the legality of proposals at the request of the Commission and cannot address the legality of the measure for the purposes of judicial review, or make an assessment as to whether a Member State has met its obligations within the context of an enforcement action.[118] Even though one of its tasks is to consider questions of fundamental rights in assessing the impact of any legislative proposal, there is presently little evidence of the Commission having consulted the Agency.

[114] M. Merlingen, M. Mudde and U. Sedelmeider, 'The Right and the Righteous? European Norms, Domestic Politics and the Sanctions Against Austria' (2001) 39 *JCMS* 59.

[115] Regulation 168/2007/EC establishing a European Union Agency for Fundamental Rights [2007] OJ L53/1. On the Agency see G. Toggenburg, 'The Role of the New EU Fundamental Rights Agency: Debating the "Sex of Angels" or Improving Europe's Human Rights Performance?' (2008) 33 *ELRev.* 385; A. v. Bogdandy and J. von Bernstoff, 'The EU Fundamental Rights Agency within the European and International Human Rights Architecture: The Legal Framework and Some Unsettled Issues in a New Field of Administrative Law' (2009) 46 *CMLRev.* 1035.

[116] Regulation 168/2007/EC article 4(1).

[117] In relation to the European Food Safety Authority, see Case T-13/99 *Pfizer Animal Health* v *Council* [2002] ECR II-3305.

[118] Regulation 168/2007/EC, article 4(2).

The Agency also has to work within the aegis of a Multi-annual Framework established by the EU political institutions, which sets out the thematic areas within which it is to function. Its work is confined either by institutional requests, in the case of opinions, or, more generally, by the political agenda of the EU institutions. This inevitably confines not only the Agency activities, but also the type of rights examined by the Agency. The Framework for 2007–2012 is a case in point. It takes a reasonably broad remit, but has excluded analysis of social rights, bioethical rights and the war on terror, all of which are touched upon significantly by Union activities.[119]

The Agency, therefore, is very much a reflection of the debate on the establishment of an EU fundamental rights policy. Its remit, as with the policy, is partial, unsteady and makes distinctions which are hard to justify. Yet, for those who advocate a fundamental rights policy, the establishment of an Agency with the legal power to police all EU legislation for compliance with fundamental rights, and with the power to act as a hub for European civil society and awareness of these matters, is indeed a powerful step forward.

FURTHER READING

P. Alston *et al.* (eds.), *The EU and Human Rights* (Oxford, Oxford University Press, 1999)

P. Alston and J. Weiler, '"An Ever Closer Union" in Need of a Human Rights Policy' (1998) 9 *European Journal of International Law* 658

M. Avbelj, *The European Court of Justice and the Question of Value Choices*, Jean Monnet Working Paper 6/04

F. Bignami, 'Creating European Rights: National Values and Supranational Interests' (2005) 11 *Columbia Journal of European Law* 241

A. v. Bogdandy, 'The European Union as a Human Rights Organization? Human Rights and the Core of the European Union' (2000) 27 *Common Market Law Review* 1307

S. Greer and A. Williams, 'Human Rights in the Council of Europe and the EU: Towards "Individual", "Constitutional" or "Institutional" Justice?' (2009) 15 *European Law Journal* 462

T. Hervey and J. Kenner (eds.), *Economic and Social Rights under the EU Charter of Fundamental Rights* (Oxford, Hart, 2003)

N. Krisch, 'The Open Architecture of European Human Rights Law' (2008) 71 *Modern Law Review* 183

B. Kunoy and A. Dawes, 'Plate Tectonics in Luxembourg: The *Ménage à Trois* between EC Law, International Law and the European Convention on Human Rights following the UN Sanctions Cases' (2009) 46 *Common Market Law Review* 73

K. Lenaerts and E. de Smijter, 'A "Bill of Rights" for the European Union' (2001) 38 *Common Market Law Review* 273

J. Liisberg, 'Does the EU Charter of Fundamental Rights Threaten the Supremacy of Community Law' (2001) 38 *Common Market Law Review* 1171

S. Peers and A. Ward (eds.), *The EU Charter of Fundamental Rights* (Oxford, Hart, 2004)

A. Williams, *EU Human Rights Policies: A Study in Irony* (Oxford, Oxford University Press, 2004)

---

[119] Decision 2008/203/EC implementing Regulation 168/2007/EC as regards the adoption of a Multi-annual Framework for the European Union Agency for Fundamental Rights for 2007–2012 [2008] OJ L63/14, article 2.

7

Rights and Remedies in National Courts

CONTENTS

1 INTRODUCTION

This chapter considers the rights and remedies that EU law allows to be invoked in national courts. It is organised as follows.

Section 2 looks at the origins of direct effect. Direct effect is the doctrine which provides for EU law to be invoked in national courts. Initially, direct effect was a 'defensive' right directed at administrations, which required them not to violate entitlements granted clearly and unconditionally to private parties by Treaty provisions.

Section 3 looks at how, over time, direct effect was reconceptualised as providing rights which generate a full set of entitlements against all parties and impose a duty on administrations and courts to protect and realise these entitlements for individuals. This led to EU Treaty provisions being capable of being invoked both against the state (vertical direct effect) and against private parties (horizontal direct effect).

Section 4 considers what remedies and procedures are available to individuals where an EU provision is invoked in a domestic court. As a general rule, these are a matter for domestic law. This autonomy is subject to two constraints. The remedies and procedures for infringement of EU law rights should be, first, no less favourable than those for similar domestic claims, and secondly, should not make it practically impossible to exercise EU rights. However, there is a right to EU remedies in four circumstances: a right to restitution for illegally levied taxes; a right to interim relief pending a preliminary reference to the Court of Justice; a right to claim damages or force repayment of illegal subsidies in the field of EU competition law; and, finally, a right to sue the state for damages where a serious breach of EU law by it has led to loss for the individual.

Section 5 considers the granting of direct effect to secondary legislation. Direct effect is granted to all binding instruments of EU law: Treaty provisions, Regulations, international agreements, Directives and Decisions. The first three sets of instruments are capable of both vertical and horizontal direct effect. Directives and Decisions are only capable of being invoked against the state. Whilst Directives are not capable of horizontal effect, like other binding instruments of EU law they can generate incidental effects for third parties. This occurs, first, where an individual invokes a Directive against the state and this imposes burdens on private parties. It occurs, secondly, where a private party challenges another under national law, and the latter invokes the Directive as a shield requiring the state to protect it from the private action under national law.

Section 6 considers the doctrine of indirect effect. As significant as direct effect, this requires national courts to interpret all national law, insofar as this is possible, in the light of all EU law. This duty encompasses non-binding instruments, such as Recommendations, as well as binding instruments. It has generated concerns about legal certainty, both as to when the duty first arises and as to the strength of the duty of interpretation.

Section 7 considers the doctrine of state liability. This requires states to compensate individuals where a breach of EU law by the state has led to loss for the individual and the provision breached creates rights for the individual. State liability covers all governmental institutions, including acts of the judiciary. If EU law allows Member States some discretion, there is a further condition to attract liability: the breach must be sufficiently serious. Typically, there are four circumstances which attract liability: failure to transpose a Directive; breach of a clear provision of EU law; failure to comply with settled case law; and failure to comply with a judgment of the Court of Justice.

Section 8 considers how the Lisbon Treaty might reshape the field through the introduction of a new provision, Article 19(1) TEU, which requires Member States to provide remedies sufficient to ensure effective legal protection in the fields covered by EU law. This might simply be a codifying provision. Alternately, it might impose a stronger duty on Member States to give effect to EU rights and to protect EU entitlements more fully.

2 DIRECT EFFECT AND THE IDEA OF A UNION RIGHT

We first considered *Van Gend en Loos* in Chapter 5. There are two central elements to that judgment.

The first concerns claims made about the quality of EU law. The Court of Justice claimed that EU law did not fall within traditional categories of international law but rather formed a new sovereign legal order with a new powerful authority. The consequences of this were addressed in Chapter 5.

The second element is the establishment of a new system of individual rights through the doctrine of direct effect. This element has different dynamics. The language of rights calls for us to rethink EU law in terms of the maximum benefits it can grant individuals, both collectively and individually. It therefore pushes for interpretations which maximise individual entitlements and autonomy. It also requires consistency in the interpretation of the Treaty. Provisions appearing on their face to grant individuals direct benefits cannot be interpreted differently, simply because the consequences for the reorganisation of legal authority between EU law and national law are too extravagant. Equally, interpretive techniques used to develop one provision cannot be denied without reason to the interpretation of another provision.

If these elements have distinct rationales, in *Van Gend en Loos* they inform one another. If the justification for the establishment of these rights is the presence of a sovereign legal order, the vehicle for the expression of this order is the development of a system of judicially protected rights.

The facts of the case have been discussed earlier.[1] At its heart, however, was the question whether the provision that is now Article 28 TFEU, prohibiting the imposition of customs duties or charges having equivalent effect on imports from other Member States, could be invoked as a matter of EU law in the Dutch court where it had been asserted.

Case 26/62 Van Gend en Loos v Nederlandse Administratie der Belastingen [1963] ECR 1

The first question ... is whether Article [28 TFEU] has direct application in national law in the sense that nationals of Member States may on the basis of this article lay claim to rights which the national court must protect.

To ascertain whether the provisions of an international treaty extend so far in their effects it is necessary to consider the spirit, the general scheme and the wording of those provisions ...

... The Community constitutes a new legal order of international law for the benefit of which the States have limited their sovereign rights, albeit within limited fields, and the subjects of which comprise not only Member States but also their nationals. Independently of the legislation of Member States, Community law therefore not only imposes obligations on individuals but is also intended to confer upon them rights which become part of their legal heritage. These rights arise not only where they are expressly granted by the Treaty, but also by reason of obligations which the Treaty imposes in a clearly defined way upon individuals as well as upon the Member States and the Institutions of the Community.

With regard to the general scheme of the Treaty as it relates to customs duties and charges having equivalent effect it must be emphasized that... [basing] the Community upon a customs union, includes as an essential provision the prohibition of these customs duties and charges. This provision is found at the beginning of the part of the Treaty which defines the foundations of the Community. It is applied and explained by Article [28 TFEU].

---

[1] See p. 14.

> The wording of Article [28 TFEU] contains a clear and unconditional prohibition which is not a positive but a negative obligation. This obligation, moreover, is not qualified by any reservation on the part of states which would make its implementation conditional upon a positive legislative measure enacted under national law. The very nature of this prohibition makes it ideally adapted to produce direct effects in the legal relationship between Member States and their subjects.
>
> The implementation of Article [28 TFEU] does not require any legislative intervention on the part of the States. The fact that under this article it is the Member States who are made the subject of the negative obligation does not imply that their nationals cannot benefit from this obligation.
>
> It follows from the foregoing considerations that according to the spirit, the general scheme and the wording of the Treaty, Article [28 TFEU] must be interpreted as producing direct effects and creating individual rights which national courts must protect.

If ground-breaking in its development of a sovereign legal order, the judgment is narrow in two respects.

First, its ambit is circumscribed. The judgment does not state that all Treaty provisions can be invoked by individuals in national courts. It only holds that some provisions, which meet certain criteria – namely that they are clear, unconditional, negatively phrased and require no legislative intervention – can be invoked by individuals. Moreover, the judgment only indicated with certainty that one provision met this: the arcane Article 28 TFEU prohibiting customs duties and charges having equivalent effect. A sovereign legal order composed solely of the individual right to import or exports goods free of customs duties is a very limited creature, indeed. This is undoubtedly why the judgment did not provoke more controversy at the time. Yet, the judgment also created instability. For *Van Gend en Loos* offered an almost endless possibility for more provisions to be found to generate individual rights. In every case where this occurs, however, there will be a renewed debate about the reorganisation of legal power entailed by this. Does it grant too much power to the Union, to judges or to particular litigants? The open-ended nature of *Van Gend en Loos* entails this will be a recurring debate that erupts whenever a provision is held to generate individual rights for the first time.

Secondly, the judgment is narrow in its understanding of what is meant by a right. To be sure, the judgment talks about the Treaty imposing obligations on others, be these national courts, administrations or private parties,[2] but it is very vague about the extent and nature of the obligations that are owed to the right-holder by others. At its narrowest, EU law may only grant certain rights vis-à-vis the state: a duty for it not to violate certain interests. Such rights are little more than an immunity from national law in which the holder can do things that others cannot (e.g. withhold taxes). A broader conception of rights involves the holder being able to call on all parties to respect, protect and make good the interests that lie at the heart of the right. Such a right can be asserted against anybody and it calls for full redress of the interests if they are infringed.

The wording of *Van Gend en Loos* suggested that it was concerned with the former type of right.[3] The stipulation that provisions be negatively phrased meant that national administrations

---

[2] For a useful discussion see T. Downes and C. Hilsom, 'Making Sense of Rights: Community Rights in EC Law' (1999) 24 *ELRev.* 121.

[3] On this early period see T. Eilmansberger, 'The Relationship Between Rights and Remedies in EC Law: In Search of the Missing Link' (2004) 41 *CMLRev.* 1199, 1202–6.

could only be called upon to refrain from doing things but not be called upon to take positive action to protect individuals. It is a duty not to violate addressed only to the national administration. Equally, the requirement of textual clarity suggested that courts could not be called upon to exercise interpretive discretion on behalf of the right-holder, as 'unclear' provisions necessitating the exercise of such discretion would simply not be directly effective. Finally, the proviso that provisions be unconditional suggested courts could not be called upon to weigh individual entitlements against other public interests if these were recognised by EU law.

Alongside this, the judgment was silent on the types of procedure, sanction or enforcement mechanism that should be deployed to protect the right. If the language of rights pushes for full protection of an individual's entitlements by all parties, it looked in *Van Gend en Loos* as if its use was somewhat rhetorical, for the Court has been much more reserved in terms of the duties it imposes on other parties. As we shall see in the rest of this chapter, the case law of the Court is marked by a push and pull between these two elements.

3 EXPLOITATION OF DIRECT EFFECT

In the 1960s, the Court applied the doctrine of direct effect to a limited number of provisions, which met the criteria set out in *Van Gend en Loos*.[4] It also did not elaborate on the implications for parties when they benefited from a directly effective provision. Most Treaty provisions only entered fully into force, however, with the end of the transitional period in 1970. In the early 1970s, the Court sought to expand direct effect in a number of directions.

(i) Relaxing the criteria: towards a test of justiciability

First, the Court began to relax the criteria for when a provision may be directly effective. In *Van Duyn*, it stated that even if the provision did not set out an absolute entitlement, it could still be invoked in national courts if any qualification or condition was subject to judicial control. As no provision or condition in the Treaty has ever been held to be outside judicial control, this effectively discarded the requirement that a provision be unconditional.[5] In *Reyners*, the Court held that what is now Article 48 TFEU, which imposes positive obligations on Member States to enable freedom of establishment, was directly effective, thereby sweeping away the insistence that only negatively phrased provisions could be invoked in national courts.[6]

If EC Treaty provisions no longer needed to be negative or unconditional to be directly effective, this begged the question which criteria they did need to meet. This issue came up most acutely in the case of *Defrenne (No. 2)*. Under Belgian law, female air stewards were required to retire at the age of 40, unlike their male counterparts. Gabrielle Defrenne had been forced to retire from the Belgian national carrier, Sabena, on this ground in 1968. She brought an action claiming that the lower pension payments this entailed breached the principle now in Article

---

[4] Case 57/65 *Lütticke* v *HZA Sarrelouis* [1966] ECR 205; Case 27/67 *Firma Fink-Frucht GmbH* v *Hauptzollamt München-Landsbergerstrasse* [1968] ECR 327; Case 13/68 *Salgoil* v *Italian Ministry of Foreign Trade* [1968] ECR 453. On the early developments see A. Dashwood, 'The Principle of Direct Effect in European Community Law' (1978) 16 *JCMS* 229; P. Craig, 'Once upon a Time in the West: Direct Effect and the Federalization of EEC Law' (1992) 12 *OJLS* 453, 460–70.

[5] Case 41/74 *Van Duyn* v *Home Office* [1974] ECR 1337.

[6] Case 2/74 *Reyners* v *Belgium* [1974] ECR 631.

157(1) TFEU that 'each Member State shall ensure and maintain the principle that men and women should receive equal pay for work of equal value'. Yet, on the face of it, there appeared to be a number of obstacles to the provision being directly effective. It was argued, first, that the provision set out general principles about the broad treatment of men and women in the workforce rather than conferring individual rights and, secondly, that it was programmatic in nature, requiring further measures for its implementation.

Case 43/75 *Defrenne* v *Sabena (No. 2)* [1976] ECR 455

16. Under the terms of the first paragraph of Article [157 TFEU], the Member States are bound to ensure and maintain 'the application of the principle that men and women should receive equal pay for equal work'...

18. For the purposes of the implementation of these provisions a distinction must be drawn within the whole area of application of Article [157 TFEU] between, first, direct and overt discrimination which may be identified solely with the aid of the criteria based on equal work and equal pay referred to by the Article in question and, secondly, indirect and disguised discrimination which can only be identified by reference to more explicit implementing provisions of a Community or national character.

19. It is impossible not to recognise that the complete implementation of the aim pursued by Article [157 TFEU], by means of the elimination of all discrimination, direct or indirect, between men and women workers, not only as regards individual undertakings but also entire branches of industry and even of the economic system as a whole, may in certain cases involve the elaboration of criteria whose implementation necessitates the taking of appropriate measures at Community and national level ...

21. Among the forms of direct discrimination which may be identified solely by reference to the criteria laid down by Article [157 TFEU] must be included in particular those which have their origin in legislative provisions or in collective labour agreements and which may be detected on the basis of a purely legal analysis of the situation.

22. This applies even more in cases where men and women receive unequal pay for equal work carried out in the same establishment or service, whether public or private.

23. As is shown by the very findings of the judgment making the reference, in such a situation the court is in a position to establish all the facts which enable it to decide whether a woman worker is receiving lower pay than a male worker performing the same tasks.

24. In such situation, at least, Article [157 TFEU] is directly [effective] and may thus give rise to individual rights which the courts must protect.

The Court gave the provision a double meaning to enable the finding of direct effect. On the one hand, it acquired a programmatic, wide-ranging, ambitious purpose, namely to secure equality between men and women within the economic system as a whole. On the other hand, the Court gave the provision a second interpretation within this, namely to prohibit pay discrimination between men and women in individual workplaces. This was considered sufficiently precise to be invoked in national courts. However one looks at it, the Court had significantly relaxed the requirement for legal clarity. To acknowledge that a provision has too uncertain an ambit to be invoked, per se, in national courts and to suggest that it has a double meaning is to indicate that it is not clear.

Since *Defrenne (No. 2)*, the Court has moved away from using the criteria set out in *Van Gend en Loos*. Instead, the test has become whether the substance of the provision is sufficiently precise and unconditional.[7] In the eyes of one judge, the invocability of Treaty provisions has now been reduced to a simple question of justiciability.[8] Yet what does this mean? The Court will not look at whether the provision is qualified by other provisions or constraints, but simply at whether the provision is 'unequivocal'.[9] This suggests that it is not important simply that a provision sets out some entitlements that are clearly for the benefit of individuals but that it also sets out direct duties on national administrations to protect these entitlements. That these may have some discretion about how to protect the entitlements is not important.[10]

(ii) The state's duty to protect individual rights and the emergence of horizontal direct effect

If *DeFrenne (No. 2)* signalled a willingness on the part of the Court to allow a wider array of Treaty provisions to be directly effective, it was also important for a second reason. It was stated earlier that if only provisions which were negatively phrased were directly effective, that doctrine only imposed a duty on Member States not to violate individual entitlements set out in the Treaty. Any positively phrased obligation, such as a duty to protect or secure, would be held not to be directly effective. While *DeFrenne (No. 2)* was not the first case to hold a positively phrased obligation to be directly effective,[11] it was the first to address the institutional implications of this for the Member States. The Belgian government argued that the discrimination was not perpetrated by it but by Sabena, a commercial operator. It therefore could not be held liable for this. By contrast, it argued that Sabena could not be liable for obligations under Article 157 TFEU, as the latter explicitly addressed these to the Member States, and only the administration was therefore bound.

Case 43/75 *Defrenne* v *Sabena (No. 2)* [1976] ECR 455

30. It is … impossible to put forward arguments based on the fact that Article [157 TFEU] only refers expressly to 'Member States'.

31. Indeed, as the Court has already found in other contexts, the fact that certain provisions of the Treaty are formally addressed to the Member States does not prevent rights from being conferred at the same time on any individual who has an interest in the performance of the duties thus laid down.

32. The very wording of Article [157 TFEU] shows that it imposes on States a duty to bring about a specific result to be mandatorily achieved within a fixed period.

33. The effectiveness of this provision cannot be affected by the fact that the duty imposed by the Treaty has not been discharged by certain Member States and that the joint institutions have not reacted sufficiently energetically against this failure to act.

---

[7] See the early Case 148/78 *Ministero Pubblico* v *Ratti* [1979] ECR 1629. In more recent times, examples include Joined Cases C-397/01–C-403/01 *Pfeiffer and Others* v *Deutsches Rotes Kreuz* [2004] ECR I-8835; Joined Cases C-152/07–154/07 *Arcor* v *Bundesrepublik Deutschland* [2008] ECR I-5959.

[8] P. Pescatore, 'The Doctrine of "Direct Effect": An Infant Disease of Community Law' (1983) 8 *ELRev.* 155, 176–7.

[9] Case C-138/07 *Belgische Staat* v *Cobelfret*, Judgment of 12 February 2009, para. 64.

[10] Case C-226/07 *Flughafen Köln/Bonn*, Judgment of 17 July 2008; Case C-138/07 *Belgische Staat* v *Cobelfret*, Judgment of 12 February 2009.

[11] Case 2/74 *Reyners* v *Belgium* [1974] ECR 631.

34. To accept the contrary view would be to risk raising the violation of the right to the status of a principle of interpretation, a position the adoption of which would not be consistent with the task assigned to the Court by Article [19(1) TEU].

35. Finally, in its reference to 'Member States', Article [157 TFEU] is alluding to those States in the exercise of all those of their functions which may usefully contribute to the implementation of the principle of equal pay.

36. Thus, contrary to the statements made in the course of the proceedings this provision is far from merely referring the matter to the powers of the national legislative authorities.

37. Therefore, the reference to 'Member States' in Article [157 TFEU] cannot be interpreted as excluding the intervention of the courts in direct application of the Treaty.

38. Furthermore it is not possible to sustain any objection that the application by national courts of the principle of equal pay would amount to modifying independent agreements concluded privately or in the sphere of industrial relations such as individual contracts and collective labour agreements.

39. In fact, since Article [157 TFEU] is mandatory in nature, the prohibition on discrimination between men and women applies not only to the action of public authorities, but also extends to all agreements which are intended to regulate paid labour collectively, as well as to contracts between individuals.

Direct effect is not therefore just about protecting individuals from states violating their rights. The doctrine also imposes duties upon the state to secure the protection of these rights. In this regard, *Defrenne (No. 2)* makes two particularly important findings. First, it reminds national courts that they are part of the state and that this duty to protect falls particularly strongly on them. Secondly, it notes from this that courts may find that Treaty provisions can be invoked against other private parties, who therefore have a duty to respect EU law. It therefore established two forms of direct effect, which have been referred to in the academic literature in the following manner:

(a) vertical direct effect: this is where a party invokes a provision of EU law in a national court against a Member State;

(b) horizontal direct effect: this is where a party invokes a provision of EU law in a national court against a private party. A corollary of this right is that private parties have responsibilities in EU law for which they can be held liable in national courts if they fail to discharge them.

From a perspective of developing individual rights, this judgment can be viewed very positively. Discrimination on grounds of gender is both egregious and a long-standing problem in the workplace. The grant to the victims of this new legal instrument to protect themselves can only be viewed positively. Moreover, in a market economy, where most employment is in the private sector, it clearly makes sense for it to be available against private employers.

At the beginning of this chapter, we also noted that the story of direct effect was one of an ongoing reorganisation of legal power. Here, the judgment in *Defrenne (No. 2)* was far more disorientating. The grant of horizontal direct effect opens the possibility for Treaty provisions to be invoked not only in the relatively limited setting of litigation of illegal behaviour by the state, but also in the much more unconfined world of private litigation. EU law would not only be deployed to govern a much wider array of disputes, but it would also provide more opportunities to challenge national law, as individuals would no longer need to seek judicial review. They could simply say that it did not govern the legal dispute between them and another private party. This was all too much for the British and Irish governments. They argued, shamefully, that to allow the principle of equal pay for men and women for work of equal value to be invoked in national courts would lead to an unmanageable disruption of economic life. The Irish government argued that the costs of compliance would exceed Irish receipts from the European Regional Development Fund for the period 1975–77 and the British government argued that it would add 3.5 per cent to labour costs – a considerable admission, it might be thought, on the part of those two governments as to the degree of exploitation of women in their respective jurisdictions!

Case 43/75 *Defrenne* v *Sabena* (*No. 2*) [1976] ECR 455

69. The Governments of Ireland and the United Kingdom have drawn the Court's attention to the possible economic consequences of attributing direct effect to the provisions of Article [157 TFEU], on the ground that such a decision might, in many branches of economic life, result in the introduction of claims dating back to the time at which such effect came into existence.

70. In view of the large number of people concerned such claims, which undertakings could not have foreseen, might seriously affect the financial situation of such undertakings and even drive some of them to bankruptcy.

71. Although the practical consequences of any judicial decision must be carefully taken into account, it would be impossible to go so far as to diminish the objectivity of the law and compromise its future application on the ground of the possible repercussions which might result, as regards the past, from such a judicial decision.

72. However, in the light of the conduct of several of the Member States ... it is appropriate to take exceptionally into account the fact that, over a prolonged period, the parties concerned have been led to continue with practices which were contrary to Article [157 TFEU], although not yet prohibited under their national law ...

74. In these circumstances, it is appropriate to determine that, as the general level at which pay would have been fixed cannot be known, important considerations of legal certainty affecting all the interests involved, both public and private, make it impossible in principle to reopen the question as regards the past.

75. Therefore, the direct effect of Article [157 TFEU] cannot be relied on in order to support claims concerning pay periods prior to the date of this judgment, except as regards those workers who have already brought legal proceedings or made an equivalent claim.

The Court gave here what is known as a prospective ruling. To manage the consequences of departing so far from Member State expectations, it said, in effect, that what is now Article 157 TFEU was subject to two interpretations. For discrimination occurring prior to the date of the judgment, the provision was interpreted as not being directly effective. The opposite was true for discrimination which occurs after the date of the judgment. The symbolism of this is considerable, however. As Rasmussen has observed, these two interpretations destroy the illusion that the Court is engaging in a neutral exercise of merely giving life to the text. It is impossible 'to maintain this myth while ruling that Article [157] was deprived of direct effects until the day of pronouncement of the Court's decision; only to produce such effects from that day onwards'.[12]

---

[12] H. Rasmussen, *On Law and Policy in the European Court of Justice* (Dordrecht, Martinus Nijhoff, 1986) 441.

4 DIRECT EFFECT AND THE DEVELOPMENT OF EU REMEDIES AND PROCEDURES

Although direct effect refers only to the right to invoke a provision in a national court, this has little substance if no remedies follow. After all, individuals go to courts for redress; thus, to be meaningful, it would seem that remedies should follow from the successful invocation of direct effect. This begs the question whether direct effect also requires national courts to put in place particular procedures and remedies. This was first broached in *Rewe*. The German authorities had unlawfully levied charges for health inspections on fruit and vegetables in this instance. Rewe, a trader, claimed a refund of these before the German Administrative Court. The German authorities argued that the limitation period for claiming a refund had passed and Rewe would not have been able to claim a refund if the measure had breached an exclusively domestic law. Rewe saw this as a denial of its rights.

Case 33/76 *Rewe-Zentralfinanz and Others* v *Landwirtschaftskammer für das Saarland* [1976] ECR 1989

5. The prohibition(s) laid down ... have a direct effect and confer on citizens rights which the national courts are required to protect.

Applying the principle of cooperation laid down in Article [4(3) TEU], it is the national courts which are entrusted with ensuring the legal protection which citizens derive from the direct effect of the provisions of Community law.

Accordingly, in the absence of Community rules on this subject, it is for the domestic legal system of each Member State to designate the courts having jurisdiction and to determine the procedural conditions governing actions at law intended to ensure the protection of the rights which citizens have from the direct effect of Community law, it being understood that such conditions cannot be less favourable than those relating to similar actions of a domestic nature.

Where necessary ... the Treaty enable[s] appropriate measures to be taken to remedy differences between the provisions laid down by law, regulation or administrative action in Member States if they are likely to distort or harm the functioning of the common market.

In the absence of such measures of harmonization the right conferred by Community law must be exercised before the national courts in accordance with the conditions laid down by national rules.

The position would be different only if the conditions and time-limits made it impossible in practice to exercise the rights which the national courts are obliged to protect. This is not the case where reasonable periods of limitation of actions are fixed. The laying down of such time-limits with regard to actions of a fiscal nature is an application of the fundamental principle of legal certainty protecting both the tax-payer and the administration concerned.

The test set out in *Rewe* is beset by contradiction. On the one hand, it argues for national procedural autonomy by saying that the question of remedies is for the national legal system to decide, subject to those for breach of directly effective provisions being no less favourable than those relating to similar domestic claims.[13] On the other hand, the requirement that national

---

[13] This constraint is known as the equivalence principle. The question of deciding whether a domestic measure is comparable to an EU measure is one for the national court but the Court of Justice has stated that they must look to the purpose and essential characteristics of the legislation to see if they are similar. Case C-261/95 *Palmisani* v *INPS* [1997] ECR I-4025; Case C-326/96 *Levez* v *Jennings* [1998] ECR I-7835. M. Dougan, *National Remedies Before the Court of Justice* (Oxford and Portland, Hart, 2004) 25–6.

procedures and remedies should not make it practically impossible to exercise EU rights pushes for the development of a Union system of remedies. This is particularly the case if we think of direct effect as enabling individuals to require courts to protect their entitlements. This is nothing if it is not a remedy! If we say that these obligations are a matter for national courts themselves to decide, then the right becomes hollow.

This tension has led to considerable complexity in the case law. Yet it is possible to discern two trends. The first trend concerns those instances where the Court of Justice will require the national court to provide, as a matter of course, a particular remedy. In such circumstances, the failure to provide this remedy is seen as a failure to secure the right provided by the directly effective provision.

The second trend concerns those instances where EU law leaves it almost entirely for national law to determine the remedies and procedures for the protection of directly effective provisions, subject to some loose EU constraints. This is less prescriptive, but it also entails that the level of protection offered and, indeed, the substance of these rights, will vary from Member State to Member State.

(i) Pan-European remedies in national courts

There are four circumstances where EU law requires particular remedies to be provided in national courts. The first of these is the principle of state liability which allows for individuals, under certain circumstances, to sue the state for damages where they have suffered loss as a result of the state's illegal behaviour. This is dealt with later in the chapter,[14] and is a self-standing procedure that is conceptually distinct from direct effect. There are, however, three circumstances where directly effective rights lead to particular remedies. These are repayment of charges or taxes levied for breach of EU law; damages and repayment for breaches of EU competition law; and the granting of interim relief where a national court wishes to make a preliminary reference to the Court of Justice.[15] Each is constrained by a particular justification. The first two types of remedy are restitutionary in nature. At their heart lies the idea that an individual or state should not be enriched as a result of its behaviour, and that to allow this would be a denial of other parties' directly effective rights. The third remedy, as we shall see, is concerned to secure the effective operation of a procedure before the Court of Justice rather than a national court, namely the preliminary reference procedure.

Repayment of charges or taxes levied contrary to EU law was considered in *San Giorgio*, the facts in which were remarkably similar to *Rewe*.[16] The Italian state had levied charges for health inspections contrary to EU law. Under Italian law, however, there was no repayment of any illegal tax where the Italian state believed that the sums involved had been passed onto other persons, typically through higher pricing. San Giorgio challenged this. The structure of the Court's reasoning in this case was different from that in *Rewe*. In *San Giorgio*, the Court held that entitlement to the repayment of charges levied contrary to EU law was 'a consequence of, and an adjunct to, the rights' conferred by EU law. Whilst the Court created some

---

[14] See pp. 301–12.

[15] There is also, of course, the remedy of state liability described above where individuals can sue states in national courts for loss suffered as a result of a state's failure to comply with EU law.

[16] Case 199/82 *Amministrazione delle Finanze dello Stato* v *San Giorgio* [1983] ECR 3595.

leeway for the national system by providing that it was for it to determine when taxes have been passed on and therefore could not be recovered, the balance drawn was very different from *Rewe*. A concrete remedy, namely the right to restitution of illegally levied taxes, was put in place.

In subsequent years, the Court has extended this remedy.[17] It applies not just to taxes levied by the state, but to taxes and charges levied by public bodies,[18] illegal requirements to pay tax in advance[19] and the levying of guarantees in breach of EU law.[20] The conditions for non-repayment have also become highly circumscribed. If charges or taxes have only partially been passed on to other persons, the Court has ruled that the national authority can only refuse to pay that part which had been passed on by the person claiming repayment.[21] To determine the amount, the Court has held that national courts must engage in economic analysis, as the degree of enrichment will be affected not just by the increase in price but also by possible decline in volume of sales as a result of that increase.[22] Finally, the Court has touched on the level of compensation that may be recovered. It has ruled that complainants are entitled not only to repayment of the tax, but also compensation for any losses that accrued as a result of not having this revenue available to them.[23]

The second type of remedy is in the field of competition. The Court has ruled that contracts which breach Article 101 TFEU, the provision prohibiting cartels and anti-competitive conduct by two or more parties, are not only void, but allow individuals to claim damages where they can show that there is a direct causal link between the harm suffered and the illegal conduct or contract.[24] Similar reasoning operates in the field of state aids. The Court has ruled that if a national court finds that an unlawful aid has been paid to an undertaking by a national authority, it must order repayment of that aid, as it is under a duty to provide protection to individuals against illegal state aids.[25] We can draw parallels with the reasoning in these cases and the reasoning deployed in cases concerning illegally levied taxes because, in addition to wishing to secure the full effect of the provisions, the Court does not wish to see the unjust enrichment of those who have benefited from illegal conduct.[26] It is thus the recipient of the illegal aid whom the national authorities must recover the money from and the Court is silent about which third party may recover compensation for loss suffered from anti-competitive practices, focusing instead on the duty of the party engaging in the illegal practice to make good.

---

[17] On this remedy see P. Wattel, 'National Procedural Autonomy and the Effectiveness of EC Law: Challenge the Charge, File For Restitution, Sue For Damages?' (2008) 35(2) *LIEI* 109.

[18] Case C-242/95 *GT-Link* v *DSB* [1997] ECR I-4449.

[19] Joined Cases C-397/98 and C-410/98 *Metallgesellschaft* v *IRC* [2001] ECR I-1727; Case C-446/04 *Test Claimants in the FII Group Litigation* v *Commissioners of Inland Revenue* [2006] ECR I-11753, para. 203.

[20] Case C-470/04 *N* v *Inspecteur van de Belastingdienst Oostkantoor Almelo* [2006] ECR I-7409.

[21] Joined Cases C-192/95–C-218/95 *Comateb and Others* [1997] ECR I-165, paras. 27 and 28.

[22] Case C-147/01 *Weber's Wine World and Others* [2003] ECR I-11365; Case C-309/06 *Marks & Spencer* v *CCE* [2008] ECR I-2283.

[23] Joined Cases C-397/98 and C-410/98 *Metallgesellschaft* v *IRC* [2001] ECR I-1727; Case C-446/04 *Test Claimants in the FII Group Litigation* v *Commissioners of Inland Revenue* [2006] ECR I-11753.

[24] Case C-453/99 *Courage Ltd* v *Crehan* [2001] ECR I-6297; Joined Cases C-295/04–C-298/04 *Vincenzo Manfredi and Others* v *Lloyd Adriatico Assicurazioni SpA and Others* [2006] ECR I-6619. For discussion see S. Drake, 'Scope of *Courage* and the Principle of "Individual Liability" for Damages: Further Development of the Principle of Effective Judicial Protection by the Court of Justice' (2006) 31 *ELRev.* 841.

[25] Case C-39/94 *SFEI* [1996] ECR I-3547; Case C-71/04 *Xunta de Galicia* [2005] ECR I-7419.

[26] Case C-453/99 *Courage Ltd* v *Crehan* [2001] ECR I-6297 (on what was then Article 81 EC); Case C-354/90 *FNCE* [1991] ECR I-5505.

The third remedy is that of interim relief sought before national courts pending a reference to the Court of Justice. In *Factortame*, a challenge was made by a number of Spanish fishermen to the United Kingdom's Merchant Shipping Act 1988. This Act made it very difficult for non-British boats to fish in British waters by imposing, most notably, a series of residence requirements as a precondition. It was argued that this violated what is now Article 49 TFEU, the provision on freedom of establishment. The national court referred the matter to the Court of Justice. In the meantime, the House of Lords found that the applicants would suffer irreparable damage if interim relief was not granted. However, the House of Lords ruled that, notwithstanding this finding, English courts had no jurisdiction to suspend the Act as the remedy was at that time barred by statute. It referred the question of whether this rule of national law should be set aside in circumstances where its application would deprive a party of the enjoyment of rights derived from EU law. The Court of Justice had little difficulty in answering in the affirmative.

Case C–213/89 *R v Secretary of State for Transport, ex parte Factortame Ltd* [1990] ECR I–2433

19. In accordance with the case law of the Court, it is for the national courts, in application of the principle of cooperation laid down in Article [4(3) TFEU], to ensure the legal protection which persons derive from the direct effect of provisions of Community law ...

20. The Court has also held that any provision of a national legal system and any legislative, administrative or judicial practice which might impair the effectiveness of Community law by withholding from the national court having jurisdiction to apply such law the power to do everything necessary at the moment of its application to set aside national legislative provisions which might prevent, even temporarily, Community rules from having full force and effect are incompatible with those requirements, which are the very essence of Community law ...

21. It must be added that the full effectiveness of Community law would be just as much impaired if a rule of national law could prevent a court seised of a dispute governed by Community law from granting interim relief in order to ensure the full effectiveness of the judgment to be given on the existence of the rights claimed under Community law. It follows that a court which in those circumstances would grant interim relief, if it were not for a rule of national law, is obliged to set aside that rule.

22. That interpretation is reinforced by the system established by Article [267 TFEU] whose effectiveness would be impaired if a national court, having stayed proceedings pending the reply by the Court of Justice to the question referred to it for a preliminary ruling, were not able to grant interim relief until it delivered its judgment following the reply given by the Court of Justice.

23. Consequently, the reply to the question raised should be that Community law must be interpreted as meaning that a national court which, in a case before it concerning Community law, considers that the sole obstacle which precludes it from granting interim relief is a rule of national law must set aside that rule.

There are two features of note to *Factortame*.

The first is that the particular remedy sought is drawn (in paragraph 21) from a new line of reasoning: that of securing the full effectiveness of EU law. It is the strongest assertion made for pan-European remedies, as it suggests that wherever there is an EU right there should be a corresponding EU remedy. After *Factortame*, it looked for a while as if the Court might be moving to develop a fully fledged system of EU remedies[27] and a number of authors argued for this on the basis of the effectiveness of EU law alone, independent of any other doctrine, requiring the development of a system of substitute remedies applicable in national courts.[28]

The second issue is a corollary of this and questions, if this is so, what principles should govern the type of remedy provided. This goes above all to the law of remedies and not the uniformity of EU law. Its difficulties were illustrated in *Factortame*. The judgment is vague about when a national law should be suspended, suggesting that it should happen whenever the effectiveness of EU law is being undermined. By contrast, the Court has operated a different set of principles when relief is sought against a national law implementing an EU measure.[29] In such circumstances, the challenge is seen as being, in reality, against the EU measure. Relief will only be granted if there is serious and irreparable damage to the applicant, and this must be weighed against other considerations such as the damage to the Union legal order and its financial interests. From the perspective of two applicants, whose interests have been damaged equally, this difference seems perverse.[30] It also illustrates the challenges for EU law in developing a system of remedies that is both uniform and sensitive to different circumstances.

There has, thus, been a firm move away from developing pan-European remedies in recent years. With the exception of the limited instances described above, EU law accepts that the development of remedies to secure direct effect is overwhelmingly a role for the national legal system. The Union will intervene only if there has been a severe failure of protection by the domestic system.

This was most strongly set out in *Unibet*. Unibet, a British gambling company, sought to advertise its Internet gambling services in the Swedish media. These gambling activities contravened Swedish law. The Swedish authorities therefore obtained injunctions and initiated criminal proceedings against those who had provided advertising space to Unibet. No action was brought against Unibet itself. However, Unibet brought an action for a declaration that the Swedish law violated what is now Article 56 TFEU, which provides for the right to provide services in another Member State. In Swedish law, no possibility existed for an individual to bring a self-standing action for a declaration that a Swedish statute was illegal in the absence of a specific legal relationship. The Swedish court asked whether effective protection of an individual's rights in EU law required the creation of a new independent remedy permitting an action for a declaration that a national law is illegal.

---

[27] D. Curtin and K. Mortelmans, 'Application and Enforcement of Community Law by the Member States: Actors in Search of a Third Generation Script' in D. Curtin and T. Heukels (eds.), *Institutional Dynamics of European Integration* (The Hague, Martinus Nijhoff, 1994).

[28] See paras. 21–2. See also Case C-208/90 *Emmott* v *Minister for Social Welfare* [1991] ECR I-4269. For an excellent discussion of the debates see T. Tridimas, 'Black, White and Shades of Grey: Horizontality of Directives Revisited' (2002) 21 *YBEL* 327; K. Lenaerts and T. Corthaut, 'Of Birds and Hedges: The Role of Primacy in Invoking Norms of EU Law' (2006) 31 *ELRev.* 287; M. Dougan, 'When Worlds Collide: Competing Visions of the Relationship Between Direct Effect and Supremacy' (2007) 44 *CMLRev.* 931.

[29] Joined Cases C-143/88 and C-92/89 *Zuckerfabrik Süderdithmarschen and Zuckerfabrik Soest* [1991] ECR I-415; Case C-465/93 *Atlanta Fruchthandelsgesellschaft and Others (No. 1)* [1995] ECR I-3761; Case C-68/95 *T. Port* [1996] ECR I-6065; Joined Cases C-453/03, C-11/04, C-12/04 and C-194/04 *Martini* v *Ministero delle Politiche Agricole e Forestali* [2005] ECR I-10423.

[30] This has already been considered in some detail at pp. 172–3.

Case C-432/05 *Unibet* v *Justitiekanslern* [2007] ECR I-2271

37. It is to be noted at the outset that, according to settled case law, the principle of effective judicial protection is a general principle of Community law stemming from the constitutional traditions common to the Member States, which has been enshrined in Articles 6 and 13 of the European Convention for the Protection of Human Rights and Fundamental Freedoms ... and which has also been reaffirmed by Article 47 of the Charter of Fundamental Rights of the European Union ...

38. Under the principle of cooperation laid down in Article [4(3) TEU], it is for the Member States to ensure judicial protection of an individual's rights under Community law ...

39. It is also to be noted that, in the absence of Community rules governing the matter, it is for the domestic legal system of each Member State to designate the courts and tribunals having jurisdiction and to lay down the detailed procedural rules governing actions for safeguarding rights which individuals derive from Community law ...

40. Although the EC Treaty has made it possible in a number of instances for private persons to bring a direct action, where appropriate, before the Community Court, it was not intended to create new remedies in the national courts to ensure the observance of Community law other than those already laid down by national law ...

41. It would be otherwise only if it were apparent from the overall scheme of the national legal system in question that no legal remedy existed which made it possible to ensure, even indirectly, respect for an individual's rights under Community law ...

42. Thus, while it is, in principle, for national law to determine an individual's standing and legal interest in bringing proceedings, Community law nevertheless requires that the national legislation does not undermine the right to effective judicial protection ...

43. In that regard, the detailed procedural rules governing actions for safeguarding an individual's rights under Community law must be no less favourable than those governing similar domestic actions (principle of equivalence) and must not render practically impossible or excessively difficult the exercise of rights conferred by Community law (principle of effectiveness) ...

44. Moreover, it is for the national courts to interpret the procedural rules governing actions brought before them, such as the requirement for there to be a specific legal relationship between the applicant and the State, in such a way as to enable those rules, wherever possible, to be implemented in such a manner as to contribute to the attainment of the objective ... of ensuring effective judicial protection of an individual's rights under Community law ...

47. In that regard, it is to be noted ... that the principle of effective judicial protection does not require it to be possible, as such, to bring a free-standing action which seeks primarily to dispute the compatibility of national provisions with Community law, provided that the principles of equivalence and effectiveness are observed in the domestic system of judicial remedies.

48. Firstly, it is apparent from the order for reference that Swedish law does not provide for such a free-standing action, regardless of whether the higher-ranking legal rule to be complied with is a national rule or a Community rule ...

53. It is necessary ... to establish whether the effect of the indirect legal remedies provided for by Swedish law for disputing the compatibility of a national provision with Community law is to render practically impossible or excessively difficult the exercise of rights conferred by Community law.

54. In that regard, each case which raises the question whether a national procedural provision renders the application of Community law impossible or excessively difficult must be analysed by reference to the role of that provision in the procedure, its progress and its special features, viewed as a whole, before the various national instances ...

55. It is apparent from the order for reference that Swedish law does not prevent a person, such as Unibet, from disputing the compatibility of national legislation, such as the Law on Lotteries, with Community law but that, on the contrary, there exist various indirect legal remedies for that purpose.

56. Thus, firstly, the Högsta domstolen states that Unibet may obtain an examination of whether the Law on Lotteries is compatible with Community law in the context of a claim for damages before the ordinary courts.

57. It is also clear from the order for reference that Unibet brought such a claim and that the Högsta domstolen found it to be admissible.

58. Consequently, where an examination of the compatibility of the Law on Lotteries with Community law takes place in the context of the determination of a claim for damages, that action constitutes a remedy which enables Unibet to ensure effective protection of the rights conferred on it by Community law.

59. It is for the Högsta domstolen to ensure that the examination of the compatibility of that law with Community law takes place irrespective of the assessment of the merits of the case with regard to the requirements for damage and a causal link in the claim for damages.

60. Secondly, the Högsta domstolen adds that, if Unibet applied to the Swedish Government for an exception to the prohibition on the promotion of its services in Sweden, any decision rejecting that application could be the subject of judicial review proceedings before the Regeringsrätten, in which Unibet would be able to argue that the provisions of the Law on Lotteries are incompatible with Community law. Where appropriate, the competent court would be required to disapply the provisions of that law that were considered to be in conflict with Community law.

61. It is to be noted that such judicial review proceedings, which would enable Unibet to obtain a judicial decision that those provisions are incompatible with Community law, constitute a legal remedy securing effective judicial protection of its rights under Community law …

62. Moreover, the Högsta domstolen states that if Unibet disregarded the provisions of the Law on Lotteries and administrative action or criminal proceedings were brought against it by the competent national authorities, it would have the opportunity, in proceedings brought before the administrative court or an ordinary court, to dispute the compatibility of those provisions with Community law. Where appropriate, the competent court would be required to disapply the provisions of that law that were considered to be in conflict with Community law.

63. In addition to the remedies referred to at paragraphs 56 and 60 above, it would therefore be possible for Unibet to claim in court proceedings against the administration or in criminal proceedings that measures taken or required to be taken against it were incompatible with Community law on account of the fact that it had not been permitted by the competent national authorities to promote its services in Sweden.

64. In any event, it is clear from paragraphs 56 to 61 above that Unibet must be regarded as having available to it legal remedies which ensure effective judicial protection of its rights under Community law. If, on the contrary, as mentioned at paragraph 62 above, it was forced to be subject to administrative or criminal proceedings and to any penalties that may result as the sole form of legal remedy for disputing the compatibility of the national provision at issue with Community law, that would not be sufficient to secure for it such effective judicial protection.

65. Accordingly, the answer to the first question must be that the principle of effective judicial protection of an individual's rights under Community law must be interpreted as meaning that it does not require the national legal order of a Member State to provide for a free-standing action for an examination of whether national provisions are compatible with Article [56 TFEU], provided that other effective legal remedies, which are no less favourable than those governing similar domestic actions, make it possible for such a question of compatibility to be determined as a preliminary issue, which is a matter for the national court to establish.

The message of the judgment is twofold. First, there will only be Union review if there has been a very strong failure of protection of the applicant or she has not been given the same level of protection as that available in a comparable domestic action. There is a presumption of trust in the national system, which involves a presumption of good faith (the equivalence principle) and a presumption of capacity (the rules that redress not be impossible or excessively difficult to obtain). Secondly, the Court will look to the local legal context to decide whether these requirements have been fulfilled. This focus on local context emphasises the reluctance of the Court to develop an autonomous system of remedies to be applied in domestic courts. For the absence of a particular remedy or procedure may indicate inadequate protection in one national legal context but not in another. In such circumstances, it is difficult to develop general rules that all Member States must provide certain forms of redress.

(ii) Union oversight of local remedies in domestic courts

Notwithstanding that remedies are predominantly for the domestic system to decide, there must still be some standard which indicates when these remedies make the exercise of EU rights 'excessively difficult'. The Court's case law is quite intricate here. It is worth looking at its approach to substantive remedies, domestic procedural rules and limitations periods separately. For its degree of intervention has been different in each of these fields.

On remedies, the Court has said very little except where a Member State limits the level or type of compensation in an *a priori* way. National measures which try to cap levels of compensation at very low levels are thus illegal[31] as are those which provide for only nominal compensation with no regard to the damage sustained.[32] Similarly, Member States are not allowed to prevent compensation for certain types of damage, notably economic loss.[33]

The Court's case law has been more extensive on procedures. The central thread here in recent times has been that judicial protection involves certain minimum fundamental rights guarantees. In *Unibet*, the Court thus roots its reasoning in the judicial guarantees provided by the European Convention on Human Rights and the EU Charter of Fundamental Rights and Freedoms. First mooted by the Court in the 1980s,[34] this reasoning has come to mean a number of things.

First, there is a requirement of judicial control so that national courts cannot be barred from considering directly effective provisions. A national requirement stating that certain forms of activities clearly falling within a Directive were not subject to judicial control was therefore found to be illegal.[35] The principle of effective judicial control also means that any decision of a professional or administrative body restricting an EU right must be subject to judicial review and, to enable that review to be meaningful, must state the reasons for the decision.[36]

---

[31] Case C-271/91 *Marshall* v *Southampton and South West Hampshire AHA* [1993] ECR I-4367.

[32] Case 14/83 *Von Colson and Kamann* v *Land Nordrhein-Westfalen* [1984] ECR 1891.

[33] Joined Cases C-46/93 and 48/93 *Brasserie du Pêcheur* v *Germany* and *R* v *Secretary of State for Transport, ex parte Factortame (No. 3)* [1996] ECR I-1029.

[34] For discussion, see A. Arnull, *The European Union and its Court of Justice* (2nd edn, Oxford, Oxford University Press, 2006) ch. 6.

[35] Case 222/84 *Johnston* v *Chief Constable of the Royal Ulster Constabulary* [1986] ECR 1651.

[36] Case 222/86 *UNECTEF* v *Heylens* [1987] ECR 4097.

Secondly, national courts must secure the proper conduct of the proceedings.[37] To that end, parties must be given a genuine opportunity to raise pleas based on EU law before them.[38] In addition to this, if parties are entitled to submit to the court observations on a piece of evidence, they must be afforded a real opportunity to comment effectively on it.[39] Parties must also be given sufficient time to prepare their defence and must be protected from abusive use of the litigation process by their adversaries.[40] Alongside this, in *Impact* v *MAFF*, although the Court did not refer to this line of reasoning, it stated that individuals should be able to bring their action before a single court for a single claim, and cannot be required to bring different elements of it before different courts.[41] The reasoning was that the procedural complications and cost thus imposed on parties made it excessively difficult for them to pursue their claims. Yet, this could be related to courts' duties to secure proper conduct of the proceedings.

There is a final category of cases, where the claimant has not pursued a claim within the limitation period set by national law or has not taken action to avert loss. In both instances, the Court of Justice has indicated that the Member State has to take action here provided it is reasonable. Reasonable limitation periods may be set[42] and Member States may impose requirements on claimants to mitigate the loss or exercise due diligence to avoid the loss.[43] Yet, as both limitation periods and due diligence preconditions can be used to bar access to courts, the Court has been willing to scrutinise the 'reasonableness' of national measures here in quite some depth.

With regard to limitation periods, the Court will look therefore at whether individuals did not bring a claim within the required time because of unconscionable behaviour by the defendant,[44] or the state,[45] which induced them to defer their action. In the field of consumer law, this has been taken a step further and also applied to failures to act, so that it is unreasonable for national limitation periods to apply if, in breach of EU legislation, vendors fail to tell consumers of their right to terminate contracts.[46] Dougan has thus talked of an estoppel principle where defendants guilty of some form of unconscionable conduct cannot benefit from national limitation periods. Yet, as he has noted, the doctrine is extremely vague as to the level of unconscionability required and the issue of when it is reasonable for the claimant to rely on it.[47] The Court of Justice will also look at the date from when the limitation period runs to ascertain that it does not start too early. It has thus held that limitation periods which begin from the day on which an anti-competitive practice is adopted might be unreasonable.[48] Similarly, it

---

[37] Case C-312/93 *Peterbroeck* v *Belgium* [1995] ECR I-4599.

[38] Joined Cases C-222/05–C-225/05 *Van der Weerd* v *Minister van Landbouw, Natuur en Voedselkwaliteit* [2007] ECR I-4233.

[39] Case C-276/01 *Steffensen* [2003] ECR I-3735.

[40] Case C-443/03 *Leffler* v *Berlin Chemie* [2005] ECR I-9611.

[41] Case C-268/06 *Impact* v *MAFF* [2008] ECR I-2483.

[42] Case C-261/95 *Palmisani* v *INPS* [1997] ECR I-4025.

[43] Joined Cases C-46/93 and C-48/93 *Brasserie du Pêcheur* v *Germany* [1996] ECR I-1029; Joined Cases C-95/07 and C-96/07 *Ecotrade* v *Agenzia delle Entrate – Ufficio di Genova*, Judgment of 21 June 2008.

[44] In *Levez*, an employer led a female employee to believe the disparity in pay between her and a male counterpart was less than it was, leading her to abstain from action until she discovered the full disparity: Case C-326/96 *Levez* v *Jennings* [1998] ECR I-7835.

[45] Case C-327/00 *Santex* v *Unità Socio Sanitaria Locale n. 42 di Pavia* [2003] ECR I-1877; Case C-241/06 *Lämmerzahl* [2007] ECR I-8415.

[46] Case C-481/99 *Heininger* [2001] ECR I-9945.

[47] Dougan, above n. 13, 280–2.

[48] Joined Cases C-295/04–C-298/04 *Vincenzo Manfredi and Others* v *Lloyd Adriatico Assicurazioni SpA and Others* [2006] ECR I-6619. Much will depend on when the harm and identity was identifiable. In *Dansk Slagterier*, the Court indicated that what will be crucial is when the injured party became aware of the loss: Case C-445/06 *Danske Slagterier* v *Germany*, Judgment of 24 March 2009.

has held that in the case of people employed on a series of short-term contracts, the limitation period begins from the end of the relationship, not the end of each of the contracts.[49]

The Court of Justice's central concern about national conditions requiring an applicant to exercise due diligence to avert loss revolves around national stipulations that an individual cannot claim for loss which would not have arisen if she had sued earlier. Initially, the Court suggested that a national requirement of due diligence could legitimately demand that parties show that they had used all legal remedies available to them before claiming for loss.[50] However, in *Metallgesellschaft*, the Court considered a British requirement that a firm could not claim for interest suffered from a tax advantage illegally denied to it on the grounds that it should have claimed and then sued. It considered that the requirement of prior litigation made the exercise of the applicant's rights excessively difficult and was therefore illegal. The Court reconciled these approaches in *Danske Slagterier*, a case concerning a German ban on uncastrated male pigs from Denmark which had lasted six years before it was challenged.[51] The Court considered that national courts could impose a duty of due diligence and this could include a requirement for the applicant to show that she had availed herself in time of all the legal remedies available. However, this requirement would not be available if use of these remedies would give rise to excessive difficulties or could not reasonably be required.

5 DIRECT EFFECT AND SECONDARY LEGISLATION

The vast bulk of EU law is contained not in the Treaties, but in secondary legislation.[52] It was not surprising, therefore, that early on after the end of the transitional period, the question arose as to whether the different types of secondary legislation were capable of direct effect.

The most straightforward case was that of Regulations. Deemed to have general application, be binding and directly applicable in all Member States, Regulations are the closest thing the Union has to domestic statutes.[53] They were therefore held to be capable of direct effect in the same way as Treaty provisions in *Leonesio*.[54]

International agreements made by the Union with non-EU states have also been held to be capable of direct effect. This will not be the case with all international agreements, however. The test is a two-tier one.[55] First, the wording, nature and purpose of the agreement is compared with some international agreements considered incapable of generating direct effect simply by virtue of their overall framework being too flexible and open-ended. Secondly, the specific provision is considered in the light of this. Only if it is sufficiently precise and unconditional will it be directly effective.

---

[49] Case C-78/98 *Preston* v *Wolverhampton Health Care Trust* [2000] ECR I-3201.

[50] Joined Cases C-46/93 and C-48/93 *Brasserie du Pêcheur* v *Germany* [1996] ECR I-1029.

[51] Case C-445/06 *Danske Slagterier* v *Germany*, Judgment of 24 March 2009.

[52] The different types of secondary legislation have been considered in Chapter 3. See pp. 98–100.

[53] Their replacements were therefore known as European laws in the failed Constitutional Treaty, Article I-33(1) CT. See also J. Winter, 'Direct Effect and Direct Applicability: Two Distinct and Different Concepts in Community Law' (1972) 9 *CMLRev.* 425.

[54] Case 93/71 *Leonesio* v *Italian Ministry of Agriculture* [1972] ECR 293. See also Case 39/72 *Commission* v *Italy (premiums for slaughtering cows)* [1973] ECR 101.

[55] The standard formulation is Case 104/81 *Hauptzollamt Mainz* v *Kupferberg* [1982] ECR 3641; Case 12/86 *Demirel* v *Stadt Schwäbisch Gmünd* [1987] ECR 2719. This test leads, in practice, to international agreements being given a wide variety of legal effects within EU law. P. Eeckhout, *External Relations of the European Union: Legal Constitutional Foundations* (Oxford, Oxford University Press, 2004) ch. 9.

(i) Establishment of the direct effect of Directives and national resistance

The position of Directives is more complicated. Directives are binding upon Member States as to the result to be achieved but leave discretion to the national authorities over how to realise this. This could lead to a number of objections being made against Directives being capable of direct effect:

- The discretion given to Member States to implement Directives should result in individuals being able to derive rights only from the acts of national authorities themselves, and not from the Directives themselves.
- To grant direct effect to Directives would blur the distinction between Directives and Regulations, a distinction clearly spelt out in Article 288 TFEU, as both would have similar legal effect.
- In numerous fields, the Union enjoys a competence to adopt Directives but not Regulations, so that according to Directives full direct effect would amount to a blurring of the distinction between the two legal forms, allowing the Union in effect to legislate through the backdoor in areas that the Treaty had not permitted through the front.[56]

Notwithstanding these arguments, the Court of Justice ruled in *Van Duyn* that Directives could generate direct effect.[57] Van Duyn was refused leave to enter the United Kingdom in order to take up an offer of a secretarial post at the Church of Scientology, as the UK government had imposed a ban on foreign scientologists entering the United Kingdom. She challenged the ban on the grounds, inter alia, that it breached Directive 64/221/EEC, which required that any ban be based upon the personal conduct of the individual. The Court considered that her association with the Church of Scientology met the requirements of the Directive. It considered, first, whether the Directive was capable of direct effect.

Case 41/74 *Van Duyn* v *Home Office* [1974] ECR 1337

12. ... It would be incompatible with the binding effect attributed to a Directive by Article [288 TFEU] to exclude, in principle, the possibility that the obligation which it imposes may be invoked by those concerned. In particular, where the Community authorities have, by Directive, imposed on Member States the obligation to pursue a particular course of conduct, the useful effect of such an act would be weakened if individuals were prevented from relying on it before their national courts and if the latter were prevented from taking it into consideration as an element of Community law. Article [267 TFEU], which empowers national courts to refer to the Court questions concerning the validity and interpretation of all acts of the Community institutions, without distinction, implies furthermore that these acts may be invoked by individuals in the national courts. It is necessary to examine, in every case, whether the nature, general scheme and wording of the provisions in question are capable of having direct effects on the relations between Member States and individuals.

---

[56] On this debate see S. Prechal, *Directives in European Community Law: A Study of Directives and their Enforcement in National Courts* (2nd edn, Oxford, Oxford University Press, 2005) 216–20.

[57] Decisions have also been held, on similar grounds, to be capable of bearing direct effect: see Case 9/70 *Grad* v *Finanzamt Traustein* [1970] ECR 838.

This reasoning is remarkably weak. It starts from an *a contrario* position of whether there is any good reason why Directives should not have direct effect. The arguments that their binding nature and their effectiveness require that they be invoked in national courts are simply *non sequiturs*. For, put simply, neither of these qualities prescribes the types of effects a Directive should have in a domestic legal system. Indeed, no less a figure than Federico Mancini, a former judge at the Court, has admitted that 'this judgment goes beyond the letter of Article [288 TFEU]', the provision that sets out the central characteristics of Regulations and Directives.[58] More significantly, the ruling provoked a strong counter-reaction from both French and German courts. The view of the French Conseil d'Etat, the highest court of administrative law in France, can be seen in its judgment in the *Cohn-Bendit* case.[59] Cohn-Bendit was a German national who had been a leader of student disturbances in 1968. He was offered a job as a broadcaster in France. The French Minister of the Interior sought to deport him. Cohn-Bendit invoked Directive 64/221/EEC stating that it required that any decision be both formally reasoned and that the grounds for the decision be made known to the immigrant. As this had not happened, the decision was illegal, he argued.

Minister of the Interior v Cohn–Bendit [1980] 1 CMLR 543

... it appears clearly from the provisions of Article [288 TFEU] that if Directives bind Member States 'with regard to the result to be achieved' and if, in order to achieve the results which they define, the national authorities of Member States are under an obligation to adapt their legislative and regulatory provisions to the directives which are addressed to them, these authorities remain the only competent authorities to determine the form to give to the implementation of these directives and to determine themselves, under the control of the national judicial authorities, their own method for producing their effect in internal national law ...

... Directives cannot be invoked by persons within the jurisdiction of those Member States in order to support a legal action undertaken against any administrative action with regard to an individual ...

... It follows from the foregoing that M. Cohn-Bendit cannot hope to succeed in his argument ... to annul the decision of the Minister of the Interior ...

The Court of Justice tried to bolster its position by resorting to a new justification in *Ratti*:[60] the estoppel argument. This states that, as Directives impose a duty upon Member States to adopt the appropriate implementing measures by a certain date, it would be wrong for Member States to be able to rely upon and gain advantage through their failure to carry out this obligation. They are thus 'estopped' or prevented from denying the direct effect of Directives once the time limit for their implementation into national law has expired. Thus, in *Ratti*, a trader was prosecuted for not labelling his solvents in accordance with Italian law. He sought to rely upon two Directives. While the transitional period for one of these had expired, it had not for the other. The Court held that he could rely only upon the first Directive. The Member State was estopped by its failure to take the necessary implementing measures from denying this

---

[58] G. Mancini and D. Keeling, 'Language, Culture and Politics in the Life of the European Court of Justice' (1995) 1 *CJEL* 397, 401.

[59] Similar reasoning by the German Bundesfinanzhof can be found in *Re Value Added Tax Directives* [1982] 1 CMLR 527.

[60] Case 148/78 *Ministero Pubblico* v *Ratti* [1979] ECR 1629. See also Case 8/81 *Becker* v *Finanzamt Münster-Innenstadt* [1982] ECR 53.

Directive's direct effect. The other Directive was not directly effective, however, as the Member State was still within its period of grace. Directives will be directly effective, therefore, only from the end of the transposition period and, even then, will be capable of direct effect only if the Member State has failed to implement them or has not implemented them correctly. Where Directives are correctly implemented, individual rights flow from the national implementing provisions and not from the Directives themselves.

(ii) Vertical direct effect of Directives

The estoppel argument has one important implication. As the direct effect of Directives is predicated on the 'fault' of the Member State, parties may invoke Directives against the state. But it does not follow from the estoppel argument that parties may invoke Directives in national legal proceedings against other private parties. In other words, the estoppel argument may be used to justify the vertical direct effect of Directives, but not their horizontal direct effect. This limitation was set out in *Marshall*. Marshall, a dietician employed by a British health authority, was dismissed at the age of 62 on the ground that she had passed the pensionable age, which was, at that time, 60 years for women. A man would not have been dismissed at that age, but Marshall had no redress under the Sex Discrimination Act 1975 because of a blanket exclusion in that Act relating to terms and conditions relating to death and retirement. She claimed that there had been a breach of article 5 of the Equal Treatment Directive 76/207/EEC, which provides for equal treatment for men and women concerning the terms and conditions of dismissal.

Case 152/84 *Marshall v Southampton and SW Hampshire Area Health Authority* [1986] ECR 723

48. With regard to the argument that a Directive may not be relied upon against an individual, it must be emphasised that according to Article [288 TFEU], the binding nature of a Directive, which constitutes the basis for the possibility of relying on the Directive before a national court, exists only in relation to 'each Member State to which it is addressed'. It follows that a Directive may not of itself impose obligations on an individual and that a provision of a Directive may not be relied upon as such against such a person.

49. In that respect it must be pointed out that where a person involved in legal proceedings is able to rely on a Directive as against the State he may do so regardless of the capacity in which the latter is acting, whether employer or public authority. In either case it is necessary to prevent the State from taking advantage of its own failure to comply with Community law ...

51. The argument submitted by the United Kingdom that the possibility of relying on provisions of the Directive against the respondent *qua* organ of the State would give rise to an arbitrary and unfair distinction between the rights of State employees and those of private employees does not justify any other conclusion. Such a distinction may easily be avoided if the Member State concerned has correctly implemented the Directive in national law.

Marshall created a distinction between Regulations and Directives by holding that only the former were capable of horizontal direct effect. This addressed some of the initial concerns about the direct effect of Directives but created problems of its own. For one thing, it generated uncertainty by begging the question as to which bodies formed part of the state and could consequently be sued. Defining the state can, to be sure, be something of a endless task. The multiple legal structures that form part of the state are frequently a consequence of historical happenstance, on the one hand, and recurring reinvention of the place of public intervention, on the other.[61]

The question was addressed most clearly in *Foster* v *British Gas*, which indicated that the test for when a body would form part of the state was one of EU law not national law. Like Marshall, Foster was forced to retire at 60 years, whereas men could continue working until aged 65. She and four other women invoked the Equal Treatment Directive against her former employer, British Gas. The latter was at the time a nationalised industry. Its board members were appointed by a British minister who could also issue to the board various directions and instruments. In addition, the board was required to submit periodic reports to the Secretary of State.

Case C-188/89 *Foster* v *British Gas* [1990] ECR I-3313

17. The Court further held in … *Marshall* that where a person is able to rely on a Directive as against the State he may do so regardless of the capacity in which the latter is acting, whether as employer or as public authority. In either case it is necessary to prevent the State from taking advantage of its own failure to comply with Community law.

18. On the basis of those considerations, the Court has held in a series of cases that unconditional and sufficiently precise provisions of a Directive could be relied on against organisations or bodies which were subject to the authority or control of the State or had special powers beyond those which result from the normal rules applicable to relations between individuals.

19. The Court has accordingly held that provisions of a directive could be relied on against tax authorities …, local or regional authorities …, constitutionally independent authorities responsible for the maintenance of public order and safety …, and public authorities providing public health services …

20. It follows… that a body, whatever its legal form, which has been made responsible, pursuant to a measure adopted by the State, for providing a public service under the control of the State and has for that purpose special powers beyond those which result from the normal rules applicable in relations between individuals, is included … among the bodies against which the provisions of a Directive capable of having direct effect may be relied upon.

The test of whether a body is part of the state is a dual one. A body may be deemed to be part of the state on functional grounds. In subsequent cases, the Court has made clear that it is sufficient that an entity is carrying out a public service and, for that reason, has special powers. Its legal form and the presence of state control is not determinative. In *Vassallo*, the Court held, therefore, that a Directive could be invoked against an Italian hospital which, although it received public funding, was not run by the Italian state but was an autonomous establishment with its own directors. In that instance, it was crucial for the Court of Justice that the hospital, notwithstanding this, was still seen by the national court as part of the public sector and performing a public service.[62]

---

[61] On this see D. Curtin, 'The Province of Government: Delimiting the Direct Effect of Directives in the Common Law Context' (1990) 15 *ELRev.* 195, 198–9.

[62] Case C-180/04 *Vassallo* v *Azienda Ospedaliera Ospedale San Martino di Genova e Cliniche Universitarie Convenzionate* [2006] ECR I-7251.

In other cases, the Court will look at the degree of state control. It has thus held that any entity which forms part of, or is subject to the authority of, public authority forms part of the state, and can be sued. In *Rohrbach*, two Austrian companies that were owned by a public authority and carried out launderette and gardening activities were held to be part of the state.[63] This was not done on the grounds that they carried out a social function (their mission was to employ people with disabilities) but purely by virtue of the local authority ownership.

The difficulties of definition were not the only problems generated by *Marshall*. Its style of analysis sits uncomfortably with *Defrenne* v *Sabena*.[64] The latter holds that obligations addressed to Member States lead, by virtue of their binding nature, to horizontal direct effect, as they require courts to apply EU law in cases before them, whereas in *Marshall* the opposite is stated. More practically, the rule in *Marshall* creates illogical outcomes: Marshall could rely on the Directive because she was employed by a public authority, a part of the state. Had she been employed by a private hospital she would not have been able to rely on the Directive. Thus, a somewhat arbitrary, two-tier legal system has been created, in which parties have greater protection against public bodies than against private ones, notwithstanding the fact that their functional relationship with the two may be the same. Finally, *Marshall* rests on a false assumption. It is difficult to see how the estoppel argument can justify reliance on a Directive against a public health authority. For, certainly, the state is responsible for implementing Directives and public health authorities are a part of the state, but there is no sense in which public health authorities are responsible for transposing the terms of equal pay Directives into national law – yet here, the Directive was held to be enforceable as against the authority.

(iii) Debate about horizontal direct effect and incidental direct effect

For the reasons outlined above, *Marshall* came under withering attack from academic commentators[65] and Advocates General[66] alike. Undoubtedly, this provided the context for some of the doctrines subsequently developed, notably indirect effect and state liability. Yet, notwithstanding this, the Court has resolutely stated that Directives are not capable of horizontal direct effect as they cannot impose obligations on individuals.[67] However, the full force of this has been overshadowed by the phenomenon of 'triangular situations' or 'incidental direct effects'. The idea of a triangular situation is that a dispute between two parties may affect the legal rights of a third party or impose a financial burden on them. This creates a dilemma: *Marshall* holds, on the one hand, that an individual can sue the state and, on the other, that it shall not impose obligations on a private party. What happens when both are present?

---

[63] Case C-297/03 *Sozialhilfeverband Rohrbach* v *Arbeiterkammer Oberösterreich* [2005] ECR I-4305.

[64] Case 43/75 *Defrenne* v *Sabena* [1976] ECR 455.

[65] D. Curtin, 'The Effectiveness of Judicial Protection of Individual Rights' (1990) 27 *CMLRev.* 709; S. Prechal, 'Remedies After Marshall' (1990) 27 *CMLRev.* 451; J. Coppell, 'Rights, Duties and the End of Marshall' (1994) 57 *MLR* 859; T. Tridimas, 'Horizontal Effect of Directives: A Missed Opportunity?' (1994) 19 *ELRev.* 621.

[66] Advocate General Van Gerven in Case C-271/91 *Marshall* v *Southampton and South-West Hampshire AHA* [1993] ECR I-4367; Advocate General Jacobs in Case C-316/93 *Vaneetveld* v *Le Foyer* [1994] ECR I-763; and Advocate General Lenz in Case C-91/92 *Faccini Dori* v *Recreb* [1994] ECR I-3325.

[67] The moment of truth is often seen as *Dori* where six governments intervened to argue against horizontal direct effect. Case C-91/92 *Faccini Dori* v *Recreb* [1994] ECR I-3325. For more recent examples see Case C-356/05 *Farrell* v *Whitty* [2007] ECR I-3067; Case C-80/06 *Carp* [2007] ECR I-4473; Joined Cases C-37/06 and C-58/06 *Viamex Agrar Handels and Others* v *Hauptzollamt Hamburg-Jonas* [2008] ECR I-69.

This was first addressed head on by the Court in *Wells*.[68] The case concerned a challenge to a British government decision authorising a quarry in Wales to carry out mining operations opposite the claimant's house without its having carried out an environmental impact assessment as required by Directive 85/337/EC.[69] The British government argued that to allow the challenge would have the effect of the Directive denying the quarry its rights under English and Welsh law. The Court was dismissive of this, stating that a Directive's having adverse repercussions on a third party could not prevent its being invoked against the state.

The Court extrapolated on this in *Arcor*. A telephone service provider challenged a decision by the German regulatory authority to allow Deutsche Telekom, the owner of the telephone network in Germany, to charge for use of that network. It was argued that two Directives precluded this charge where the network was run by a market dominant business, as was the case here, and the fees were unrelated to the costs of connection. Whilst the case was brought against the German regulators, its central target was, of course, Deutsche Telekom and the fees it was charging.

Joined Cases C-152/07–C-154/07 *Arcor* v *Bundesrepublik Deutschland* [2008] ECR I-5959

35. It should be recalled that, according to settled case-law, a directive cannot of itself impose obligations on an individual, but can only confer rights. Consequently, an individual may not rely on a directive against a Member State where it is a matter of a State obligation directly linked to the performance of another obligation falling, pursuant to that directive, on a third party ...

36. On the other hand, mere adverse repercussions on the rights of third parties, even if the repercussions are certain, do not justify preventing an individual from relying on the provisions of a directive against the Member State concerned ...

37. In the main proceedings ... the actions before the referring court have been brought by private persons against the Member State concerned, represented by the national regulatory authority which made the contested decision and has sole competence to set the rates of both the connection charge at issue in the main proceedings and the interconnection charge to which the former is added.

38. It is clear that Deutsche Telekom is a third party in relation to the dispute before the referring court and is only capable of suffering adverse repercussions because it levied the connection charge at issue in the main proceedings and because, if that charge were removed, it would have to increase its own subscribers' rates. Such a removal of benefits cannot be regarded as an obligation falling on a third party pursuant to the directives relied on before the referring court by the appellants in the main proceedings.

If *Arcor* held that additional costs or removal of benefits for a third party were not a reason to prevent an individual invoking a Directive in national courts, it was still opaque about when Directives can be invoked in national courts.[70] Nyssens and Lackhoff suggest that there are three circumstances. The first is when a Directive entitles an individual to require the Member State to do something but this places a burden on another party. This is uncontroversial. It happens when individuals invoke Directives requiring local authorities to set things out properly

---

[68] It had been touched on but not addressed in a number of cases, with the first being Case C-431/91 *Commission v Germany* [1995] ECR I-2189. For a review of these see H. Nyssens and K. Lackhoff, 'Direct Effect of Directives in Triangular Situations' (1998) 23 *ELRev.* 397; D. Colgan, 'Triangular Situations: The Coup de Grâce for the Denial of Horizontal Direct Effect of Community Directives' (2002) 8 *EPL* 545; F. Becker and A. Campbell, 'The Direct Effect of European Directives: Towards the Final Act?' (2007) 13 *CJEL* 401.

[69] Case C-201/02 *R* v *Secretary of State for Transport, Local Government and the Regions, ex parte Wells* [2004] ECR I-723.

[70] On this see Advocate General Mazák in Case C-411/05 *Félix Palacios de la Villa* v *Cortefiel Servicios SA* [2007] ECR I-8531, paras. 123–7.

for public tender. Such tenders require significant information from other companies and are costly.[71] The second is where Directives require states to impose a burden on third parties 'whilst not allowing any third party the symmetrical right to require that they do so. Nevertheless, any such third party might be able to invoke the provisions of a Directive in a national administrative court.'[72] This was the situation in *Wells* and *Arcor*. Neither of the applicants had an ex ante right to compel a decision to be taken, but once one was taken in breach of the Directive which affected their interests they were able to challenge it. The third situation is the most controversial. It occurs where a Directive grants a party a legal right to shield itself from certain activities by the Member State. In defiance of this, the Member State engages in these activities in such a way that they create rights in national law for third parties. Can the Directive be invoked by the individual in litigation with these third parties?

This happened in *CIA*. Signalson and Securitel sought to restrain CIA Security from marketing an alarm system on the grounds that it had not received authorisation as required by Belgian law. This requirement of prior authorisation breached EU law, however, as, under Directive 83/189/EC, it should have been notified to the Commission. This had not happened and CIA therefore argued that the national law was inapplicable.

Case C-194/94 *CIA Security International* v *Signalson & Securitel* [1996] ECR I-2201

44. That view cannot be adopted. Articles 8 and 9 of Directive 83/189 lay down a precise obligation on Member States to notify draft technical regulations to the Commission before they are adopted. Being, accordingly, unconditional and sufficiently precise in terms of their content, those articles may be relied on by individuals before national courts.

45. It remains to examine the legal consequences to be drawn from a breach by Member States of their obligation to notify and, more precisely, whether Directive 83/189 is to be interpreted as meaning that a breach of the obligation to notify, constituting a procedural defect in the adoption of the technical regulations concerned, renders such technical regulations inapplicable so that they may not be enforced against individuals.

46. The German and Netherlands Governments and the United Kingdom consider that Directive 83/189 is solely concerned with relations between the Member States and the Commission, that it merely creates procedural obligations which the Member States must observe when adopting technical regulations, their competence to adopt the regulations in question after expiry of the suspension period being, however, unaffected, and, finally, that it contains no express provision relating to any effects attaching to non-compliance with those procedural obligations.

47. The Court observes first of all in this context that none of those factors prevents non-compliance with Directive 83/189 from rendering the technical regulations in question inapplicable.

48. For such a consequence to arise from a breach of the obligations laid down by Directive 83/189, an express provision to this effect is not required. As pointed out above, it is undisputed that the aim of the directive is to protect freedom of movement for goods by means of preventive control and that the obligation to notify is essential for achieving such Community control. The effectiveness of Community control will be that much greater if the directive is interpreted as meaning that breach of the obligation to notify constitutes a substantial procedural defect such as to render the technical regulations in question inapplicable to individuals.

---

[71] Case 103/88 *Fratelli Costanzo* v *Milano* [1989] ECR 1839.
[72] Nyssens and Lackhoff, above n. 68, 402.

Whilst *CIA* was decided prior to *Arcor*, the latter reinforces it conceptually. If a Directive grants directly effective rights, no enforcement actions can be taken using state apparatus, be it through the courts, the administration or the police, to rob the individual of the benefit of these rights. It does not matter whether it is another private party asking the state to take this action or whether the administration does it at its own behest. Turned around, this means that whilst an individual cannot lodge a claim against another party invoking a Directive, by virtue of the lack of horizontal direct effect, she can always use the Directive as a shield to protect herself from actions brought against her by other parties.

If this does not result in Directives placing obligations on private parties, it does result in their affecting the latter's entitlements and rights significantly, and the question has to be asked how this is consistent with the ethos of *Marshall*, which is that states should bear the burden of unimplemented Directives as these are addressed to them.[73]

The other challenge is a substantive one. It is that of 'regulatory gaps'. If a Directive can be invoked to prevent a national law being applied but cannot be fully applied itself, this leaves a 'lawless' situation, where the public good at the heart of the dispute is unprotected. This arose in *Lemmens*. Lemmens was breathalysed by Dutch police, who used a breathalyser conforming to Dutch regulations, which had not been notified to the Commission as required by Directive 83/189/EC.[74] He challenged his ensuing conviction on the basis that a lawful test had not taken place, as the regulations authorising use of this breathalyser were illegal. The Court found that the Dutch regulations could be enforced against Lemmens. It observed that the purpose of the Directive was to facilitate free movement of goods. Whilst this required that an unnotified technical regulation would be unenforceable wherever it hindered the use or marketing of a product, it did not render regulations inapplicable where this was not the case. *Unilever* elaborated on this.[75] Unilever had delivered some Italian olive oil to Central Food. A condition of the contract was that the oil should be labelled in accordance with Italian law. Central Food refused to accept the oil as it did not comply with a 1998 Decree stating that olive oil could not be termed 'Italian' unless the entire cycle of harvesting, production, processing and packaging had taken place in Italy. This Decree had been notified to the Commission, but had been too quickly implemented. The Court stated that this illegal implementation meant that the law in question would be unenforceable against individuals if it hindered the marketing or use of a product. This was the case here. Marketing was hindered not merely where a good was directly prevented from being sold by a technical regulation but could also occur indirectly, where a regulation was used to allow a party in civil proceedings to revoke a contract and thereby prevent a good from being marketed.

These two cases limit but do not resolve the problem of the regulatory gap. To be sure, claims must be brought with the purpose of marketing goods. Yet, even where this is the motivation for the litigation, there is still the problem that public goods, such as protection of the consumer or the environment, will be unprotected once the national measure is declared invalid. In *Unilever*, for example, it is possible to argue that an effect of the judgment was to weaken consumer protection by leaving the consumers of this oil uninformed as to its origin.

---

[73] S. Weatherill, 'Breach of Directives and Breach of Contract' (2001) 26 *ELRev.* 177, 182–3.
[74] Case C-226/97 *Lemmens* [1998] ECR I-3711.
[75] Case C-443/98 *Unilever SpA* v *Central Food SpA* [2000] ECR I-7535.

6 INDIRECT EFFECT

Direct effect has, in the last twenty years, become merely one route amongst others through which individuals may invoke EU law in national courts. It is arguable, indeed, that it is no longer even the predominant doctrine in that regard – this may be the doctrine of indirect effect. As the development of direct effect has faltered, the doctrine of indirect effect has expanded. Back in 1998, an empirical study found that it was deployed more widely in British courts than direct effect.[76] Despite the greater academic attention that is generally given to direct effect, it has therefore been argued persuasively that indirect effect 'is currently the main form of ensuring effect of Directives whether correctly, incorrectly or not transposed at all'.[77]

(i) Arrival of indirect effect

Indirect effect began inauspiciously in *Von Colson*.[78] Two female social workers were refused employment in a German prison by virtue of their sex. They sued in the German labour court relying on the German law implementing Directive 76/207/EEC, the Equal Treatment Directive. Under that, the German court could only order that they be compensated for such losses as they had suffered as a result of applying for the positions which had been denied them, in this case the travel expenses to the interviews. The national court referred the question of whether such a restriction in the availability of compensation was compatible with EU law, in particular article 6 of the Directive, which required persons who considered themselves wronged to be able to pursue their claims by judicial process. The relevant provision was insufficiently clear and unconditional to satisfy the test for direct effect. However, the Court of Justice ruled that this did not necessarily mean that the Directive could be of no assistance to the claimants.

Case 14/83 *Von Colson & Kamann* v *Land Nordrhein–Westfalen* [1984] ECR 1891

22. It is impossible to establish real equality of opportunity without an appropriate system of sanctions. That follows not only from the actual purpose of the Directive but more specifically from Article 6 thereof which, by granting applicants for a post who have been discriminated against recourse to the courts, acknowledges that those candidates have rights of which they may avail themselves before the courts.

23. Although ... full implementation of the Directive does not require any specific form of sanction for unlawful discrimination, it does entail that that sanction be such as to guarantee real and effective judicial protection. Moreover it must also have a real deterrent effect on the employer. It follows that where a Member State chooses to penalize the breach of the prohibition of discrimination by the award of compensation, that compensation must in any event be adequate in relation to the damage sustained.

24. In consequence it appears that national provisions limiting the right to compensation of persons who have been discriminated against as regards access to employment to a purely nominal amount, such as, for example, the reimbursement of expenses incurred by them in submitting their application, would not satisfy the requirements of an effective transposition of the Directive ...

---

[76] D. Chalmers, 'The Positioning of EU Judicial Politics within the United Kingdom' (2000) 23 *WEP* 169, 190.
[77] G. Betlem, 'The Doctrine of Consistent Interpretation: Managing Legal Uncertainty' (2002) 22 *OJLS* 397, 399.
[78] See also Case 79/83 *Harz* v *Deutsche Tradax* [1984] ECR 192.

26. ... The Member States' obligation arising from a Directive to achieve the result envisaged by the Directive and their duty under Article [4(3) TEU] to take all appropriate measures, whether general or particular, to ensure the fulfilment of that obligation, is binding on all the authorities of Member States including, for matters within their jurisdiction, the courts. It follows that, in applying the national law and in particular the provisions of national law specifically introduced in order to implement Directive 76/207, national courts are required to interpret their national law in the light of the wording and purpose of the Directive ...

For many years, it seemed the application of the doctrine of indirect effect – the duty to interpret national law in accordance with EU law – was quite limited. Following *Von Colson*, the doctrine only applied where national laws were implementing Directives and a provision was highly ambiguous. However, such an interpretation was scotched by the Court in its ruling in *Marleasing*. Marleasing brought an action against La Comercial in order to have the latter's articles of association declared void as having been created for the sole purpose of defrauding and evading creditors. The Spanish Civil Code stated that contracts made with 'lack of cause' were void. Directive 68/151/EEC contained an exhaustive list of reasons under which companies could be declared void. Avoidance of creditors was not on that list.

Case C–106/89 *Marleasing SA* v *La Comercial Internacionale de Alimentación SA* [1990] ECR I–4135

8   as the Court pointed out in its judgment in *Von Colson* ..., the Member States' obligation arising from a Directive to achieve the result envisaged by the Directive and their duty under Article [4(3) TEU] to take all appropriate measures, whether general or particular, to ensure the fulfilment of that obligation, is binding on all the authorities of Member States including, for matters within their jurisdiction, the courts. It follows that, in applying national law, whether the provisions in question were adopted before or after the Directive, the national court called upon to interpret it is required to do so, as far as possible, in the light of the wording and the purpose of the Directive in order to achieve the result pursued by the latter and thereby comply with the third paragraph of Article [288 TFEU].

Marleasing expanded the law of indirect effect in two ways. First, it required *all* national legislation to be interpreted in the light of EU law, irrespective of whether it is implementing legislation or not, and irrespective of whether it was enacted prior or subsequent to the provision of EU law in question. In this instance, the Spanish Civil Code, which concerned civil/contract law, had to be interpreted in the light of a subsequent piece of EU company legislation. Secondly, it strengthened the national courts' interpretive duty. As Docksey and Fitzpatrick observed 'it is no longer sufficient for a national court to turn to Community law only if the national provision is "ambiguous". Its priority must be to establish the meaning of the Union obligation and only then to conclude whether it is possible to achieve the necessary reconciliation with the national law.'[79]

The *Marleasing* judgment narrowed the gap that the Court of Justice had created in *Marshall*, where it held that Directives only had vertical direct effect. For the expansion of the duty of

[79] C. Docksey and B. Fitzpatrick, 'The Duty of National Courts to Interpret Provisions of National Law in Accordance with Community Law' (1991) 20 *ILJ* 113, 119.

consistent interpretation allowed Directives to govern the substance of disputes between private parties. As long as there was a national law which allowed some room for interpretation, it could be manoeuvred to comply with the Directive, thereby allowing it to determine the dispute 'indirectly' via the medium of the national law. It is to be emphasised, therefore, that *Marleasing* concerned a dispute between two private parties. While *Marleasing* allows for Directives to be involved in the adjudication of relations between private parties, the judgment does not go so far as to insist that Directives should govern such relations in an exclusive manner. Instead, it creates a new form of what might be termed 'inter-legality', in which a mix of national and EU law regulates a dispute, with the EU element opening up adjudication to wider norms and concerns, whilst the national law element ensures that the local traditions and trajectories surrounding the dispute are not overlooked.

M. Amstutz, 'In-Between Worlds: *Marleasing* and the Emergence of Interlegality in Legal Reasoning' (2005) 11 *European Law Journal* 766, 781–2

The internal culture-specific 'constraints' on national adjudication remain unaffected by the requirement for interpretation in conformity with Directives; local specificities of the various legal discourses are not pushed aside, say, by rational arguments that in the end are always weaker than the constraints of organically grown legal cultures. For ultimately it is the legal policies present in the private law of the individual Member States that act as 'regulators' in the process of incorporating Community private-law positions into the national legal discourses. They are ensuring that two separate sets of norms do not emerge in Member States' civil legal systems – one deriving from the historical trajectory of the State concerned, the other dictated by the Community. They alone can offer guarantees for a Community private law integrated into the national legal culture, and this fact immediately makes it clear how they ensure the evolutionary capacity of national law in the biotope of the European Community: by on the one hand – as artful combinations of 'flexible' and 'fixed' control parameters – blocking the propagation of the 'perturbations' from European law throughout the national private law, without on the other losing the national law's responsiveness to EC law.

Although some have argued that *Marleasing* created a skilful new balance between EU and national law, others have criticised the judgment for generating considerable uncertainty.[80] The sources of this uncertainty are twofold. The first stems from the strength of the duty of interpretation. It is clearly strong but the extent of that strength is uncertain. It is something stronger than giving effect to EU law-compliant interpretations when there are two equally plausible interpretations. It is something less than requiring national law to be overridden. Between these poles, however, it is very unclear whether the national judge is to give more weight to the national law or EU law provisions in question. The second derives from the duty to interpret the national law in the light of all EU law. Put simply, there is so much of the latter and it is so wide-ranging that it is very difficult for national lawyers or judges to consider any Union provision that might cut across some national dispute in an incidental manner.

The risks posed to legal certainty have been partially recognised by the Court of Justice. It has held that indirect effect does not require *contra legem* interpretations of national law. That is to say, the strength of the interpretive obligation is not so strong as to require a provision of

---

[80] G. de Búrca, 'Giving Effect to European Community Directives' (1992) 55 *MLR* 215.

national law to be given a meaning that contradicts its 'ordinary' meaning.[81] Furthermore, the Court has been particularly wary of using the doctrine in the field of criminal law, where the liberties of the individual are at stake, or where it seems that the effect will be to impose strong obligations on individuals. In *Arcaro*, the Court stated:

> The obligation of the national court to refer to the content of the Directive when interpreting the relevant rules of its own national law reaches a limit where such an interpretation leads to the imposition on an individual of an obligation laid down by a Directive which has not been transposed or, more especially, where it has the effect of determining or aggravating, on the basis of the Directive and in the absence of a law enacted for its implementation, the liability in criminal law of persons who act in contravention of that Directive's provisions.[82]

Notwithstanding this, the Court has continued to regard indirect effect as being as important as ever and, in recent years, as illustrated below, it has sought to expand it.[83]

(ii) When does the duty of indirect effect arise?

The date from when direct effect takes effect varies. For Regulations, it is stated in the Regulation or, failing that, twenty days after publication.[84] In the case of Directives, we saw that a Directive may have direct effect only after the date has passed by which Member States are required to transpose it into national law, and only if they have failed to do so.[85] However, the basis for indirect effect is different from direct effect. In the case of Directives it derives not from the state's failure to comply with EU law but rather from the duty in what is now Article 4(3) TEU to take all measures to ensure compliance with EU law.[86] This begs the question as to whether there is a different starting date for indirect effect.

This became an issue in *Mangold*.[87] In 2003, Mangold, who was 56 years old, entered into an eight month fixed-term employment contract with Helm, a German lawyer. He subsequently challenged the fixed term nature of this contract on the grounds that it contravened Directive 2000/78/EC which, inter alia, prohibited discrimination on grounds of age. The basis was that Germany introduced a 2002 law which only allowed fixed term contracts for workers younger than 52 years old in exceptional circumstances, whereas this restriction did not apply for older workers. Although adopted in 2000, the Directive was not due to be transposed until December 2003, and Member States could even request (provided they made annual reports to the Commission) that transposition not occur until December 2006. The German government argued that it had a freedom, and that the Directive could not generate legal effects, prior to that date. The Court disagreed. It stated that it was the duty of the national court to set aside

---

[81] Most notably, Case C-334/92 *Wagner-Miret* v *Fondo de Garantia Salarial* [1993] ECR I-6911.

[82] Case C-168/95 *Arcaro* [1996] ECR I-4705, para. 42. See also Case C-321/05 *Kofoed* v *Skatteministeriet* [2007] ECR I-5795. On this see P. Craig, 'The Legal Effects of Directives: Policy, Rules and Exceptions' (2009) 34 *ELRev*. 349, 360–4.

[83] Affirmations have included Joined Cases C-397/01–C-403/01 *Pfeiffer and Others* v *Deutsches Rotes Kreuz* [2004] ECR I-8835; Case C-212/04 *Adeneler and Others* v *ELOG (Ellinikos Organismos Galaktos)* [2006] ECR I-6057; Joined Cases C-378/07–C-380/07 *Angelidaki* v *ONAR*, Judgment of 23 April 2009. For analysis, see S. Drake, 'Twenty Years after *Von Colson*: The Impact of "Indirect Effect" on the Protection of the Individual's Community Rights' (2005) 30 *ELRev*. 329.

[84] Article 297 TFEU.

[85] See pp. 287–8.

[86] On this see Advocate General Kokott in Case C-212/04 *Adeneler and Others* v *ELOG (Ellinikos Organismos Galaktos)* [2006] ECR I-6057, paras. 47–50.

[87] Case C-144/04 *Mangold* v *Helm* [2005] ECR I-9981.

any provision of national law which conflicted with the Directive even if the time limit for transposition had not passed. Its reasoning was twofold. First, it argued that Member States were under a duty to refrain from taking any measures liable seriously to compromise the attainment of the result prescribed by the Directive. This was reinforced by the terms of the Directive, which provided for an exceptional period for transposition to enable progressive realisation of the measures necessary to meet its objectives. The 2002 law, insofar as it exacerbated age discrimination, violated this duty. Secondly, the Directive gave effect to a fundamental principle of EU law, that of non-discrimination. Observance of this principle could not be conditional simply upon expiry of a transposition period. The judgment was heavily criticised both within the Court and by academics for its opaque reasoning.[88] It was unclear whether the judgment's reasoning was confined to the particular Directive in question or what the underlying basis was for this new obligation.

The position was clarified in *Adeneler*. Eighteen employers were on a variety of fixed term contracts with the Greek milk board which came to an end between June and September 2003. Greece was due to have implemented Directive 1999/70/EC on fixed term work by July 2002, which provided that fixed term contracts would only be allowed if there were objective reasons. This had been interpreted to mean that there had to be precise and concrete circumstances which provided a need for a fixed term contract. The Greek court asked from what moment a national court was required to interpret the Directive.

Case C–212/04 *Adeneler and Others* v *ELOG (Ellinikos Organismos Galaktos)* [2006] ECR I–6057

113. With a view, more specifically, to determining the date from which national courts are to apply the principle that national law must be interpreted in conformity with Community law, it should be noted that that obligation, arising from the second paragraph of Article [4(3) TEU], the third paragraph of Article [288 TFEU] and the directive in question itself, has been imposed in particular where a provision of a directive lacks direct effect, be it that the relevant provision is not sufficiently clear, precise and unconditional to produce direct effect or that the dispute is exclusively between individuals.

114. Also, before the period for transposition of a directive has expired, Member States cannot be reproached for not having yet adopted measures implementing it in national law...

115. Accordingly, where a directive is transposed belatedly, the general obligation owed by national courts to interpret domestic law in conformity with the directive exists only once the period for its transposition has expired.

116. It necessarily follows from the foregoing that, where a directive is transposed belatedly, the date... on which the national implementing measures actually enter into force in the Member State concerned does not constitute the relevant point in time. Such a solution would be liable seriously to jeopardise the full effectiveness of Community law and its uniform application by means, in particular, of directives.

117. In addition, ... it should be pointed out that it is already clear from the Court's case law that the obligation on Member States, under the second paragraph of Article [4(3) TEU], the third paragraph of Article [288 TFEU] and the directive in question itself, to take all the measures necessary to achieve the

---

[88] For different views see A. Dashwood, 'From *Van Duyn* to *Mangold* via *Marshall*: Reducing Direct Effect to Absurdity?' (2006–07) 9 *CYELS* 81; C. Tobler, 'Putting *Mangold* in Perspective: In Response to *Editorial Comments*, Horizontal Direct Effect – A Law of Diminishing Coherence?' (2007) 44 *CMLRev.* 1177.

result prescribed by the directive is binding on all national authorities, including, for matters within their jurisdiction, the courts...

118. Also, directives are either (i) published in the *Official Journal of the European Communities* in accordance with Article [297 TFEU] and, in that case, enter into force on the date specified in them or, in the absence thereof, on the 20th day following that of their publication, or (ii) notified to those to whom they are addressed, in which case they take effect upon such notification, in accordance with Article [297(2) TFEU].

119. It follows that a directive produces legal effects for a Member State to which it is addressed – and, therefore, for all the national authorities – following its publication or from the date of its notification, as the case may be.

120. In the present instance, Directive 1999/70 states, in Article 3, that it was to enter into force on the day of its publication in the *Official Journal of the European Communities*, namely 10 July 1999.

121. In accordance with the Court's settled case law, it follows from [Article 4(3) TEU] in conjunction with the third paragraph of Article [288 TFEU] and the directive in question itself that, during the period prescribed for transposition of a directive, the Member States to which it is addressed must refrain from taking any measures liable seriously to compromise the attainment of the result prescribed by it... In this connection it is immaterial whether or not the provision of national law at issue which has been adopted after the directive in question entered into force is concerned with the transposition of the directive...

122. Given that all the authorities of the Member States are subject to the obligation to ensure that provisions of Community law take full effect... the obligation to refrain from taking measures, as set out in the previous paragraph, applies just as much to national courts.

123. It follows that, from the date upon which a directive has entered into force, the courts of the Member States must refrain as far as possible from interpreting domestic law in a manner which might seriously compromise, after the period for transposition has expired, attainment of the objective pursued by that directive.

There is, thus, a tiered obligation on national courts. The full force of the duty to interpret only takes effect from the date of transposition. Prior to that, there is a more limited duty. National courts must interpret national law in such a manner that it does not compromise realisation of a directive's objective from the end of the transposition period. The meaning of this obligation is very unclear. In *VTB-VAB* Advocate General Trstenjak stated:

> If ... the national court cannot avoid the suspicion that a piece of national legislation is liable to prevent the achievement of the result prescribed by a directive which is imminently due to be implemented once the period for transposition has expired, it is obliged to take the necessary measures even before the transposition phase has ended. Such measures also include, in principle, the possibility of disapplying the offending national law if an interpretation of the current law in conformity with the directive is out of the question.[89]

Asking, however, a national court to engage with a particular form of interpretation on the basis of a suspicion is a real threat to legal certainty. The concrete circumstances in which this will occur will invariably always be difficult to ascertain and the strength of interpretive obligation is extremely hazy. It is difficult to reconcile this with the Court's repeated concern that

[89] Joined Cases C-261/07 and C-299/07 *VTB-VAB* v *Total*, Judgment of 29 April 2009, para. 62.

Directives should not place obligations on individuals. For the latter now live under a shadow where they do not know what obligations Directives impose, and this can only have a chilling effect on their behaviour.

(iii) Range of measures that national courts must take into account

A final issue to be addressed is the question of which instruments national courts are required to consider. It might have been thought, in the wake of *Von Colson*, that national courts would be required to consider only such instruments as may be directly enforceable in national courts (i.e. Treaty provisions, Regulations, Decisions and Directives). As early as 1989, however, the Court established that the duty of consistent interpretation was a free-standing principle in its own right. It may have been *developed* in the context of seeking ways to make Directives effective before national courts, but from as early as 1989 that has not been its sole purpose. In *Grimaldi*,[90] the Court held that national courts were to take account not just of 'hard law' but also of legally non-binding recommendations.

More dramatic was the Court's ruling in *Pupino*, which controversially extended indirect effect to the third pillar of the European Union.[91] *Pupino* arose out of a dispute relating to the interpretation by an Italian criminal court of Council Framework Decision 2001/220/JHA, concerning the safeguards afforded to vulnerable victims when they appear as witnesses in criminal proceedings. Framework Decisions were pieces of legislation that existed under the third pillar of the original TEU. They were to be 'binding upon the Member States as to the result to be achieved but shall leave to the national authorities the choice of form and methods. They shall not entail direct effect.'[92] The Court noted, notwithstanding this, that the language of this provision is similar to that used by what is now Article 288(3) TFEU for Directives. The British and Italian governments argued, however, that this could not be the case as there was no third pillar equivalent of the duty of cooperation which was then set out in Article 10 EC, and is now contained in Article 4(3) TEU. The Court rejected this. It noted that what is now Article 1(2) TEU stated that the Treaty marked a new stage in the process of ever closer union and that the task of the Union was to organise, in a manner demonstrating consistency and solidarity, relations between the Member States and between their peoples. It stated this would be difficult if the principle of loyal cooperation did not apply to the third pillar. National courts were therefore under an obligation to interpret national law in the light of Framework Decisions.

With the coming into force of Lisbon, *Pupino* must be seen in a new light. Framework Decisions no longer exist, and there is no pillar structure in the previously understood sense. The decision's significance lies in the reasoning used. It provides an alternate basis for indirect effect: the general obligation residing in the objective of ever closer union set out in Article 1(2) TEU. This is intriguing and concerning. The language is vague and open-ended. It suggests that the duties of indirect effect might simply be part of a parcel of duties on Member States which is continually evolving and thus never fully known.

---

[90] Case 322/88 *Grimaldi* v *Fonds des Maladies Professionelles* [1989] ECR 4407.

[91] Case C-105/03 *Pupino* [2005] ECR I-5285. For analysis see M. Fletcher, 'Extending "Indirect Effect" to the Third Pillar: The Significance of Pupino' (2005) 30 *ELRev.* 862; S. Peers, 'Salvation Outside the Church: Judicial Protection in the Third Pillar After the *Pupino* and *Segi* Judgments' (2007) 44 *CMLRev.* 885; E. Spaventa, 'Opening Pandora's Box: Some Reflections on the Constitutional Effects of the Ruling in Pupino' (2007) 3 *European Constitutional Law Review* 5.

[92] Article 34(2)(b) TEU(M). On this see A. Hinarejos, 'On the Legal Effects of Framework Decisions and Decisions: Directly Applicable, Directly Effective, Self Executing, Supreme?' (2008) 14 *ELJ* 620.

7 STATE LIABILITY

(i) Arrival and challenges of state liability

The doctrine of indirect effect only partially addresses the 'gap' left by Directives only having vertical direct effect. There are two circumstances where it will not come to the rescue of individuals granted entitlements by Directives. One is where there is no national measure to interpret, and the other is where the national legislation contradicts the Directive. In each instance there is a problem, as there is nothing to interpret – so the individual cannot be helped – but these cases represent the most flagrant violations of EU law by Member States.

This scenario arose in *Francovich*. Italy had persistently failed to implement the terms of Directive 80/987/EC, a measure that was intended to guarantee to employees a minimum level of protection under Community law in the event of the insolvency of their employer. The Directive provided in particular for specific guarantees of payment of unpaid wage claims. It should have been implemented by October 1983, and in 1987 the Commission brought a successful enforcement action against the Italian government for its failure to transpose the Directive.[93] Even after the judgment, there was still no transposition. *Francovich* concerned an action by thirty-four employees, who were owed back-pay by employers that had now gone bankrupt, against the Italian state for the losses they had suffered as a consequence of its failure to transpose the Directive.

Joined Cases C-6/90 and C-9/90 Francovich and Bonifaci v Italy [1991] ECR I-5357

31. It should be borne in mind at the outset that the EEC Treaty has created its own legal system, which is integrated into the legal systems of the Member States and which their courts are bound to apply. The subjects of that legal system are not only the Member States but also their nationals. Just as it imposes burdens on individuals, Community law is also intended to give rise to rights which become part of their legal patrimony. Those rights arise not only where they are expressly granted by the Treaty but also by virtue of obligations which the Treaty imposes in a clearly defined manner both on individuals and on the Member States and the Community institutions ...

32. Furthermore, it has been consistently held that the national courts whose task it is to apply the provisions of Community law in areas within their jurisdiction must ensure that those rules take full effect and must protect the rights which they confer on individuals ...

33. The full effectiveness of Community rules would be impaired and the protection of the rights which they grant would be weakened if individuals were unable to obtain redress when their rights are infringed by a breach of Community law for which a Member State can be held responsible.

34. The possibility of obtaining redress from the Member State is particularly indispensable where, as in this case, the full effectiveness of Community rules is subject to prior action on the part of the State and where, consequently, in the absence of such action, individuals cannot enforce before the national courts the rights conferred upon them by Community law.

35. It follows that the principle whereby a State must be liable for loss and damage caused to individuals as a result of breaches of Community law for which the State can be held responsible is inherent in the system of the Treaty.

---

[93] Case 22/87 *Commission v Italy* [1989] ECR 143.

36. A further basis for the obligation of Member States to make good such loss and damage is to be found in Article [4(3) TEU], under which the Member States are required to take all appropriate measures, whether general or particular, to ensure fulfilment of their obligations under Community law. Among these is the obligation to nullify the unlawful consequences of a breach of Community law ...

37. It follows from all the foregoing that it is a principle of Community law that the Member States are obliged to make good loss and damage caused to individuals by breaches of Community law for which they can be held responsible.

38. Although State liability is thus required by Community law, the conditions under which that liability gives rise to a right to reparation depend on the nature of the breach of Community law giving rise to the loss and damage.

39. Where, as in this case, a Member State fails to fulfil its obligation under the third paragraph of Article [288 TFEU] to take all the measures necessary to achieve the result prescribed by a Directive, the full effectiveness of that rule of Community law requires that there should be a right to reparation provided that three conditions are fulfilled.

40. The first of those conditions is that the result prescribed by the Directive should entail the grant of rights to individuals. The second condition is that it should be possible to identify the content of those rights on the basis of the provisions of the Directive. Finally, the third condition is the existence of a causal link between the breach of the State's obligation and the loss and damage suffered by the injured parties.

41. Those conditions are sufficient to give rise to a right on the part of individuals to obtain reparation, a right founded directly on Community law.

42. Subject to that reservation, it is on the basis of the rules of national law on liability that the State must make reparation for the consequences of the loss and damage caused. In the absence of Community legislation, it is for the internal legal order of each Member State to designate the competent courts and lay down the detailed procedural rules for legal proceedings intended fully to safeguard the rights which individuals derive from Community law ...

43. Further, the substantive and procedural conditions for reparation of loss and damage laid down by the national law of the Member States must not be less favourable than those relating to similar domestic claims and must not be so framed as to make it virtually impossible or excessively difficult to obtain reparation ...

Francovich was seen as a seminal judgment.[94] At that time, most states did not provide a system of governmental liability for equivalent breaches of national law, and, in the negotiations leading up to Maastricht, drew the line at the notion that national courts should be able to award damages against the state for breach of Community law.[95] Notwithstanding this, most academic commentators welcomed the decision on the grounds that it would lead to better enforcement of EU law[96] and greater citizen empowerment.[97] Yet individual litigation has rarely

[94] The academic literature is voluminous. P. Craig, '*Francovich*, Remedies and the Scope of Damages Liability' (1993) 109 *LQR* 595; R. Caranta, 'Governmental Liability After *Francovich*' (1993) *CLJ* 272 and M. Ross, 'Beyond *Francovich*' (1993) 56 *MLR* 55; E. Szyszczak, 'Making Europe More Relevant to its Citizens' (1996) 21 *ELRev.* 35; J. Steiner, 'From Direct Effects to *Francovich*: More Effective Means of Enforcement of Community Law' (1993) 18 *ELRev.* 3; R. Caranta, 'Judicial Protection Against Member States: A New *jus commune* Takes Shape' (1995) 32 *CMLRev.* 703.

[95] J. Tallberg, 'Supranational Influence in EU Enforcement: The ECJ and the Principle of State Liability' (2000) 7 *JEPP* 104, 114–16.

[96] Caranta, above n. 94, 710.

[97] See e.g. E. Szyszczak, 'Making Europe More Relevant to its Citizens' (1996) 21 *ELRev.* 35; Steiner, above n. 94.

been seen as the most effective route to regulatory enforcement, and there was scepticism, particularly as Member States were being asked, for the most part, to establish a new form of remedy and this might lead to national resistance.[98]

The most wide-ranging study, by Marie-Pierre Granger, found this to be unfounded.[99] All Member States had adopted the principle, normally in adopting their tort laws, and national courts had not been hesitant to award substantial damages.[100] The only qualification to this picture was in cases of legislative liability, where a parliament has passed a law contradicting EU law. In such circumstances, there was widespread evasion, with decisions by courts in Belgium, Greece, France and Italy all giving cause for concern.[101]

Many of the actions cited by Granger involved group actions or actions by large undertakings and this begged the question of who is empowered by *Francovich*. One of the most powerful critiques of *Francovich* was offered by Harlow. She argued that no thought had been given to the question of who would actually benefit from the imposition of state liability and who would lose from it.

C. Harlow, '*Francovich* and the Problem of the Disobedient State' (1996) 2 *European Law Journal* 199, 204

At the outset we should dismiss the vision of a squad of citizen policemen engaged in law enforcement. There are, of course, actions fought by individuals or groups of individuals. *Marshall* falls into this category; *Francovich* ... and *Faccini Dori* may. In the field of environmental law, we find a developing pattern derived from human rights law, where a number of specialist organisations (NGOs) dedicated to the enforcement of human rights through courts operate; in Article [288] cases, their place has largely been assumed by State-funded agencies. Whether or not these groups and agencies can be said to represent 'citizens' is a moot point but they do embody the private enforcement machinery to which the ECJ apparently aspires. This is not to imply, however, that the model of 'politics through law' espoused by the ECJ is best pursued through the medium of the action for damages; ... there is much to be said in favour of judicial review as the standard procedure, with annulment or declaratory orders as the standard remedy, in this type of citizen enforcement. In other areas, citizen enforcement is in any event a fantasy ... [A]n overwhelming majority of actions against the Community are brought by corporations ... [in litigation that] typically involves licences and other economic interests ...

This was particularly apposite, she argued, because systems of government liability locked courts into tragic choices. Awarding compensation was never simply granting compensation to a plaintiff from some limitless budget. Instead, as states invariably never increased taxes to pay for liability claims, claims awarded to plaintiffs were awarded at the expense of other public goods – typically, as welfare spending is the highest proportion of national budgets, money intended for the old, the sick and the poor. She wondered whether a distributive exercise was best achieved through the happenstance of individual litigation.[102]

---

[98] Tallberg, above n. 95, 110–11.

[99] M.-P. Granger, '*Francovich* and the Construction of a European Administrative *ius commune*' (2007) 32 *ELRev.* 157.

[100] The most widely reported was a fine of 26.4 million euros imposed by the Spanish Supreme Court in 2003 for failure to comply with EU broadcasting law: Tribunal Supremo, 12 June 2003, *CanalSatelite Digital* v *State Attorney* [2005] 5 *EuroCL* 33. S. Lage and H. Brokelmann, 'The Liability of the Spanish State for Breach of EC law: The Landmark Ruling of the Spanish Tribunal Supremo in the *Canal Satelite Digital* Case' (2004) 24 *ELRev.* 530.

[101] Granger, above n. 99, 163–7.

[102] *Ibid.* 210–12.

Both Granger's and Harlow's work assumes that formal legal structures lead to particular forms of enforcement. More recent work challenges this and argues that even when these are in place, widespread variation takes place. A series of case studies carried out by Slepcevic of public interest litigation in relation to nature protection Directives in the Netherlands, France and Germany found widespread variation.[103] He concluded that decentralised enforcement relied on a series of features, which were rarely all in place at the same time. These included organisational capacity of groups to litigate, effective access to courts unimpeded by standing rulings or financial restrictions, willingness by courts to give full interpretations, and preparedness of the administration to implement court rulings fully and quickly. In very few states can all these matters be taken for granted.

(ii) Conditions of liability

Francovich only considered the narrow circumstances of when a Member State had failed to transpose a Directive. Its language was wider than that, and this left open the question of when a Member State would be held liable for breaching EU law: a question that exercised all the national governments in the run up to the Treaty of Amsterdam.[104] This was addressed in *Brasserie du Pêcheur* and *Factortame III*. These joined cases were referred in 1993 but, aware of their sensitivity, the Court did not decide them until 1996. Brasserie du Pêcheur, a French firm, had been forced to discontinue exports of beer to Germany in 1981 by virtue of a German 'purity law' which prohibited beers being marketed as beer if they contained additives. This law was declared illegal in 1987 on the ground that it contravened Article 34 TFEU, the provision outlawing quantitative restrictions or measures having equivalent effect on the free movement of goods.[105] Brasserie du Pêcheur sought compensation of DM1,800,000 for the loss of sales between 1981 and 1987. The facts of *Factortame* were given above.[106] After the system of registration contained in the Merchant Shipping Act 1988 had been declared illegal, the applicants claimed for damages against the British government.

Joined Cases C–46/93 and C–48/93 *Brasserie du Pêcheur* v *Germany* and *R* v *Secretary of State for Transport, ex parte Factortame (No. 3)* [1996] ECR I–1029

38. Although Community law imposes State liability, the conditions under which that liability gives rise to a right to reparation depend on the nature of the breach of Community law giving rise to the loss and damage ...

39. In order to determine those conditions, account should first be taken of the principles inherent in the Community legal order which form the basis for State liability, namely first, the full effectiveness of Community rules and the effective protection of the rights which they confer and, second, the obligation to cooperate imposed on Member States by Article [4(3) TEU] ...

40. In addition ... it is pertinent to refer to the Court's case law on non-contractual liability on the part of the Community.

---

[103] R. Slepcevic, 'The Judicial Enforcement of EU Law through National Courts: Possibilities and Limits' (2009) 16 *JEPP* 378.

[104] See, in particular, the Memorandum to the 1996 Intergovernmental Conference by the United Kingdom on the Court of Justice (London, FCO, 1996) 2.

[105] Case 178/84 *Commission* v *Germany (German beer)* [1987] ECR 1227.

[106] See p. 279.

41. First, ... Article [340 TFEU] refers as regards the non-contractual liability of the Community, to the general principles common to the laws of the Member States, from which, in the absence of written rules, the Court also draws inspiration in other areas of Community law.

42. Second, the conditions under which the State may incur liability for damage caused to individuals by a breach of Community law cannot, in the absence of particular justification, differ from those governing the liability of the Community in like circumstances. The protection of the rights which individuals derive from Community law cannot vary depending on whether a national authority or a Community authority is responsible for the damage.

43. The system of rules which the Court has worked out with regard to Article [340 TFEU], particularly in relation to liability for legislative measures, takes into account, inter alia, the complexity of the situations to be regulated, difficulties in the application or interpretation of the texts and, more particularly, the margin of discretion available to the author of the act in question.

44. Thus, in developing its case law on the non-contractual liability of the Community, in particular as regards legislative measures involving choices of economic policy, the Court has had regard to the wide discretion available to the institutions in implementing Community policies.

45. The strict approach taken towards the liability of the Community in the exercise of its legislative activities is due to two considerations. First, even where the legality of measures is subject to judicial review, exercise of the legislative function must not be hindered by the prospect of actions for damages whenever the general interest of the Community requires legislative measures to be adopted which may adversely affect individual interests. Second, in a legislative context characterised by the exercise of a wide discretion, which is essential for implementing a Community policy, the Community cannot incur liability unless the institution concerned has manifestly and gravely disregarded the limits on the exercise of its powers ...

46. That said, the national legislature – like the Community institutions – does not systematically have a wide discretion when it acts in a field governed by Community law. Community law may impose upon it obligations to achieve a particular result or obligations to act or refrain from acting which reduce its margin of discretion, sometimes to a considerable degree. This is so, for instance, where, as in the circumstances to which the judgment in *Francovich* relates, Article [288 TFEU] places the Member State under an obligation to take, within a given period, all the measures needed in order to achieve the result required by a directive. In such a case, the fact that it is for the national legislature to take the necessary measures has no bearing on the member State's liability for failing to transpose the directive.

47. In contrast, where a Member State acts in a field where it has a wide discretion, comparable to that of the Community institutions in implementing Community policies, the conditions under which it may incur liability must, in principle, be the same as those under which the Community institutions incur liability in a comparable situation.

48. In the case which gave rise to the reference in Case C–46/93, the German legislature had legislated in the field of foodstuffs, specifically beer. In the absence of Community harmonization, the national legislature had a wide discretion in that sphere in laying down rules on the quality of beer put on the market.

49. As regards the facts of Case C–48/93, the United Kingdom legislature also had a wide discretion. The legislation at issue was concerned, first, with the registration of vessels, a field which, in view of the state of development of Community law, falls within the jurisdiction of the Member States and, secondly, with regulating fishing, a sector in which implementation of the common fisheries policy leaves a margin of discretion to the Member States.

50. Consequently, in each case the German and United Kingdom legislatures were faced with situations involving choices comparable to those made by the Community institutions when they adopt legislative measures pursuant to a Community policy.

51. In such circumstances, Community law confers a right to reparation where three conditions are met: the rule of law infringed must be intended to confer rights on individuals; the breach must be sufficiently serious; and there must be a direct causal link between the breach of the obligation resting on the State and the damage sustained by the injured parties...

54. The first condition is manifestly satisfied in the case of Article [34 TFEU], the relevant provision in Case C-46/93, and in the case of Article [49 TFEU], the relevant provision in Case C-48/93 ...

55. As to the second condition, as regards both Community liability under Article [340 TFEU] and Member State liability for breaches of Community law, the decisive test for finding that a breach of Community law is sufficiently serious is whether the Member State or the Community institution concerned manifestly and gravely disregarded the limits of its discretion.

56. The factors which the competent court may take into consideration include the clarity and precision of the rule breached, the measure of discretion left by that rule to the national or Community authorities, whether the infringement and the damage caused was intentional or involuntary, whether any error of law was excusable or inexcusable, the fact that the position taken by a Community institution may have contributed towards the omission, and the adoption or retention of national measures or practices contrary to Community law.

57. On any view, a breach of Community law will clearly be sufficiently serious if it has persisted despite a judgment finding the infringement in question to be established, or a preliminary ruling or settled case law of the Court on the matter from which it is clear that the conduct in question constituted an infringement...

65. As for the third condition, it is for the national courts to determine whether there is a direct causal link between the breach of the obligation borne by the State and the damage sustained by the injured parties.

67. As appears from ... *Francovich*, subject to the right to reparation which flows directly from Community law where the conditions referred to in the preceding paragraph are satisfied, the State must make reparation for the consequences of the loss and damage caused in accordance with the domestic rules on liability, provided that the conditions for reparation of loss and damage laid down by national law must not be less favourable than those relating to similar domestic claims and must not be such as in practice to make it impossible or excessively difficult to obtain reparation ...

82. Reparation for loss or damage caused to individuals as a result of breaches of Community law must be commensurate with the loss or damage sustained so as to ensure the effective protection for their rights.

83. In the absence of relevant Community provisions, it is for the domestic legal system of each Member State to set the criteria for determining the extent of reparation. However, those criteria must not be less favourable than those applying to similar claims based on domestic law and must not be such as in practice to make it impossible or excessively difficult to obtain reparation.

The Court's judgment suggests a distinction between contexts where Member States have some discretion and contexts where they do not. In the latter contexts, three criteria must be met for liability:

- the provision must be intended to confer rights on individuals;
- the breach must be sufficiently serious; and
- there must be a direct causal link between the breach of the obligation resting on the state and the damage sustained by the injured parties. In the former contexts, there is no

requirement for the breach to be sufficiently serious. It suffices that the provision be intended to confer rights and that there be a causal link between the breach of EU law and the individual damage sustained.

Yet, in determining whether a breach is sufficiently serious to justify liability, the Court will look at the degree of discretion afforded by EU law. If there is little or no discretion, the Court will treat the breach as sufficiently serious to incur liability. This has led to the categories being fluid in recent years. It appears Member States will be deemed to have no discretion where they fail to transpose a Directive in any way at all.[107] In recent years, the Court has indicated these are not the only circumstances. In *AGM-COS.MET*, the Court held that a failure by the Finnish government to let machines, which complied with EU law, onto its market, led to liability without the need to consider the question of the seriousness of the breach. This was because the relevant EU Directive contained a market access clause requiring the machines to be allowed to be marketed, and this gave the Member States no discretion.[108] By contrast, in *Synthon*, the British government was held liable for refusing to recognise the marketing authorisation of a drug certified by the Dutch authorities on the ground that the breach was a sufficiently serious one.[109] It was held that it was sufficiently serious as the provision allowed states no discretion to refuse mutual recognition unless they followed a special procedure which had not been invoked by the British government in that case.

In such circumstances, it makes more sense to consider the precise circumstances when liability will be found. *Francovich* and *Brasserie du Pêcheur* suggest three circumstances where liability will be easily found. These are:

- a complete failure to transpose a Directive;
- breach of an order of the Court of Justice;
- breach of settled case law.

There are a whole host of other circumstances where liability might be incurred.[110] These include breach of an EU legal norm; breach of case law that is not completely settled; and inadequate transposition of or compliance with a Directive. In all these circumstances, the Court looks at the clarity of the provision or law. If it was reasonably capable of bearing the meaning understood by the Member State[111] or if there is no consensus as to the meaning of the provision, then no liability will be found.[112] In short, liability occurs only when Member States are breaching EU law in a manner that must be obvious to them and one which leaves little room for doubt. State liability is thus a backstop measure. It is there to penalise the very wayward state rather than to be concerned with redress for litigants. For, if it were the latter, there would be little justification for such a restrictive test. This, in turn, raises an important question: is it really for the Court of Justice to decide whether punitive measures should be attached to the Treaty?

---

[107] Joined Cases C-6/90 and C-9/90 *Francovich and Bonifaci* v *Italy* [1991] ECR I-5357.

[108] Case C-470/03 *AGM-COS.MET Srl* v *Suomen valtio and Tarmo Lehtinen* [2007] ECR I-2749.

[109] Case C-452/06 *R* v *Licensing Authority of the Department of Health, ex parte Synthon* [2008] ECR I-7681.

[110] For a discussion of the cases following *Brasserie du Pêcheur* see T. Tridimas, 'Liability for Breach of Community Law: Growing Up and Mellowing Down?' (2001) 38 *CMLRev.* 301, 310.

[111] Case C-392/93 *R* v *HM Treasury, ex parte British Telecommunications* [1996] ECR I-1631.

[112] Case C-278/05 *Robins* v *Secretary of State for Work and Pensions* [2007] ECR I-1053.

(iii) Liability of judicial institutions

Brasserie du Pêcheur indicated that states were liable for acts of all public institutions. This has led to arguably the most interesting and certainly the most challenging dimension to state liability, liability for rulings by national courts. This arose in *Köbler* v *Austria*.[113] Köbler was a professor employed in an Austrian university. Part of his salary was based on length of service, but periods of employment in universities in Member States other than Austria did not count towards this aspect of his salary. The Austrian Administrative Court initially decided to refer the matter to the Court of Justice, but then withdrew the reference on the grounds that the matter had already been decided by the Court, which had ruled it lawful.[114] Köbler brought an action in damages, arguing that the state was liable in respect of the court's ruling on the grounds that it failed to refer the matter when obliged to do so and had given an erroneous ruling. The Court of Justice agreed that the measure violated Article 45 TFEU on freedom of movement of workers. It considered whether this gave grounds for liability.

Case C–224/01 *Köbler* v *Austria* [2003] ECR I–239

33. In the light of the essential role played by the judiciary in the protection of the rights derived by individuals from Community rules, the full effectiveness of those rules would be called in question and the protection of those rights would be weakened if individuals were precluded from being able, under certain conditions, to obtain reparation when their rights are affected by an infringement of Community law attributable to a decision of a court of a Member State adjudicating at last instance.

34. It must be stressed, in that context, that a court adjudicating at last instance is by definition the last judicial body before which individuals may assert the rights conferred on them by Community law. Since an infringement of those rights by a final decision of such a court cannot thereafter normally be corrected, individuals cannot be deprived of the possibility of rendering the State liable in order in that way to obtain legal protection of their rights.

35. Moreover, it is, in particular, in order to prevent rights conferred on individuals by Community law from being infringed that under the third paragraph of Article [267 TFEU] a court against whose decisions there is no judicial remedy under national law is required to make a reference to the Court of Justice.

36. Consequently, it follows from the requirements inherent in the protection of the rights of individuals relying on Community law that they must have the possibility of obtaining redress in the national courts for the damage caused by the infringement of those rights owing to a decision of a court adjudicating at last instance ...

37. Certain of the governments which submitted observations in these proceedings claimed that the principle of State liability for damage caused to individuals by infringements of Community law could not be applied to decisions of a national court adjudicating at last instance. In that connection arguments were put forward based, in particular, on the principle of legal certainty and, more specifically, the principle of *res judicata*, the independence and authority of the judiciary and the absence of a court competent to determine disputes relating to State liability for such decisions.

38. In that regard the importance of the principle of *res judicata* cannot be disputed ... In order to ensure both stability of the law and legal relations and the sound administration of justice, it is important that

---

[113] P. Wattel, '*Köbler, CILFIT* and *Welthgrove*: We Can't Go on Meeting Like This' (2004) 41 *CMLRev.* 177.

[114] The Austrian court sought to rely on the Court of Justice's ruling in Case C–15/96 *Schöning-Kougebetopoulou* [1998] ECR I–47.

judicial decisions which have become definitive after all rights of appeal have been exhausted or after expiry of the time-limits provided for in that connection can no longer be called in question.

39. However, it should be borne in mind that recognition of the principle of State liability for a decision of a court adjudicating at last instance does not in itself have the consequence of calling in question that decision as *res judicata*. Proceedings seeking to render the State liable do not have the same purpose and do not necessarily involve the same parties as the proceedings resulting in the decision which has acquired the status of *res judicata*. The applicant in an action to establish the liability of the State will, if successful, secure an order against it for reparation of the damage incurred but not necessarily a declaration invalidating the status of *res judicata* of the judicial decision which was responsible for the damage. In any event, the principle of State liability inherent in the Community legal order requires such reparation, but not revision of the judicial decision which was responsible for the damage.

40. It follows that the principle of *res judicata* does not preclude recognition of the principle of State liability for the decision of a court adjudicating at last instance.

41. Nor can the arguments based on the independence and authority of the judiciary be upheld.

42. As to the independence of the judiciary, the principle of liability in question concerns not the personal liability of the judge but that of the State. The possibility that under certain conditions the State may be rendered liable for judicial decisions contrary to Community law does not appear to entail any particular risk that the independence of a court adjudicating at last instance will be called in question.

43. As to the argument based on the risk of a diminution of the authority of a court adjudicating at last instance owing to the fact that its final decisions could by implication be called in question in proceedings in which the State may be rendered liable for such decisions, the existence of a right of action that affords, under certain conditions, reparation of the injurious effects of an erroneous judicial decision could also be regarded as enhancing the quality of a legal system and thus in the long run the authority of the judiciary.

44. Several governments also argued that application of the principle of State liability to decisions of a national court adjudicating at last instance was precluded by the difficulty of designating a court competent to determine disputes concerning the reparation of damage resulting from such decisions.

45. In that connection, given that, for reasons essentially connected with the need to secure for individuals protection of the rights conferred on them by Community rules, the principle of State liability inherent in the Community legal order must apply in regard to decisions of a national court adjudicating at last instance, it is for the Member States to enable those affected to rely on that principle by affording them an appropriate right of action. Application of that principle cannot be compromised by the absence of a competent court ...

51. As to the conditions to be satisfied for a Member State to be required to make reparation for loss and damage caused to individuals as a result of breaches of Community law for which the State is responsible, the Court has held that these are threefold: the rule of law infringed must be intended to confer rights on individuals; the breach must be sufficiently serious; and there must be a direct causal link between the breach of the obligation incumbent on the State and the loss or damage sustained by the injured parties ...

52. State liability for loss or damage caused by a decision of a national court adjudicating at last instance which infringes a rule of Community law is governed by the same conditions.

53. With regard more particularly to the second of those conditions and its application with a view to establishing possible State liability owing to a decision of a national court adjudicating at last instance, regard must be had to the specific nature of the judicial function and to the legitimate requirements of legal certainty, as the Member States which submitted observations in this case have also contended. State liability for an infringement of Community law by a decision of a national court adjudicating at

last instance can be incurred only in the exceptional case where the court has manifestly infringed the applicable law.

54. In order to determine whether that condition is satisfied, the national court hearing a claim for reparation must take account of all the factors which characterise the situation put before it.

55. Those factors include, in particular, the degree of clarity and precision of the rule infringed, whether the infringement was intentional, whether the error of law was excusable or inexcusable, the position taken, where applicable, by a Community institution and non-compliance by the court in question with its obligation to make a reference for a preliminary ruling under [Article 267(3) TFEU].

56. In any event, an infringement of Community law will be sufficiently serious where the decision concerned was made in manifest breach of the case law of the Court in the matter …

122. Community law does not expressly cover the point whether a measure for rewarding an employee's loyalty to his employer, such as a loyalty bonus, which entails an obstacle to freedom of movement for workers, can be justified and thus be in conformity with Community law. No reply was to be found to that question in the Court's case law. Nor, moreover, was that reply obvious.

123. In the second place, the fact that the national court in question ought to have maintained its request for a preliminary ruling … is not of such a nature as to invalidate that conclusion. In the present case the Verwaltungsgerichtshof had decided to withdraw the request for a preliminary ruling, on the view that the reply to the question of Community law to be resolved had already been given in the judgment in *Schöning-Kougebetopoulou* …Thus, it was owing to its incorrect reading of that judgment that the Verwaltungsgerichtshof no longer considered it necessary to refer that question of interpretation to the Court.

124. In those circumstances and in the light of the circumstances of the case, the infringement … cannot be regarded as being manifest in nature and thus as sufficiently serious.

At the time, only Spain and Austria has systems of liability for judicial decisions in place. As illustrated below, the judgment raised questions about legal certainty and traditional judicial hierarchies.

H. Scott and N. Barber, 'State Liability under *Francovich* for Decisions of National Courts' (2004) 120 *Law Quarterly Review* 403, 404–5

The extension of *Francovich* liability to courts of final decision has profound implications for the domestic legal hierarchy. After *Köbler* the English High Court could find itself compelled to pass judgment on a decision of the English House of Lords. A litigant disappointed by the House of Lords' decision could start a fresh action against the United Kingdom. The High Court, a few months later, would then be called on to assess whether the House of Lords had made an error of law that was sufficiently serious to warrant damages. The High Court would, almost certainly, refer the question to the ECJ under Article [267 TFEU] if it thought there was any doubt as to the correctness of the Lords' ruling. In response to such a reference the ECJ would give a ruling on the content of European law …

This prospect raises a number of problems for domestic legal systems. First, and most superficially, it reduces legal certainty. This is not, as some in *Köbler* tried to argue, because it allows the reopening of concluded cases. Once the State's highest court has ruled, the judgment is definitive between the parties and cannot be challenged; the principle of *res judicata* is not affected. The *Francovich* action is a separate legal right and is directed against the State; a body which, ordinarily, would not have been a party to the original action. However, *Köbler* does have the effect of allowing litigants a second chance to raise the legal question apparently resolved in the primary action: frustrated in the House of Lords, the litigant could re-start the process through *Francovich* in the High Court. Secondly, the decision upsets the domestic legal hierarchy. The High Court would be obliged to question the correctness of a decision of the House of Lords made a few months earlier: it would have to decide whether there was a sufficient chance of error to warrant a reference to the ECJ, and, when this ruling was returned, how severe the error had been. Further problems might arise as this secondary action progressed up the legal order, perhaps ending with one group of Law Lords ruling on the judgment of their colleagues. Thirdly, the decision has the potential to create serious constitutional conflict within the domestic legal order. The German Constitutional Court has ruled that in exceptional cases it might refuse to accept rulings of the ECJ (see *Brunner* [1994] 1 CMLR 57). If such a decision was then challenged under *Francovich*, a first instance judge might be forced to choose between loyalty to the final court of appeal and to the ECJ.

Köbler was challenged in *Traghetti*.[115] The Italian Court of Cassation, the top civil court, had ruled in a dispute between ferry operators that a subsidy granted to a ferry operation did not violate EU law on state aids as it followed the Court of Justice's settled case law. Traghetti, the ferry operator bringing the proceedings, had meanwhile gone into liquidation. Its administrator considered that the Court of Cassation had misapplied the law and brought an action for damages. However, Italian law excluded liability for damage where any infringement was the result of a court of last instance's interpretation of the law or assessment of the facts and evidence. The Court of Justice reiterated that the *Köbler* judgment applied to all courts, including courts of last instance, and that it applied not just to refusals to apply EU law but also to poor interpretations of EU law. This raised the question of what was the basis of such liability: was there a requirement for intentional fault and serious misconduct on the part of the court or was it sufficient that it was incompetent?

Case C-173/03 *Traghetti del Mediterraneo v Italy* [2006] ECR I-5177

42. With regard, finally, to the limitation of State liability to cases of intentional fault and serious misconduct on the part of the court, it should be recalled … that the Court held, in the *Köbler* judgment, that State liability for damage caused to individuals by reason of an infringement of Community law attributable to a national court adjudicating at last instance could be incurred in the exceptional case where that court manifestly infringed the applicable law.

43. Such manifest infringement is to be assessed, inter alia, in the light of a number of criteria, such as the degree of clarity and precision of the rule infringed, whether the infringement was intentional, whether the error of law was excusable or inexcusable, and the non-compliance by the court in question with its obligation to make a reference for a preliminary ruling under the third paragraph of Article [267 TFEU]; it is in any event presumed where the decision involved is made in manifest disregard of the case law of the Court on the subject …

44. Accordingly, although it remains possible for national law to define the criteria relating to the nature or degree of the infringement which must be met before State liability can be incurred for an infringement of Community law attributable to a national court adjudicating at last instance, under no circumstances may such criteria impose requirements stricter than that of a manifest infringement of the applicable law …

---

[115] D. Nassimpian, ' … And We Keep on Meeting: (De)fragmenting State Liability' (2007) 32 *ELRev*. 819.

Aside from reaffirming *Köbler*, *Traghetti* indicates liability is to be determined on the basis of a competence-based rather than fault-based test. It will be incurred not merely where a national court of last resort deliberately flouts EU law, but also where it fails to interpret EU law in the manner that one would expect of a reasonable court. To be sure, it is too simplistic to argue the test is merely one of whether a court could reasonably have come to the interpretation it did, and if not then the state is liable for damages. Yet, the test, namely whether the interpretation was manifestly inappropriate, is not so different from the standard applied to the notionally competent court. The relevant question would then be how far the national court must fall below that standard in order to attract state liability.[116] On this basis, an action for state liability may involve an action before a court of first instance attacking the most senior court in the land for behaving not just incompetently but very incompetently! This raises all kinds of questions about conflict of interest and about the actual competence of the junior court to hear the action. More structurally, there is the question of whether fining states is the best way to go about improving weak, often poorly funded judiciaries.

8 DRAWING THE THREADS TOGETHER

As mentioned at the beginning of this chapter, this field sits atop two tectonic plates. On the one hand, there is the logic of competing legal orders. This pushes for the primacy of EU law but acknowledges the autonomy of local legal orders, the sensitivities involved, and the difficulties of imposing uniform and centralised solutions. On the other, there is the logic of individual rights which pushes for the full protection of individual entitlements. If, at any moment, most notably over Directives but also over the question of remedies, one of these logics prevails, the other re-emerges through the establishment of a new doctrine.

Further uncertainty has been added by the Lisbon Treaty, which questions whether the balance needs to be readdressed with the introduction of the following provision.

Article 19(1) TEU

Member States shall provide remedies sufficient to ensure effective legal protection in the fields covered by Union law.

On the one hand, the appearance of this provision is that of a codifying provision. It seems to ask no more of Member States than the current case law, namely that they give effective protection to EU rights. In that sense, you might expect it to be no more than a rearticulation of existing case law. On the other hand, it might be thought that if a new provision is added, there has to be a reason for this. This reason might be to emphasise a stronger idea of effectiveness, in which the need for remedies is made more salient as a position of EU law, and in which a tighter, more overarching link is made between the grant of rights and the provision of remedies. It might be (and we cannot yet know) that it effects a revolution in which the logic of rights is made to prevail over that of the balance of legal orders.

---

[116] The general view is that the standard is quite low and that liability will be found only in exceptional cases.
B. Beutler, 'State Liability for Breaches of Community Law by National Courts: Is the Requirement of a Manifest Infringement of the Applicable Law an Insurmountable Obstacle?' (2009) 46 *CMLRev.* 773.

T. Eilmansberger, 'The Relationship Between Rights and Remedies in EC Law: In Search of the Missing Link' (2004) 41 *Common Market Law Review* 1199, 1238–9

The characteristic feature of an *absolute* subjective right is the imposition of an obligation on everybody to abstain from any acts considered to interfere with that right. The types of rights primarily of interest in the Community law context are more '*relative*' in nature, meaning that they create specific obligations between certain persons. These obligations, and corresponding rights, notably comprise (i) obligations to perform in a certain way (e.g. obligations to provide certain services, grant specific benefits, or effect equal treatment), furthermore (ii) (secondary) obligations to make good damage or restitute assets received without valid title, and, finally, (iii) obligations to abstain from certain conduct including the commitment of delicts.

With regard to remedies, the decisive point now is this: if the legal obligation making up the right is established in a clear and unequivocal manner, the necessary remedy for the protection of this right is equally apparent. This is so because this obligation can be directly translated into (or actually constitutes) a concrete claim. Such 'claim rights', in other words, automatically imply the appropriate remedy and cause of action required for its enforcement. Thus, once it is established that a private actor or the State is under an obligation towards certain persons to make good harm caused by illegal conduct, to repay money collected though not being due, or to abstain from or to commit certain acts, it follows that the beneficiaries have according rights, or to be more precise, claims. These claims to compensation, repayment or abstainment also constitute the respective components of these remedies. These remedies have a procedural component as well in that they represent the claims in a legally enforceable form, i.e. in a form which allows its enforcement by a (national) court. If the claim right and resulting remedy is established by Community law, the division of labour between Community law and national law in the enforcement of individual rights becomes, in principle, clear. Exclusively Community law determines the existence of the remedy. National law would have a merely auxiliary function. It would designate the competent courts to adjudicate the substantive claims in question and provide the appropriate procedural framework.

FURTHER READING

G. Betlem, 'The Doctrine of Consistent Interpretation: Managing Legal Uncertainty' (2002) 22 *Oxford Journal of Legal Studies* 397

B. Beutler, 'State Liability for Breaches of Community Law by National Courts: Is the Requirement of a Manifest Infringement of the Applicable Law an Insurmountable Obstacle?' (2009) 46 *Common Market Law Review* 773

P. Craig, 'The Legal Effects of Directives: Policy Rules and Exceptions' (2009) 34 *European Law Review* 349

A. Dashwood, 'From *Van Duyn* to *Mangold* via *Marshall*: Reducing Direct Effect to Absurdity?' (2006–07) 9 *Cambridge Yearbook of European Legal Studies* 81

M. Dougan, *National Remedies Before the Court of Justice* (Oxford, Hart, 2005)
  'When Worlds Collide: Competing Visions of the Relationship Between Direct Effect and Supremacy' (2007) 44 *Common Market Law Review* 931

S. Drake, 'Twenty Years After *Von Colson*: The Impact of "Indirect Effect" on the Protection of the Individual's Community Rights' (2005) 30 *European Law Review* 329

W. van Gerven, 'Bridging the Unbridgeable: Community and National Tort Laws After *Francovich* and *Brasserie*' (1996) 45 *International and Comparative Law Quarterly* 507

M.-P. Granger, '*Francovich* and the Construction of a European Administrative *ius commune*' (2007) 32 *European Law Review* 157

K. Lenaerts and T. Corthaut, 'Of Birds and Hedges: The Role of Primacy in Invoking Norms of EU Law' (2006) 31 *European Law Review* 287

S. Prechal, *Directives in EC Law* (2nd edn, Oxford, Oxford University Press, 2005)

J. Tallberg, 'Supranational Influence in EU Enforcement: the ECJ and the Principle of State Liability' (2000) 7 *Journal of European Public Policy* 104

8

Infringement Proceedings

CONTENTS

1 INTRODUCTION

This chapter considers the infringement proceedings that the Commission may bring against Member States for failure by the latter to comply with EU law. It is organised as follows.

Section 2 considers the main features of the infringement proceedings set out in Articles 258 to 260 TFEU. The central provision is Article 258 TFEU and it allows the Commission to take the Member State to the Court of Justice and to obtain a ruling that it has failed to comply with EU law. The roles of such proceedings are threefold: to secure the rule of EU law; as a public policy instrument to contribute to the effective functioning of EU policies; and as a public law arena, in which the different interests of the EU institutions, Member States, complainants and

EU citizens can be mediated. All three roles are important and there is a danger in overemphasising any one.

Section 3 considers the scope of Member States' responsibilities under Article 258 TFEU. Actions can be brought only against the state, but they can be brought for the failure of any state agency, including courts and local and regional government, even if it is constitutionally independent of the central government which is, in practice, the body against whom the action is taken. The state is also responsible not just for legal instruments that conflict with EU law but also administrative practices that conflict with EU law. These usually have to be general and consistent in nature to attract liability. The state is finally under a duty to secure and police the effective functioning of EU law, and will be held liable for a failure to do so.

Section 4 considers the stages of the Article 258 TFEU procedure. This will be begun following either a Commission investigation or, more often, a complaint by a third party. The procedure is a seven stage one, designed to give the Member State plenty of time to comply and plenty of scope for submitting observations on the Commission's complaint. Typically, it takes close to two years to complete. However, the overwhelming majority of cases are settled at the first stage where the Commission sends an informal letter to the Member State concerned. In addition, there are now moves to ascertain, where the procedure derives from a complaint, whether the complaint can be mediated between the complainant and the Member State without the Commission needing to be involved.

Section 5 considers the responsibilities and discretion of the Commission in the process. The Commission has complete freedom to decide whether to start the proceedings or to cease them. This has raised concerns about transparency, insufficiently rigorous prosecution by the Commission of EU law and, above all, exclusion of the complainant from the process. Following repeated criticism by the European Ombudsman, the Commission adopted a Communication in 2002, which grants the complainant some modest procedural guarantees. Centrally, there is a commitment to keep the complainant informed about the process and to reach a decision about whether to close a file or to instigate proceedings within twelve months.

Section 6 considers the sanctions that may be imposed. Following the Lisbon Treaty, the Court of Justice may impose a fine on the Member State under Article 258 TFEU where the proceedings concern a failure by the Member State to communicate national transposition of a Directive. For all other infringements, a second proceeding under Article 260 TFEU must be instigated. The Court may impose two types of fine. The lump sum penalises the state for non-compliance with the original judgment given under Article 258 TFEU. The penalty payment is calculated at a daily rate and is to induce the state to comply with the subsequent judgment given under Article 260 TFEU. The size of the fine is determined by the duration of the infringement, its seriousness and the capacity of the state to pay. Important guidelines were set out in a 2005 Commission Communication, although this does not bind the Court. In all cases, both the Commission and the Court will additionally look at what is needed to secure compliance and the overall proportionality of the sanction.

2 THE DIFFERENT ROLES OF INFRINGEMENT PROCEEDINGS

The enforcement of EU law through the assertion of individual rights before national courts discussed in the previous chapter is an important and distinctive feature of EU law. However, the enforcement of the EU legal order here is only seen as a byproduct of the assertion of individual rights. The primary focus is to secure individual redress and the question of enforcement is tailored around this. The judgment might thus address only some features of the illegality. The status of the Court of Justice might mean that its rulings are not binding or even persuasive for other courts in that state, and they will certainly not bind courts in other Member States. Most importantly, the EU law in question must give rise to rights and somebody must be willing to litigate those rights. If it does not, there can be no enforcement. As we saw, only a very small proportion of EU law is litigated regularly in national courts.[1]

With that in mind, it is worth turning our attention to the centralised procedures that exist for the enforcement of EU law against the Member States: the bodies that have the most extensive responsibilities for the administration of EU law in the Union. The principal procedures are set out in Article 258 TFEU.

Article 258 TFEU

If the Commission considers that a Member State has failed to fulfil an obligation under the Treaties, it shall deliver a reasoned opinion on the matter after giving the State concerned the opportunity to submit its observations.

If the State concerned does not comply with the opinion within the period laid down by the Commission, the latter may bring the matter before the Court of Justice of the European Union.

There are a number of other provisions which allow legal proceedings to be brought against Member States for breaches of EU law. Article 259 TFEU allows Member States to take other Member States before the Court of Justice for failure to comply with EU law. Its use has been rare, Member States preferring to leave it to the Commission to take action rather than to institute legal proceedings themselves.[2] Article 108(2) TFEU allows legal proceedings to be brought against Member States for breach of the EU law provisions on state aids. However, it is Article 258 TFEU which plays the central role. At the end of 2007, the Commission was looking at 3,400 cases under it.[3] In 2008 alone, the Commission filed 207 cases. Except for Bulgaria and Romania, actions were brought in that year against all states other than Denmark and Latvia.[4] The actions also cover all sectors of EU law. In its 2008 report, the Commission reported that it had to police the Treaties, 10,000 Regulations and over 1,700 Directives under the procedure. It was active in most sectors of EU activity:

> There continues to be a significant complaints and infringements case-load in environment, internal market, taxation and customs union, energy, transport and employment, social affairs and equal opportunities as well as health and consumer affairs and justice, freedom and security, with a rapidly increasing body of legislation of high interest to citizens.[5]

[1] See p. 157.

[2] Examples are rare. See Case 141/78 *France* v *United Kingdom* [1979] ECR 2923; Case C-388/95 *Belgium* v *Spain* [2000] ECR I-3123; Case C-145/04 *Spain* v *United Kingdom* [2006] ECR I-7917.

[3] European Commission, *25th Annual Report from the Commission on the Monitoring of Community Law*, COM (2008)777, 3.

[4] Court of Justice, *Annual Report for 2008* (Luxembourg, Court of Justice, 2009) 85–6. Bulgaria and Romania having only just acceded to the Union, there had not yet been time to consider whether there had been any infringements by them.

[5] See above n. 3, 2–3.

The use of Article 258 TFEU is wide-ranging and significant but its place within the architecture of EU law is far from settled. There are a number of different perspectives on the role it serves within the EU institutional settlement. Before going on to consider its legal dynamics, it is worth considering these perspectives not only for their own sake but because they shape analysis of the minutiae of the procedures themselves.

(i) Article 258 TFEU and the rule of law

The first view of Article 258 TFEU is that it is the procedure through which the Commission exercises its role as guardian of the Treaties. It is a policing procedure to secure the rule of EU law within the European Union. This is the view expressed in much legal scholarship.[6] As we shall see in the judgment below, it is also the view of the Court of Justice. In *Commission v Germany*, the government of Lower Saxony concluded a contract for the collection of waste water which broke EU law on public procurement. The German government admitted it violated EU law but stated that the contract could not be terminated without payment of substantial compensation to the contractor. The Commission brought the infringement before the Court. The German government argued that it was inadmissible as there was no good reason for the Commission's action. It had admitted its guilt and the payment of compensation was disproportionately large when put next to the benefits of securing the EU law in question.[7]

Joined Cases C–20/01 and C–28/01 *Commission v Germany* [2003] ECR I–3609

29. ... in exercising its powers under Article [258 TFEU] the Commission does not have to show that there is a specific interest in bringing an action. The provision is not intended to protect the Commission's own rights. The Commission's function, in the general interest of the Community, is to ensure that the Member States give effect to the Treaty and the provisions adopted by the institutions thereunder and to obtain a declaration of any failure to fulfil the obligations deriving therefrom with a view to bringing it to an end.

30. Given its role as guardian of the Treaty, the Commission alone is therefore competent to decide whether it is appropriate to bring proceedings against a Member State for failure to fulfil its obligations and to determine the conduct or omission attributable to the Member State concerned on the basis of which those proceedings should be brought. It may therefore ask the Court to find that, in not having achieved, in a specific case, the result intended by the directive, a Member State has failed to fulfil its obligations ...

41. The Court has already held that it is responsible for determining whether or not the alleged breach of obligations exists, even if the State concerned no longer denies the breach and recognises that any individuals who have suffered damage because of it have a right to compensation ...

42. Since the finding of failure by a Member State to fulfil its obligations is not bound up with a finding as to the damage flowing therefrom ... the Federal Republic of Germany may not rely on the fact that no third party has suffered damage ...

44. In the light of the foregoing, the actions brought by the Commission must be held to be admissible.

---

[6] A. Evans, 'The Enforcement Procedure of Article 169 EEC: Commission Discretion' (1979) 4 *ELRev.* 442; A. Dashwood and R. White, 'Enforcement Actions under Article 169 and 170 EEC' (1989) 14 *ELRev.* 388. For a differentiated account that still falls within this school see A. Gil Ibañez, *The Administrative Supervision and Enforcement of EC Law, Powers, Procedures and Limits* (Oxford and Portland, Hart, 1999) especially 26–35.

[7] For similar reasoning see Case C-76/08 *Commission v Malta*, Judgment of 10 September 2009.

The securing of the rule of law is an important function. As was stated above, Article 258 TFEU is the only institutional mechanism that gives practical legal support to many fields of EU law. It also has the advantage that it is, potentially at least, quite an egalitarian mechanism. The Commission, not private parties, bears the cost of litigation. It can therefore act for those who do not have resources or do not have standing, and also in cases where particularly large numbers of legal interests are adversely affected. There are, however, reservations to adopting such a view wholeheartedly.

First, conceiving the procedure in these terms is overly dogmatic. It can be excessively doctrinaire in individual cases. *Commission* v *Germany* is a case in point. The German government argued that there was no practical way for them to rescind the contract: it would violate individuals' property rights; it would disrupt construction of the waste water system as everything would have to be restarted; it would lead to the public authorities having to pay large amounts of compensation. The German government did not implement the judgment. It was then successfully prosecuted by the Commission under Article 260 TFEU and, finally, rescinded the contract.[8] The problems still remained, however.

There is a second danger. Protecting the rule of law is valuable. It is not, however, an exclusive value. There are other values that may sometimes have to be weighed against it, particularly as in most cases we are not talking here about 'law' or 'no law' but rather 'EU law' or 'national law'. This is not just an ethical question but also a problem of mischaracterising the procedure. As *Commission* v *Germany* indicates, the Commission has a discretion whether or not to prosecute. The presence of that discretion indicates that other values and considerations can be taken into account by the Commission. As Börzel has noted, the mission of Article 258 TFEU is to consider whether 'the observed level of non-compliance is considered as a serious problem for a community'.[9] The rule of law analysis treats this process as a black box, and this is questionable given its centrality in the process.

Thirdly, the analysis misdescribes the law. Article 258 TFEU does not permit the Commission to seek to secure 100 per cent compliance with EU law 100 per cent of the time. There seems to be a threshold of illegality where the breach must be of a certain gravity before proceedings can be launched. The Court of Justice has been far from clear on the level of this threshold. In a number of cases, it has intimated that the Commission may initiate proceedings against a Member State for violation of EU law even in a specific case.[10] The cases in which this has happened have all concerned residence or expulsion of non-nationals,[11] or public procurement.[12] The former often have particular civil liberties concerns, while the latter involve significant purchases whose tenders are necessarily very specific and in which it is difficult to look for a general practice. More often, the Court will find that the Commission may only bring an action if either the national law conflicts with EU law or there is a general and consistent administrative practice breaching EU law.

---

[8] Case C-503/04 *Commission* v *Germany* [2007] ECR I-6153.

[9] T. Börzel, 'Non Compliance in the European Union: Pathology or Statistical Artefact?' (2001) 8 *JEPP* 803, 818.

[10] Case C-441/02 *Commission* v *Germany* [2006] ECR I-3449; Case C-157/03 *Commission* v *Spain* [2005] ECR I-2911.

[11] See, in addition to the cases cited above n. 10, Case C-503/03 *Commission* v *Spain* [2006] ECR I-1097.

[12] Joined Cases C-20/01 and C-28/01 *Commission* v *Germany* [2003] ECR I-3609 is an example of the latter category.

In *Commission* v *Greece*, the Commission brought an action against Greece on the ground that its hospitals, in their tendering procedures for medical devices, were excluding devices that met EU law and standards. The Greek government claimed that it had transposed the relevant Directives into EU law and that it had sent a circular to Greek hospitals reminding them of their obligations under EU law. The Court nevertheless found a breach of EU law.

Case C–489/06 *Commission* v *Greece*, Judgment of 19 March 2009

46. ... even if the applicable national legislation itself complies with Community law, a failure to fulfil obligations may arise due to the existence of an administrative practice which infringes that law ...

48. In order for a failure to fulfil obligations to be found on the basis of the administrative practice followed in a Member State, the Court has held that the failure to fulfil obligations can be established only by means of sufficiently documented and detailed proof of the alleged practice; that administrative practice must be, to some degree, of a consistent and general nature; and, in order to find that there has been a general and consistent practice, the Commission may not rely on any presumption ...

49. It must be pointed out that, according to the information in the file before the Court, the products in question are products fulfilling the requirements of the European Pharmacopoeia technical standard and must, by their very nature, be purchased repeatedly and regularly by hospitals and, consequently, with an established degree of regularity.

50. None the less, at least 16 hospital contracting authorities rejected the medical devices in question, during tendering procedures, including the hospitals of Komotiní, Messolonghi, Agios Nikolaos of Crete, Venizeleio-Pananeio of Heraklion, Attica, Agios Savvas, Elpis, Argos, Korgialenio-Benakio, Geniko Nosokomio of Kalamata, Nauplie, P. & A. Kyriakou, Sparta, Panakardiko of Tripoli, Elena Venizelou and Asklipiio Voula.

51. The list of the hospitals mentioned by the Commission shows a variety in the size of the establishments, since some of the largest Greek hospitals such as Agios Savvas, Kyriakou and Asklipiio Voula are referred to, as well as medium-sized hospitals such as Argos, Agios Nikolaos of Crete or Sparta.

52. Moreover, that list refers to establishments with a geographical coverage encompassing the entire country with, in particular, hospitals in Athens, in the Peloponnese and on Crete, but concerns also a wide field of competence, including general hospitals, a children's hospital, a hospital treating cancer-related illnesses and a maternity hospital.

53. Therefore, it can be deduced that the administrative practice of the contracting authorities in question, ... demonstrates a certain degree of consistency and generality.

(ii) Article 258 TFEU as a public policy instrument

It has been suggested that in determining whether an infringement can be pursued, regard will have to be had to the duration, geographical spread and number of infringements.[13] As an overall statement, this might be right. Looking at the case law in the round, there seems to be policy sensitivity to whether a case can be pursued. It is not simply that within certain

---

[13] P. Wennerås, 'A New Dawn for Commission Enforcement under Articles 226 and 228: General and Persistent (GAP) Infringements, Lump Sums and Penalty Payments' (2006) 43 *CMLRev.* 31, 38. This article provides an excellent analysis of the development of this line of reasoning.

sectors a single breach will be sufficient whilst in others it will not. Different approaches are taken within individual sectors. Both *Commission* v *Germany* and *Commission* v *Greece* concerned public procurement but the latter looked for a general and consistent practice whereas the former did not. It is possible that this had to do with the size and scale of the tender in the first instance.

This suggests a second function to Article 258 TFEU: that of being a public policy tool. Such a conception sees its dominant role as being to secure the effective functioning of EU policies. To be sure, realising the rule of law is part of this but only insofar as it is instrumental to bringing about a successful policy.[14]

On such a view, there would be a gradated view to enforcement. If a Member State's laws fail to comply formally with EU law, then there is no hope of realising the policy. There must always be the possibility of prosecution, as no policy can be realised if not even the formal norms are in place. In other fields such as human rights, prosecution may be desirable for individual breaches as these are not measured simply in terms of general compliance but individual violations are seen as, per se, egregious, by virtue of the importance of these for the human condition. For other matters, prosecution only takes place where the alleged illegal behaviour seriously impedes the functioning of the policy. The Commission set out such a prioritisation in 2002.

European Commission, *Better Monitoring of the Application of Community Law*, COM(2002)725 final/4, 11–12

The Commission, in its White Paper on Governance,[15] announced that it would conduct surveillance and bring proceedings against infringements effectively and fairly by applying priority criteria reflecting the seriousness of the potential or known failure to comply with the legislation. Filling in the framework sketched out by the White Paper, the criteria are based on accumulated experience. They rank the following infringements as serious:

(a) Infringements that undermine the foundations of the rule of law
- Breaches of the principles of the primacy and uniform application of Community law (systemic infringements that impede the procedure for preliminary rulings by the Court of Justice or prevent the national courts from acknowledging the primacy of Community law, or provide for no redress procedures in national law: examples include the failure to apply the redress procedures in a Member State and national court rulings that conflict with Community law as interpreted by the Court of Justice).
- Violations of the human rights or fundamental freedoms enshrined in substantive Community law (e.g. interference with the exercise by European citizens of their right to vote, refusal of access to employment or social welfare rights conferred by Community law, threats to human health and damage to the environment with implications for human health).
- Serious damage to the Community's financial interests (fraud with implications for the Community budget, or violation of Community law in relation to a project receiving financial support from the Community budget).

---

[14] On this dimension see M. Mendrinou, 'Non-compliance and the Commission's Role in Integration' (1996) 3 *JEPP* 1; M. Smith, *Centralised Enforcement, Legitimacy and Good Governance in the EU* (Abingdon, Routledge, 2009) 10–15, 114–17.
[15] On this see pp. 352–61.

(b) Infringements that undermine the smooth functioning of the Community legal system
- Action in violation of an exclusive European Union power in an area such as the common commercial policy; serious obstruction of the implementation of a common policy.
- Repetition of an infringement in the same Member State within a given period or in relation to the same piece of Community legislation; these are mainly cases of systematic incorrect application detected by a series of separate complaints by individuals.
- Cross-border infringements, where this aspect makes it more complicated for European citizens to assert their rights.
- Failure to comply with a judgment given by the Court of Justice against a Member State on an application from the Commission for failure to comply with Community law.

(c) Infringements consisting in the failure to transpose or the incorrect transposal of directives which can in reality deprive large segments of the public of access to Community law and actually are a common source of infringements.

The above criteria will help the Commission to make the best use of the various mechanisms designed to restore a situation in line with the Treaties as rapidly as possible, bearing in mind that the Commission's purpose in monitoring the application of Community law and bringing proceedings against infringements is not to 'punish' a Member State, but to ensure that Community law is applied correctly.

In practice, where it is found that an infringement meets these priority criteria, infringement proceedings will be commenced immediately unless the situation can be remedied more rapidly by some other means. Other cases – of lower priority – will be handled on the basis of complementary mechanisms[16] ... which does not rule out the possibility of bringing proceedings for failure to fulfil an obligation. This approach will meet a concern for efficiency – more rapid and effective intervention including where proceedings for failure to fulfil an obligation would not be the most appropriate mechanism – while ensuring equal treatment for the Member States and for the different channels for identifying presumed infringements (complaints, cases identified by the Commission itself, cases referred by the European Parliament or the European Ombudsman).

These criteria indicate a willingness to prioritise cases according to policy needs but they have not been interpreted too strictly. Protection of the environment and public health are mentioned as top priorities in the communication. However, this was not strictly followed. In the years following the communication, environment was the sector in which the Commission examined most cases, followed by internal market, energy, tax and employment.[17]

If Article 258 TFEU is used as a policy tool, however, that means that it cannot just be deployed strategically across sectors or against states, but it also has to be receptive to national capacities to realise a policy. Pragmatism is the order of the day, as its role is that of a regulatory tool deployed as part of the policy to secure the best possible results for the policy. Its use takes place against a context where it is not possible in any Member State to realise perfect application of EU law on the ground on a day-to-day basis.[18] This derives from many

---

[16] See pp. 333–4.
[17] Smith, above n.14, 123–31.
[18] For a case study of British, German, Spanish and Dutch application (or non-application!) of Directive 91/155/EC, the Safety Data Sheets Directive, see E. Versluis, 'Even Rules, Uneven Practices: Opening the "Black Box" of EU Law in Action' (2007) 30 *WEP* 50.

things, not least administrative resources and the general law-abidingness of the society. Public policy specialists have therefore noted in detailed and wide-ranging case studies that the capacity of states to implement EU law falls into a number of categories.[19]

G. Falkner and O. Treib, 'Three Worlds of Compliance or Four? The EU-15 Compared to New Member States' (2008) 46 *Journal of Common Market Studies* 293, 296–7, 308–9

In the *world of law observance*, the compliance goal typically overrides domestic concerns. Even if there are conflicting national policy styles, interests or ideologies, transposition of EU Directives is usually both in time and correct. This is supported by a 'compliance culture' in the sense of an issue-specific 'shared interpretive scheme' ..., a 'set of cognitive rules and recipes' ... Application and enforcement of the national implementation laws is also characteristically successful, as the transposition laws tend to be well considered and well adapted to the specific circumstances and enforcement agencies as well as court systems are generally well-organized and equipped with sufficient resources to fulfil their tasks. Non-compliance, by contrast, typically occurs only rarely and not without fundamental domestic traditions or basic regulatory philosophies being at stake. In addition, instances of non-compliance tend to be remedied rather quickly ...

Obeying EU rules is at best one goal among many in the *world of domestic politics*. Domestic concerns frequently prevail if there is a conflict of interests, and each single act of transposing an EU Directive tends to happen on the basis of a fresh cost-benefit analysis. Transposition is likely to be timely and correct where no domestic concerns dominate over the fragile aspiration to comply. In cases of a manifest clash between EU requirements and domestic interest politics, non-compliance is the likely outcome. While in the countries belonging to the world of law observance breaking EU law would not be a socially acceptable state of affairs, it is much less of a problem in one of the countries in this second category. At times, their politicians or major interest groups even openly call for disobedience with European duties – an appeal that is not met with much serious condemnation in these countries. Since administrations and judiciaries generally work effectively, application and enforcement of transposition laws are not a major problem in this world – the main obstacle to compliance is political resistance at the transposition stage ...

In the countries forming the *world of transposition neglect*, compliance with EU law is not a goal in itself. Those domestic actors who call for more obedience thus have even less of a sound cultural basis for doing so than in the world of domestic politics. At least as long as there is no powerful action by supranational actors, transposition obligations are often not recognized at all in these 'neglecting' countries. A posture of 'national arrogance' (in the sense that indigenous standards are typically expected to be superior) may support this, as may administrative inefficiency. In these cases, the typical reaction to an EU-related implementation duty is inactivity. After an intervention by the European Commission, the transposition process may finally be initiated and may even proceed rather swiftly. The result, however, is often correct only on the surface. Where literal translation of EU Directives takes place at the expense of careful adaptation to domestic conditions, for example, shortcomings in enforcement and application are a frequent phenomenon. Potential deficiencies of this type, however, do not belong to the defining characteristics of the world of transposition neglect ...

---

[19] Most extensively see G. Falkner *et al.*, *Complying with Europe: EU Harmonisation and Soft Law in the Member States* (Cambridge, Cambridge University Press, 2005).

> ... we suggest a fourth category: the 'world of dead letters'. Countries belonging to this cluster of our typology may transpose EU Directives in a compliant manner, depending on the prevalent political constellation among domestic actors, but then there is non-compliance at the later stage of monitoring and enforcement. In this group of countries, what is written on the statute books simply does not become effective in practice. Shortcomings in the court systems, the labour inspections and finally also in civil society systems are among the detrimental factors accounting for this.

Public policy analyses of Article 258 TFEU would have it be sensitive to the domestic environment with its deployment, mindful that it can only stimulate limited change and that use in the wrong circumstances could be counter-productive, leading to domestic counter-reactions or impoverishment of resources.[20] There is much in such approaches but there are difficulties with overemphasising this dimension. First, it is not clear whether an overcharacterisation of Article 258 TFEU is not taking place here. This is a relatively crude instrument in regulatory terms which ends up (as we shall see later) with the national government being fined under Article 260 TFEU if there is no compliance. To argue for its regulatory sensitivity is perhaps to argue for something that it is not. Secondly, as with all public policy instruments, there are concerns about things getting lost along the way. Regard to overarching Commission priorities can lead to local concerns which rely on Article 258 TFEU for protection getting lost. Finally, there is the law of perverse consequences. If one looks at the models of compliance suggested by Falkner and Treib, the lesson would be to punish the law-abiding states more harshly through Article 258 TFEU as they are the ones who will respond best to it. By contrast, the fourth class should be left alone, as no amount of judgments will remedy the structural flaws of poor court systems or weak labour inspections. Yet, it is not clear that Article 258 TFEU is there to reinforce a world in which states are categorised into those seeking perfection, on the one hand, and those damned by their lack of resources, on the other.

(iii) Article 258 TFEU as a public law arena

Concerns about the dogmatism of the rule of law approach and the instrumentalism of the public policy approach have led to a third conception of the Article 258 TFEU procedure. In this, Article 258 TFEU is characterised not 'simply as single-faceted legal provision, but also a unique space of interaction for a multitude of actors'.[21] The procedure is a legal procedure involving national governments and the Commission. As we shall see, it involves other EU institutions, notably the Ombudsman, and EU subjects, be they complainants or those affected by national compliance or non-compliance with EU law. It is thus both a forum for interaction between the institutions and a forum for interaction between institutions and citizens. It is also

[20] A study of environmental and social policy case studies in Germany found that enforcement proceedings could stimulate compliance by shaming the national administration and mobilising social groups in favour of change. It was not always effective and could stimulate a backlash, however. D. Panke, 'The European Court of Justice as an Agent of Europeanization? Restoring Compliance with EU Law' (2007) 14 *JEPP* 847.
[21] Smith, above n. 14, 17.

a procedure that involves the exercise of considerable administrative power. Successful Commission proceedings can change the quality of people's lives significantly.[22]

All these dimensions mean that there is a politics to Article 258 TFEU that must be regulated and constrained through public law, and that the need for public law constraints is as pressing as with any powerful administrative process.

Such constraints would focus, first, on public participation in the process itself and the public accountability of the Commission for its action or inaction.[23] This is discussed in more detail when we examine the responsibilities of the Commission under the procedures themselves. As we shall see, whilst there are some constraints to enable some participation and accountability, there is a consensus amongst analysts that these are weak.

The constraints would focus, secondly, on the constraint of administrative power. US scholars have suggested that, if the American experience is anything to go by, a central constraint on competence creep and the misuse of powers are what they describe as techniques of process. In the United States, the key ingredient in the protection of the various states against the legislative powers of the national government is the extreme difficulty of the process of passing federal law. Obtaining the agreement of the President and of sufficient numbers of Senators and Congressmen is, most of the time, far from straightforward. In the European Union, they suggest, the most effective check on excessive law-making may well lie in the fact that the vast bulk of EU law is administered, not by a pan-European executive, but by national and regional authorities within Member States.[24]

On such a view, the Article 258 TFEU procedure is Janus-faced. It can be conceived as a threat to local autonomy and democracy by being the remorseless, insensitive instrument that enforces unjust, intrusive or unnecessary EU laws. Alternatively, it can be conceived as a political arena, where the implications of an EU law for a Member State are considered in the light of the local, regional or national implications that have come to the fore. It is one of the few places where national democracy can meet Union democracy, namely that German or Slovenian citizens can discuss how an EU measure affects Germany or Slovenia, respectively. To be sure, it may be argued that this also takes place when a state transposes a Directive. In the latter case, however, the norms are already set. There is a debate about how to manoeuvre around within them. The type of debate is different in the former context. It is the discussion about how to mitigate the rigour of the norms, possibly the case for selective non-enforcement of some of them, which cause most difficulties. The other feature of such a debate at this stage is that it is a debate ex post facto, where the implications of an EU law on the ground are now more imminent and local concerns more focused.

This role for Article 258 TFEU is not yet formalised. However, the question of whether the rigour of EU law could be mitigated for non-legal reasons was addressed in *Commission* v *Poland*. The Commission brought an action against a Polish law, the Law on Seeds, which, in effect, prohibited the marketing of genetically modified seeds in Poland. This violated Directive 2001/18/EC on the deliberate release into the environment of genetically modified organisms,

---

[22] *Ibid.* 15–20 and ch. 7. Smith's book is unrivalled as a study of the process and the context to the process.

[23] The starting point for such an analysis is R. Rawlings, 'Engaged Elites: Citizen Action and Institutional Attitudes in Commission Enforcement' (2000) 6 *ELJ* 4.

[24] E. Young, 'Protecting Member State Autonomy in the European Union: Some Cautionary Tales from American Federalism' (2002) 77 *New York University Law Review* 1612, 1736; G. Bermann, 'Taking Subsidiarity Seriously: Federalism in the European Community and the United States' (1994) 94 *Colum. L Rev.* 331, 399.

which allowed the marketing of these where they had been authorised by EU authorities. The Polish government justified its non-compliance by challenging both the ethics of genetically modified food and by arguing that their release violated important tenets of Catholic thought.

Case C-165/08 *Commission* v *Poland*, Judgment of 16 July 2009

49. In its defence and its rejoinder, the Republic of Poland concentrated its arguments wholly on the ethical or religious considerations on which the contested national provisions are based …

56. However, a Member State cannot rely in that manner on the views of a section of public opinion in order unilaterally to challenge a harmonising measure adopted by the Community institutions … As the Court observed in a case specifically concerning Directive 2001/18, a Member State may not plead difficulties of implementation which emerge at the stage when a Community measure is put into effect, such as difficulties relating to opposition on the part of certain individuals, to justify a failure to comply with obligations and time-limits laid down by Community law …

57. Secondly, and as regards the more specifically religious or ethical arguments put forward by the Republic of Poland for the first time in the defence and rejoinder submitted to the Court, it must be held that that Member State has failed to establish that the contested national provisions were in fact adopted on the basis of such considerations.

58. The Republic of Poland essentially referred to a sort of general presumption according to which it can come as no surprise that such provisions were adopted in the present case. First, the Republic of Poland relies on the fact that it is well known that Polish society attaches great importance to Christian and Roman Catholic values. Secondly, it states that the political parties with a majority in the Polish Parliament at the time when the contested national provisions were adopted specifically called for adherence to such values. In those circumstances, according to that Member State, it is reasonable to take the view that the Members of Parliament, who do not, as a general rule, have scientific training, are more likely to be influenced by the religious or ethical ideas which inspire their political actions, rather than by other considerations, in particular, those linked to the complex scientific assessments relating to the protection of the environment or of human health.

59. However, such considerations are not sufficient to establish that the adoption of the contested national provisions was in fact inspired by the ethical and religious considerations described in the defence and the rejoinder, especially since the Republic of Poland had, in the pre-litigation procedure, based its defence mainly on the shortcomings allegedly affecting Directive 2001/18, regard being had to the precautionary principle and to the risks posed by that directive to both the environment and human health.

The reasoning is finely textured. It holds that Poland has failed to meet its obligations in EU law. However, whilst it holds that a state cannot defy EU law for populist reasons, it leaves open the question whether a state can do so for ethical or religious reasons. It does suggest that if such a defence does exist, it must be argued from the start and that the law or administrative practice in question must be justified on those grounds. Leaving open the possibility of such a defence is not the same thing as suggesting that there is such a defence. We will have to await further clarification. At the moment, however, an opening is suggested for public deliberation at a local level where, if a state or locality comes to a view that an EU law poses insurmountable ethical or religious difficulties for it, and it wishes to protect a domestic provision on these grounds, this might not be incompatible with EU law.

Like the other two dimensions to Article 258 TFEU, there is a danger of focusing exclusively on it as 'public law' process. To do so would fail to distinguish Article 258 TFEU from other administrative processes. It clearly has distinctive functions of its own: namely, upholding the rule of EU law and contributing to the effective functioning of EU policies. There is also an internal tension in this vision of Article 258 TFEU. In some circumstances, it may seek to compel enforcement, namely where citizens adversely affected by illegal national behaviour press for enforcement action. In other circumstances, there is an idea that there should be constraints on enforcement action to allow local democracy to flourish. It is a challenge to know how to mediate between these tensions other than to suggest somewhat vaguely and unsatisfactorily that the procedure should be sensitive to both.

3 SCOPE OF MEMBER STATE RESPONSIBILITIES

One feature of the Article 258 TFEU process is that it may be used only against Member States. Although, formally, actions are brought against the state, in practice it is the central government which is proceeded against. This prompts two questions: first what is considered to be state action for the purposes of Article 258 TFEU; and secondly, what capacities and responsibilities are assumed of the state, in particular whether it should be accountable for everything that happens within its territory.

(i) Acts and omissions of all state agencies

The consistent position of the Court is that it is the state, not the government, which is responsible. From this it has derived two related doctrines.[25] First, it is the acts and omissions of state agencies, and only these acts and omissions, which attract liability. Secondly, the state is responsible for these agencies even if these are constitutionally independent.

The conception of a state agency is considered to comprise institutions from all tiers of government, be they national, regional or local.[26] It also comprises certain bodies that are not formally part of the state but which are subject to public authority.[27] Regulatory agencies, even if set up as independent private bodies, have therefore been held on this basis to be part of the state.[28] Private companies will be held to be a state agency if the government exercises considerable influence over them. In *CMA*, a public body financed by a levy on the German food and agriculture sector, the Fund, was set up to promote German agriculture. A private company, the CMA, was further established to realise the objectives of the Fund. It had to observe the latter's guidelines and was financed by it. The CMA adopted a quality label certifying the qualities of produce from Germany. The Commission argued this label violated the EU provisions on free movement, as it was only available to German produce. The German government argued, to no avail, that the CMA was a private body and, it, therefore, was not responsible.

---

[25] Case 77/69 *Commission v Belgium* [1970] ECR 237.
[26] Case 199/85 *Commission v Italy* [1987] ECR 1039.
[27] Case 249/81 *Commission v Ireland* [1982] ECR 4005; Case 222/82 *Apple & Pear Development Council* [1983] ECR 4083.
[28] Case T-187/06 *Netherlands v Commission* [2008] ECR II-3151.

Case C–325/00 *Commission* v *Germany (CMA)* [2002] ECR I-9977

17. In that regard, it must be recalled that the CMA, although set up as a private company, is
    - established on the basis of a law…is characterised by that law as a central economic body and has, among the objects assigned to it by that law, the promotion, at central level, of the marketing and exploitation of German agricultural and food products;
    - is bound, according to its Articles of Association, originally approved by the competent federal minister, to observe the rules of the Fund, itself a public body, and additionally to be guided, in particular in relation to the commitment of its financial resources, by the general interest of the German agricultural and food sector;
    - is financed, according to the rules laid down by the AFG, by a compulsory contribution by all the undertakings in the sectors concerned.

18. Such a body, which is set up by a national law of a Member State and which is financed by a contribution imposed on producers, cannot, under Community law, enjoy the same freedom as regards the promotion of national production as that enjoyed by producers themselves or producers' associations of a voluntary character … Thus it is obliged to respect the basic rules of the Treaty on the free movement of goods when it sets up a scheme, open to all undertakings of the sectors concerned, which can have effects on intra-Community trade similar to those arising under the scheme adopted by the public authorities.

19. Furthermore, it must be observed that:
    - the Fund is a public law body;
    - the CMA is required to respect the Fund's guidelines;
    - the financing of the CMA's activities, under legislation, comes from resources which are granted to it through the Fund, and
    - the Fund supervises the CMA's activities and the proper management of the finances which are granted to it by the Fund.

20. In those circumstances, it must be held that the Commission could rightly take the view that the contested scheme is ascribable to the State.

21. Thus it follows that the contested scheme must be considered to be a public measure … ascribable to the State.

Although it has never been raised in infringement proceedings under Article 258 TFEU, it seems that a body will be considered a state agency even if it is not subject to public authority but is performing a public service and, for that reason, has special powers.[29]

This wide definition of the state to include private bodies subject to state influence or performing a public service and enjoying special powers makes sense from all three perspectives set out above. For the purposes of securing the 'rule of law', the state should not be able to evade its responsibilities by contracting-out tasks. In terms of realising the public policy objectives of the Union, it is important, on the one hand, that States be able to organise themselves in the most efficient and effective manner possible, and this may involve privatisation. It is important, however, that their responsibility to secure a policy is not lost in this and their

---

[29] Case C-180/04 *Vassallo* v *Azienda Ospedaliera Ospedale San Martino di Genova e Cliniche Universitarie Convenzionate* [2006] ECR I-7251. This is dealt with in more detail in Chapter 7 at pp. 288–9.

responsibility to coordinate different organisations is not fragmented. Finally, in terms of public and democratic control, exposing the actions of private entities to public law procedures holds them accountable and subject to scrutiny.

The second dimension of the doctrine of state responsibility, that the government be responsible for the actions of constitutionally independent units, is more controversial. It has led to governments being accountable when they were unable, despite their best intentions, to get legislation through parliament.[30] It also has led to central governments being responsible for the actions of regional authorities even when the former do not have the power under their constitutions to compel action by the latter.[31] The most controversial application of this doctrine is holding states accountable for the actions of national courts. In *Commission* v *Italy*, infringement proceedings were brought against a series of decisions by the Italian Court of Cassation, the highest Italian civil court, in which the latter had consistently interpreted Italian law on customs duties in a way that conflicted with EU law.

Case C-129/00 *Commission* v *Italy* [2003] ECR I-14637

29. A Member State's failure to fulfil obligations may, in principle, be established under Article [258 TFEU] whatever the agency of that State whose action or inaction is the cause of the failure to fulfil its obligations, even in the case of a constitutionally independent institution ...

30. The scope of national laws, regulations or administrative provisions must be assessed in the light of the interpretation given to them by national courts ...

31. In this case what is at issue is Article 29(2) of Law No. 428/1990 which provides that duties and charges levied under national provisions incompatible with Community legislation are to be repaid, unless the amount thereof has been passed on to others. Such a provision is in itself neutral in respect of Community law in relation both to the burden of proof that the charge has been passed on to other persons and to the evidence which is admissible to prove it. Its effect must be determined in the light of the construction which the national courts give it.

32. In that regard, isolated or numerically insignificant judicial decisions in the context of case law taking a different direction, or still more a construction disowned by the national supreme court, cannot be taken into account. That is not true of a widely-held judicial construction which has not been disowned by the supreme court, but rather confirmed by it.

33. Where national legislation has been the subject of different relevant judicial constructions, some leading to the application of that legislation in compliance with Community law, others leading to the opposite application, it must be held that, at the very least, such legislation is not sufficiently clear to ensure its application in compliance with Community law.

There is an element of disingenuousness to the judgment. The problem is framed as one of poor Italian legislation rather than as one of judicial practice which fails to comply with EU law. It was the Italian Court of Cassation's interpretation of these laws which generated the problem, however. The disingenuousness was in order to avoid directly confronting national

---

[30] Case 77/69 *Commission* v *Belgium* [1970] ECR 237.
[31] Case 1/86 *Commission* v *Belgium* [1987] ECR 2797.

courts. A holding that national courts were in breach of EU law would have posed difficulties for the principle of judicial independence and *res judicata*, as it would have required the national government to intervene to suspend the judgments and would have thrown into doubt the binding effects of the judgment.[32]

If the challenge is most intense for breaches by the judiciary, it exists in relation to all constitutionally independent arms of government. The central authorities are being enjoined to trespass beyond their domestic constitutional limits to secure compliance with EU law. The problem arises from the fiction of the unitary state. In domestic law, individuals rarely sue the state but rather the agency which they allege is harming their interests. Litigation against the state in these instances causes many problems. Whilst it places duties on central authorities to uphold the rule of law, the constitutional independence of other actors may prevent effective measures by central government. They can only uphold the rule of law by violating domestic constitutional arrangements, thereby creating difficulties for the domestic rule of law. In public policy terms, a system of perverse incentives is established. As other governmental actors will not be litigated against, there is simply no reason for them to take measures to comply with EU law, as they know that central government (with whom they are often in competition) will be held accountable.[33] Finally, this can hardly be good for local democracy. Powers of enforcement are used to justify central intervention at the domestic level to secure compliance, thereby curbing local self-government.

(ii) Accountability of state actors

State agencies are clearly responsible for actions that violate EU law. The state will be responsible for any measure that formally conflicts with EU law, be it a law, statutory instrument or judgment. This is not completely clear-cut. It is for the Commission to prove that the national law conflicts with EU law. It is insufficient that it is ambiguous. The Court of Justice will therefore often insist that there be interpretations by national courts of the measure which conflict with EU law before holding that there is a violation.[34]

The state is also responsible for administrative practices conflicting with EU law. As we have seen, in some cases, a specific act may be sufficient whilst, in others, the Court will look for a generalised practice.[35] These practices can also consist of omissions and failures to act, for state agencies are under positive duties to secure the effective functioning of EU law. These duties have been developed through the interpretation of the fidelity principle, Article 4(3) TEU, and they have been explored in more detail in Chapter 5.[36] To recap, briefly, however, the central duties for which states can be subject to infringement proceedings are:

---

[32] Compare Case C-224/01 *Köbler* v *Austria* [2003] ECR I-239, discussed at pp. 308–11.

[33] In Belgium, for example, administrative coordination was so difficult and there was so much mistrust that the Wallonian regional government actually took the Flemish regional government to the Court of Justice through the preliminary reference procedure for its failure to observe the free movement provisions. Case C-212/06 *Government of the French Community and Walloon Government* v *Flemish Government (Flemish Insurance Case)* [2008] ECR I-1683.

[34] Case C-300/95 *Commission* v *United Kingdom* [1997] ECR I-2649; Case C-418/04 *Commission* v *Ireland* [2007] ECR I-10947.

[35] See pp. 319–20.

[36] See pp. 223–7.

- the duty to secure legal certainty for EU law;[37]
- the duty actively to police EU law;[38]
- the duty to penalise infringements of EU law under analogous conditions applicable to infringements of national law of a similar nature and importance[39] and to ensure that penalties for breach of EU law are effective, proportionate and dissuasive;[40]
- the duty to notify the Commission of any problems applying or enforcing EU law.[41]

These are general duties reflecting assumptions about state capacity and good faith in EU law. They apply with particular force in the case of enforcement proceedings, as it is here, in the context of an alleged failure by the state, that they are explored at most length. There is, however, one particular duty which is specific to the Article 258 TFEU procedure itself and relates to the question of the burden of proof. If the Commission notifies the state of a possible breach of EU law and provides sufficient evidence of that breach, the duty is on the state to investigate that breach in order to prove otherwise.

In *Commission* v *Ireland*, the Commission received twelve complaints of illegal dumping of waste or operating unlicensed waste dumps across Ireland in breach of EU environmental law. It wrote to the Irish government but received only limited replies. The Irish government argued that the Commission had failed to provide sufficient proof of its infringements.

Case C-494/01 *Commission* v *Ireland* [2005] ECR I-3331

41. ... In proceedings under Article [258 TFEU] for failure to fulfil obligations it is incumbent upon the Commission to prove the allegation that the obligation has not been fulfilled. It is the Commission's responsibility to place before the Court the information needed to enable the Court to establish that the obligation has not been fulfilled, and in so doing the Commission may not rely on any presumption ...

42. However, the Member States are required, under Article [4(3) TEU], to facilitate the achievement of the Commission's tasks, which consist in particular, pursuant to Article [17(1) TEU], in ensuring that the provisions of the Treaty and the measures taken by the institutions pursuant thereto are applied ...

43. In this context, account should be taken of the fact that, where it is a question of checking that the national provisions intended to ensure effective implementation of the directive are applied correctly in practice, the Commission which ... does not have investigative powers of its own in the matter, is largely reliant on the information provided by any complainants and by the Member State concerned ...

44. It follows in particular that, where the Commission has adduced sufficient evidence of certain matters in the territory of the defendant Member State, it is incumbent on the latter to challenge in substance and in detail the information produced and the consequences flowing therefrom ...

45. In such circumstances, it is indeed primarily for the national authorities to conduct the necessary on-the-spot investigations, in a spirit of genuine cooperation and mindful of each Member State's duty, recalled in paragraph 42 of the present judgment, to facilitate the general task of the Commission ...

---

[37] Case C-159/99 *Commission* v *Italy (conservation of wild birds)* [2001] ECR I-4007.
[38] Case C-265/95 *Commission* v *France (Spanish strawberries)* [1997] ECR I-6959.
[39] Case C-180/95 *Draehmpaehl* v *Urania Immobilienservice* [1997] ECR I-2195.
[40] Case 68/88 *Commission* v *Greece* [1989] ECR 2965.
[41] Case C-105/02 *Commission* v *Germany* [2006] ECR I-9659.

46. Thus, where the Commission relies on detailed complaints revealing repeated failures to comply with the provisions of the directive, it is incumbent on the Member State to contest specifically the facts alleged in those complaints ...

47. Likewise, where the Commission has adduced sufficient evidence to show that a Member State's authorities have developed a repeated and persistent practice which is contrary to the provisions of a directive, it is incumbent on that Member State to challenge in substance and in detail the information produced and the consequences flowing therefrom.

The onus on the Commission, in the case of administrative failure to comply with EU law, is to make no more than a prima facie case. It must provide sufficient evidence for it to be plausible that there has been non-compliance. Whilst this question appears just to be an evidentiary one, its consequence is to impose some investigatory duties on the Member States, which stem from the duty of cooperation in Article 4(3) TEU.[42] They must know what is going on in their own backyard. If they do not, they are responsible for the consequences. A lower threshold of proof will be adduced to show non-compliance.

4 THE DIFFERENT STAGES OF INFRINGEMENT PROCEEDINGS

The infringement proceedings are best seen as a series of stages which, extrapolated out, comprise:

- an informal letter to the Member State;
- a letter of formal notice to the Member State that it is in breach of EU law;
- the submission of observations by the Member State;
- the issuing of a reasoned opinion by the Commission setting out the breach of EU law;
- a period for the Member State to comply with the reasoned opinion and submit observations;
- referral to the Court by the Commission;
- judgment by the Court.

The process is arduous and time-consuming. In 2007, the average time taken was twenty-three months.[43] There are three central points in the process. These are the initial informal contacts between the Commission and the Member State; the letter of formal notice setting out the breach and the Member State's observations on this (sometimes known as the administrative stage); and the issue of a reasoned Opinion by the Commission with possible referral to the Court if the Member State does not comply with that Opinion.

(i) Informal letter

There are two procedures for detecting a complaint. The Commission may discover something problematic through its own investigations ('own initiative'), or it may receive a complaint of an infringement from a third party. Although this varies from year to year, in 2006, a not untypical

---

[42] See also Case C-135/05 *Commission* v *Italy* [2007] ECR I-3475.
[43] European Commission, *25th Annual Report on Monitoring the Application of Community Law*, COM(2008)777, 2.

year, the latter accounted for 35.9 per cent of detections of infringements.[44] This figure understates the role of complainants, however. Many infringement proceedings are begun because Member States have not communicated information that they have transposed an EU law to the Commission, as is required of them. When these are taken into account, complaints are the main way for the Commission of finding out what is happening on the ground.

Historically, whether on the basis of its own investigation or on the basis of receiving a complaint, the Commission then sets out the reasons why it suspects an infringement has taken place to the Member State concerned. The Member State government is invited to reply and to supply further information. Around 70 per cent of proceedings are closed at this stage.[45] In 2007, concerned that it was letting its enforcement strategy be determined by which complaints arrived at its door, the Commission changed tack. Own initiative proceedings would continue to be resolved in the traditional way. Complaints by third parties were to be treated, in the first place, as a matter of dispute settlement with the State concerned. The State would commit itself to resolve the dispute, with the Commission only stepping in and commencing proceedings if resolution was not possible. The approach is set out below.

European Commission, *A Europe of Results: Applying Community Law*, COM(2007)502, 7–8

As is the case now, enquiries and complaints raising a question of the correct application of Community law sent to the Commission would continue to be registered and acknowledged and the Commission would provide explanations of Community law. Where an issue requires clarification of the factual or legal position in the Member State, it would be transmitted to the Member State concerned. Unless urgency requires immediate action and when the Commission considers that the contact with the Member State can contribute to an efficient solution, the Member States would be given a short deadline to provide the necessary clarifications, information and solutions directly to the citizens or business concerned and inform the Commission. When the issue amounts to a breach of Community law, Member States would be expected to remedy, or offer a remedy, within set deadlines. When no solution is proposed, the Commission would follow-up, taking any further action, including through infringement proceedings, in accordance with existing practice.

In this way, Member States would have the opportunity to resolve issues arising within this agreed framework, operating at the point closest to the citizen within its national legal and institutional context, in conformity with the requirements of Community law. With the necessary commitment, there would be a greater possibility for enquiries and complaints to be seen through to an early conclusion.

Transmission mechanisms would be established between the Commission and Member States. A central contact point within the Member State would have to process incoming enquiries and outgoing responses. This contact point would encourage the appropriate authority in the Member State to respond constructively, providing information, solving the problem or at least explaining its position.

The outcome of cases would be recorded to enable reporting on performance and any follow up, including the registration and initiation of infringement proceedings. This reporting would identify the volume, nature and seriousness of problems remaining unresolved, indicating if additional specific problem-solving mechanisms or more tailored sector initiatives are needed.

---

[44] *Ibid.* 3.
[45] *Ibid.* 2.

These procedures are currently being tested in fifteen states but they move the Article 258 TFEU procedure away from the traditional paradigm of securing the rule of EU law. For, in instances where individuals settle with the Member State, that settlement may not address the wider legal issues that extend beyond the dispute. Enforcement would be privatised to the extent that complainant satisfaction would be the primary benchmark of whether the state had done enough legally. It is also to be wondered what this form of alternate dispute resolution will do in terms of securing the effective functioning of EU policies. These are something to be assessed in the round from a panoramic perspective, rather than from the point of view of tailoring them around the circumstances of individual disputes, which pull policy this way and that. This is particularly significant in the light of the large proportion of proceedings both instigated by complainants and resolved at this stage. It might be considered that Article 258 TFEU is here moving towards a role of facilitating local democracy and national accountability, whereby pressure groups and citizens can wave the sword of EU law against abusive state action that is harming their interests. Yet, the procedure is flawed even from this perspective, as the extract below suggests.

M. Smith, 'Enforcement, Monitoring, Verification, Outsourcing: The Decline and Decline of the Infringement Process' (2008) 33 *European Law Review* 777, 798

There are several worrying implications that flow from the adoption of the new 'pilot scheme'. The most obvious is that the already protracted 'normal' Article 226 procedure will be prolonged even further because if the Member State does not resolve the complaint to the Commission's satisfaction, the regular Article 226 process may be initiated (i.e. investigation, negotiation, formal letter, etc). Even if the complaint has already been through the pilot system it will not bypass any of the existing steps in the process. Another consequence of this elongated process is that complainants will no doubt suffer 'complaint fatigue' and simply give up pursuing the alleged infraction. This undermines the Commission's statements that the legitimacy of the Union depends on the continued participation of the citizen.

Despite this the Commission contends that 'with the necessary commitment' from the Member States, the pilot scheme will lead to a faster resolution of infractions. It is difficult to see how. If the Commission itself, with all its political and institutional weight, cannot easily obtain the information it requires from offending Member States, it is difficult to see how the citizen will manage this in its place. It is also possible that this will lead to a disparate enforcement of EC law across the Union depending on the administrative sophistication and the internal (political) characteristics of each Member State. It is unlikely that this new initiative will increase either the efficiency or effectiveness of the enforcement mechanism: it simply draws out the administrative phase even further, presenting the Member States with a greater opportunity to avoid their legal responsibilities.

The second major implication is that the Commission's new pilot scheme has the result of outsourcing its responsibility to deal with complainants *to the very entity committing the alleged infraction*. Whilst the Commission wishes to preserve its status as initial contact and registration point (to retain the 'information fodder' aspect of the complainant which is vital to the Commission's ability to detect infringements), the complainant will thereafter have been referred to the Member State and the Commission will play no further part.

(ii) Letter of formal notice and Member State observations

The process begins with the Commission issuing a letter of formal notice. The reason for this is that Article 258 TFEU only allows the Commission to issue a reasoned Opinion once the Member State concerned has had the opportunity to submit observations. For the latter to be able to do this, there must be a letter of formal notice upon which it can submit observations. As the letter of formal notice is seen as central to safeguarding the rights of defence, it is also seen as framing the dispute. The Commission can only take complaints to a Member State that are specifically set out in the letter of formal notice. A sense of the role of the letter of formal notice is provided in *Commission* v *Denmark*. The Commission brought an action against the Danish government for failing to transpose Directive 76/891/EC on electrical energy meters into Danish law. The Danish government claimed that the letter of formal notice was insufficient as it had merely noted Denmark's failure to act and not set out what positive steps the Danish government needed to take to remedy the breach.

Case 211/81 *Commission* v *Denmark* [1982] ECR 4547

8. It follows from the purpose assigned to the pre-contentious stage of the proceedings for failure of a state to fulfil its obligations that a letter giving formal notice is intended to delimit the subject matter of the dispute and to indicate to the Member State which is invited to submit its observations the factors enabling it to prepare its defence.

9. ... the opportunity for the Member State concerned to submit its observations constitutes an essential guarantee required by the Treaty and, even if the Member State does not consider it necessary to avail itself thereof, observance of that guarantee is an essential formal requirement of the procedure under Article [258 TFEU].

10. It appears from the documents before the Court that by a letter dated 23 May 1979 giving formal notice the Commission merely asserted that in its view the Danish Government had not put into force the measures necessary to transpose Directive 76/891 into national law but refrained from specifying the obligations which, in its view, were imposed on that State by virtue of the directive and which had been disregarded.

11. In the present case, however, that fact did not have the effect of depriving the Danish Government of the opportunity of submitting its observations to good effect. On 7 June 1978 the Commission had addressed to the Danish Government a letter setting out the precise reasons which led it to conclude that the Kingdom of Denmark had failed to fulfil one of the obligations imposed on it by Directive 76/891. It was by reference to the position adopted by the Commission in that letter of 7 June 1978 that the Danish Government submitted its observations on 22 August 1979.

Whilst the Commission does not have to set out what Member States need to do to comply with EU law, it must set out all legal complaints in the letter of formal notice. Anything not mentioned there will be deemed inadmissible.[46] However, the Commission can subsequently bring in new evidence to clarify the grounds on which it is making the complaint on condition that this does not alter the subject-matter of the dispute.[47]

---

[46] Case C-371/04 *Commission* v *Italy* [2006] ECR I-10257.
[47] Case C-494/01 *Commission* v *Ireland* [2005] ECR I-3331.

(iii) Reasoned Opinion and the period for national compliance

If, after the Member State has submitted its observations on the letter of formal notice, agreement is still not reached, the Commission will issue a reasoned Opinion. As the subject-matter of the dispute is delimited by the formal letter of notice, the reasoned Opinion cannot modify the subject-matter of the dispute by introducing new claims.[48] It should therefore not amend conclusions contained in the letter of notice. However, account can be taken of changes in circumstances. In *Commission* v *Belgium*, the Commission challenged, in its letter of formal notice, a 1987 broadcasting law passed by the Flemish Communities.[49] The 1987 law was then replaced by a 1994 law. This latter law was challenged in the reasoned Opinion. The Court rejected a Belgian claim that this amendment compromised the latter's rights of defence, noting that the national provisions mentioned need not be identical if the change in legislation resulted in the system as a whole not being altered.

The Commission has less room for manoeuvre in the reasoned Opinion than in the letter of formal notice. Whilst the latter need do no more than give a summary of the complaints, the reasoned Opinion must give a coherent and detailed statement of reasons that led the Commission to believe that the Member State has breached EU law. This should include a detailed statement of the legal and factual context to the dispute and take account of any resolutions submitted by the Member State.[50] Finally, and importantly, the reasoned Opinion must also set out a reasonable period for compliance by the Member State. The following extract summarises the current position.

Case C–350/02 *Commission* v *Netherlands* [2004] ECR I–6213

18. In ... an action for failure to fulfil obligations the purpose of the pre-litigation procedure is to give the Member State concerned an opportunity, on the one hand, to comply with its obligations under Community law and, on the other, to avail itself of its right to defend itself against the charges formulated by the Commission ...

19. The proper conduct of that procedure constitutes an essential guarantee required by the Treaty not only in order to protect the rights of the Member State concerned, but also so as to ensure that any contentious procedure will have a clearly defined dispute as its subject-matter ...

20. It follows that the subject-matter of proceedings under Article [258 TFEU] is delimited by the pre-litigation procedure governed by that provision. The Commission's reasoned opinion and the application must be based on the same grounds and pleas, with the result that the Court cannot examine a ground of complaint which was not formulated in the reasoned opinion ... which for its part must contain a cogent and detailed exposition of the reasons which led the Commission to the conclusion that the Member State concerned had failed to fulfil one of its obligations under the Treaty ...

21. It should also be emphasised that, whilst the formal letter of notice, which comprises an initial succinct résumé of the alleged infringement, may be useful in construing the reasoned opinion, the Commission

---

[48] Case 278/85 *Commission* v *Denmark* [1987] ECR 4065.
[49] Case C-11/95 *Commission* v *Belgium* [1996] ECR I-4115.
[50] Case C-266/94 *Commission* v *Spain* [1995] ECR I-1975.

is none the less obliged to specify precisely in that opinion the grounds of complaint which it already raised more generally in the letter of formal notice and alleges against the Member State concerned, after taking cognizance of any observations submitted by it under the first paragraph of Article [258 TFEU]. That requirement is essential in order to delimit the subject-matter of the dispute prior to any initiation of the contentious procedure provided for in the second paragraph of Article [258 TFEU] and in order to ensure that the Member State in question is accurately apprised of the grounds of complaint maintained against it by the Commission and can thus bring an end to the alleged infringements or put forward its arguments in defence prior to any application to the Court by the Commission.

Once the reasoned Opinion has been issued, the Commission must afford Member States sufficient time both to respond to the views it sets out and to comply with the Opinion.[51] The minimum time limit laid down will depend upon a number of factors. These include the urgency of the matter and when the matter was first brought to the attention of the Member State by the Commission.[52]

Perhaps the most stark example of what circumstances might be taken into account is *Commission* v *Belgium*. Under a 1985 law, Belgian universities were authorised to charge a supplementary fee (a 'minerval') on nationals from other Member States who enrolled with them. The Commission considered such action to be illegal following the *Gravier* judgment, given on 13 February 1985.[53] It had an informal meeting with Belgian officials on 25 June 1985, where it expressed that view but also stated that it was still considering the effects of the judgment. On 17 July 1985, it issued a letter of formal notice stating that, in view of the onset of the new academic year, the Belgian government should submit its observations within eight days. The Belgian authorities asked for more time. On 23 August 1985, the Commission issued a reasoned Opinion, with the Belgian government being given fifteen days to comply. The Belgian government claimed that the action was inadmissible given the limited time periods allowed for compliance.

Case 293/85 *Commission* v *Belgium (Gravier)* [1988] ECR 305

13. It should be pointed out first that the purpose of the pre-litigation procedure is to give the Member State concerned an opportunity, on the one hand, to comply with its obligations under Community law and, on the other, to avail itself of its right to defend itself against the complaints made by the Commission.

14. In view of that dual purpose the Commission must allow Member States a reasonable period to reply to the letter of formal notice and to comply with a reasoned opinion, or, where appropriate, to prepare their defence. In order to determine whether the period allowed is reasonable, account must be taken of all the circumstances of the case. Thus, very short periods may be justified in particular circumstances, especially where there is an urgent need to remedy a breach or where the Member State concerned is fully aware of the Commission's views long before the procedure starts.

---

[51] See e.g. Case 211/81 *Commission* v *Denmark* [1982] ECR 4547.
[52] In determining this, account is taken not of when the letter of formal notice was sent but when informal contacts were first made. Case C-56/90 *Commission* v *United Kingdom* [1993] ECR I-4109; Case C-473/93 *Commission* v *Luxembourg* [1996] ECR I-3207.
[53] Case 293/83 *Gravier* v *City of Liège* [1985] ECR 593.

15. It is therefore necessary to examine whether the shortness of the periods set by the Commission was justified in view of the particular circumstances of this case ...

16. ... the imminent start of the 1985 academic year may indeed be regarded as a special circumstance justifying a short time limit. However, the Commission could have taken action long before the start of the academic year because the major part of the Belgian provisions were already part of its legislation before the law of 21 June 1985. They were therefore known to the Commission at the latest when the judgment of 13 February 1985 was delivered, which was six months before the start of the 1985 academic year. Furthermore, it should be noted that at the time the Commission had not made any criticism of the minerval and had even given the impression, prior to the entry into force of the law in question, that it accepted that the minerval was compatible with Community law. In those circumstances the Commission cannot rely on urgency which it itself created by failing to take action earlier.

17. As for the Commission's alternative argument that the time limits laid down were not absolute and that consequently replies given after their expiry would have been accepted, it should be remarked that that factor is not relevant. A Member State to which a measure subject to a time limit is addressed cannot know in advance whether, and to what extent, the Commission will if necessary grant it an extension of that time limit. In this case, moreover, the Commission did not reply to the Kingdom of Belgium's request for an extension of time.

18. As regards the question whether the Kingdom of Belgium was aware sufficiently in advance of the Commission's views, it is common ground that although the commission had expressed its views to the competent officials of the Belgian ministries of national education on 25 June 1985, at a meeting of the education committee of 27 and 28 June 1985 it stated that it was still considering the effects of the judgments of the Court in the field of university education. It follows that the Kingdom of Belgium was not fully informed of the definitive views of the Commission before these proceedings were brought against it.

It is only if compliance with the reasoned Opinion does not occur that the matter may be brought before the Court. Indeed, once the period set out in the reasoned Opinion has elapsed there is nothing a Member State can do to prevent the matter being heard by the Court. The latter has repeatedly stated that it will consider the position at the end of the period laid down in the reasoned Opinion, and will not take account of subsequent changes.[54] Compliance by the Member State with the reasoned Opinion after the deadline set out in the latter but before judgment will not therefore prevent the Court's declaring that the Member State has acted illegally.[55] The reasons are, first, that the unwieldy nature of the procedure would, otherwise, be unable to capture breaches of a relatively short duration,[56] and, secondly, that Member States could, otherwise, manipulate the procedures by simply bringing their conduct to an end shortly before judgment was given.[57]

[54] See e.g. Case C-200/88 *Commission* v *Greece* [1990] ECR I-4299; Case C-133/94 *Commission* v *Belgium* [1996] ECR I-2323.

[55] See e.g. Case C-446/01 *Commission* v *Spain* [2003] ECR I-6053.

[56] Advocate General Lenz in Case 240/86 *Commission* v *Greece* [1988] ECR 1835.

[57] Advocate General Lagrange in Case 7/61 *Commission* v *Italy* [1961] ECR 317.

5 ADMINISTRATION OF INFRINGEMENT PROCEEDINGS

(i) The Commission's discretion

There are a number of remarkable features about the Article 258 TFEU process. The first is how few actions reach the Court of Justice. According to Commission figures, in 2007, only 7 per cent of proceedings reached the Court.[58] The heart of the infringement procedure is thus an administrative process, with judicial proceedings predominantly acting as a backdrop to structure the negotiations between the Commission and the Member States. Secondly, the Commission wins the overwhelming majority of cases that reach the Court. In 2008, for example, ninety-four Commission actions were successful and nine dismissed.[59] This is not atypical, with the Commission typically winning over 90 per cent of the cases arriving before the Court: a staggeringly high proportion when it is remembered that the case can be dismissed not just on substantive but also on procedural grounds.[60] The third feature is that the instigation and cessation of proceedings is entirely a matter of Commission discretion.[61] Its motives for starting or stopping proceedings cannot be challenged[62] and neither can protracted administrative delays in instigating proceedings unless they are so extreme that they would infringe the Member State's procedural rights by making it more difficult for the state concerned to refute the Commission's arguments.[63]

These three features have raised a number of concerns.[64] From the perspective of securing the rule of EU law, there is simply a concern about Commission leniency. It might not take up proceedings where there is a serious infraction of EU law and the statistics suggest that it may well cease proceedings when national compliance is still far from perfect. Indeed, in 2006, the European Parliament deployed strong words in its assessment of the Commission's exercise of its discretion. In its report on the Commission's 2004 and 2005 Annual Reports, the European Parliament stated that it:

> Calls on the Commission to place the principle of the rule of law and citizens' experience above purely economic criteria and evaluations; urges the Commission to monitor carefully the respect of the fundamental freedoms and general principles of the Treaty as well as the respect of regulations and framework directives; invites the Commission to use secondary legislation as a criterion for determining whether there has been an infringement of fundamental freedoms; [and]

> Calls on the Commission seriously to reassess its indulgence of Member States when it comes to the deadlines for submitting requested information to the Commission, adopting and communicating national implementing measures and correctly applying Community legislation at national, regional and local levels.[65]

---

[58] European Commission, *25th Annual Report*, above n. 3, 2.
[59] *Annual Report of the Court of Justice 2008* (Luxembourg, Office for Official Publications of the European Communities, 2009) 93.
[60] D. Chalmers, 'Judicial Authority and the Constitutional Treaty' (2005) 4 *ICON* 448, 452–3.
[61] Case 48/65 *Lütticke* v *Commission* [1965] ECR 19. More recently see Case C-205/98 *Commission* v *Austria* [2000] ECR I-7367.
[62] Case 416/84 *Commission* v *United Kingdom* [1988] ECR 3127.
[63] Case C-96/89 *Commission* v *Netherlands (own resources: manioc from Thailand)* [1991] ECR I-2461.
[64] For academic commentary see R. Mastroianni, 'The Enforcement Procedure under Article 169 of the EC Treaty and the Powers of the European Commission: *Quis Custodiet Custodes?*' (1995) 1 *EPL* 535; I. Harden, 'What Future for the Centralised Enforcement of Community Law?' (2002) 55 *CLP* 495.
[65] European Parliament, *Report on the Commission's 21st and 22nd Annual Reports on Monitoring the Application of Community Law (2003 and 2004)*, A6–0089/2006, paras, 13, 15.

Whilst this is something of an isolated condemnation, subsequent reports repeatedly focus on the lack of transparency of the process.[66] This is also of concern as it has led to abuse, with one celebrated instance of condemnation of the Commission by the Ombudsman in a case where a Greek official publicly involved with a Greek political party chose not to take action against the Greek government. The Ombudsman noted that it would be difficult for anybody not to doubt the impartiality of the Commission in this instance and to question whether it was acting in the Union interest.[67]

There is also a concern from a public policy perspective about what checks and balances are in place to ensure that the Commission acts in a coherent and systematic manner in this field. In principle, the Commission investigates and prosecutes proceedings on the basis of the priority criteria set out in its 2002 Communication on better monitoring of the application of Community law described above. Yet, as Smith has observed, enforcement policy owes as much to the structures and politics of the organisation as anything else.

M. Smith, *Centralised Enforcement, Legitimacy and Good Governance in the EU* (Abingdon, Routledge, 2009) 136–7

When assessing the statistical information produced by the Commission, it must be acknowledged that there does seem to be a coherent output of the enforcement policy, although not one that necessarily matches the stated policy criteria. Whatever the stated approach to the enforcement policy, the result appears to guarantee that the environment sector always produces the greatest number of investigations and referrals to the ECJ. This sector is followed by cases on the internal market and/ or energy and transport, although neither of these sectors are mentioned in the priority criteria at all. This of course may not be a result of the policy on enforcement, but rather the particular organisation of the Commission and the way in which each DG mobilises its resources to combat infringements. For instance, DG Environment is one of the few DGs that contain a unit specifically responsible for dealing with infringements, as opposed to (say) DG Justice, Freedom and Security, which has no such department and generates very few infringement cases. It may be that the type of legislation produced by DG Environment (predominantly directives) is particularly prone to generating infractions (which appears to be confirmed by the Commission's Annual Reports), or it may be that the subject matter is particularly unpopular with Member States. It could be that DG Environment is particularly focused upon enforcement more than other DGs.

The final concern is that this is an administrative process seemingly unconstrained by the usual public law disciplines of participation, accountability and transparency. The process has traditionally been an executive to executive one in which the only players were the central governments and the Commission. The Commission, as we shall see, was until recently not really publicly accountable for any of its actions. Finally, the process is secret. The General Court has held that Member States are entitled to expect that all documents relating to the investigative procedure as well as the reasoned Opinion remain confidential. They can therefore oppose

---

[66] See e.g. European Parliament, *Report on the 25th Annual Report from the Commission on Monitoring the Application of Community Law (2007)*, A6–0245/2009, para. 13.

[67] EO Decision on Complaint 1288/99/OV. For analysis of this see Smith, above n. 14, 175–83.

any publication by the Commission or dissemination to third parties. The reason, according to the General Court, is that such confidentiality facilitates amicable resolution of the dispute.[68] Nevertheless, it also creates a climate of public suspicion, as outsiders have no idea of what is being discussed or agreed, or even what conduct, however egregious, the Commission has discovered.

In recent years, there have been attempts to put some constraints on the exercise of Commission discretion in this area. These are, however, quite limited.

(ii) Complainants and Article 258 TFEU

Notwithstanding the key role which they play, complainants are frozen out of the procedure. They have no right to require the Commission to commence proceedings or to be involved in the dispute. In *Star Fruit*, a Belgian banana trader alleged that it had been prejudiced by the organisation of the French banana market, which it believed was contrary to EU law. The trader complained to the Commission but the latter did not commence proceedings against France. Star Fruit sought to take the Commission to court for failure to act. The Court of Justice ruled that the action was inadmissible.

Case 247/87 *Star Fruit* v Commission [1989] ECR 291

11. ... it is clear from the scheme of Article [258 TFEU] that the Commission is not bound to commence the proceedings provided for in that provision but in this regard has a discretion which excludes the right for individuals to require that institution to adopt a specific position.

12. It is only if it considers that the Member State in question has failed to fulfil one of its obligations that the Commission delivers a reasoned opinion. Furthermore, in the event that the State does not comply with the opinion within the period allowed, the institution has in any event the right, but not the duty, to apply to the Court of Justice for a declaration that the alleged breach of obligations has occurred.

13. It must also be observed that in requesting the Commission to commence proceedings pursuant to Article [258 TFEU] the applicant is in fact seeking the adoption of acts which are not of direct and individual concern to it within the meaning of the second paragraph of Article [263(4) TFEU] and which it could not therefore challenge by means of an action for annulment in any event.[69]

14. Consequently, the applicant cannot be entitled to raise the objection that the Commission failed to commence proceedings against the French Republic pursuant to Article [258 TFEU].

This freezing out is controversial even within the EU judiciary. It excludes parties who are not merely at the centre of proceedings in that they are the impetus for them, but who are also often suffering significant adversity because of illegal acts by national governments. In *max. mobil* the General Court held that the 'principle of sound administration' required complainants to be able to seek judicial review of Commission decisions not to take action against Member States under Article 106(3) TFEU, the provision that allows the Commission to require Member

---

[68] Case T-191/99 *Petrie* v *Commission* [2001] ECR II-3677.

[69] These are the *locus standi* requirements for challenging EU acts. They are discussed at pp. 414–24.

States to bring public undertakings into line with EU law.[70] Even though the General Court distinguished this provision from Article 258 TFEU by suggesting (possibly for the moment) that this duty does not apply to the latter, the General Court was clearly laying the way for it to do so. It was the first time that it had been suggested that an individual could compel the Commission to take an action against a Member State and that the principle of sound administration is a general principle of EU law. The Court of Justice was, however, having none of it and, on appeal, overturned the judgments. It held that the Commission was not required to bring proceedings and that individuals could not require the Commission to take a position on a specific issue.[71]

This lack of success before the Union courts led complainants during the 1990s to turn to the European Ombudsman.[72] Sufficiently concerned by the complaints it was receiving, the Ombudsman launched in 1997 an 'own initiative' enquiry into the Commission's handling of individual complaints of a breach of EU law by a national government. In its report it observed:

> [T]he Ombudsman has received many complaints concerning the administrative procedures used by the Commission in dealing with complaints lodged by private citizens concerning Member States' failure to fulfil their Community law obligations. The object of these complaints was ... the administrative process which takes place before judicial proceedings may begin. The allegations ... concerned, in particular, excessive time taken to process complaints, lack of information about the ongoing treatment of the complaints and not receiving any reasoning as to how the Commission had reached a conclusion that there was no infringement.[73]

Matters reached a nadir in 2001 with the *Macedonian Metro* Decision. This concerned a complaint that the Greek authorities had violated EU public procurement law in a tender they had put out for construction of a metro in Thessaloniki. The Ombudsman found that there had been acts of maladministration, first, because the Commission had indicated to the complainant that it was closing the file because there was no breach of EU law. In fact, it had not told the truth. It closed the file as an act of political discretion rather than because of any finding as to the law.[74] Secondly, it found that the Commission had violated the complainant's right to be heard as it had sent its provisional views to the complainant eight days before closing the file and at the beginning of the summer holidays. This clearly gave the latter insufficient time.[75] As a consequence, in 2002, the Commission adopted a Communication setting out certain procedural entitlements for complainants.[76] This Communication includes the following central principles:

- Anybody may bring a complaint free of charge without having to prove an interest.
- All correspondence must be recorded. It will not be investigable if it is anonymous; fails to refer to a Member State; denounces private parties unless public authorities are involved or

---

[70] Case T-54/99 *max.mobil* v *Commission* [2002] ECR II-313.

[71] Case C-141/02 P *Commission* v *max.mobil* [2005] ECR I-1283.

[72] On these early years see Rawlings, above n. 23.

[73] European Ombudsman, *Own-Initiative Inquiry into the Commission's Administrative Procedures for Dealing with Complaints under Article 226 [now Article 258 TFEU]*, EO Annual Report 1997, 270.

[74] Decision of the European Ombudsman on Complaint 995/98/OV against the European Commission, 31 January 2001, 3.1–3.7, www.ombudsman.europa.eu/cases/decision.faces/en/1088/html.bookmark (accessed 1 September 2009).

[75] *Ibid.* paras. 4.1–4.6.

[76] European Commission, *On Relations with the Complainant in respect of Infringements of Community Law*, COM(2002)141.

fail to act; fails to set out a grievance or sets out a grievance on which the Commission has adopted a clear, public, consistent position or which falls outside EU law.

- The Commission Departments will communicate with the complainant and inform them after each Commission Decision of the steps taken in response to the complaint.
- The Commission will endeavour to close the case or issue a formal notice within one year from registering the complaint.
- If the Commission closes the case, unless there are exceptional circumstances, the Commission will give the complainant four weeks to submit comments having set out the reasons for its Decision.

Whilst all this brings some transparency to the processes, the Commission makes it clear that it still has complete discretion as to whether to initiate proceedings, and that any infringement action is a bilateral matter between it and the Member State concerned. It also leaves a number of procedural matters unaddressed. Rawlings has noted, for example, that citizen participation is left until very late in the day – four weeks before the closing of the file – and this rarely allows for effective input. He also noted that the commitment to close a file within a reasonable period of time tells us nothing about how the file is handled subsequent to a letter of formal notice being issued.[77] Smith has likewise noted that there is no commitment to fairness and non-discrimination in the investigation of the complaint and subsequent follow-up. She also wonders whether, significant though they are, these organisational changes are bringing any attitudinal change in the Commission.[78]

6 SANCTIONS

(i) Article 260 TFEU and the Lisbon reforms

The procedure in Article 258 TFEU is long and cumbersome. At the end of it there is a simple declaration by the Court of Justice that the Member State has breached EU law. Member States are given plenty of time before having to comply and plenty of time to negotiate a good deal. Furthermore, the effect of a Court ruling is uncertain. Research by Chalmers found that in 2002, Member States had failed to comply with 37.33 per cent of the judgments given against them within twelve months.[79] Legal commentators have claimed that this is because of the absence of sanctions in the procedure.[80] At Maastricht, a procedure was therefore introduced whereby the Commission could take non-compliant states back to the Court to have them fined. The procedure prior to Lisbon was a repeat of that in Article 258 TFEU. There would be a new informal letter, a letter of formal notice, Member State observations, etc.[81] This entailed a total of fourteen stages from the first registration by the Commission of the breach before a sanction was introduced. The procedure was amended by the Lisbon Treaty and is now contained in Article 260 TFEU.

---

[77] Rawlings, above n. 23, 18.
[78] Smith, above n. 14, 191–4.
[79] Chalmers, above n. 60, 453.
[80] E. Szyszczak, 'EC Law: New Remedies, New Directions?' (1992) 55 *MLR* 690, 691; J. Steiner, 'From Direct Effects to *Francovich*: Shifting Means of Enforcement of Community Law' (1993) 18 *ELRev*. 3.
[81] This was formerly Article 228 EC.

> ### Article 260 TFEU
>
> 1. If the Court of Justice of the European Union finds that a Member State has failed to fulfil an obligation under the Treaties, the State shall be required to take the necessary measures to comply with the judgment of the Court.
> 2. If the Commission considers that the Member State concerned has not taken the necessary measures to comply with the judgment of the Court, it may bring the case before the Court after giving that State the opportunity to submit its observations. It shall specify the amount of the lump sum or penalty payment to be paid by the Member State concerned which it considers appropriate in the circumstances.
>   If the Court finds that the Member State concerned has not complied with its judgment it may impose a lump sum or penalty payment on it.
>   This procedure shall be without prejudice to Article 259.
> 3. When the Commission brings a case before the Court pursuant to Article 258 on the grounds that the Member State concerned has failed to fulfil its obligation to notify measures transposing a directive adopted under a legislative procedure, it may, when it deems appropriate, specify the amount of the lump sum or penalty payment to be paid by the Member State concerned which it considers appropriate in the circumstances.
>   If the Court finds that there is an infringement it may impose a lump sum or penalty payment on the Member State concerned not exceeding the amount specified by the Commission. The payment obligation shall take effect on the date set by the Court in its judgment.

The new provision introduces two significant procedural amendments to the previous position.

The first is in Article 260(3) TFEU. When an infringement proceeding is brought for failure to notify measures transposing a Directive, it is unnecessary to go through the procedures set out in Article 260(2) TFEU. Instead, the Court can impose a sanction at the same time that it rules against the Member State under Article 258 TFEU.

The second concerns the procedure in Article 260(2) TFEU for other forms of breach of EU law. This has been truncated. There is no need for the Commission to issue a reasoned Opinion. It will still have to issue a Member State a letter of formal notice on which the latter can submit observations, but after that it can refer the matter to the Court. This does raise the question whether the letter of formal notice here is subject to the same legal constraints as the reasoned Opinion (but not the letter of formal notice) in Article 258 TFEU, namely whether it must give a statement of the reasons why there is still non-compliance and whether it must set out a reasonable period for compliance before the matter can be referred back to the Court. In *Commission v Portugal*, the Court stated that the opportunity for Member States to submit observations was an essential guarantee of both procedures.[82] It would appear from this, therefore, that the Commission could not subsequently include complaints that were not in the original letter of formal notice and is under a duty both to consider national observations submitted in response

---

[82] Case C-457/07 *Commission* v *Portugal*, Judgment of 10 September 2009.

to it and to give Member States a date for compliance. Otherwise, it would seem to prejudice these essential rights of defence. In short, therefore, the letter of formal notice would have to adopt the same features as the reasoned opinion in Article 258 TFEU.

Whilst these amendments speed up the procedure, there is the question of the distinction between breaches for non-notification of Directives and other breaches of EU law. For the latter, the requirement to go, first, through Article 258 TFEU and then through Article 260 TFEU renders prosecution of breaches still extremely cumbersome. The reason lies in national government opposition; this issue was discussed at the Future of Europe Convention, with national governments opposing the simultaneous imposition of sanctions for anything other than non-communication of measures transposing Directives.[83] Yet, given the length of the Article 258 TFEU procedure, it might be questioned where exactly their worries lie, and whether, at heart, they simply do not want EU law to be policed too vigorously. The length of the procedure limits the capacity of the proceedings both to uphold the rule of EU law and to be an effective and responsive public policy tool.

Finally, the effectiveness of the penalty payment should not be assumed. In the following extract, Harlow and Rawlings examined the impact of the first Article 260 TFEU case to reach the Court of Justice.[84]

C. Harlow and R. Rawlings, 'Accountability and Law Enforcement: The Centralised EU Infringement Procedure' (2006) 31 *European Law Review* 447, 462–3

The first case to reach the Court involved Greece and concerned a toxic waste dump at Kouroupitos (Chania) in Crete. On the basis of five years' non-compliance with an ECJ ruling, it ended in the imposition of a daily penalty payment of €20,000 coupled with an order to close the dump. Yet the penalty itself proved to be only a first step towards compliance. Six months later, when Greece began payment under threat that the Commission would otherwise withhold its aid payments, nothing had been done to remove the offending dump that was the subject of the proceedings. Six months later again, when the European Parliament's Environment Committee met in Brussels, it heard that Greece, which by now owed €4.20 million, had paid off €2.98 million, though otherwise the position had not changed; the fines were now remitted with a promise of rehabilitation. By keeping the matter as a constant agenda item, the Committee helped to secure closure of the dump. But the Committee had to return to Kouroupitos in 2005, when it learned from the Commission that the new site was not functioning properly and that a formal notice had been served on the Greek authorities. These dismal facts underscore the difficulties associated with forcing governments into 'remedial action'.

This case appears to be a healthy reminder to lawyers that a problem is not cured just because there is a court ruling. Court judgments are not self-executing and the judicial enforce*ability* of the law can sometimes be a quite different thing from its judicial enforce*ment*.

---

[83] See *Final Report of the Discussion Circle on the Court of Justice*, CONV 636/03.

[84] Case C-387/97 *Commission v Greece (waste disposal: Kouroupitos)* [2000] ECR I-5047. For further analysis, see M. Theodossiou, 'An Analysis of the Recent Response of the Community to Non-compliance with Court of Justice Judgments: Article 228(2) EC' (2002) 27 *ELRev.* 25.

(ii) Types of sanction levied under Article 260 TFEU

Two types of financial sanction are mentioned in Article 260(3) TFEU: the lump sum and the penalty payment. The Commission has characterised these in the following way. The lump sum is a single one-off sanction that penalises the state for its non-compliance between the date of the original judgment given under Article 258 TFEU and the subsequent judgment given under Article 260 TFEU. The penalty payment is a sanction which applies to each day of delay in compliance after the judgment given under Article 260 TFEU. It is thus calculated at a daily rate. It applies from the date of the second judgment under Article 260 TFEU and goes on indefinitely (in theory at least) or until state compliance.[85]

The wording of Article 260(3) TFEU states that a lump sum *or* a penalty payment can be imposed. This would seem to suggest quite clearly that the Court cannot impose both in the same judgment. It must be one or the other. This assumption was overturned in *Commission* v *France*.[86] In 1991, the Court upheld a Commission complaint that France had failed to comply with EU fisheries law between 1984 and 1987 by not sufficiently carrying out inspections or monitoring the mesh sizes of nets and by allowing undersized fish to be sold. Following a series of inspections of French ports during the 1990s, the Commission considered that very little was being done to comply with the judgment. It instigated Article 260 TFEU proceedings. The Commission asked for both a lump sum sanction and penalty payment to be imposed. The reason, it argued, was that they pursued different functions: the former was to punish the Member State for its behaviour prior to the Article 260 TFEU judgment; the latter was to induce the Member State to comply with that judgment as quickly as possible following its pronouncement.

Case C–304/02 *Commission* v *France (non-compliance with Judgment)* [2005] ECR I-6263

80. The procedure laid down in Article [260 TFEU] has the objective of inducing a defaulting Member State to comply with a judgment establishing a breach of obligations and thereby of ensuring that Community law is in fact applied. The measures provided for by that provision, namely a lump sum and a penalty payment, are both intended to achieve this objective.

81. Application of each of those measures depends on their respective ability to meet the objective pursued according to the circumstances of the case. While the imposition of a penalty payment seems particularly suited to inducing a Member State to put an end as soon as possible to a breach of obligations which, in the absence of such a measure, would tend to persist, the imposition of a lump sum is based more on assessment of the effects on public and private interests of the failure of the Member State concerned to comply with its obligations, in particular where the breach has persisted for a long period since the judgment which initially established it.

82. That being so, recourse to both types of penalty provided for in Article [260(2) TFEU] is not precluded, in particular where the breach of obligations both has continued for a long period and is inclined to persist.

---

[85] European Commission, Application of Article 228 EC, SEC(2005)1658, para. 10.3.
[86] Case C-64/88 *Commission* v *France* [1991] ECR I-2727.

83. This interpretation cannot be countered by reference to the use in Article [260(2) TFEU] of the conjunction 'or' to link the financial penalties capable of being imposed. As the Commission and the Danish, Netherlands, Finnish and United Kingdom Governments have submitted, that conjunction may, linguistically, have an alternative or a cumulative sense and must therefore be read in the context in which it is used. In light of the objective pursued by Article [260 TFEU], the conjunction 'or' in Article [260(2) TFEU] must be understood as being used in a cumulative sense ...

91. ...The procedure provided for in Article [260(2) TFEU] is a special judicial procedure, peculiar to Community law, which cannot be equated with a civil procedure. The order imposing a penalty payment and/or a lump sum is not intended to compensate for damage caused by the Member State concerned, but to place it under economic pressure which induces it to put an end to the breach established. The financial penalties imposed must therefore be decided upon according to the degree of persuasion needed in order for the Member State in question to alter its conduct ...

103. As to those submissions, while it is clear that a penalty payment is likely to encourage the defaulting Member State to put an end as soon as possible to the breach that has been established...it should be remembered that the Commission's suggestions cannot bind the Court and are only a useful point of reference ... In exercising its discretion, it is for the Court to set the penalty payment so that it is appropriate to the circumstances and proportionate both to the breach that has been established and to the ability to pay of the Member State concerned ...

104. In that light, and as the Commission has suggested in its communication of 28 February 1997, the basic criteria which must be taken into account in order to ensure that penalty payments have coercive force and Community law is applied uniformly and effectively are, in principle, the duration of the infringement, its degree of seriousness and the ability of the Member State to pay. In applying those criteria, regard should be had in particular to the effects of failure to comply on private and public interests and to the urgency of getting the Member State concerned to fulfil its obligations

113. ... the French Republic should be ordered to pay to the Commission, into the account 'European Community own resources', a penalty payment of 182.5 x EUR 316 500, that is to say of EUR 57 761 250, for each period of six months from delivery of the present judgment at the end of which the judgment in Case C-64/88 *Commission* v *France* has not yet been fully complied with.

114. In a situation such as that which is the subject of the present judgment, in light of the fact that the breach of obligations has persisted for a long period since the judgment which initially established it and of the public and private interests at issue, it is essential to order payment of a lump sum (see paragraph 81 of the present judgment).

115. The specific circumstances of the case are fairly assessed by setting the amount of the lump sum which the French Republic will have to pay at EUR 20 000 000.

The reference point for determining when there has been a failure to fulfil obligations under Article 260 TFEU and for prescribing sanctions is the date of expiry given in the letter of formal notice.[87] From that point on, there is discretion to impose both a lump sum payment and a penalty payment. The Commission indicated in a Communication following the judgment that, as a general rule, it will press for both.[88] Yet, the two have different functions, and this limits

---

[87] It used to be the date in the reasoned Opinion: Case C-304/02 *Commission* v *France* [2005] ECR I-6263, para. 30.
[88] European Commission Communication, n. 85 above, paras. 10.3, 10.4.

when this can be done. The lump sum punishes the earlier non-compliance whilst the periodic payment is intended to secure compliance with the final ruling under Article 260 TFEU. The Court has therefore indicated that it will not impose a penalty payment where the state concerned did not comply by the date set out in the letter of formal notice but has complied by the time of its ruling.[89] It may, however, impose a lump sum in such circumstances.

There is a discretion not to apply a sanction at all. The Court has indicated that the question of whether to impose a sanction is a matter for its decision. In deciding whether to impose a fine it will look at what is appropriate in the circumstances and proportionate both to the breach and the state's capacity to pay.[90] With respect to the lump sum, it will look at how long the breach persisted since the original judgment and its effect on public and private interests.

(iii) Level of fines imposed

The final amendment introduced by the Lisbon Treaty is set out in the final paragraph of Article 260(3) TFEU. This states that the Court cannot impose a fine in excess of that suggested by the Commission.[91] This amendment reinforces the importance of the guidelines announced by the Commission on 13 December 2005.[92]

On the penalty payment, the Communication sets out a two stage formula. The first stage is a daily flat rate of €600 per day multiplied by a coefficient for seriousness (on a scale 1–20) and a coefficient for duration (on a scale 1–3). The coefficient for duration will be 0.10 for each month of continued infringement after the Article 260 TFEU judgment. The coefficient for seriousness is determined by the importance of the provision breached[93] and the impact on particular and general interests. The second stage will apply a multiplier, n, to the amount reached in the first stage. This multiplier is based on the capacity of a state to pay and its votes in the Council, and ranges from 0.36 for Malta to 25.40 for Germany.

As regards the lump sum, the Communication suggests a minimum sum for each Member State based on the fault of the state in not complying with the initial judgment. These range from €180,000 for Malta to €12,700,000 for Germany. In addition, to calculate the lump sum a daily rate will be applied if its amount exceeds that of the minimum sum. This rate, which starts from the date of the Article 258 TFEU judgment, is €200 per day multiplied by the same coefficient for seriousness and by the same n multiplier as that described above.

The Commission acknowledges these formulae must operate in light of the proportionality principle. There may be times, therefore, when it has to depart from them. It may ask only for a lump sum penalty where the Member State has taken all the necessary measures but some time is needed for the results to be realised. Similarly, it acknowledges that more lenient treatment may be appropriate where a Member State has made 'best efforts': it has taken all

---

[89] Case C-177/04 *Commission* v *France* [2006] ECR I-2461. This is also acknowledged in the European Commission Communication, above n. 85, para. 10.5.

[90] Case C-121/07 *Commission* v *France*, Judgment of 9 December 2008.

[91] Previously, the Court considered it could impose a greater penalty than in the Commission's guidelines: Case C-177/04 *Commission* v *France* [2006] ECR I-2461.

[92] European Commission Communication, above n. 85.

[93] Importance is determined not by whether it is a Treaty provision or secondary legislation but by the perceived nature of the rules, so violations of fundamental rights or economic rights are always treated as very serious breaches. *Ibid.* para. 16.1.

practical steps but is still not yet fully compliant. There may also be times where the Commission has to suspend penalties to verify whether compliance has taken place or where it may only be practicable to award periodic penalties based on monthly intervals. The proportionality principle cuts both ways, however, and can be used to increase penalties. The Communication, therefore, indicates that where there are several heads of infringement, the Commission will ask for penalties, both the lump sum and daily penalty, to be applied to each one separately.

Whilst the Lisbon Treaty indicates that the Court cannot impose more severe penalties than those requested by the Commission, it can impose more lenient ones. The Court uses the same methodology as the Commission Communication but does not see it as binding. In cases brought before it, it reserves the right to apply the criteria in a manner independent from the Commission. This has resulted in its imposing alternative levels of fine from that proposed by the Commission where it sees issues such as the duration of the breach or its seriousness differently.[94]

FURTHER READING

G. Falkner *et al.*, *Complying with Europe: EU Harmonisation and Soft Law in the Member States* (Cambridge, Cambridge University Press, 2005)

A. Gil Ibañez, *The Administrative Supervision and Enforcement of EC Law, Powers, Procedures and Limits* (Oxford and Portland, Hart, 1999)

I. Harden, 'What Future for the Centralised Enforcement of Community Law?' (2002) 55 *Current Legal Problems* 495

C. Harlow and R. Rawlings 'Accountability and Law Enforcement: The Centralised EU Infringement Procedure' (2006) 31 *European Law Review* 447

M. Mendrinou, 'Non compliance and the Commission's Role in Integration' (1996) 3 *Journal of European Public Policy* 1

R. Rawlings, 'Engaged Elites: Citizen Action and Institutional Attitudes in Commission Enforcement' (2000) 6 *European Law Journal* 4

M. Smith, *Centralised Enforcement, Legitimacy and Good Governance in the EU* (Abingdon, Routledge, 2009)

E. Versluis, 'Even Rules, Uneven Practices: Opening the "Black Box" of EU Law in Action' (2007) 30 *West European Politics* 50

R. White and A. Dashwood, 'Enforcement Actions under Article 169 and 170 EEC' (1989) 14 *European Law Review* 388

---

[94] Most recently see Case C-70/06 *Commission* v *Portugal* [2008] ECR I-1.

9

Governance

CONTENTS

1 INTRODUCTION

This chapter considers EU governance. It is organised as follows.

Section 2 considers the nature of EU governance. Governance was set out at greatest length in the 2001 Commission White Paper. It comprises, in the first place, a series of norms guiding the exercise of Union power. These norms are openness, participation, accountability, effectiveness, coherence, subsidiarity and proportionality. The governance agenda in the White Paper also sets out an ethos as to how the European Union is to govern and when it is to govern. It suggests that the central mission of the Union is to solve problems that cannot be resolved by the Member States unilaterally. There is flexibility about the legal instruments to be deployed, as what matters is that the problem be resolved. The concern that the problem be resolved effectively and coherently also leads to a priority being given to expert knowledge, on the one hand, as this is seen as central to knowing the problem and the solution, and to impact assessment, on the other, as this requires policy-makers to anticipate the effects of the policy on others. Finally, the commitment to openness and participation has led to an engagement by the Union with the idea of a pan-European civil society.

Section 3 examines the principles of subsidiarity and proportionality. Subsidiarity sets out when, acting within its powers, the Union should intervene. It is based around two logics. One is concerned with protecting national identities from Union intrusion and is concerned with the loss of tradition and self-government. The other looks at whether a measure can, by reason of its scale and effects, be better realised at EU rather than national level. The two logics are difficult to combine and the Court of Justice has yet to strike down an EU measure for violating the principle of subsidiarity. The proportionality principle guides the quality of Union intervention. It states that EU measures shall not exceed what is necessary to realise the objectives of the Treaties. In practice, the Union courts will only intervene when the Union measure is manifestly inappropriate. This has resulted in the central importance of the proportionality principle being its reshaping of the EU legislative culture. The 2003 InterInstitutional Agreement on Better Law-Making led to a commitment to consider non-legislative instruments wherever these would be equally effective, and these have become pervasive in recent years.

Section 4 considers the principle that EU institutions should consult widely before taking any legislative action. Set out in Article 11 TEU and a 2002 Commission Communication, there is a commitment that the consultation should involve dialogue, be transparent and be plural. Whilst there is a duty to give reasons for any measure, this duty is a weak one, which allows EU institutions to give reasons in very general terms and does not require them to respond to particular observations. This has limited the requirement on them to engage in active dialogue rather than merely take views. The commitment to transparent consultation is expressed in a Register of lobbyists, all of whom must observe a Code of Conduct specifying certain standards. Whilst the EU institutions commit themselves to inclusive consultation, a central challenge is that most of the lobbyists in Brussels represent either corporate groups or are pan-European associations, often heavily funded by the Commission.

Section 5 considers the role of knowledge in the decision-making processes. EU institutions are neither free to adopt measures without taking scientific advice nor free to ignore it. They must take it from an independent body that is regarded as excellent and transparent, usually an EU agency, and can only not adopt it if it shows different advice from a body of equal scientific standing. The other role of knowledge in the process is the commitment to use impact assessments prior to developing proposals on significant legislative measures. These seek to anticipate the economic, social and environmental impacts of a measure.

Section 6 considers the transparency principle. Central to securing the accountability of EU institutions, its central expression is Regulation 1049/2001/EC. This secures transparency through an electronic register or through allowing individuals to seek access from EU bodies to documents in their possession. The central justifications for refusing access are the exceptions set out in article 4 of the Regulation. These fall into three categories. First, there are exceptions where the institution must refuse access to a document. Here, Union courts will look merely to see whether there has been a manifest error of assessment and whether accurate reasons have been given. Secondly, there are exceptions where EU institutions have a discretion and can grant access where disclosure is in the overriding public interest. Courts will engage in much stronger review here, starting from a presumption that there is always a public interest in disclosure and that institutions must explain quite specifically how disclosure would undermine a particular interest. Finally, there are documents originating from Member States. Member States can refuse to consent to a document being released if it falls within one of the categories justifying non-release of EU documents but they must also provide reasons.

2 THE GOVERNANCE AGENDA

The term 'governance' came to the fore in the Union as a consequence of the biggest administrative scandal to hit the European Union. In 1998, a series of allegations about fraud and financial mismanagement by the Santer Commission were made to the European Parliament. It established a Committee of Independent Experts to examine fraud, mismanagement and nepotism.[1] The report was damning. On its publication in March 1999, the entire College of Commissioners resigned.[2] To counter the damage, the incoming Prodi Commission published a series of Codes of Conduct and consultation papers on Commission reform and accountability which culminated in the White Paper on European Governance.[3] The document is an attempt to regain the high ground and recapture popular legitimacy through a commitment to exercise power in a particular way in the future:[4]

> The White Paper on European Governance concerns the way in which the Union uses the powers given by its citizens. Reform must be started now, so that people see changes well before further modification of the EU Treaties.
>
> The White Paper proposes opening up the policy-making process to get more people and organisations involved in shaping and delivering EU policy. It promotes greater openness, accountability and responsibility for all those involved. This should help people to see how Member States, by acting together within the Union, are able to tackle their concerns more effectively.[5]

To this end, the *White Paper* understands governance as:

> the rules, processes and behaviour that affect the way in which powers are exercised at European level, particularly as regards openness, participation, accountability, effectiveness and coherence.

Although terse, this definition hints at two dimensions to the governance agenda. First, it is about setting norms that justify and guide EU decision-making. Criteria are set for acceptable

---

[1] Committee of Independent Experts, *First Report on Allegations regarding Fraud, Mismanagement and Nepotism in the European Commission* (15 March 1999) para. 9.4.25. Both this report and the committee's second report (see below) are available at www.europarl.eu.int/experts/.

[2] For commentary, see A. Tomkins, 'Responsibility and Resignation in the European Commission' (1999) 62 *MLR* 744; P. Craig, 'The Fall and Renewal of the Commission: Accountability, Contract and Administrative Organisation' (2000) 6 *ELJ* 98; V. Mehde, 'Responsibility and Accountability in the European Commission' (2003) 40 *CMLRev*. 423.

[3] European Commission, *European Governance: A White Paper*, COM(2001)428.

[4] For criticism, see L. Metcalfe, 'Reforming the European Governance: Old Problems or New Principles?' (2001) 67 *International Review of Administrative Sciences* 415; F. Scharpf, 'European Governance: Common Concerns vs. the Challenge of Diversity' in C. Joerges *et al.* (eds.), *Mountain or Molehill: Critical Appraisal of the Commission White Paper on Governance*, Jean Monnet Working Paper 6/01 (New York, New York University, 2001).

[5] Above n. 3, 3.

behaviour and legal standards and procedures established on the basis of them. Secondly, governance is also a description of how the Union is to go about its decision-making. To that end, it sets out a mode of governing which prescribes a number of features that EU decision-making should incorporate. We shall now consider each of these in further detail.

(i) The norms of governance

The White Paper sets out seven principles of governance. In addition to the ones above, it sets out those of subsidiarity and proportionality. It then elaborates on these.

European Commission, *European Governance: A White Paper* COM(2001)428, 10–11

Openness. The Institutions should work in a more open manner. Together with the Member States, they should actively communicate about what the EU does and the decisions it takes. They should use language that is accessible and understandable for the general public. This is of particular importance in order to improve the confidence in complex institutions.

Participation. The quality, relevance and effectiveness of EU policies depend on ensuring wide participation throughout the policy chain – from conception to implementation. Improved participation is likely to create more confidence in the end result and in the Institutions which deliver policies. Participation crucially depends on central governments following an inclusive approach when developing and implementing EU policies.

Accountability. Roles in the legislative and executive processes need to be clearer. Each of the EU Institutions must explain and take responsibility for what it does in Europe. But there is also a need for greater clarity and responsibility from Member States and all those involved in developing and implementing EU policy at whatever level.

Effectiveness. Policies must be effective and timely, delivering what is needed on the basis of clear objectives, an evaluation of future impact and, where available, of past experience. Effectiveness also depends on implementing EU policies in a proportionate manner and on taking decisions at the most appropriate level.

Coherence. Policies and action must be coherent and easily understood. The need for coherence in the Union is increasing: the range of tasks has grown; enlargement will increase diversity; challenges such as climate and demographic change cross the boundaries of the sectoral policies on which the Union has been built; regional and local authorities are increasingly involved in EU policies. Coherence requires political leadership and a strong responsibility on the part of the Institutions to ensure a consistent approach within a complex system.

The application of these five principles reinforces those of *proportionality and subsidiarity*. From the conception of policy to its implementation, the choice of the level at which action is taken (from EU to local) and the selection of the instruments used must be in proportion to the objectives pursued. This means that before launching an initiative, it is essential to check systematically (a) if public action is really necessary, (b) if the European level is the most appropriate one, and (c) if the measures chosen are proportionate to those objectives.

These principles constrain Union decision-making in that it must respect them. It is important to note that they formulate a vision of Union decision-making, in that the principles also prescribe goals it must realise. That is to say, it must be as accountable, open, coherent, etc. as possible. A further feature of the governance agenda is its informality. It does not set out these principles as legally binding norms but rather as general principles to be realised in a number of ways. Care has to be taken in analysing them, as the devil lies in the detail and how they are institutionalised: be it through legal norms, new procedures or new institutions. Only through consideration of these will it be possible to see if these principles are met and also to observe whether there are any other consequences as a result.

(ii) The traits of governance

A feature of the White Paper is that it also describes how the Union is to govern. Union decision-making is to be marked by a number of traits.

First, Union decision-making is characterised as being about problem-solving. The question becomes how to solve the identified problem in a way that meets the governance criteria. It is a test that conceives the measure of Union performance as whether it is fit for purpose. Joseph Weiler has described this in the following way:

> The refocusing of the Commission's tasks proposed here takes on board the vision of a Union concentrating on the realisation of a few major projects with widespread appeal. It is by rallying support for such projects rather than seeking to replace national allegiances by a wider collective identity that we will encourage the people of the Union – in existing Member States and applicant countries alike – to see themselves as Europeans. Taking this line of thinking a step further, the political purpose of the Union is not to supplant the existing States with a new super-State, but to establish a system of shared legislative powers in order to carry through common projects.[6]

Weiler has lambasted this approach.

J. Weiler, 'The Commission as Euro-Skeptic: A Task Oriented Commission for a Project-Based Union, a Comment on the First Version of the White Paper' in C. Joerges *et al.* (eds.), *Symposium: Mountain or Molehill? A Critical Appraisal of the Commission White Paper on Governance*, Jean Monnet Working Paper 6/01 (EUI and NYU, 2002)

6. The thinking is clear: Concentration on 'a few major projects' will bring clarity – the lack of which is identified as one key to public confusion and disenchantment. The major projects the Union selects must have 'widespread appeal' which in turn will 'rally support' and such support, in its turn, will encourage people to see themselves as Europeans rather than by seeking to replace national allegiances by a wider European collective identity. Not a new super-State but a system to carry through common projects.

7. In similar manner, the principal strategy of restoring Commission legitimacy hearkens to its glorious past. It would consist of a '... a return to the original notion of a task oriented administration...' which evidently had been lost along the way. A Commission which is selective about that which it does is what is wanted. The implicit model being rejected is a Commission with plenary governance functions: a Commission-government. The Commission is about governance, not government.

---

[6] European Commission, Draft Memorandum to the Commission: Approaches to European Governance for Democratic European Governance, 10 March 2001, para. 2.4. This can be found at www.jeanmonnetprogram.org/papers/01/firstdraftwhitepaper.rtf (accessed 25 September 2009).

8. The Union is not a state and the Commission is not a government – it is instead a mere functional 'system of sharing or legislative powers to carry through common projects'. It is hard to recall, even in the most Euro-skeptic British or Danish literature, a more functionalist and impoverished conception and self-understanding of Europe.

9. The nostalgic harping back to the past which is evident in the rhetoric of the Draft is also the source of the biggest flaw in its legitimacy strategy: The false dichotomy which is set up in the understanding of Europe. The early functionalist and neo-functionalist theories also suggested a project based Community with an efficient task oriented Community. They predicted and hoped that it would result in a shift of allegiance and a replacement of national identity (the famous 'spillover'). The 'modernized' version presented by the Draft *rightly* abandons the notions of allegiance and all that. But then, amazingly, the alternative presented is the same old functionalism simply stripped of the early fanciful 'spillover' notions. The European construct is presented as a two-way choice between *either* a statal vision in which European legitimacy has to rest on a nation-like collective identity which would replace Member State national identities and allegiances *or* a rather bare pragmatic functionalism.

   In its opening paragraphs the Draft calls for a clarification and '[u]nderstanding what Europe is all about'. When you strip away the verbiage what is the answer given? Europe is about (appealing) projects. And what is the Commission about? An efficient and task oriented instrument for realizing these projects.

10. One should reject this 'either or' picture. It is possible to reject as undesirable and unfeasible a statal conception of Europe and a national conception of European identity and allegiance without going to the other extreme functionalist and reductionist approach presented here.

11. I can understand the temptation of packaging Europe as consisting of some well defined 'appealing' projects and the Commission as simply a friendly, attentive and responsive body concerned with the task of effectively realizing these projects. It can produce some important and immediate political capital. Who can, after all, object to appealing projects and such a minimalist conception of the Commission?

12. But it comes with some notable longer term dangers and costs. And in part it also leads to some naïve positions which will not be taken seriously by large constituencies. Let me explain.

13. There have always been two principal strands in the European debate which has taken place from time to time (and in some national quarters endlessly). In some Member States the debate has mostly followed functionalist premises: Whether or not Europe serves the national interest. 'What's-in-it-for-us?' Where that has been the premise of the debate (and it is not necessary to mention Member States by name) the legitimacy of the very European construct has remained contingent, subject to a continuous assessment and re-assessment of the 'appeal' of Europe and the extent that it continued to serve interests. Under this conception a failure of the Commission, like the Santer Commission, calls into question the very legitimacy of Europe itself. Europe under this form of discourse is analogous to a politician in power whose policies and efficiency in implementing these policies are subject to contingent acceptance and rejection. Europe becomes a continuous experiment not fully integrated into the political culture in the same way that some German historians claimed that in Post War Germany, democracy itself was treated as a contingent proposition, the approval of which was dependent on its success.

   This position is the hall mark of classical Euro-Skepticism.

14. The other strand, and this is the one that (inadvertently) has been sacrificed in the Draft, does not regard Europe only in functionalist terms. Under this strand Europe is not, for sure, considered as a proto-state or a would-be state nor is European identity conceived with a vocabulary associated with national identity and allegiance. But Europe is much more than project oriented. It is process oriented and above all it is a Community of Values the principal one of which is an historical commitment to a different, more civil, process of inter-statal intercourse, to a different, more civil, method of drawing boundaries

between states and nations, to a different, more civil, way of managing certain domains of the public sphere. To be European, under this conception, is a commitment to 'doing things' (hence process) in a different, European, way – *whatever the current major appealing project happens to be*. To be European is essentially about the way we do things, rather than what we do.

Secondly, the success of governance is measured by whether an external observer would consider that the Union measure in question meets the various criteria set out.[7] The assumption is that an observer can know what is good policy. This is expressed in the commitment to 'Better Policies, Regulation and Delivery', suggesting there is a verifiable good, better, best out there. It leads to faith being placed in what are perceived as external sources of truth: expertise and feedback.

European Commission, *European Governance: A White Paper* **COM(2001)428, 18–22**

..., the Union needs to boost confidence in the expert advice that informs its policy. It needs to improve the quality of its legislation, including better implementation and enforcement.

Confidence in expert advice ...

Scientific and other experts play an increasingly significant role in preparing and monitoring decisions. From human and animal health to social legislation, the Institutions rely on specialist expertise to anticipate and identify the nature of the problems and uncertainties that the Union faces, to take decisions and to ensure that risks can be explained clearly and simply to the public ...

In many other areas, networking at European and even global level shows clear benefits. Expertise, however, is usually organised at a national level. It is essential that resources be put together and work better in the common interest of EU citizens. Such structured and open networks should form a scientific reference system to support EU policy-making. ...

At the same time, the Union must be able to react more rapidly to changing market conditions and new problems by reducing the long delays associated with the adoption and implementation of Community rules. In many cases these may run to three years or more. A tension between faster decisions and better, but time consuming consultation is not necessarily a problem: investment in good consultation 'upstream' may produce better legislation which is adopted more rapidly and easier to apply and enforce. ...

... proposals must be prepared on the basis of *an effective analysis* of whether it is appropriate to intervene at EU level and whether regulatory intervention is needed. If so, the analysis must also assess the potential economic, social and environmental impact, as well as the costs and benefits of that particular approach. A key element in such an assessment is ensuring that the objectives of any proposal are clearly identified. ...

...a stronger culture of *evaluation and feedback* is needed in order to learn from the successes and mistakes of the past. This will help to ensure that proposals do not over-regulate and that decisions are taken and implemented at the appropriate level.

Thirdly, governance is blind to the institutions or forms of norm deployed to realise its goals. These can be public institutions, private ones, binding instruments or soft law or a mix of all these.

---

[7] C. Möllers, 'European Governance: Meaning and Value of a Concept' (2006) 43 *CMLRev.* 313, 315–18.

European Commission, *European Governance: A White Paper* COM(2001)428, 20–22

The European Union will rightly continue to be judged by the impact of its regulation on the ground. It must pay constant attention to *improving the quality, effectiveness and simplicity of regulatory acts.* Effective decision-making also requires the combination of different policy instruments (various forms of legislation, programmes, guidelines, use of structural funding, etc.) to meet Treaty objectives ...

... *legislation is often only part of a broader solution* combining formal rules with other non-binding tools such as recommendations, guidelines, or even self-regulation within a commonly agreed framework. This highlights the need for close coherence between the use of different policy instruments and for more thought to be given to their selection.

... the *right type of instrument* must be used whenever legislation is needed to achieve the Union's objectives:

- The *use of regulations* should be considered in cases with a need for uniform application and legal certainty across the Union. This can be particularly important for the completion of the internal market and has the advantage of avoiding the delays associated with transposition of directives into national legislation.
- So-called '*framework directives*' should be used more often. Such texts are less heavy-handed, offer greater flexibility as to their implementation, and tend to be agreed more quickly by the Council and the European Parliament.

Whichever form of legislative instrument is chosen, *more use should be made of 'primary' legislation* limited to essential elements (basic rights and obligations, conditions to implement them), leaving the executive to fill in the technical detail via implementing 'secondary' rules.

... under certain conditions, implementing measures may be prepared within the *framework of co-regulation.* Co-regulation combines binding legislative and regulatory action with actions taken by the actors most concerned, drawing on their practical expertise. The result is wider ownership of the policies in question by involving those most affected by implementing rules in their preparation and enforcement. This often achieves better compliance, even where the detailed rules are non-binding.

- It has already been used, for example, in areas such as the internal market (agreeing product standards under the so-called 'New Approach' directives)[8] and the environment sector (reducing car emissions).
- The exact shape of co-regulation, the way in which legal and non-legal instruments are combined and who launches the initiative — stakeholders or the Commission — will vary from sector to sector...

... in other areas, Community action may be complemented or reinforced by the use of the so-called '*open method of co-ordination*', which can already involve the applicant countries in some cases.

- The open method of co-ordination is used on a case by case basis. It is a way of encouraging co-operation, the exchange of best practice and agreeing common targets and guidelines for Member States, sometimes backed up by national action plans as in the case of employment and social exclusion. It relies on regular monitoring of progress to meet those targets, allowing Member States to compare their efforts and learn from the experience of others.

In some areas, such as employment and social policy or immigration policy, it sits alongside the programme-based and legislative approach; in others, it adds value at a European level where there is little scope for legislative solutions. This is the case, for example, with work at a European level defining future objectives for national education systems.

---

[8] See pp. 696–700.

A perusal of any field of EU policy therefore finds that, typically, an Action Plan or programme has been agreed which sets out the legal instruments needed to realise a policy and range of goals.[9] These instruments will usually include Regulations and Directives, but also soft law instruments, such as Recommendations, benchmarks or Codes of Conduct[10] and standards set up by private or professional bodies.[11] To many, this adaptability, flexibility and responsiveness is highly desirable. EU law is no longer simply about telling people what they do. Instead, it acquires a more enabling role. The formal norms provide a backdrop against which informal, collective arrangements are put in place, be it through soft law or other informal instruments, bringing actors together both to maximise their resources and to develop shared commitments to resolving common problems on the basis of shared criteria.[12]

C. Sabel and J. Zeitlin, 'Learning from Difference: The New Architecture of Experimentalist Governance in the EU' (2008) 14 *European Law Journal* 271, 307–8

This 'shadow of hierarchy' view extends to EU governance a trope originally developed to explain collective bargaining and neo-corporatist concertation between the state, labour and capital. The core idea is that the state or public hierarchy more generally is limited – perhaps because of the volatility of the situation in which it acts – in its ability to secure the outcomes that it prefers, or would prefer if it could identify them in advance. Given this limitation, the state enlists non-state actors who do command the necessary capacities in its problem solving by proposing an exchange: in return for their promise to bargain with one another fairly and in a public-regarding way, the relevant parties are endowed with a semi-constitutional authority to speak on behalf of their members and the assurance that their agreements will be backed by the authority of the state, provided only that they respect the conditions of the founding bargain itself. Parties to such agreements are thus reasonably said to be 'bargaining in the shadow of the state' and acting in some sense as its authorised agents or deputies in reaching solutions not directly available to the authorities themselves. Seen this way, the new architecture that we describe might be thought to be simply a capacity-increasing extension of the EU's formal hierarchical decision-making apparatus rather than a networked, deliberative alternative to it. At the limit, this argument simply applies to governance an idea familiar from organisational sociology, in which the capacities of a rigid formal organisation are rendered flexible by connecting it to an informal network over which the official hierarchy maintains control.

This view, however, is not uncontroversial and others have pointed to the dangers of too much informality.[13]

---

[9] On the single market, see European Commission, *A Single Market for 21st Century Europe*, COM(2007)724; on the Area of Freedom, Security and Justice, see European Commission, *An Area of Freedom, Security and Justice Serving the Citizen*, COM(2009)262. On the environment, see Decision 1600/2002/EC of the European Parliament and of the Council of 22 July 2002 laying down the Sixth Community Environment Action Programme [2002] OJ L242/1.

[10] See pp. 101–3.

[11] On the variety of these, see D. Chalmers, 'Private Power and Public Authority in European Union Law' (2005–06) 8 *CYELS* 59; D. Schiek, 'Private Rule-making and European Governance: Issues of Legitimacy' (2007) 32 *ELRev.* 443.

[12] The work of Chuck Sabel and Jonathan Zeitlin has been particularly pioneering and influential here. In addition, see J. Scott and D. Trubek, 'Mind the Gap: Law and New Approaches to Governance in the European Union' (2002) 8 *ELJ* 1; G. de Búrca and J. Scott (eds.), *Law and New Governance in the EU and the US* (Oxford and Portland, Hart, 2006).

[13] See also I. Chiu, 'On the Identification of an EU Legal Norm' (2007) 26 *YBEL* 193.

C. Joerges, 'Integration Through De-legalisation?' (2008) 33 *European Law Review* 291, 310

Iterative benchmarking of national practices, the management of national states to agree upon guidelines and the mutual learning thereby stimulated are seen as genuinely democratic processes through which a problem-related *demos* articulates itself. These are fascinating and highly conditioned perspectives which provoke sceptical questions: How can transnational criteria that enable and legitimate a benchmarking of national experience, national history and national expectations be found? Why can we reliably expect that confrontation with the experience of others will change national perceptions and practices so as to lead to coordinated policies? And if indeed learning occurs in some quarters, how is its successful implementation conceivable if we are confronted not only with extremely complex fields of social policy but also with vested interests? There are no valid reasons which could be put forward against transnational exchanges of ideas among bureaucracies and expert communities. What seems risky, however, is the delegation of quasi-regulatory tasks to such networks. This sort of governance would be considered 'soft' to the extent that it is no longer dependent on binding law. But it might be considered 'strong' because its informality permits its evasion of risks of being tied down and controlled by the regular political process including the constraints of the rule of law.

How to reconcile such different views? It is best to see each as characterisations which point to the potential advantages and risks of governance. In practice, many regimes will be set up in such a way that they are a little bit more prescriptive and a little less facilitative than their advocates would have it. By contrast, many will have checks and balances that will limit some of the risks.

The final feature of governance is a commitment to what the White Paper calls better involvement. This includes, inter alia, greater consultation, transparency and a stronger mobilisation of civil society.[14]

European Commission, *European Governance: A White Paper* COM(2001)428, 14–16

Democracy depends on people being able to take part in public debate. To do this, they must have access to reliable information on European issues and be able to scrutinise the policy process in its various stages ...

Providing more information and more effective communication are a pre-condition for generating a sense of belonging to Europe. The aim should be to create a trans-national 'space' where citizens from different countries can discuss what they perceive as being the important challenges for the Union. This should help policy makers to stay in touch with European public opinion, and could guide them in identifying European projects which mobilise public support ...

Involving civil society ...
Civil society plays an important role in giving voice to the concerns of citizens and delivering services that meet people's needs. Churches and religious communities have a particular contribution to make.

---

[14] On civil society and the European Union more generally, see M. Wilkinson, 'Civil Society and the Re-imagination of European Constitutionalism' (2003) 9 *ELJ* 451; C. Ruzza, *Europe and Civil Society* (Manchester, Manchester University Press, 2004).

The organisations which make up civil society mobilise people and support, for instance, those suffering from exclusion or discrimination …

Trade unions and employers' organisations have a particular role and influence. The EC Treaty requires the Commission to consult management and labour in preparing proposals, in particular in the social policy field. Under certain conditions, they can reach binding agreements that are subsequently turned into Community law (within the social dialogue). The social partners should be further encouraged to use the powers given under the Treaty to conclude voluntary agreements.

Civil society increasingly sees Europe as offering a good platform to change policy orientations and society. This offers a real potential to broaden the debate on Europe's role. It is a chance to get citizens more actively involved in achieving the Union's objectives and to offer them a structured channel for feedback, criticism and protest.

With better involvement comes greater responsibility. Civil society must itself follow the principles of good governance, which include accountability and openness. The Commission intends to establish, before the end of this year, a comprehensive on-line database with details of civil society organisations active at European level, which should act as a catalyst to improve their internal organisation.

What is needed is a *reinforced culture of consultation and dialogue*; a culture which is adopted by all European Institutions and which associates particularly the European Parliament in the consultative process, given its role in representing the citizen. The European Parliament should play a prominent role, for instance, by reinforcing its use of public hearings. European political parties are an important factor in European integration and contribute to European awareness and voicing the concerns of citizens.

Once again, this seems all highly desirable but it begs the question as to whom one is involving and who constitutes this civil society. As Armstrong suggests below, this is, itself, an uneasy question.[15]

K. Armstrong, 'Rediscovering Civil Society: The European Union and the White Paper on Governance' (2002) 8 *European Law Journal* 102, 114–15

It is one thing to seek to bridge the gap between society and transnational governance through a differentiated civic demos rooted in the structures and traditions of national civil society actors (even if they choose to cooperate transnationally). It is another to seek to bridge that gap through transnational structures that owe their legitimacy to their transnational functionality and authority. This latter position is less about European civil society's bridging the gap between society and governance, and more its jumping the gap to support the legitimation of transnational governance through transnational structures. The normative case for transnational civil society … lies in the inclusion of a new constituency of voices, interests and expertise within transnational governance.

The difficulty is that in seeking to build a transnational civil society in its normative variant, civil society is subject to three processes, which, while contributing to the inclusion of the voice of civil society within governance, nonetheless sit uneasily with the democratic turn to civil society in the

---

[15] See also S. Smismans, 'European Civil Society: Shaped by Discourses and Institutional Interests' (2003) 9 *ELJ* 473.

first place. These processes are the 'Europeanisation' of civil society; its 'automatisation', and its 'governmentalisation'. By Europeanisation, I refer to processes by which civil society actors organise in larger, transnational structures not merely to act as a vehicle for national members, but in order to give an authoritatively, representative European voice. Plural voices are replaced by authoritative European voices. 'Autonomisation' is the process by which transnational structures develop their strategies autonomously from the direct control of constituency members. Governmentalisation refers not only to external pressures from government for changes to the organisational structures and strategies of civil society, but also the internal self-organisation of civil society as it takes on tasks of policy – influencing, decision-making and service-delivery.

Each of these processes is relative and each can positively contribute towards enhancing something that we might call the voice of European civil society. But in jumping rather than bridging the gap between society and transnational structures of governance, there is the danger that a transnationalised civil society suffers from the same sort of democratic defects as transnational governance itself. First, there is a *static* problem that the voices of national civil society actors may be lost or excluded as civil society becomes Europeanised and autonomised. Second, there is a more dynamic problem that legitimation through transnational civil society cannot make up on the transnational swings what is lost on the national roundabouts of the erosion of national structures of representative and participative democracy.

3 SUBSIDIARITY AND PROPORTIONALITY

Having looked at the general norms and traits of governance, it is now time to turn our attention to the individual principles and their interpretation and application. We shall look, first, at subsidiarity and proportionality as these go to when and how the Union intervenes.

(i) An outline of the subsidiarity and proportionality principles

The central elements of the subsidiarity and proportionality principles are set out in Article 5 TEU.

Article 5(3), (4) TEU

3. Under the principle of subsidiarity, in areas which do not fall within its exclusive competence, the Union shall act only if and insofar as the objectives of the proposed action cannot be sufficiently achieved by the Member States, either at central level or at regional and local level, but can rather, by reason of the scale or effects of the proposed action, be better achieved at Union level.

    The institutions of the Union shall apply the principle of subsidiarity as laid down in the Protocol on the application of the principles of subsidiarity and proportionality. National Parliaments ensure compliance with the principle of subsidiarity in accordance with the procedure set out in that Protocol.
4. Under the principle of proportionality, the content and form of Union action shall not exceed what is necessary to achieve the objectives of the Treaties.

On their face, the principles do two very different things.

The subsidiarity principle goes to when the Union should intervene. It expresses the political philosophy of self-government. The Preamble to the Treaty captures this by stating that the Member States are 'resolved to continue the process of creating an ever closer union among the peoples of Europe, in which decisions are taken as closely as possible to the citizen in accordance with the principle of subsidiarity'. Local decisions are, in principle, better than regional ones and national decisions are, likewise, better than international ones:[16] the closer to the people decisions are made, the more the people will be able to participate and the more responsive to the people's concerns the decisions will be.[17]

The proportionality principle goes, by contrast, not to when to intervene, but to the quality of that intervention. It is concerned with the density and intrusiveness of EU law. Originating in Prussia in the late nineteenth century, its philosophy is a presumption in favour of private autonomy and that state intrusion into that should always be justified.[18] This has led to three tenets within it. First, the measure must be suitable for realising the objectives set by the administration. This will only be the case if it is necessary for achieving the objectives in question. Secondly, of several equally suitable measures, the one chosen should be that which imposes the fewest constraints on individuals. Thirdly, the means should not be out of proportion to the ends sought.

As they seek different goals, the subsidiarity and proportionality principles have to be treated separately. Yet, as we shall see, they have been conflated in recent years by the governance agenda, and this also has to be considered. This conflation is even present in the central provision in the Protocol on the application of the principles of subsidiarity and proportionality.

Protocol on the application of the principles of subsidiarity and proportionality, Article 5

Draft legislative acts shall be justified with regard to the principles of subsidiarity and proportionality. Any draft legislative act should contain a detailed statement making it possible to appraise compliance with the principles of subsidiarity and proportionality. This statement should contain some assessment of the proposal's financial impact and, in the case of a directive, of its implications for the rules to be put in place by Member States, including, where necessary, the regional legislation. The reasons for concluding that an objective of the Union can be better achieved at the level of the Union shall be substantiated by qualitative and, wherever possible, quantitative indicators. Draft legislative acts shall take account of the need for any burden, whether financial or administrative, falling upon the Union, national governments, regional or local authorities, economic operators and citizens, to be minimised and commensurate with the objective to be achieved.

There are thus two strands in the provision. On the one hand, the Union has to justify the relative efficacy of EU legislation vis-à-vis its national or regional alternatives. On the other, there is a concern with the regulatory weight of EU legislation. Its financial and administrative impacts should be minimised and attention should be addressed to the legislative disturbance that it will cause.

---

[16] In its consultations on any legislative proposal, the Commission is required (where appropriate) to take into account the regional and local dimension of the action envisaged: Protocol on the application of the principles of subsidiarity and proportionality, Article 2.

[17] A. Follesdal, 'Subsidiarity' (1998) 6 *Journal of Political Philosophy* 190; Y. Soudan, 'Subsidiarity and Community in Europe' (1998) 5 *Ethical Perspectives* 177; N. Barber, 'The Limited Modesty of Subsidiarity' (2005) 11 *ELJ* 308.

[18] J. Schwarze, *European Administrative Law* (London, Sweet & Maxwell, 1992) 685.

(ii) Subsidiarity

Two logics sit at the heart of the subsidiarity principle.

The first logic expresses a concern that the Union should not intrude on national, regional and local political and cultural identities. It is directed at policing and limiting the reach and levels of EU legislation. Although the idea goes back to the mid-1970s,[19] it was first made a Treaty provision at Maastricht. This was in response to the perceived explosive growth in the quantity of EU legislation from 1984 onwards, which trebled between 1984 and 1992. Fligstein and McNichol estimated that just under 400 binding acts were adopted in 1984, while nearly 2,500 were adopted in 1992.[20] Estella, more conservatively, estimates that 254 binding acts were adopted in 1984 and 752 in 1992.[21] There has been a concern ever since that time with the amount of legislation produced by the Union.[22]

This logic is reflected in the first part of the test in Article 5(3) TEU: namely that the Union should only act if objectives of the proposed action cannot be sufficiently achieved by the Member States. This test is one of local self-government. It is not based on the efficiency of the measure but relates more to how the measure forms part of the national cultural identity. The British decision to drive on the left-hand side of the road is thus an expression of quirky Britishness. Left is chosen rather than right not because one is safer than the other but because that is the tradition within the United Kingdom and this tradition asserts British distinctiveness. There is no feeling that one has to justify why left is better than right, or vice versa. It is nevertheless felt to go to what it means to live in the United Kingdom.

The second logic emanates from that of comparative federalism. All federal systems have a principle mediating the relationship between federal and local government, and when it is appropriate for the central federal authorities to intervene and when it is not. A good example is that provided in article 72(2) of the German Basic Law.

> ### Article 72(2)
>
> In this field the [federal authorities] will have the right to legislate if federal legal regulation is needed:
> (1) because a matter could not be settled effectively by the legislation of the various *Länder* [regions], or
> (2) because the regulation of a matter by the law of a *Land* [region] could affect the interests of other or all *Länder*, or
> (3) to safeguard the legal or economic unity, and in particular, to safeguard the homogeneity of the living conditions beyond the territory of a *Land*.

---

[19] *Tindemans Report on European Union, EC Bulletin* Supplement 1/76.

[20] N. Fligstein and J. McNichol, 'The Institutional Terrain of the European Union' in W. Sandholtz and A. Stone Sweet (eds.), *European Integration and Supranational Governance* (Oxford, Oxford University Press, 1998) 76.

[21] A. Estella, *The EU Principle of Subsidiarity and its Critique* (Oxford, Oxford University Press, 2002) 20.

[22] The British House of Commons noted that in 2006, 3,255 legal instruments were adopted by the Union. It quoted estimates suggesting that about half of all legislation affecting business and the voluntary sector stemmed from EU legislation and about 9 per cent of all statutory instruments. House of Commons Library, *EU Legislation*, Standard Note SN/IA/2888, 23 April 2007, 9–11.

The logic of comparative federalism is different. Everybody is part of a unitary legal and political order. Both the federal and regional authorities in Germany are thus assumed to be German! The test is therefore one of comparative efficiency, namely could the measure be more effectively resolved by central rather than local legislation. Article 72(2) therefore sets out three types of circumstance where that is the case. No regional authority in Germany would claim therefore to require drivers to drive on the left when in the rest of Germany they drive on the right. It would prevent an integrated road system and a national car industry, and concerns would be expressed about the effect on road safety if drivers suddenly had to swap from one side to the other.

This logic of comparative federalism is adopted in the second part of the test in Article 5(3) TEU and the indicators set out in article 5 of the Protocol on the application of the principles of subsidiarity and proportionality. This is that the objects of a measure can, by reason of its scale or effects, be better achieved at EU level. The test is essentially one of comparative efficiency: would one central measure be better than twenty-seven different ones? In this, it is highly centralising. For it is always possible to argue that one standard will generate economies of scale in that operators need only have one standard for their workplaces and that twenty-seven standards lead to problems of alignment and coordination. On this test, for example, it is very difficult to argue that the Union should not harmonise the side of the road on which people drive, for example.

The logic of each test slides past the other. One is about expression of cultural identity; the other is about realisation of economies of scale and minimising disruptions caused by different laws. Scharpf has talked, therefore, of the subsidiarity principle putting in place a bipolar constitutional logic.[23] The aim of the subsidiarity principle can never be for things to be decided according to one style of reasoning or the other. Instead, it must be to secure mutual accommodation and balance between the two logics.

This is a very difficult task for a court. The test is a struggle to apply in any one instance, and the Court of Justice must do so in a context where it may have to come to a different conclusion on the need for a measure after all three political institutions had indicated their support for a measure. It would be difficult for the Court to tell them that they were all wrong.[24] Although the principle of subsidiarity has regularly been invoked before the Court of Justice, the Court has yet to annul a measure for breach of the principle. An illustration of the lightness of touch is the judgment in *Netherlands* v *European Parliament and Council*, which concerns a Directive requiring Member States to protect biotechnological inventions by patents.[25] The Dutch government challenged this on the grounds that the Directive provided few reasons why its objectives were better realised at EU level and in the light of what is now Article 345 TFEU, which stipulates that nothing in the Treaties should prejudice national rules governing the system of property ownership.[26]

---

[23] F. Scharpf, 'Community and Autonomy: Multi-level Policy Making in the European Union' (1994) 1 *JEPP* 219, 225–6.

[24] It has thus been argued that subsidiarity is necessarily a centralising notion. G. Davies, 'Subsidiarity: The Wrong Idea, in the Wrong Place, at the Wrong Time' (2006) 43 *CMLRev.* 63.

[25] See to similar effect Case C-84/94 *United Kingdom* v *Council* [1996] ECR I-5755; Case C-491/01 *British American Tobacco* [2002] ECR I-11453; Joined Cases C-154/04 and C-155/04 *R* v *Secretary of State for Health, ex parte Alliance for Natural Health* [2005] ECR I-6451.

[26] The situation has been changed in this regard by the Lisbon Treaty which explicitly provides for the first time for some harmonisation of intellectual property rights: Article 118 TFEU.

Case C-377/98 *Netherlands* v *European Parliament and Council (Biotechnology Directive)* [2001] ECR I-7079

2. The Directive was adopted on the basis of Article [114 TFEU], and its purpose is to require the Member States, through their patent laws, to protect biotechnological inventions, whilst complying with their international obligations.

3. To that end the Directive determines inter alia which inventions involving plants, animals or the human body may or may not be patented ...

30. The applicant submits that the Directive breaches the principle of subsidiarity ... and, in the alternative, that it does not state sufficient reasons to establish that this requirement was taken into account ...

32. The objective pursued by the Directive, to ensure smooth operation of the internal market by preventing or eliminating differences between the legislation and practice of the various Member States in the area of the protection of biotechnological inventions, could not be achieved by action taken by the Member States alone. As the scope of that protection has immediate effects on trade, and, accordingly, on intra-Community trade, it is clear that, given the scale and effects of the proposed action, the objective in question could be better achieved by the Community.

33. Compliance with the principle of subsidiarity is necessarily implicit in the fifth, sixth and seventh recitals of the preamble to the Directive, which state that, in the absence of action at Community level, the development of the laws and practices of the different Member States impedes the proper functioning of the internal market. It thus appears that the Directive states sufficient reasons on that point.

Commentators have, therefore, suggested a variety of institutional innovations to compensate for this. Weiler has argued for the creation of a European Constitutional Court, presided over by the President of the European Court of Justice and comprising judges drawn from the constitutional courts or their equivalents in the various Member States.[27] He considers that only a body comprising the most senior judges in the European Union would have the authority and confidence to police the limits of Community powers. Others think the task should not be in the hands of judges. In 1994, the then British Commissioner, Leon Brittan, proposed the creation of a chamber of national parliamentarians who would vet the Union's legislative proposals on grounds of subsidiarity before they became law.[28] It is this latter suggestion which has been taken up in the Treaty of Lisbon. As was seen earlier,[29] a central function of national parliaments is now to patrol Commission drafts for verification with the principle of subsidiarity. This process is, of course, untested, and we will have wait and see whether the parliaments do it more effectively than the Court of Justice.

If it is difficult for the Court to engage in a substantive view in this field, it should be possible for it to verify that the legislative institutions address the question meaningfully. Article 5 of the Protocol on the application of the principles of subsidiarity and proportionality requires that any proposal be 'justified' (contain reasons) with regard to those principles.[30] The quality of the justification – whether the reasons given are consistent, properly considered and accurately

---

[27] J. Weiler, 'The European Union Belongs to its Citizens: Three Immodest Proposals' (1997) 22 *ELRev.* 150, 155–6.

[28] L. Brittan, *The Europe We Need* (London, Hamilton, 1994).

[29] See pp. 129–32.

[30] On this see G. Bermann, 'Taking Subsidiarity Seriously: Federalism in the EC and in the USA' (1994) 94 *Columbia Law Review* 331, 391–5; G. de Búrca, *Reappraising Subsidiarity's Significance after Amsterdam*, Jean Monnet Working Paper 7/99, http://centers.law.nyu.edu/jeanmonnet (accessed 21 November 2009).

reflected the legal text – is something that the Court ought to be able to monitor relatively easily. Crucial, however, is the extent to which the Court has the will to examine the detail of the reasons offered by the political institutions. In *Germany* v *European Parliament and Council*, Germany challenged Directive 94/19/EC, the Deposit Guarantee Directive. This required all credit institutions to have guarantee schemes for depositors which would provide the latter with some coverage if the institution ran into trouble. The German government argued that the compulsory nature of the scheme had insufficient regard to established national practices. It was forcing Germany to scrap an effective voluntary scheme. The German government argued that insufficient reasons were provided in the Directive why a binding EU scheme was necessary. The Court did not accept Germany's arguments and the Directive survived.

Case C-233/94 *Germany* v *European Parliament and Council* ('Deposit Guarantee Directive')' [1997] ECR I-2405

22. The German Government claims that the Directive must be annulled because it fails to state the reasons on which it is based ... It does not explain how it is compatible with the principle of subsidiarity ...

23. As to the precise terms of the obligation to state reasons in the light of the principle of subsidiarity, the German Government states that the Community institutions must give detailed reasons to explain why only the Community, to the exclusion of the Member States, is empowered to act in the area in question. In the present case, the Directive does not indicate in what respect its objectives could not have been sufficiently attained by action at Member State level or the grounds which militated in favour of Community action ...

26. In the present case, the Parliament and the Council stated in the second recital in the preamble to the Directive that 'consideration should be given to the situation which might arise if deposits in a credit institution that has branches in other Member States became unavailable' and that it was 'indispensable to ensure a harmonized minimum level of deposit protection wherever deposits are located in the Community'. This shows that, in the Community legislature's view, the aim of its action could, because of the dimensions of the intended action, be best achieved at Community level. The same reasoning appears in the third recital, from which it is clear that the decision regarding the guarantee scheme which is competent in the event of the insolvency of a branch situated in a Member State other than that in which the credit institution has its head office has repercussions which are felt outside the borders of each Member State.

27. Furthermore, in the fifth recital the Parliament and the Council stated that the action taken by the Member States in response to [a] Commission Recommendation has not fully achieved the desired result. The Community legislature therefore found that the objective of its action could not be achieved sufficiently by the Member States.

28. Consequently, it is apparent that, on any view, the Parliament and the Council did explain why they considered that their action was in conformity with the principle of subsidiarity and, accordingly, that they complied with the obligation to give reasons ... An express reference to that principle cannot be required.

The Court's failure to take seriously Germany's arguments in this case is worrying. The judgment suggests that the procedural requirements will be held to have been complied with even where there is no evidence to suppose that the institutions actually considered whether the measure satisfied the principle of subsidiarity and notwithstanding the fact that no part of the measure in question specifically refers to it. As Dashwood has concluded, the Court has shown that 'while the justiciability of the principle cannot any longer be doubted, the case law indicates equally clearly that annulment of a measure on the ground that it offends against subsidiarity is likely to occur only in extreme circumstances'.[31]

(iii) Proportionality

As set out in Article 5(4) TEU, the proportionality principle requires that the content and form of Union action shall not exceed what is necessary to achieve the objectives of the Treaties.[32] There is a long lineage of Court of Justice case law on the proportionality principle, however.[33] The modern formulation of the doctrine is set out in *Fedesa*, which concerned a challenge to a Directive that prohibited the use of certain hormonal substances in livestock farming.

> **Case C–331/88 *R* v *Minister of Agriculture, Fisheries and Food, ex parte Fedesa* [1990] ECR I–4023**
>
> 12. It was argued that the directive at issue infringes the principle of proportionality in three respects. In the first place, the outright prohibition on the administration of the five hormones in question is inappropriate in order to attain the declared objectives, since it is impossible to apply in practice and leads to the creation of a dangerous black market. In the second place, outright prohibition is not necessary because consumer anxieties can be allayed simply by the dissemination of information and advice. Finally, the prohibition in question entails excessive disadvantages, in particular considerable financial losses on the part of the traders concerned, in relation to the alleged benefits accruing to the general interest.
> 13. The Court has consistently held that the principle of proportionality is one of the general principles of Community law. By virtue of that principle, the lawfulness of the prohibition of an economic activity is subject to the condition that the prohibitory measures are appropriate and necessary in order to achieve the objectives legitimately pursued by the legislation in question; when there is a choice between several appropriate measures recourse must be had to the least onerous, and the disadvantages caused must not be disproportionate to the aims pursued.

From this formulation it has been argued that the doctrine of proportionality entails a three-part test: (1) Is the measure suitable to achieve a legitimate aim? (2) Is the measure necessary to achieve that aim? (3) Does the measure have an excessive effect on the applicant's interests?[34]

---

[31] A. Dashwood, 'The Relationship between the Member States and the European Union/European Community' (2004) 41 *CMLRev.* 355, 368.

[32] For detailed analysis and commentary, see N. Emiliou, *The Principle of Proportionality in European Law* (Deventer, Kluwer, 1996); E. Ellis (ed.), *The Principle of Proportionality in the Laws of Europe* (Oxford, Oxford University Press, 1999); G. de Búrca, 'The Principle of Proportionality and its Application in EC Law' (1993) 13 *YEL* 105; P. Craig, *EU Administrative Law* (Oxford, Oxford University Press, 2006) chs. 17 and 18.

[33] The principle was stated to be a general principle of law in Case 11/70 *Internationale Handelsgesellschaft* v *Einfuhr- und Vorratstelle für Getreide und Futtermittel* [1970] ECR 1125.

[34] See de Búrca, above n. 32, 113; Emiliou, above n. 32, 24.

Tridimas has argued, by contrast, that the courts do not really distinguish between the second and third tests.[35]

> **T. Tridimas, *The General Principles of EU Law* (2nd edn, Oxford, Oxford University Press, 2006) 139**
>
> ... proportionality requires that a measure must be appropriate and necessary to achieve its objectives. According to the standard formula used by the Court, in order to establish whether a provision of Community law is consonant with the principle of proportionality, it is necessary to establish whether the means it employs to achieve the aim correspond to the importance of the aim and whether they are necessary for its achievement. Thus, the principle comprises two tests: a test of suitability and a test of necessity. The first refers to the relationship between the means and the end ... The second is one of weighing competing interests.

Considerably more important than determining whether the doctrine of proportionality consists of two, three, or more tests is understanding what the doctrine actually enables the courts to do in judicial review cases.

> **T. Tridimas, *The General Principles of EU Law* (2nd edn, Oxford, Oxford University Press, 2006) 140**
>
> The application of the tests of suitability and necessity enable the Court to review not only the legality but also, to some extent, the merits of legislative and administrative measures. Because of that distinct characteristic, proportionality is often perceived to be the most far-reaching ground of review, the most potent weapon in the arsenal of the public law judge. It will be noted, however, that much depends on how strictly a court applies the tests of suitability and necessity and how far it is prepared to defer to the choices of the authority which has adopted the measure in issue ... [I]n Community law, far from dictating a uniform test, proportionality is a flexible principle which is used in different contexts to protect different interests and entails varying degrees of judicial scrutiny.

There is a marked contrast in the case law of the courts between the application of proportionality with regard to the Member States and its application with regard to the EU institutions. A strict test is applied to Member States' actions. If a party considers that a national authority has restricted its access to a market and argues that the restriction is disproportionate, the Court of Justice will hold that the national measure is unlawful unless the Member State can establish that it is necessary to achieve a legitimate aim and that no less restrictive alternative exists. The application of the proportionality principle to the EU institutions is, by contrast, much more lenient.

---

[35] T. Tridimas, *The General Principles of EU Law* (2nd edn, Oxford, Oxford University Press, 2006) 139.

Case C-331/88 *R* v *Minister of Agriculture, Fisheries and Food, ex parte Fedesa* [1990] ECR I-4023

14. ... with regard to judicial review ... it must be stated that in matters concerning the common agricultural policy the Community legislature has a discretionary power which corresponds to the political responsibilities given to it by ... the Treaty. Consequently, the legality of a measure adopted in that sphere can be affected only if the measure is manifestly inappropriate having regard to the objective which the competent institution is seeking to pursue ...

15. On the question whether or not the prohibition is appropriate in the present case, it should first be stated that even if the presence of natural hormones in all meat prevents detection of the presence of prohibited hormones by tests on animals or on meat, other control methods may be used and indeed were imposed on the Member States by [other legislation]. It is not obvious that the authorization of only those hormones described as 'natural' would be likely to prevent the emergence of a black market for dangerous but less expensive substances. Moreover, according to the Council, which was not contradicted on that point, any system of partial authorization would require costly control measures whose effectiveness would not be guaranteed. It follows that the prohibition at issue cannot be regarded as a manifestly inappropriate measure.

16. As regards the arguments which have been advanced in support of the claim that the prohibition in question is not necessary, those arguments are in fact based on the premise that the contested measure is inappropriate for attaining objectives other than that of allaying consumer anxieties which are said to be unfounded. Since the Council committed no manifest error in that respect, it was also entitled to take the view that, regard being had to the requirements of health protection, the removal of barriers to trade and distortions of competition could not be achieved by means of less onerous measures such as the dissemination of information to consumers and the labelling of meat.

17. Finally, it must be stated that the importance of the objectives pursued is such as to justify even substantial negative financial consequences for certain traders.

18. Consequently, the principle of proportionality has not been infringed.

The test that Union measures will only be illegal if the action is 'manifestly inappropriate' seems a weak one.[36] However, the impact of the proportionality principle may be felt not so much for the possibility of judicial review provided by it, but, instead, for its contribution to a change in legislative culture. In 2003, in an Inter-institutional Agreement on Better Law-Making, the EU institutions committed themselves to move away from a process of law-making to a process of regulation.[37] The latter process involves considering which is the best type of regulatory instrument to realise a task. This may be legislation or it may be

[36] The test is a standard one. See e.g. Case C-84/94 *United Kingdom* v *Council* [1996] ECR I-5755; Case C-233/94 *Germany* v *European Parliament and Council ('Deposit Guarantee Directive')* [1997] ECR I-2405; Case C-157/96 *National Farmers' Union and Others* [1998] ECR I-2211; Case C-491/01 *British American Tobacco (Investments) and Imperial Tobacco* [2002] ECR I-11453; Case C-210/03 *R* v *Secretary of State for Health, ex parte Swedish Match* [2004] ECR I-11893; Case C-380/03 *Germany* v *Parliament and Council (Tobacco Advertising II)* [2006] ECR I-11573. For detailed discussion see Craig, above n. 32, 658–72.

[37] On the shift to this, see A. Héritier, 'New Modes of Governance in Europe: Policy-Making Without Legislating' in A. Héritier (ed.), *Common Goods: Reinventing European and International Governance* (Lanham, Rowman & Littlefield, 2002); J. Caporaso and J. Wittenbrink, 'The New Modes of Governance and Political Authority in Europe' (2006) 13 *JEPP* 471.

co-regulation (the delegation to private parties to agree norms according to EU set criteria) or self-regulation (the possibility for any area to be regulated entirely by private operators).

Inter-institutional Agreement on Better Law-Making [2003] OJ C321/01

16. The three Institutions recall the Community's obligation to legislate only where it is necessary, in accordance with the Protocol on the application of the principles of subsidiarity and proportionality. They recognise the need to use, in suitable cases or where the Treaty does not specifically require the use of a legal instrument, alternative regulation mechanisms.

17. The Commission will ensure that any use of co-regulation or self-regulation is always consistent with Community law and that it meets the criteria of transparency (in particular the publicising of agreements) and representativeness of the parties involved. It must also represent added value for the general interest. These mechanisms will not be applicable where fundamental rights or important political options are at stake or in situations where the rules must be applied in a uniform fashion in all Member States. They must ensure swift and flexible regulation which does not affect the principles of competition or the unity of the internal market.

Co-regulation

18. Co-regulation means the mechanism whereby a Community legislative act entrusts the attainment of the objectives defined by the legislative authority to parties which are recognised in the field (such as economic operators, the social partners, non-governmental organisations, or associations). This mechanism may be used on the basis of criteria defined in the legislative act so as to enable the legislation to be adapted to the problems and sectors concerned, to reduce the legislative burden by concentrating on essential aspects and to draw on the experience of the parties concerned ...

20. In the context defined by the basic legislative act, the parties affected by that act may conclude voluntary agreements for the purpose of determining practical arrangements. The draft agreements will be forwarded by the Commission to the legislative authority. In accordance with its responsibilities, the Commission will verify whether or not those draft agreements comply with Community law (and, in particular, with the basic legislative act).

    At the request of inter alia the European Parliament or of the Council, on a case-by-case basis and depending on the subject, the basic legislative act may include a provision for a two-month period of grace following notification of a draft agreement to the European Parliament and the Council. During that period, each Institution may either suggest amendments, if it is considered that the draft agreement does not meet the objectives laid down by the legislative authority, or object to the entry into force of that agreement and, possibly, ask the Commission to submit a proposal for a legislative act.

21. A legislative act which serves as the basis for a co-regulation mechanism will indicate the possible extent of co-regulation in the area concerned. The competent legislative authority will define in the act the relevant measures to be taken in order to follow up its application, in the event of non-compliance by one or more parties or if the agreement fails. These measures may provide, for example, for the regular supply of information by the Commission to the legislative authority on follow-up to application or for a revision clause under which the Commission will report at the end of a specific period and, where necessary, propose an amendment to the legislative act or any other appropriate legislative measure.

Self-regulation

22. Self-regulation is defined as the possibility for economic operators, the social partners, non-governmental organisations or associations to adopt amongst themselves and for themselves common guidelines at European level (particularly codes of practice or sectoral agreements). As a general rule, this type of voluntary initiative does not imply that the Institutions have adopted any particular stance, in particular where such initiatives are undertaken in areas which are not covered by the Treaties or in which the Union has not hitherto legislated. As one of its responsibilities, the Commission will scrutinise self-regulation practices in order to verify that they comply with the provisions of the EC Treaty.

The use of co-regulation, in particular, is widespread with private standards deployed as a substitute for legislation across wide swathes of Union activity. They are prevalent in the fields of the internal market, employment and social policy, protection of the environment, financial services, information and communications technology, fighting crime and consumer protection.[38] The justification is that they enable market participants to decide the level and form of regulation in a manner suitable for them and in a way that minimises adjustment and financial costs. Yet such arrangements bring a host of unanswered questions: in particular there is a concern that by contracting out law-making, many of its checks and balances are being lost.[39]

D. Chalmers, 'Private Power and Public Authority in European Union Law' (2005–06) 8 *Cambridge Yearbook of European Legal Studies* 59, 79

[These] regimes consequently generate a number of possible difficulties. The first is with the protection of public goods, such as protection of the environment, administration of justice or an effective financial system. They are set up to protect these public goods, but, invariably, the questions arise as to how effectively they do it and whether they are ambitious enough in their reach. The second is the protection of so called 'credential goods'. Credential goods deal with problems of asymmetries of information. Professional regimes are, for example, typically justified on the ground that consumers will know little about the quality of services provided by professionals, and it is, therefore, important to have a professional regime to regulate them. Yet all problem-solving regimes surround the individual with a bewildering array of semi-formal structures, which open up some possibilities, whilst closing off others. The forms of advertising she sees; her Internet provision; the quality and price of the goods and services she buys; access to professional help; and much of her natural environment: all are governed by this twilight zone of EU private law making. An individual goes to replace a part in her car, but can no longer obtain it because a manufacturer has discontinued it to meet its CO_2 obligations under the Union agreements, and she is, therefore, unable to drive any more. She has no redress, no sense

---

[38] For a survey see Chalmers, above n. 11, 64–73.

[39] See also L. Senden, 'Soft Law, Self-regulation and Co-regulation in European Law: Where do They Meet?' (2005) 9 *Electronic Journal of Comparative Law* No. 1; P. Verbruggen, 'Does Co-Regulation Strengthen EU Legitimacy?' (2009) 15 *ELJ* 425.

of transparency, and no sense of identifying who is responsible for this significant change in her life. Moreover, in contrast to parliamentary statutes or case law, the opacity of her entitlements undermines her ability to feel comfortable about and trust her surrounding environment, and her sense of social status, self-esteem and confidence to make choices. The final difficulty is distributive asymmetries. Problem-solving regimes may benefit some participants at the expense of others, and the entitlements they provide for third parties may benefit some more than others or actually disadvantage some parties by withdrawing entitlements they might otherwise have had.

(iv) Subsidiarity, proportionality and 'better regulation'

The subsidiarity and proportionality principles were brought together in a 2005 Commission initiative. Concern with the impact of EU legislation on the competitiveness of enterprises in the Union led the Commission to identify 'simplification' of EU legislation as a priority action for the Union.[40] There was, in particular, a concern that, if not properly formulated, EU legislation could generate unnecessary costs, restrict business activities and limit efficiency and innovation. A Communication was therefore adopted whose objective was to establish a 'European regulatory framework that fulfils the highest standards of law making respecting the principles of subsidiarity and proportionality'.[41]

European Commission, *Implementing the Community Lisbon Programme: A Strategy for the Simplification of the Regulatory Environment*, COM(2005)535, 2–3

Following these principles, the EU should only regulate if a proposed action can be better achieved at EU level. Any such action should not go beyond what is necessary to achieve the policy objectives pursued. It needs to be cost efficient and take the lightest form of regulation called for. In this respect simplification intends to make legislation at both Community and national level less burdensome, easier to apply and thereby more effective in achieving their goals.

The development of the European Union over the last half century has produced a large body of Community legislation, the Community 'acquis', which has often replaced 25 sets of rules with one and thereby offered business a more certain legal environment and a level playing field in which to operate. This stock of legislation has been essential, for example, in establishing the single market, developing EU environmental policy and in setting EU wide levels for the protection of workers and consumers. At the same time, legislation can also entail costs, hamper business, channel resources away from more efficient uses and in some cases act as a constraint to innovation, productivity and growth. The challenge is to get the balance right so as to ensure that the regulatory environment is necessary, simple and effective ...

Better regulation is however not de-regulation. Simplification at Community and national level means making things easier for citizens and operators. In turn, this should lead to a more effective legislative framework which is better suited to delivering the policy objectives of the Community.

---

[40] European Commission, *Better Regulation for Growth and Jobs*, COM(2005)97.
[41] European Commission, *Implementing the Community Lisbon Programme: A Strategy for the Simplification of the Regulatory Environment*, COM(2005)535.

The commitment to EU regulation only where it is necessary, simple and effective led the Commission to propose a simplification strategy whose five central points were the following:

- repeal of all legislative acts that are irrelevant or obsolete. The Commission will introduce review clauses to all legislation to ensure that new legislation is reviewed within a particular time-frame (typically three to five years);
- codification of existing EU legislation into more readable, coherent texts;
- recasting of legislation; this is different from codification as it involves the merging of legal texts so as to increase consistency and minimise overlaps;
- modification of the regulatory approach to make more use of co-regulation;
- greater use of Regulations rather than Directives as the former are seen as having immediate application, guaranteeing that all actors are subject to the same rules at the same time, and focusing attention on the concrete enforcement of EU rules.[42]

The impact of this in quantitative terms has been significant. By January 2009, about 600 legal acts amounting to about 6,500 pages of the Official Journal had been repealed. Codification had led to 729 previous acts being replaced by 229 pieces of legislation. The Commission estimated that this reduced the acquis, the amount of EU law, by about 10 per cent.[43] In addition, many proposals were withdrawn: 108 between 2005 and the end of 2008.[44]

To be sure, the dismantling of unnecessary legislation is not to be decried. It runs the risk, however, of deregulatory bias. In this, there is a worrying lack of transparency about the process. It is not clear how measures are deemed obsolete. The American author Wiener has observed that the criteria for determining this will be central, and that in the case of the Union the simple idea of disuse for a long time as a criterion is too vague and invites selective enforcement. He observes, for example, that whilst some laws may be obsolete it may be the case with others that they are 'dormant' because they are widely accepted and rarely violated.[45] In short, as one would not accept a process for law enactment whose criteria and procedures are so opaque, it is unclear why it is deemed sufficient for the repeal of legislation.

4 CONSULTATION

(i) General standards and minimum principles for consultation

A central concern of governance is that EU institutions should consult widely before taking any legislative action.[46] This is contained in Article 11 TEU which also sets out three underlying principles – dialogue, transparency and pluralism – that must inform such consultations.

---

[42] *Ibid.* 6–9.

[43] European Commission, *Third Progress Report on the Strategy for Simplifying the Regulatory Environment*, COM(2009)19, 2–3.

[44] European Commission, *Third Strategic Review of Better Regulation in the European Union*, COM(2009)15, 3.

[45] J. Wiener, 'Better Regulation in Europe' (2006) 59 *CLP* 447, 503.

[46] On the evolution of the Commission's and Court's approaches to consultation, see F. Bignami, 'Three Generations of Participation Rights Before the Commission' (2004) 68 *Law and Contemporary Problems* 61.

> **Article 11 TEU**
>
> 1. The institutions shall, by appropriate means, give citizens and representative associations the opportunity to make known and publicly exchange their views in all areas of Union action.
> 2. The institutions shall maintain an open, transparent and regular dialogue with representative associations and civil society.
> 3. The European Commission shall carry out broad consultations with parties concerned in order to ensure that the Union's actions are coherent and transparent.

These principles are detailed in the 2002 Commission Communication on general principles and minimum standards for consultation.[47] This sets out the following responsibilities for the Commission.

Content of consultation is to be clear   The Commission should set out a summary of the context, scope and objectives of consultation, including a description of the specific issues open for discussion or questions with particular importance for the Commission. It should make available details of any hearings, meetings or conferences, as well as contact details and information on deadlines. It should provide explanation of the Commission processes for dealing with contributions, what feedback to expect and details of the next stages involved in the development of the policy.

Relevant parties should have an opportunity to express their opinions   In its consultations, the Commission should ensure adequate coverage of those affected by the policy, those who will be involved in implementation of the policy, or bodies that have stated objectives giving them a direct interest in the policy. In determining the relevant parties for consultation, it should take into account the impact of the policy on other policy areas, the need for specific experience, expertise or technical knowledge and the need to involve non-organised interests. It should consider the track record of participants in previous consultations as well as the need for a proper balance between representatives of social and economic bodies, large and small organisations or companies, wider constituencies (such as churches and religious communities) and specific target groups (for example women, the elderly, the unemployed, or ethnic minorities).

The Commission should publish consultations widely   This is via the web portal, 'Your Voice in Europe',[48] which is the Commission's single access point for consultation.

Participants are to be given sufficient time to respond   The Commission should allow at least eight weeks for reception of responses to written public consultations and twenty working days' notice for meetings.

---

[47] European Commission, *General Principles and Minimum Standards for Consultation of Interested Parties by the Commission*, COM(2002)704. See D. Obradovic and J. Alonso, 'Good Governance Requirements Concerning the Participation of Interest Groups in EU Consultations' (2006) 43 *CMLRev.* 1049.

[48] See http://ec.europa.eu/yourvoice/consultations/index_en.htm (accessed 1 September 2009).

Acknowledgement and adequate feedback is to be provided   Receipt of contributions should be acknowledged and the results displayed on websites. Explanatory memoranda accompanying legislative proposals following a consultation process must include the results of these consultations, an explanation as to how these were conducted and how the results were taken into account in the proposal.

Like any procedures, there is a danger that these criteria are just paper obligations and are no more than hoops to climb through. To assess their bite, it is necessary to consider the surrounding legal context to see whether it gives rise to the dialogue, transparency and pluralism alluded to in Article 11 TEU.

(ii) Dialogue within the consultation process

Dialogue, to be meaningful, has to be a commitment to do more than merely talk; for one can talk forever without its necessarily having any bearing on the subsequent legislation. To be significant, dialogue has therefore to be similar to the notion of accountability used by Bovens in which he describes it as 'a relationship between an actor and a forum in which the actor has an obligation to explain and justify his or her conduct, the forum can pose questions and pass judgment and the actor may face consequences'.[49] The duty on EU institutions to give reasons is central to such a dialogue. It imposes duties on them to justify themselves, to be questioned and to be held to account for the reasons they present. There is, indeed, a duty to provide reasons which is set out in Article 296 TFEU.

> **Article 296(2) TFEU**
>
> Legal acts shall state the reasons on which they are based and shall refer to any proposals, initiatives, recommendations, requests or opinions required by the Treaties.

The duty is not a strong one, however. The reasons given can be quite general and they do not have to respond to points made by those who have been consulted. A good example is *Commission* v *Spain*.[50] Aid had been granted to farmers in Extremadura, one of the poorest areas of Spain. The aid to each farmer was for relatively small amounts and applied to just nine products, with the aid paid in the case of most of the vegetables only if they were to be used for processing. The Commission argued that, in the light of the significant trade in vegetables between Spain and the other states, the aid could distort competition and affect trade between Member States by virtue of the subsidy to production costs for Spanish undertakings. It declared the aid illegal. The Spanish government stated that the reasons were inadequate on a number of grounds. First, the decision looked at the market for all green vegetables rather than the nine vegetables in question. Secondly, it did not look at the share of Extremaduran produce in the national market and its contribution to trade within the Union. Finally, there was no explanation of the relationship between the total volume of trade between Spain and the other Member States and the quantity of aid in question, in particular it was not shown how

---

[49] M. Bovens, 'Analysing and Assessing Accountability: A Conceptual Framework' (2007) 13 *ELJ* 447, 450.

[50] In like vein, see Joined Cases C-346/03 and C-529/03 *Atzeni and Others* v *Regione autonoma della Sardegna* [2006] ECR I-1875; Case T-271/03 *Deutsche Telekom* v *Commission* [2008] ECR II-477.

the latter affected the former. These points had previously been made to the Commission by the Spanish government, and the latter's failure to address them was quite an indictment. The Court of Justice nevertheless held that the Commission's reasoning was sufficient.

Case C–113/00 *Spain v Commission* [2002] ECR I–7601

47. It should first of all be observed that the obligation to provide a statement of reasons laid down in Article [296(2) TFEU] is an essential procedural requirement, as distinct from the question whether the reasons given are correct, which goes to the substantive legality of the contested measure. Accordingly, the statement of reasons required by Article [296(2) TFEU] must be appropriate to the act at issue and must disclose in a clear and unequivocal fashion the reasoning followed by the institution which adopted the measure in question in such a way as to enable the persons concerned to ascertain the reasons for the measure and to enable the competent court to exercise its power of review.

48. Furthermore, that requirement must be appraised by reference to the circumstances of each case, in particular the content of the measure, the nature of the reasons given and the interest which the addressees of the measure, or other parties to whom it is of direct and individual concern, may have in obtaining explanations. It is not necessary for the reasoning to go into all the relevant facts and points of law, since the question whether the statement of reasons meets the requirements of Article [296(2) TFEU] must be assessed with regard not only to its wording but also to its context and to all the legal rules governing the matter in question.

49. In the light of that case law, it does not appear that the Commission failed in this case to fulfil its obligation to provide an adequate statement of reasons in the contested decision for the finding that the aid in question affects trade between Member States.

50. First of all … the Commission provides figures on the total quantity of vegetables produced in Spain and on the volume of trade in vegetables between Spain and the other Member States in 1998. It is clear from this information that a sizeable portion of Spanish horticultural goods is exported to other Member States. Whilst the Commission did not provide detailed figures on exports of those vegetables to which the aid scheme in question applies, it none the less noted that the overall context in which the scheme operates is one of a high level of trade between Member States of products in the horticultural sector.

51. Next … the Commission refers to the direct and immediate effect of the aid measures on the production costs of undertakings producing and processing fruit and vegetables in Spain, and to the economic advantage that they confer on such undertakings over those that do not have access to comparable aid in other Member States.

52. … the Commission also refers explicitly to Regulation No. 2200/96 which established a common organisation of the market in the fruit and vegetable sector. The Spanish Government could therefore not be unaware that the Commission's assessment of the aid scheme in question, including its finding that trade between Member States was affected by it, necessarily had to be viewed in the context of the rules on the common organisation of the markets.

53. In that connection it must be pointed out that the regime under Regulation No. 2200/96, which contains a set of uniform rules on production, marketing and competition between the economic operators concerned, benefits both trade in the fruit and vegetable sector and the development and maintenance of effective competition at Community level.

54. Finally, whilst it is common ground that in the statement of reasons for its decision the Commission is bound to refer at least to the circumstances in which aid has been granted where those circumstances show that the aid is such as to affect trade between Member States … it is not bound to demonstrate the real effect of aid already granted …

The Commission is let off with very thin reasoning and with providing little engagement with the issues raised by the Spanish government. This derives from the functions that are ascribed to the duty to give reasons. It is not there to require EU institutions to enter into dialogue with and justify themselves to interested parties. Instead, as paragraph 47 sets out, it is merely there to enable the Court of Justice to orient the Decision. The duty to state reasons is therefore stated to be important to discover the rationale for the measure and to enable judicial review. The reasons do little more than serve as a context for understanding the Decision.

The consequence is that there is a very light onus on EU institutions to be responsive to the consultation. This is reflected in how the Commission treats the results of its consultations. Typically, a synthesis is brought together of all the central views. This synthesis will set out the views but will rarely express a Commission opinion. It is entirely descriptive in nature. The question of how these views inform any Commission proposal or how the Commission will respond to any of them is left completely opaque.[51] The Commission is also of the view that it is under no legal obligation to consult an individual party or to respond or give individual feedback to a particular view.[52]

(iii) Transparency of the consultation process

A central concern within the consultation process is knowing who the lobbyists are and who they represent. The 2002 Communication, thus, imposes some responsibilities on lobbyists. Representative institutions must set out which interests they represent and how inclusive that representation is.[53] If they fail to do so, their submission, though not disqualified, will be treated as an individual submission and given less weight. In a review of the procedure, the Commission identified the thinness of these responsibilities as the central weakness in the lobbying system.[54] It has therefore established a voluntary register for lobbyists.[55] Membership is only available to those who observe a Code of Conduct set out in the Register. This requires the lobbyist:

- to identify themselves by name and the entity they work for or represent;
- not to misrepresent themselves so as to mislead third parties and/or EU staff;
- to declare the interests, and where applicable the clients or the members, which they represent;
- to ensure that, to the best of their knowledge, information which they provide is unbiased, complete, up-to-date and not misleading;
- not to obtain or try to obtain information, or any decision, dishonestly;
- not to induce EU staff to contravene rules and standards of behaviour applicable to them;
- if employing former EU staff, to respect their obligation to abide by the rules and confidentiality requirements which apply to them.

---

[51] A good example is the Commission Consultation on the European Commission, *Green Paper on Agricultural Product Quality: Product Standards, Farming Requirements and Quality Schemes*, COM(2008)641. This elicited 560 responses. The Commission Conclusions on them are available at http://ec.europa.eu/agriculture/quality/policy/privstat_en.pdf (accessed 1 October 2009).

[52] For a description of the evolution of Commission views, see Obradovic and Alonso, above n. 48, 1059–61.

[53] European Commission, above n. 48, 17.

[54] European Commission, *Follow-up to the Green Paper: European Transparency Initiative*, COM(2007)127, 3–4.

[55] European Commission, *European Transparency Initiative: A Framework for Relations with Interest Representatives (Register and Code of Conduct)*, COM(2008)323.

Whilst membership is voluntary, the Register had more than 1,000 members after one year.[56] That said, it is not clear how some of the more wide-ranging transparency concerns will be policed. These include the presentation of distorted information by lobbyists to the EU institutions and the manufacture of organising campaigns exaggerating popular support for an initiative.[57]

(iv) Inclusiveness of EU consultation

The final question is the pluralism of the processes: to whom do the EU institutions talk and to whom do they listen? Clearly, it is undesirable that they only listen to a limited number of groups and that they listen to these groups exclusively and recurrently. There is a danger of 'capture', with the EU institutions possibly promoting policies that are too closely aligned to the interests of a particular constituency, and a problem of credibility with their not being perceived to act in the wider public interest. In its 2002 Communication, the Commission stated that it wished to be as inclusive as possible, but there were practical limits.

European Commission, *General Principles and Minimum Standards for Consultation of Interested Parties by the Commission*, COM(2002)704, 11–12

The Commission wishes to stress that it will maintain an inclusive approach in line with the principle of open governance: Every individual citizen, enterprise or association will continue to be able to provide the Commission with input. In other words, the Commission does not intend to create new bureaucratic hurdles in order to restrict the number of those that can participate in consultation processes.

However, two additional considerations must be taken into account in this context. First, best practice requires that the target group should be clearly defined prior to the launch of a consultation process. In other words, the Commission should actively seek input from relevant interested parties, so these will have to be targeted on the basis of sound criteria. Second, clear selection criteria are also necessary where access to consultation is limited for practical reasons. This is especially the case for the participation of interested parties in advisory bodies or at hearings.

The Commission would like to underline the importance it attaches to input from representative European organisations. However, the issue of representativeness at European level should not be used as the only criterion when assessing the relevance or quality of comments. The Commission will avoid consultation processes which could give the impression that 'Brussels is only talking to Brussels', as one person put it. In many cases, national and regional viewpoints can be equally important in taking into account the diversity of situations in the Member States. Moreover, minority views can also form an essential dimension of open discourse on policies. On the other hand, it is important for the Commission to consider how representative views are when taking a political decision following a consultation process.

---

[56] See http://ec.europa.eu/transparency/index_en.htm (accessed 6 October 2009).
[57] European Commission, *Green Paper: European Transparency Initiative*, COM(2006)194, 6.

EU institutions face two challenges to this ethos of inclusiveness. The first is the heavy predominance of corporate lobbyists. Economic interests are seen as having resources not available to other groups and a particularly strong presence in Brussels.[58] The second concerns the role of pan-European organisations. There is the issue of how representative these are. In the 2002 Communication, the Commission stated that they must have a permanent pan-European interest, represent general interests and have a presence in most Member States. Yet doubts have been raised about the representative nature of even the most well-known of these. In 1998, UEAPME, the pan-European organisation representing small and medium-sized enterprises, challenged an agreement on parental leave between UNICE, the main pan-European industrial association, and ETUC, the pan-European association representing the trade unions, on the grounds that it excluded them. Whilst the application before the General Court was unsuccessful, it indicated the difficulties involved, as it is hard to argue that small and medium-sized enterprises might not have a particular view on the particular issue that should be heard.[59] The other problem is that, as Greenwood has noted, 'extended partnership arrangements have become established as de facto practice' between the Commission and these pan-European groups.[60] In other words, particular attention is paid to their views. This is problematic not simply because they are best at representing concerns of a more universal nature, rather than particular local ones, but because many are funded by the Commission. In his 2007 article, Greenwood noted that the Commission spends around €1 billion annually in funding interest-group activities. Almost all the 300 pan-European citizen interest groups received funding, with this being 80–90 per cent of the income for prominent groups such as the European Network Against Racism and the European Social Platform.[61]

5 THE PRIORITY OF KNOWLEDGE

Central principles of the White Paper are that Union decision-making be effective and coherent. In part, this relates to regulatory responsiveness and the 'better regulation' strategy. Attention must be paid to the choice of regulatory instrument, the level of intervention and regular review of the measure. It also relates, however, to the use of knowledge to inform the policy-making process.

Knowledge is used here in two ways. First, expert knowledge is used to inform the policy-making process so the policy is based on the best we know. Secondly, knowledge is used to assess the impacts of the policy: what do we know about how this will affect us? This latter process, impact assessment, relies, of course, on expertise but is a slightly wider process as it is not simply looking at whether a policy will work but what its wider effects will be.

---

[58] This is acknowledged in European Commission, *ibid.* 6. See also for an overview S. Sarugger, 'Interest Groups and Democracy in the European Union' (2008) 31 *WEP* 1274, 1280–5.

[59] Case T-135/96 *UEAPME* v *Commission* [1998] ECR II-2335. For comment see N. Bernard, 'UEAPME and the Social Dialogue' in J. Shaw (ed.), *Social Law and Policy in an Evolving European Union* (Oxford and Portland, Hart, 2000); S. Smismans, 'The European Social Dialogue in the Shadow of Hierarchy' (2008) 28 *Journal of Public Policy* 161, 167–70.

[60] J. Greenwood, 'Organised Civil Society and Democratic Legitimacy in the European Union' (2007) 37 *BJPS* 333, 346.

[61] *Ibid.* 343.

(i) Expertise and the policy-making process

EU institutions are neither free to take measures without taking scientific advice nor free to ignore it. Any measure failing to give weight to scientific evidence is likely to be regarded as a breach of the proportionality principle insofar as it will be argued that it imposes an unnecessary constraint on an operator without a sound reason. The institutional implications of this were explored at greatest length in *Pfizer*. A ban was placed on virginiamycin, an antibiotic used in animal feeding stuffs, which had been lawfully marketed in the European Union for a number of years. The ban followed a conference in Copenhagen, which concluded that it could lead to new viruses which were resistant to antibiotics. The Danish government, therefore, asked for virginiamycin to be banned. The Commission consulted the Standing Committee on Animal Nutrition (SCAN), which considered that the scientific evidence did not justify a ban. The Council nevertheless decided to ban the antibiotic. Pfizer, the sole producer of the antibiotic, argued that such a measure was illegal as it lacked any scientific basis.

T–13/99 *Pfizer Animal Health* v *Council* [2002] ECR II–3305

149. ... risk assessment includes for the competent public authority, in this instance the Community institutions, a two-fold task, whose components are complementary and may overlap but, by reason of their different roles, must not be confused. Risk assessment involves, first, determining what level of risk is deemed unacceptable and, second, conducting a scientific assessment of the risks. ...

151. In that regard, it is for the Community institutions to determine the level of protection which they deem appropriate for society. It is by reference to that level of protection that they must then, while dealing with the first component of the risk assessment, determine the level of risk – i.e. the critical probability threshold for adverse effects on human health and for the seriousness of those possible effects – which in their judgment is no longer acceptable for society and above which it is necessary, in the interests of protecting human health, to take preventive measures in spite of any existing scientific uncertainty ... Therefore, determining the level of risk deemed unacceptable involves the Community institutions in defining the political objectives to be pursued under the powers conferred on them by the Treaty.

152. Although they may not take a purely hypothetical approach to risk and may not base their decisions on a zero-risk ... the Community institutions must nevertheless take account of their obligation under the first subparagraph of Article [168 TFEU] to ensure a high level of human health protection, which, to be compatible with that provision, does not necessarily have to be the highest that is technically possible ...

153. The level of risk deemed unacceptable will depend on the assessment made by the competent public authority of the particular circumstances of each individual case. In that regard, the authority may take account, inter alia, of the severity of the impact on human health were the risk to occur, including the extent of possible adverse effects, the persistency or reversibility of those effects and the possibility of delayed effects as well as of the more or less concrete perception of the risk based on available scientific knowledge.

154. As regards the second component of risk assessment, the Court of Justice has already had occasion to note that in matters relating to additives in feeding stuffs the Community institutions are responsible for carrying out complex technical and scientific assessments (see Case 14/78 *Denkavit* v *Commission* [1978] ECR 2497, paragraph 20). The Council itself has drawn attention in its arguments to the fact that the decision to withdraw the authorisation of virginiamycin was based on extremely complex scientific and technical assessments over which scientists have widely diverging views ...

155. In such circumstances a scientific risk assessment must be carried out before any preventive measures are taken.

156. A scientific risk assessment is commonly defined, at both international level ... and Community level ... as a scientific process consisting in the identification and characterisation of a hazard, the assessment of exposure to the hazard and the characterisation of the risk.

157. In that regard, it is appropriate to point out, first, that, when a scientific process is at issue, the competent public authority must, in compliance with the relevant provisions, entrust a scientific risk assessment to experts who, once the scientific process is completed, will provide it with scientific advice.

158. As the Commission pointed out in its Communication on Consumer Health and Food Safety ... scientific advice is of the utmost importance at all stages of the drawing up of new legislation and for the execution and management of existing legislation... Furthermore, the Commission stated there that it will use this advice for the benefit of the consumer in order to ensure a high level of protection of health (*ibid*). The duty imposed on the Community institutions by the first subparagraph of Article [168 TFEU] to ensure a high level of human health protection means that they must ensure that their decisions are taken in the light of the best scientific information available and that they are based on the most recent results of international research, as the Commission has itself emphasised in the Communication on Consumer Health and Food Safety.

159. Thus, in order to fulfil its function, scientific advice on matters relating to consumer health must, in the interests of consumers and industry, be based on the principles of excellence, independence and transparency ...

169. ... in this case, in which the Community Institutions were required to undertake a scientific risk assessment and to evaluate highly complex scientific and technical facts, judicial review of the way in which they did so must be limited. The Community Judicature is not entitled to substitute its assessment of the facts for that of the Community institutions, on which the Treaty confers sole responsibility for that duty. Instead, it must confine itself to ascertaining whether the exercise by the institutions of their discretion in that regard is vitiated by a manifest error or a misuse of powers or whether the institutions clearly exceeded the bounds of their discretion.

170. In particular, under the precautionary principle the Community institutions are entitled, in the interests of human health, to adopt, on the basis of as yet incomplete scientific knowledge, protective measures which may seriously harm legally protected positions, and they enjoy a broad discretion in that regard.

171. However, according to ... settled case law... in such circumstances, the guarantees conferred by the Community legal order in administrative proceedings are of even more fundamental importance. Those guarantees include, in particular, the duty of the competent institution to examine carefully and impartially all the relevant aspects of the individual case ...

172. It follows that a scientific risk assessment carried out as thoroughly as possible on the basis of scientific advice founded on the principles of excellence, transparency and independence is an important procedural guarantee whose purpose is to ensure the scientific objectivity of the measures adopted and preclude any arbitrary measures ...

197. ... the role played by a committee of experts, such as SCAN, in a procedure designed to culminate in a decision or a legislative measure, is restricted, as regards the answer to the questions which the competent institution has asked it, to providing a reasoned analysis of the relevant facts of the case in the light of current knowledge about the subject, in order to provide the institution with the factual knowledge which will enable it to take an informed decision.

198. However, the competent Community institution must, first, prepare for the committee of experts the factual questions which need to be answered before it can adopt a decision and, second, assess the probative value of the opinion delivered by the committee. In that regard, the Community institution must ensure that the reasoning in the opinion is full, consistent and relevant.

199. To the extent to which the Community institution opts to disregard the opinion, it must provide specific reasons for its findings by comparison with those made in the opinion and its statement of reasons must explain why it is disregarding the latter. The statement of reasons must be of a scientific level at least commensurate with that of the opinion in question. In such a case, the institution may take as its basis either a supplementary opinion from the same committee of experts or other evidence, whose probative value is at least commensurate with that of the opinion concerned. In the event that the Community institution disregards only part of the opinion, it may also avail itself of those parts of the scientific reasoning which it does not dispute.

On the one hand, the judgment pays lip-service to the discretion enjoyed by policy-makers in how they treat scientific expertise.[62] A division is made between risk assessment and risk management. The former identifies and characterises the hazard (paragraph 156) while the latter determines how much exposure there should be to the risk. This is a matter for EU decision-makers (paragraph 151). Yet this discretion is more apparent than real. In areas characterised by scientific complexity, they must consult scientific bodies, which are marked by 'excellence, independence and transparency' (paragraph 172). This advice is not neutral in that it will characterise the hazard in terms of its danger (e.g. dangerous, not dangerous, high or low level of risk). Whilst the legislature is free not to follow the advice, it can only depart from it if it provides scientific evidence of equivalent authority as a justification for doing so (paragraph 199). In practice, it invariably follows it. This makes the scientific bodies very powerful as, in effect, they determine the body of the law in such cases.

Historically, as was the case in *Pfizer*, this process was carried out through the establishment of Scientific Committees which, whilst embedded within the institutional structures of the Commission, were often composed of outside experts. The governance agenda changed this. It proposed that the place of these be taken by new regulatory agencies which will be responsible for the carrying out of risk assessment.[63] The establishment of these has been discussed in Chapter 2.[64] There, an extract from Shapiro was considered about how this leads to government by technocracy and integration by stealth with deeply contentious issues reduced to questions of scientific expertise. Joerges has raised another issue, which is the ideological neutrality of these agencies. Frequently, the safety standards considered by these are industry standards based on industry research. He points out that they provide a venue for private interests free from traditional political scrutiny.

[62] For some of the wider implications of the judgment, see J. Scott and S. Sturm, 'Courts as Catalysts: Rethinking the Judicial Role in New Governance' (2007) 13 *CJEL* 565.
[63] European Commission White Paper, above n. 3, 23–4.
[64] See pp. 66–7.

> **C. Joerges, 'The Law's Problems with the Governance of the Single European Market'**
> **in C. Joerges and R. Dehousse (eds.) *Good Governance in Europe's Integrated Market***
> **(Oxford, Oxford University Press, 2002) 1, 17**
>
> Charged with market entry/exit regulation and more general, informal, information-gathering and policy-informing duties, the new European agencies apparently meet a purely technical demand for market-corrective and sector-specific regulation. This seemingly technocratic and semi-autonomous status implicitly provides private market interests with a voice, and this gives credence to the lingering notion that internal market regulation has more to do with 'neutral' sustenance of individual economic enterprise than with the imposition of (collective) political/social direction. Notwithstanding their placement under the Commission's institutional structure and the presence of national representatives within their management structures, their founding statutes (Council Directives and Regulations), permanent staff, organizational independence, varying degrees of budgetary autonomy and direct networking with national administrators largely shield these agencies from explicitly political processes.

(ii) Impact assessment

In the White Paper, the Commission stated that the quality of EU policy proposals would be improved not only by reliance on expert advice but also through impact assessment.[65] This has been described by the Commission in the following terms:

> the process of systematic analysis of the likely impacts of intervention by public authorities. It is as such an integral part of the process of designing policy proposals and making decision-makers and the public aware of the likely impacts.[66]

It is a process whereby the EU institutions try to anticipate the social, economic and environmental impacts of different policy options, and model their choices accordingly. There is a tension here, as this suggests that impact assessment is about finding the best choice economically, ecologically and socially. The Commission, however, indicates that it is not to be so prescriptive and that it is an aid to, rather than a substitute for, policy planning.[67] As the procedure is time-consuming, it is not applied to all Commission proposals. Instead, the Commission will only use it if the proposal results in substantial economic, environmental and/or social impacts on a specific sector or sectors, has a significant impact on major interested parties, or represents a major policy reform.[68] That said, the number of assessments carried out is still significant, with 135 being formulated in 2008.[69] The procedure is a six stage one that takes place before the Commission makes its proposal. It is carried out in the first instance by the unit in the Commission developing the proposal and involves the following steps:

- identification of the problem: this will include the nature and extent of the procedure and the key players;
- defining the objectives of any action: this must consider in particular whether they are coherent, comply with other EU policies, and respect the European Union Charter of Fundamental Rights;

[65] European Commission White Paper, above n. 3, 30.
[66] European Commission, *Impact Assessment*, COM(2002)276, 3.
[67] *Ibid.* 9–10.
[68] *Ibid.* 7.
[69] European Commission, *Impact Assessment Board Report for 2008*, SEC(2009)55, 2.

- development of the main policy options: the development of these options must consider whether regulatory or non-regulatory choices should be adopted and compliance with the proportionality principle;
- analysis of the social, economic and environmental impacts of the options: this should be done in qualitative and, where possible, quantitative and monetary terms;
- comparison of the options: this involves looking at the impacts of the different options and selecting, if possible, a preferred one;
- outlining of policy monitoring and evaluation: this will look at the arrangements and the indicators used to inform the assessment.[70]

There should be consultation with stakeholders throughout the process.[71] In 2006, an external evaluation was carried out of the process. It found consultation was good but there was little evidence that impact assessment had much influence on policy proposals; strong resistance within the Commission to it; and the reports were of variable quality.[72] An Impact Assessment Board was therefore established to monitor the quality of the assessments done by the different parts of the Commission and to provide support. The effect of this Board is difficult to gauge. It reported in 2009 that many assessments it saw were sub-standard. It also stated that whilst in about 40 per cent of cases the Commission unit substantially revised its communication after the opinion of the Board, there were only minor or no changes in about 25 per cent of cases.[73]

The question of the effect of impact assessment on EU decision-making is thus still open. Yet, it can also be questioned as a policy tool. Radaelli has pointed to a number of concerns that are present in the regulation literature about impact assessment.[74] First, it can lead to an overly empirical analysis. In fields such as the environment, there is a real question as to how quality of life or ecological perspectives can be measured. Secondly, there is a danger of overstatement. Often, advocacy papers can be put forward as impact assessments. A position will be put forward as a truth that one option has less negative impacts than another, but the biases that lead to this view can be hidden. Finally, it is problematic for measuring or subsequently evaluating fast-changing regulatory regimes that involve a range of instruments and have to adapt continually to changing circumstances. For impact assessments are quite static processes that rely above all on an anticipation of what will happen, and this anticipation will invariably involve a number of assumptions.

6 TRANSPARENCY

The final virtue set out in the White Paper is that of accountability. Views on the meaning of accountability vary considerably. Earlier, a definition by Bovens was set out in which accountability was described as a relationship in which actors have to explain and justify their conduct, be questioned on it and face the consequences for it.[75] As important as the definition is

---

[70] European Commission, *Impact Assessment Guidelines*, SEC(2009)92, 4–5.
[71] *Ibid.* 19.
[72] The Evaluation Partnership, *Evaluation of the Commission's Impact Assessment System: Final Report* (April 2007), available at http://ec.europa.eu/governance/impact/key_docs/docs/tep_eias_final_report.pdf (accessed 5 October 2009).
[73] European Commission, *Impact Assessment Board Report*, above n. 70, 8–11.
[74] C. Radaelli, 'Whither Better Regulation for the Lisbon Agenda?' (2007) 14 *JEPP* 190.
[75] See p. 375.

the medium through which this accountability takes place. Harlow talks therefore of financial, legal and political accountability with different mechanisms (audit procedures, the courts, the political and administrative process) for securing institutional behaviour.[76] The White Paper is much blander. It sets out two ideas of accountability.[77]

First, it states that the institutional roles in the legislative and executive processes need to be clearer. This relates to the institutional checks and balances and the accountability institutions owe to each other. This is set out in Chapters 2 and 3 on institutional relations and the legislative procedures. In Chapter 10 we shall also consider the processes of institutional review, be it through the Ombudsman or the General Court. Secondly, each of the EU institutions must explain and take responsibility for what they do. In part, this is done through the duty to give reasons, which was discussed earlier.[78] More generally, this is secured through providing information on what they do. The principle of transparency is set out in Article 15(3) TFEU.[79]

Article 15(3) TFEU

Any citizen of the Union, and any natural or legal person residing or having its registered office in a Member State, shall have a right of access to documents of the Union institutions, bodies, offices and agencies, whatever their medium, subject to the principles and the conditions to be defined in accordance with this paragraph.

General principles and limits on grounds of public or private interest governing this right of access to documents shall be determined by the European Parliament and the Council, acting by means of regulations in accordance with the ordinary legislative procedure.

Each institution, body, office or agency shall ensure that its proceedings are transparent and shall elaborate in its own Rules of Procedure specific provisions regarding access to its documents, in accordance with the regulations referred to in the second subparagraph.

Article 15(3) TFEU is a framework provision. It sets out a principle of a right of access to EU documents and of transparency of procedures. However, the modalities are to be set out in secondary legislation. The central instrument is Regulation 1049/2001/EC.[80] However, there is currently a Commission proposal to amend this Regulation, and the two documents, the Regulation and the proposed amendment, should be read side by side.[81]

---

[76] C. Harlow, *Accountability in the European Union* (Oxford, Oxford University Press, 2002) ch. 1.
[77] European Commission White Paper, above n. 3, 10.
[78] See pp. 375–7.
[79] On the development of the principle in EU law, see A. Tomkins, 'Transparency and the Emergence of a European Administrative Law' (1999) 19 *YBEL* 217. The principle is also contained in Article 42 of the European Charter on Fundamental Rights and Freedoms.
[80] Regulation 1049/2001/EC regarding public access to European Parliament, Council and Commission documents [2001] OJ L145/43. See M. De Leeuw, 'The Regulation on Public Access to European Parliament, Council and Commission Documents in the European Union: Are Citizens Better Off?' (2003) 28 *ELRev.* 324.
[81] The latest Commission amended proposal is European Commission, Proposal for a Regulation regarding public access to European Parliament, Council and Commission documents, COM(2008)229. For discussion, see I. Harden, 'The Revision of Regulation 1049/2001 on Public Access to Documents' (2009) 15 *EPL* 239.

(i) Scope of the right to access to documents

The central entitlement is set out in article 2 of the Regulation.

Article 2

1. Any citizen of the Union, and any natural or legal person residing or having its registered office in a Member State, has a right of access to documents of the institutions, subject to the principles, conditions and limits defined in this Regulation.
2. The institutions may, subject to the same principles, conditions and limits, grant access to documents to any natural or legal person not residing or not having its registered office in a Member State.
3. This Regulation shall apply to all documents held by an institution, that is to say, documents drawn up or received by it and in its possession, in all areas of activity of the European Union.

This access is provided in two ways. First, all EU institutions are required to keep up-to-date electronic registers of documents to which the public should have access.[82] In debates surrounding amendment of the Regulation, this register was not seen as particularly user-friendly and was seen as incomplete, excluding many preparatory documents in particular. There is a commitment, therefore, that these should be placed on the register and where possible in an electronic form. If a document is not on the register, the latter should, if possible, indicate where it is located.[83]

Secondly, parties can request access to particular information. The number of requests have risen from year to year, with 3,841 requests in 2006, 4,196 in 2007 and 5,197 in 2008.[84] If this is about increasing popular engagement with the European Union, its impact appears extremely limited. It is not simply that the overall numbers are very small for a polity of close to half a billion people. The composition of those requesting is very skewed. 31 per cent of requests were from academics and 17.5 per cent from public institutions. Only 16.75 per cent were from members of the public and 18.26 per cent from civil society.[85] It is the latter two groups that would be particularly important in the context of public engagement, and it is concerning that they make up only around one-third of all requests for information.

Any request must be made in writing and must be sufficiently precise to enable the institution to identify the document.[86] If the application is not sufficiently precise, the institution must ask the applicant to clarify the application and should provide assistance to enable her to do so.[87] There is a more general duty on the EU institutions to provide information and assistance on how and where applications are to be made.[88] Institutions must acknowledge receipt of any application and, within fifteen days, provide either access to the documents or reasons for refusing access.[89] If the application is for a very long document or a very large number

---

[82] Regulation 1049/2001, art. 11.
[83] European Commission Proposal, above n. 82, art. 12.
[84] European Commission, *Report on the Application in 2008 of Regulation 1049/2001*, COM(2009)331, 10.
[85] *Ibid.* 13.
[86] Regulation 1049/2001, art. 6(1).
[87] *Ibid.* art. 6(2).
[88] *Ibid.* art. 6(4).
[89] *Ibid.* art. 7.

of documents, the institution may confer with the applicant informally to find a fair solution about what should be supplied.[90]

This raises the question about what happens when the institution feels unable to supply the documents. This was explored at most length in *Williams*. The applicant was writing a doctorate at the Free University of Brussels. She asked for all internal documentation within the Commission on six pieces of legislation that constituted the heart of the Union's regime on genetically modified organisms. The Commission stated that the request was very wide-ranging. Williams met with the Commission and agreed to her request being split into six, with a priority being made between the six. In relation to the first request, the Commission refused access to twenty-three documents. Before the General Court, one of the arguments raised by the Commission was that the request was too imprecise and wide-ranging.[91] This was rejected by the Court.

Case T–42/05 *Williams* v *Commission* [2008] ECR II–156

85. It must be observed that the Court has already had occasion (Case T-2/03 *Verein für Konsumenteninformation* v *Commission* [2005] ECR II-1121) to note that it is necessary to bear in mind that an applicant may make a request for access, under Regulation No. 1049/2001, relating to a manifestly unreasonable number of documents, perhaps for trivial reasons, thus imposing a volume of work for processing of his request which could very substantially paralyse the proper working of the Institution. The Court also noted in the same judgment that, in such a case, the institution's right to seek a 'fair solution' together with the applicant, pursuant to Article 6(3) of Regulation No. 1049/2001, reflects the possibility of account being taken, albeit in a particularly limited way, of the need to reconcile the interests of the applicant with those of good administration. The Court concluded from this that an institution therefore had to retain the right, in particular cases where concrete, individual examination of the documents would entail an unreasonable amount of administrative work, to balance the interest in public access to the documents against the burden of work so caused, in order to safeguard, in those particular cases, the interests of good administration.

86. The Court stated, however, that that possibility was applicable only in exceptional cases, in view, in particular, of the fact that it is not, in principle, appropriate that account should be taken of the amount of work entailed by the exercise of the applicant's right of access and its interest in order to vary the scope of that right... In addition, in so far as the right of access to documents held by the institutions constitutes an approach to be adopted in principle, the institution relying on the unreasonableness of the task entailed by the request bears the burden of proof of the scale of that task...

87. In the present case, first of all, it must be noted that the Commission availed itself of the possibility provided by Article 6(3) of Regulation No. 1049/2001, which enabled it to divide the applicant's initial request into six. Accordingly, in the contested decision, the Commission replied only to the first of the applicant's requests — whereby the applicant sought access to preparatory documents relating to Directive 2001/18 — which means that the request cannot be regarded as very wide-ranging. Furthermore, there is nothing in the contested decision to suggest that the handling of that request

---

[90] *Ibid.* art. 6(3).
[91] For debate, see J. Helikoski and P. Leino, 'Darkness at the Break of Noon: The Case Law on Regulation No.1049/2001 on Access to Documents' (2006) 43 *CMLRev.* 735, 756–60; H. Kraneborg, 'Is it Time to Revise the European Regulation on Public Access to Documents?' (2006) 12 *EPL* 251, 267–71.

88. ... the fact that neither the initial request nor the confirmatory application mentions specific documents cannot be regarded as having prevented the Commission from understanding that the applicant wished to have access to all preparatory documents relating to the legislation on GMOs ... Nor can the Commission reasonably rely on that fact in support of its contention that the burden of work imposed by the handling of the first request was unreasonable and that, in those circumstances, if it was to observe the principle of good administration, it could not – due to its limited resources – be required, under the principle of transparency, to consider the disclosure of each and every document held by it that could be relevant to such a request.

89. In that regard, it is sufficient to note that the Commission confined itself in its written pleadings to maintaining that the first request amounted to an exceptional situation because it was actually not possible, on account of its imprecise and undefined nature, to calculate the number of files and documents liable to fall within its scope. Such an argument cannot be upheld, since the request was clear in referring to access to all preparatory documents relating to Directive 2001/18 and therefore the absence of a list of specific documents could have an impact only on the time-limits for reply – an issue which was resolved by the fair solution – but not on the scope of the request for access.

It would seem, therefore, that whilst the institution may refuse unreasonable requests for absurd levels of documentation for trivial reasons, this will be highly unusual. There has to be a consideration whether the request can be broken down, and provided it seems (according to paragraph 89) the documents are identifiable, it is not sufficient for the institution to refuse a request because it cannot calculate the number of files.

The duties on the other side are less. There is no duty on the party to state the reason for the application, to provide any justification or to declare its interest in any way at all. It is therefore possible for those who are subject to disciplinary investigations by the Commission to ask for documents. The current reasoning is that if this will undermine an investigation, then justification must be sought in one of the exceptions rather than an exclusion that will prevent the party from having information about the nature of the proceedings against them.[92] Yet the proposed amendments suggest this will be reversed. Access to information is to be excluded on investigations or proceedings concerning an act of individual scope until the proceedings are closed or a definitive act taken.[93]

There are a number of further things to note about what can be sought, who can seek it and from whom.

First, Article 2(3) of the Regulation makes clear that applicants can ask not just for documents drawn up by the EU institutions but also those that fall into their possession. This widens the scope of available information considerably, as the Commission, in particular, acts very much as a clearing house, receiving documentation from private parties, other institutions and, above all, national governments. All these can be requested. Alongside this, the right of access to documents is a right of access to the information in the document itself. As a consequence,

---

[92] Joined Cases T-391/03 and T-70/04 *Franchet and Byk* v *Commission* [2006] ECR II-2023.
[93] European Commission Proposal, above n. 82, art. 2(6). See also p. 7 of the proposal for an explanation.

the institution has to consider whether to give partial access to a document, that is it must give access to all information that does not fall within an exception.[94]

Secondly, at the moment, Article 2(1) allows only EU residents or EU citizens to make a request for information. This is seen as too narrow, and the amendments propose that any natural or legal person should be able to seek access to EU institutions' documents, irrespective of nationality or residence.[95]

Thirdly, prior to the Lisbon Treaty, the right of access to documents could only be invoked against EU institutions themselves. Whilst Article 2(1) and the proposed amendments still hold that to be the case, this has to be read in the light of Article 15(3) TFEU, which extends this right to be applied against EU bodies, offices and agencies. The Union courts are not mentioned in Article 15(3) TFEU, however. The proposed amendments suggest that it should not apply to documents submitted to them by parties other than the institutions.[96] It is difficult to see the rationale for this. If there is a concern about the administration of justice, then this applies to all parties involved, including the institutions. Otherwise, it is not clear why judicial proceedings are treated differently from any other context.

(ii) Exceptions to the right to access to information

Most litigation has not focused on the extent of the right of access to information but rather the exceptions to this right, which allow access to be refused. These are set out in article 4 of Regulation 1049/2001/EC. On its face, it may seem an arcane business, to ponder over and again the meaning of this provision. Yet, it has proved central as these exceptions are formulated in such a way as to cover whole fields of Union governmental or legislative activity. Debates about the remit of article 4 raise questions as to whether we can be denied access to knowledge about the way in which an entire field of EU law or politics is being conducted. In this regard, the rate of refusal is quite high, with 13.99 per cent of requests for information being refused in 2008, with a further 3.33 per cent only being given partial access.[97]

> ### Article 4
>
> 1. The institutions shall refuse access to a document where disclosure would undermine the protection of:
>   (a) the public interest as regards:
>   - public security,
>   - defence and military matters,
>   - international relations,
>   - the financial, monetary or economic policy of the Community or a Member State;
>   (b) privacy and the integrity of the individual, in particular in accordance with Community legislation regarding the protection of personal data.
> 2. The institutions shall refuse access to a document where disclosure would undermine the protection of:
>   - commercial interests of a natural or legal person, including intellectual property,

---

[94] Case C-353/99 P *Council* v *Hautala* [2001] ECR I-9565.
[95] European Commission Proposal, above n. 82, art. 2(1).
[96] *Ibid.* art. 2(5).
[97] European Commission, above n. 85, 10.

  – court proceedings and legal advice,
  – the purpose of inspections, investigations and audits, unless there is an overriding public interest in disclosure.

3. Access to a document, drawn up by an institution for internal use or received by an institution, which relates to a matter where the decision has not been taken by the institution, shall be refused if disclosure of the document would seriously undermine the institution's decision-making process, unless there is an overriding public interest in disclosure.

   Access to a document containing opinions for internal use as part of deliberations and preliminary consultations within the institution concerned shall be refused even after the decision has been taken if disclosure of the document would seriously undermine the institution's decision-making process, unless there is an overriding public interest in disclosure.

4. As regards third-party documents, the institution shall consult the third party with a view to assessing whether an exception in paragraph 1 or 2 is applicable, unless it is clear that the document shall or shall not be disclosed.

5. A Member State may request the institution not to disclose a document originating from that Member State without its prior agreement.

6. If only parts of the requested document are covered by any of the exceptions, the remaining parts of the document shall be released.

There has been extensive case law on these exceptions, and only some of the more salient issues will be addressed here.[98] The starting point of the Union courts is that, as the public right of access to the documents is connected with the democratic nature of the EU institutions, the Regulation intends to give the public the widest access. The exceptions must therefore be interpreted and applied strictly.[99] This statement is, however, little more than rhetorical, particularly as the exceptions are grouped into three categories.

• The first category set out in article 4(1) of the Regulation is mandatory. It requires the institution to refuse access to the document if it falls within that category. The proposed amendments to the Regulation would create one further exception here relating to the public interest as regards the 'the environment, such as breeding sites of rare species'.[100] It deletes the privacy exception set out in the current Regulation, replacing it with a new exception which requires EU institutions only to disclose personal data in accordance with EU legislation on data protection.[101]

• The second exception set out in article 4(2) and (3) gives the EU institutions a discretion to grant access to a document if, notwithstanding that it falls within one of the categories, there is an overriding public interest. This category has been extended by the proposed amendments to include arbitration and dispute settlement proceedings and the objectivity and impartiality of selection procedures.

---

[98] For more extensive treatment, see D. Adamski, 'How Wide is the "Widest Possible"? Judicial Interpretation of the Exceptions to the Right of Access to Official Documents' (2009) 46 *CMLRev*. 521.
[99] See e.g. Case C-266/05 P *Sison* v *Council* [2007] ECR I-1233.
[100] European Commission Proposal, above n. 82, art. 4(1)(e).
[101] *Ibid*. art. 4(5).

- The third exception, in article 4(5), relates to documents originating from a Member State. In such instances, there is a requirement of prior agreement.

The Regulation, thus, sets out three tests of review. This is not uncontroversial, as it is hard to see why an overriding public interest can never exist in relation to the first or the third category. There may, for example, be 'security' documents or national documents whose disclosure makes the decision-maker uncomfortable, but which are nevertheless essential for public debate.

With regard to the mandatory exceptions, the courts apply a test of marginal review. That is to say that they accept that the issue will often be sensitive and the institution in question must have discretion over the matter. The courts will thus not substitute their judgement for that of the institution but confine themselves to seeing whether accurate reasons have been given for the refusal and whether there has been a manifest error of assessment. A recent example is *WWF European Policy Programme*. The WWF, an environmental NGO, asked for documents concerning international trade negotiations taking place within the World Trade Organization. These documents set out other states' positions as well as that of the Union in the negotiations, and also the minutes of the meetings. The Council refused to disclose under article 4(1)(a), arguing that this undermined the Union's commercial interests and would be prejudicial to its relations with other states.

Case T-264/04 *WWF European Policy Programme* v Council [2007] ECR II-911

39. ... the rule is that the public is to have access to the documents of the institutions and refusal of access is the exception to that rule. Consequently, the provisions sanctioning a refusal must be construed and applied strictly so as not to defeat the application of the rule. Moreover, an institution is obliged to consider in respect of each document to which access is sought whether, in the light of the information available to that institution, disclosure of the document is in fact likely to undermine one of the public interests protected by the exceptions which permit refusal of access. In order for those exceptions to be applicable, the risk of the public interest being undermined must therefore be reasonably foreseeable and not purely hypothetical ...

40. It is also apparent from the case law that the institutions enjoy a wide discretion when considering whether access to a document may undermine the public interest and, consequently, that the Court's review of the legality of the institutions' decisions refusing access to documents on the basis of the mandatory exceptions relating to the public interest must be limited to verifying whether the procedural rules and the duty to state reasons have been complied with, the facts have been accurately stated, and whether there has been a manifest error of assessment of the facts or a misuse of powers ...

41. As to whether there was a manifest error of assessment of the facts, as the applicant essentially submits is the case, it must be noted that the Council refused to grant access to the note so as not to risk upsetting the negotiations that were taking place at that time in a sensitive context, which was characterised by resistance on the part of both the developing and the developed countries and the difficulty in reaching an agreement, as illustrated by the breakdown of negotiations at the WTO Ministerial Conference in Cancun in September 2003. Thus, in considering that disclosure of that note could have undermined relations with the third countries which are referred to in the note and the room for negotiation needed by the Community and its Member States to bring those negotiations to a conclusion, the Council did not commit a manifest error of assessment and was right to consider that disclosure of the note would have entailed the risk of undermining the public interest as regards international relations and the Community's financial, monetary and economic policy, which was reasonably foreseeable and not purely hypothetical.

In this instance, the review was quite thin. The General Court defers to the Council's assessment in paragraph 41 that providing the information will upset negotiation. However, it has not been consistent and, in some instances, the review of whether there has been a manifest error of assessment will be quite exacting. In *Kuijer*, a university lecturer challenged a decision by the Council to refuse him access to human rights reports on a number of countries that had been prepared for CIREA, an EU body that compiled documentation and exchanged information on asylum.[102] As some of these were quite damning, the Council refused on the grounds that this would damage relations with these countries. The General Court did not agree with this characterisation and overturned the Council's decision. It held that refusal had to be made by reference to the specific content and context of each human rights report. These reports contained general information on the protection of human rights which had already been made public and did not involve any politically sensitive appraisal of the state by the Council itself. The Court held, therefore, that neither the content nor the nature of the reports justified a refusal to grant access.

In the case of the discretionary category in article 4(2) and (3) of the Regulation, EU institutions must allow access to a document if, notwithstanding that it falls within one of these categories, there is an overriding public interest which justifies disclosure. The strongest example of judicial review of this is *Turco*. Turco, an MEP, sought access to legal advice the Council had received from its legal services on the proposed Directive laying down minimum standards for the reception of applicants for asylum in Member States. This was refused under the legal advice exception in article 4(2). The Council stated that greater transparency alone was not an overriding public interest, and this view was upheld by the General Court. Turco and the Swedish government appealed to the Court of Justice, who upheld his appeal. Having found that the advice constituted legal advice for the purposes of article 4(2), the Court went on to assess whether there was an overriding public interest justifying disclosure.

Joined Cases C–39/05 and C–52/05 *Sweden and Turco* v *Council* [2008] ECR I–4723

44. ... if the Council takes the view that disclosure of a document would undermine the protection of legal advice as defined above, it is incumbent on the Council to ascertain whether there is any overriding public interest justifying disclosure despite the fact that its ability to seek legal advice and receive frank, objective and comprehensive advice would thereby be undermined.

45. In that respect, it is for the Council to balance the particular interest to be protected by non-disclosure of the document concerned against, inter alia, the public interest in the document being made accessible in the light of the advantages stemming, as noted in recital 2 of the preamble to Regulation No. 1049/2001, from increased openness, in that this enables citizens to participate more closely in the decision-making process and guarantees that the administration enjoys greater legitimacy and is more effective and more accountable to the citizen in a democratic system.

46. Those considerations are clearly of particular relevance where the Council is acting in its legislative capacity, as is apparent from recital 6 of the preamble to Regulation No. 1049/2001, according to which wider access must be granted to documents in precisely such cases. Openness in that respect contributes to strengthening democracy by allowing citizens to scrutinize all the information which

---

[102] Case T-211/00 *Kuijer* v *Council* [2002] ECR II-485.

has formed the basis of a legislative act. The possibility for citizens to find out the considerations underpinning legislative action is a precondition for the effective exercise of their democratic rights.

47. It is also worth noting that, under [Article 16(8) TEU], the Council is required to define the cases in which it is to be regarded as acting in its legislative capacity, with a view to allowing greater access to documents in such cases. Similarly, Article 12(2) of Regulation No. 1049/2001 acknowledges the specific nature of the legislative process by providing that documents drawn up or received in the course of procedures for the adoption of acts which are legally binding in or for the Member States should be made directly accessible.

The requirements to be satisfied by the statement of reasons

48. The reasons for any decision of the Council in respect of the exceptions set out in Article 4 of Regulation No. 1049/2001 must be stated.

49. If the Council decides to refuse access to a document which it has been asked to disclose, it must explain, first, how access to that document could specifically and effectively undermine the interest protected by an exception laid down in Article 4 of Regulation No. 1049/2001 relied on by that institution and, secondly, in the situations referred to in Article 4(2) and (3) of that Regulation, whether or not there is an overriding public interest that might nevertheless justify disclosure of the document concerned.

50. It is, in principle, open to the Council to base its decisions in that regard on general presumptions which apply to certain categories of documents, as considerations of a generally similar kind are likely to apply to requests for disclosure relating to documents of the same nature. However, it is incumbent on the Council to establish in each case whether the general considerations normally applicable to a particular type of document are in fact applicable to a specific document which it has been asked to disclose.

The judgment has been described as 'spectacularly progressive' by Adamski.[103] Certainly, it must be seen in its context which is that of an elected representative, an MEP, asking about an instrument which raised strong human rights concerns. Yet, the reasoning of the Court is general in nature and imposes significant constraints, both substantively and procedurally. It suggests that where disclosure enables increased participation in decision-making or greater accountability, then there is already the makings of a case of an overriding public interest (paragraph 45). Yet, disclosure will in many cases enable this. The procedural constraints are also quite precise. It is not enough simply to mention a category and leave it at that. The institution must explain specifically how the interest is undermined and whether or not there is a public interest.

The final exception is set out in article 4(5) and concerns documents originating from a Member State. The traditional view is that the state concerned can veto any disclosure.[104] This changed in *Sweden* v *Commission*,[105] where Sweden appealed against the *IFAW* decision of the General Court to the Court of Justice.[106] IFAW, a German NGO concerned with nature conservation, sought disclosure of certain documents relating to the reclaiming of part of an estuary for the construction of a runway that originated in Germany. The General Court held that if

---

[103] Adamski, above n. 99, 536.
[104] Case T-76/02 *Messina* v *Commission* [2003] ECR II-3203.
[105] Case C-64/05 P *Sweden* v *Commission* [2007] ECR I-11389.
[106] Case T-168/02 *IFAW Internationaler Tierschutz-Fonds* v *Commission* [2004] ECR II-4135.

a Member State requested, as Germany did here, that the document not be disclosed, then it should not be disclosed. The Member State need not give reasons and the question would be decided exclusively by the national law of that state. The Swedish government appealed. The Court of Justice upheld the appeal. It held that to give a national veto over documents originating from a Member State would be incompatible with the purpose of the Regulation, which was to grant the widest possible access to documents by allowing that right to be frustrated without any objective reason. It would also introduce arbitrary distinctions whereby documents of a similar kind held by the EU institutions would have different rules applying to them depending on the origin of the document. The national veto applied, therefore, only if the document fell within one of the categories set out in article 4(1)–(3) of the Regulation. If an EU institution received a request for a national document, it was required to open a dialogue with the Member State, which could only refuse disclosure if it provided reasons why the document fell within one of the exceptions set out in article 4(1)–(3).

The judgment indicates that the same substantive principles concerning grounds for disclosure will apply whatever the provenance of the document. In this way, it significantly expands the remit of the principle in that whole fields of activity, in which the predominant players are Member States, will now be subject to far greater scrutiny. It has led to a reaction, however. The proposed amendments suggest a new article 5(2).

Article 5(2)

Where an application concerns a document originating from a Member State, other than documents transmitted in the framework of procedures leading to a legislative act or a non-legislative act of general application, the authorities of that Member State shall be consulted. The institution holding the document shall disclose it unless the Member State gives reasons for withholding it, based on the exceptions referred to in Article 4 or on specific provisions in its own legislation preventing disclosure of the document concerned. The institution shall appreciate the adequacy of reasons given by the Member State insofar as they are based on exceptions laid down in this Regulation.

Two qualifications to the *Sweden* v *Commission* judgment are thus added, both of which narrow the scope of access. First, the substance of the national reasons cannot be second-guessed by the EU institution. Even if it disagrees with them, it must respect them and not disclose the document if that is what is requested. It may be open to the applicant to challenge the Member State's refusal but it can only do this before a national court, as it does not have standing to challenge Member States before the Court of Justice. Secondly, a further exception is added, namely exceptions allowed under national legislation. In this way, Member States can, if they so wish, restrict the access considerably by simply passing very draconian legislation.

FURTHER READING

D. Adamski, 'How Wide is the "Widest Possible"? Judicial Interpretation of the Exceptions to the Right of Access to Official Documents' (2009) 46 *Common Market Law Review* 521

G. Davies, 'Subsidiarity: The Wrong Idea, in the Wrong Place, at the Wrong Time' (2006) 43 *Common Market Law Review* 63

C. Joerges, 'Integration Through De-legalisation?' (2008) 33 *European Law Review* 291

C. Joerges, Y. Mény and J. Weiler (eds.), *Mountain or Molehill? A Critical Appraisal of the Commission White Paper on Governance* (EUI and NYU, 2002), available at www.jeanmonnetprogram.org/papers/01/010601.html

C. Möllers, 'European Governance: Meaning and Value of a Concept' (2006) 43 *Common Market Law Review* 313

D. Obradovic and J. Alonso, 'Good Governance Requirements Concerning the Participation of Interest Groups in EU Consultations' (2006) 43 *Common Market Law Review* 1049

C. Radaelli, 'Whither Better Regulation for the Lisbon Agenda?' (2007) 14 *Journal of European Public Policy* 190

J. Scott and D. Trubek, 'Mind the Gap: Law and New Approaches to Governance in the European Union' (2002) 8 *European Law Journal* 1

S. Smismans, 'New Governance: The Solution for Active European Citizenship, or the End of Citizenship?' (2007) 13 *Columbia Journal of European Law* 595

J. Wiener, 'Better Regulation in Europe' (2006) 59 *Current Legal Problems* 447

10

Judicial Review

CONTENTS

1 INTRODUCTION

This chapter considers judicial review by the European Court of Justice. It is organised as follows.

Section 2 considers the scope of Article 263 TFEU, the central provision governing direct actions for judicial review of Union measures before the General Court and the Court of Justice. It has been amended by the Lisbon Treaty to allow not just the traditional institutions to be reviewed but also the European Council and EU agencies, offices and bodies. The measures susceptible to review include not just formal legal acts but any measure intended to produce legal effects. This will be any measure which is clear, definitive and produces a change in the applicant's legal situation.

Section 3 considers the grounds for review. A measure will be annulled, first, if the institution does not have the formal competence to adopt it. Review is possible, secondly, if the institution has misused its power. This may be an abuse of power where a power is used for purposes other than that for which it was granted. More common is a manifest error of assessment. This requires Union measures to be substantiated by the evidence provided, and for that evidence to be accurate, reliable, consistent and sufficiently complete. The third heading of review is 'rights of process'. These include the right to know the reasons for a legal measure, the rights to a hearing where one's interests are restricted, protection of one's rights of defence in the case of possible sanction, and, finally, the right to administration of one's affairs with due care by the EU institutions. The final heading of review is infringement of the Treaties or any rule of law relating to its application. This includes breach of any substantive provision of EU law and violation of fundamental rights. It also encompasses EU legal principles developed by the Court of Justice, namely non-discrimination, proportionality, legal certainty and protection of legitimate expectations.

Section 4 considers the standing requirements for bringing an action under Article 263 TFEU. Privileged applicants – the Member States, Parliament, the Commission and Council – have unlimited standing to challenge a measure subject to their observance of the time limits. Semi-privileged applicants – the Court of Auditors, European Central Bank and Committee of the Regions – may bring an action to protect their institutional prerogatives. All other parties have standing to bring an action against a regulatory act if it is of direct concern to them and against other measures if these are of direct and individual concern to them. This distinction between regulatory and other acts is new. The best interpretation is to see regulatory acts as any non-legislative act. Direct concern will be established where the Union measure directly affects a legal entitlement of the applicant without any significant intermediation by another party. Individual concern is governed by the *Plaumann* formula. This requires the interest affected to belong to a fixed, ascertainable and limited group of interests which is not capable, even hypothetically, of being added to. This is a highly restrictive test and has been criticised for making economically arbitrary distinctions and for favouring private interests over public ones.

Section 5 considers Article 265 TFEU and the failure to act. This complements Article 263 TFEU and allows parties to challenge omissions by EU institutions where these are under a duty to act. The standing requirements are similar in the two provisions. However, an action under Article 265 TFEU can only be commenced against an EU institution if it is under a duty to perform a task. If there is only a discretion, no remedy exists. Secondly, an institution, if called upon to act, avoids any further action if it defines its position within two months. Finally, the institution must be called upon to act by the applicant before any action can be commenced.

Section 6 considers the plea of illegality set out in Article 277 TFEU. This is not an independent action, but in an action against a measure brought under another provision (e.g. Article 263 TFEU) it allows challenge of a parent measure. It is subject to two constraints. It cannot be brought where the measure is being challenged before a court elsewhere by the parties, and it cannot be brought by parties who have already had the opportunity to challenge the measure but did not take up that opportunity.

Section 7 considers the action for non-contractual liability under Article 340(2) TFEU. Parties can sue EU institutions for damages where three conditions are met: first, that the institution has infringed a rule of law intended to confer rights on individuals; secondly, that the breach is sufficiently serious; and finally, that there is a direct causal link between the breach and the damage sustained by the applicant. In fields where EU institutions enjoy no discretion, a simple breach of EU law or failure to exercise reasonable care will be sufficient to establish liability. In fields where they enjoy some discretion, liability will only exist if they manifestly and gravely disregard the limits of their discretion.

Section 8 considers the consequences of a finding of annulment. Such a ruling is binding on all institutional actors in the Union. A measure found to be illegal continues to have legal effects until it is withdrawn by the EU institution, albeit the latter is under a duty to withdraw the measure following a Court judgment. However, if the measure is so tainted with irregularity, the Court has the power to declare it void and without legal effects.

2 SCOPE OF JUDICIAL REVIEW AND ARTICLE 263 TFEU

There are four sets of issues that must be addressed with judicial review. These are: (i) who may be reviewed; (ii) the range of acts subject to review; (iii) the grounds of review; and (iv) the standing of various parties to seek judicial review. The starting point for consideration of all of these is Article 263 TFEU.

Article 263 TFEU

The Court of Justice of the European Union shall review the legality of legislative acts, of acts of the Council, of the Commission and of the European Central Bank, other than recommendations and opinions, and of acts of the European Parliament and of the European Council intended to produce legal effects vis-à-vis third parties. It shall also review the legality of acts of bodies, offices or agencies of the Union intended to produce legal effects vis-à-vis third parties.

It shall for this purpose have jurisdiction in actions brought by a Member State, the European Parliament, the Council or the Commission on grounds of lack of competence, infringement of an essential procedural requirement, infringement of the Treaties or of any rule of law relating to their application, or misuse of powers.

The Court shall have jurisdiction under the same conditions in actions brought by the Court of Auditors, by the European Central Bank and by the Committee of the Regions for the purpose of protecting their prerogatives.

Any natural or legal person may, under the conditions referred to in the first and second subparagraphs, institute proceedings against an act addressed to that person or which is of direct and individual concern to them, and against a regulatory act which is of direct concern to them and does not entail implementing measures.

Acts setting up bodies, offices and agencies of the Union may lay down specific conditions and arrangements concerning actions brought by natural or legal persons against acts of these bodies, offices or agencies intended to produce legal effects in relation to them.

The new provision widens the range of the bodies and institutions susceptible to judicial review by including not just the long-standing EU institutions but also the European Council and EU agencies as bodies whose acts can be challenged. As stated in Chapter 1, the inclusion of the European Council is potentially significant as the decision to subject the agreements of twenty-seven Heads of Government to judicial challenge is unprecedented and illustrates the symbolic importance attached to the rule of law in the European Union.[1] In a different way, the clarification as to the accountability of EU agencies is of equal significance. In recent years, agencies have proliferated.[2] Though their powers vary considerably, most dominate their fields through establishing technical norms or patterns of coordination between national agencies. There has been particular concern over their accountability, most notably in the field of policing and judicial cooperation in criminal matters.[3]

The wider range of actors subject to review raises new questions about the range of acts subject to review. The European Council cannot adopt legislative measures and very few agencies have the power to adopt legally binding decisions.[4] If the Court adopts a narrow view in which 'acts' capable of being reviewed must bring about a change in a party's legal position, then most of the activity of these bodies would fall outside the radar. This would be a pity, as European Council guidelines are intended to inform legal changes, while EU institutions invariably not only follow the expert opinions of agencies in setting out legal norms, but are also obliged to do so unless they can find a substitute expert body and provide reasons for following the opinion of the latter.[5] There are, therefore, strong arguments for the accountability of these activities.

Article 263(1) TFEU uses a formula that was first used in the *ERTA* judgment for determining when a measure is subject to review.[6] A measure will be reviewable not merely when it is a formal legal act but, notwithstanding its form, when it is intended to produce legal effects. When will this be the case? In *IBM*, the company IBM challenged a Commission Decision indicating that it had initiated proceedings against it to determine whether IBM was in breach of EU competition law. The Commission argued that the Decision to open proceedings was not a formal act in any way and was not therefore reviewable.

Case 60/81 *IBM v Commission* [1981] ECR 2639

8. According to Article[263 TFEU] proceedings may be brought for a declaration that acts of the council and the commission other than recommendations or opinions are void. That remedy is available in order to ensure, as required by Article [19(1) TEU], that in the interpretation and application of the Treaty the law is observed, and it would be inconsistent with that objective to interpret restrictively the conditions under which the action is admissible by limiting its scope merely to the categories of measures referred to in Article [288 TFEU].

9. In order to ascertain whether the measures in question are acts within the meaning of Article [263] it is necessary, therefore, to look to their substance ... any measure the legal effects of which are binding on, and capable of affecting the interests of, the applicant by bringing about a distinct change in his legal position is an act or decision which may be the subject of an action under Article [263] for a declaration that it is void. However, the form in which such acts or decisions are cast is, in principle, immaterial as regards the question whether they are open to challenge under that Article.

---

[1] On the organisation of the European Council see pp. 78–81.
[2] See pp. 66–7.
[3] Case C-160/03 *Spain* v *Eurojust* [2005] ECR I-2077; Case T-411/06 *Sogelma* v *EAR* [2008] ECR II-2771.
[4] Article 15(1) TEU.
[5] Case T-13/99 *Pfizer Animal Health* v *Council* [2002] ECR II-3305.
[6] Case 22/70 *Commission* v *Council (ERTA)* [1971] ECR 263.

10. In the case of acts or decisions adopted by a procedure involving several stages, in particular where they are the culmination of an internal procedure, it is clear from the case law that in principle an act is open to review only if it is a measure definitively laying down the position of the Commission or the Council on the conclusion of that procedure, and not a provisional measure intended to pave the way for the final decision.

11. It would be otherwise only if acts or decisions adopted in the course of the preparatory proceedings not only bore all the legal characteristics referred to above but in addition were themselves the culmination of a special procedure distinct from that intended to permit the Commission or the Council to take a decision on the substance of the case.

12. Furthermore, it must be noted that whilst measures of a purely preparatory character may not themselves be the subject of an application for a declaration that they are void, any legal defects therein may be relied upon in an action directed against the definitive act for which they represent a preparatory step.

The measure will therefore be reviewable if it brings about a change in the applicant's legal position. However, in *IBM*, the Court found that the decision to initiate proceedings was just a preparatory measure. It did not compromise IBM's rights of defence which were safeguarded later in the procedure. Central to the Court's reasoning was that the Commission had not yet taken a 'definitive position' (paragraph 12). What does this mean?

First, there will be no 'definitive position' and no reviewable act if the institution does not have the competence to adopt the act. In *Sunzest*, the Commission instructed the Belgian authorities at Antwerp that they should not recognise certificates issued by the 'Turkish Federated State of Cyprus' certifying the fitness of citrus fruit from Northern Cyprus.[7] Whilst the language of the Commission's letter was mandatory in nature, the Court did not recognise it as producing legal effects. It noted that the national authorities had exclusive responsibility under the Directive to apply protective measures against fruit from third countries. The Commission, in the Court's view, could only have been expressing an opinion. Such opinions were not reviewable.[8] The challenge with this is that it will often be difficult to know if the institution has some competence or not, and everything will hang on fine-grained interpretations of whether it has the power to do something or not.[9]

Secondly, the act is likely only to be considered definitive if the language is both reasonably imperative and alters the institution's position. Thus, restating an existing position is not reviewable.[10] Conversely, indicating no more than an intention to follow a particular line of conduct will not be reviewable.[11] There must be some stronger reorientation. This is often difficult to predict. In *Commission* v *Netherlands*, the Court held that the Code of Conduct on Public Access to Documents was not a reviewable act.[12] It considered it to be no more than a voluntary coordination between the Council and the Commission to ensure their approaches did not diverge, which did no more than set out general principles. This was notwithstanding

7 Case C-50/90 *Sunzest* v *Commission* [1991] ECR I-2917.
8 More recently Case T-212/06 *Bowland Dairy Products* v *Commission*, Judgment of 29 October 2009.
9 For different views of the same measure by the General Court and Court of Justice see Case T-185/94 *Geotronics* v *Commission* [1995] ECR II-2795; Case C-395/95 *Geotronics* v *Commission* [1997] ECR I-2271.
10 Case T-351/02 *Deutsche Bahn* v *Commission* [2006] ECR II-1047.
11 Case T-185/05 *Italy* v *Commission* [2008] ECR II-3207.
12 Case C-58/94 *Netherlands* v *Council* [1996] ECR I-2169.

that the Code was actually a detailed document which is not much further elaborated in either the Council or Commission Decisions implementing it.

Thirdly, the Court is more likely to find an act reviewable if it brings to an end or suspends some decision-making procedure. Whilst in *IBM*, therefore, the Decision to initiate competition proceedings was not reviewable, the position is different if the Commission decides *not* to initiate proceedings.[13] In *Air France*, the Commission issued an oral statement that it had no jurisdiction to consider a takeover of Dan Air by British Airways.[14] There was no text nor was the oral statement addressed to anyone. Furthermore, the statement did not follow any notification of the takeover by British Airways to the Commission, as required by the then Merger Regulation 4064/89/EC. The Court considered the statement to be reviewable, claiming that the measure had legal effects by reaffirming national jurisdiction over the merger and absolving the parties of their duty to notify the takeover under the Merger Regulation.

A similar approach was shown in *Commission* v *Council (Stability and Growth Pact)*.[15] This case concerned the stability and growth pact which requires those states who have the euro as their currency to maintain fiscal discipline and avoid excessive government deficits. The Commission reported both France and Germany to the Council for running excessive budgetary deficits. The Council did two things. First, it decided not to follow the Commission's recommendations to impose sanctions on France and Germany. Secondly, it stated that the procedure would be held in abeyance. Germany and France had made certain commitments. The Council stated that if these were not met, the procedure could be continued. The Commission sought judicial review of the Council's two measures.

On the first measure, the Court of Justice ruled that there had simply been no decision. In its view, there was not the majority to act on the Commission's recommendations, and therefore nothing had taken place. There was thus nothing to review. It came to a different view on the second measure. It noted that this was not merely confirming the existing position but making it conditional on Germany and France meeting certain commitments. It was altering a defined position, and it was intended to change the legal responsibilities of those two states. The measure was therefore reviewable.

Whilst it is possible to rationalise the decisions of the Court, the case law is confusing and arbitrary. The two measures in *Commission* v *Council* were, in practice, part and package of the same thing, and it makes no sense to look at one but not the other. Similarly, the distinction between decisions to start and not to start competition investigations is economic nonsense. This confusion also holds out little prospect that the new actors, the European Council and the agencies, will be held to account.

3 GROUNDS OF REVIEW

Four grounds of review are formally listed in Article 263 TFEU: lack of competence; infringement of an essential procedural requirement; infringement of the Treaty or of any rule of law relating to its application; and misuse of power. These have been subject to significant case law and, over time, the grounds have been reconfigured around four headings:

---

[13] Case C-39/93 P *SFEI* v *Commission* [1994] ECR I-2681.

[14] Case T-3/93 *Air France* v *Commission* [1994] ECR II-121. R. Greaves, 'The Nature and Binding Effect of Decisions under Article 189 EC' (1996) 21 *ELRev*. 3, 9–10.

[15] Case C-27/04 *Commission* v *Council (Stability and Growth Pact)* [2004] ECR I-6649.

in its review of legality ... the Community judicature conducts a full review as to whether the Commission applied properly the relevant rules of law. On the other hand, the [General Court] cannot take the place of the Commission on issues where the latter must carry out complex economic and ecological assessments ... In this respect, the Court is obliged to confine itself to verifying that the measure in question is not vitiated by a manifest error or a misuse of powers, that the competent authority did not clearly exceed the bounds of its discretion and that the procedural guarantees, which are of particularly fundamental importance in this context, have been fully observed.[16]

Rearranging the order of these groupings, they can be categorised in the following way:

(i) the institution in question must not exceed the power granted to it;

(ii) it must not abuse the discretion granted to it by a manifest error of assessment or an abuse of power;

(iii) there must not be a breach of process; this will involve all cases of a failure to give reasons but it will also involve violation of the rights of defence of parties that are subject to administrative proceedings;

(iv) there must be no breach of the substantive obligations imposed by EU law. This comprises not just explicit provisions of EU law, but also fundamental rights[17] and certain principles on which there has been extensive case law: those of legal certainty, non-discrimination and proportionality.[18]

(i) Lack of competence

An EU institution will be found to have acted illegally if it has exceeded the legal powers granted to it. This is relatively rare. The Union has very broad powers, most notably in Article 352 TFEU, the flexibility provision, which allows it to take action necessary to realise the objectives of the Union where no other legislative procedure is available.[19] An EU institution will, therefore, rarely be found to have taken action which is not available to the Union.[20] Instead, there tend to be two circumstances where an EU institution is found to have exceeded its powers: first, if it has taken action that should have been taken by other EU institutions and, secondly, if it has exceeded delegated powers granted to it by a piece of EU legislation.

The first goes to institutional balance, preserving both the institutional checks and balances within the Treaties and protecting the prerogatives of the different institutions. This is addressed in part through the case law on whether legislation has been adopted under the appropriate legal base.[21] In institutional terms, this case law is above all about whether the legislative powers of the different institutions have been respected.

---

[16] Case T-263/07 *Estonia* v *Commission*, Judgment of 23 September 2009.

[17] See Chapter 6.

[18] These have traditionally been known as general principles of law. This will not be possible after the Lisbon Treaty as this term is now used for all the case law of the Court on fundamental rights which is inspired by the ECHR and the constitutional traditions of Member States, Article 6(3) TEU.

[19] See pp. 214–19.

[20] The only example is Opinion 2/94 *Re Accession of the Community to the ECHR* [1996] ECR I-1759.

[21] See pp. 95–8.

Occasionally, however, an institution adopts a unilateral measure which should have been adopted by another. In *Safe Countries of Origin*,[22] under the legal regime at the time, EU legislation on the granting or withdrawal of refugee status had to be based on the ordinary legislative procedure if there were already common rules in force. In 2005, a Directive was adopted setting out principles for the grant and withdrawal of refugee status. Provision was made in it for the idea of safe country of origin. Persons coming from such countries were presumed not to be entitled to refugee status. The Directive stated that the Council would draw up a list of safe countries of origin having consulted the Parliament. The Parliament challenged this procedure. It argued that as EU legislation was now in force, further rules on what was a safe country of origin could only be drawn up through the ordinary legislative procedure. The Council did not have competence to agree them unilaterally. The Court agreed. It held the rules regarding the manner in which EU institutions made decisions were set by the Treaty alone and were not at the disposal of the institutions or Member States. To allow the Council to set new procedures would undermine the institutional balance in the Treaty and the Council did not have the competence to do this.

The second context in which institutions are found to have formally exceeded their powers is where the Commission is delegated certain powers and acts outside these powers. *Boyle* concerned the common fisheries policies.[23] Funding was received from the Union but a number of conditions were attached to it, notably a concern not to increase the overall national fishing capacities. To this end, the Council delegated to the Commission powers to determine when modernisation of fishing vessels was appropriate. This was allowed, above all, for modernisation and safety reasons. The applicants, a group of Irish fishermen, successfully challenged a Commission Decision which introduced new criteria that were not in the parent instrument, namely that the boat be registered, be at least five years old and the works concern a particular part of the boat. It was argued successfully that nothing in the original legislation gave the Commission the power to introduce additional criteria, and these were therefore illegal.

(ii) Manifest error of assessment and abuse of power

More common than a lack of competence is an abuse of discretion. This will happen in two circumstances: where there has been a manifest error of assessment and where there has been an abuse of power.

The central judgment on manifest error of assessment is *Tetra Laval*. The case concerned a conglomerate merger between Tetra Laval, the world-leader for carton packaging, and Sidel, a company specialising in PET packaging.[24] This was a form of packaging composed of a resin through which oxygen and light can pass. The Commission disallowed the merger on the grounds that Tetra Laval would leverage its dominant position on the market for cartons to persuade its customers on that market switching to PET to use Sidel's goods, thereby eliminating competition in that market. The General Court found that the Commission had committed a manifest error of assessment in that it had used reports which overestimated the possibility for leveraging and the possibility for growth in the PET market. The Commission appealed to the Court of Justice.

---

[22] Case C-133/06 *Parliament v Council (safe countries of origin)*, Judgment of 6 May 2008.
[23] Joined Cases T-218/03–T-240/03 *Boyle v Commission* [2006] ECR II-1699. For another instance see also Case T-263/07 *Estonia v Commission*, Judgment of 23 September 2009.
[24] A conglomerate merger is a merger between firms engaged in unrelated business activities: here cartons and PET.

Case C–12/03 P *Commission* v *Tetra Laval* [2005] ECR I–987

39. Whilst the Court recognises that the Commission has a margin of discretion with regard to economic matters, that does not mean that the Community Courts must refrain from reviewing the Commission's interpretation of information of an economic nature. Not only must the Community Courts, inter alia, establish whether the evidence relied on is factually accurate, reliable and consistent but also whether that evidence contains all the information which must be taken into account in order to assess a complex situation and whether it is capable of substantiating the conclusions drawn from it ...

41. Although the [General Court] stated ... that proof of anti-competitive conglomerate effects of a merger of the kind notified calls for a precise examination, supported by convincing evidence, of the circumstances which allegedly produce those effects, it by no means added a condition relating to the requisite standard of proof but merely drew attention to the essential function of evidence, which is to establish convincingly the merits of an argument or, as in the present case, of a decision on a merger...

44. The analysis of a 'conglomerate-type' concentration is a prospective analysis in which, first, the consideration of a lengthy period of time in the future and, secondly, the leveraging necessary to give rise to a significant impediment to effective competition mean that the chains of cause and effect are dimly discernible, uncertain and difficult to establish. That being so, the quality of the evidence produced by the Commission in order to establish that it is necessary to adopt a decision declaring the concentration incompatible with the common market is particularly important, since that evidence must support the Commission's conclusion that, if such a decision were not adopted, the economic development envisaged by it would be plausible.

45. It follows from those various factors that the [General Court] did not err in law when it set out the tests to be applied in the exercise of its power of judicial review or when it specified the quality of the evidence which the Commission is required to produce in order to demonstrate that the requirements ... of the Regulation are satisfied.

46. With respect to the particular case of judicial review exercised by the [General Court] in the judgment under appeal, it is not apparent from the example given by the Commission, which relates to the growth in the use of PET packaging for sensitive products, that [General Court] exceeded the limits applicable to the review of an administrative decision by the Community Courts. Contrary to what the Commission claims, paragraph 211 of the judgment under appeal merely restates more concisely, in the form of a finding by the [General Court], the admission made by the Commission at the hearing ... that its forecast in the contested decision with regard to the increase in the use of PET for packaging UHT milk was exaggerated. In paragraph 212 of the judgment under appeal, the [General Court] gave the reasons for its finding that the evidence produced by the Commission was unfounded by stating that, of the three independent reports cited by the Commission, only the PCI report contained information on the use of PET for milk packaging. It went on, in that paragraph, to show that the evidence produced by the Commission was unconvincing by pointing out that the increase forecast in the PCI report was of little significance and that the Commission's forecast was inconsistent with the undisputed figures ... contained in the other reports. In paragraph 213 of the judgment under appeal, the [General Court] merely stated that the Commission's analysis was incomplete, which made it impossible to confirm its forecasts, given the differences between those forecasts and the forecasts made in the other reports ...

48. It follows from these examples that the [General Court] carried out its review in the manner required of it, as set out in paragraph 39 of this judgment. It explained and set out the reasons why the Commission's conclusions seemed to it to be inaccurate in that they were based on insufficient, incomplete, insignificant and inconsistent evidence.

The Court went on to dismiss the Commission's appeal. The Court was here stating that it will not substitute its assessment for that of the institutions but will check that any measure is sufficiently substantiated by the evidence provided, and the evidence deployed must be accurate, reliable, consistent and sufficiently complete. A distinction is therefore drawn between the assessment of the institution (not reviewable) and the grounds for the assessment (reviewable). Yet, the demanding level of evidence that must be presented leads, as Craig suggests, to the distinction being eroded.

> **P. Craig, *EU Administrative Law* (Oxford, Oxford University Press, 2006) 470**
>
> The determination of whether the evidence is factually accurate, reliable and consistent requires evaluation, not simply observation. This is *a fortiori* so in relation to issues such as whether the evidence contains all the information that must be taken into account in order to assess a complex situation and whether the evidence is capable of sustaining the conclusions drawn from it. The need for complex assessment is equally present when deciding on the 'various chains of cause with a view to ascertaining which of them are most likely'.[25] It is, however, precisely in relation to these more complex findings, where the facts are multifaceted and difficult, requiring a greater degree of evaluative judgment, that there can be real differences of view as to the facts and possible consequences flowing from them.

If, as Craig persuasively argues, the Union courts are constraining the discretion of the institutions here, this raises the question of what is really taking place. It is probably overstating the argument to say unconditionally that they intervene to replace the view of the latter with their own view. In *Tetra Laval*, neither Union court, for example, sets out a positive thesis on the anti-competitive effects of conglomerate mergers. Instead, they look at whether the argument of the EU institution is more plausible than that of the applicant. Whilst there may be a presumption that it is, it would appear from *Tetra Laval* that this is fairly easy to rebut. Furthermore, the difficulty with a test of comparative plausibility is its inherent instability. Every applicant will believe its arguments are better than those of the EU institution, and every EU institution will be wary about how Union courts measure this.[26]

In contrast to the doctrine of manifest error of assessment, that of misuse of powers can be mentioned almost as a postscript. It arises if it appears:

> on the basis of objective, relevant and consistent indications to have been adopted to achieve purposes other than those for which it was intended.[27]

However, the principle has rarely brought joy to applicants. First, as the test is essentially a subjective one it has proved difficult for applicants to prove the necessary bad faith on the part of the institution. Secondly, the threshold is further raised by the requirement that the decision

---

[25] Case C-12/03 P *Commission v Tetra Laval* [2005] ECR I-987, para. 43.

[26] An indication of the challenges can be found in the field of cartels. A study of challenges to Commission Decisions between 1995 and 2004 found that they were only fully successful in 6 per cent of cases. There were partially successful in securing a reduction of the fine in 122 cases (61 per cent). The predominant ground was insufficient evidence (manifest error of assessment) provided by the Commission. The Union courts were, thus, finding in these cases that it erred in some of its reasoning but not in all of it – a very woolly scenario. C. Harding and A. Gibbs, 'Why Go to Court in Europe? An Analysis of Cartel Appeals 1995–2004' (2005) 30 *ELRev.* 349, 365–7.

[27] Case C-323/88 *Sermes v Directeur de Service des Douanes de Strasbourg* [1990] ECR I-3027.

challenged must have been guided exclusively or predominantly by the motivation to use the power for purposes other than those for which they were conferred.[28] This is difficult to prove and, outside two staff cases,[29] the principle has only been successfully invoked once.[30]

(iii) Rights of process

There are, to be sure, procedures set out throughout the Treaties and also through secondary legislation. These are to secure institutional balance and to enable particular actors to have a voice. Breach of these is a violation of rights of process but is also a breach of substantial provisions of EU law. There are, however, more general rights of process in EU law which exist in the absence of specific guarantees. These include the right to know the reasons for a legal measure, the rights to a hearing where one's interests are restricted, and particular rights of defence. It is this latter group that is being considered here. Such rights of process are seen as having a dual function in EU law. Process is seen, first, as important for understanding the basis for the decision and whether this is lawful, and secondly, to enable parties to defend entitlements granted to them.

The rationale for both functions lies in that of securing effective judicial review of the acts of other EU institutions. This was set out most explicitly in *Kadi*. The judgment, addressed in Chapter 5,[31] concerned a challenge to an EU Regulation implementing UN sanctions restricting financial and material resources to individuals who were on a list of people suspected of associating with Usama Bin Laden and Al Qaeda. Kadi was on this list, which was contained in Annex I to the Regulation. He challenged the Regulation, claiming that due process had been ignored, in that he had been given no opportunity to make a case as to why he should not be on that list, nor to challenge the grounds for placing him on the list.

Joined Cases C–402/05 P and C–415/05 P *Kadi and Al Barakaat International Foundation* **v** *Council*, **Judgment of 8 November 2008**

335. According to settled case law, the principle of effective judicial protection is a general principle of Community law stemming from the constitutional traditions common to the Member States, which has been enshrined in Articles 6 and 13 ECHR, this principle having furthermore been reaffirmed by Article 47 EUCFR ...

336. In addition, having regard to the Court's case law in other fields ... it must be held in this instance that the effectiveness of judicial review, which it must be possible to apply to the lawfulness of the grounds on which, in these cases, the name of a person or entity is included in the list forming Annex I to the contested Regulation and leading to the imposition on those persons or entities of a body of restrictive measures, means that the Community authority in question is bound to communicate those grounds to the person or entity concerned, so far as possible, either when that inclusion is decided on or, at

---

[28] Case C-48/96 P *Windpark Groothusen* v *Commission* [1998] ECR I-2873; Case C-407/04 P *Dalmine SpA* v *Commission* [2007] ECR I-829.

[29] Joined Cases 18/65 and 35/65 *Gutmann* v *Commission* [1966] ECR 103; Case 105/75 *Giuffrida* v *Council* [1976] ECR 1395.

[30] Joined Cases 351/85 and 360/85 *Fabrique de Fer de Charleroi* v *Commission* [1987] ECR 3639.

[31] See pp. 217–19.

the very least, as swiftly as possible after that decision in order to enable those persons or entities to exercise, within the periods prescribed, their right to bring an action.

337. Observance of that obligation to communicate the grounds is necessary both to enable the persons to whom restrictive measures are addressed to defend their rights in the best possible conditions and to decide, with full knowledge of the relevant facts, whether there is any point in their applying to the Community judicature ... and to put the latter fully in a position in which it may carry out the review of the lawfulness of the Community measure in question which is its duty under the EC Treaty.

The Court went on to find a breach of Kadi's rights of defence. According to *Kadi*, the requirement of judicial control is satisfied, first, through the duty, set out in Article 296(2) TFEU, for all EU legal acts to provide the reasons on which they are based. As we have seen in Chapter 9, this relationship is not unproblematic. As the duty to give reasons is simply about enabling parties to know their rights and courts to know the basis for the measure, the reasons need be no more detailed than required for that purpose.[32]

It is satisfied, secondly, through parties being able to 'defend their rights in the best possible fashion, with full knowledge of the relevant facts' (paragraph 337). However, if the duty to provide reasons is a general duty in EU law, there is not an equivalent right for all actors to have a hearing in all circumstances. *Kadi* refers to it being present whenever restrictive measures are taken against the actors in question. The meaning of this is uncertain. The fact that a measure adversely affects a party's interests is insufficient to grant them a hearing.[33] However, if a party is named or addressed in a Union measure and their interests are significantly affected, they are entitled to a hearing.[34]

There is an intermediate category where a party is not named in a measure but nevertheless has standing under Article 263(4) TFEU. In *Al Jubail*, the Court stated that if a measure directly and individually concerned an undertaking, that undertaking would be entitled to a hearing.[35] By contrast, parties will not necessarily have a right to a hearing where they complain to the Commission about a state aid or anti-competitive practice. In such circumstances, the Court has ruled they are doing no more than provide information, and this is insufficient to justify a hearing.[36] They will have no right to a hearing unless secondary legislation requires it.[37]

Turning to the substance of the right, the right to be heard encompasses an obligation on the institution to make its case known to the party concerned, and the right of that party to reply.[38] There is a right to be heard on all matters of fact and law which form the basis for the

---

[32] Case C-113/00 *Spain* v *Commission* [2002] ECR I-7601.

[33] Case T-37/92 *BEUC and NCC* v *Commission* [1994] ECR II-285.

[34] Case C-32/95 P *Commission* v *Lisrestal and Others* [1996] ECR I-5373. See also recently Case C-141/08 P *Foshan Shunde Yongjian Housewares and Hardware Co.* v *Commission*, Judgment of 1 October 2009.

[35] Case C-49/88 *Al-Jubail* v *Council* [1991] ECR I-3187. It may be that this formulation will be changed for regulatory acts following the Lisbon Treaty. As these only have to be of direct concern to undertakings for the latter to have standing, it would make sense that undertakings need only be directly concerned by a measure to have a right to a hearing.

[36] Case T-198/01 *Technische Glaswerke Ilmenau* v *Commission* [2004] ECR II-2717.

[37] There is limited provision for this in the case of competition under Regulation 1/2003/EC on the implementation of the rules on competition [2003] OJ L1/1, article 27(3) and in the case of mergers under Regulation 139/2004/EC on the control of concentrations by undertakings [2004] OJ L24/22, article 18(4).

[38] Joined Cases 56/64 and 58/64 *Consten and Grundig* v *Commission* [1966] ECR 299.

measure but not on the final position which the administration intends to adopt.[39] The institution is thus not obliged to hear an applicant with regard to a factual assessment which forms part of its final decision.[40]

The rights of defence are distinct from the right to be heard as it applies where EU institutions are to impose some sanction on a party.[41] The rights of defence include the opportunity for the applicant to make known their views on the truth and relevance of the facts alleged;[42] a duty to set out to the applicant the presumed facts justifying the investigation;[43] prosecution only for criminal or administrative penalties that are clearly and unambiguously defined (*nullum crimen, nulla poena sine lege*);[44] the presumption of innocence;[45] the right not to be tried twice for the same facts (*ne bis in idem*);[46] the right to judicial review of any sanction;[47] the right to legal assistance and the right for all lawyer-client communications prepared for the purpose of defence to be privileged;[48] the right to be heard in one's own defence before any administrative sanction is imposed;[49] protection from self-incrimination,[50] and access to the file setting out the allegations.[51]

These rights of process have in recent years increasingly been subsumed within a new right, which is that of observance of the principle of sound administration.[52] There is a dual element to this principle. First, as set out by the General Court recently in *Holland Malt*:

> observance of that principle requires a diligent and impartial investigation by the Commission of the measure at issue. The Commission is therefore under an obligation to obtain all the necessary points of view, in particular by requesting information... in order to make a finding in full knowledge of all the facts relevant at the time of adoption of its decision.[53]

This imposes a duty of care on the institutions, which has both a substantive and procedural element. Substantively, the Commission must act in good faith[54] and give due consideration and attention both to all the arguments presented[55] and to the task in hand.[56] At the very least,

---

[39] Case T-16/02 *Audi* v *OHIM (TDI)* [2003] ECR II-5167.

[40] Case T-458/05 *Tegometall International* v *OHIM – Wuppermann (TEK)* [2007] ECR II-4721.

[41] They cover all proceedings leading up to this sanction, no matter how preparatory: Case 46/87 *Hoechst AG* v *Commission* [1989] ECR 2859.

[42] Joined Cases C-204/00 P, C-205/00 P, C-211/00 P, C-213/00 P, C-217/00 P and C-219/00 P *Aalborg Portland A/S and Others* v *Commission* [2004] ECR I-123.

[43] Joined Cases 46/87 and 227/88 *Hoechst AG* v *Commission* [1989] ECR 2859; Case T-99/04 *Treuhand* v *Commission*, Judgment of 8 July 2008.

[44] Case C-303/05 *Advocaten voor de Wereld* v *Leden van de Ministerraad* [2007] ECR I-3633.

[45] Case C-344/08 *Rubach*, Judgment of 16 July 2009.

[46] Case C-469/03 *Miraglia* [2005] ECR I-2009.

[47] Case 222/86 *UNECTEF* v *Heylens* [1987] ECR 4097.

[48] Case 155/79 *AM & S Europe Ltd* v *Commission* [1982] ECR 1575; Joined Cases T-125/03 and T-253/03 *Akzo Nobel Chemicals Ltd and Akcros Chemicals Ltd* v *Commission* [2007] ECR II-3523.

[49] Case 17/74 *Transocean Marine Paint* v *Commission* [1974] ECR 1063.

[50] Case 374/87 *Orkem* v *Commission* [1989] ECR 3283.

[51] This is not an unqualified right. It is subject to the principle that confidential information supplied by third parties be respected. Furthermore, only failure to disclose inculpatory information will render a measure automatically illegal. Failure to disclose exculpatory information will only render any measure illegal if it effectively hinders the applicant's rights of defence: Case T-30/91 *Solvay SA* v *Commission* [1995] ECR II-1775.

[52] On the evolution of this right, see H.-P. Nehl, *Principles of Administrative Procedure in EC Law* (Oxford and Portland, Hart, 1999) 127–49; P. Craig, *EU Administrative Law* (Oxford, Oxford University Press, 2006) 373–81.

[53] Case T-369/06 *Holland Malt* v *Commission*, Judgment of 9 September 2009, para. 195. See also Case T-198/01 *Technische Glaswerke Ilmenau* v *Commission* [2004] ECR II-2717.

[54] For a failure here see Case T-410/03 *Hoechst* v *Commission* [2008] ECR II-881.

[55] Case 210/81 *Demo-Studio Schmidt* v *Commission* [1983] ECR 3045.

[56] Case C-16/90 *Nölle* v *Hauptzollamt Bremen-Freihafen* [1991] ECR I-5163.

it must be able to show the basis for its decision and how this relates to the information provided to it. This extends beyond merely providing reasons for the measure. Those reasons must be coherent, take account of the evidence provided and form the basis for the measure itself.[57] Procedurally, the principle of sound administration requires EU institutions to be proactive in gathering information. There is, in particular, a duty to fill in gaps in information through seeking it from parties who have a right to a hearing.[58] However, it does not appear to give new rights to new parties, and goes more to the type of information that EU institutions can request of parties who are being offered a hearing.[59]

The second dimension to the principle of sound administration is that EU institutions must exercise their powers within a reasonable period of time.[60] The delay must not be such as to compromise the rights of defence.[61] The reasonableness of the time taken will, however, be assessed in relation to the particular circumstances of each case: its background, complexity, the procedural stages followed and its importance for the various parties involved.[62] These conditions can be read separately, so the complexity of a case may justify a lengthy investigation.[63] This has resulted in the Union courts taking a very relaxed view of what is an unreasonable period of time. Whilst, where the case seems uncomplicated, they have ruled that twenty-six months is excessive,[64] in other cases where the applicant has contributed to the delay or the matter has had to go through the domestic courts, they have not found seven or twelve years unduly long.[65]

(iv) Infringement of the Treaties or of any rule of law relating to their application

The final set of grounds for review relate to infringement of the Treaties or any rule relating to their application. This can be a breach of a substantive piece of EU law, be it a provision of the Treaties or a piece of secondary legislation that binds the institution in question.[66] It can also be a breach of a number of other types of norm:

- fundamental rights: the substance of these were set out in more detail in Chapter 6;[67]
- proportionality: this is also discussed in more detail elsewhere in Chapter 9. Insofar as it governs the behaviour of EU institutions, in fields where these enjoy discretion, measures will only be unlawful if the courts consider these to be manifestly inappropriate with regard to the objective in hand;[68]

---

[57] Case T 263/07 *Estonia* v *Commission*, Judgment of 23 September 2009.
[58] Case T-420/05 *Vischim* v *Commission*, Judgment of 7 October 2009.
[59] Case C-367/95 P *Commission* v *Sytraval* [1998] ECR I-1719.
[60] Joined Cases C-74/00 P and C-75/00 P *Falck and Acciaierie di Bolzano* v *Commission* [2002] ECR I-7869; Joined Cases C-346/03 and C-529/03 *Atzeni and Others* v *Regione autonoma della Sardegna* [2006] ECR I-1875.
[61] Joined Cases C-238/99 P, C-244/99 P, C-245/99 P, C-247/99 P, C-250/99 P–C-252/99 P and C-254/99 P *Limburgse Vinyl Maatschappij NV and Others* v *Commission* [2003] ECR I-8375.
[62] Case T-73/95 *Oliveira* v *Commission* [1997] ECR II-381.
[63] Joined Cases C-322/07 P, C-327/07 P and C-338/07 P *Papierfabrik August Koehler* v *Commission*, Judgment of 3 September 2009.
[64] Case 223/85 *RSV* v *Commission* [1987] ECR 4617.
[65] Joined Cases T-30/01–T-32/01 and T-86/02–T-88/02 *Diputación Foral de Álava* v *Commission*, Judgment of 9 September 2009; Case T-347/03 *Branco* v *Commission* [2005] ECR II-2555.
[66] There is one exception to this. The Court of Justice will not allow judicial review of a Union measure for non-compliance with the WTO agreement on the grounds that the agreement is not such as to generate rights for individuals. Case C-377/02 *Van Parys* v *BIRB* [2005] ECR I-1465.
[67] See pp. 248–52 in particular.
[68] Case C-331/88 *R* v *MAFF, ex parte Fedesa* [1990] ECR I-4023.

- non-discrimination;
- legal certainty;
- legitimate expectations.

As the first two of these have been addressed in detail elsewhere, this section will focus on the latter three norms: non-discrimination, legal certainty and legitimate expectations. Readers are asked, however, to refer to the other sections of the book for discussion of fundamental rights and proportionality.

(a) Non-discrimination

EU law protects against certain status harms, where parties are disadvantaged on grounds of their enjoying a particular status, be it gender, ethnicity, race, age, disability, religion, belief or sexual orientation. These are set out in Articles 10 and 19 TFEU. Beyond these, there is a general principle that like cases be treated alike. The seminal case is *Ruckdeschel*. It concerned identical subsidies that were historically granted to starch and quellmehl producers by the EU institutions. The reason was that the two products were seen as economically substitutable. The quellmehl subsidy was withdrawn. Ruckdeschel, a producer, challenged this, arguing that there was a discrimination between it and starch producers. The Court of Justice agreed.

Joined Cases 117/76 and 16/77 *Ruckdeschel v Council* [1977] ECR 1753

7. The second subparagraph of [Article 40(2) TFEU] provides that the common organization of agricultural markets 'shall exclude any discrimination between producers or consumers within the [Union]'.

   Whilst this wording undoubtedly prohibits any discrimination between producers of the same product it does not refer in such clear terms to the relationship between different industrial or trade sectors in the sphere of processed agricultural products. This does not alter the fact that the prohibition of discrimination laid down in the aforesaid provision is merely a specific enunciation of the general principle of equality which is one of the fundamental principles of Community law.

   This principle requires that similar situations shall not be treated differently unless differentiation is objectively justified.

8. It must therefore be ascertained whether quellmehl and starch are in a comparable situation, in particular in the sense that starch can be substituted for quellmehl in the specific use to which the latter product is traditionally put.

   In this connexion it must first be noted that the Community Regulations were, until 1974, based on the assertion that such substitution was possible …

   While the Council and the Commission have given detailed information on the manufacture and sale of the products in question, they have produced no new technical or economic data which appreciably change the previous assessment of the position. It has not therefore been established that, so far as the Community system of production refunds is concerned, quellmehl and starch are no longer in comparable situations.

   Consequently, these products must be treated in the same manner unless differentiation is objectively justified.

The prohibition on discrimination will prohibit not just like cases being treated differently but also different cases being treated in a like manner.[69] In practice, however, it is rare that there will be a finding of discrimination. Often, where there is differential treatment the Court will simply state that the cases are not alike. This will always be the case where the EU institution can justify the differential treatment (e.g. there is a different basis for the treatment of each). In *Melli Bank*, for example, an Iranian bank pleaded discrimination on the grounds that Union sanctions had targeted it but not other British subsidiaries of Iranian banks.[70] The General Court had little difficulty in finding that there was no discrimination. It noted that the Regulation in question implemented a UN Security Council Resolution which targeted financial institutions engaged in assisting nuclear proliferation. For the Court this rationale provided a basis for the differential treatment.

The Court is thus engaged here in looking at the reasonableness of the Union measure. There is, correspondingly, less intense review where EU institutions enjoy a margin of discretion. Discrimination will only be found if the conduct borders on the 'arbitrary'.[71] In these circumstances the non-discrimination principle seems to add little to the proportionality principle.[72]

(b) Legal certainty

The principle of legal certainty has been protected within EU law for some time.[73] In *Heinrich*, it was stated as requiring that:

> Community rules enable those concerned to know precisely the extent of the obligations which are imposed on them. Individuals must be able to ascertain unequivocally what their rights and obligations are and take steps accordingly.[74]

The first dimension to this is a temporal one. There is a prohibition against retroactivity. A measure must not take effect prior to its publication.[75] It will thus not be retroactive if it regulates the future effects of situations which arose prior to publication. It will only be retroactive if it applies to events which have already been concluded.[76]

The principle is absolute in relation to penal measures.[77] The Court has also indicated that it should be observed strictly where the rules are liable to have financial consequences.[78] Other measures may exceptionally take effect before publication where the purpose to be achieved so demands and where the legitimate concerns of those concerned are respected. In *Fedesa*, following the annulment of a Directive outlawing the use of certain hormones, the subsequent Directive, which was published on 7 March 1988, stipulated that it was to take effect from the beginning of that year.[79] The reason was to prevent the market being unregulated for the period prior to March as a consequence of the annulment of an earlier Directive. The Court

---

[69] Joined Cases T-222/99, T-327/99 and T-329/99 *Martinez and Others* v *Parliament* [2001] ECR II-2823.
[70] Joined Cases T-246/08 and T-332/08 *Melli Bank* v *Council*, Judgment of 9 July 2009.
[71] Case 245/81 *Edeka* v *Commission* [1982] ECR 2745; Case C-479/93 *Francovich* v *Italian Republic (Francovich II)* [1995] ECR I-3843.
[72] M. Herdegen, 'The Equation Between the Principles of Equality and Proportionality' (1985) 22 *CMLRev.* 683.
[73] It was first set out in Joined Cases 42/59 and 49/59 *SNUPAT* v *High Authority* [1961] ECR 109.
[74] Case C-345/06 *Heinrich*, Judgment of 10 March 2009, para. 44.
[75] Case 84/78 *Tomadini* v *Amministrazione delle Finanze dello Stato* [1979] ECR 1801.
[76] Case 63/83 *R* v *Kent Kirk* [1984] ECR 2689.
[77] Case C-331/88 *R* v *MAFF, ex parte Fedesa* [1990] ECR I-4023.
[78] Case C-94/05 *Emsland-Stärke* [2006] ECR I-2619.
[79] Case C-331/88 *R* v *MAFF, ex parte Fedesa* [1990] ECR I-4023.

considered there to be no breach of the principle of the legal certainty in light of the short time-span between the annulment of the first Directive and the publication of the second.

The second dimension to legal certainty is that of clarity: enabling the subjects of EU law to know their rights and obligations. At the very least, this means that the EU law in question must be published. In *Heinrich*, an unpublished Annex to a Regulation which prohibited tennis rackets from being taken on civil air aircraft was found to be void because it had not been published.[80] Alongside this, the Court has repeatedly stated that EU legislation must be clear and its application foreseeable.[81] This would suggest that if a Union measure is obscure it could be struck down. However, this has yet to happen.

(c) Legitimate expectations

The principle of legitimate expectations is often linked to that of legal certainty. However, its roots lie in the concept of good faith and require that, having induced an operator to take one course of action, the administration should not then renege on that, so that the individual suffers loss.[82]

An example of how this might be claimed arose in *Branco*. Branco was awarded funding under the European Social Fund for the training of young adults. The training was certified by the Portuguese ministry who sent a request to the Commission for payment. The ministry subsequently found irregularities in the performance of Branco's duties under the contract. The Commission refused to make the final payment and sought repayment of the funds already granted. Branco claimed a violation of the principle of legitimate expectations in that the work had been certified by the Portuguese ministry in question. The General Court made the following observation:

> Three conditions must be satisfied in order to claim entitlement to the protection of legitimate expectations. First, precise, unconditional and consistent assurances originating from authorised and reliable sources must have been given to the person concerned by the Community authorities. Second, those assurances must be such as to give rise to a legitimate expectation on the part of the person to whom they are addressed. Third, the assurances given must comply with the applicable rules.[83]

In *Branco*, the General Court found that the action failed on the first condition. It noted that the decision to authorise payment was one for the Commission and not the Portuguese authorities, and it had given no assurances here. Even if assurances are made, they must create an expectation on the part of the applicant. This is not simply a subjective test. The expectation must be legitimate and Court will look to whether an ordinary, prudent trader would have relied on it on the basis of the institution's representation.[84] Finally, the Union measure in question must not be illegal. If it is, it will not generate any protected expectation.[85]

Although *Branco* refers to a precise, unconditional and consistent assurance, this assurance does not have to be individualised in the sense that the applicant must be named. It can be a

---

[80] Case C-345/06 *Heinrich*, Judgment of 10 March 2009. See also Case T-115/94 *Opel Austria* v *Council* [1997] ECR II-39.

[81] Case 325/85 *Ireland* v *Commission* [1987] ECR 5041; Case C-301/97 *Netherlands* v *Council* [2001] ECR I-8853.

[82] See generally S. Schonberg, *Legitimate Expectations in Administrative Law* (Oxford, Oxford University Press, 2000).

[83] Case T-347/03 *Branco* v *Commission* [2005] ECR II-255, para. 102.

[84] Case 265/85 *Van den Bergh en Jurgens* v *Commission* [1987] ECR 1155. On this see E. Sharpston, 'Legitimate Expectations and Economic Reality' (1990) 15 *ELRev*. 103, 108–15.

[85] Case T-336/94 *Efisol* v *Commission* [1996] ECR II-1343.

general statement or even a particular course of conduct which encourages certain expectations. In *Mulder*, farmers were paid by the Union to take land out of milk production to reduce milk surpluses. Mulder took his land out of production under the scheme but when he sought to resume milk production without paying a levy, he was refused on the ground that this possibility was only available to those who had produced milk in the preceding year. He argued that he had been encouraged to take his land out of production by the Union offering him premiums. This had led him to believe that there would be no penalties for his action. The Court of Justice agreed, ruling that:

> where a producer ... has been encouraged by a Community measure to suspend marketing for a limited period in the general interest ... he may legitimately expect not to be subject, upon the expiry of his undertaking, to restrictions which specifically affect him precisely because he availed himself of the possibilities offered by the Community provisions.[86]

In *Mulder*, the penalty was simply inconsistent with the existing policy framework. The question does arise, however, as to whether a reversal of policy could violate legitimate expectations.[87] The steady view of the Court is that it will not. Instead, there is a presumption of a freedom to legislate, as the Court considers that prudent traders ought to be able to take into account the possibility that the law might change.[88] In only one case has a reversal in policy given rise to a successful claim in legitimate expectations. In *CNTA*, the Commission suddenly stopped granting monetary compensation amounts (MCAs) in the colza and rape seed sectors.[89] MCAs are subsidies granted to traders designed to protect them against loss from currency fluctuations. This was a clear reversal of policy, which was unusual in that it was a sudden withdrawal of a subsidy. The financial effects were therefore immediate and unexpected. The Court found that there had been a breach of legitimate expectations in this case. Whilst MCAs could not be considered a guarantee against risks on the exchange rate, nevertheless, they meant, in practice, that a prudent trader might not insure himself against the risk. In the absence of an overriding public interest, the Court considered that the immediate withdrawal of MCAs with no provision for transitional measures breached EU law.

4 STANDING UNDER ARTICLE 263 TFEU

(i) Privileged and semi-privileged applicants

By virtue of Article 263(1) TFEU, the so-called privileged applicants – the Member States, the Commission, the Council and the European Parliament – have a general power to seek judicial review against acts of the EU institutions. This grants them general, unrestrained policing powers against the EU institutions, subject to the observance of the time limits set out in the final paragraph of Article 263 TFEU. The justification for this power to monitor and constrain is that each of these represents an important public interest that must be legally protected: the Member States represent individual national interests, the Council collective national interests,

---

[86] Case 120/86 *Mulder* v *Minister van Landbouw en Visserij* [1988] ECR 2321.
[87] For an argument that occasionally it should, see P. Craig, 'Substantive Legitimate Expectations in Domestic and Community Law' (1996) 55 *CLJ* 289, 299.
[88] Case 52/81 *Faust* v *Commission* [1982] ECR 3745.
[89] Case 74/74 *CNTA* v *Commission* [1975] ECR 533.

the European Parliament a pan-European democratic voice and the Commission a pan-European non-governmental public interest.

The actors in Article 263(2) TFEU – the European Central Bank, the Court of Auditors and the Committee of the Regions – are semi-privileged applicants. The justification for their interest in litigation is different. It is not to police generally but rather to protect their institutional prerogatives. It is a defensive power to ensure that other institutions do not trespass on their legal entitlements.

Infringement of these prerogatives can occur in three ways. First, an institution may fail to observe a procedure at the expense of another institution.[90] Secondly, an institution may use one procedure when it should have used another procedure which gives another institution greater entitlements:[91] so, for example, use of the consultation procedure rather than the ordinary legislative procedure. The final circumstance is when the institutional balance is shifted through the delegation of broad powers to the Commission at the expense of the primary legislative procedures. As this pre-empts other institutions' entitlements, they can challenge the delegation.

(ii) Non-privileged applicants

(a) Regulatory acts and legislative acts

Historically, most debate has centred around the circumstances under which private parties, so-called non-privileged applicants, can seek judicial review of acts of EU institutions. This is set out in Article 263(4) TFEU which introduces two amendments to the prior Treaty Article governing the same.

First, Article 263(4) TFEU provides that any natural or legal person may institute proceedings against an *act* which is either addressed to them or of direct and individual concern to them. This replaces an unhappy formulation which allowed individuals to challenge decisions addressed to them or decisions, which although in the form of regulation, were of direct and individual concern.[92] Over time, the Court focused attention away from the form of the act and more to the test of direct and individual concern. The procedure could therefore be used to challenge not only Decisions but also Regulations and Directives.[93] Yet the amendment represents a welcome and overdue clarification. It may also herald a slightly more expansive approach for, on its face, it allows instruments such as the Conclusions of the European Council or international agreements to be challenged by individuals, something that has not happened hitherto.

The second amendment concerns the establishment of a distinction between regulatory and other acts. To challenge regulatory acts individuals need only establish direct concern.[94] For other acts they must establish direct and individual concern. The distinction is therefore an

---

[90] Case C-65/90 *Parliament v Council* [1992] ECR I-4593.

[91] Case 70/88 *European Parliament v Council ('Chernobyl')* [1990] ECR 2041.

[92] On this see R. Greaves, 'Locus Standi under Article 173 EEC when Seeking Annulment of Regulation' (1986) 11 *ELRev*. 119.

[93] Case C-309/89 *Cordorníu v Council* [1994] ECR I-1853; Case C-10/95 P *Asocarne v Council and Commission* [1995] ECR I-4149; Case T-420/05 *Vischim v Commission*, Judgment of 7 October 2009.

[94] Prior to the Lisbon Treaty, the Court of Justice had already introduced more relaxed standing requirements in fields characterised by wide Commission regulatory powers (e.g. competition, state aids and anti-dumping). The change is part of a progression, therefore. On the earlier regime see A. Arnull, 'Challenging EC Anti-Dumping Regulations: The Problem of Admissibility' (1992) 13 *ECLR* 73.

axiomatic one. Unfortunately, whilst a distinction is made between legislative acts and non-legislative acts, with the latter comprising delegated acts and implementing acts,[95] no definition is provided of regulatory acts.

Some help can be found in the Future of Europe Convention that preceded the Constitutional Treaty. A Discussion Circle there considered the situation of the Court of Justice. In its Final Report, the *locus standi* requirements for non-privileged applicants were addressed:

> 22. A majority of those members who wanted the [provision] to be amended would prefer the option mentioning 'an act of general application'. However, some members felt that it would be more appropriate to choose the words 'a regulatory act', enabling a distinction to be established between legislative acts and regulatory acts, adopting, as the President of the Court had suggested, a restrictive approach to proceedings by private individuals against legislative acts (where the condition 'of direct and individual concern' still applies) and a more open approach as regards proceedings against regulatory acts.[96]

It seems that regulatory acts are intended to be non-legislative acts. Indeed, a strong case can be made for subjecting non-legislative acts to greater judicial scrutiny than legislative acts. The latter involve representative institutions. This is not the case with non-legislative acts taken by non-majoritarian institutions, such as the Commission or agencies. Judicial review can provide an opportunity for popular scrutiny and constraints that is lacking in non-legislative processes.

Yet, this begs the question as to what counts as a legislative act. Article 289(3) TFEU defines a legal act as anything adopted by one of the EU legislative procedures. This would leave all delegated and implementing acts as regulatory acts. This definition would make a lot of sense, as it suggests that any act not adopted by one of the legislative procedures should be subject to greater scrutiny precisely because it has not come through those procedures with their greater checks and balances and arguably greater legitimacy. However, historically, the Court of Justice has adopted a different definition of a legislative act: it is any measure that is couched in general and abstract terms.[97] In this regard, it is the phraseology that is important, as all that matters is the level of abstraction of the text rather than the number of interests affected or the procedure used.[98] It would be regrettable if such a test was adopted. It would allow EU institutions to escape judicial review through the formulation of the wording they deploy. More importantly, it would not address the justifications for increased judicial review. This is that processes have been used that do not involve representative institutions, and, in such circumstances, courts have to be particularly vigilant against executive abuse and more willing to consider the arguments of citizens who have not had the chance to press their arguments through their representatives.

(b) Direct concern

Historically, the case law on direct concern has been limited. This is because the greater impediment to standing for non-privileged applicants has been that of individual concern. This may change following the Lisbon Treaty. As we shall see, going through the case law, a high

---

[95] Articles 289–91 TFEU.
[96] The European Convention Secretariat, *Final Report of the Discussion Circle on the Court of Justice*, CONV 636/03.
[97] Joined Cases 16/62 and 17/62 *Confédération Nationale des Producteurs de Fruits et Légumes and Others* v *Council* [1962] ECR 471.
[98] Case C-10/95 P *Asocarne* v *Council and Commission* [1995] ECR I-4149.

proportion of the measures challenged may now be classified as regulatory acts. If that is so, direct concern will be the sole test for determining standing to challenge these measures. One would therefore expect considerably more litigation on its meaning and remit.

There are two dimensions to direct concern. The first involves causation. There must be a direct link between the act of the EU institution and the damage inflicted on the applicant. The second involves the nature of the interest affected by the Union measure. It must be a legal entitlement rather than any other form of interest.

Turning to the first of these, direct concern means that the measure which the applicant wishes to challenge must affect her legal position directly. It must be the Union measure that caused the change in her position:

> The contested measure must directly produce effects on the legal situation of the person concerned and its implementation must be purely automatic and follow solely from the [Union] rules, without the application of other intermediate measures.[99]

If the measure leaves the national authorities of a Member State a degree of discretion as to its implementation, this may be sufficient to break the chain of causation as it will be argued that it is the national measure not the Union one that inflicts the damage. In determining whether there is discretion, the Court will look, however, not merely to the leeway afforded by the Union measure but whether in practice the national authorities will exercise that discretion.

In *Piraiki-Pitraiki*, some Greek cotton exporters challenged a restriction on exporting to other parts of the Union that was applied to them after Greek accession to the European Union but during the transitional period when some restrictions were allowed.[100] The background was that the French government applied a pre-existing regime restricting cotton imports from Greece. It came to the Commission, as required by EU law, to ask for an authorisation to continue it. This was granted. When the exporters challenged this authorisation, the Commission argued that as the authorisation did not compel the French authorities to do anything, the applicants were not directly concerned by it. The Court of Justice rejected this argument. It noted the pre-existing French regime, and stated that there was no more than a theoretical possibility that the French would not continue it. The Commission authorisation, therefore, directly concerned the applicants by legalising a national regime.[101]

This stance is not uncontroversial, as the issue is about allocation of responsibilities. The test for direct concern is that actions should be brought against the EU institutions only if they have exclusive responsibility for the measure as the national authorities had no discretion over the matter. This is a high threshold, indeed. It could be argued that in many cases where the latter had some discretion, there is a shared responsibility in that national authorities would not have taken the action but for the Union measure. In such circumstances, it would seem more appropriate that if both parties are responsible, any action should lie against both of them.

---

[99] Case T-29/03 *BUPA and Others* v *Commission* [2008] ECR II-81. For an early ruling on this see Case 69/69 *Alcan* v *Commission* [1970] ECR 385.

[100] Case 11/82 *Piraiki-Pitraiki* v *Commission* [1985] ECR 207.

[101] That said, it will only be in exceptional circumstances that the Court will be willing to make inferences about behaviour by national authorities. It will normally therefore assume that if they have been granted a discretion, they will exercise it. Joined Cases C-445/07 P and C-455/07 P *Commission* v *Ente per le Ville Vesuviane*, Judgment of 10 September 2009.

The second dimension to direct concern is that the measure must adversely affect the applicant's legal position. If it affects an interest not recognised by the Court of Justice as being legally protected, the applicant will not be directly concerned. This is neatly illustrated in *Front National*. Most MEPs are members of a political group, for example the Socialist group, or the Green group. A few independent MEPs, including a number of far-right Front National MEPs, belonged to no group, meaning that they suffered some disadvantages in the European Parliament, particularly with regard to secretarial support. Accordingly, they sought to establish a *groupe mixte*, known as the TDI group. Other political groups objected and the European Parliament chose not to grant it group status. The decision was challenged by a number of MEPs individually and by the Front National. The General Court held that both sets of applicants were directly concerned, but that the applicants' substantive arguments were not made out.[102] The Front National appealed to the Court of Justice who overturned the decision of the General Court and ruled that it was not directly concerned by the European Parliament decision.

Case C–486/01 P *Front National* v *European Parliament* [2004] ECR I-6289

34. ... the condition that the decision forming the subject-matter of [annulment] proceedings must be of 'direct concern' ... requires the Community measure complained of to affect directly the legal situation of the individual and leave no discretion to the addressees of that measure, who are entrusted with the task of implementing it, such implementation being purely automatic and resulting from Community rules without the application of other intermediate rules ...

35. In this instance there is no question that the contested act – to the extent to which it deprived the Members having declared the formation of the TDI Group, and in particular the Members from the Front National's list, of the opportunity of forming ... a political group ... – affected those Members directly. As the [General Court] rightly pointed out ... those Members were in fact prevented, solely because of the contested act, from forming themselves into a political group and were henceforth deemed to be non-attached Members ...; as a result, they were afforded more limited parliamentary rights and lesser material and financial advantages than those they would have enjoyed had they been members of a political group ...

36. Such a conclusion cannot be drawn, however, in relation to a national political party such as the Front National. ... [A]lthough it is natural for a national political party which puts up candidates in the European elections to want its candidates, once elected, to exercise their mandate under the same conditions as the other Members of the Parliament, that aspiration does not confer on it any right for its elected representatives to form their own group or to become members of one of the groups being formed within the Parliament. ...

39. ... the [General Court] admittedly found that, since the contested act deprived the Members concerned, particularly those elected from the Front National's list, of the opportunity to organise themselves into a political group, it directly impinged on the promotion of the ideas and projects of the party which they represented in the European Parliament and, hence, on the attainment of that political party's stipulated object at European level, the reason why the Front National was directly affected by the act.

40. Such effects, however, cannot be regarded as directly caused by the contested act.

---

[102] See Joined Cases T-222/99, T-327/99 and T-329/99 *Martinez and Others* v *Parliament* [2001] ECR II-2823.

The Front National was held not to be directly concerned because there was, according to the Court, no legal right directly infringed by the measure. This was because the former had no right to form its own grouping or to join another grouping (paragraph 38). The requirement that the measure must directly affect the legal situation of the applicant is, however, a very uncertain test. It has proved difficult to apply, as the presence of a legal entitlement is not always clear. In *Regione Siciliana*, the General Court and the Court of Justice disagreed about when this would be so. The Commission had cancelled regional assistance for the construction of a dam in Sicily. The Region of Sicily, named in the document as the authority to administer the assistance, challenged this. The General Court stated that the measure directly concerned the region by depriving it of assistance it would have otherwise received and requiring it to repay money already received.[103] The sums combined came to over €48 million. The Court of Justice overturned this. It stated that the region had no right in EU law to the assistance as, although it was noted as the administering authority, it was the Italian Republic which had made the application.[104] As the region had no legal entitlement to the assistance, in the Court of Justice's view, notwithstanding the financial impact, it could not be said to be directly concerned.

(c) Individual concern and the *Plaumann* formula

The other part of the test is that of individual concern. The seminal ruling is *Plaumann*. The German authorities wished to suspend customs duty, an import tax, on importation of clementines. They needed, under EU law, authorisation from the Commission. It refused them this. The applicant, an importer of clementines, sought judicial review of the Commission Decision. He had to show individual concern as the Decision had been addressed to the German authorities and not to him. The Court of Justice ruled that the applicant lacked standing.

Case 25/62 *Plaumann & Co.* v *Commission* [1963] ECR 95

Persons other than those to whom a decision is addressed may only claim to be individually concerned if that decision affects them by reason of certain attributes which are peculiar to them or by reason of circumstances in which they are differentiated from all other persons and by virtue of these factors distinguishes them individually just as in the case of the person addressed. In the present case the applicant is affected by the disputed Decision as an importer of clementines, that is to say, by reason of a commercial activity which may at any time be practised by any person and is not therefore such as to distinguish the applicant in relation to the contested Decision as in the case of the addressee.

The test is both restrictive and cryptic. It needs dissecting. *Plaumann* states that private parties will be able to seek judicial review of Decisions not expressly addressed to them only if they can distinguish themselves by virtue of certain attributes or circumstances from all other persons. Although not explicitly stated, these attributes/circumstances must be fixed and determinate and distinguish members from the rest of the world. Craig has observed that the test could have chosen three dates for deciding when this was the case. The first is the date of the measure. This would involve simply looking at the number of traders importing clementines

---

[103] Case T-60/03 *Regione Siciliana* v *Commission* [2005] ECR II-4139.
[104] Case C-15/06 P *Regione Siciliana* v *Commission* [2007] ECR I-2591.

into Germany at the date of the Commission Decision. This would be fixed. The simple question would be whether the number was sufficiently limited. The second would be the date of the challenge. This would involve an identical calculation but at the date when the application was made before the Court. The third date is any date in the future. The test becomes therefore whether there is a possibility that the group may cease to be fixed and determinate at some future, undefined date.

Plaumann adopted this last position.[105] The test was whether, even though not many of us are in fact engaged in the business of importing clementines, any of us could, in theory become clementine importers. As a consequence, Plaumann was part of a group that anybody could join and did not have attributes or circumstances that distinguished him from others. Hartley has therefore talked of *Plaumann* drawing a distinction between open categories and fixed categories.[106] An open category is one where the membership is not fixed and determined when the measure comes into force. A closed one is one where the membership is fixed and determined in such a way that it cannot be added to. Applicants can only claim individual concern if they fall into a closed category.

An example of the difference between the two is provided in *Koninklijke Friesland Campina*. A 1996 Dutch law created a scheme to give tax benefits to Dutch companies providing international financing activities (the GFA scheme). In 2000, Koninklijke Friesland Campina (KFC) applied for authorisation to join the scheme. In 2001, the Commission announced it was investigating the scheme to see if it was illegal state aid. Following this, the Dutch government announced it would not admit any more undertakings to the scheme, and would not, therefore, admit KFC to the scheme. In 2003, the Commission declared the scheme illegal but stated that all undertakings who were currently members of the scheme could continue to enjoy its benefits. KFC successfully challenged the Commission Decision before the General Court. The Commission successfully appealed this before the Court of Justice. One of the Commission's arguments, which was unsuccessful, was that KFC was not individually concerned.

Case C–519/07 P *Commission* v *Koninklijke Friesland Campina*, Judgment of 17 September 2009

52. … natural or legal persons may claim that a contested provision is of individual concern to them only if it affects them by reason of certain attributes which are peculiar to them or by reason of circumstances in which they are differentiated from all other persons …

53. An undertaking cannot, in principle, contest a Commission decision prohibiting a sectoral aid scheme if it is concerned by that decision solely by virtue of belonging to the sector in question and being a potential beneficiary of the scheme. Such a decision is, vis-à-vis that undertaking, a measure of general application covering situations which are determined objectively and entails legal effects for a class of persons envisaged in a general and abstract manner …

54. By contrast, the Court has held that, where a contested measure affects a group of persons who were identified or identifiable when that measure was adopted by reason of criteria specific to the members

---

[105] P. Craig, 'Legality, Standing and Substantive Review in Community Law' (1994) 14 *OJLS* 507, 509–10.

[106] T. Hartley, *The Foundations of European Community Law: An Introduction to the Constitutional and Administrative Law of the European Community* (6th edn, Oxford, Oxford University Press, 2007) 348.

of the group, those persons might be individually concerned by that measure inasmuch as they form part of a limited class of traders ...

55. It is not in dispute, first, that the contested decision had the effect that requests for first GFA authorisation, which were pending on the date of notification of the contested decision, were rejected without being examined and, second, that the undertakings concerned were easily identifiable, owing to the very existence of such a request, at the time when that decision was adopted. In that regard, it should be recalled that KFC was part of a group of, at most, 14 applicants for first GFA authorisation, whose requests were pending at the time of the 11 July 2001 decision, that those requests were suspended following that decision, and that the Netherlands authorities announced on 5 December 2002 that they would be ceasing, with immediate effect, to consider any new requests for the application of the GFA scheme.

56. Thus, ... KFC formed part of a closed group of undertakings – and not of an indefinite number of undertakings belonging to the sector concerned – specifically affected by the contested decision.

57. It should be borne in mind that, in order to benefit from the GFA scheme, an undertaking which had made a request for first GFA authorisation must have already taken the necessary measures in order to fulfil the criteria required for that scheme. Furthermore, as the Netherlands authorities did not have any discretion in that regard, they were obliged to grant such an authorisation if those criteria were fulfilled. Thus, the undertakings whose requests for first GFA authorisation were pending must be regarded as being concerned by the contested decision, by reason of attributes which are peculiar to them and by reason of circumstances in which they are differentiated from every other undertaking in that sector which had not lodged a request for first GFA authorisation.

58. It follows that those undertakings have standing to bring an individual action against the contested decision.

A distinction is thus made between an open category and a closed category. The open category is that of companies engaging in international financial activities. In principle, anybody could engage in this category (hence its openness) and it is not enough to sustain individual concern. The closed category is composed of undertakings who have already made an application to join the GFA scheme at the time of the Commission Decision. This is closed in that nobody can join that category of pending applications prior to the Commission Decision, as once the Decision is taken the category closes definitively.

In practice, this means that closed categories comprise parties who are limited in number and have some special pre-existing legal relationship disrupted by the Union measure. In *KFC*, it was a formal application for tax exemption. Possibly crucial here was the fact that if a trader met the criteria they had an automatic right to join the scheme, so the application carried with it a certain legal entitlement. In other instances, the Court has found traders who had pre-existing contracts which could not be carried out because of a Commission Decision to be individually concerned.[107] It has also found traders to be concerned where they were part of a small group given a tax exemption in a particular year for a limited period by a Member State which was then subsequently withdrawn because of a Commission Decision.[108]

The applicant will also be individually concerned if, notwithstanding that they would otherwise be in an open category, they are part of a fixed group granted certain procedural safeguards. In

---

[107] Case 11/82 *Piraiki-Patraiki and Others* v *Commission* [1985] ECR 207; Case C-152/88 *Sofrimport* v *Commission* [1990] ECR I-2477.

[108] Joined Cases C-182/03 and C-217/03 *Belgium and Forum 187* v *Commission* [2006] ECR I-5479.

Vischim, EU legislation provided for the phasing out of certain plant protection products.[109] During a transitional period, manufacturers were invited to present dossiers setting out the qualities of these products. Vischim was one of sixteen who presented dossiers in relation to a product, chlorothalonil. A Directive was duly introduced prohibiting it. The General Court held that as Vischim was provided procedural safeguards by the original legislation it was individually concerned.

How to explain this standing rule? Two justifications are deployed. The first is that allowing too many challenges by private parties will unduly disrupt Union decision-making processes. A reason why this argument might have particular force in the EU setting is that Union decisions necessarily involve a delicate balance between many actors, which involve all the Member States and the central EU institutions. Exposing them to wide-ranging and incessant legal challenges ignores the precarious nature of this process and would make the job of realising this balance even harder..[110]

The second justification provided for such limited standing requirements is to protect the status of the Court of Justice. It has been argued that restrictive *locus standi* requirements have been used to channel applicants to challenge Union measures before national courts in the first resort. These then act as a filter for the Court of Justice.[111] This view re-emerged in the Discussion Circle on the Court of Justice at the Future of Europe Convention, with one group within the discussion arguing against reform on this basis.

The European Convention Secretariat, *Final Report of the Discussion Circle on the Court of Justice*, CONV 636/03 (2003)

18. It emerged from the discussion that the circle was clearly divided into two groups. For the first group, the current wording of the provision satisfied the essential requirements of providing effective judicial protection of the rights of litigants, taking account of the fact that, in the present decentralised system based on the subsidiarity principle, it was mainly national courts which were called upon to defend the rights of individuals and which might (or should, if at last instance) refer questions to the Court for a preliminary ruling on the validity of a Union act; it would therefore not be necessary to make any substantive changes to [Article 263(4) TFEU]. These members felt, on the other hand, that it would be appropriate for the Constitution to mention explicitly that, in accordance with the principle of loyal cooperation as interpreted by the Court of Justice, national courts are required, so far as possible, to interpret and apply national procedural rules governing the exercise of rights of action in a way that enables natural and legal persons to challenge before the courts the legality of any decision or other national measure relative to the application to them of a Community act of general application, by pleading the invalidity of such an act. It is in fact for the Member States to establish a system of legal remedies and procedures which ensures respect for the right of individuals to effective judicial protection as regards rights resulting from Union law ...

---

[109] Case T-420/05 *Vischim v Commission*, Judgment of 7 October 2009. See also Case T-13/99 *Pfizer Animal Health v Council* [2002] ECR II-3305.

[110] On this see A. Arnull, 'Private Applicants and the Action for Annulment under Article 173 of the EC Treaty' (1995) 32 *CMLRev*. 7, 46; C. Harding, 'The Private Interest in Challenging Community Action' (1980) 5 *ELRev*. 354. Arnull is very critical of this argument. For excellent coverage of the different arguments, see A. Arnull, *The European Union and its Court of Justice* (2nd edn, Oxford, Oxford University Press, 2006) 91–4.

[111] This was first deployed by Rasmussen who argued that it was a strategy to transform the Court of Justice into a European Court of Appeal. H. Rasmussen, 'Why is Article 173 Interpreted Against Private Plaintiffs?' (1980) 5 *ELRev*. 112. For a defence of this argument, see J. Usher, 'Direct and Individual Concern: An Effective Remedy or a Conventional Solution?' (2003) 28 *ELRev*. 575.

Even on their own terms, both these arguments are highly problematic.

Taking first the argument about not disrupting EU decision-making processes: this may be an argument for restrictive rules of standing but it does not explain the arbitrariness of the current test and the obscure world of the difference between open and closed categories. The Court has ruled that a party is not individually concerned by a Union measure where it is the only party affected by it on the grounds that it belongs to an open category which others could potentially join.[112] If the rules on standing are concerned solely with restricting applicants, they could look at those actually affected by a measure, and confine standing to a very limited group and not those affected speculatively.

Turning to the argument about the preliminary reference procedure as the central route for judicial review, this begs the question whether national courts would be effective filters.[113] In principle, following the *Fotofrost* doctrine, they should refer everything to the Court as they are not allowed to declare a Union measure invalid themselves.[114] It could therefore become a free-for-all with the only question being whether the applicant has standing domestically. In some instances, this may be very liberal, whereas conversely, there may not even be a domestic measure that can be the subject of a challenge. There is, moreover, an institutional contradiction in this argument, as the procedures send the applicant to different courts. An action under Article 263(4) TFEU is brought before the General Court whilst a reference goes to the Court of Justice.[115] It would be absurd if the clear Treaty preference for individual administrative challenges to be the main concern of the General Court was undermined in this way. Viewed more broadly, there are further disadvantages to this vision. Legal proceedings would be highly protracted with all the disadvantages for legal certainty and costs.

The bulk of the academic literature has thus been highly critical of the *Plaumann* formula. It is viewed, in the first place, as highly restrictive, preventing applicants adversely affected by Union measures from any effective judicial redress. There is also a sense that it is textually unjustified.[116] The text of Article 263 TFEU clearly does not *require* it. Nor does it justify it. There is nothing in the Treaty to imply that the phrase 'direct and individual concern' should be interpreted as narrowly as the Court chose to in *Plaumann*.

The most robust critique of the *Plaumann* formula is that of Advocate General Jacobs in *UPA*. UPA, a Spanish trade association representing the interests of Spanish farmers, sought judicial review of a 1998 Council Regulation which abolished many forms of financial aid to olive oil farmers and producers. It was impossible to challenge this Regulation before the Spanish courts. The General Court dismissed the application for the reason that UPA lacked standing. UPA appealed to the Court of Justice. In his Opinion, Advocate General Jacobs set out a series of reasons why, in his view, the current law was in need of reform. Underlying the Advocate General's analysis was the idea that judicial review must be informed by the 'principle of effective judicial protection'.

---

[112] Case 231/82 *Spijker* v *Commission* [1983] ECR 2559.

[113] For a particularly thorough critique of the undesirability of this route, see the Opinion of Advocate General Jacobs in Case C-50/00 P *Unión de Pequeños Agricultores* v *Council* [2002] ECR I-6677, paras. 41–9.

[114] Case 314/85 *Firma Fotofrost* v *Hauptzollamt Lübeck-Ost* [1987] ECR 4199.

[115] Article 256(1) TFEU.

[116] A. Barav, 'Direct and Individual Concern: An Almost Insurmountable Barrier to the Admissibility of Individual Appeal to the EEC Court' (1974) 11 *CMLRev.* 191; A. Arnull, 'Private Applicants and the Action for Annulment since *Codorníu*' (2001) 38 *CML Rev.* 7; K. Lenaerts and T. Corthaut, 'Judicial Review as a Contribution to the Development of European Constitutionalism' (2003) 22 *YBEL* 1; P. Craig, *EU Administrative Law* (Oxford, Oxford University Press, 2006) 340–4.

Case C-50/00 P *Unión de Pequeños Agricultores* v *Council* [2002] ECR I-6677, Opinion of Advocate General Jacobs

38. As is common ground in the present case, the case law of the Court of Justice acknowledges the principle that an individual who considers himself wronged by a measure which deprives him of a right or advantage under Community law must have access to a remedy against that measure and be able to obtain complete judicial protection.

39. That principle is, as the Court has repeatedly stated, grounded in the constitutional traditions common to the Member States and in Articles 6 and 13 of the European Convention on Human Rights. Moreover, the Charter of Fundamental Rights of the European Union, while itself not legally binding, proclaims a generally recognised principle in stating in Article 47 that '[e]veryone whose rights and freedoms guaranteed by the law of the Union are violated has the right to an effective remedy before a tribunal'...

Suggested solution: a new interpretation of the notion of individual concern

59. The key to the problem of judicial protection against unlawful Community acts lies therefore, in my view, in the notion of individual concern laid down in the fourth paragraph of Article [263 TFEU]. There are no compelling reasons to read into that notion a requirement that an individual applicant seeking to challenge a general measure must be differentiated from all others affected by it in the same way as an addressee. On that reading, the greater the number of persons affected by a measure the less likely it is that judicial review under the fourth paragraph of Article [263 TFEU] will be made available. The fact that a measure adversely affects a large number of individuals, causing wide-spread rather than limited harm, provides however to my mind a positive reason for accepting a direct challenge by one or more of those individuals.

60. In my opinion, it should therefore be accepted that a person is to be regarded as individually concerned by a Community measure where, by reason of his particular circumstances, the measure has, or is liable to have, a substantial adverse effect on his interests.

61. A development along those lines of the case law on the interpretation of Article [263 TFEU] would have several very substantial advantages.

62. First ... [it avoids] what may in some cases be a total lack of judicial protection – a *déni de justice*.

63. Second, the suggested interpretation of the notion of individual concern would considerably improve judicial protection. By laying down a more generous test for standing for individual applicants than that adopted by the Court in the existing case law, it would not only ensure that individual applicants who are directly and adversely affected by Community measures are never left without a judicial remedy; it would also allow issues of validity of general measures to be addressed in the context of the procedure which is best suited to resolving them, and in which effective interim relief is available.

64. Third, it would also have the great advantage of providing clarity to a body of case law which has often, and rightly in my view, been criticised for its complexity and lack of coherence, and which may make it difficult for practitioners to advise in what court to take proceedings, or even lead them to take parallel proceedings in the national courts and the [General Court].

65. Fourth, by ruling that individual applicants are individually concerned by general measures which affect them adversely, the Court of Justice would encourage the use of direct actions to resolve issues of validity, thus limiting the number of challenges raised via Article [267 TFEU]. That would, as explained above, be beneficial for legal certainty and the uniform application of Community law ...

> 66. A point of equal, or even greater, importance is that the interpretation of Article [263 TFEU] which I propose would shift the emphasis of judicial review from questions of admissibility to questions of substance. While it may be accepted that the Community legislative process should be protected against undue judicial intervention, such protection can be more properly achieved by the application of substantive standards of judicial review which allow the institutions an appropriate margin of appreciation in the exercise of their powers than by the application of strict rules on admissibility which have the effect of blindly excluding applicants without consideration of the merits of the arguments they put forward.

Shortly after this Opinion was handed down, the General Court applied its reasoning in *Jégo Quéré*.[117] But when *UPA* was considered by the Court of Justice, it chose not to follow the advice of its Advocate General. The Court insisted on the continuing force of the *Plaumann* formula, stating that any reform to the law of standing must come not from the Court, but from the Member States. It has since then insisted resolutely on the *Plaumann* formula.[118] The Opinion of Advocate General Jacobs must be seen, therefore, as a critique of the existing law rather than anything more.

The debate about widening standing rules is monolithic and too black and white. It revolves around general statements about having either relaxed rules or restrictive rules. If standing requirements are relaxed they may, of course, address the concerns surrounding restrictive requirements. However, they open the door to other concerns. These involve disruption of the legislative process and government by courts. Significant numbers of Union measures will go up before the courts, with a danger of the latter substituting their views for those of the legislature. There is also the concern about capture of courts by minority interests. Groups unable to secure agreement for their view elsewhere may simply bombard the courts with actions as a way of undermining the legislative procedures and as a strategy for securing what they could not achieve elsewhere.

The strength of these arguments will vary according to the context. In some instances, the argument for efficient judicial protection might seem strong, whilst in others the case for restrictive standing is apparent. In this regard, the amendments introduced by Lisbon between regulatory and legislative acts in Article 263(4) TFEU are pertinent. In instances where there is EU legislation, there is restricted standing. In the case of administrative acts, individual concern is abolished and there is liberalised standing. This ethos is reinforced by Article 263(5) TFEU which provides that the acts setting up EU agencies and bodies may lay down specific arrangements allowing acts of these bodies to be challenged. The philosophy is clear. Non-legislative acts are taken by non-representative institutions and therefore there are less strong concerns about democratic process being disrupted by judicial challenge. Furthermore, there are strong reasons why questions of due process and the reach of executive power should be more actively policed. These institutions are not subject to the same levels of public debate and scrutiny as the legislative process, and, therefore, judicial review intervenes to substitute for that.

---

[117] Case T-177/01 *Jégo Quéré v Commission* [2002] ECR II-2365.
[118] See e.g. Joined Cases C-373/06 P, C-379/06 P and C-382/06 P *Flaherty and Others v Commission* [2008] ECR I-2649; Case C-362/06 P *Sahlstedt v Commission*, Judgment of 23 April 2009.

(d) Standing and interest groups

A further criticism of *Plaumann* is that the test of 'individual concern' is easier to meet for those who can point to some individual financial or material interest that has been prejudiced. It thus benefits trading interests over groups representing public interests such as the environment, the regions or the consumer. This is particularly problematic if judicial review is seen as also having a function of allowing different social groups to challenge legislative or administrative abuse. It cannot be right if this is only available to some interests or traders and not to others.

Interest groups will be granted standing if they are seen as having been granted certain procedural entitlements. This will be where they have been given certain procedural rights or privileges either by EU law or through the practice of the EU institutions. The argument is that this recognition by the political process confers a parallel entitlement to protection of this before the courts. The position was set out most cogently in *Associazione Nazionale Bieticoltori*. In this instance, Associazione Nazionale Bieticoltori (ANB), a trade association representing Italian sugar beet producers, brought an action against a Regulation that granted aid to their Portuguese counterparts whilst reducing aid for the Italian growers. It was found to lack standing.

> **Case T–38/98 *Associazione Nazionale Bieticoltori v Council* [1998] ECR II–4191**
>
> 25. It should be pointed out, second, that an application for annulment lodged by an association may be admissible in three types of situation, namely:
>   (a) where a legislative provision expressly confers a range of procedural powers on trade associations ...
>   (b) where the association represents the interests of undertakings having *locus standi* to seek the annulment of the provision in question ...
>   (c) where the association is distinguished because its own interests as an association are affected, in particular because its position as a negotiator has been affected by the measure whose annulment is sought ...
> 26. In those three types of situation the Court of Justice and the [General Court] have also taken into account the participation of the associations in question in the procedure ...
> 27. As regards the first type of situation, mentioned above, it is sufficient to point out that the regulations on the common organisation of the markets in the sugar sector do not recognise that associations have any right of a procedural nature.
> 28. As regards the second of the abovementioned types of situation, it should be observed that the fact that the contested provision will affect sugar beet producers whose interests are represented by the Associazione Nazionale Bieticoltori is not such as to differentiate those producers from all other persons, since they are in a situation which is comparable to that of any other operator who may enter the same market ...
> 29. As regards, last, the third type of situation referred to above, it should be pointed out that, according to a consistent line of decisions, an association formed to promote the collective interests of a category of persons cannot be regarded as individually concerned by a measure affecting the general interests of that category, and is therefore not entitled to bring an action for annulment where its members may not do so individually ... None the less, the existence of particular circumstances, such as the role played by an association in a procedure leading to the adoption of an act within the meaning of Article [263 TFEU], may justify admitting an action brought by an association whose members are not directly and individually concerned by the act at issue, particularly when its position as negotiator is affected by it ...

Such procedural entitlements will be rare, and they will only be given to 'insider' groups who have good relationships with the EU institutions. These are likely to be the last people who wish to challenge a measure as their privileged position in negotiations or consultations is likely to have already secured some influence for them.

More interesting, therefore, is whether other interest groups with a strong stake in a measure can challenge it. In *Greenpeace*, three environmental campaigning groups and several individuals resident on the Canary Islands challenged the legality of a series of Commission Decisions granting aid from the European Regional Development Fund (ERDF) to assist with the construction of two power stations, one on Gran Canaria and the other on Tenerife. The General Court ruled that neither the associations nor the individuals had standing.[119]

Case T–585/93 *Greenpeace and Others* v *Commission* [1995] ECR II–2205

32. The applicants ask the Court to adopt a liberal approach on this issue and recognize that, in the present case, their *locus standi* can depend not on a purely economic interest but on their interest in the protection of the environment ...

39. In the alternative, the applicants submit that the representative environmental organizations should be considered to be individually concerned by reason of the particularly important role they have to play in the process of legal control by representing the general interests shared by a number of individuals in a focused and coordinated manner. ...

56. Nor can the fact that [certain of the] applicants have submitted a complaint to the Commission constitute a special circumstance distinguishing them individually from all other persons and thereby giving them *locus standi* to bring an action under Article [263]. No specific procedures are provided for whereby individuals may be associated with the adoption, implementation and monitoring of decisions taken in the field of financial assistance granted by the ERDF. Merely submitting a complaint and subsequently exchanging correspondence with the Commission cannot therefore give a complainant *locus standi* to bring an action under Article [263] ...

59. ... [S]pecial circumstances such as the role played by an association in a procedure which led to the adoption of an act within the meaning of Article [263] may justify holding admissible an action brought by an association whose members are not directly and individually concerned by the contested measure ...

60. The three applicant associations ... claim that they represent the general interest, in the matter of environmental protection, of people residing on Gran Canaria and Tenerife and that their members are affected by the contested decision; they do not, however, adduce any special circumstances to demonstrate the individual interest of their members as opposed to any other person residing in those areas. The possible effect on the legal position of the members of the applicant associations cannot, therefore, be any different from that alleged here by the applicants who are private individuals. Consequently, in so far as the applicants in the present case who are private individuals cannot, as the Court has held, be considered to be individually concerned by the contested decision, nor can the members of the applicant associations, as local residents of Gran Canaria and Tenerife ...

62. In the present case ... the Commission did not, prior to the adoption of the contested decision, initiate any procedure in which Greenpeace participated; nor was Greenpeace in any way the interlocutor of the Commission with regard to the adoption of the ... decision. Greenpeace cannot, therefore, claim to have any specific interest distinct from that of its members to justify its *locus standi*.

---

[119] The judgment was affirmed on appeal. Case C-321/95 P *Greenpeace and Others* v *Commission* [1998] ECR I-1651.

Public interest associations will therefore only be able to seek judicial review of measures not addressed to them if they are granted specific procedural privileges or safeguards; their members are individually concerned; or in negotiations they are recognised by the EU institutions as the central interlocutor of particular interests. It will be rare that any of these conditions will be met. Since *Greenpeace*, the Court has consistently refused to relax standing requirements for public interest litigation.[120] EU law has therefore been criticised as resulting in diffuse public interests being less well protected than private interests.[121]

Whilst apparently attractive, this argument must be treated cautiously. There are dangers in substituting judicial review for political accountability. Take the *Greenpeace* case, for example: why should it be characterised as being a *legal* concern to decide whether European funds should be allocated to the environmentally controversial construction of a new power station? Is this not precisely the sort of question which is best resolved politically?

C. Harlow, 'Public Law and Popular Justice' (2002) 65 *Modern Law Review* 1, 13

In public interest litigation, campaigning groups can be treated as experts provided their hidden agenda is overtly recognised. Alternatively, they can be treated as single issue political parties, in which case their presence as advocates in the legal process needs a different justification. Otherwise ... the triumph of pressure groups or factions or special interests will mark a corruption of the legal process. To put this important point differently, too close a relationship between courts and campaigning groups may result in a dilution of the neutrality and objectivity of law.

Harlow suggests, therefore, that a middle way might be to give public interest groups wider rights of intervention in proceedings. As she makes clear, this has not yet happened.

C. Harlow, 'Towards a Theory of Access for the European Court of Justice' (1992) 12 *Yearbook of European Law* 213, 247–8

The most economical way to increase interest representation without overloading the Court is, however, undoubtedly through intervention procedure. Many modern courts feel able to allow intervention freely and interventions by interest groups are particularly a feature of constitutional courts. In the Court of Justice, in sharp contrast, group interventions are rare and Articles 37 and 20[122] of the Statute are largely the preserve of the privileged applicants.

---

[120] Case T-461/93 *An Taisce* v *Commission* [1994] ECR II-733; Case T-219/95 R *Danielsson and Others* v *Commission* [1995] ECR II-3051.

[121] M. Führ *et al.*, 'Access to Justice: Legal Standing for Environmental Associations in the European Union' in D. Robinson and J. Dunkley (eds.), *Public Interest Perspectives in Environmental Law* (Chichester, Chancery, 1995); L. Krämer, 'Public Interest Litigation in Environmental Matters before European Courts' (1996) 8 *JEL* 1; N. Gerard, 'Access to Justice on Environmental Matters: A Case of Double Standards?' (1996) 8 *JEL* 139.

[122] The right to intervene is now set out in article 40 of the current Statute of the Court of Justice which gives that right to all Member States and EU institutions. Others may intervene if they can show an interest and the dispute is not between Member States, EU institutions or between a Member State and an EU institution.

The Court's distinctive inquisitorial procedures could be used to design an appropriate intervention procedure without adding to burdens on applicants in the shape of greater expense or delay. Strict time-limits can already be imposed for interventions with limited rights of contradiction and oral observations already require the Court's permission. Submissions could be limited as to length. Increased use could be made of the *juge rapporteur* if orality were thought necessary; alternatively, they could be collected and evaluated by the Advocate General, forming part of his Opinion.

5 ARTICLE 265 TFEU AND THE FAILURE TO ACT

In certain circumstances positive duties are placed by EU law upon the EU institutions to act. They are under a duty to realise some Treaty objectives[123] and secondary legislation often places duties upon the institutions.[124] The conditions for bringing an action if an institution fails to act in such circumstances are set out in Article 265 TFEU.

Article 265 TFEU

Should the European Parliament, the European Council, the Council, the Commission or the European Central Bank, in infringement of the Treaties, fail to act, the Member States and the other institutions of the Union may bring an action before the Court of Justice to have the infringement established. This Article shall apply, under the same conditions, to bodies, offices and agencies of the Union which fail to act.

The action shall be admissible only if the institution, body, office or agency concerned has first been called upon to act. If, within two months of being so called upon, the institution, body, office or agency concerned has not defined its position, the action may be brought within a further period of two months.

Any natural or legal person may, under the conditions laid down in the preceding paragraphs, complain to the Court that an institution, body, office or agency of the Union has failed to address to that person any act other than a recommendation or an opinion.

There is a similar distinction between privileged and non-privileged applicants as in Article 263 TFEU, with the former laid out in Article 265(1) TFEU and the latter in 265(3). Privileged applicants comprise a wider group under Article 265 TFEU than under Article 263 TFEU, as all EU institutions and Member States are granted that status, whilst under the latter provision it is available just to Member States, the Commission, the Parliament and the Council. The European Council, the European Central Bank and (hypothetically) the Court of Justice all have a wider standing, therefore, under Article 265 TFEU.[125]

---

[123] On the common transport policy, see Case 13/83 *Parliament* v *Council* [1985] ECR 1513.

[124] For example, the Commission is required to examine the factual and legal particulars of any complaint about a breach of EU competition law which is made by a person with a legitimate interest: Case T-24/90 *Automec Srl* v *Commission (Automec II)* [1992] ECR II-2223.

[125] The list of institutions is set out in Article 13 TEU.

Quirks are also added to the provision by the Lisbon Treaty. Prior to the Treaty, only the Parliament, Council and Commission were institutions against whom an action could be brought. Two further institutions have been added to this: the European Council and the European Central Bank. The second paragraph, however, refers to an action only being available if the 'institution, body or agency' has been called upon to act. This suggests that, in principle, the action should be available against EU agencies, bodies and offices as well in the same way as Article 263 TFEU is available against acts taken by these. This is the preferable interpretation. It not only secures consistency between the provisions but also ensures that there is no lacuna in the rule whereby an EU body or agency can escape judicial scrutiny by simply doing nothing.[126]

Articles 263 and 265 TFEU were described in an early judgment as prescribing 'one and the same method of recourse'.[127] This means, as one author put it, that:

> the system of remedies … would be incomplete if Community institutions were subject to judicial control only in respect of their positive actions while they could evade the obligations imposed upon them by simply failing to act.[128]

It also means that the provisions should be interpreted in a parallel manner. There is thus a similar distinction between privileged and non-privileged applicants. Non-privileged applicants can only invoke Article 265 TFEU if they would be directly concerned by the regulatory act or directly and individually concerned by the non-regulatory act which has not been adopted.[129]

However, there are some lacunae in this coverage.

First, an action under Article 265 TFEU can only be commenced against an EU institution if it is under a duty to perform a task. If there is only a discretion, no remedy exists. The decision of the Court to rule in some circumstances that the matter is one of discretion rather than obligation has been controversial as it creates a gap in protection. We saw in Chapter 8 how the decision to hold that the Commission had complete discretion whether to launch enforcement proceedings against a Member State under Article 258 TFEU for infringement of EU law has led to private parties being largely excluded from this important process.[130]

Secondly, an institution, if called upon to act,[131] avoids any further action if it defines its position within two months. The principle of complementarity would require that this position be an act capable of being reviewed under Article 263 TFEU. However, an institution can define its position without adopting an act that is reviewable under that provision.[132] It can also act in a different way from that in which it was called upon to act.[133]

Finally, the institution must be called upon to act by the applicant. If this does not happen, there will be no action.[134] Whilst the Article sets no time limit within which an action must

---

[126] Case T-411/06 *Sogelma* v *EAR* [2008] ECR II-2771.

[127] Case 15/70 *Chevalley* v *Commission* [1970] ECR 979.

[128] A. Toth, 'The Law as it Stands on the Appeal for Failure to Act' (1975) 2 *LIEI* 65.

[129] Case T-395/04 *Air One* v *Commission* [2006] ECR II-1343; Case T-167/04 *Asklepios Kliniken* v *Commission* [2007] ECR II-2379.

[130] Case 247/87 *Star Fruit* v *Commission* [1989] ECR 291. See pp. 341–3.

[131] Joined Cases T-30/01–T-32/01 and T-86/02–T-88/02 *Diputación Foral de Álava* v *Commission*, Judgment of 9 September 2009.

[132] Case 377/87 *Parliament* v *Council* [1988] ECR 4017; Case 302/87 *European Parliament* v *Council* [1988] ECR 561; Case T-186/94 *Guérin Automobiles* v *Commission* [1995] ECR II-1753.

[133] Case C-25/91 *Pesqueras Echebastar* v *Commission* [1993] ECR I-1719; Case T-420/05 *Vischim* v *Commission*, Judgment of 7 October 2009.

[134] Joined Cases T-30/01–T-32/01 and T-86/02–T-88/02 *Diputación Foral de Álava* v *Commission*, Judgment of 9 September 2009.

be brought, if the institution's position on the matter is clear to the applicant, it must bring the request for action within a reasonable period. In *Netherlands* v *Commission*, a case which involved Article 35 ECSC, the parallel provision to Article 265 TFEU in the ECSC Treaty, the Commission informed the Dutch government that a French restructuring plan did not violate the Treaty provisions on state aids.[135] The Dutch government waited a further eighteen months before requesting the Commission to act. The Court, reasoning from the principle of legal certainty, stated that an applicant did not have a right to raise the matter with the Commission indefinitely and had delayed too long in this instance.

6 THE PLEA OF ILLEGALITY

Particularly in areas where the Commission enjoys delegated powers, parties face a problem if they want to challenge an act. The Commission measure may be addressed to them or be of direct and individual concern to them, but they may want to challenge the act on the basis that the parent measure is illegal. They may face difficulties here because the time limits have passed, or because they may not satisfy the *locus standi* requirements in relation to the parent instrument. The plea of illegality addresses this by allowing a party in proceedings against a measure to plead the inapplicability of its parent measure.

Article 277 TFEU

Notwithstanding the expiry of the period laid down in Article 263, fifth paragraph, any party may, in proceedings in which an act of general application adopted by an institution, body, office or agency of the Union is at issue, plead the grounds specified in Article 263, second paragraph, in order to invoke before the Court of Justice of the European Union the inapplicability of that act.

The plea of illegality is a parasitic procedure. It cannot be brought as an independent action but can only be invoked in the context of proceedings brought under some other provisions of the Treaties. To that end, the party must secure *locus standi* under the other procedure and observe the time limits set out in that procedure, albeit that the time limits for challenging the parent measure may have lapsed.[136] To give an example, a party might want to challenge a Decision on the grounds that the enabling Regulation was illegal. It would have to show that it had *locus standi* under Article 263 TFEU to challenge the Decision, and that it observed the time limits set out there for challenging the Decision within two months of its publication. It does not matter that it is more than two months since the Regulation was adopted.

The concern with the plea of illegality is that it should not lead to an abuse of process where it is used to subvert other procedures. This has led to two refinements.

First, a plea of illegality may not be invoked where a matter is pending before another court or in another action before the same court.[137] For this to be the case, it must be considered to be *lis pendens*. This will only happen if three conditions are met. The action must be between the same parties, must seek the same object and must do so on the basis of the same

---

[135] Case 59/70 *Netherlands* v *Commission* [1971] ECR 639.
[136] Joined Cases 31/62 and 33/62 *Wöhrmann* v *Commission* [1962] ECR 506.
[137] Joined Cases T-246/08 and T-332/08 *Melli Bank* v *Council*, Judgment of 9 July 2009.

submissions. This will very rarely be the case. Even if the substance of the dispute is similar, the litigation before the courts may look at slightly different dimensions, and parties will, in any case, often use different arguments.

Secondly, a party who had an earlier opportunity to challenge the parent measure cannot subsequently raise the plea of illegality.[138] The most obvious example is privileged parties under Article 263 TFEU who had unlimited standing to challenge the parent measure at the time of adoption. If they could subsequently raise a plea of illegality, this would allow them to evade the time limits in that procedure and generate uncertainty. In *Spain* v *Commission*, the Court refused to allow a Spanish challenge to a 1992 Commission Decision extending the regime on subsidies to the motor vehicle industry.[139] For the basis of the Spanish challenge was that the initial 1990 regime on which the 1993 Decision was based was illegal. The Court ruled that as Spain had not challenged the 1990 regime at the time, it could not subsequently raise a plea of illegality.

However, the principle applies not just to privileged parties but to any party who had an earlier opportunity to bring the matter directly to the Court of Justice. In *TWD (No. 2)*, a 1986 Commission Decision that a subsidy from the German *Land* of Bavaria to the applicant, a textile company, was illegal was not challenged.[140] A new subsidy was authorised by a second Commission Decision on condition that the initial subsidy granted to the applicant be repaid. The applicant challenged the 1986 Decision, under a plea of illegality, claiming that its economic effects only became apparent following the second Decision. The General Court deemed this inadmissible, noting that, as the applicant could have challenged the first Decision using Article 263 TFEU, it was debarred now from bringing a challenge under Article 277 TFEU.

7 NON-CONTRACTUAL LIABILITY

The final head of action under which Union measures can be reviewed is that of non-contractual liability. In such circumstances, the applicant will not be seeking merely annulment of the measure but also damages from the EU institutions. This is governed by Article 340(2) TFEU.

Article 340(2) TFEU

In the case of non-contractual liability, the Union shall, in accordance with the general principles common to the laws of the Member States, make good any damage caused by its institutions or by its servants in the performance of their duties.

Although an equivalent Treaty provision has been present since the Treaty of Rome in the 1950s, the law on the non-contractual liability of EU institutions was reshaped by the *Brasserie du Pêcheur* judgment.[141] This judgment, it will be remembered, set out the circumstances in

---

[138] On the early debate surrounding this, see G. Bebr, 'Judicial Remedy of Private Parties Against Normative Acts of the European Communities: The Role of the Exception of Illegality' (1966) 4 *CMLRev.* 7; A. Barav, 'The Exception of Illegality in Community Law: A Critical Analysis' (1974) 11 *CMLRev.* 366.

[139] Case C-135/93 *Spain v Commission* [1995] ECR I-1651.

[140] Joined Cases T-244 and T-486/93 *TWD Textilwerke Deggendorf v Commission* [1995] ECR I-2265.

[141] Joined Cases C-24/93 and C-48/93 *Brasserie du Pêcheur v Germany* [1996] ECR I-1029. See pp. 304–7. See also T. Tridimas, 'Liability for Breach of Community Law: Growing Up and Mellowing Down?' (2001) 38 *CMLRev.* 301.

which Member States could be liable for individual loss that arose from their failure to comply with EU law. Aware of the inconsistencies that might otherwise arise, the Court stated that the same criteria set out in that case delimiting Member State liability should also govern the liability of EU institutions under Article 340(2) TFEU.[142] To be sure, it has proved difficult for the Court of Justice to apply these parallels too formulaically but it has tried to reason from similar principles for both.

(i) Nature of the liability

The leading case following *Brasserie du Pêcheur* in which the Court considered the liability of the EU institutions was *Bergaderm*. A Commission Decision banned the use of a chemical, bergapten, in sun oil on the ground that it was carcinogenic. Bergaderm was the only company that produced sun oil using this chemical. Following the Decision, it went into liquidation. It sued the Commission, claiming that the latter had misinterpreted the scientific evidence. The application failed, but the Court set out new parameters for Article 340(2) TFEU.

Case C–352/98 P *Laboratoires Pharmaceutiques Bergaderm* v *Commission* [2000] ECR I–5291

39. [Article 340(2) TFEU] provides that, in the case of non-contractual liability, the Community is, in accordance with the general principles common to the laws of the Member States, to make good any damage caused by its institutions or by its servants in the performance of their duties.

40. The system of rules which the Court has worked out with regard to that provision takes into account, inter alia, the complexity of the situations to be regulated, difficulties in the application or interpretation of the texts and, more particularly, the margin of discretion available to the author of the act in question ...

41. The Court has stated that the conditions under which the State may incur liability for damage caused to individuals by a breach of Community law cannot, in the absence of particular justification, differ from those governing the liability of the Community in like circumstances. The protection of the rights which individuals derive from Community law cannot vary depending on whether a national authority or a Community authority is responsible for the damage ...

42. As regards Member State liability for damage caused to individuals, the Court has held that Community law confers a right to reparation where three conditions are met: the rule of law infringed must be intended to confer rights on individuals; the breach must be sufficiently serious; and there must be a direct causal link between the breach of the obligation resting on the State and the damage sustained by the injured parties ...

43. As to the second condition, as regards both Community liability under Article [288(2), the predecessor to 340(2) TFEU] and Member State liability for breaches of Community law, the decisive test for finding that a breach of Community law is sufficiently serious is whether the Member State or the Community institution concerned manifestly and gravely disregarded the limits on its discretion ...

44. Where the Member State or the institution in question has only considerably reduced, or even no, discretion, the mere infringement of Community law may be sufficient to establish the existence of a sufficiently serious breach ...

46. In that regard, the Court finds that the general or individual nature of a measure taken by an institution is not a decisive criterion for identifying the limits of the discretion enjoyed by the institution in question.

---

[142] *Brasserie du Pêcheur*, paras. 40–7.

The judgment sets out three conditions which must be met for the institutions to incur liability (paragraph 42). These are:

- the conduct of the institution must infringe a rule of law intended to confer rights on individuals;
- the breach of EU law must be sufficiently serious;
- there must be a direct causal link between the breach by the EU institution and the damage sustained by the applicant.

As there was no liability in *Bergaderm*, the Court did not address in detail the third condition but only the first two. In this, it recast a distinction that it had previously made between legislative acts involving economic policy choices and other acts, with a far higher degree of fault required for liability for the former.[143] In *Bergaderm*, the Court indicated that it will operate a single test which makes no distinction between the types of act being challenged. Within this single test, there will be a spectrum of cases. These will range from situations where the EU institutions are faced with complex choices and where they enjoy a fair degree of discretion, to more straightforward scenarios where they have little or no discretion. Questions of complexity and discretion will be central to determining the standard of liability in each case.

On relatively straightforward matters or where the EU institution has little or no discretion, the Court has stated, in regard to the first test that a superior rule must be breached, that the norm must grant rights for individuals. Breach of an instrument, such as the WTO agreement, that does not do this will not lead to liability.[144] Beyond that, any breach of any EU legal obligation, be it substantive or procedural, will be sufficient.[145] A failure to exercise due diligence will also incur liability.[146] With regard to the second head of the test, in such circumstances mere illegality or failure to exercise due diligence will be sufficient.

The situation is different where the EU institutions enjoy a measure of discretion. With regard to the first part of the test, general principles of EU law, fundamental rights and the doctrine of misuse of powers have been held to be norms that will lead to liability.[147] The duty to give reasons, on the other hand, is not regarded as having that status, so a failure to give reasons cannot give rise to an action under Article 340(2) TFEU.[148] Similarly a failure of due diligence, be it in the form of an error of assessment or a failure to consider evidence that should have been considered, will not be sufficient to incur liability.[149]

With regard to the second heading, *Bergaderm* indicated that a simple breach of EU law by an EU institution would not be sufficient for it to incur liability. The breach must be sufficiently serious and that would involve the EU institution 'manifestly and gravely' exceeding the limits on its discretion (paragraph 43). The meaning of this was addressed in most detail in *Schneider*. Schneider and Legrand were two companies specialising in electrical distribution and low voltage installations who merged into a single company. The Commission declared

---

[143] Case 5/71 *Aktien-Zuckerfabrik Schöppenstedt* v *Council* [1971] ECR 975. For an excellent discussion of the position since *Bergaderm*, see C. Hilson, 'The Role of Discretion in EC Law on Non-contractual Liability' (2005) 42 *CMLRev*. 677.

[144] Joined Cases C-120/06 and C-121/06 *FIAMM and Others* v *Council and Commission*, Judgment of 9 September 2008.

[145] Case T-351/03 *Schneider* v *Commission* [2007] ECR II-2237. The most extensive list of grounds can be found in Case T-48/05 *Franchet and Byk* v *Commission* [2008] ECR II-1585.

[146] Case T-178/98 *Fresh Marine* v *Commission* [2000] ECR II-3331.

[147] For a summary of the position, see Joined Cases T-481/93 and T-484/93 *Vereniging van Exporteurs in Levende Varkens* v *Commission* [1995] ECR II-2941.

[148] See e.g. Case C-76/01 P *Eurocoton* v *Council* [2003] ECR I-10091, para. 98 and the case law cited therein.

[149] Case T-212/03 *MyTravel* v *Commission*, Judgment of 9 September 2008.

the merger incompatible with the common market and ordered a break-up of the company. In 2002, the General Court found the Commission decision to be illegal on two grounds.[150] First, there were errors in its economic analysis of all the national markets other than the French market. Notwithstanding this, the General Court held that the competition effects on the French market were sufficient for the merger to be declared incompatible with the single market. In addition, in its initial statement of objections, the Commission had failed to tell Schneider in sufficiently clear terms what measures it needed to take to avoid the merger being declared illegal. Schneider then brought an action under Article 340(2) TFEU.

Case T–351/03 *Schneider v Commission* [2007] ECR II–2237

116. The system of rules which the Court of Justice has worked out in relation to the non-contractual liability of the Community takes into account, inter alia, the complexity of the situations to be regulated, difficulties in the application or interpretation of the legislation and, more particularly, the margin of discretion available to the author of the act in question …

121. In that context, the Commission contends that, if it were to incur financial liability in circumstances such as those of this case, its capacity fully to function as a regulator of competition, a task entrusted to it by the EC Treaty, would be compromised as a result of the possible inhibiting effect that the risk of having to bear damages alleged by the undertakings concerned might have on the control of concentrations.

122. It must be conceded that such an effect, contrary to the general Community interest, might arise if the concept of a serious breach of Community law were construed as comprising all errors or mistakes which, even if of some gravity, are not by their nature or extent alien to the normal conduct of an institution entrusted with the task of overseeing the application of competition rules, which are complex, delicate and subject to a considerable degree of discretion.

123. Therefore, a sufficiently serious breach of Community law, for the purposes of establishing the non-contractual liability of the Community, cannot be constituted by failure to fulfil a legal obligation, which, regrettable though it may be, can be explained by the objective constraints to which the institution and its officials are subject as a result of the provisions governing the control of concentrations.

124. On the other hand, the right to compensation for damage resulting from the conduct of the institution becomes available where such conduct takes the form of action manifestly contrary to the rule of law and seriously detrimental to the interests of persons outside the institution and cannot be justified or accounted for by the particular constraints to which the staff of the institution, operating normally, is objectively subject.

125. Such a definition of the threshold for the establishment of non-contractual liability of the Community is conducive to protection of the room for manoeuvre and freedom of assessment which must, in the general interest, be enjoyed by the Community regulator of competition, both in its discretionary decisions and in its interpretation and application of the relevant provisions of primary and secondary Community law, without thereby leaving third parties to bear the consequences of flagrant and inexcusable misconduct …

129. In principle, the possibility cannot be ruled out that manifest and serious defects affecting the economic analysis underlying competition policy decisions may constitute sufficiently serious breaches of a rule of law to cause the Community to incur non-contractual liability.

---

[150] Case T-310/01 *Schneider Electric SA* v *Commission* [2002] ECR II-4071.

130. However, for such a finding to be made it is first necessary to verify that the rule infringed by the incorrect analysis is intended to confer rights on individuals. Whilst certain principles and certain rules which must be observed in any competitive analysis are indeed rules intended to confer rights on individuals, not all norms, whether of primary or secondary law or deriving from case law, which the Commission must observe in its economic assessments can be automatically held to be rules of that kind.

131. Next, it must be noted that the economic analyses necessary for the classification, under competition law, of a given situation or transaction are generally, as regards both the facts and the reasoning based on the account of the facts, complex and difficult intellectual formulas, which may inadvertently contain certain inadequacies, such as approximations, inconsistencies, or indeed certain omissions, in view of the time constraints to which the institution is subject. That is even more so where, as in the case of the control of concentrations, the analysis has a prospective element. The gravity of a documentary or logical inadequacy, in such circumstances, may not always constitute a sufficient circumstance to cause the Community to incur liability.

132. Last, it must be borne in mind that the Commission enjoys discretion in maintaining control over Community competition policy, which means that rigorously consistent and invariable practice in implementing the relevant rules cannot be expected of it, and, as a corollary, that it enjoys a degree of latitude regarding the choice of the econometric instruments available to it and the choice of the appropriate approach to the study of any matter (see, for example, regarding the definition of the relevant market, ...) provided that those choices are not manifestly contrary to the accepted rules of economic discipline and are applied consistently.

In *Schneider*, the General Court went on to find that there was liability because the Commission had violated Schneider's rights of defence by not telling it what corrective action it needed to take. It saw this question as unrelated to the complexity of the assessment, and therefore simple breach was sufficient to justify liability.[151]

The Court could have used a risk-based test. This would have involved the Court deciding, in conditions of uncertainty, whether EU institutions or private parties would be better equipped to bear responsibility for the costs of things going wrong. Misbehaviour by EU institutions would have been irrelevant to this test. Instead, the Court chose to apply a fault-based test. The virtues of such a test are that it carries with it a duty of care on the part of EU institutions to those affected by their actions. This test is not, however, without its own challenges. In this regard, EU law suggests a paradoxical standard. With regard to substantive obligations, only the most flagrant violations of clear obligations or arbitrary conduct will incur liability – a very narrow fault test indeed. As regards matters of process, the situation is reversed, with relatively small failures to observe due process or rights of defence being likely to lead to liability. The difficulty with this is that it provides incentives for EU institutions to focus on process in their activities at the expense of substance.

---

[151] The decision of the General Court on these points was upheld on appeal. Case C-440/07 P *Commission v Schneider Electric*, Judgment of 16 July 2009.

(ii) Presence of loss caused by the Union

The final condition for liability is the presence of a direct causal link between the breach of EU law and the damage. The range of types of loss that may be covered is, in principle, considerable. The position on the types of loss which may be recovered was most clearly set out by Advocate General Capotorti in *Ireks-Arkady*:

> It is well known that the legal concept of 'damage' covers both a material loss *stricto sensu*, that is to say, a reduction in the person's assets and also the loss of an increase in those assets which would have occurred if the harmful act had not taken place (these two alternatives are known respectively as *damnum emergens* and *lucrum cessans*)... The object of compensation is to restore the assets of the victim to the condition in which they would have been apart from the unlawful act, or at least to the condition closest to that which would have been produced if the unlawful act had not taken place: the hypothetical nature of that restoration often entails a certain degree of approximation.[152]

The Court has thus taken a broad view of which loss may be recovered. It will include any incidental loss, such as penalties the applicant had to pay as a result of having to repudiate a contract,[153] or bank interest as a result of loans taken out to pay money wrongfully levied.[154] The Court has also been ready to award compensation for non-pecuniary loss such as anxiety, hurt feelings[155] and slurs on professional reputation.[156] The 'expectation interest' will also be protected. Compensation will be awarded, therefore, for loss of profits.[157]

However, the establishment of loss is often a significant hurdle, in practice, for applicants.

The first problem is that of joint or concurrent liability: situations where both an EU institution and a Member State may be liable.[158] There are two situations where this may occur.[159] The first is where a national authority implements or administers an unlawful Union measure, such as the transposition of a Directive or the collection of agricultural levies. The second is where a decision is taken jointly by a Member State and an institution, such as in the field of external trade, where Member States are permitted to restrict imports of third country goods once they have received the permission of the Commission. The most equitable solution would be to establish a system of joint and several liability. The applicant could choose whom to sue, with unsuccessful defendants recovering contributions from each other afterwards. Such a scheme, however, has not been established in EU law. Instead, the Court presumes that parties should first exhaust remedies in domestic courts,[160] although the presumption is rebuttable where it would be impossible for an applicant to obtain a remedy in a national court.[161]

---

[152] Case 238/78 *Ireks-Arkady* v *Council and Commission* [1979] ECR 2955, 2998–9.

[153] Case 74/74 *CNTA* v *Commission* [1975] ECR 533.

[154] Case T-167/94 *Nölle* v *Council and Commission* [1995] ECR II-2589.

[155] Case 110/63 *Willame* v *Commission* [1965] ECR 649.

[156] Case T- 48/05 *Franchet and Byk* v *Commission* [2008] ECR II-1585.

[157] Joined Cases 56/74–60/74 *Kampffmeyer* v *Commission and Council* [1976] ECR 711; Joined Cases C-104/89 and C-37/90 *Mulder* v *Council and Commission* [1992] ECR I-3061.

[158] For detailed critique see A. Ward, *Judicial Review and the Rights of Private Parties in EU Law* (2nd edn, Oxford, Oxford University Press, 2007) 375–90.

[159] W. Wils, 'Concurrent Liability of the Community and a Member State' (1992) 17 *ELRev.* 191, 194–8.

[160] Case 96/71 *Haegeman* v *Commission* [1972] ECR 1005.

[161] Case 281/82 *Unifrex* v *Commission and Council* [1984] ECR 1969.

This has resulted in unsatisfactory and needless complexity, requiring, in some instances, that applicants simultaneously commence actions in both the domestic courts and the Court of Justice.[162]

Secondly, the burden of proof is upon applicants to show a direct causal link between the loss and the illegal act.[163] The chain of causation can thus be severed by third parties, such as by an independent act of a Member State.[164] It is not sufficient to prove that the loss would not have occurred but for the illegal act.[165] There must a sufficient proximity between the illegal act and the loss suffered.[166] In practice, this has made it very difficult for applicants to claim for loss of profits as these will often be too remote or speculative. For the Court has stated that it will only compensate damage that is actual and certain.[167] Even where a causal link is established between the loss suffered and the illegal act, the applicant might still not recover full compensation. This may be, first, as a result of the doctrine of contributory negligence, where the applicant is considered to have contributed to the damage as a result of a failure to take due care.[168] Secondly, the applicant is under a duty to mitigate any loss suffered. A failure to do so will result in compensation being reduced.[169] Finally, compensation will be reduced if there is evidence that the applicant has, or could have, passed the loss on to somebody else.[170]

8 CONSEQUENCES OF ANNULMENT

The consequences of a finding of illegality are set out in Article 264 TFEU.

Article 264 TFEU

If the action is well founded, the Court of Justice shall declare the act concerned to be void.

In the case of a regulation, however, the Court of Justice shall, if it considers this necessary, state which of the effects of the regulation which it has declared void shall be considered as definitive.

A finding of invalidity can be made not just on the basis of Article 263 TFEU and under the plea of illegality, but also under a claim brought for damages.[171] This has *erga omnes* effect by binding all national courts in the European Union.[172] In *BASF*, the Court ruled that 'acts of the Community institutions are in principle presumed to be lawful and accordingly produce

---

[162] Case T-167/94 *Nölle* v *Council and Commission* [1995] ECR II-2589.

[163] Case T-168/94 *Blackspur DIY* v *Council and Commission* [1995] ECR II-2627. On this see A. Toth, 'The Concepts of Damage and Causality as Elements of Non-Contractual Liability' in H. Schermers *et al.* (eds.), *Non-Contractual Liability of the European Communities* (Dordrecht, Martinus Nijhoff, 1988).

[164] Case 132/77 *Société pour l'Exportation des Sucres SA* v *Commission* [1978] ECR 1061.

[165] This is, however, a *sine qua non*: Case T-478/93 *Wafer Zoo* v *Commission* [1995] ECR II-1479.

[166] Joined Cases 64/76, 113/76, 167/78, 239/78, 27/79, 28/79 and 45/79 *Dumortier Frères* v *Council* [1979] ECR 3091.

[167] Joined Cases T-3/00 and T-337/04 *Pitsiorlas* v *Council and ECB* [2007] ECR II-4779.

[168] Case 145/83 *Adams* v *Commission* [1985] ECR 3539.

[169] Joined Cases C-104/89 and C-37/90 *Mulder* v *Council and Commission* [1992] ECR I-3061.

[170] Case 238/78 *Ireks-Arkady* v *Council and Commission* [1979] ECR 2955.

[171] Joined Cases 5/66, 7/66, 13/66–24/66 *Kampfmeyer* v *Commission* [1967] ECR 245.

[172] See Case 66/80 *International Chemical Corporation* v *Amministrazione delle Finanze* [1981] ECR 1191.

legal effects, even if they are tainted by irregularities, until such time as they are annulled or withdrawn'.[173] The Court went on to add the following rider:

> by way of exception to that principle, acts tainted by an irregularity whose gravity is so obvious that it cannot be tolerated by the Community legal order must be treated as having no legal effect, even provisional, that is to say that they must be regarded as legally non-existent. The purpose of this exception is to maintain a balance between two fundamental, but sometimes conflicting, requirements with which a legal order must comply, namely stability of legal relations and respect for legality.[174]

A ruling to that effect will have the consequence of releasing all parties from any obligation to which they might have thought themselves subject under the measure. Otherwise, the effects will vary according to the measure declared invalid. A Regulation declared invalid is void not just between the parties to the dispute, but also in respect of third parties. While the presumption in the first paragraph of Article 264 TFEU is that it is void *ab initio*, considerable discretion is given to the Court under the second paragraph of Article 264 TFEU, enabling it to determine the effects of its ruling. Accordingly, the Court may declare that only part of a measure is void, maintaining in place other aspects of it. Temporal limitations may also be placed upon an annulment, meaning that the legislation will remain in force until new legislation is passed to replace it.[175]

FURTHER READING

A. Arnull, 'Private Applicants and the Action for Annulment Since *Codorníu*' (2001) 38 *Common Market Law Review* 7

The European Union and its Court of Justice (2nd edn, Oxford, Oxford University Press, 2006) ch. 3

P. Craig, *EU Administrative Law* (Oxford, Oxford University Press, 2006) chs. 10, 13, 20

C. Harlow, 'Towards a Theory of Access for the European Court of Justice' (1992) 12 *Yearbook of European Law* 213

C. Hilson, 'The Role of Discretion in EC Law on Non-contractual Liability' (2005) 42 *Common Market Law Review* 677

H. Nehl, *Principles of Administrative Procedure in EC Law* (Oxford, Oxford University Press, 1999)

E. Sharpston, 'Legitimate Expectations and Economic Reality' (1990) 15 *European Law Review* 103

T. Tridimas, 'Liability for Breach of Community Law: Growing Up and Mellowing Down?' (2001) 38 *Common Market Law Review* 301

The General Principles of EU Law (2nd edn, Oxford, Oxford University Press, 2006)

M. Vogt, 'Indirect Judicial Protection in EC Law: The Case of the Plea of Illegality' (2006) 31 *European Law Review* 364

A. Ward, *Judicial Review and the Rights of Private Parties in EU Law* (2nd edn, Oxford, Oxford University Press, 2007) chs. 6, 8

W. Wils, 'Concurrent Liability of the Community and a Member State' (1992) 17 *European Law Review* 191

---

[173] See Case C-137/92 P *Commission v BASF* [1994] ECR I-2555.
[174] *Ibid.* para. 49.
[175] See e.g. Case C-392/95 *Parliament v Council* [1997] ECR I-3213.

Index